Rhetoric
in
Civic Life

Rhetoric in Civic Life

third edition

Catherine Helen Palczewski
University of Northern Iowa

Richard Ice
College of St. Benedict | St. John's University

John Fritch
University of Northern Iowa

Ryan McGeough
University of Northern Iowa

Strata Publishing, Inc.
State College, Pennsylvania

Strata Publishing, Inc.
P.O. 1303
State College, PA 16804
USA

Telephone: 814-234-8545

Web site: www.stratapub.com

Printed and bound in the United States by Sheridan.

Cover printed in the United States by Phoenix Color.

Image on cover: *abstract colorful city skyline pattern background for design* by iStock.com/naqiewei

Credits and acknowledgments appear on pages 351–352 and on this page by reference.

The URLs in this book were accurate as of the date cited or the date of publication. Neither the authors nor Strata guarantee the accuracy of information provided in websites listed.

ISBN: 978-1-891136-51-1

to Arnie, Jeanne, Trudy and Danielle
our partners in life
who have enacted with us
the possibility of disagreeing
without being disagreeable

Brief Contents

Contents

Preface

The third edition of *Rhetoric in Civic Life* continues our commitment to developing students' habits of rhetorical engagement. Now, more than ever, developing and practicing the rhetorical skills of political friendship, stranger sociability, careful analysis, and civic responsibility are essential. The revisions in this edition are designed to speak to current and enduring concerns of rhetoric as civic engagement.

The text is intended for introductory rhetorical theory courses; courses on rhetoric, civic life, and civic engagement; persuasion courses that adopt a rhetorical approach; rhetorical criticism courses that approach criticism as an inventional practice; and other courses that are concerned with rhetoric in public life. It could also be used for advanced rhetorical theory courses, perhaps supplemented with primary texts from core theorists.

The impetus for writing this book came from our desire for a textbook for our own courses that would approach rhetoric from a conceptual perspective, rather than unfolding chronologically or focusing on key theorists. We wanted to provide our students with a sense of the disciplinary evolution of rhetorical concepts, but with an emphasis on the concepts rather than on who said what and when.

The impetus for the third edition was our desire to update the book to reflect current issues and events, including the increasing role of digital and social media in public discourse; incorporate recent theoretical perspectives on the role of the rhetor in a digital and postmodern world; expand on the centrality of race and gender to understanding rhetoric; recognize the emergence of networked public spheres; attend to the importance of emotion in public life; and explore emerging perspectives on looking practices in visual culture. We emphasize that it takes practice to develop the rhetorical habits necessary for democracy.

The new edition continues our commitment to provide examples that make rhetorical theories and concepts come alive. It also continues our commitment to work closely with our peers and colleagues who have used the book, reviewed our ideas for revisions, and recommended changes on the basis of their own classroom needs and experiences. We have sought to incorporate the feedback we have received in ways that would make the book accessible yet thoughtful; timely, yet building on historical as well as contemporary examples; and relevant, while also engaging the timeless concepts of rhetoric.

Our goal with this edition, as with the first two, was to help students understand how rhetoric shapes and creates meaning in the full range of civic life, from the instrumental rhetoric of deliberative and electoral politics to the constitutive rhetoric of epideictic public memory and identity formation. We wanted a textbook that students would find useful and engaging, and that also presented scholarship clearly and substantively, describing complex theories with the nuance and subtlety they deserve. We reference a range of classical and contemporary theories and theorists, comparing and interweaving ideas from the rise of ancient Greek democracy (Aristotle, Plato, Isocrates, and the Sophists), to twentieth-century theorists (including Kenneth Burke, Susanne K. Langer, Lucie Olbrechts-Tyteca, and Chaïm Perelman), to the most recent cutting-edge research appearing in the books and journals of the discipline. We wrote this book from the perspective that rhetoric—verbal, visual, embodied, argumentative, narrative—is symbolic action with consequences and, as such, deserves careful study.

We strove for writing that is clear and concise, but not oversimplified, providing extensive documentation through endnotes. We endeavored to define terms and concepts clearly and to provide an abundance of detailed examples that would resonate with students. By including extended examples and short texts, for which we offer brief analyses that deploy the concepts covered, we attempted to show students how a rhetorical approach offers an enhanced understanding of how social reality is created, maintained, and challenged.

FEATURES OF THE BOOK

This new edition retains the central features of the previous editions.

Conceptual approach: We have attempted to provide a heuristic vocabulary that will help students make sense of the forms, functions, and consequences of rhetoric. The book explores theories and theorists from an integrated, topical perspective. Thus, the contributions of some theorists appear in multiple chapters. We do not dictate a particular methodological approach, but rather offer a range of concepts that enable more subtle and nuanced analyses of symbolic action. We hope these concepts will enable students to ask smarter questions about the symbolic actions they produce and encounter.

Expansive range of rhetorical theories: The textbook grounds each chapter in traditional rhetorical theories, describing the core concept (rhetor, audience, argument, and so on), then extends the study of that concept by drawing from recent scholarship. For example, in the discussion of rhetors, we cover the classical conceptions of ethos, but also problematize the very notion of the rhetor with a careful consideration of the role of authorial intent in meaning making, the ways rhetors may both invent and be invented by rhetoric, and the possibility of rhetoric without rhetors in an age of algorithms. We also focus on identity as intersectional (rather than essential) and the possibilities of using strategic essentialism as a rhetorical resource. This approach enables the study of rhetorical forms from legislative debates and public address to vernacular body argument and visual rhetorics.

Emphasis on civic life and civic advocacy: Although the book discusses rhetoric across its many theoretical, cultural, and practical contexts, the central emphasis is on rhetoric in civic life and the inextricable connections between deliberative debates about policy and epideictic debates about civic identity. We want students to understand that all members of a public have a role to play in civic life, and to understand the range of, and limits on, each person's power. We want them to understand that rhetoric has consequences—particularly for identity, power, memory, and ideology—and, thus, shapes social reality. We foreground the need to practice rhetoric in order to develop civic habits.

Detailed examples: Abundant historical and contemporary examples show how words, images, arguments, and stories have consequences. These examples, many of which are new to this edition, include recent activism in response to school shootings, videos of police violence against Black people, #NoKidsInCages guerrilla art installations, school dress codes, COVID-19, presidential speeches in times of crisis, reparations, New Orleans Mayor Landrieu's speech about Confederate monuments, media coverage of the opioid epidemic, Greta Thunberg's activism on the climate crisis, abolitionist speakers who caused northerners to think of enslaved people as suffering human beings, political campaigns, national monuments that celebrate a shared history and reinforce a shared set of values, public debates over issues such as health care and immigration, and events and issues in students' personal and campus lives.

FEATURES OF THE NEW EDITION

As with every edition, we have updated examples, refined theory, and expanded our attention to race, gender, sexuality, and other vectors of marginalization. We have also updated the book in several significant respects. Major revisions include:

Updated discussions of current theory: The third edition pays particular attention to recent advances in rhetorical theory and evolving conceptions of rhetoric in a digital age. For example, a new section in Chapter 4 on the ethics of looking grapples with the way visual culture presumes a right to look and the dynamics of invisibility/visibility/hypervisibility. We have integrated new literature on passing (Chapter 8), circulation (Chapter 4), and an evolving conceptualization of the rhetorical situation in a digital and networked age (Chapter 9), among other updates.

Enhanced emphasis on the civic functions of rhetoric: The introductory chapter of the previous editions has been divided into two chapters, allowing Chapter 1 to focus fully on rhetoric as a form of civic action. The reconfigured argument chapter (now Chapter 5) foregrounds the civic possibilities of debate and overtly argues for argument as a form that has unique possibilities in democracy. Related updates include a new section on political friendship (Chapter 1) and theoretical implications of civic action in the digital age (Chapter 10). Throughout the book, we emphasize the need to practice rhetoric and argument in order to develop the habits of civic engagement and interaction.

Updated implications of digital media: Reflecting the increasingly complex nature of public discourse in our mass-mediated and digitally connected world, this edition includes discussions of the evolving conceptualization of the rhetorical situation in a digital age (Chapter 9), and of networked publics, public screens, networked activism, and slacktivism (Chapter 10). Numerous examples throughout the book are drawn from Twitter, Facebook, and YouTube campaigns.

New appendix on rhetorical history: We have added a new appendix on rhetorical thought in classical Greece and the Haudenosaunee Confederacy, as well as other traditions that influenced the formation of US democracy. For those who seek to ground their courses in these traditions, the appendix complements the first chapter. Alternatively, the appendix can be introduced later in the semester, after students have been introduced to general concepts of rhetoric.

Updated examples reflecting current issues, controversies, and events: Continuing our focus on providing examples that are both timeless and timely, the new edition has numerous new examples that illustrate the value of civic diversity and the manner in which people come to understand their world through rhetoric. Many of the examples that begin chapters are new, including new extended examples on Parkland students' activism concerning school shootings, sit-ins as a tactic of civil rights activism, the 1619 Project, and youth activism in response to dress codes.

We are committed to keeping the cost of the textbook reasonable by limiting the amount of money needed for permissions fees. (For example, even short quotations from news stories can cost $250–$500 each.) Although, as rhetoricians, we realize that every word matters, that every sentence can construct meaning, and that a verbal description of a visual artifact is always incomplete, we often had to paraphrase and cut quotations or choose not to include an image, a Tweet, or an Instagram post because of exorbitant permission fees. However, we tried to provide citations so that people can track down the rhetorical artifacts we reference and, when we think seeing or hearing the complete artifact is important, we note that in the text.

Although we wanted to include more memes, tweets, and other social media examples, the challenge and expense of copyright permissions made this impossible. In many cases, copyright holders could not (or did not want to) be identified and so garnering permission was impossible. Similar challenges arose when we wanted to include longer passages or complete speeches. Our dilemma in this respect offers an interesting example of how broader institutional structures contribute to the amplification and preservation of some voices and not others.

ORGANIZATION

The book is composed of ten chapters, organized into four parts according to the central facets of rhetorical form and function, plus an appendix. The organization is flexible: we believe instructors can teach the chapters in any order they wish, according to their own classroom needs.

Part I, "Introduction," consists of two chapters. In response to suggestions from colleagues who have used this textbook, we have split the original introductory chapter into two chapters.

Chapter 1, "Rhetoric as Civic Action," defines rhetoric and explains its historical foundation in democratic traditions. The chapter explains rhetoric as a form of symbolic action and as a central means of enacting civic engagement. It explores the rhetorical functions of generating identification, constituting identity, and constructing social reality. A new section on political friendship helps foreground the idea that civic engagement requires the development and practice of several rhetorical habits.

Chapter 2, "Core Concepts in Rhetoric," identifies the central feature of rhetoric as addressed. It also offers the persuasive continuum as a means of understanding a range of rhetorical effects and identifies rhetoric as both a creator and a practice of culture, ideology, public memory, and power.

Part II, "Modes of Symbolic Action," includes four chapters.

Chapter 3, "Language," introduces language as symbolic action, a novel idea for many students. Drawing on theories of linguistic relativity, semiotics, and dramatism, the chapter shows that language is not merely a means by which humans transmit information; it also constitutes social reality. The chapter explores the ways that a public vocabulary forms social reality through characterizations, metaphors, and ideographs, as well as the possibilities of resignification.

Chapter 4, "Visual Rhetoric," encourages students to ask not just "What does an image mean?" but also "What does an image do?" It grounds visual rhetoric in an understanding of visual culture and examines the power of three categories of visual rhetoric: iconic photographs, monuments, and bodies. New sections articulate the importance of circulation to understanding rhetoric and offer ethical considerations about whether (or not) to look.

Chapter 5, "Argument," describes the role of argument in civic life. It explores argument as a thing and as an interactional process, drawing on the Toulmin model and on theory about spheres of argument (technical, personal, and public). This chapter has been substantially revised in order to articulate more clearly the importance of public argument, particularly policy argument, to civic life. New extended examples illustrate major concepts. The chapter also explores ways to address challenges to public argument, including fake news and confirmation bias.

Chapter 6, "Narrative," is informed by Walter Fisher's narrative paradigm and by Kenneth Burke's comic/tragic frames, providing students with a critical approach to understanding narrative and the role it plays in forming memory and creating culture.

Part III, "Generators of Symbolic Action," includes two chapters.

Chapter 7, "Rhetors," explores the concept of the rhetor as both producing and produced by rhetorical action. The chapter introduces students to the idea of persona and its various facets, explains identity as a social construction and as intersectional, and explores the complex roles and functions of rhetors, with particular attention to how rhetors function in a postmodern world. The chapter also explores the role of authorial intent in making meaning, the ways in which rhetors may both invent and be invented by rhetoric, and the possibility of rhetoric without rhetors in an age of algorithms.

Chapter 8, "Audiences," revisits the basic premise that rhetoric is, at its core, addressed, and that the audience is both the receiver and the product of rhetorical action. The chapter shows that when one audience is created (a second persona), another may be denied existence (a third persona), and yet another may emerge as eavesdropping or silently complicit (a fourth persona). In this new edition, the chapter also attempts to build a better understanding of public emotion, audience agency, and passing.

Part IV, "Contexts for Symbolic Action," includes two chapters.

Chapter 9, "Rhetorical Situations," takes a synergistic approach, drawing on Bitzer's discussion of the basic components of the rhetorical situation and on his argument that rhetoric is situational, and on Vatz's counterargument that situations are rhetorical. The chapter also explores Branham and Pearce's discussion of the various ways that a rhetor may react to a situation. A new section on rhetorical ecologies explores evolving conceptualizations of the rhetorical situation in a digital age.

Chapter 10, "Publics and Counterpublics," introduces students to current theories of public sphere discourse, beginning with Habermas's basic model and incorporating current theories that recognize the possibility and productivity of multiple publics, as well as ways in which digital technologies have complicated traditional understandings of what constitutes a public and how publics emerge.

Appendix, Rhetorical Traditions and Democracy, is new to this edition. It offers a history of rhetoric and democracy, including the influences of classical Greece and the Haudenosaunee Confederacy on US democracy. It shows that both the benefits and exclusions of the classical tradition are still visible today, and that realizing the promise of democracy demands awareness and active corrections to sex- and race-based exclusions.

PEDAGOGICAL RESOURCES

Key Concepts: Every chapter opens with a list of terms for key concepts. Within the chapter, each of these terms is boldfaced and defined, then followed by examples.

Discussion Questions: Each chapter ends with a series of questions that guide discussion and encourage students to apply concepts to the use of rhetoric in civic life.

Recommended Readings: Every chapter ends with a short list of recommended readings that students can use to explore the foundational literature of the field.

ACKNOWLEDGMENTS

Scholarship is never an isolated endeavor. We are not, and should not be, confined to an ivory tower. Conversations with colleagues, fellow scholars, and friends always enliven our writing and thinking. Many of the examples and felicitous phrasings come from conversations with members of our intellectual family. Their influence on earlier editions continue to resonate in this edition, even as new influences also deserve recognition. In particular, we want to thank Robert Asen and Daniel Brouwer for help with all things public and counterpublic; G. Thomas Goodnight for help with all things rhetoric; Donn Parson, Arnie Madsen, and David Williams for help with all things Burke; Damien Pfister for help with all things networked; Karma Chávez for constant questioning of citizenship as a frame; E Cram for feedback about material and visual rhetorics; Sam Perry for feedback concerning lynching; Annie Hill for brilliant edits on the visual ethics section; Jeff Jarman for all things confirmation bias; Fernando Ismael Quiñones Valdivia for all things Pepe and memes; Cecilia Cerja for all things popular culture; Francesca Soans for help with obscure but apt examples; Christopher Martin and Bettina Fabos for conversations about current events and media fluency; Terence Check and Jeanmarie Cook for their conversations about pedagogy; Isaac West for refining our understanding of identification; Bonnie Dow and Roseann Mandziuk for correcting our misrepresentation of Sojourner Truth; Christian O. Lundberg and Joshua G. Gunn for help with all things post-humanist; Carole Blair for help with all things material and monumental; Brenda J. Allen for help with expanding the diversity of our examples; and Heather Bart for thoughtful examples. The colleagues listed above come from a range of institutions and career locations. But they all share one thing in common: whenever we sent a message asking for a bibliography on a topic, a review of new content, a conversation about a thorny theoretical issue, a confirmation that we got their research right, or just a word of encouragement, they delivered.

Richard thanks the College of St. Benedict and St. John's University for a generous sabbatical leave that enabled him to work on the first edition of this book. Richard, John, and Ryan also would like to thank their children (Hannah, Noah, Garrett, Byron, Harper, and Ada) for being tolerant and supportive throughout this process. We also want to recognize students who introduced us to some of the powerful examples we used across editions: Fernando Ismael Quiñones Valdivia, Nicole Brennan, Zoe Russell, and Evan Schares.

Previous editions of this book were transformed throughout the writing process as a result of feedback from numerous reviewers: Lin Allen, University of Northern Colorado; Jennifer Asenas, California State University, Long Beach; Linda Czuba Brigance, State University of New York, Fredonia; Bonnie Dow, Vanderbilt University; Janis L. Edwards, University of Alabama; Pat J. Gehrke, University of South Carolina; Zac Gershberg, Keene State College; Ron Greene, University of Minnesota; Alina Haliliuc, Denison University; Judith Hendry, University of New Mexico; Brandon Inabinet, Furman University; Jack Kay, Eastern Michigan University; Jim A. Kuypers, Virginia Polytechnic Institute and State University; Lenore Langsdorf, Southern Illinois University; Ilon Lauer, Western Illinois University; Heather Lettner-Rust, Longwood University; David M. Lucas, Ohio University; Noemi Marin, Florida Atlantic University; Michael McFarland, Stetson University; Jerry Miller, Ohio University; Billie Murray, Villanova University; Tony Palmeri, University of Wisconsin–Oshkosh; Emily Plec, Western Oregon University; Lawrence Prelli, University of New Hampshire; Jennifer Reem, Nova Southeastern University; Kara Shultz, Bloomsburg University; Steven Schwarze, University of Montana; John M. Sloop, Vanderbilt University; Matthew J. Sobnosky, Hofstra University; Stacey K. Sowards, University of Texas at El Paso; Nathan Stormer, University of Maine; Elizabeth Chiseri Strater, University of North Carolina–Greensboro; Richard Vatz, Towson University; Isaac West, Vanderbilt University; and Dylan Wolfe, Clemson University. Their challenges, corrections, and questions made the book immeasurably better. Any errors that remain are ours, not theirs.

Faculty who used previous editions of the book were extremely helpful in providing feedback through survey responses and conversations about the text. This edition was shaped by their generous sharing of their experiences: Pat Arneson, Duquesne University; Keely R. Austin, Carnegie Mellon University; Elizabeth Benacka, Lake Forest College; E. Tristan Booth, Arizona State University; Brandon Bumstead, City Colleges of Chicago; Anthony Chiaviello, University of Houston Downtown; Adam J. Gaffey, Winona State University; Heather A. Hayes, Whitman College; Spoma Jovanovic, University of North Carolina at Greensboro; Margret McCue-Enser, St. Catherine University; Angela McGowan-Kirsch, The State University of New York at Fredonia; Jan Osborn, Chapman University; Tony Palmeri, University of Wisconsin–Oshkosh; J. Blake Scott, University of Central Florida; Shana Scudder, University of North Carolina Greensboro; John W. Self, Truman State University; Samantha Senda-Cook,

Creighton University; Elizabeth Chiseri Strater, University of North Carolina Greensboro; David Supp-Montgomerie, University of Iowa; and Anke Wolbert, Eastern Michigan University.

We also would like to thank the people who reviewed the proposal and/or the manuscript for the third edition. Their insights helped shape the text in a number of ways, both in our explanations of large concepts and in our attention to detail in many of the examples: Kamran Afary, California State University, Los Angeles; E. Tristan Booth, Arizona State University; Jonathan L. Bradshaw, Western Carolina University; Kundai Chirindo, Lewis & Clark College; Daniel Grano, University of North Carolina at Charlotte; Elif Guler, Longwood University; Christine Harold, University of Washington; Spoma Jovanovic, University of North Carolina at Greensboro; Casey Kelly, University of Nebraska–Lincoln; Randall Lake, University of Southern California; Angela McGowan-Kirsch, The State University of New York at Fredonia; Jonathan Rossing, Gonzaga University; J. Blake Scott, University of Central Florida; John W. Self, Truman State University; Samantha Senda-Cook, Creighton University; Paul Stob, Vanderbilt University; David Supp-Montgomerie, University of Iowa; and J. Thomas Wright, University of Central Florida.

We would like to remember the contributions of Jack Kay, Arnie Madsen, and Dan Brouwer. Not only in places where we footnote, but throughout the book, their influence is pronounced. Their thoughtfulness and brilliance is missed.

Jack passed away in early 2015. His influence on one of the authors, John, began when Jack was John's undergraduate director of forensics. His influence is seen in the textbook in many of the examples and understandings of rhetoric. During his final months, he helped us by providing examples and thoughts about the book and the direction of culture.

Arnie Madsen died in September 2017. Cate's partner and John's friend, Arnie was a source of knowledge on all things related to political campaigns, argument, and Kenneth Burke. Arnie and Cate's relationship proved argument could be a source of delight, play, and relationship maintenance. Cate's work on this edition was made much more challenging without an editor and sounding board sitting on the couch next to her.

Dan Brouwer died in May 2021. His constant, delightful, and always brilliant support over the years influenced this book in profound ways. The many seminars and conversations Cate had with him resonate throughout the publics and counterpublics chapter. The discipline has lost a central voice in public sphere theory that constantly challenged us to hear the marginalized, the vernacular, and the embodied.

We honor these three rhetoricians by offering a book that strives to live up to their intellectual brilliance, delight in rhetoric, and commitment to democratic practice.

We also thank our editor and publisher, Kathleen Domenig, for her patience and guidance throughout the writing of this book. We are sure that working with an authorial quadumvirate is an editorial nightmare. We hope the end result made the hundreds, if not thousands, of emails worth it.

Part I
Introduction

Chapter 1
Rhetoric as Civic Action

Civic life can be full of moments of joy, play, exuberance, contentment, and pride. It can also contain moments of grief, labor, remorse, discontent, and shame. Because civic life is full of both celebrations and challenges, the topics we explore in this book are, too. We do not shy away from the difficult. It is in moments of difficulty when rhetoric in civic life is most needed. One such moment occurred on February 14, 2018, when a shooter opened fire at Marjory Stoneman Douglas High School in Parkland, Florida, murdering seventeen people.

In the wake of the shooting, Vice President Mike Pence tweeted that "these students, teachers, administrators, & families will all remain in our prayers." President Trump tweeted "prayers and condolences."[1] Florida Representatives also responded with tweets: Matt Gaetz tweeted "thoughts and prayers"; Charlie Crist was "praying for the safety" of those affected; and Daniel Webster wrote "my prayers are with them."[2]

Responding to politicians' offers of "thoughts and prayers," Parkland students instead demanded legislative and governmental actions. The students lobbied for changes through interactions with media and debate with legislators. They were prepared to do this because their high school foregrounded civic skills,[3] the same skills we seek to help you develop. These students were part of their school's debate, journalism, and drama programs. They were taught to value public advocacy and use their communication skills to move others, and they practiced those skills in a variety of forums. They were trained to function as members of a democratic community.

They engaged in collective action, working with people across the nation, to demand institutional change.

On February 18, Parkland students announced that they were organizing a March for Our Lives in Washington, DC.[4] In addition to raising $2 million in private donations from celebrities and media executives, their GoFundMe campaign received $3.5 million from other donors.[5] The students also spoke directly to state legislators. On February 21, more than a hundred survivors of the Parkland shooting went to the Florida state capitol to rally for gun control.[6]

The Parkland students also made numerous media appearances. On the Saturday after the shooting, John Barnitt, a Parkland high school junior, gave an estimated thirty-five interviews. On April 2, Jaclyn Corin, Cameron Kasky, Emma González, David Hogg, and Alex Wind were on the cover of *Time*. They and other Parkland survivors spoke on various television shows, including *Dr. Phil, Ellen,* and *Real Time with Bill Maher.* Kasky also challenged Senator Marco Rubio in a CNN town hall on February 21, asking whether Rubio would refuse NRA donations.[7]

In addition to mourning their own losses, the Parkland students sought to draw attention to other, less publicized teen deaths that had been caused by gun violence across the United States. For perspective, consider that in the thirty-seven days after the Parkland school shooting, seventy-three more US teens were shot to death.[8] Meeting with students from Chicago schools, the Parkland students argued that all deaths caused by gun violence deserved attention. With nationwide death tolls in mind, the students stated their mission, in their March 2018 web page, as seeking legislation that addressed "gun violence issues that are rampant in our country." They added, "We demand morally just leaders to rise up from both parties in order to ensure public safety." The legislative actions they called for included comprehensive and universal background checks; changes in policies of the Bureau of Alcohol, Tobacco, Firearms and Explosives; funding for research on the "gun violence epidemic"; and bans on assault weapons.[9]

The March for Our Lives took place on March 24, 2018. The crowd in Washington, DC, was estimated at two hundred thousand people.[10] Over eight hundred sibling marches occurred across the United States and world.

Not everyone approved of the students' advocacy. The day after the march, former senator and presidential candidate Rick Santorum suggested that the students should focus "internally" on their individual failures, instead of "protesting and saying, 'Oh, someone else needs to pass a law.'" He suggested that the students take CPR classes, act to stop bullying, or learn what they could do to intercept a shooter. He criticized them for not asking themselves how each one of them, "as an individual," could solve the problem of school shootings.[11] (We encourage you to watch the video to see Santorum's complete statement at https://www.youtube.com/watch?v=PWMsCO-Icg4, or search "Santorum Parkland CPR video.") Santorum's focus was not on civic action, legal changes, or institutional responses, but instead on individual solutions.

Individual responsibility is necessary, but it is not sufficient to solve the problems of a society. Our focus in this book is on how communication skills can be used to organize collective action, form identity, and guide and demand systemic solutions to systemic problems. For a democracy to work and for civic life to be vibrant, attention to entities larger than the individual (communities, cities, states, nations, collectives) must be embraced.

This book encourages a civic, rather than personal and individual, orientation. Central to that orientation is rhetoric, and all of its confusions, ambiguities, and frustrations. The rest of this chapter explains in more detail why we believe rhetoric is central to civic life. When you choose to participate in civic life, rhetoric equips you to do so more productively and helps you to understand the communities of which you are a part.

DEFINING RHETORIC

You have probably heard the word "rhetoric" before, most likely in a negative context. In contemporary situations, people often use the term to describe something as untrue, misleading, or manipulative. Yet, the term originally had none of these connotations. It comes from the ancient Greek word *rhetor*, which meant "public speaker." The Greek term *rhetorike* referred to the art of public speaking, meaning speaking to a broader audience than one's family or friends and about issues of public, rather than personal, concern.[12]

Rhetoric is *the use of symbols (words and images) to share ideas, enabling people to work together to make decisions about matters of common concern, create identity, and construct social reality.* It is the means by which people make meaning of and affect the world in which they live. Throughout this book, we use the term **rhetor** to mean *any person, group, or institution that uses rhetoric.* We use the term **rhetorician** to describe *a person who studies rhetoric.*

Although the Greeks coined the term "rhetorike," the practice of eloquent or effective public speaking was a feature of many ancient cultures.[13] Various forms of rhetoric existed in the oral cultures of ancient China, Egypt, Israel, and Mesopotamia.[14] The Arabic tradition of *balagha* has emphasized rhetoric and eloquence for over fourteen hundred years.[15] India is the home of a tradition of argument stretching back millennia.[16] Even before these places and cultures developed concepts of rhetoric, they used it to construct their civilizations. Broadly speaking, rhetoric has been present since the first time some humans tried to get others to see the world the same way they did and to act accordingly. Rhetoric has become an essential part of how people use symbols to work together in a democratic culture and of how they understand themselves and their world.

Understanding rhetoric, whether you are producing or consuming it, is valuable in many facets of life. Messages from political candidates, social media posts from advocacy groups, and news stories are rhetorical. You cannot log onto social media or watch a sporting event without receiving a variety of messages designed to get you to spend money on various products. The message in this book also is rhetorical. Analyzing how different messages are intended to persuade can help you make more informed decisions. The ability to produce skillful rhetoric of your own is also valuable in a variety of personal, professional, and public settings. Rhetoric can persuade, bring people to agreement on complex issues, and transform how they see themselves and the world. Our goal with this text is to provide you with the knowledge to produce rhetoric more skillfully, use it ethically, and analyze it critically.

RHETORIC AS SYMBOLIC ACTION

Human beings make sense of their interactions with the world and with each other through the symbols (words and images) they attach to their experiences. Words (language) and images (icons, pictures, photos, bodies, architectural structures) are not merely a means to transmit information; they are the grounds for the judgments people make about things, events, and other people. Quite simply, symbols matter.

How many people do you know who went home from grade school crying because of something another person said or a mean picture another person drew? Even if some children shouted, "Sticks and stones may break my bones, but words will never hurt me" through tear-stained faces, they recognized the immense power of words and symbols to hurt. People's symbol use makes a difference in interpersonal relationships, too.

Symbols matter. Your professional self-image is influenced by how others describe you. If you have received a positive job review, you know the power of words to make you feel better about yourself. If you grew up in the United States and have been in a serious relationship, you know the power of the words "I love you" or the significance of a gold band worn on the ring finger. Most people do not speak the words lightly. The symbolism of a ring extends far beyond the typical meaning of an expensive gift of jewelry. The value of the ring is far more than its weight in gold.

People's symbol use also makes a difference in public communication. The words of public figures, as well as symbols of citizenship, possess the power to lead, reflect, inspire, praise, unite, confront, provoke, and entertain.

Words led a nation to reflect on the effects of racism when Martin Luther King, Jr., at the 1963 March on Washington, said, "I have a dream that one day on the red hills of Georgia, the sons of former slaves and the sons of former slave owners will be able to sit down together at the table of brotherhood."[17]

Words spoken from a very particular body inspired the world to fight for education when Malala Yousafzai, the youngest Nobel Laureate in history, delivered her Nobel Prize acceptance speech. After the Taliban took over Pakistan's Swat Valley, Yousafzai, then a fifteen-year-old schoolgirl and already an activist for girls' education, was shot in the face by a gunman who boarded her school bus and asked for her by name. In her speech, Yousafzai described the changes that the Swat Valley had undergone, then the changes experienced by schoolgirls:

> Girls were stopped from going to school. When my world suddenly
> changed, my priorities changed too. I had two options. One was to remain
> silent and wait to be killed. And the second was to speak up and then be
> killed. I chose the second one. I decided to speak up. . . . The terrorists
> tried to stop us and attacked me and my friends . . . on our school bus in
> 2012, but neither their ideas nor their bullets could win. We survived. And
> since that day, our voices have grown louder and louder. I tell my story, not
> because it is unique, but because it is not. It is the story of many girls.[18]

Words praised sacrifice and outlined a course for the future when Abraham Lincoln, in remarks at the Gettysburg battlefield in 1863, said, "But in a larger sense we cannot dedicate, we cannot consecrate, we cannot hallow this ground. The brave men, living and dead, who struggled here, have consecrated it far above our power to add or detract."[19] Theodore Sorensen, speech writer for President John F. Kennedy, described Lincoln's Gettysburg Address as the "greatest example of American public speech."[20]

Words united a nation when President George W. Bush, on September 11, 2001, said, "None of us will ever forget this day, yet we go forward to defend freedom and all that is good and just in our world."[21]

Words confronted a nation when Malcolm X, speaking out against the Senate filibuster of the Civil Rights Act of 1964, said "No, if you never see me another time in your life, if I die in the morning, I'll die saying one thing: the ballot or the bullet, the ballot or the bullet."[22]

Rhetorical action is not confined to politicians. Although those who have institutional power were long the focus of study, it is as important to study the rhetoric of those without access to the halls of power, political leadership positions, or the platforms to deliver public addresses to which audiences feel obliged to listen.[23] Tweets, Facebook posts, testimony to legislative hearings, conversations, and memes are just a few examples of rhetoric. The point is: Every person uses rhetoric in civic life.

Spoken words are not the only form of rhetoric. Visual symbols, too, can enrage and provoke, as when Andres Serrano placed a crucifix in a jar of urine as a work of art.[24] Images can also induce us to see the world in different ways. For example, US presidential election maps that color states red and blue might create the wrong impression that one side won because more of the map is in that color. Such maps also create the impression of total agreement within a state. However, if you redraw the map based on population or electoral votes, it becomes clearer which color won the most votes, rather than just the most land mass as represented by state borders.[25]

What people communicate, and how they communicate it, has real effects on others and their perceptions. People cannot know what things or events mean until they have the symbols to attach meaning to them.

Because symbols have power and are grounded in ideas, people can use them to induce others to take ethical, as well as unethical, actions. During World War II, Winston Churchill delivered speeches to the British people to rally them to defend democracy and to US audiences to encourage them to become involved in the war. In the wake of British Prime Minister Neville Chamberlain's appeasement of Adolf Hitler on September 30, 1938, and German troops' occupation of the Sudetenland on October 15, Churchill, who at that time served no official role in the British government, sought to persuade the United States to defend democracy. On October 16, Churchill warned, "The lights are going out. . . . We need the swift gathering of forces to confront not only military but moral aggression." He appealed to "English-speaking peoples" and "all the nations, great and small, who wish to walk with them. Their faithful and zealous comradeship would almost between night and morning clear the path of progress and banish from all our lives the fear which already darkens the sunlight to hundreds of millions of men."[26] He painted Hitler's forces as a darkness, smothering the lights of freedom; only the help of the United States could guarantee that Europeans would again see the sunlight of living in a free land. Churchill's speeches would help frame understandings of what the war in Europe meant to people living in the United States.

At the same time, Adolph Hitler was persuading the German people to engage in horrific crimes against humanity and to wage total war. Using the metaphor of disease, Hitler announced on April 1, 1939: "Only when this Jewish bacillus infecting the life of peoples has been removed can one hope to establish a cooperation amongst the nations which shall be built up on a lasting understanding."[27] The vileness of this metaphor becomes clear in Hitler's call for an absolute eradication of the "Jewish bacillus" in order to save the German fatherland from disease. Infection can only be stopped when all the infection is removed. Hitler's use of language was dastardly as it sought the "perfection" of an Aryan nation. For Hitler, the Aryan race could only be saved if all Jewish people were eradicated.

These examples illustrate why rhetoric is profoundly important to civic life. Rhetoric can enlighten and confuse, reveal and hide. Churchill and Hitler both used rhetoric, but for very different purposes. Accordingly, the study of rhetoric involves not only an assessment of its effects (both Churchill and Hitler were effective) but also of its ethics. (Churchill sought to defend freedom; Hitler sought the genocidal destruction of an entire people.) Rhetoric is more than just words or images; it is a form of symbolic action.

Symbols

A **symbol** is *an arbitrary representation of something else: a word, an image, or an artifact that represents a thing, thought, or action.* The symbol $ represents the US dollar, although the symbol ∂ could just as easily be used. The US flag represents the nation and its values. A cross represents belief in a Christian faith; a Star of David, in Judaism; and a crescent moon, in Islam. Sports teams are often identified by their mascots or symbols. The logo of the Alabama Crimson Tide is an elephant![28] Sports teams' logos change. For instance, the Nebraska Cornhuskers were originally the Nebraska Bug Eaters. The logo for the Kansas Jayhawks has changed at least six times over the years.[29] These symbols or logos could have been almost anything. However, fans of the Crimson Tide, the Cornhuskers, or the Jayhawks typically feel strong connections to those symbols.

Symbols can be verbal, visual, or multisensory. **Verbal symbols** are *symbols found in language* (whether spoken or written). Every word is a symbol insofar as it stands for something other than itself. When you use the term "dog," the word stands for an animal in the canine family. Other languages also have words for "dog" (perro/perra, suka, псина, 狗, chien, cane, hund, سگ). Symbols are by nature human constructions rather than innate to the things symbolized. Although people often think of symbols as abstractions, they may not think of words as symbolic. Yet, language is inherently a symbol system, with written languages using alphabets and with spoken languages using sounds to form words that name and represent things, ideas, and people. Every word you use is a symbol.

Visual symbols are *symbols such as pictures, images, objects, artifacts, and embodied actions.* Examples include photographs, religious icons, tattoos, statues, flags, bodies, movies, YouTube clips, and even the acts of kneeling or marching.

The US flag is a banner of three colors sewn together, yet it is more than just a piece of fabric; it symbolically represents the nation. Symbols convey meaning and, in the process, influence how people encounter the world.[30] Although scholars for many years confined the study of rhetoric to the study of verbal symbols, they now recognize the importance of visual symbols.[31]

The meaning of a symbol is not the same for everyone. The fluidity of meaning is clear even when you consider language-based symbols. For example, the word "apple" can refer to a fruit or to a technology company. If the word is used to refer to the technology company, people will still have quite different responses to it. Some people will stand in line for hours to buy the newest Apple products because they believe the company is innovative, cutting edge, and cool. Some are hostile to the company and would never buy an Apple product. Others are indifferent.

Although we describe verbal and visual symbols separately, almost all symbolic action is a mix of verbal and visual symbols. People listen to—and watch—speeches. People read—and look at—magazines and websites. People hear—and gaze at—movies.

Symbolic Action

When people use symbols, they engage in action. Our definition of rhetoric focuses on the fact that humans use symbols to engage in actions with consequences. For example, when people exchange marriage vows and rings in a wedding ceremony, their actions create a new social relationship. The symbolic actions that compose a marriage ceremony (clothing, ring, vows, witnesses) create meaning beyond the wedding license the couple signs.

Things around you engage in motion: trees are moved by the wind, water by the tide, and earth by quakes (even if human actions such as the production of greenhouse gases, destruction of wetland coastal buffers, and fracking contribute to these events). What distinguishes human action from these motions is that it involves some level of intent and can be communicated about and reflected upon.[32] Human beings act on their environment in a variety of ways, such as by walking, driving, planting a garden, and eating food. All these actions are instrumental—specific actions taken in order to cause an effect. Human action is almost always more than instrumental, however. It is also expressive and meaning-making: It is symbolic.

Symbolic action is *expressive human action, the rhetorical mobilization of symbols to act in and affect the world.* Symbolic actions include, but are not limited to, speeches, silent marches, movies, memes, documentaries, plays, blogs, newspaper articles, advertisements, photographs, sit-ins, personal testimonies, monuments, YouTube videos, tweets, Instagram posts, and street theatre. People act in the world through symbol use that induces cooperation, generates identification, produces division, enables persuasion, and constitutes identity. Thus, when people study rhetoric, they need to ask not only what a rhetorical action *means,* but also what it *does.* Because rhetoric is the study of symbolic action, it studies not only symbols and their meanings, but also their consequences.[33]

FUNCTIONS OF SYMBOLIC ACTION

Rhetoric as symbolic action does many things. A few specific functions of rhetoric are to create identification, constitute identity, and construct social reality.

Identification

Rhetorical critic Kenneth Burke, an influential twentieth-century scholar, argues that two things distinguish rhetoric: it requires an audience and it creates a sense of connection between the rhetor and the audience. Burke argues that the creation of identification between rhetor and audience is an essential characteristic of rhetoric and an integral element of persuasion. **Identification** is *a communicative process through which people are unified into a whole on the basis of common interests or characteristics.*[34]

Burke believes identification is central to rhetoric because "there is no chance of keeping apart the meaning of persuasion, identification ('consubstantiality') and communication (the nature of rhetoric as 'addressed' [to other people])."[35] If rhetoric is about addressing audiences, then the relationship of the audience to the rhetor must be considered; identification becomes a central rhetorical concept. To make decisions about matters of common concern, people need to be able to identify what they have in common. According to Burke, once "their interests are joined, A is *identified* with B."[36] Identification does not automatically exist; it is created through symbolic action.

Given the influence of Aristotle, the classical Greek philosopher who first systematized the study of rhetoric in a treatise titled *On Rhetoric,* attention to "persuasion" long dominated studies of rhetoric. Now, "identification" is a key term for what is known as "the new rhetoric."[37] With identification, the focus is less on how one person can "deliberate[ly] design" symbolic action as a stimulus to persuade other people as the provoked response, and more on how symbolic actions "spontaneously, intuitively, and often unconsciously act upon" people to create a sense of collective identity.[38]

Identification can be created on the basis of demographic characteristics over which a person has limited control (sex, ethnicity, racial category, class, sexual orientation) or on the basis of common interests (such as improving elementary and secondary education, lowering college tuition, or ending discrimination). Although Burke notes that "in forming ideas of our personal identity, we spontaneously identify ourselves with family, nation, political or cultural cause, church and so on," he also recognizes that rhetors induce listeners to feel identification with them.[39] The rhetor and audience become "consubstantial," or "substantially one."[40] In ways that matter, they share substance; they are connected.

Burke does not say that people who identify with each other become identical; indeed, identification allows for the maintenance of distinctions even as it creates a sense of unity. Burke explains that when identification makes a person "substantially one" with another, "at the same time [the person] remains unique, an individual locus of motives. Thus, [the person] is both joined and separate, at once a distinct substance and consubstantial with another."[41] Identification "does not deny [people's] distinctness."[42] People often assume identification means that people who identify with one another are identical, but in a complex society, such a perspective on collective and collaborative action is doomed to fail. For example, a metaphor often used for the people of the United States is "melting pot," which implies that all the people who come here are blended into one indistinguishable mass. But becoming one is not the only way to identify with another person.

Communication professor Isaac West uses political theorist Danielle Allen's work to explain how people seek to share identification through citizenship by thinking about "wholeness, as opposed to oneness."[43] Distinct people, when they identify with one another, become a consubstantial *whole,* not an indistinguishable *one.* When you identify with other people, you do not transform into them, but you do share something important with them.

For example, what does it mean to identify as being part of a people? Allen details how a metaphor of "oneness"—of being identical *to* rather than identifying *with* others—has long dominated the way persons in the United States have thought of themselves as one people.[44] The ideal of the melting pot, references to assimilation creating "one people," the pledge to "one nation under God," or the invocation of *e pluribus unum* (out of many, one) on the national seal, and many other messages induce people to see themselves through the lens of oneness.

However, Allen details how, in the history of segregation and reservations in the United States, "division, not unity, has marked" individuals' lived experiences. Writing about the desegregation of Central High School in Little Rock, Arkansas, in September 1957, Allen notes that at that time the people of the United States were not one people, "but at least two, and maybe three, four, or more, peoples." What distinguished these peoples from each other? Because of Jim Crow and reservation systems, Blacks and Native Americans lived under "different laws, with differential rights and powers, with different habitual practices of citizenship."[45]

Allen offers *wholeness* as an alternative to *oneness* because it recognizes the multiplicity that is typical of democracies. In democracies, the goal is not "homogeneity," but the "coherence and integrity" of connections among all the people, as diverse as they might be, who form the polity.[46] The goal is identification across differences, not the suppression and homogenization of differences. Thus, West argues, when people seek to identify on the basis of shared citizenship, they do not have to "rely on an either/or logic of assimilation" or radical difference. Instead, they can think of citizenship as "both/and." A person might "desire to be a citizen like everyone else even as an individual wants to preserve [their] difference."[47] Thus, alternative metaphors such as "quilt" or "mosaic" may make more sense than "melting pot" to represent the shared US identity.

People can communicate and persuade most effectively when they induce their audiences to identify with them. For example, abolitionist Angelina Grimké Weld used identification when facing mob violence in Philadelphia on May 16, 1838, during her speech to an antislavery convention. The challenge to the audience was to consider whether they wanted to identify with Grimké Weld and enslaved people, or with the angry mob outside. While Grimké Weld was being introduced to the audience of three thousand men and women, "bricks crashed through the windows and glass fell to the floor."[48] As she spoke, the mob outside the hall grew increasingly agitated, throwing stones and screaming during the hour-long speech. Although the audience inside the hall was receptive to the message because they already opposed slavery, the mob outside felt threatened by the argument that slavery was not an objective fact, but an immoral choice. Not wanting the mob to weaken the audience's resolve, Grimké Weld artistically turned the mob response into proof that slavery should be abolished. She challenged the audience to use their fear of the mob as a basis for identifying with enslaved people's fear of violence from their masters:

> What is a mob? What would the breaking of every window be? What would the levelling of this Hall be? Any evidence that we are wrong, or that slavery is a good and wholesome institution? What if the mob should now burst in upon us, break up our meeting and commit violence upon our persons—would this be anything compared with what the slaves endure? No, no: and we do not remember them "as bound with them" [Heb. 13:3], if we shrink in the time of peril, or feel unwilling to sacrifice ourselves, if need be, for their sake. (*Great noise.*) I thank the Lord that there is yet life left enough to feel the truth, even though it rages at it—that conscience is not so completely seared as to be unmoved by the truth of the living God.[49]

By comparing the threat of mob violence to the constant threat of violence under which enslaved people lived, Grimké Weld used the moment to induce the audience to identify with enslaved people.[50] The argument was not that Whites' experience was identical to enslaved people's experiences, but that all, White and Black, free and enslaved, were part of a larger whole of humanity.

Identification that provides a sense of wholeness can bring people together to address and solve common problems. Identification based on a sense of oneness, though, can separate people by constructing "us" versus "them" dichotomies. If being identical is required for identification, then any difference becomes suspect. For instance, Adolf Hitler induced non-Jewish German people to identify themselves as members of a superior race, an Aryan nation, thus dividing themselves from Jewish German people.

Identification can function for good or ill, unity or division. It can be used to recognize common concerns or disguise them, to solve common concerns or create new concerns.

Constitutive Rhetoric

A specific term is used to name how identification can be used to create a people, nation, or collective. Literary and legal scholar James Boyd White defines **constitutive rhetoric** as "*the art of constituting character, community, and culture in language.*"[51] Here, "constituting" means forming or creating. For example, drafting and ratifying a constitution forms, or creates, a nation. As communication scholar James Jasinski writes, constitutive rhetoric works by inviting an "audience to experience the world in certain ways."[52] It invites them to see the character of a people, the membership in a community, or the qualities of a culture in a particular way.

Group identity is rhetorically constructed rather than an unchanging and innate sense of self, group, and nation. Thus, rhetoric scholar Maurice Charland says, students of rhetoric should ask "how those in Athens [or Texas, the United States, Ukraine, or Russia] come to experience themselves as Athenians [or Texans, Americans, Ukrainians, or Russians]."[53] Charland explains that in constitutive rhetoric, "the very boundary of whom the term ['people'] includes and excludes is rhetorically constructed."[54] A particular identity may actually exclude some people from membership. Sometimes the very identity is based on exclusions, or on what Judith Butler and others refer to as the "constitutive outside."[55]

For example, consider how national identity is constituted. Max Fisher, the *New York Times* host of "The Interpreter," explains "Nationality feels so powerful. We fight for our country, we cheer for it, we draw our values from it. It's a big way many of us describe who we are."[56] But identifying with others on the basis of national borders is a relatively recent phenomenon. Historically, people identified on the basis of smaller groups such as clans, religion, or family. Now, though, millions of strangers identify on the basis of borders, which create a "made-up" commonality. Because language and ethnicity do not align with borders, nations use constitutive rhetoric to create a national identity that generates a sense of cohesion. National identity "changes our reality; we experience whatever happens to our nation as if it happened to us."[57] The reality constituted by national identity involves not only internal cohesion but also external exclusion, and thus "primes us for dictatorship, racism, genocide."[58]

Understanding symbolic action as constitutive encourages thinking about how rhetoric creates people's understanding of themselves, their relations to each other, and the world. According to Jasinski, that understanding moves the effects of rhetoric "beyond a narrow causal model of influence."[59] Studying rhetoric is not about identifying a stimulus and a response, but about discovering how meaning is created, maintained, and changed. The power of rhetoric to shape people's ideas of themselves, each other, and the world around them inspired Burke to define human beings as the "symbol-using (symbol-making, symbol-misusing) animal."[60] Thus, the study of rhetoric provides insights into what it means to be human. For Burke, rhetoric is rooted in *the use of language as a symbolic means of inducing cooperation in beings that by nature respond to symbols.*"[61] Because we respond to symbols, it is important to understand how symbols do what they do.

Constructing Social Reality

Rhetoric is more than a means to transmit information or persuade. When people engage in symbolic action, they participate in the construction of social reality. Saying that rhetoric "constructs social reality" does not mean that people and things do not exist prior to human symbolic action. Rather, the *meaning* people ascribe to the things in their world is not predetermined, but created by symbolic action. Although people may know things exist apart from their symbol systems, they cannot know what those things mean or how to react to them except through the symbol system. Thus, social reality is constructed—it is made and not given.

Social reality is *reality as understood through the symbols humans use to represent it.* People create social reality as they name objects, actions, concepts, and each other. Although a material world exists from which human beings receive sensory data, they do not know how to interact with that world until symbolic action gives meaning to that data. People's only access to reality is through symbols.

Communication scholar Barry Brummett argues that "experience is sensation plus meaning" and "reality is meaning."[62] For example, a study in the *Journal of Consumer Research* found that when a dish is called "pasta" rather than a "salad" (even though the ingredients are identical), dieters (who are motivated to identify "forbidden foods") "perceive the item to be less healthful and less tasty than do nondieters."[63] Similar effects were found in comparing perceptions of the terms "candy chews" and "fruit chews." The researchers found "the effect of food name on perceptions of healthfulness is pervasive; it does not subside with the presentation of pictures of food items and their ingredients, nor does it diminish when consumers have an opportunity to consume the product."[64] The name determines the meaning of the sensations, regardless of sensory input of taste, sight, smell, and touch, and regardless of people's objective knowledge of ingredients.

Symbolic action—words, images, and artifacts—construct, maintain, and transform social reality. Communication scholar Kevin Michael DeLuca argues that people should understand rhetoric as "discerning [studying] and deploying [using] the available contingent means of constructing, maintaining, and transforming social reality in a particular context."[65] Imagine if you lived in a world devoid of symbolic action. You could not speak, upload video on social media, send a selfie, post a meme, draw, pray, or engage in any action with symbolic importance. You also could not read, listen to music, watch videos, or receive others' symbolic actions. You would still have sensory experiences, but those experiences would be deprived of meaning. Would you still feel human? Would you still possess the characteristics that make you human? Would you know how to act in the world or react to others? Symbolic action is not just an instrumental means to transmit information; it is central to making meaning of, and in, the world.

CIVIC ENGAGEMENT

Our definition of rhetoric focuses on the use of symbolic action to identify and solve issues of common concern, and to construct social reality. A key aspect of that definition is that rhetoric is a social activity, meaning that it occurs among people. Thus, rhetoric has always been linked to social action and civic engagement.

Civic engagement is *people's participation in individual or collective action to construct identity and develop solutions to social, economic, and political challenges in their communities, states, nations, and world.* It includes talking with others about ballot initiatives or pending legislation, using social networking sites for activism, volunteering with community organizations, being present in places from which others have excluded you, testifying to a city council or board of trustees, participating in parades (whether celebratory or protest), working for electoral campaigns, wearing T-shirts with political messages, signing petitions, voting, writing letters to the editor, engaging in buycotts and boycotts, and posting to blogs. Change (and maintenance) of social, political, and economic structures is accomplished through civic engagement, and civic engagement is accomplished through rhetoric.

Rhetorician Gerard A. Hauser reviewed the scholarly research on why citizens engage in civic action in their communities, and found consensus that the absolutely necessary requirement for "a well-functioning civic community is engagement in the . . . rhetoric of civil society."[66] The use of rhetoric is not confined to people campaigning for office, nor are citizens' roles in rhetorical action confined to membership in audiences. Civic engagement helps each person understand who they are. Rhetorician Bruce Gronbeck argued that "civic engagement . . . is as much a matter of understanding the building and maintenance of political identity . . . as it is about getting legislation passed."[67] People use rhetoric as they develop identity (as individuals, citizens, and members of groups) and determine what should be done (by them as individuals and for them through legislation). They use rhetoric as they develop conceptions of themselves as individuals, group members, and citizens, all of whom can make a claim on others and on the government to act legislatively.

The root word of "civic" is the Latin term *civis,* which means "citizen" or "city." We emphasize the root meaning "city": a collection of people bound together in space and time, strangers who need to learn to live together. We are inspired by rhetorician Karma Chávez's call to avoid orienting rhetoric toward the "legal and administrative designation" of citizenship, but to honor and witness the "civic, community, and activist practices" and "the lives, experiences, and practices of numerous collectives and individuals" who use rhetoric.[68] Regardless of citizenship status, people participate in civic engagement. The examples we use throughout the book are meant to celebrate civic rhetorical practices.

Rhetorical engagement in a democratic society is essential to the decision-making process in situations as mundane as a group of people deciding where to eat dinner (at a national chain or at a restaurant that supports local farmers) to situations as serious as determining which campus groups are funded, which laws are passed, and which wars are declared. Although people's reasons for doing things can be personal, those reasons can be expressed to and contested with other people. To truly enter the realm of rhetoric, people must be open to having their minds changed and to providing the reasons for their beliefs. They must engage with others. When they do, they must be willing to provide reasons, listen, and modify their positions. This process of interaction and modification of positions is essential to decision making in an open society.

For example, if members of a campus group disagreed about how to spend a thousand dollars, it would not be productive if each person simply stated: I want the money spent *this* way, period. Instead, for the group to decide collectively what to do, each person would have to articulate the reason the money should be spent in a particular way. As people gave their reasons, some shared interests might become clear, at which point each person could see the merits in others' ideas. As the discussion proceeded, agreement might emerge. Or, it might become clear that the group members had totally competing interests, so that agreement could never be reached. At that point, they may find that the disagreement is less about what to do with the money (policy) and more about what it means to be a member of the group (identity).

Unfortunately, modern society increasingly allows people to refuse such interactions. The fragmentation of media enables you to seek out and listen only to those with whom you agree. When exchanges of diverse opinions do occur, it is becoming more common to hear people refuse to participate. You probably have heard comments such as "we'll just have to agree to disagree," or "it works for me," or "I don't have time to get involved," or even just "whatever." These comments are a way of ending discussion and debate about differing opinions and ideas, rather than actually engaging people. They are antithetical to decision making based on the principles of rhetoric. Social media make it easy to block, mute, or unfollow people with whom you disagree. Agreeing to disagree, or ignoring those with whom you disagree, is not always a viable option. Sometime, people need to choose between competing options and ideas.

What differentiates an open and free society from a closed, fascist, and dictatorial society is its willingness to tolerate the open expression of differing ideas and beliefs. In an open society, communication serves personal, epistemological, and political functions. It serves a personal function when it enables people to express themselves, communicating and developing their senses of self. It serves an epistemological function when it enables people to test their ideas and to develop knowledge. It serves a political function when it enables people to participate in the processes of governance.

All of these functions, however, rely on an embrace of "**stranger relationality**,"[69] *a willingness to communicate with others to develop "collective self-understanding that acknowledges mutual interdependence with strangers" and in ways that focus on the public good instead of simply seeing one's self as "seeking to maximize individual power" through purchasing and economic decisions.*[70] Although you may know everyone in your family, you probably do not know everyone in your city. To be civic, to be of a city, you need to be comfortable with those who are strangers. President Abraham Lincoln's ideal of a "government of the people, by the people, for the people" cannot be realized if the people do not participate in civic life where they see themselves as part of a whole people.[71]

Open communication is not to be feared. Ideas with which you disagree should not be avoided or suppressed. Instead, all people should develop the critical faculties that enable them to judge which ideas are persuasive, which expressions are worthy of assent, and which ideas should define their characters. People need the right to express their opinions, the skills and knowledge to do so, and a government and society willing to consider and respond to those opinions. Democracies require habits of rhetorical engagement.

Your own rhetoric and your ability to listen to the rhetoric of others are essential to an open society. Thus, a free press and its ability to report on public issues fulfills a political function when it serves as a check on government abuses. For these reasons, the United States has a long tradition of protecting open communication, which it codified in the First Amendment to the Constitution. Supreme Court Justice Holmes articulated this trust in freely exchanged ideas in 1919:

> [T]he ultimate good desired is better reached by free trade in ideas—that the best test of truth is the power of the thought to get itself accepted in the competition of the market, and that truth is the only ground upon which their wishes safely can be carried out. That, at any rate, is the theory of our Constitution. It is an experiment, as all life is an experiment. Every year, if not every day, we have to wager our salvation upon some prophecy based upon imperfect knowledge. While that experiment is part of our system, I think that we should be eternally vigilant against attempts to check the expression of opinions that we loathe and believe to be fraught with death, unless they so imminently threaten immediate interference with the lawful and pressing purposes of the law that an immediate check is required to save the country.[72]

Whenever you engage in this free exchange of ideas, you act, meaning you exercise rhetorical agency. The habits you take to those interactions are central to whether civic life is vibrant or not. Thus, we encourage you to develop habits of political friendship. We explore these concepts in the following sections.

Rhetorical Agency

When you study rhetoric you study how people act rhetorically on each other, as well as how rhetoric acts on people. In other words, you study **rhetorical agency,** which rhetorician Karlyn Kohrs Campbell defines as *"the capacity to act, that is, to have the competence to speak or write [or engage in any form of symbolic action] in a way that will be recognized or heeded by others in one's community."*[73] Individuals are capable of intentional symbolic action, but that action occurs within a larger web of symbolic action that may help or hinder willingness to recognize or heed other people's messages. Whether someone's message is "recognized or heeded" by others in the community is affected by many things, including who is considered a part of the community, previous rhetorical actions, communication technologies, public vocabularies, and shared social values.

For many years, approaches to rhetorical agency came from the humanist tradition, which focuses on an ideal of an autonomous human agent engaging in action.[74] In this tradition, people studied individual speakers to see what choices they made and how those choices influenced other choices. More recently, rhetorical scholars have recognized that no one is an island. Because humans are isolated neither from one another nor from history, rhetorical agency is better understood as existing within a larger system of interactions.

Rhetorician Christian O. Lundberg notes, "The human is not the only or even primary agent in the rhetorical situation."[75] This view operates within the **posthumanist theory of agency,** which, rhetorician Sarah Hallenbeck explains, is *a theory that "rejects the human agent as the primary source of change but* *redeems that agent as a participant in the larger network of which [they are] a part."* Hallenbeck claims that the choices individuals make are circumscribed by a variety of factors, ranging from socioeconomic conditions, to language constraints, to the people with whom the individuals are interacting. "Hence," Hallenbeck explains, "agency occurs not solely within the realm of human intention or as the direct result of human action but somewhat outside of human control."[76] A rhetor has agency in any given rhetorical action, but so do others involved in that action.

Put simply, much is outside the control of rhetors. To understand rhetoric, scholars must account for the factors over which rhetors lack control and also for the factors that control the rhetor. Posthumanist theories incorporate these assumptions, arguing that rhetorical scholars should move beyond an exclusive focus on the individual human agent and, instead, attend to the multiple forces at play in rhetorical agency. Thinking about agency as a complex interplay of forces means studying how the rhetor came to be perceived as the rhetor, as well as how symbolic action circulates through groups of people, structures of language, technology, and other things[77] that constrain, produce, and condition the possibility for the human to be an agent.

Consider the hand gesture that once meant "OK" (the index and thumb forming a circle while the three other fingers stick up). In 2017, some people tried to stage a hoax on the 4chan website by falsely claiming that the sign did not signify "OK," but "WP" for "white power" (the three upright fingers forming the W, the circle and wrist forming the P). They were trying to induce an overreaction from people who oppose white supremacy, making them appear foolish when they reacted to people who were only using the OK symbol. Then white supremacists actually started using the sign in selfies or in public. In March 2019, an "Australian white supremacist . . . flashed the symbol during . . . a courtroom appearance" after being arrested "for allegedly murdering 50 people in a shooting spree at mosques in Christchurch, New Zealand."[78] (In August 2020, the shooter was convicted and sentenced to life without parole.)

Even though the original posters' intent was to create a hoax, they actually created a rhetorical action that came to signify adherence to white supremacy. In May 2019 the Chicago Cubs organization banned a person from Wrigley Field for life after he flashed the sign behind NBC sports reporter Doug Glanville.[79] Even though the evidence convinced the Cubs organization that the fan meant the sign as a racist taunt against the reporter, some people did not understand why "just an OK sign" might get a person banned from a stadium for life.[80] As this example illustrates, the meaning of a symbol is not necessarily determined by the rhetor or by the audience; moreover, the meaning of a symbol can change across time. This example might also induce you to be careful about using the gesture, lest it be understood in ways you never intended.

Political Friendship

A commitment to rhetoric as civic action, as well as the ability to see themselves as agents of action, enabled high school students who survived a school shooting to become activists to address a problem. Even former senator Santorum's argument against them—that they should not respond by seeking to get laws passed—was rhetorical: Santorum attempted to persuade the audience of what was, or was not, an appropriate response and offered alternative responses. His response, however, failed to recognize what those who study rhetoric have known since the inception of that study: the value of public deliberation. Santorum did not argue that institutional policies, such as universal background checks or allowing the Centers for Disease Control to research gun violence, were ineffective. Instead, he exhorted the students to focus on individual and internal actions. In other words, he called for the student activists from to step out of public participation and back into private life. Such downsizing of democracy sacrifices one of the central benefits of civic culture: the process of engaged, democratic deliberation among people with competing ideas leads to wiser solutions.

Particularly on issues with personal connections, such as gun control or abortion, engaging in such debates can be challenging. How might people argue productively about issues that seem irresolvable? Aristotle, who authored treatises on rhetoric and politics, offered a valuable perspective on how members of a civic culture might communicate with one another: not only as equals, but as friends. In the contemporary political landscape, the idea of treating people on other parts of the political spectrum as friends may seem unpleasant, offensive, or hopelessly naïve. But Aristotle was writing in an Athens that was no more ideal than today: this was a city that literally made an elderly teacher, Socrates, drink poison for saying things with which the city leaders disagreed.

Yet, consider how seeing those with whom you argue as friends might change how you engage them. We encourage an ethic of **political friendship,** *a set of habits people use in civic spaces to interact and make decisions with people who might be strangers or who have different identities, interests, or needs.* These habits guide attitudes and practices.

In contrast to attempts to achieve the power to accomplish an agenda, friendship is based on a willingness to compromise. If every time you met with friends, they were only willing to talk about what they wanted to discuss, eat only at their favorite restaurant, and do only the things they wanted, you would probably not continue being friends. Friends share power within a relationship: you talk about topics on all your minds, you consider options until you find a restaurant you can all enjoy, you take turns doing the activities you each want. Nor do you demand that your friends tone-check everything they say to you; you are willing to engage with your friends even when they present arguments in what you might deem an "inappropriate" way. You are probably willing to make these compromises because your commitment to the relationship is greater than your desire to always get your way. If the commitment is reciprocal, you see that your friends are also willing to compromise, because the benefits of the relationship outweigh the cost of not always getting your own way. Aristotle saw such a commitment as essential to political friendship.[81]

This is not to say all citizens will or should enjoy spending time with one another. Aristotle recognized that political friendships lack the emotional component of other forms of friendship, but the commitment to maintain them is mutually beneficial.[82] This recognition informs philosopher Hannah Arendt's belief that healthy democracy necessitates that people engage one another with political respect, "a kind of friendship without intimacy and without closeness."[83]

We turn to political theorist Danielle Allen to translate these historical concepts into the contemporary moment. Allen recognizes that Aristotle's idea of political friendship requires that people interact with those whom they may not know (people who are strangers) in the same way they would interact with people whom they do know (people who are friends), in ways that look and sound the same.[84] She is not saying all people should "just be friends" or that the goal is to make friends with strangers on the basis of something you have in common. Political friendship is not about feelings but practices—habits—of interaction:

> Friendship is not an emotion, but a practice, a set of hard-won,
> complicated habits that are used to bridge trouble, difficulty, and
> differences of personality, experience, and aspiration. Friendship is not
> easy, nor is democracy. Friendship begins in the recognition that friends
> have a *shared* life—not a "common" nor an identical life—only one
> with common events, climates, built-environments, fixations of the
> imagination, and social structures.[85]

The habits that guide how you treat friends enable those relationships to weather disagreements and allow you to understand one another better. Seeing others as friends does not require you to see them as the same as you; in fact, it is more interesting to think about which practices of citizenship enable identification that makes a people whole rather than one, that enable people to identify with one another while not denying their differences.[86]

The practice of political friendship requires a willingness to listen, take turns, compromise, and make sacrifices for one another based on a mutual commitment to the relationship. Friendship is not a shallow performance of civility. It allows for honest judgments and criticisms of ideas, so long as they are communicated with the same grace that you would show a friend.

Such a commitment can require substantial changes in how people engage in rhetoric. In a moment of increasing political polarization, imagine the potential benefits of speaking and listening to one another as friends: of listening even when it is uncomfortable. You would not dismiss friends who refuse to say only things you want to hear; sometimes, a friend is the only one who will confront you with your deepest failings. Make sure, though, that just as you might seek to correct a friend who has made a mistake, you are willing to correct the mistakes of the society in which you live.[87]

We are persuaded by Allen's argument that citizenship is not just voting, paying taxes, or serving on juries (although it does include all these things). Allen does not tie citizenship to only a legal status. Instead, she argues that citizenship is a set of "long-enduring habits of interaction" that shape civic life and people's understanding of their role in it.[88] She calls for civic habits that are not limited to formal interactions in legislative chambers, but that are also a part of daily interactions. She notes that "citizens enact what they are to each other ... when, as strangers, they speak to one another, or don't, or otherwise respond to each other's presence."[89] Engaging with one another, responding to each other's presence, is central to civic engagement. Civic engagement occurs in places of recognized political power, such as legislative assemblies and hearings, but also in our daily interactions. This book explores how to *do* citizenship, how civic engagement requires practice to become a habit.[90] We explore habits of rhetoric in civic life.

Civic engagement and practices of citizenship were long defined narrowly in terms of the specific acts of voting and civic organization membership.[91] Research using this approach tends to see civic engagement as on the decline, as fewer people vote or belong to civic organizations. Rhetorician Robert Asen is not so pessimistic. He advocates a different perspective, arguing that analysis of citizenship should focus, not on citizenship as an act, but as a process of action. Thus, the question is: How do people enact citizenship and civic engagement? The answer is: through rhetoric. Civic engagement as a process, a "mode of public engagement," means that participation in society has many different forms, all of which involve rhetorical habits.[92]

Asen argues that rhetoric is central to civic engagement because it is an act of interacting and engaging with others: "Engagement positions people as rhetorical agents hoping to persuade and/or seek recognition from others of their views, even as it recognizes that others hope to do the same. Commitment thus extends to a commitment to interaction itself."[93] Thus, to understand citizenship as more than just a legal status, Asen examines the processes by which people engage and interact with each other. He explores how people come to understand themselves—through rhetoric—as members of groups and as individuals, and how "actions that begin on a small scale may spread across social, cultural, and political sites."[94] Civic engagement occurs when people engage in communication that generates new areas for discussion, when they are willing to accept the risk of being wrong (and accept correction of their views), when they affirm a commitment to engage one another in discourse, and when they engage in creative forms of communication that build social connections.

CONCLUSION

Our goal in this book is to introduce you to some of the joys and responsibilities of rhetorical action in civic life. Democracy is not a spectator sport, nor is life. To be able to participate, you need to understand how rhetoric works, and that it is at work in a variety of places: politics, religion, family, sports, entertainment, small town life, and workplaces. The ability to attach meaning to the world and to make sense of that meaning requires an understanding of rhetoric.

Rhetoric is essential to the functioning of civic culture. Rhetoric in open societies enables citizens to challenge the actions of those in power and to engage each other in discussions and debates over what is right—for individuals, communities, the nation, and the world. Civic engagement is much more than the act of voting. It necessitates that you engage with other people, that you treat strangers as political friends, and that you participate in symbolic actions that constitute your identity as a person, a group member, and a citizen.

DISCUSSION QUESTIONS

1. Give examples of ways people are civically engaged outside the traditional electoral process. Explain how rhetoric is involved with these forms of engagement.
2. Have you ever argued about a contentious issue with a close friend? How do you engage in that argument differently from the way you would with a classmate or stranger?
3. What is rhetorical agency? How does a posthumanist theory change how agency is understood?

RECOMMENDED READINGS

Allen, Danielle S. *Talking to Strangers*. Chicago: University of Chicago Press, 2004.

Aristotle. *On Rhetoric*. Translated by George A. Kennedy. New York: Oxford University Press, 1991.

Asen, Robert. "A Discourse Theory of Citizenship." *Quarterly Journal of Speech* 90, no. 2 (2004): 189–211.

Charland, Maurice. "Constitutive Rhetoric: The Case of the *Peuple Québécois*." *Quarterly Journal of Speech* 73, no. 2 (May 1987): 133–150.

Fisher, Max, Josh Keller, Mae Ryan, and Shane O'Neill. The Interpreter, Episode 2, "National Identity is Made Up." *New York Times*, 2018. https://www.nytimes.com/2018/02/28/world/national-identity-myth.html.

Hauser, Gerard A. "Rhetorical Democracy and Civic Engagement." In *Rhetorical Democracy: Discursive Practices of Civic Engagement,* edited by Gerard A. Hauser and Amy Grim, 1–16. Mahwah, NJ: Erlbaum, 2004.

ENDNOTES

[1] Quoted in AJ Willingham, "How 'Thoughts and Prayers' Went from Common Condolence to Cynical Meme," CNN, March 24, 2018, https://www.cnn.com/2018/02/20/us/thoughts-and-prayers-florida-school-shooting-trnd/index.html.

[2] Quoted in Eli Watkins, "Lawmakers Express Sadness after Florida School Shooting," CNNPolitics, February 14, 2018, https://www.cnn.com/2018/02/14/politics/congress-reaction-florida-shooting/index.html.

[3] Dahlia Lithwick, "They Were Trained for This Moment," Slate.com, February 28, 2018, https://slate.com/news-and-politics/2018/02/the-student-activists-of-marjory-stoneman-douglas-high-demonstrate-the-power-of-a-full-education.html.

[4] Emanuella Grinberg and Nadeem Muaddi, "How the Parkland Students Pulled Off a Massive National Protest in Only 5 Weeks," CNN.com, March 26, 2018, https://www.cnn.com/2018/03/26/us/march-for-our-lives/index.html.

[5] Grinberg and Muaddi, "How the Parkland Students."

[6] Mary Ellen Klas and Kyra Gurney, "Parkland Students and Parents Decided 'This Time Must Be Different.' And It Was," *Miami Herald,* March 11, 2018, http://www.miamiherald.com/news/politics-government/state-politics/article204511654.html.

[7] Daniella Diaz, "6 Things Marco Rubio Said at the CNN Town Hall That Made News in the US Gun Debate," CNN, February 22, 2018, https://www.cnn.com/2018/02/22/politics/marco-rubio-gun-debate-cnn-town-hall/index.html.

8 Nick Wing, "73 Teens Shot to Death in the 37 Days since the Parkland Massacre," *Huffington Post,* March 24, 2018, https://www.huffingtonpost.com/entry /teens-killed-since-parkland_us_5ab54cd5e4b0decad049d34c.

9 March for Our Lives, "Mission Statement," accessed March 28, 2018, https://marchforourlives.com/mission-statement; archived at https://web.archive .org/web/20180329070937/https://marchforourlives.com/mission-statement/.

10 "How Many People Attended March for Our Lives? Crowd in D.C. Estimated at 200,000," CBS News, March 25, 2018, https://www.cbsnews.com/news /march-for-our-lives-crowd-size-estimated-200000-people-attended-d-c-march/.

11 For full video, see "Santorum Rips Kids Calling for Gun Laws: They Should Take CPR Classes Instead," CNN State of the Union, YouTube, March 25, 2018, https://www.youtube.com/watch?v=PWMsCO-Icg4. See also Eli Watkins, "Santorum: Instead of Calling for Gun Laws, Kids Should Take CPR Classes," CNN.com, March 26, 2018, https://www.cnn.com/2018/03/25/politics/rick-santorum-guns -cnntv/index.html; Jaime Ducharme, "Former Sen. Rick Santorum Said Kids Should Be Learning CPR Instead of Protesting Gun Violence," March 25, 2018, *Time.com*, http://time.com/5214844/rick-santorum-cpr-gun-protests/.

12 George A. Kennedy, *A New History of Classical Rhetoric* (Princeton, NJ: Princeton University Press, 1994), 7.

13 Edward Schiappa, *Protagoras and Logos: A Study in Greek Philosophy and Rhetoric* (Columbia: University of South Carolina Press, 1991).

14 Carol Lipson and Roberta A. Binkley, *Rhetoric before and beyond the Greeks* (Albany: State University of New York Press, 2004); see also David Hutto, "Ancient Egyptian Rhetoric in the Old and Middle Kingdoms," *Rhetorica: A Journal of the History of Rhetoric* 20, No. 3, (2002): 213–233, DOI: 10.1525/rh.2002.20.3.213.

15 Loubna A. Youssef, "*Balāgha* or Rhetoric? The Language of the Tahrir Square Revolution," in *Toward, around, and away from Tahrir: Tracking Emerging Expressions of Egyptian Identity,* ed. Emily Golson, Loubna Youssef, and Amanda Fields (Newcastle upon Tyne, England: Cambridge Scholars, 2014), 9–28; Philip Halldén, "What Is Arab Islamic Rhetoric? Rethinking the History of Muslim Oratory Art and Homiletics," *International Journal of Middle East Studies,* 37, no. 1 (February 2005): 19–38.

16 Amartya Sen, *The Argumentative Indian* (New York: Farrar, Strauss and Giroux, 2005).

17 Martin Luther King, Jr., "I Have a Dream," August 28, 1963, http://www.americanrhetoric.com/speeches/mlkihaveadream.htm.

18 Malala Yousafzai, "Nobel Lecture," Oslo, December 10, 2014, http://www.nobelprize .org/nobel_prizes/peace/laureates/2014/yousafzai-lecture_en.html.

19 Abraham Lincoln, Abraham Lincoln Online, http://www.abrahamlincolnonline.org /lincoln/speeches/gettysburg.htm, Bancroft copy, accessed September 10, 2021.

20 Theodore C. Sorensen, "Ted Sorensen on Abraham Lincoln: A Man of His Words," Smithsonian.com, http://www.smithsonianmag.com/history/ted-sorensen -on-abraham-lincoln-a-man-of-his-words-12048177/?page=2.

21 George W. Bush, "The Text of President Bush's Address Tuesday Night, after Terrorist Attacks on New York and Washington," CNN.com, http://edition.cnn.com/2001 /US/09/11/bush.speech.text.

22 Malcolm X, "The Ballot or the Bullet," April 3, 1964, http://www.edchange.org /multicultural/speeches/malcolm_x_ballot.html.

23 Ekaterina Haskins, *Popular Memories* (Columbia: University of South Carolina Press, 2015); Gerard A. Hauser, *Vernacular Voices: The Rhetoric of Publics and Public Spheres* (Columbia: University of South Carolina Press, 2008).

[24] Joan Bakewell, "Arts under Siege," *Sunday Times* (London), June 10, 1990, LexisNexis.

[25] "Beyond Red and Blue: 7 Ways to View the Presidential Election Map," *Scientific American,* 2008, https://www.scientificamerican.com/slideshow/electoral-results -maps/; Mark Wilson, "U.S. Election Maps Are Wildly Misleading, So This Designer Fixed Them," *Fast Company,* November 5, 2020, https://www.fastcompany.com /90572489/u-s-election-maps-are-wildly-misleading-so-this-designer-fixed-them.

[26] Winston S. Churchill, "The Lights Are Going Out," *Never Give In: The Best of Winston Churchill's Speeches* (New York: Hyperion, 2003), 182–185.

[27] Adolf Hitler, *The Speeches of Adolf Hitler,* vol. 1, ed. N. H. Baynes (Oxford, UK: Oxford University Press, 1942), 743.

[28] "Traditions: The Elephant Story," accessed July 14, 2014, http://www.rolltide.com/trads /elephant.html.

[29] "The Jayhawk," University of Kansas, accessed July 14, 2014, http://www.ku.edu/about /traditions/jayhawk.

[30] Michael Osborn, *Michael Osborn on Metaphor and Style* (East Lansing: Michigan State University Press, 2018), xxi.

[31] Charles A. Hill and Marguerite Helmers, eds., *Defining Visual Rhetorics* (Mahwah, NJ: Erlbaum, 2004); Diane S. Hope, ed., *Visual Communication: Perception, Rhetoric, and Technology* (Cresskill, NJ: Hampton, 2006); Lawrence J. Prelli, ed., *Rhetorics of Display* (Columbia: University of South Carolina Press, 2006).

[32] Kenneth Burke, "Dramatism," in *International Encyclopedia of the Social Sciences,* vol. 7, ed. David L. Sills (New York: Macmillan and Free Press, 1968), 447.

[33] Carole Blair, "Contemporary U.S. Memorial Sites as Exemplars of Rhetoric's Materiality," in *Rhetorical Bodies,* ed. Jack Selzer and Sharon Crowley (Madison: University of Wisconsin Press, 1999), 16–57, 19.

[34] Burke, *A Rhetoric of Motives* (Berkeley: University of California Press, 1969), 20.

[35] Burke, *A Rhetoric of Motives,* 46.

[36] Burke, *A Rhetoric of Motives,* 20.

[37] Jasinski, *Sourcebook on Rhetoric: Key Concepts in Contemporary Rhetorical Studies* (Thousand Oaks, CA: Sage, 2001), 305.

[38] Kenneth Burke, *Development and Design* (Worcester, MA: Clark University Press, 1972), 27–28.

[39] Burke, *Language as Symbolic Action* (Berkeley: University of California Press, 1969), 301.

[40] Burke, *A Rhetoric of Motives,* 21.

[41] Burke, *A Rhetoric of Motives,* 21.

[42] Burke, *A Rhetoric of Motives,* 21.

[43] Isaac West, *Transforming Citizenships: Transgender Articulations of the Law* (New York: New York University Press, 2014), 28. See also Danielle Allen, *Talking to Strangers: Anxieties of Citizenship since Brown v. Board of Education* (Chicago: University of Chicago Press, 2004).

[44] Danielle Allen, *Talking to Strangers.*

[45] Allen, *Talking to Strangers,* 15.

[46] Allen, *Talking to Strangers,* 17.

[47] West, *Transforming Citizenships,* 28.

[48] Gerda Lerner, *The Grimké Sisters from South Carolina* (New York: Schocken, 1967), 245.

[49] Angelina Grimké [Weld], Address at Pennsylvania Hall, 1838, in Karlyn Kohrs Campbell, ed., *Man Cannot Speak for Her,* vol. 2 (New York: Praeger, 1989), 27.

[50] Karlyn Kohrs Campbell, *Man Cannot Speak for Her,* vol. 1 (New York: Praeger, 1989), 30. See also Stephen H. Browne, "Encountering Angelina Grimké: Violence, Identity,

and the Creation of Radical Community," *Quarterly Journal of Speech* 82, no. 1 (February 1996): 55–73, 70, for a discussion of how Grimké saw "not the repression of public discourse but an opportunity for it" in violent reactions to abolitionists.

[51] James Boyd White, *Heracles' Bow: Essays on the Rhetoric and Poetics of Law* (Madison: University of Wisconsin Press, 1989), x.

[52] James Jasinski, "A Constitutive Framework for Rhetorical Historiography: Toward an Understanding of the Discursive (Re)Constitution of 'Constitution' in *The Federalist Papers*," in *Doing Rhetorical History: Cases and Concepts,* ed. Kathleen J. Turner (Tuscaloosa: University of Alabama Press, 1998), 74–75.

[53] Maurice Charland, "Constitutive Rhetoric: The Case of the *Peuple Québécois*," *Quarterly Journal of Speech* 73, no. 2 (May 1987): 133–150, 134.

[54] Charland, "Constitutive Rhetoric," 136.

[55] Judith Butler, *Bodies That Matter* (New York: Routledge, 1993), 8.

[56] Max Fisher, Josh Keller, Mae Ryan, and Shane O'Neill, "National Identity is Made Up," The Interpreter, *New York Times,* 2019, https://www.nytimes.com/video/world /100000005660651/national-identity.html.

[57] Fisher et al., "National Identity."

[58] Fisher et al., "National Identity."

[59] James Jasinski, *Sourcebook on Rhetoric,* 106.

[60] Kenneth Burke, *Language as Symbolic Action,* 16. Original is in italics.

[61] Kenneth Burke, *A Rhetoric of Motives,* 43.

[62] Barry Brummett, "Some Implications of 'Process' or 'Intersubjectivity': Postmodern Rhetoric," *Philosophy and Rhetoric* 9, no. 1 (1976): 21–53, 28–29.

[63] Caglar Irmak, Beth Vallen, and Stefanie Rosen Robinson, "The Impact of Product Names on Dieters' and Nondieters' Food Evaluations and Consumption," *Journal of Consumer Research* 38 (August 2011): 390.

[64] Irmak et al., "The Impact of Product Names," 401.

[65] Kevin Michael DeLuca, "The Speed of Immanent Images: The Dangers of Reading Photographs," in Hope, *Visual Communication,* 81.

[66] Gerard A. Hauser, "Rhetorical Democracy and Civic Engagement," in *Rhetorical Democracy: Discursive Practices of Civic Engagement,* ed. Gerard A. Hauser and Amy Grim, 1–16 (Mahwah, NJ: Erlbaum, 2004), 11.

[67] Bruce Gronbeck, "Citizen Voices in Cyberpolitical Culture," in Hauser and Grim, *Rhetorical Democracy,* 17–32, 28.

[68] Karma Chávez, "Beyond Inclusion: Rethinking Rhetoric's Historical Narrative, *Quarterly Journal of Speech* 101, no. 1 (2015): 162–172, 165.

[69] Michael Warner, *Publics and Counterpublics* (Brooklyn, NY: Zone, 2002), 75, 84.

[70] Damien Smith Pfister, "Technoliberal Rhetoric, Civic Attention, and Common Sensation in Sergey Brin's 'Why Google Glass?,'" *Quarterly Journal of Speech* 105, no. 2 (2019): 182–203, 184.

[71] Abraham Lincoln, "Gettysburg Address," November 19, 1863, http://www.americanrhetoric.com/speeches/gettysburgaddress.htm.

[72] Justice Oliver Wendell Holmes, *Abrams v. United States* 250 US 616, argued October 21–22, 1919, decided November 10, 1919, http://www.tedford-herbeck-free -speech.com/abrams.html.

[73] Karlyn Kohrs Campbell, "Agency: Promiscuous and Protean," *Communication and Critical/Cultural Studies* 2 (2005): 3, italics added.

[74] Christian Lundberg and Joshua Gunn, "'Ouija Board, Are There Any Communications?' Agency, Ontotheology, and the Death of the Humanist Subject, or, Continuing the ARS Conversations," *Rhetoric Society Quarterly* 35, no. 4 (Fall 2005): 83–105.

75 Christian O. Lundberg, email to Catherine Palczewski, July 16, 2014. Correspondence with Lundberg and Joshua G. Gunn was extremely helpful regarding agency.

76 Sarah Hallenbeck, "Toward a Posthuman Perspective: Feminist Rhetorical Methodologies and Everyday Practices," *Advances in the History of Rhetoric* 15 (2012): 19.

77 Lundberg and Gunn, "'Ouija Board,'" 98.

78 "Okay Hand Gesture," Anti-Defamation League, 2019, https://www.adl.org/education/references/hate-symbols/okay-hand-gesture.

79 Andrew Joseph, "Cubs Ban the Fan Who Flashed a Racist Gesture behind Reporter Doug Glanville," May 8, 2019, *USA Today,* https://ftw.usatoday.com/2019/05/cubs-fan-racist-gesture-white-power-ok-sign-banned-glanville-mlb.

80 Joseph, "Cubs Ban the Fan."

81 Aristotle, *Nicomachean Ethics,* 8.9 [1160a-22], trans. W. D. Ross, classics.mit.edu/Aristotle/nicomachaean.html, accessed September 13, 2021.

82 Allen, *Talking to Strangers,* 127.

83 Hannah Arendt, *The Human Condition* (Chicago: University of Chicago Press, 1958), 243.

84 Allen, *Talking to Strangers,* 127.

85 Allen, *Talking to Strangers,* xxi-xxii.

86 Allen, *Talking to Strangers,* 19.

87 Allen, *Talking to Strangers,* xxii.

88 Allen, *Talking to Strangers,* 10.

89 Allen, *Talking to Strangers,* 10.

90 Allen, *Talking to Strangers,* 12, 18.

91 Robert Asen, "A Discourse Theory of Citizenship," *Quarterly Journal of Speech* 90, no. 2 (2004): 189–211.

92 Asen, "A Discourse Theory," 191.

93 Asen, "A Discourse Theory," 201.

94 Asen, "A Discourse Theory," 195.

Chapter 2
Rhetorical Resources and Constraints

KEY CONCEPTS

collective memory

culture

hegemony

ideology

power

public memory

July 4 is a day like any other. Because the Continental Congress formally adopted the final version of its Declaration of Independence from Great Britain on July 4, 1776, however, the date has taken on immense symbolic importance in the United States. The day is no longer July 4, but is instead the Fourth of July, one of ten federal holidays (established in 1870), marked by speeches, parades, concerts, firework displays, and the rereading of the Declaration on media outlets such as National Public Radio. Individually, people mark the event with displays of the US flag. In the United States, the Fourth of July is an occasion for intense celebrations of patriotism.

If you were asked to deliver a speech on the Fourth of July, you would likely embrace a celebratory tone that draws the audience members together in their shared love of country. That is how most speakers approach the event.[1] However, the Fourth of July could mean something else.

When the Rochester, New York, Ladies' Anti-Slavery Society invited famed abolitionist, woman's rights activist, and former enslaved person Frederick Douglass to deliver a Fourth of July oration in 1852, Douglass chose to redefine the situation from one of celebration to condemnation. Speaking as "the most powerful black man in the nation" at that time,[2] Douglass reviewed US history and the significance of the day and, using second person pronouns, made it clear it was a celebration for some, but not all: "This, for the purpose of this celebration, is the Fourth of July. It is the birthday of *your* National Independence, and of *your* political freedom. . . . Pride and patriotism, not less than gratitude, prompt *you* to celebrate and to hold it

27

in perpetual remembrance."[3] Speaking thirteen years before the end of the Civil War and the adoption of the Thirteenth Amendment, which officially abolished slavery in the United States, Douglass used the day not to celebrate the ideals of the nation, but to condemn the nation for not living up to its ideals. Douglass asked:

> Fellow-citizens, pardon me, allow me to ask, why am I called upon to speak here to-day? What have I, or those I represent, to do with your national independence? Are the great principles of political freedom and of natural justice, embodied in that Declaration of Independence, extended to us? . . . I am not included within the pale of this glorious anniversary! . . . Fellow-citizens; above your national, tumultuous joy, I hear the mournful wail of millions! whose chains, heavy and grievous yesterday, are, to-day, rendered more intolerable by the jubilee shouts that reach them.[4]

For White people the situation may have called for the celebration of liberty, but for Black people the day simply placed into stark relief the monstrous inequalities and violence inherent in White enslavement of Black people.

This example illustrates many of the characteristics of rhetoric in civic life discussed in chapter 1. Douglass's challenge to the audience was a form of civic engagement. It asked the audience to see and care about the concerns of others, of strangers. The celebration of the Fourth of July also makes clear the power of symbolic action, as does Douglass's brilliant speech. It matters that the Fourth of July is celebrated through words and images and that the audience could see *and* hear Douglass. His words were powerful because they were delivered from the body of a formerly enslaved person.

The example also illustrates some of the core concepts we discuss in this chapter. Despite its eloquence, the speech did not cause the end of White enslavement of Black people, but that does not mean it was ineffective or unpersuasive. To understand how rhetoric as civic engagement works, you need to think about the audience, the larger context, and the constraints rhetors face. Rhetorical action requires a rhetor *and* an audience, and audiences' interpretations of meaning are influenced by social factors. Not every symbolic action will be completely and immediately understood by everyone hearing or seeing it, or accepted even if it is understood. Douglass was not arguing simply against a law that allowed enslavement but also against a dominant ideology that divided people from one another on the basis of color. Your familiarity with this speech also is a point of interest. When people think about United States history, is Douglass's story part of that history? You likely know the names of Washington, Adams, and Lincoln, but do you know the name of Douglass? The interplay between remembering and forgetting, woven into the history you learn, illustrates how power matters to people's understanding of themselves.

In this chapter, we discuss some of the limits on and resources for what rhetoric can accomplish. We start by clarifying what it means to say rhetoric is "addressed" to an audience. We next identify the range of rhetorical purposes by describing the persuasive continuum. We then turn to a discussion of culture, public memory, power, ideology, and hegemony. This list of resources and constraints is not exhaustive, but it does constitute overarching constraints and resources that influence most aspects of rhetorical engagement in civic life. Our goal is to assist you in understanding that rhetoric is always a collective enterprise, implicated with power, constitutive of social reality and identity, and relevant to questions of how to act in the world.

RHETORIC AS ADDRESSED

In his treatise *On Rhetoric,* Aristotle defined rhetoric as "an ability in each [particular] case, to see the available means of persuasion."[5] Notice that the definition says that rhetoric is an *ability to see.* Thus, using rhetoric requires analysis of a situation in order to determine how to persuade. For Aristotle, a rhetorical situation "consists of three things: a speaker and a subject on which he speaks and someone addressed, and the objective of the speech relates to the last."[6] Rhetoric is addressed to particular people, on particular occasions, in particular times and societies, about particular issues.

For Kenneth Burke, a twentieth-century rhetorical theorist who deeply influenced the study, the nature of rhetoric "as addressed" to others is one of its definitive characteristics (in addition to identification, as discussed in the preceding chapter).[7] Humans use rhetoric to communicate *with* one another. Although communication clearly has an individual expressive component, rhetoricians emphasize how some communication, though still expressive, is more than individuals expressing their thoughts and feelings. Rhetoric is the communication that occurs between people, between a rhetor and an audience. It always involves an audience, even if that audience is not immediately present. Thus, the making of meaning is interactive: it occurs between people.

Because rhetors and audiences coproduce meaning, rhetorical agency belongs not only to rhetors but also to audiences. As we discussed in the preceding chapter, agency includes the ability to construct and interpret symbolic actions, and to take action in response to those interpretations. Campbell describes agency as "communal, social, cooperative, and participatory and, simultaneously, constituted and constrained by the material and symbolic elements of context and culture."[8] In other words, people make meaning through a social, and not just individual, process. When you interpret messages or decode images, you do not use only those resources that you alone possess. Instead, you rely on a complex set of contextual and cultural symbols.

Rhetoric is an action that creates meaning, informing human beings about how to understand and react to the world. It is not merely a mechanism of information transmission, but a means by which human beings construct social reality. The political, personal, and meaning-creating functions highlight how rhetoric affects what laws are passed, how people see themselves, and what people think they know. Because rhetoric fulfills all these functions, it is important to understand that rhetoric is far more than persuading another person to do something you want them to do.

PERSUASIVE CONTINUUM

Because of limits on persuasion stemming from an audience, a topic, or even the rhetor, persuasion is seldom absolutely achieved or an argument completely dismissed. An audience is neither totally persuaded nor completely unconvinced by a single rhetorical action. When people think of persuasion, they often think of it as intentionally trying to change another person's actions or beliefs (sometimes against the other person's will), but not all rhetoric has such goals.

Communication scholar Karlyn Kohrs Campbell describes persuasive purposes in terms of a continuum:[9]

In many cases, changing a person's mind is not possible with a single rhetorical action. Beliefs can be so deeply ingrained that an audience may not even recognize that alternative beliefs exist. In such a case, a rhetor's goal may be to create a virtual experience for audience members, so they come to feel they have experienced something they never thought possible. For example, when African American activist Mary Church Terrell wrote about the effects of Jim Crow segregation laws in her 1906 magazine essay "What It Means to Be Colored in the Capital of the United States,"[10] she *created a virtual experience* of what it was like to live under Jim Crow segregation laws. Writing to a primarily White, northern audience, she provided example after example of the segregation African Americans faced in what was thought to be the cradle of liberty and equality: Washington, DC. Moving from finding shelter, to finding food, to finding a place to worship, work, and be entertained and educated, the essay created for the White audience members the virtual experience of being "colored in the capital of the United States" and enabled them to identify with African Americans.

The virtual experience need not be based in material reality. For example, readers of the Harry Potter novels are transported to places that never actually existed. The books create a virtual experience for readers through detailed descriptions of the characters and settings for the stories. For some readers, the characters and locations were defined in their minds even before the Harry Potter movies were produced. One critic wrote, "Disappointingly, some of the clever nuances from the book don't come through in the film. Harry's miserable home life, which was vibrantly written, is forgettable here."[11] For those readers, the movie, with its reliance on the visual, did not produce the same effect as the written word, which created characters and scenes that allowed the audience to experience an imaginary world.

If rhetors can create virtual experiences for audience members, they might be able to *alter their perceptions,* or at least introduce them to new perspectives. For example, Ida B. Wells, a journalist and long-time activist for African American rights, fought against lynching. In an essay written in 1892 (also delivered as a speech), "Southern Horrors: Lynch Law in All Its Phases," Wells attempted to alter audience members' perception that Black men were lynched because they were accused of raping White women.[12] She made clear that, as reported by White sources, the real reason White people lynched Black people was economic. White businesspeople resented Black people's economic success. Wells also pointed out that Black children and Black women had been murdered by White lynch mobs, but no White man had ever been lynched for raping a Black woman, or even a Black eight-year-old child, showing that the fear of rape was an inadequate explanation for lynching. Although she may not have been able to convince the audience that all lynching was wrong, Wells at least opened their minds to an alternative perspective on lynching—that it was an economically and racially motivated crime of hate, rather than an act defending fragile White women's honor. She sought to create divisions between White people who lynched and those who would oppose lynching, and to foster identification between White people and Black people.

If audience members are willing to entertain the possibility of an alternative perception, a speaker can then *explain* reasons behind that perception. Wells explained the reasons to oppose lynching, to demand that northerners condemn the act, and to support African Americans arming themselves in self-defense. She ended by explaining: "Of the many inhuman outrages of this present year, the only case where the proposed lynching did *not* occur, was where the men armed themselves in Jacksonville, Fla., and Paducah, Ky., and prevented it. The only times an Afro-American who was assaulted got away has been when he had a gun and used it in self-defense."[13]

Another example of explanation, this time not tied to altering perception, can be found in the comments made about COVID-19 by Dr. Anthony Fauci, director of the National Institute of Allergy and Infectious Diseases. When the novel coronavirus (2019-nCoV) emerged in late 2019 and continued to spread in 2020, the challenge was to explain new and constantly evolving technical information to the broader public: what caused the virus, how it spread, what public health measures were possible to slow the spread, what treatments worked, and what was involved in developing, testing, and distributing a vaccine. Fauci became "the explainer-in-chief of the coronavirus epidemic" because of an "ability to explain science without talking down to his audience" and a willingness to talk with anyone.[14] His explanations appeared on numerous TV shows, including *The Daily Show* with Trevor Noah. When the White House stopped approving requests for television interviews,[15] Fauci spoke on Julia Roberts's Instagram livestream and on podcasts with Lil Wayne and Rashida Jones. When Boston pastor Liz Walker of Roxbury Presbyterian Church invited Fauci to speak to the congregation in a November 2020 Zoom meeting, Fauci agreed. Across all these platforms, he sought to explain the science behind vaccine development and why public health measures (such as mask wearing and social distancing) were effective and necessary.

Rhetors might seek not only to alter perceptions or explain, but to *formulate beliefs*. As a result of speeches and essays, Ida B. Wells and other rhetors were able to begin formulating the beliefs in audience's minds that lynching was a criminal act that violated Black people's rights and that lynchers should face the most severe legal punishments possible. It took time to formulate those beliefs. Lynching persisted well into the 1950s. A federal antilynching law was not even proposed until 1900 (and then received only three votes) and no federal anti-lynching law was ever passed, an oversight for which the US Senate apologized in 2005.[16] Dr. Fauci, in addition to explaining why masks were important and a vaccine was necessary, sought to induce people to believe mask-wearing was good and vaccines were effective and safe.

Formulating belief is not the only possible goal for a rhetorician. In many cases, audience members seek out speakers in order to reaffirm their own beliefs. For example, people attend religious services to have their beliefs reaffirmed and attend political rallies for candidates they already support in order to maintain (and demonstrate) their belief in a candidate.

Having beliefs does not necessarily mean people act on them. In recent years, social media has been used to *initiate action*. The revolutions during the Arab Spring in the early 2010s were facilitated by social media. The revolution in Tunisia relied heavily on Facebook; the revolution in Egypt on Twitter.[17] The use of social media may not have caused the revolutions, but it allowed "unprecedented waves of spread" that allowed the revolutions to evolve more quickly.[18] Messages and images on Twitter and Facebook can seek to initiate action by people who share similar beliefs. They also raise the possibility of a "leaderless revolution," in which groups of people organize based on spontaneity, homogeneity, and synchronicity of actions, catalyzed by social media.[19]

When a movement or campaign achieves success, members must be reminded that there is more work to be done. Since 2000, for example, nine states have done away with the death penalty (for a total of twenty-two states).[20] Groups that wish to see it abolished entirely hope to see further successes. In early 2014, three executions by lethal injection did not go as planned. In the third case, it took two hours for a man convicted of a double murder in Arizona to die.[21] Abolitionists quickly took to Twitter, using #DeathPenalty to mark their tweets. Ed Pilkington of *The Guardian* (@Edpilkington) tweeted, "If you care about the #deathpenalty in US u need to pay attention to Arizona right now—the mother of all botched executions is unfolding."[22] ACLU National (@ACLU) sent out a tweet referring to the death penalty as a constitutionally prohibited form of cruel and unusual punishment.[23] Messages opposing the death penalty continue.

CULTURE

Rhetoric and civic engagement occur within particular cultures. According to anthropologist Clifford Geertz, **culture** is the *"historically transmitted pattern of meanings embodied in symbols, a system of inherited conceptions expressed in symbolic forms by means of which [people] communicate, perpetuate, and develop their knowledge about and attitudes toward life."*[24] Culture is composed of knowledge, experiences, beliefs, values, attitudes, meanings, hierarchies, religions, conceptions of time, social roles, worldviews, myths, and even the material possessions or artifacts acquired by a group of people, the meanings of which are transmitted through symbols. Your culture frames how you interpret rhetorical messages.

For example, in an individualist culture, appeals to individual rights may carry more weight than in a more communitarian culture that places the concerns of the group ahead of individuals' rights.[25] In their study of the famous image of the man standing in front of the tank during the 1989 Tiananmen Square protests, communication scholars Robert Hariman and John L. Lucaites argue that Western media sources made that image, rather than images of massive crowds, emblematic of the event because the lone individual confronting the power of the state made sense to Western cultures that emphasize liberal individualism.[26]

Geertz uses the metaphor of a spiderweb to explain the complex relationship between culture and symbol use: he says that humans are "suspended in webs of significance" they themselves "have spun."[27] For Geertz, symbols do not literally bring something into existence, but locate it within systems, or webs, of meaning. Patriotism, the love of or devotion to a country, is an example of a cultural system of meaning. In the US patriotic web of significance, key words such as "freedom," "equality," and "liberty"; visual symbols such as the US flag; holidays such as the Fourth of July; and icons such as Uncle Sam and the Statue of Liberty have come to symbolize the country. People who are citizens come to understand who they are because of their relationship to the United States, to which they pledge allegiance. Expressions of patriotism (such as Lee Greenwood's 1984 song "God Bless the USA," which played at the Republican National Convention that year, increased in popularity during Operation Desert Storm in 1991, then regained popularity in the wake of the 9/11 attacks in 2001) create a sense of identification among many citizens.

As that sense of identification develops so, too, does a sense of differentiation and exclusion. Even as people create identification (a sense of "us"), they also create division (a sense of "them"). Identification is meant to counteract the feeling of division, but even as it does so it tends to recreate divisions along new lines. Patriotism normalizes the idea that some people deserve rights in a country because they "belong" while others do not because they do not belong. Patriotism also normalizes the idea that a fellow citizen's loss of life counts more than another person's death.[28] Patriotism gives a particular meaning to being a citizen of a country. The words and symbols interweave so that to attack one of them (freedom) means you have attacked all of them (attacking freedom means you are attacking all the United States stands for). Sometimes dissent is called unpatriotic because it means not supporting the country unconditionally. Patriotism is a web of significance in which people are suspended and that they, themselves, have spun.

Geertz's definition of culture includes "a system of inherited conceptions expressed in symbolic forms,"[29] which means that the web of significance is learned. Communication scholars Judith N. Martin and Thomas K. Nakayama state that culture is comprised of "learned patterns of behavior and attitudes shared by a group of people."[30] The primary functions of culture are to teach shared meanings, share views of the world, and create group identity. Through these functions, cultures also help reduce uncertainty and chaos, largely by socializing their members to behave in prescribed ways.

Rhetoric is constrained by culture, but also constructs culture. It is constrained by culture because people's interpretations of symbolic action depend on the culture in which they participate. What is persuasive to a rural, midwestern, US audience might not be persuasive to an audience in another nation, or even another part of the United States. Yet, rhetoric can be used to change culture. For example, in the United States, women were once considered inferior and thus were systematically denied the right to vote. This state of affairs was considered "normal" in the eighteenth and nineteenth centuries. Yet, in the twenty-first-century United States, if someone advocated denying women the right to vote, you would probably think that person was irrational. Women achieved their current role through rhetoric and civic engagement that altered the culture.

PUBLIC AND COLLECTIVE MEMORY

In referring to "a historically transmitted pattern of meanings," Geertz points to the link between culture and memory, including cultural memory that resides in the web of significance. If culture is learned patterns, where do people learn those patterns? A person does not inherit a chest of drawers that contains the culture. Instead, people develop their culture as they inherit symbol systems that contain memories.

Memories are maintained through symbolic actions. Sociologist Barry Schwartz explains, "Recollection of the past is an active, constructive process, not a simple matter of retrieving information. To remember is to place a part of the past in the service of conceptions and needs of the present."[31] Memories do not just exist: remembering requires human symbols to re-present memory. Communication scholar Carole Blair explains: "memory is based on the capacity to *re-present* an event, a place, a person, or an idea that one has already encountered."[32] People engage in the act of remembering, and in doing so develop a sense of collective identity.

Memory can exist at the personal level, as when family members recall past experiences with each other. It can also exist at the cultural level, when people engage in the memory work that sustains them as a culture. **Collective memory** is *memory that is not simply an individualized process, but a shared and constructed creation of a group.*[33] **Public memory** is *a particular type of collective memory that combines the memories of the dominant culture and fragments of marginalized groups' memories, and enables a public to make sense of the past, present, and future.*[34] Memory is the product of rhetorical action even as it constrains the rhetorical actions of anyone who would challenge the dominant memory.

Citizens of a nation maintain and construct public memory through the stories they tell, the heroes they revere, and the monuments and memorials they choose to erect. In the process, they construct an identity for themselves. In the United States, the Lincoln Memorial, Washington Monument, Vietnam Veterans

Memorial, National World War II Memorial, and Korean War Veterans Memorial all construct particular memories of the nation's past. The addition in 2011 of the Martin Luther King, Jr., National Memorial expanded the story when it became the first monument on the National Mall that was dedicated to an African American.

Public memories give identity to a particular society. You personally have no memory of national events such as the American Revolution, but through your education and your participation in Fourth of July celebrations, through national monuments and speeches, you participate in a public memory of the events of the American Revolution, memories the Tea Party movement sought to revivify when it launched in 2009. Thus, an individual's memories of such events do not really make sense unless situated within a larger collective. Communication scholar Iwona Irwin-Zarecka writes, "'Collective memory'—as a set of ideas, images, feelings about the past—is best located not in the minds of individuals, but in the resources they share."[35]

Collective memory may be controversial because remembering always involves forgetting. Collective remembering is always intimately linked to collective forgetfulness. No single version of the past exists, and dominant interpretations of past events can "wip[e] out many of the others."[36] Thus, rhetorical action may focus on which things to remember and how to remember them.

For example, memorial depictions of Christopher Columbus illustrate both the amount of work done to maintain collective memory and the way memory always induces forgetfulness. Symbols in the form of statues and images, poems, stories, and named holidays all sought to fix collective memory of Columbus as defining the US identity as a nation of explorers. Columbus has been celebrated as an American mythic hero since the genesis of the nation, partly because the revolutionary leaders were reluctant to ascend the pedestal in a country that ostensibly was built on democratic principles.[37] Into this void people placed Columbus. In the years during and immediately after the Revolutionary War, numerous poetic histories and references to Columbus emerged, including Phillis Wheatley's 1775 innovation of the poetic device "Columbia" as a symbol of both Columbus and America.[38] In 1792, the new capital in Washington was subtitled the District of Columbia. These acts of rhetoric participated in the creation and maintenance of public memory.

The original narrative of Columbus-the-discoverer was woven into and stabilized US public memory without opposition for many years. Regardless of whether Columbus was the first to land in the Americas, Columbus Day is the day celebrated; Columbus's image is immortalized in the US capitol; over 150 Columbus statues have been erected across 26 states and Washington, DC; and Columbus's story is told in textbooks and movies. In other words, all available anchoring devices for collective memory have been used to fix Columbus-the-discoverer in US public memory. During the process of commemorating Columbus, however, much faded in memory.

The Columbian quincentenary in 1992 provided a unique moment to highlight the connection between collective forgetting and collective remembering. Native American and indigenous protests against Columbus Day parades offered a way to materialize grievances, as well as to challenge collective memory and public memorializing practices. A leading scholar on indigenous Latin American peoples, José Barreiro, introduced a special issue of the *Northeast Indian Quarterly* that was dedicated to "American Indian Perspectives on the Quincentenary." Barreiro explained the rhetorical significance of the quincentenary: "To the degree that the Quincentenary spectacle exalts Columbus as a metaphor for the expansion of Western materialist culture[,] a debate is joined that focuses issues of cultural values survival, environmental ethics and practice[,] and sustainability in economic activity."[39]

The celebration of Columbus's memory provided a focal point through which to reframe the nation's understanding of discovery and settlement. The reframing was not to be achieved by a single protest or a single text. For Native Americans, the issue was not the accurate chronicling of history, although that was a part of it, but the effects of commemorative holidays and parades on the memory of what was done to the indigenous peoples following Columbus's landfall. The aim of reframing was to remind others that Columbus did not "discover" an empty land, but claimed a land populated by many different peoples. The memory of Columbus is rhetorical insofar as it exhorts people in the United States to perceive their identity as explorers. Native Americans countered that rhetorical exhortation by depicting Columbus not as an explorer but as a colonizer and murderer. The criticisms of Columbus's actions have led to calls to remove his statues.

Memories, even those enshrined in memorials, monuments, parades, and holidays, do not proceed uncontested. Memory can be a site of rhetorical conflict precisely because of the necessary relationship between remembering and forgetting. Those with power tend to shape public memory; those with less power must contest the absence left by the partial memory of the powerful.

Memory work, the contestation and rehearsal of collective memory, is important to an evolving civic culture. Cultural studies scholar Henry Giroux argues that "organized forgetting" has become a form of weaponized ignorance, a "refusal to acknowledge the violence of the past" that "revels in a culture of media spectacles in which public concerns are translated into private obsessions, consumerism and fatuous entertainment."[40] Organized forgetting is another manifestation of the downsizing of democracy; it shifts attention away from public concerns and toward private pleasures. Public memory work, then, is a way to practice civic habits as it offers people a chance to witness and acknowledge moments where the people and the nation could have, and should have, done better.

POWER, IDEOLOGY, AND HEGEMONY

Power, as defined by feminist scholars Cheris Kramarae and Paula A. Triechler, is *"the ability to get things done."*[41] Power to do something is not inherently bad, but when it transforms into power over others, problems arise. Power is a social phenomenon: people have power in relation to others. Class, gender/sex, race, citizenship, political affiliation, education, sexuality, and religion all influence the cultural resources that rhetors may access and thus how much rhetorical power they have.

Communication scholars John Louis Lucaites and Celeste Michelle Condit point out that people who study rhetoric need to consider the "systems of social conditions and their impact on public discourse."[42] Not all people have equal access to the public podium, because rhetorical actions occur in culturally and historically specific contexts in which power is apportioned unequally. Lucaites and Condit posit a refined definition of rhetoric that "portrays significant rhetors as those able to realign material life experiences and cultural symbols through the artful use of the available means of persuasion."[43] This definition of rhetoric highlights the role of people in shaping experiences and symbols. Such shaping is an art form. However, not all people have the same experiences nor do all people have access to the same symbols. The means of persuasion available to a US president differ from those available to an unemployed steelworker, or from those available to an immigrant living and working in the United States without documentation. When you are part of an audience, it is important to consider these things before judging a rhetor to be a failure or success.

Power is also central to the study of rhetoric because rhetoric is, itself, a form of power. Philosopher Michel Foucault, who wrote extensively about power, notes that "as history constantly teaches us, discourse is not simply that which translates struggles or systems of domination, but is the thing for which and by which there is struggle, discourse is the power which is to be seized."[44] In other words, rhetoric is both the object of power over which people struggle and the means by which people engage in a struggle for power.

Foucault theorized that some of the most oppressive power is that which people internalize. He examined British philosopher Jeremy Bentham's panopticon—a jail with prisoners in individual cells arranged around a guard at the center, so that prisoners could not see each other or the guard, but the guard could always see all the prisoners. Because it was always possible that they were being watched, the prisoners acted *as if* they were always being watched; they disciplined themselves. Foucault says the power of the panopticon "makes it possible to perfect the exercise of power" because

> it can reduce the number of those who exercise it, while increasing
> the number of those on whom it is exercised. Because it is possible to
> intervene at any moment and because the constant pressure acts even
> before the offences, mistakes or crimes have been committed. Because,
> in these conditions, its strength is that it never intervenes, it is exercised
> spontaneously and without noise, it constitutes a mechanism whose effects
> follow from one another. Because, without any physical instrument other
> than architecture and geometry, it acts directly on individuals; it gives
> "power of mind over mind."[45]

In other words, a guard does not need to stand over you with a gun in order to generate your compliance: if you believe you are being watched, you behave. You internalize the rules, accepting them as the way things are, and act accordingly. You watch yourself.

As an example, think about how, and whether, you choose to talk. Even though the United States valorizes freedom of expression, people are often reluctant to speak out for fear of what might happen. Someone might be listening who will discipline them by showing they are wrong, or disagreeing, or judging them to be weird. In a classroom, students often self-censor for fear of not giving the answer the professor wants, even when the professor makes clear there are no wrong answers. In these examples, there is no guard to discipline you; instead, you have internalized an ideology that induces you to discipline yourself.

Power is not simply something that one entity has over another, or that flows from those at the top of the hierarchy to those at the bottom. Foucault emphasizes that power neither resides in only one location nor moves in only one direction: "Power is everywhere, not because it embraces everything, but because it comes from everywhere . . . power is not an institution, and not a structure; neither is it a certain strength we are endowed with."[46]

The guard in the prison does not possess absolute power over the inmates. Foucault writes that power is "a mechanism whose effects flow from one another," meaning power is not located in one place, but in relationships, and that "in the relations of power, there is necessarily the possibility of resistance."[47] Political scientist Michael Dutton writes, "the prisoner in the cell has 'all the time in the world' to map the cracks in the wall that offer the opportunity to escape, for . . . even panoptic power must blink."[48]

Power manifests itself rhetorically through the creation of a dominant **ideology,** which can be defined as *the ideas, values, beliefs, perceptions, and understandings that are known to members of a society and that guide their behaviors.* In *Making Sense of Political Ideology,* communication scholars Bernard L. Brock, Mark E. Huglen, James F. Klumpp, and Sharon Howell describe ideology as "typical ways of thinking about the world [that] help shape human action"[49] because it normalizes "day-to-day social, political, economic, and cultural structures" by making them appear natural and inevitable.[50] In short, ideology is a symbol system that explains why society is the way it is. Geertz identifies ideology as one example of a web of significance, because "the inherent elusiveness of ideological thought" is "expressed as it is in intricate symbolic webs as vaguely defined as they are emotionally charged."[51] Ideology is created and maintained through symbol use, but the ideological content of symbols is often difficult to track.

Ideology becomes most powerful when humans forget it is socially constructed and give it "the status of objective reality."[52] For example, marriage ceremonies are socially constructed rituals, but people forget these ceremonies are choices and begin to think they must be performed a particular way in order to be real. Cultural ideology about marriage ceremonies explains why the average cost of a US wedding tops $33,900, a hefty sum for a couple starting out, which might be better spent to make a down payment on a house or to pay off debts.[53] You might even hear someone complain at a nontraditional (or less expensive) wedding that it was "not right" or "unnatural." Such comments indicate the existence of cultural ideology.

Rhetorician Kenneth Burke offers a metaphorical description of how words operate together to constitute an ideology, as well as how that ideology induces people to act in certain ways: "An 'ideology' is like a spirit taking up its abode in a body: it makes that body hop around in certain ways; and that same body would have hopped around in different ways had a different ideology [or set of terms] happened to inhabit it."[54] In the case of the mob violence targeted at abolitionists, white supremacist ideology made the mob hop in a particularly violent way, legitimating the violence of slavery and the violence targeted at those who would challenge slavery. Ideology is not neutral, but tends to normalize the possession of power by the "haves" and the denial of power to the "have-nots."

British cultural studies scholar Stuart Hall argues that dominant cultural ideology influences how people come to perceive reality.[55] For example, capitalism is not only an economic system, but also a dominant ideology in the United States that undergirds the values and behaviors that support competition, individualism, and consumerism, and that enables money to determine status and power. Hall's argument does not mean that every person in US culture embraces the ideology unquestioningly, but it does explain the predominant US culture. As a result of this dominant cultural ideology, many people think the more expensive something is, or the more a job pays, the better it is.

Hegemony is *the dominant ideology of a society, exerting social control over people without the use of force.*[56] Philosopher Rosemary Hennessy explains that hegemony is not a form of power that controls through overt violence. Rather, it subtly controls by determining what makes sense: "Hegemony is the process whereby the interests of a ruling group come to dominate by establishing the common sense, that is, those values, beliefs, and knowledges that go without saying."[57]

Hegemony is constructed and maintained by rhetorical actions. Communication scholars draw on Italian political theorist Antonio Gramsci's concept of hegemonic ideology.[58] Gramsci argues that social control is primarily accomplished through the control of ideas. People are encouraged to see an idea as common sense, even if it conflicts with their own experiences. By following the cultural norms that guide behaviors, members of the culture uphold the ideology.

Hegemony reduces people's agency by limiting the choices that make sense to a rhetor or audience. For example, because capitalism is the hegemonic US ideology, most people in the United States believe in free and open markets and in the freedom of consumers to choose where to shop and what to buy. Recently, in a small town where two locally owned restaurants were located next to a park, a multinational fast-food restaurant offered to buy the park land and pay to relocate the park so it could build a restaurant on that location. The town council held an open meeting to discuss the proposal. Some members of the community opposed the fast-food restaurant, arguing that it would put the locally owned restaurants out of business and destroy the community by taking away a valuable central public meeting place. These community members were accused of being "anti-development" and "against the free enterprise system." One council member said, "If you do not like fast food, then don't eat there. The other restaurants need to learn to compete. It's a free country." These statements did not really answer the opponents' arguments but sought to silence the opposition by making them seem un-American, opposed to competition and freedom.

Because hegemony is embedded within symbolic actions, rhetorical critics need to learn how to read through it. Media scholar Stuart Hall identifies three positions from which audiences can decode a text: dominant or preferred (hegemonic) reading, negotiated reading, and oppositional (counterhegemonic) reading.[59] Different people in any given time have different resources available for oppositional readings, and have to expend more or less effort to construct them. Communication scholar Bonnie Dow observes that it is easy to "acquire the codes necessary for preferred readings" while "the acquisition of codes for negotiated or oppositional readings is more difficult and less common."[60] This text is intended to provide you with the code, or vocabulary, with which to understand rhetoric critically and oppositionally.

CONCLUSION

As we discussed in Chapter 1, rhetoric is the use of symbolic action to share ideas, enabling people to work together to make decisions about matters of common concern, to constitute identity, and to construct social reality. What this definition makes clear, and Aristotle's does not, is that rhetoric is much more than a tool of information transmission or persuasion. Through rhetoric, people construct culture, maintain and challenge memory, and develop and sustain ideology. As a result, they are able to identify, maintain, and counter hegemonic power.

When studying rhetoric, scholars do not really use a *single* approach or a preset step-by-step method. Instead, they use what communication scholars William L. Nothstine, Carole Blair, and Gary A. Copeland refer to as "conceptual heuristics or vocabularies."[61] Throughout the chapters that follow, we present additional vocabulary that describes the modes, generators, and contexts of rhetoric, and that should enable you to explain rhetoric's power to liberate *and* subordinate. We introduce you to diverse modes of symbolic action, including language, visual rhetoric, argument, and narrative. We show you ways to analyze rhetorical action as generated by rhetors and audiences. We end with a discussion of contexts for studying rhetoric—rhetorical situations and publics—and show how you can identify yourself as an agent of civic action.

DISCUSSION QUESTIONS

1. Identify the ways in which you participate in civic engagement. Where do each of those actions fit on the persuasive continuum?
2. What is power? Give examples of how it functions in politics, the law, and your daily life.
3. Identify a hegemonic ideology. What are some of the rhetorical engines that sustain it?
4. Recently, extensive debate over whether statues valorizing Confederate generals should be removed has occurred. How do these memorials participate in collective remembering and forgetting?

RECOMMENDED READINGS

Blair, Carole. "Communication as Collective Memory." In *Communication as . . . : Perspectives on Theory*, edited by Gregory J. Shepherd, Jeffrey St. John, and Ted Striphas, 51–59. Thousand Oaks, CA: Sage, 2006.

Brock, Bernard L., Mark E. Huglen, James F. Klumpp, and Sharon Howell. *Making Sense of Political Ideology: The Power of Language in Democracy*. New York: Rowman and Littlefield, 2005.

Burke, Kenneth. "Dramatism." In *International Encyclopedia of the Social Sciences*, vol. 7, edited by David L. Sills, 445–452. New York: Macmillan and Free Press, 1968.

Douglass, Frederick. "What to the Slave Is the Fourth of July?" July 5, 1852, *Teaching American History*. https://teachingamericanhistory.org/library/document/what-to-the-slave-is-the-fourth-of-july/.

Hall, Stuart. "Ideology and Communication Theory." In *Rethinking Communication Theory*, vol. 1, edited by Brenda Dervin, Larry Grossberg, Barbara O'Keefe, and Ellen Wartella, 40–52. Newbury Park, CA: Sage, 1989.

ENDNOTES

[1] Cedric Larson, "Patriotism in Carmine: 162 Years of July 4th Oratory," *Quarterly Journal of Speech* 26, no. 1 (1940): 12–25.

[2] Robert E. Terrill, "Irony, Silence, and Time: Frederick Douglass on the Fifth of July," *Quarterly Journal of Speech* 89, no. 3 (August 2003): 216–234.

[3] Frederick Douglass, "What to the Slave Is the Fourth of July?," July 5, 1852, *Teaching American History*, https://teachingamericanhistory.org/library/document/what-to-the-slave-is-the-fourth-of-july/, italics added.

[4] Douglass, "What to the Slave?"

[5] Aristotle, *On Rhetoric*, 1.2.1 [1355], trans. George Kennedy (Cambridge, MA: Oxford University Press, 2007).

[6] Aristotle, *On Rhetoric*, 1.3 [1358b].

[7] Burke, *A Rhetoric of Motives* (Berkeley: University of California Press, 1969), 37–46.

[8] Karlyn Kohrs Campbell, "Agency: Promiscuous and Protean," *Communication and Critical/Cultural Studies* 2 (2005): 1–19, 3.

[9] Karlyn Kohrs Campbell, *The Rhetorical Act*, 2nd ed. (Belmont, CA: Wadsworth, 1996), 9–17.

[10] Mary Church Terrell, "What It Means to Be Colored in the Capital of the United States," in Karlyn Kohrs Campbell, *Man Cannot Speak for Her*, vol. 2 (New York: Praeger, 1989), 421–432.

[11] US Catholic Conference, quoted in Jeffrey Overstreet, "Harry Potter and the Sorcerer's Stone," *Christianity Today*, January 1, 2001, http://www.christianitytoday.com/ct/2001/januaryweb-only/harrypotter.html?paging=off.

[12] Ida B. Wells, "Southern Horrors: Lynch Law in All Its Phases," in Campbell, *Man Cannot Speak for Her*, vol. 2, 385–420.

[13] Wells, "Southern Horrors."

[14] Denise Grady, "Not His First Epidemic: Dr. Fauci Sticks to the Facts," *New York Times*, March 8, 2020, https://www.nytimes.com/2020/03/08/health/fauci-coronavirus.html.

15 Jim Acosta and Brian Stelter, "White House Hasn't Approved Requests for TV Interviews with Fauci, Official Says," CNN, July 3, 2020, https://www.cnn.com /2020/07/03/media/fauci-network-tv-appearances/index.html.

16 Avis Thomas-Lester, "A Senate Apology for History on Lynching," *Washington Post,* June 14, 2005, http://www.washingtonpost.com/wp-dyn/content/article/2005/06/13 /AR2005061301720.html.

17 Yousri Marzouki and Oliver Oullier, "Revolutionizing Revolutions: Virtual Collective Consciousness and the Arab Spring," Huffington Post, http://www.huffingtonpost .com/yousri-marzouki/revolutionizing-revolutio_b_1679181.html.

18 Marzouki and Oullier, "Revolutionizing Revolutions."

19 Marzouki and Oullier, "Revolutionizing Revolutions."

20 Ashby Jones and Jacob Gershman, "Lengthy Arizona Execution Heightens Lethal-Injection Questions: Condemned Man Dies Two Hours after Drugs Were Administered," *Wall Street Journal,* July 25, 2014, http://online.wsj.com/articles /lengthy-arizona-execution-heightens-lethal-injection-questions-1406213831.

21 Jones and Gershman, "Lengthy Arizona Execution."

22 Ed Pilkington (@Edpilkington), Twitter, July 23, 2014.

23 ACLU National (@ACLU), Twitter, July 24, 2014.

24 Clifford Geertz, *The Interpretation of Cultures* (New York: Basic Books, 1973), 89, italics added.

25 William B. Gudykunst, "Individualistic and Collectivistic Perspectives on Communication: An Introduction," *International Journal of Intercultural Relations,* 22 (1998): 107–134.

26 Robert Hariman and John Louis Lucaites, "Liberal Representation and Global Order: The Iconic Photograph from Tiananmen Square," in Lawrence Prelli, ed., *Rhetorics of Display* (Columbia: University of South Carolina Press, 2006), 121–138. Image at http://www.sbs.com.au/news/article/1171447/-Tank-man-photo-on-Google-China.

27 Geertz, *The Interpretation of Cultures,* 5.

28 Judith Butler, *Precarious Life: The Power of Mourning and Violence* (New York: Verso, 2004); and Steven Johnston, *The Truth about Patriotism* (Durham, NC: Duke University Press, 2007).

29 Geertz, *The Interpretation of Cultures,* 89.

30 Judith N. Martin and Thomas K. Nakayama, *Intercultural Communication in Contexts,* 3rd ed. (Boston: McGraw-Hill, 2004), 3.

31 Barry Schwartz, "The Social Context of Commemoration: A Study of Collective Memory," *Social Forces* 61 (1982): 374.

32 Carole Blair, "Communication as Collective Memory," in *Communication as . . . Perspectives on Theory,* ed. Gregory J. Shepherd, Jeffrey St. John, and Ted Striphas (Thousand Oaks, CA: Sage, 2006), 52.

33 Maurice Halbwachs, *On Collective Memory* (Chicago, University of Chicago Press, 1992).

34 Richard Morris, *Sinners, Lovers, and Heroes* (Albany: State University of New York Press, 1997), 26.

35 Iwona Irwin-Zarecka, *Frames of Remembrance: The Dynamics of Collective Memory* (New Brunswick, NJ: Transaction, 1994), 4.

36 Irwin-Zarecka, *Frames of Remembrance,* 217.

37 Michael Kammen, *The Mystic Chords of Memory: The Transformation of Tradition in American Culture* (New York: Knopf, 1991), 27.

38 Thomas J. Steele, S.J., "The Figure of Columbia: Phillis Wheatley plus George Washington," *The New England Quarterly: A Historical Review of New England Life and Letters* 54, no. 2 (1981): 264–266.

[39] José Barreiro, ed., *Northeast Indian Quarterly: View from the Shore: American Indian Perspectives on the Quincentenary* 7 (Fall 1990): 2. See also José Barreiro, "What 1992 Means to American Indians," in *Without Discovery: A Native Response to Columbus,* ed. Ray Gonzales (Seattle: Broken Moon, 1992), 57–60.

[40] Henry Giroux, in interview with Brad Evans, "The Violence of Forgetting," *New York Times,* June 20, 2016, https://www.nytimes.com/2016/06/20/opinion/the-violence-of -forgetting.html?smprod=nytcore-iphone&smid=nytcore-iphone-share.

[41] Cheris Kramarae and Paula A. Triechler, *Amazons, Bluestockings and Crones: A Feminist Dictionary,* 2nd ed. (London: Pandora, 1992), 351, italics added.

[42] John Louis Lucaites and Celeste Michelle Condit, "Reconstructing <Equality>: Culturetypal and Counter-Cultural Rhetorics in the Martyred Black Vision," *Communication Monographs* 57 (March 1990): 21, n3.

[43] Lucaites and Condit, "Reconstructing <Equality>," 6.

[44] Michel Foucault, "The Order of Discourse," in *Language and Politics,* ed. Michael J. Shapiro (New York: New York University Press, 1984), 110.

[45] Michel Foucault, *Discipline and Punish: The Birth of the Prison,* 2nd ed. (New York: Vintage, 1995), 206.

[46] Michel Foucault, *The History of Sexuality* (New York: Vintage, 1980), 93.

[47] Michel Foucault, *The Final Foucault,* ed. James Bernauer and David Rasmussen (Cambridge, MA: MIT Press, 1987), 12.

[48] Michael Dutton, "Street Scenes of Subalternity: China, Globalization, and Rights," *Social Text* 60 (1999): 65.

[49] Bernard L. Brock, Mark E. Huglen, James F. Klumpp, and Sharon Howell, *Making Sense of Political Ideology: The Power of Language in Democracy* (New York: Rowman and Littlefield, 2005), 39.

[50] Brock et al., *Making Sense,* 39.

[51] Geertz, *The Interpretation of Cultures,* 195.

[52] Peter Berger defines legitimation in this way. We see ideology as legitimizing the social order. See Berger, *The Sacred Canopy,* 4, 9, 29.

[53] Anna Hecht, "Here's How Much the Average Wedding Cost in 2019," CNBC.com, February 14, 2020, cnbc.com/2020/02/13/how-much-the-average-wedding-cost-in-2019.html.

[54] Kenneth Burke, *Language as Symbolic Action: Essays on Life, Literature, and Method* (Berkeley: University of California Press, 1966), 6.

[55] Stuart Hall, "Ideology and Communication Theory," in *Rethinking Communication Theory,* vol. 1, ed. Brenda Dervin, Larry Grossberg, Barbara O'Keefe, and Ellen Wartella (Newbury Park, CA: Sage, 1989), 40–52.

[56] Antonio Gramsci, *Selections from the Prison Notebooks of Antonio Gramsci,* trans. and ed. Quintin Hoare and Geoffrey Nowell Smith (New York: International Publishers, 1971), 12–13.

[57] Rosemary Hennessy, "Subjects, Knowledges, ... and All the Rest: Speaking for What," *Who Can Speak? Authority and Critical Identity,* ed. Judith Roof and Robyn Weigman (Urbana: University of Illinois Press, 1995), 145–146.

[58] Joseph P. Zompetti, "Toward a Gramscian Critical Rhetoric," *Western Journal of Communication* 61, no. 1 (Winter 1997): 66–86, and John M. Murphy, "Domesticating Dissent: The Kennedys and the Freedom Rides," *Communication Monographs* 59, no. 1 (March 1992): 61–78.

[59] Stuart Hall, "Encoding, Decoding," *The Cultural Studies Reader,* ed. Simon During (London: Routledge, 1993), 98–102.

[60] Bonnie J. Dow, *Prime-Time Feminism* (Philadelphia: University of Pennsylvania Press, 1996), 13.

[61] William L. Nothstine, Carole Blair, and Gary A. Copeland, *Critical Questions: Invention, Creativity, and the Criticism of Discourse and Media* (New York: St. Martin's, 1994), 40.

Part II
Modes of Symbolic Action

Chapter 3
Language

The power of a single word was demonstrated on comedian Bill Maher's HBO show *Real Time* in May 2017. During an interview, Senator Ben Sasse invited Maher to come work in Nebraska's fields. Maher responded: "Work in the fields? Senator, I'm a house n*****."[1] Sasse remained silent while some in the audience groaned, to which Maher responded: "No, it's a joke."[2] HBO issued a statement calling the slur "inexcusable and tasteless" and bleeped the remark during rebroadcasts of the show.[3] Maher issued an apology, saying the term was "offensive" and expressing "regret" for "saying it."[4] Sasse tweeted that his own minimal reaction, a cringe, "wasn't good enough," and that he should have instead said "Hold up" and asked Maher why he thought that using the term was acceptable. Sasse said the word attacks "universal human dignity" and thus attacks "the American Creed." His final words: "Don't use it."[5]

During the *Real Time* show the following week, Maher had a lengthy conversation with rapper, producer, writer, and actor Ice Cube, who was ideally situated to critique Maher's use of the word. As a founding member of the 1990s rap group N.W.A., Ice Cube is seen as "the rapper most responsible for making the n-word a celebrated part of today's lexicon."[6] When Ice Cube asked Maher why he thought he could use the term, Maher said "there was no thought put into it" and reiterated the apology. Ice Cube accepted Maher's apology and then offered a nuanced and thorough explanation of why White people using the n-word were different from Black people saying it. He used the metaphor of "knife" to describe the n-word when used by a White person, explaining that the term can be used "as a weapon, or you can use it as a tool." When Black people say it, Ice Cube said, "it don't feel like venom," but when White people use the term "it feels like that knife stabbing me, even if they don't mean it."[7] He made clear that the word coming from a White body functioned very differently (as a venomous weapon) from the way it functioned when coming from a Black body (as a tool). We encourage you to watch Ice Cube's comments in full at https://www.youtube.com/watch?v= gnwiYdFaRfk, or search "Ice Cube Maher").

The power of the n-word and the debates over who can use it show the power of language to liberate and to subordinate, to injure and to heal. In a series of experiments, psychology researchers tested the healing effect on marginalized people when they reacted to a derogatory slur used by the dominant culture by taking the term and using it in a new way. The researchers found that that reaction can "weaken the label's stigmatizing force."[8]

Language can elicit a complex range of responses in people: it can induce fear; it can awe; it can make people weep with sadness or with joy; it can motivate people to action; or it can bore them into a stupor. Language is a tool with which to transmit information, but it is also a rich, complex, transactional web that defines who you are and how you see the people, objects, and actions that enmesh you in daily life.

If you doubt the importance of language, think about times when disagreement arises over what word to use to name a particular individual or action. Depending on how you name people's actions, your reaction to the people and their actions shifts. A crime is viewed as worthy of punishment because it is an instance in which one human being, motivated by personal gain or animosity, harmed another. An act of terrorism is viewed as worthy of even greater condemnation because it is an instance in which one human being, motivated by hatred of a group, harmed another human being in order to terrorize all members of the group to which that person belonged. A crime affects the person attacked (and that person's friends and family); an act of terrorism also affects the larger social group to which the person belongs.

Even words whose connotations seem less intense can illustrate the power of language. "Illegal" is a word that could be merely descriptive and connotatively neutral, but its use in relation to immigration has induced a more careful analysis of its use. Colorlines, a daily news site that foregrounds issues of race, began a "Drop the I-word" campaign in September 2010.[9] Claiming that "illegal" was an inaccurate and dehumanizing way to describe people who immigrate into the United States without required documentation, Colorlines sought to change the way news outlets talked about immigration. By Spring 2013, several news outlets (*USA Today,* the *Los Angeles Times,* and the *San Francisco Chronicle*) had agreed to stop using the "I-word." The Associated Press (AP) altered its stylebook, a major guide for US newspapers, to change "how we describe people living in a country illegally."[10] The AP Stylebook directs writers not to use "illegal" as an adjective for a person, but only for an action. Thus, a person might immigrate illegally, but should not be called an illegal immigrant; instead, you might use the phrase "undocumented immigrant."[11] By keeping the focus on the action, and not the person, the AP guidelines remind people "no human being is illegal."[12] Usage of the term "illegal" to describe a person declined during 2013, particularly among outlets that committed to end their usage of the term, but began to spike in 2015, causing a reinvigoration of the campaign.[13]

We open this chapter with a discussion of theories that describe how language constructs social reality. We then identify four concepts that offer a vocabulary with which to describe how language functions as symbolic action: terministic screens, public vocabulary, discursive and presentational forms, and resignification. Finally, we examine some ways in which language can be misused. This chapter demonstrates that language is more than a tool to transmit information about the world in which you live. It is a way in which you make that world.

LANGUAGE AND THE CONSTRUCTION OF SOCIAL REALITY

Early studies of language relied on the correspondence theory, which assumes that each word corresponds to some thing in the world. For example, the word "dog" corresponds to a barking, wagging, furry member of the family *Canidae*. Understanding between people using the word "dog" is based on each person's ability to know the meaning of the word and to what thing in the world it corresponds.

Although one basic function of communication is information transmission, the correspondence theory fails to fully explain the power of language, especially because subtle differences in meaning emerge for a word. Theorists now see language as much more than a tool to reference specific things in the world. People use language to construct social reality, not just to refer to reality. In the following sections, we describe theories that explain how language makes meaning.

Semiotics

In the mid-1800s, US philosopher Charles Sanders Peirce coined the term **semiotics** to describe *the relationship among signs, meanings, and referents.* Around the same time, Swiss linguist Ferdinand de Saussure pushed forcefully for a semiotic approach to studying language, arguing that a science that "studies the role of signs as part of social life" should be a part of psychology and linguistics.[14] Semiotics rejects the correspondence theory of language. It urges people to consider signifying practices—to consider that language does not *have* meaning but, as a social practice, *makes* meaning.

Semiotics recognizes a relationship between a sign and a referent, but that relationship is rather complex. Semiotics defines a sign as composed of two parts: the signifier (the sound/image of the sign or the form it takes) and the signified (the concept referenced by the signifier).[15] A sign still refers to some thing in the world (the creature wagging its tail), but it is composed of the signifier (the word "dog") and the signified. (The idea of what a dog is never corresponds perfectly to the creature wagging its tail. Otherwise, how can a Great Dane and a teacup

Chihuahua both be dogs?) In semiotics, people understand the meaning of a sign by decoding the concept that is signified, not just what the sign refers to.

The semiotic recognition of the signified enables a distinction between the denotation of a word and its connotation. **Denotation** is *the literal, common-sense meaning of a sign, ostensibly value-free and objective.* "Dog" would denote a domesticated, carnivorous, four-legged, hair-covered mammal of the family *Canidae.* If this definition sounds like something you would find in a dictionary, it is because dictionary definitions attempt to provide the denotative meaning of a word. Denotation is where the correspondence theory of meaning stops in its explanation.

Connotation is *the emotional or cultural meaning attached to a sign; it is what is signified.* Connotative meanings are usage-specific. They emerge when the sign's denotative meaning is not sufficient to completely communicate a concept. Even though the same canine can serve as the referent for "dog," "cur," "mutt," "pet," and "stray," the change in what is signified influences your understanding of that canine. "Dog" and "pet" likely induce a neutral or positive valuation, while "cur," "mutt," and "stray" would induce a negative valuation. The denotations of signs may be easily decoded, but their connotations require a more nuanced process of decoding.

The same term can have very different connotations in different contexts, because a sign does not correspond to a single concept or thing. For example, at a dog show, different categories of competition exist for each breed, including puppy dog, American-bred dog, open dog, puppy bitch, American-bred bitch, and open bitch. In that context, "bitch" has a very specific denotative meaning: a female canine. Because the word carries no negative connotation, it is common to hear a person comment to another: "Your Brittany bitch is gorgeous." In another context, "bitch" carries very negative connotations. When used as a derogatory term for a woman, it likens a human woman to a vicious and moody female canine.

Linguistic Relativity

Attention to the way that language structures meaning led to the development of the Sapir-Whorf hypothesis, also known as the **theory of linguistic relativity:** *the idea that the structure of a language influences the way people perceive the world.* Anthropologist and linguist Edward Sapir explains that a person lives in both an objective reality and a social reality constructed through language. Thus, multiple social realities exist. Sapir explains:

> Human beings . . . are very much at the mercy of the particular language which has become the medium of expression for their society. It is quite an illusion to imagine . . . that language is merely an incidental means of solving specific problems of communication or reflection. The fact of the matter is that the "real world" is to a large extent unconsciously built upon the language habits of the group. . . . The worlds in which different societies live are distinct worlds, not merely the same world with different

labels attached . . . . We see and hear and otherwise experience very largely as we do because the language habits of our community predispose certain choices of interpretation.[16]

Although people may know things exist apart from their language, they do not know what those things mean, or how to react to them, except through language. In other words, meanings are relative to the symbol system, or code, that produces them.

Many studies on the linguistic relativity theory support the idea that people's language does, indeed, affect their perceptions. For example, the range of linguistic categories for color affect whether a person sees changes in hues.[17]

An example from the art community also illustrates the power of language to structure meaning. Artist Marcel Duchamp is credited with developing the form of art known as "readymade," in which an artist elevates a found object to the highest levels of art "by the simple performative utterance of calling it 'art.'"[18] In 1916, Duchamp became a member of the Society of Independent Artists, "founded in that year with the express purpose of holding exhibitions for any artist who cared to exhibit something. There were no juries, and no work would be refused."[19] To test the group's conception of art and its purpose, Duchamp submitted, under a pseudonym, an upended urinal titled "Fountain." The committee rejected the piece. Duchamp resigned in protest because the group had violated its own commitment to accept all submissions.

This story illustrates the power of naming: a committee was given the power to determine what was art and was not. The example also raises the possibility that what people think of as a discarded urinal could be called art, and that as a result their reactions to that object—what it means to them—could change. In fact, even though "Fountain" originally was rejected as a work of art, its importance to contemporary art has attached both meaning and value to it. It is now recognized as a piece of art so important it sold in a 1997 Sotheby's auction for $1,762,500.[20] The symbolic act of Duchamp calling it "Fountain" and the ensuing controversy made a urinal into art.

People are capable of thinking beyond the limits set by language, but it takes effort. Sapir writes that "language is . . . a prepared road or groove."[21] Feminist lexicographer Julia Penelope explains that a person's language creates paths of least resistance through which they can understand the world. The more a person travels those paths, the deeper the grooves become and the more difficult it becomes to think outside of them, because "language focuses our attention on what we believe we know . . . and we neglect to glance aside at . . . the much larger, but apparently formless lands of all that we do not, but might know if we stepped outside the mainstream."[22] For example, even though language habits in the 1800s named enslaved Black people as less than fully human, activists such as British parliamentarian William Wilberforce, the Quaker Grimké sisters, former enslaved people Sojourner Truth and Frederick Douglass, and US social reformer William Lloyd Garrison were able to see outside of the groove of white supremacy to name the immanent humanity of all people, regardless of color.

LANGUAGE AS SYMBOLIC ACTION

Kenneth Burke, one of the most significant rhetorical theorists of the twentieth century, described himself as a "word-man."[23] Burke's writing on language continues to influence scholars in communication studies, English, philosophy, theatre, and sociology. His theory of rhetoric is known as **dramatism,** *an idea that is premised on two interlocking assumptions: (1) "language is primarily a species of action . . . rather than an instrument of definition," and (2) the best way to understand human relations and motives is through an analysis of symbolic action.*[24] When people use symbols, they engage in a form of human action that relies on the mobilization of symbols, rather than physical force, to act in the world. When they use language, people *do* things: they induce cooperation, foment division, create identification, constitute identity, and shape social reality.

Burke's dramatistic approach offers many concepts to explain the power of language and inspires scholars to develop even more. A few key concepts that share Burke's basic assumption that language is a species of action include terministic screens, public vocabulary, discursive and presentational forms, and resignification.

Terministic Screens

Words can shape human beings as much as human beings use words to shape the world. Burke asks: "Do we simply use words, or do they not also use us?"[25] The ability language has to use human beings is explained by the idea of a **terministic screen,** which Burke describes as *a screen composed of terms through which humans perceive the world, and that directs attention away from some interpretations and toward others.* For Burke, language always acts to direct attention, making all communication persuasive because "even if any given terminology is a *reflection* of reality, by its very nature as a terminology it must be a *selection* of reality; and to this extent it must function also as a *deflection* of reality."[26] In other words, your words screen what you see.

We explain Burke's concept with the terms "sex" and "race," and with the idea of money. People think of sex and race as purely biological, but they are not. How people see other human beings in terms of sex and race is a social construction achieved through symbolic action. People think of monetary valuation as objective; it is not. We end with an example of how two competing screens direct attention in two completely different ways.

Sex. The English language has long described the sexes of human beings in a binary and dichotomous way: male or female—and those sexes are "opposite," as in the phrase "opposite sex." More than two sexes exist, however. Many recent medical studies have determined that about one in two thousand babies are born both/and or neither/nor, and that even more people have more subtle sex anatomy variations that do not appear until later.[27] This example shows how words begin to "use us" when you consider what was done to babies who did not fit into the male/female binary. From the 1950s (when surgical intervention became a possibility) to the 1990s, doctors embraced the concealment model, which calls for radical surgical intervention. In many cases, doctors did not even consult the parents but simply made surgical adjustments to make a baby's body fit the sex the doctor "assigned."[28] Literally, babies' bodies were surgically altered to fit the linguistic binary.[29] Since the early 1990s, new language has emerged that makes space for bodies that the sex binary does not name, starting with biology professor Anne Fausto-Sterling's declaration that at least five sexes exist along a continuum (male, merm, herm, ferm, female).[30] Activists embraced the term "intersex" to describe a person who "is born with a reproductive or sexual anatomy that doesn't seem to fit the typical definitions of female or male."[31] They also demanded a shift from a concealment approach to a more patient-centered model. Language has power to reinforce binaries that use people in real ways.

Race. People often assume that race, like sex, is a biological (and hence objective and unchanging) designation, but history and recent studies prove that race is socially constructed and "not a biological fact."[32] Historian Noel Ignatiev's book, *How the Irish Became White,*[33] opens by clarifying "no biologist has ever been able to provide a satisfactory definition of 'race' . . . . The only logical conclusion is that people are members of different races because they have been assigned to them."[34] Sociologist Estelle Disch agrees: "Genetically, there is currently no such thing as 'race' and the category makes little or no sense from a scientific standpoint. What is essential, of course, is the meaning that people in various cultural contexts attribute to differences in skin color or other physical characteristics."[35] To illustrate, consider that after the great migration of the early 1900s and up to the 1960s, Germans, Irish, Italians, and Russians (who are now considered White in the United States) were considered "colored or other."[36] The rhetorical construct of race is a powerful terministic screen through which people look and that induces them to see differences that do not really exist. Where did that screen come from?

In a documentary titled *The Invention of Race,* scholars provide a detailed description of how race became so embedded in terministic screens.

During the 1400s, 1500s, and early 1600s when people emigrated to the Americas, their primary identification was according to religion and secondarily by country or region of origin (such as English, Dutch, or African). Initially, no official distinctions based on race were codified in laws.

But race would soon become an integral part of how colonists saw the world. The colonists constructed their own terministic screens. *The Invention of Race* describes how a "totalitarian framework based on rigid notions of race and sex . . . was constructed on this continent . . . plank by plank. That process started not too long after the first African people landed in Jamestown on a Dutch ship in 1619—about twenty people, stolen from Angola. But the project took decades to complete."[37] This origin is important because "the innovations that built slavery American style are inseparable from the construction of Blackness and Whiteness as we know them today."[38]

Africans initially came to the Americas as free people or indentured servants, as did many European colonists. In 1640, however, after three indentured servants (one of whom was African, one Dutch, and one Scottish) ran away from their servitude, colonial officials declared legal distinctions that infused race into terministic screens. After being caught, the Dutch and Scottish servants were sentenced to four additional years of service. The African, named John Punch, was sentenced to "labor for his master for the rest of his days," the first case of perpetual servitude codified in the colonies.[39] This differential treatment was important because most people in the colonies were poor laborers and were beginning to engage in uprisings against the wealthy landowners. Landowners created a distinction between laborers who looked like the landowners and people from Africa, which gave poor workers of European descent a small advantage. As a consequence, they "switched their allegiance from the people in their same circumstance to the people at the top. It eventually created a multi-class coalition of people who would later come to be called white."[40]

Later in the 1640s, Virginia changed its laws so that the status of a child was derived from its mother. Why? Elizabeth Key, the daughter of a free White man and an enslaved African woman, had sued for freedom on the grounds that her father was a free man. In English common law, the status of a child derived from its father. Key won freedom. In response, Virginia changed the law.

"White," as a concept, did not appear in law until the 1690s. The Virginia House of Burgesses, "the first legislative body in Colonial America" debated who would and would not be considered White. In 1682 "the Burgesses passed a law limiting citizenship to Europeans. It made all non-Europeans—'Negroes, Moors, Mollatoes, and Indians,' as the law put it—quote, 'slaves to all intents and purposes.'"[41] In 1691, they passed a law that "included the first documented use in the English-speaking colonies of the word 'white'—as opposed to English, European, or Christian—to describe the people considered full citizens. That is, the people who got to remain citizens so long as they didn't marry outside of their so-called race. The law read, quote: 'Whatsoever English or other white man or woman . . . being free . . . shall intermarry with a negro, mullato, or Indian man or woman . . . bond or free . . . shall within three months after marriage be banished and removed from this dominion forever.'"[42]

A range of official acts solidified the concept of White being different from Black. The Virginia Slave Codes of 1705 defined enslaved people of color as property. The US Census of 1790, the first national census, counted these categories: White males 16 years and older, White males under sixteen, White females, all other free persons, and slaves (each of whom counted only as three-fifths of a person for the purpose of apportioning Congressional representation). The census did not count Native Americans. The Naturalization Act of 1790 declared that only "white" people could be naturalized as citizens. Thus, only Whites could own land, vote, start a business, or serve on a jury.

Slavery has been around for millennia, but the concept of race has not. History demonstrates that race has been institutionalized—fixed into the terministic screen in the United States—at a very specific historical moment, and tied to power: who could be free, be a citizen, own land, and have legal rights. Race was incorporated into the nation's terministic screen in order to guarantee cheap labor. Race is about power, not skin pigmentation.

Even though race is part of the terministic screen and presented as though it is a biological fact, its malleability demonstrates how the term may be using people as much as people use the term. Recent studies show that "how individuals are racially classified by others and how they identify themselves...both change over time."[43] In a series of studies, sociologists Andrew M. Penner, Aliya Saperstein, and their colleagues discovered the following:

- "Cirrhosis decedents are more likely to be recorded as American Indian on their death certificates, and homicide victims are more likely to be recorded as Black [by medical examiners and funeral directors, even if they were not identified as such by next of kin], . . . suggest[ing] that seemingly non-racial characteristics, such as cause of death, affect how people are racially perceived by others and thus shape U.S. official statistics."[44]

- "Individuals who are unemployed, incarcerated, or impoverished are more likely to be seen and identify as Black and less likely to be seen and identify as White, regardless of how they were classified or identified previously."[45]

- "Incarceration increase[s] the likelihood that people are racially classified by others as black, and decreas[es] the likelihood that they are classified as White." Moreover, "even one arrest significantly increases the odds of subsequently being classified as Black, and decreases the odds of being classified as White or Asian."[46]

These researchers explain the role of daily communicative interactions on people's understanding of race: "Our results emphasize not only that racial divisions are drawn by macro-level decision making but that race and racial inequality are constantly created and renegotiated in everyday interactions."[47] National Public Radio science desk correspondent Shankar Vedantam notes, "Strong stereotypes [link] race with crime. . . . this research suggests it's not just our perceptions of race that drive our stereotypes, but our stereotypes that drive our perceptions of race." The existence of race in terministic screens directs people's attention so that they see some things and not others. Such studies illustrate the social nature of race: it is a concept developed by people rather than a function of biology.[48]

We go into this detail about race to make two things clear. First, race, itself, is rhetorical. Second, to understand rhetoric you must study race. Rhetoric scholar Lisa Flores notes that to study the "impact, influence, or circulation" of rhetoric and to understand "argument and audience," you "cannot ignore race. Rhetorical meanings, as they circulate on and around bodies, are already raced. Bodies that speak and listen, that exhort and cajole, that desire and hate are already raced."[49] Race is rhetorically constructed and, in turn, constructs the bodies of human beings so that the rhetorical actions they produce are always already perceived through senses attuned to race. Race is not just something that is. Race is made, and in its making, it infuses "dominant discourses and public vocabularies"— narratives, metaphors, and ideographs—with "racial and racist ideologies."[50] Understanding that race is rhetorical can help you understand how language maintains racist ideology.

Every single time you think about something, the words you use to articulate your thoughts have directed your attention in one way rather than another. The terms "male," "female," and "opposite sex" contribute to a terministic screen that induces humans to see only males or females. Without terms such as "intersex" and "trans," the recognition of the existence of people who do not fit the sex binary is deflected. Terms such as "Black," "White," and "Indian" also induce people to see a person's race first, as a thing that differentiates one person from others, rather than to see people's shared humanity. Because people tend to associate some races with crime and others with alcoholism, if a person is a criminal, they might see the person as Black. If the person dies from a drinking-related disease, they might see the person as a Native American. Because people also tend to think in binaries in terms of race, they see someone as *either* Black *or* White.

Money. Because US society has symbols that stand for money (currency), people tend to judge the quality of an item through its monetary value: attention is directed to the cost of a thing, rather than to its intrinsic characteristics. The monetary symbol system directs people's attention so powerfully that people judge the same thing to be of a higher quality when *only* the price assigned to it is changed. In a study that tested the power of marketing, researchers at the California Institute of Technology and Stanford University told volunteer subjects they would be tasting different wines sold at different prices. Actually, they were given the same wine over and over. Not only did the subjects indicate that the supposedly more expensive wine tasted better, their medial orbitofrontal cortexes (the part of the brain that processes feelings of pleasantness) reacted differently.[51] Because the dollar symbol directed their attention to see "more expensive" as "better quality," they were not able to see (or taste, smell, or feel) what their own senses could have imparted—that all the wine was exactly the same.

Competing Terministic Screens. Another example of the effect of terministic screens comes from the reproductive freedom and abortion controversy, a rhetorically charged issue in the contemporary United States. Two main sides have long dominated the controversy: pro-life and pro-choice. People who are pro-life tend to refer to the reality as a "baby" while those who are pro-choice tend to refer to the reality as a "fetus." Each term selects, deflects, and reflects reality in a particular way, and calls forth different clusters of terms that flesh out the contours of the screen.[52]

"Baby" accurately reflects reality inasmuch as people often ask "when is the baby due?" and feel pain at miscarriages as the loss of a baby. The term also selects a particular aspect of reality to highlight: it focuses your attention on the idea that the reality is a fully formed human being, separable from its gestational location. A person could leave a baby in a room unattended (though safely ensconced in a crib). However, when the baby is in the womb, it cannot be separated from its location. The term also selects a particular type of relationship to other human beings: babies have mothers and fathers, not women and men. "Baby" also calls forth positive associations because US culture is pronatal—it celebrates the arrival of babies—and perceives babies as innocent and pure. Once people think of the reality as a separate and distinct human being, to terminate its existence means that someone has murdered the baby. Babies can be murdered. People do not talk about "terminating" babies.

In selecting some parts of reality to highlight, the term "baby" also deflects part of reality. It deflects that the reality is located within a person's body, as well as the possibility that such a person can be anything more than a mother. It also deflects the fact that recognized development stages occur during the gestation process: from zygote, to blastocyst, to embryo, to fetus.

In the same way that "baby" reflects, deflects, and selects parts of reality, so too does the term "fetus," which selects those parts of reality that "baby" deflects. "Fetus" notes that the reality is described in medical and scientific terms, that gestational stages occur through which the fetus eventually becomes a complete human being, and that a fetus cannot exist without a person to carry it. In fact, "fetus" reverses the order of the relationship created by "baby": babies have mothers; women carry fetuses. A baby is an entity that has agency and rights—a baby has a mother, and focus is literally on the baby first. With "fetus," the woman is the entity that has agency and rights—a woman carries the fetus, and focus is on the woman first.

In selecting the medical reality of the fetus, the term highlights that the fetus is not a complete human being. Although people may think fondly of sitting in a rocking chair and cuddling with a baby, the image of cuddling with a fetus is not quite the same.

In the process of selecting, "fetus" also deflects attention away from things the term "baby" selects. "Fetus" deflects the emotional attachments people have to small human forms, as well as the idea that the fetus can be murdered. Fetuses are not murdered; instead, pregnancies are terminated.

The clusters of terms around "baby" and "fetus" form terministic screens through which individuals construct and view reality. Those screens form a context that infuses the terms with particular connotations, even though each term ostensibly refers to the same referent. As terms direct people's attention in one way rather than another, they "affect the nature of our observations." Burke posits that "much that we take as observations about 'reality' may be but the spinning out of possibilities implicit in our particular choice of terms."[53]

Public Vocabulary

Because rhetoric constructs, maintains, and transforms your understanding of reality, to understand some event in the world or some policy enacted by the government, one must ask not just "What is it?" but also "How do we talk about it?" Communication scholar Celeste Michelle Condit argues that the "process of convincing" involves more than just acceptance of a particular policy; it also requires "that a given vocabulary (or set of understandings) be integrated into the public repertoire."[54] John Louis Lucaites and Celeste Michelle Condit describe a **public vocabulary** as the *"culturally established and sanctioned"* terms *that compose people's taken-for-granted understanding of the world.*[55] A public vocabulary forms a society's terministic screen. Daily, people in a community call upon this vocabulary to justify social actions, but when conditions call for social change, "the public vocabulary needs to be managed and reconstituted in ways that require" rhetorical skill.[56] Rhetors can try to "rearrange and revivify" the existing vocabulary, or they can introduce new vocabulary.[57] Ideographs, characterizations, narratives, and metaphors are key elements of the public vocabulary.

Ideographs. Michael Calvin McGee, a communication scholar, coined the term **ideograph** to represent "*an ordinary language term found in political discourse. It is a high-order abstraction representing collective commitment to a particular but equivocal and ill-defined normative goal. It warrants the use of power, excuses behavior and belief which might otherwise be perceived as eccentric or antisocial, and guides behavior and belief into channels easily recognized by a community as acceptable or laudable.*"[58] Words such as "freedom" and "security" are examples of ideographs: they are abstract words, used in ordinary language, that warrant the use of power. People cannot point at freedom or security, yet US troops are ready to give their lives to defend them. On September 11, 2001, when physical structures (the World Trade Center and the Pentagon) had been attacked, President George W. Bush used abstract language to declare: "our very freedom came under attack."[59] Because freedom was under attack and US security was undermined, Bush called for a collective commitment to the "war on terror" in a clear attempt to warrant the use of presidential power, both in the invasion of Afghanistan and the later attack on Iraq.

It may seem strange to think of military action as antisocial, but consider this: typically, we do not condone one person taking the life of another and, hence, name it "murder." In a time of war, however, people do condone taking lives and tend to speak of it as killing (the enemy) rather than as murder. Killing in the name of freedom is not murder. An antisocial behavior is condoned, in part because the abstraction calls for the people to condone the use of that power.

Scholars have studied a range of ideographs, including family values,[60] equality,[61] choice, and life.[62] In each case, the word offers a way to track ideology as expressed through language.

Characterizations and Narratives. Characterizations are *the labels and descriptions rhetors attach to acts, agencies, agents, scenes, and purposes.* These five terms constitute what Burke calls the dramatistic pentad. An *act* is "what took place, in thought or deed"; *scene* is "the background of the act, the situation in which it occurred"; *agent* is the "person or kind of person" who "performed the act"; *agency* is the means by which the act was accomplished; and *purpose* is the justification for the act.[63] Whenever you analyze a rhetorical act, you should be able to identify the way a rhetor characterizes each of these elements.

Simply changing a word from a noun to an adjective can direct attention in a different direction by reconfiguring the relationship between agents and acts. Songwriter and musician Rhiannon Giddens explains how Edward E. Baptist's book *The Half Has Never Been Told: Slavery and the Making of American Capitalism,* clarified this:

> I'm finding a lot of strength and power in not saying *slave* and saying *enslaved person.* . . . it really makes a difference in how you look at it because you're not born a slave. You know, you're born a person, and

somebody decides to enslave you. . . . It is done to you. It is not an integral part of who you are. So that's something I'm trying to change . . . as I think about it because I found the change after I read that book . . . really powerful.[64]

In Burkean terms, referring to a person as a slave puts all the focus on the enslaved person as the agent. It is who they are. But the phrase "enslaved person" makes clear another agent is involved, the enslaver. "Enslaved" reminds the audience of the act, enslavement, that was done to one person by another person. As Giddens points out, this single shift in characterization "really makes a difference in how you look at" slavery.

By exploring where differences arise among rhetors' characterizations of act, agent, agency, scene, and purpose, you can identify motives and reasons for disagreement. Burke explains that people "may violently disagree about the purposes behind a given act, or about the character of the [people] who did it, or how [they] did it, or in what kind of situation [they] acted; or they may even insist upon totally different words to name the act itself."[65] Thus, to understand human communication, you need to understand the stories told and how the elements of the stories are characterized. Characterizations are never neutral; according to Lucaites and Condit, they "integrate cultural connotations and denotations while ascribing a typical and pervasive nature to the entity described."[66] Depending on how an agent, scene, or act is characterized, your reactions to that agent, scene, or act may change.

The various ways drug crises have been characterized illustrate the power of narratives and characterizations to frame public debate. Michael Shaw, in an article in the *Columbia Journalism Review,* explored how the opioid crisis, which predominantly impacts nonurban White people, "is being treated with a drastically different attitude and approach in words and imagery than those used to characterize heroin use in the 1970s, crack cocaine in the late 1980s, and the drug problem plaguing America's people of color and urban poor today."[67] In both verbal reporting and visual images, and in contrast to reporting on previous drug crises that focused on scenes of squalor, sociopathy, and criminality, "the opioid crisis has been framed as a threat from outside, with drug users facing an 'illness' or a 'disease' rather than a personal moral shortcoming."[68] Our point is not about whether this kinder and gentler approach is right or wrong; rather, we are pointing out that the characterization of a drug crisis that predominately affects rural and suburban Whites is quite different from the characterization of a crisis that affects urban people of color. Coverage of the crack and heroin crises characterizes users as immoral criminals and the scene as squalid cities. Coverage of the opioid crisis characterizes users as ill and the scene as regular homes.

These characterizations matter. Nearly fifty years later, the same characteristics continue. Researchers gathered one hundred popular press articles that were published between 2001 and 2011. Fifty of these focused on heroin users; fifty on prescription opioid users. In analyzing these articles, the researchers found "a consistent contrast between *criminalized* urban black and Latino heroin injectors with *sympathetic* portrayals of suburban white prescription opioid users."[69] White drug users' addiction was described "in ways that often leaves them blameless or at least sympathetic to the reader." White addicts were not described as agents; instead, something happened to them. In contrast, in the articles "about black and Latino people who use drugs, the criminality of their actions is the story"; Black and Latino people were agents who engaged in criminal actions. These characterizations matter because, as the authors of the study note, "These representational tropes reinforce racially disparate policy responses." Although people of color and Whites use illegal drugs at similar rates, people considered Black are "6–10 times more likely to be incarcerated for drug offenses."[70]

Characterizations are the building blocks of narratives, or stories. Narratives direct people to see particular relationships among characterizations and, thus, offer explanations about how reality makes sense and works.[71] You tell stories about family members, daily events, classroom incidents, and yourself. People's reliance on stories to understand the world in which they live led moral philosopher Alasdair MacIntyre to describe the human being as "a story-telling animal."[72]

Narratives play a significant role in public communication. They form and maintain public memory and teach cultural values. Communication scholar Walter Fisher identifies the ways that narratives offer good reasons in public deliberation and help people make sense of the world.[73] The dominant social narrative that informs the US public vocabulary is the American Dream, most vividly illustrated by Horatio Alger's stories. Alger wrote hundreds of books in the 1800s about young working-class men pulling themselves up by their bootstraps in order to improve their positions in life and achieving rags-to-riches success. These stories embodied the US ideal that regardless of where people start out, if they work hard enough, they can achieve success. Rhetorical critics Robert C. Rowland and John M. Jones suggest that when public figures refer to the "American Dream," they tap into this narrative and its characterization of the people in the United States as being "on a progressive journey to a better society."[74] (Chapter 6 explores narratives in more depth.)

Metaphors. A **metaphor** is *a figure of speech in which two dissimilar things are said to be similar, offering a new perspective on a known issue.* Burke explains that a metaphor provides "perspective" insofar as it is "a device for seeing something *in terms of* something else. It brings out the thisness of a that, or the thatness of a this."[75] For example, when Plato's *Republic* refers to government as the ship of state,[76] "ship" is a metaphor for government. People learn something about government by looking at it as a ship; they gain perspective on the ship-ness of government. By thinking about government as a ship, and not just the administrative arm of the state, you begin to think about government as having a direction, navigating through troubled waters, and needing a captain.

Insofar as metaphors enable you to see one thing in terms of something else, linguistics professor George Lakoff and philosophy professor Mark Johnson believe metaphors enable a person to "elaborate a concept . . . in considerable detail" and "find appropriate means for highlighting some aspects of it and hiding others."[77] Burke's observation that language selects and deflects is echoed by Lakoff and Johnson's description of how metaphors function.

A range of metaphors populates language ("range" and "populate" both being metaphors themselves). Lakoff and Johnson argue that metaphor is not only a "device of the poetic imagination" but a matter of "ordinary language."[78] They believe people's "ordinary conceptual system is metaphorical in nature,"[79] which means you cannot understand language unless you understand metaphor. Nearly every sentence you use contains metaphors. In the previous sentence, "contains" is a metaphor. Sentences are words, and cannot really contain anything; but if you think of a sentence as a structure with sides, it can hold other things ("structure," "sides," and "hold" all being extensions of the metaphor "contains").

The power of metaphor resides in its ability to structure thought and make sense of the world.[80] Lakoff explores the metaphors "tax relief" and "tax burden" to demonstrate this power. According to Lakoff, "relief" implies that a person has some affliction. In this case taxes are a burden, from which people need to be relieved. Within this metaphor, the person who relieves another of a burden is a hero, while anyone who would interfere with relief is a villain. What if, instead, people think of taxes as a patriotic obligation for living in the United States and reaping the benefits of its infrastructure? Lakoff points out:

> As Oliver Wendell Holmes famously said, taxes are the price of civilization. They are what you pay to live in America—your dues—to have democracy, opportunity and access to all the infrastructure that previous taxpayers have built up and made available to you: highways, the internet, weather reports, parks, the stock market, scientific research, Social Security, rural electrification, communications satellites, and on and on. If you belong to America, you pay a membership fee and you get all that infrastructure plus government services: flood control, air-traffic control, the Food and Drug Administration, the Centers for Disease Control and so on. . . . It is an issue of patriotism! Are you paying your dues, or are you trying to get something for free at the expense of your country? It's about being a member.[81]

Metaphors are ubiquitous and inconspicuous at the same time. They populate language, yet few people are aware of their presence. The stealth nature of metaphor is part of its power to structure thought. Political scientist Riikka Kuusisto warns that if people do not recognize that metaphors express a particular and necessarily limited perspective, they may be heard as "objective factual descriptions and come to define the only way of seeing and doing things in a specific situation."[82] Instead of offering *a* perspective, the metaphor comes to be *the* perspective. If you do not hear how metaphors direct your attention, you will begin to accept a metaphorical interpretation of the world as fixed and objective reality.

In an analysis of Western metaphors concerning the 1998–1999 war in Kosovo, Kuusisto identifies the ways US President Bill Clinton, British Prime Minister Tony Blair, and French President Jacques Chirac described the conflict through the metaphors of heroic fairy tale, athletic game, and business deal. All these metaphors operated in subtle ways to structure people's understanding of the conflict: "They made participation in the conflict chivalrous and reassuring (heroic tales), exciting and fun (games), and profitable and rational (trading)."[83] In the process, the metaphors downplayed "the misery, pain, and turbulence often associated with deadly quarrels."[84] Kuusisto concludes the metaphors "brought the complicated and destructive conflict into the sphere of the well-known and harmless."[85] The metaphors enabled people who lived outside the conflict zone and had no direct experience of the horrors to understand the war, but also provided a very particular understanding, one that "tied the progression of the events to a logic of responding and accepting the challenge, a logic that could not easily be reversed into negotiating or giving the enemy a second chance."[86] The metaphors of war as fairy tale, game, and trading directed attention toward reassurance, fun, and rationality. These metaphors also deflected attention away from the horror of war.

Discursive and Presentational Forms

Philosopher Susanne Langer significantly contributed to understanding the primary role symbols play in constructing meaning within cultures and individuals, and how rhetors and audiences achieve meaning collaboratively.[87] Langer explored all forms of symbol use, including those related to art, myth, ritual, and science. To highlight the diverse functions that symbols perform, she advanced an important distinction between two types of symbols: discursive and presentational.

Discursive symbolism is *language use with a linear structure that operates through reason and not intuition.* Discursive form breaks down complex relationships into an easy-to-follow linear structure, such as problem/cause/solution. In contrast, **presentational symbolism** is *"a direct presentation of an individual object"* that *"widens our conception of rationality far beyond the traditional boundaries, yet never breaks faith with logic in the strictest sense."*[88] Langer used art and music as the primary examples of presentational symbolism, but also highlighted how some uses of language participated in presentational form. Both verbal and visual forms can be presentational and discursive. In this chapter, we focus on the verbal.

Langer uses the metaphor of clothing to explain the differences between the two forms:

> All language has a form which requires us to string out our ideas even though their objects rest one within the other; as pieces of clothing that are actually worn one over the other have to be strung side by side on the clothesline. This property of verbal symbolism is known as *discursiveness:* by reason of it, only thoughts which can be arranged in this peculiar order can be spoken at all; any idea which does not lend itself to this "projection" is ineffable, incommunicable by means of words.[89]

If you wanted to share your experience of seeing a moose in the wild, you could do so discursively or presentationally. Discursively, you would articulate what you saw in a linear format, word after word, breaking down the experience into a description of the time, the place, the sounds, the smells, and your emotions. The experience would unfold bit by bit. In contrast, presentationally, you could offer a painting or a photograph—a virtual experience of the moose all at once, the time, place, sounds, and your emotions all contained in the presentational form, taken in by your audience not over time as your words unfold, but all at once as they look at the image. You could also use a metaphor and say that seeing the moose was a "thrill ride."

Metaphors are verbal symbolic acts that function on a level beyond the discursive and, thus, are presentational. Even though metaphors are presented in discursive form (through language), they operate presentationally. In fact, Langer argues, "Metaphor is our most striking evidence of *abstractive seeing*, of the power of human minds to use presentational symbols."[90] As metaphors encourage people to see one thing in terms of something else, they collapse all the points made about the thing, rather than stringing them out on a line. A metaphor takes a complex subject with many components (say, war) and collapses them into a single easy-to-grasp concept (say, fairy tale). Langer's main argument is that discursive action is not the only form of "articulate symbolism."[91] Presentational symbols that operate on the level of intuition and the gestalt can be both articulate and reasonable.

The German word "Gestalt" refers to a shape or form. In contemporary English usage, **gestalt** is *a pattern or structure whose parts are so integrated that one cannot really describe the pattern simply by referring to the parts.* Langer explains, "The symbolic materials given to our senses, the *Gestalten* or fundamental perceptual forms which invite us to construe the pandemonium of sheer impression into a world of things and occasions, belong to the 'presentational' order."[92] An example often used to illustrate how human beings make sense of random impression is the "dog picture" attributed to R. C. James. At first glance, the picture appears to be a random series of dots, but because the human brain possesses the perceptual form of "dog," the image of a Dalmatian emerges. (For an example of the image, see http://psychology.jrank.org/pages/1286/6-Some -principles-with-examples.html, or search "dalmation gestalt picture.")

Presentational form helps people make sense of a barrage of impressions by ordering them into a form, but a form that is more than just the sum of its parts. Just as language can name and condense a large category of things into a single term, presentational symbolism can "telescope" many concepts into a single image that psychoanalysts call a condensation symbol.[93] In relation to civic discourse, political science scholar Doris Graber defines a **condensation symbol** as *"a name, word, phrase, or maxim which stirs vivid impressions involving the listener's most basic values" and readies the listener for action.*[94]

Within rhetoric, scholars study ideographs, as well as god and devil terms, as the primary forms of condensation symbols.[95] Rhetorician Richard Weaver describes **god terms** as *"expression[s] about which all other expressions are ranked as subordinate,"* and that have the *"capacity to demand sacrifice."*[96] In contrast, **devil terms** are *"terms of repulsion."*[97] Langer's emphasis on presentational symbols shows how symbolic action always involves emotional appeals and not merely rational claims.

Condensation symbols, including ideographs, god terms, and devil terms, whether verbal or visual, operate presentationally because they do not lay out a series of ideas side by side, but instead condense them into an inseparable whole. "My country," "Old Glory," "American Dream," "un-American," and "family values" are examples of presentational form because they create a picture of the referent that possesses intense emotional or affective power. Groups often try to use such forms to advance a cause. For example, the Human Rights Campaign, the largest national lesbian, gay, bisexual, and transgender (LGBT) civil rights organization, uses the verbal condensation symbols of "Human Rights" and "Equal Rights" in its campaigns.[98] Those who oppose extending legal protections to LGBT people often refer to those legal protections as "special rights."[99] To counter the idea that those rights are special, the Human Rights Campaign highlights that the rights it fights for are human rights and *equal* rights. It supplements these powerful terms with a mathematical symbol that condenses their meaning into a symbolic form: the "=" symbol, which the campaign hopes will appeal to the historic commitment to equality in the United States.

We end our discussion of discursive and presentational symbolism with an example that highlights the difference between them. On July 9, 2011, Regan Bienvenue posted a four minute and forty-one second, black-and-white video, titled "Retarded," to YouTube.[100] As of August 10, 2021, the video had over 105,800 views and numerous repostings on Pinterest, other websites, and blogs. Throughout the video, the Rocket Summer's song "Walls" plays. During the first four minutes and twenty seconds, Regan silently holds fifty-three handwritten sticky notes up to the camera. The notes mostly contain terms such as "waste of time," "awful," "ugly," "beastly," "crap," "loser," and "worthless." The notes then tell viewers all these words are related to one word, "retarded" and, thus, to one person: "my brother," Russell. The next note says that on urbandictionary.com, these are the top-voted definitions for "retarted" (misspelled on the video) and that Russell will never be able to speak to Regan, but because Russell means the world to Regan, Regan will be Russell's voice. The last notes ask people to think about what "retarded" (and "retarted") mean before using the word. The last twenty seconds of the video show Regan interacting with Russell, who has Down Syndrome and autism. On the YouTube page, Regan asks viewers to go to urbandictionary.com to vote down these definitions.

If you watch the video, think about how our discursive description cannot really capture its presentational power. Although the words Regan presents are central to the video, more is going on than the discursive request to stop using the term and to vote down the definitions. Note after note after note with pejorative terms builds an impression of hurt and pain. Regan's distraught face, the accumulation of the notes, and the mournful music all build an impression that exceeds the words themselves. In fact, even the words are more than discursive symbols: the hurtful power of the words is made present by their accumulation. The video ending, with Russell laughing and smiling, shows that Regan's brother is not worthless. In reducing the video to only the words used, to the discursive appeal, you miss the power of the video as a presentational whole.

Viewers responded by voting down the definitions on urbandictionary.com. Regan thanked them in a follow-up video.[101] If you visited urbandictionary.com in

June 2014, the top definition of "retarted" focused on the hurt and pain that the word causes even when it is spelled correctly. Entries on the site also encouraged people to stop using the word in hurtful ways and to join the Spread the Word to End the Word movement.[102] If you visit urbandictionary.com now, though, the definitions have reverted to the ones Regan criticized.

Resignification

The concepts of terministic screens, public vocabulary, and discursive and presentational form explain how language constructs social meaning and effects social change. Language itself can also be the focus of change—where the meanings of words, as words, are challenged and transformed. Burke noted this possibility: "A Dramatistic approach to the analysis of language starts with problems of terministic catharsis," as "when a major term is found somehow to have moved on, and thus to have in effect changed its nature either by adding new meanings to its old nature, or by yielding place to some other term that henceforth takes over its functions wholly or in part."[103] A term might "move on" when its connotations are challenged.

Resignification is *a process in which people reject the connotation of a symbol, expose how the meaning of the symbol is constructed, and attempt to change its connotation (and maybe even its denotation).* If a group is labeled with a particular word, it can reject the sign, saying "That word does not accurately denote us," or resignify the sign, saying "That word does denote our group, but its connotation is one we reject." Thus, when you seek to change the meaning of a sign, or to resignify it, you need to think about both the connotational and denotational meanings. A few examples illustrate the possibilities and perils of resignification.

Lawyer and civic activist Urvashi Vaid, in an analysis of lesbian and gay rights, found that gay men originally used the word "queer" as a form of self-naming. By the 1920s, men who thought of themselves as different because of their homosexual attraction to other men called themselves "queer."[104] The term later developed its negative connotation, when it began to be used as an epithet. This connotation did not develop overnight. As rhetorician Judith Butler explains, "'Queer' derives its force precisely through the repeated invocation by which it has become linked to accusation, pathologization, insult."[105] "Queer" came not only to denote sexuality, but also to connote something negative, immoral, and wrong. The connotation of a term is not an inherent or fixed part of it: what is signified develops over time, as people repeatedly use the term in contexts that infuse it with negative (or positive) meaning.

The fact that terms have histories explains the difficulty involved in resignifying them. People cannot simply decree that the connotation of a term change. If a connotation develops as the result of repeated usage that derogates, it can only change as the result of repeated usage that infuses the term with new, positive connotations. Resignification requires the repeated invocation of a term, linking it to praise, normalization, and celebration. The meaning of "queer," for example, has altered with the emergence of queer theory and queer studies in the academy, Queer Nation's chant "We're here! We're queer! Get used to it!" and queer theory scholars such as Vaid reclaiming the term. Instead of unreflexively using language, resignifiers "seek to recite language oppositionally so that hegemonic terms take on alternative, counter-hegemonic meanings."[106] Words are consciously used as a way to challenge dominant meanings. Unfortunately, even when a term is resignified within a group, its new meaning may not carry beyond that group, which is why "queer" is still used as an epithet against people. Even though resignification is possible, it is difficult.

SlutWalks are another example of resignification.[107] Historically, the word "slut" referred to a slovenly girl; in contemporary usage, it has risen to the status of a "four-letter word"[108] that accuses a woman of being sexually promiscuous and impure. For example, in January 2011 a police officer at a York University (Canada) panel on campus safety said women should stop dressing like "sluts" if they wanted to avoid sexual assault.[109] Instead of saying "I am not a slut" or "we don't dress like sluts," which communication scholar Annie Hill points out would have "affirm[ed] the stigmatic division of women operative in rape logic,"[110] campus activists embraced the term "slut" and responded by planning SlutWalks. Organizers signaled that they could be both prosex and antirape.[111] Planners rejected the division of women into good and bad, slut and pure, and so refused victim-blaming and slut-shaming.[112] Organizers of SlutWalk Seattle made clear the importance of the term: "One of the most effective ways to fight hate is to disarm the derogatory terms employed by the haters, embracing them and giving them positive connotations."[113] SlutWalks and the surrounding activism have embraced the term "slut" and sought to change its meaning.[114]

Resistance to reclaiming "slut" illustrates the complexity of resignification. Sociology professor Gail Dines and law professor Wendy J. Murphy describe the attempt to change the meaning as a "waste of precious feminist resources," because the term is "so saturated with the ideology that female sexual energy deserves punishment."[115] A group of Black women also challenge the SlutWalk movement to rename and rebrand itself. Calling for an intersectional approach, they argue: "As Black women, we do not have the privilege . . . to play on destructive representations burned in our collective minds, on our bodies and souls for generations."[116] They explain that, given the power of historical and contemporary stereotypes about Black women's sexuality, the word "slut" carries more intense emotional baggage for them and, thus, is less open to being resignified when applied to Black women's bodies. HuffPost writer Zeba Blay argues that Amber Rose's October 2015 SlutWalk in Los Angeles marked a turning point in the debate. Because that event was organized by a woman of color for women of color, and included people with diverse genders, it addressed the myriad forms "of slut-shaming and victim blaming" and made clear "There *is* room for women of color in the SlutWalk movement—and it has to be on our terms."[117] When organizing a protest around sexual violence, one could not assume all women, or all people, experience sexual violence in the same way. Sexual violence and racialized violence intersect.

Although resignification is possible, it is not easy. Rhetors cannot simply snap their fingers and declare that the connotation of a word has changed. As the opening example of this chapter illustrates, who uses the term, in what context, and to what end, all matter, as does the repeated use of the word by others whose politics and terministic screens may not align with the politics and terministic screens of the resignifiers.

When a dominant group has used a term to injure and marginalize another group, a repetition of that term by the dominant group can repeat that injury. This does not mean that some terms should be legally banned, but rather that people should think carefully about what it means to use a term. Are you the group to whom the term is applied? Or are you part of the group that has repeated that term as a way to injure others? Judith Butler explains that "The resignification of speech requires opening new contexts, speaking in ways that have never been legitimated, and hence producing legitimation in new and future forms."[118] In other words, human beings who have been used by language must be the ones to use it in new ways. Resignification is not achieved with a single utterance. Instead, it requires using the term in new ways, in new contexts, and in ways that challenge dominant meanings. And, slowly, the meaning of the resignified term is given legitimacy, is given meaning.

As an illustration, many of those who participated in the 2017 Women's March made signs in response to Donald Trump's 2005 hot-mic comment about how "when you're a star, they let you do it. You can do anything. . . Grab them by the pussy. You can do anything."[119] Trump used "pussy" in a way that injures, reducing women to a body part that he could grab without consent. During the Women's March on Washington, and around the country and globe, many wore pink "pussy hats" (knitted and stitched to look like cat ears) and held up signs declaring "This pussy grabs back." Actress and political activist Ashley Judd recited nineteen-year-old Nina Donovan's poem "Nasty Woman," which declared, "And our pussies ain't for grabbing. . . . . Our pussies are for our pleasure. They are for birthing new generations of filthy, vulgar, nasty, proud, Christian, Muslim, Buddhist, Sikh, you name it, for new generations of nasty women."[120]

In response to the signs, TV host and lawyer Michael Smerconish asked documentarian Michael Moore "Has the word been normalized?"[121] Moore answered "Women have normalized it and owned it." Smerconish said, "But not us." Moore emphatically replied "No! No! . . . . it's time to show some respect but let them own the word."[122]

Even when words are reclaimed, they might (intentionally or unintentionally) create other exclusions. At the 2017 Women's March on Washington, reclaiming "pussy," for example, reasserted the assumption that having a vagina is essential to womanhood. As a result, many trans women felt excluded from the event. Resignification is a difficult and complicated process.

THE MISUSE OF LANGUAGE

Burke's description of human beings as "symbol-making, symbol-using, symbol-misusing,"[123] means that symbol use is not neutral. Symbols can be used to create differences among people, or to denigrate groups or individuals. They can be used to damage people, ideas, or institutions. In this section, we discuss some misuses of language and ways to identify them. We do not provide an exhaustive list of ethically questionable rhetoric but introduce you to some of the unscrupulous ways that language can be used: doublespeak; truncated passives; and people, places, and topics of silence. Most of this book celebrates the positive uses of rhetoric as symbolic action, but language can also be used to deceive and silence people.

Doublespeak

In the insightful novel *1984* (written in 1949), George Orwell depicted a society misled by language. Orwell's fictional society developed a new form of English, "Newspeak." In the novel, dictionaries were rewritten and words changed to alter people's thinking. Orwell described this new language in the appendix of the novel: "The purpose of Newspeak was not only to provide a medium of expression for the world-view and mental habits proper [for society], but to make all other modes of thought impossible."[124] Through the use of deliberately ambiguous language, it became possible to hold views that were otherwise contradictory, enabling the ruling party of the state to have as the state slogan: "War is peace; freedom is slavery; ignorance is strength." Orwell's conception of language is similar to the one we have laid out in this chapter: language and thought are linked, so the way to manipulate thought is to manipulate language.

Unfortunately, Newspeak is not limited to the fictional world. Hitler's concentration camps used the slogan "work will set you free," even though no one was freed and the work was forced labor. The Obama administration was accused of using "newspeak" to explain its use of drones in the "war on terror."[125] In 2009, the United States intensified the war in Afghanistan with a surge in troop deployments and by "shifting use of Remote Piloted Aircraft—drones—from surveillance to targeted killing."[126] Although the killing was supposedly targeted, in Pakistan alone, in the ten-year span between 2004 and 2014, drones killed 2310 to 3743 people, of whom 416 to 957 were civilians and 168 to 202 were children. Apparently the drones missed their targets over 20 percent of the time.[127] The decision on whom to "target" (meaning "kill") was based on a "disposition matrix," which journalist Glenn Greenwald called an "Orwellian euphemism for due-process-free presidential assassinations."[128]

Taking a cue from Orwell, English professor William Lutz wrote about **doublespeak,** *language used in the real world to confuse or deliberately distort its actual meaning rather than to achieve understanding.* Lutz explained doublespeak this way:

> Doublespeak is language that pretends to communicate but really doesn't. It is language that makes the bad seem good, the negative appear positive, the unpleasant appear attractive or at least tolerable. Doublespeak is language that avoids or shifts responsibility, language that is at variance with its real or purported meaning. It is language that conceals or prevents thought; rather than extending thought, doublespeak limits it.[129]

Lutz identifies two types of doublespeak: euphemism and inflated language.

A **euphemism** is *a word used to denote a thing in a way that avoids connotations of harshness or unpleasantness.* Consider the way people talk about lying. A plethora of words are available in English to describe dishonesty or degrees of lying, most of which enable people to avoid saying that they lied: "white lie," "deception," "dishonesty," "untruth," "evasion," "falsehood," "fib," "fiction," "conceal," "hyperbole," "guile," "prevarication," "tall tale," "misstatement," "omission," "misleading," and so on. Very few words exist for honesty: the main examples are "blunt," "candid," and "frank."[130] Most news fact-checkers avoid using the word "lie" because it focuses on the intent of the speaker, and instead use terms such as "false" or "misleading" that focus on the claim. Glenn Kessler, the fact-checker at the *Washington Post,* documented more than "4,000 false or misleading claims" by Trump after January 2017, but did not use "lie" until August 2018,[131] when he reported that former Trump attorney Michael Cohen's plea deal offered "indisputable evidence that Trump and his allies have been deliberately dishonest" regarding hush money it had paid regarding Trump's relationships with two women.[132]

Euphemisms can be unethical because they tend to lessen the harshness of something that probably should be judged harshly. Even though the full horror of the Holocaust is known, even now public officials use euphemisms to describe it. In 2017, for example, then–press secretary Sean Spicer tried to justify US air strikes against Syria by arguing that Assad's use of chemical weapons was worse than Hitler's atrocities because Assad dropped chemical weapons onto towns, whereas Hitler used them in what Spicer called a "Holocaust center." Instead of naming "concentration camps" or "death camps," Spicer used the more neutral term "center."[133]

Inflated language, Lutz explains, is *"language designed to make the ordinary seem extraordinary; to make everyday things seem impressive; to give an air of importance to people, situations, or things that would not normally be considered important; to make the simple seem complex."*[134] Inflated language is clearly evident in advertising. For instance, if you go to the store and see food labeled as "home-style," the language seems to suggest a type of food preparation. In reality the term is meaningless because it can be used to mean various things.[135] When television channels declare they are about to air a "special encore presentation," they are using inflated language to describe a rerun. People sometimes use inflated language on résumés to try to make their jobs sound more impressive, for example, "cleaning specialist" instead of "janitor," or "special administrative assistant" instead of "work-study student worker." (Just to be clear: you should not use inflated language on your résumé. Employers are very critical of inflated language.)

Truncated Passives

The power of language resides in its grammatical structure as well as in the individual words. Julia Penelope, a linguist who focuses on language structures, reminds people "languages are much more than the words in their vocabularies. They are systems of rules."[136] Those rules, themselves, contain political consequences. In particular, Penelope encourages people to watch out for **truncated passives,** *sentences that use a passive verb in order to delete the agent of action.* A sentence uses passive voice when it combines some "to be" verb with another verb and no do-er of the action appears in the sentence. Using the passive voice "The toy was broken" instead of the active voice "I broke the toy" enables the speaker to leave out the phrase ". . . by me."

People who attempt to avoid responsibility for the consequences of their actions use truncated passives. When a communicator deletes the agent of action, then only the object on which the agent acted is present in the sentence. In this way, Penelope says, "Passives without agents foreground the objects (victims) in our minds so that we tend to forget that some human agent is responsible for performing the action,"[137] as in "mistakes were made."[138]

In the 2014 "Bridgegate" scandal, New Jersey Governor Chris Christie's close aides, as a form of political retribution, allegedly ordered lanes to the George Washington Bridge to be closed, resulting in a massive traffic jam. Christie, in his State of the State address, said of the debacle, "Mistakes were clearly made."[139] This phrase begs the question: mistakes were made *by whom?* Instead of saying "I made mistakes," or "This person made mistakes," Christie's language suggested that the mistakes happened outside of human control.

Penelope explains, "Agentless passives conceal and deceive when it doesn't suit speakers' or writers' purposes to make agency explicit. . . . This makes it easy to suppress responsibility" and, thus, results in "protection of the guilty and denial of responsibility, . . . the pretense of objectivity, . . . and trivialization."[140] Identifying truncated passives is one way to identify hidden power. Once you identify a truncated passive, you can begin to ask who had the power to do this thing that happened.

Penelope's insight can be used to explain the way language structures the way people think about sexual violence. Antiviolence educator Jackson Katz uses this example:

John beat Mary. [active voice]

Mary was beaten by John. [passive voice]

Mary was beaten. [truncated passive]

Mary was battered. [truncated passive]

Mary is a battered woman.[141]

Each sentence is grammatically correct but offers a different characterization of the event. When a rhetor uses an active verb, the agent is foregrounded: the agent begins the sentence. When a rhetor uses passive voice, the victim is foregrounded: the victim becomes the first potential agent. The final sentence completely removes the agent, and instead characterizes Mary as a particular type of person instead of being someone who was acted upon. Rhetors using the truncated passive enable blaming the victim because the victim is the only one present in the sentence. Katz explains "the political effect has been to shift the focus from John to Mary."[142] Psychology research confirms that the use of the passive voice when discussing sexual violence correlates with acceptance of rape myths. The more someone uses the passive voice when describing an assault, the less likely they are to see the assailant as the responsible agent of action.[143]

PEOPLE, PLACES, AND TOPICS OF SILENCE

Language is not only a collection of words, but a system of rules with political consequences. Language rules influence who can speak, about what, and where. To truly understand language, people need to understand that it is a form of power and a place where power is contested. French philosopher Michel Foucault believed it was possible to trace power by analyzing language. He wrote about language rules governing people, places, and topics in the essay "The Discourse on Language," which outlined "rules of exclusion" that control people's use of language:

> We know perfectly well that we are not free to say just anything, that we cannot simply speak of anything, when we like or where we like; not just anyone, finally, may speak of just anything. We have three types of prohibition, covering objects, ritual with its surrounding circumstances, the privileged or exclusive right to speak of a particular subject; these prohibitions interrelate, reinforce and complement each other, forming a complex web, continually subject to modification.[144]

Foucault recognized that people are not allowed to speak about certain topics, that cultural practices limit what people speak about and how they can speak, and that certain topics may only be addressed by particular people (such as experts). These prohibitions also interact to create additional constraints. Who speaks, where, and about what is governed by rules of discourse. If you analyze language, then, you can discover people, places, and topics of silence.

Think about how these rules govern language use in a classroom. If a class is discussing a particular topic and a class member starts talking about something that goes beyond that topic, the other students might experience discomfort or irritation. Constraints on whose speech matters in the classroom also make power dynamics visible. For example, students rarely take notes when other students speak; nor do they direct their comments to other students, but instead funnel them through the instructor. In the classroom, the teacher is accorded credibility to speak. When students do formal presentations, they often move to the podium. People in the United States have been acculturated to the rules of discourse to recognize that the podium is a location that accords a person more power.

The rules governing people, places, and topics are in constant flux. For example, a significant revision of the rules of discourse in the public sphere occurred as part of the US struggle to abolish slavery during the 1800s. Initially, slavery was viewed as a private economic matter, not an issue of public concern. The language of the time reflected this view. Additionally, when it came to debating issues in the public sphere, women and African Americans were not granted access. Thus, women and African Americans who were abolitionists had to justify their right to speak even before broaching the topic of slavery. They challenged the rules about who was allowed to speak. Their eloquence and rational arguments made clear their brains were not inferior. Women's and African Americans' struggle for the podium, for the right to speak, was a challenge to the rules that governed communication in the public sphere.

The first US-born woman known to speak in public to a mixed-sex audience was African American Maria W. Miller Stewart, who addressed Boston's African American abolitionist community between 1831 and 1833.[145] Later, White Quaker sisters Sarah and Angelina Grimké spoke against slavery and argued that the era's dictates on womanhood were contradictory. Historian Barbara Welter, in the influential book *Dimity Convictions,* notes that during this time period, women were expected to be pure, pious, domestic, and submissive.[146] If women believed slavery was an affront to piety, however, they had to leave the domestic sphere to agitate against it. Ultimately, the rules governing discourse in the public sphere shifted. Slavery became a topic open to debate; women and African Americans were slowly recognized as legitimate participants in this debate; and the evidence they brought from their own experience began to count.

CONCLUSION

Language is messy, unpredictable, and fascinating. Language is a symbol system through which human beings construct, maintain, and transform social reality. It forms the terministic screens through which people observe and understand reality, and composes the public vocabulary central to public policy and identity formation. The role language plays in symbolic action is complex because language can operate both discursively and presentationally. Because it can operate presentationally—through metaphors and condensation symbols—it can become emotionally charged. Language is so central to reality that words, themselves, become a site for struggle, as in the case of resignification.

Language defines what people know. It both enables and restrains; it makes sense of the world and imposes a particular sense on the world. It limits what you know, but also provides the possibility of seeing beyond the limits. Language does more than correspond to reality; it allows human beings to imagine a reality that may not yet exist. It allows human beings to imagine, hope, and hypothesize.

Even though people tend to think public deliberation is at its best when purely logical and rational, in reality, the artistry of language affects its persuasiveness. Public discourse occurs within a larger cultural and symbolic context, or public vocabulary, and calls on taken-for-granted assumptions about the world. To convince people, you need to think about your vocabulary as much as your goal.

When responding to rhetoric and formulating rhetorical messages, people must understand, analyze, critique, and consider the language choices involved. The use of language to communicate is a symbolic action; consequently, individuals exercise choice about the nature of that action and about whether to use or misuse it.

The analysis of language requires nuanced thinking and facile imaginations. People must think not only about what was said, but what else could have been said. Why was one word chosen, and how did it direct your attention differently from the way another word might have? Identifying the difference between what was said and what could have been said will help identify the subtle ways in which rhetoric is at work. Identifying silences (of people, about topics, and in places) also enables you to identify the way language and power interact. Because language is a way to exercise power, and because power resides in language, understanding locations of silence is important.

DISCUSSION QUESTIONS

1. Can you think of an example where two different terms for the same thing direct your attention in different ways, selecting, reflecting, or deflecting different aspects of "reality"?
2. Can you think of examples of metaphors that have become so ingrained in the English language that people do not even think of them as metaphors?
3. Discuss how people, places, actions, and events are characterized in news coverage of a recent event. How were the people characterized? How did language shape the way the events, places, actions, and people were interpreted?
4. Identify an example of a term undergoing resignification. How has its connotation changed? Has its denotation changed?

RECOMMENDED READINGS

Burke, Kenneth. "Dramatism." In *International Encyclopedia of the Social Sciences,* vol. 7, edited by David L. Sills, 445–452. New York: Macmillan and Free Press, 1968.

Burke, Kenneth. "Terministic Screens." In *Language as Symbolic Action,* 44–62. Berkeley: University of California Press, 1966.

Condit, Celeste Michelle, and John Louis Lucaites. "Preface: Toward Consideration of the Rhetorical Culture of Equality." In *Crafting Equality: America's Anglo-African Word,* ix–xix. Chicago: University of Chicago Press, 1993.

Fisher, Walter R. "Narration as a Human Communication Paradigm: The Case of Public Moral Argument." *Communication Monographs* 51, no. 1 (March 1984): 1–22.

Kuusisto, Riikka. "Heroic Tale, Game, and Business Deal? Western Metaphors in Action in Kosovo." *Quarterly Journal of Speech* 88, no. 1 (February 2002): 50–68.

Lucaites, John Louis, and Celeste Michelle Condit. "Reconstructing <Equality>: Culturetypal and Counter-Cultural Rhetorics in the Martyred Black Vision." *Communication Monographs* 57 (March 1990): 5–24.

ENDNOTES

[1] Maher said the complete word. We have chosen to not spell it out precisely because of its power to injure.

[2] "Growing Outrage over Bill Maher's Racial Slur on Live Television," *ABC News,* June 3, 2017, https://www.youtube.com/watch?v=2z8ybuZ5aMc.

[3] Kory Grow, "Ice Cube on Bill Maher Racial Slur: 'You Gotta Know When to Shut Up,'" *Rolling Stone,* June 8, 2017, https://www.rollingstone.com/music/news/ice-cube -on-bill-maher-n-word-know-when-to-shut-up-w486487.

[4] Nicole Chavez, "Bill Maher Apologizes for Using Racial Slur during 'Real Time' Interview," CNN, June 3, 2017, https://www.cnn.com/2017/06/03/entertainment/bill-maher-racial-slur-sasse-interview/index.html.

[5] Chavez, "Bill Maher Apologizes."

[6] Rodney Carmichael, "Ice Cube Leaves Bill Maher Shaken and Stirred over the N-Word," NPR, June 12, 2017, https://www.npr.org/sections/therecord/2017/06/12/532474238/ice-cube-leaves-bill-maher-shaken-and-stirred-over-the-n-word.

[7] *Real Time with Bill Maher,* season 15, episode 18, aired June 9, 2017, HBO, https://www.hbo.com/real-time-with-bill-maher/2017/18-episode-428; and *Real Time with Bill Maher,* "Ice Cube and Symone Sanders on White Privilege," video, aired June 9, 2017, HBO, https://www.youtube.com/watch?v=gnwiYdFaRfk.

[8] Adam D. Galinsky, Synthia S. Wang, Jennifer A. Whitson, Eric M. Anicich, Kurt Hugenberg, and Galen V. Bodenhausen, "The Reappropriation of Stigmatizing Labels: The Reciprocal Relationship between Power and Self-Labeling," *Psychological Science* 24, no. 10 (2013): 2020.

[9] "Drop the I-Word," Colorlines, 2013, http://colorlines.com/droptheiword.

[10] Paul Colford, "'Illegal Immigrant' No More," *AP: The Definitive Source* (blog), April 2, 2013, http://blog.ap.org/2013/04/02/illegal-immigrant-no-more.

[11] As cited in Colford, "'Illegal Immigrant' No More."

[12] Jose Antonio Vargas, quoted in Rachel Weiner, "AP Drops 'Illegal Immigrant' from Stylebook," *Washington Post,* April 2, 2013, http://www.washingtonpost.com/blogs/post-politics/wp/2013/04/02/ap-drops-illegal-immigrant-from-stylebook.

[13] Rinku Sen, "Let's Drop the I-Word Again," Colorlines, November 6, 2015, https://www.colorlines.com/articles/lets-drop-i-word%E2%80%94again.

[14] Ferdinand de Saussure, quoted in Daniel Chandler, *Semiotics: The Basics* (New York: Routledge, 2007), 2–4.

[15] Sonya Andermahr, Terry Lovell, and Carol Wolkowitz, *A Glossary of Feminist Theory* (New York: Oxford University Press, 2000), 240.

[16] Edward Sapir, "The Status of Linguistics as a Science," *Language* 5, no. 4 (1929): 209–210.

[17] Julia M. Penn, *Linguistic Relativity versus Innate Ideas* (Paris: Mouton, 1972), 39.

[18] Michael Mackenzie, "Marcel Duchamp and the Antimonies of Art Historical and Art Critical Discourse," *Modernism/Modernity* 7, no. 11 (2000): 154.

[19] Mackenzie, "Marcel Duchamp," 154.

[20] Francis M. Naumann, "The Art of Defying the Art Market," *Tout-Fait: The Marcel Duchamp Studies Online Journal* 2, no. 5 (April 2003), http://www.toutfait.com/issues/volume2/issue_5/news/naumann/naumann1.htm.

[21] Edward Sapir, *Language: An Introduction to the Study of Speech* (New York: BiblioBazaar, 1921/1939/2007), 23.

[22] Julia Penelope, *Speaking Freely* (New York: Pergamon, 1990), 203.

[23] David Blakesley, "Introduction: Kenneth Burke, Word-Man," in Kenneth Burke, *Late Poems, 1968–1993: Attitudinizing Verse-Wise, while Fending for One's Selph, and in a Style Somewhat Artificially Colloquial* (Columbia: University of South Carolina Press, 2005), xvii.

[24] Kenneth Burke, "Dramatism," in *International Encyclopedia of the Social Sciences,* vol. 7, ed. David L. Sills (New York: Macmillan and Free Press, 1968), 447, italics added.

[25] Kenneth Burke, "Definition of Man," in *Language as Symbolic Action,* (Berkeley: University of California Press, 1966), 6.

[26] Burke, "Terministic Screens," in *Language as Symbolic Action,* 45.

[27] Melanie Blackless, Anthony Charuvastra, Amanda Derryck, Anne Fausto-Sterling, Karl Lauzanne, and Ellen Lee, "How Sexually Dimorphic Are We? Review and Synthesis," *American Journal of Human Biology* 12 (2000): 151–166. See also Julie A. Greenberg, "Defining Male and Female: Intersexuality and the Collision between Law and Biology," *Arizona Law Review* 41 (Summer 1999): 265–328.

[28] Anne Tamar-Mattis, "Medical Decision Making and the Child with a DSD," *Endocrine Today,* November 10, 2008, http://endocrinetoday.com/view.aspx?rid=32542.

[29] Suzanne J. Kessler, "The Medical Construction of Gender: Case Management of Intersexed Infants," *Signs* 16, no. 1 (Autumn 1990): 3–26.

[30] Anne Fausto-Sterling, "The Five Sexes," *The Sciences* 33, no. 2 (March/April 1993): 20–24.

[31] Intersex Society of North America, "What is Intersex?" 2008, http://www.isna.org/faq /what_is_intersex.

[32] Nell Irvin Painter, quoted in John Biewen (producer), *The Invention of Race, MPR News,* December 5, 2017, https://www.mprnews.org/story/2017/12/05/the_invention_of _race.

[33] Noel Ignatiev, *How the Irish Became White* (New York: Routledge, 2009).

[34] Ignatiev, *How the Irish,* 1.

[35] Estelle Disch, *Reconstructing Gender: A Multicultural Anthology,* 5th ed. (Boston: McGraw-Hill, 2009), 22.

[36] Nancy Foner and George M. Fredrickson, Eds., *Not Just Black and White: Historical and Contemporary Perspectives on Immigration, Race and Ethnicity in the United States* (New York: Russell Sage Foundation, 2005).

[37] Biewen, *The Invention of Race.*

[38] Biewen, *The Invention of Race.*

[39] Biewen, *The Invention of Race.*

[40] Biewen, *The Invention of Race.*

[41] Biewen, *The Invention of Race.*

[42] Biewen, *The Invention of Race.*

[43] Andrew M. Penner and Aliya Saperstein, "How Social Status Shapes Race," *Proceedings of the National Academy of Sciences* 105, no. 50 (2008): 19628–19630.

[44] Andrew Noymer, Andrew M. Penner, and Aliya Saperstein, "Cause of Death Affects Racial Classification on Death Certificates," *PLoS One* 6, no. 1 (2011): e15812.

[45] Penner and Saperstein, "How Social Status," 19628.

[46] Aliya Saperstein, Andrew M. Penner, and Jessica M. Kizer, "The Criminal Justice System and the Racialization of Perceptions," *Annals of the American Academy of Political and Social Sciences* 651 (2014): 104–121. See also Aliya Saperstein and Andrew M. Penner, "Beyond the Looking Glass: Exploring Fluidity in Racial Self-Identification and Interviewer Classification," *Sociological Perspectives* 57 (2014): 186–207.

[47] Aliya Saperstein and Andrew M. Penner, "Racial Fluidity and Inequality in the United States," *American Journal of Sociology* 118, no. 3 (November 2012): 712.

[48] Shankar Vedantam, "Study: Stereotypes Drive Perceptions of Race," *Code Switch,* NPR, February 11, 2014, http://www.npr.org/blogs/codeswitch/2014/02/11/275087586 /study-stereotypes-drive-perceptions-of-race?utm_medium=Email&utm _source=share&utm_campaign.

[49] Lisa A. Flores, "Between Abundance and Marginalization: The Imperative of Racial Rhetorical Criticism," *Review of Communication* 16, no. 1 (2016), 4–24, 7.

[50] Flores, "Between Abundance and Marginalization," 13.

51 Hilke Plassmann, John O'Doherty, Baba Shiv, and Antonio Rangel, "Marketing Actions Can Modulate Neural Representations of Experienced Pleasantness," *Proceedings of the National Academy of Sciences* 105, no. 3 (January 22, 2008): 1050–1054.

52 The description of "fetus" and "baby" as illustrations of terministic screens first appeared in Victoria Pruin DeFrancisco and Catherine Helen Palczewski, *Communicating Gender Diversity* (Thousand Oaks, CA: Sage, 2007), 110–111.

53 Burke, "Terministic Screens," 46.

54 Celeste Michelle Condit, *Decoding Abortion Rhetoric: Communicating Social Change* (Urbana: University of Illinois Press, 1990), 6.

55 John Louis Lucaites and Celeste Michelle Condit, "Reconstructing <Equality>: Culturetypal and Counter-Cultural Rhetorics in the Martyred Black Vision," *Communication Monographs* 57 (March 1990): 8.

56 Lucaites and Condit, "Reconstructing <Equality>," 8.

57 Lucaites and Condit, "Reconstructing <Equality>," 8.

58 Michael Calvin McGee, "The 'Ideograph': A Link between Rhetoric and Ideology," *Quarterly Journal of Speech* 66 (February 1980): 15, italics added.

59 George W. Bush, "Address to the Nation by President George W. Bush regarding Terrorist Attacks on the World Trade Center and the Pentagon," Federal News Service, September 11, 2001, LexisNexis.

60 Dana L. Cloud, "The Rhetoric of <Family Values>: Scapegoating, Utopia, and the Privatization of Social Responsibility," *Western Journal of Communication* 62, no. 4 (Fall 1998): 387–419.

61 Celeste Michelle Condit and John Louis Lucaites, *Crafting Equality: America's Anglo-African Word* (Chicago: University of Chicago Press, 1993).

62 Celeste Condit Railsback, "The Contemporary American Abortion Controversy: Stages in the Argument," *Quarterly Journal of Speech* 70, no. 4 (November 1984): 410–424.

63 Kenneth Burke, *A Grammar of Motives* (Berkeley: University of California Press, 1969), xv.

64 Quoted in Terry Gross, "Rhiannon Giddens Speaks for the Silenced," *Fresh Air,* NPR, May 11, 2017, https://www.npr.org/templates/transcript/transcript.php?storyId =527911058.

65 Burke, *A Grammar of Motives,* xv.

66 Lucaites and Condit, "Reconstructing <Equality>," 7.

67 Michael Shaw, "Photos Reveal Media's Softer Tone on Opioid Crisis," *Columbia Journalism Review,* July 26, 2017, https://www.cjr.org/criticism/opioid-crisis-photos .php.

68 Shaw, "Photos Reveal."

69 Julie Netherland and Helena B. Hansen, "The War on Drugs That Wasn't: Wasted Whiteness, 'Dirty Doctors,' and Race in Media Coverage of Prescription Opioid Misuse," *Culture, Medicine and Psychiatry* 40, no. 4 (2016): 664–686, doi:10.1007/ s11013-016-9496-5. Emphasis added.

70 Netherland and Hansen, "War on Drugs."

71 Lucaites and Condit, "Reconstructing <Equality>," 8.

72 Alasdair MacIntyre, *After Virtue: A Study in Moral Theory,* 3rd ed. (Notre Dame, IN: University of Notre Dame Press, 2007), 216.

73 Walter Fisher, "Narration as a Human Communication Paradigm: The Case of Public Moral Argument," *Communication Monographs* 51, no. 1 (March 1984): 1–22.

74 Robert C. Rowland and John M. Jones, "Recasting the American Dream and American Politics: Barack Obama's Keynote Address to the 2004 Democratic National Convention," *Quarterly Journal of Speech* 93, no. 4 (November 2007): 430.

[75] Burke, *A Grammar of Motives,* 503.

[76] Plato, *The Republic,* trans. Benjamin Jowett, book vi, http://classics.mit.edu/Plato/republic.7.vi.html.

[77] George Lakoff and Mark Johnson, *Metaphors We Live By* (Chicago: University of Chicago Press, 1980), 61.

[78] Lakoff and Johnson, *Metaphors We Live By,* 3.

[79] Lakoff and Johnson, *Metaphors We Live By,* 4.

[80] Michael Osborn, *Michael Osborn on Metaphor and Style* (East Lansing: Michigan State University Press, 2018).

[81] George Lakoff, "Framing the Dems," *American Prospect* 14, no. 8 (September 2003), http://www.prospect.org/cs/articles?article=framing_the_dems.

[82] Riikka Kuusisto, "Heroic Tale, Game, and Business Deal? Western Metaphors in Action in Kosovo," *Quarterly Journal of Speech* 88, no. 1 (February 2002): 54.

[83] Kuusisto, "Heroic Tale," 62.

[84] Kuusisto, "Heroic Tale," 62.

[85] Kuusisto, "Heroic Tale," 62.

[86] Kuusisto, "Heroic Tale," 62.

[87] For more on Langer's contribution to rhetorical theory, see Arabella Lyon, "Susanne K. Langer, Mother and Midwife at the Rebirth of Rhetoric," in *Reclaiming Rhetorica: Women in the Rhetorical Tradition,* ed. Andrea A. Lunsford, (Pittsburgh: University of Pittsburgh Press, 1995), 265–284.

[88] Susanne K. Langer, *Philosophy in a New Key,* 3rd ed. (Cambridge, MA: Harvard University Press, 1957), 96–97, italics added.

[89] Langer, *Philosophy in a New Key,* 81–82.

[90] Langer, *Philosophy in a New Key,* 141.

[91] Langer, *Philosophy in a New Key,* 88.

[92] Langer, *Philosophy in a New Key,* 98.

[93] Langer, *Philosophy in a New Key,* 191.

[94] Doris Graber, *Verbal Behavior and Politics* (Urbana: University of Illinois Press, 1976), 289, italics added.

[95] Murray Edelman, *The Symbolic Uses of Politics* (Urbana: University of Illinois Press, 1972), 6. See also David S. Kaufer and Kathleen M. Carley, "Condensation Symbols: Their Variety and Rhetorical Function in Political Discourse," *Philosophy and Rhetoric* 26, no. 3 (1993): 201–226.

[96] Richard M. Weaver, *The Ethics of Rhetoric* (Davis, CA: Hermagoras, 1985), 212, 214. See also Randall A. Lake, "The Metaethical Framework of Anti-Abortion Rhetoric," *Signs* 11, no. 3 (Spring 1986): 478–499.

[97] Weaver, *The Ethics of Rhetoric,* 222.

[98] Human Rights Campaign, http://www.hrc.org (accessed May 1, 2009).

[99] See, for example, *Gay Rights/Special Rights—Inside the Homosexual Agenda,* Jeremiah Films, 1993, uploaded July 26, 2006, http://video.google.com/videoplay?docid=7664929225320091404.

[100] RayMay52, "Retarded," YouTube.com, July 9, 2011, http://www.youtube.com/watch?v=1iSlok6muY0.

[101] RayMay52, "Thank You," YouTube.com, October 18, 2011, http://www.youtube.com/watch?v=U5f5EohyhCo&list=UUxVwpX0Sjs38WHbmrlgogVA.

[102] "Retarded," UrbanDictionary.com, http://www.urbandictionary.com/define.php?term=retarded.

[103] Burke, "What are the Signs of What?" in *Language in Thought and Action,* 367.

[104] Urvashi Vaid, *Virtual Equality* (New York: Anchor, 1995), 42.

[105] Judith Butler, *Bodies That Matter: On the Discursive Limits of "Sex"* (New York: Routledge, 1993), 226.

[106] Moya Lloyd, "Radical Democratic Activism and the Politics of Resignification," *Constellations* 14, no. 1 (2007): 129–146, 129.

[107] This example is based on a similar section in Victoria Pruin DeFrancisco, Catherine Helen Palczewski, and Danielle Dick McGeough, *Gender in Communication,* 2nd ed. (Thousand Oaks, CA: Sage, 2014), 119–120.

[108] Geoff Nunberg, "Slut: The Other Four Letter S-Word," *Fresh Air,* NPR, March 13, 2012, http://www.npr.org/2012/03/13/148295582/slut-the-other-four-letter-s-word.

[109] Quoted in "Officer Tells Students Don't Dress Like a 'Slut,'" *MacLeans.ca,* February 17, 2011, http://www.macleans.ca/education/uniandcollege/officer-tells-students-dont-dress-like-a-slut.

[110] Annie Hill, "SlutWalk as a Perifeminist Response to Rape Logic: The Politics of Reclaiming a Name," *Communication & Critical/Cultural Studies* 13, no. 1 (2016): 32.

[111] Deborah Tuerkheimer, "Slutwalking in the Shadow of the Law," *Minnesota Law Review* 98 (2014): 1453–1511.

[112] Hill, "Slutwalk."

[113] Quoted in Christie Thompson, "Taking *Slut* for a Walk," *Ms.* (Summer 2011), 14.

[114] Ratna Kapur, "Pink Chaddis and SlutWalk Couture: The Postcolonial Politics of Feminism Lite," *Feminist Legal Studies* 20 (2012): 1–20.

[115] Gail Dines and Wendy J. Murphy, "SlutWalk is Not Sexual Liberation," *Guardian,* May 8, 2011, http://www.guardian.co.uk/commentisfree/2011/may/08/slutwalk-not-sexual-liberation.

[116] "An Open Letter from Black Women to the SlutWalk," *Huffington Post,* September 23, 2011, http://www.huffingtonpost.com/susan-brison/slutwalk-black-women_b_980215.html.

[117] Zeba Blay, "Reclaiming the Word 'Slut' Is an Entirely Different Beast for Black Women," HuffPost, October 2, 2015, https://www.huffpost.com/entry/reclaiming-the-word-slut-is-an-entirely-different-beast-for-black-women_n_56128706e4b0af3706e14d49.

[118] Judith Butler, *Excitable Speech: A Politics of the Performative* (New York: Routledge, 1997), 41.

[119] "Transcript: Donald Trump's Taped Comments about Women," *New York Times,* October 8, 2016, https://www.nytimes.com/2016/10/08/us/donald-trump-tape-transcript.html. See also David A. Fahrenthold, "Trump Recorded Having Extremely Lewd Conversations about Women in 2005," *Washington Post,* October 8, 2016, https://www.washingtonpost.com/politics/trump-recorded-having-extremely-lewd-conversation-about-women-in-2005/2016/10/07/3b9ce776-8cb4-11e6-bf8a-3d26847eeed4_story.html.

[120] Quoted in Christopher Rosen, "Ashley Judd Recites Powerful 'Nasty Woman' Poem at Women's March," *Entertainment Weekly,* January 23, 2017, http://ew.com/news/2017/01/21/womens-march-ashley-judd-nasty-woman-poem/.

[121] Michael Moore, "Interview with Smerconish," CNN, January 22, 2017, transcribed from http://www.cnn.com/videos/tv/2017/01/22/moore-trump-sounds-like-guy-who-lost.cnn.

[122] This example is borrowed from Palczewski, DeFrancisco, and McGeough, *Gender in Communication.*

[123] Burke, "Definition of Man," 16.

[124] George Orwell, *1984,* ed. Irving Howe (New York: Harcourt, Brace, Jovanovich, 1982), 198.

125 Andrew O'Hehir, "How Do You Explain Drone Killings? With Post-Orwellian 'Newspeak,'" Salon.com, February 9, 2013, http://www.salon.com/2013/02/09/how _do_you_explain_drone_killings_with_post_orwellian_newspeak.

126 G. Thomas Goodnight and Gordon R. Mitchell, "Drones: Argumentation in a Communication Control Society," in *Disturbing Argument,* ed. Catherine H. Palczewski (New York: Routledge, 2015).

127 Bureau of Investigative Journalism, "Get the Data: Drone Wars: Casualty Estimates: Pakistan 2004–2014 CIS Drone Strikes," 2014, http://www.thebureauinvestigates.com /category/projects/drones/drones-graphs.

128 Glenn Greenwald, "Obama Moves to Make the War on Terror Permanent," *Guardian,* October 24, 2012, http://www.theguardian.com/commentisfree/2012/oct/24/obama -terrorism-kill-list.

129 William Lutz, *Doublespeak* (New York: Harper and Row, 1989), 1.

130 William Lutz, *Doublespeak,* 1.

131 Reported in David Bauder, "News Media Hesitate to Use 'Lie' for Trump's Misstatements," AP News, August 29, 2018, https://www.apnews.com /88675d3fdd674c7c9ec70f170f6e4a1a.

132 Glenn Kessler, "Not Just Misleading. Not Merely False. A Lie," *Washington Post,* August 22, 2018, https://www.apnews.com/88675d3fdd674c7c9ec70f170f6e4a1a.

133 Erik Wemple, "The Daily Spicer: 'Holocaust Center.' Yes, the Press Secretary Used That Term," *Washington Post,* April 7, 2017, https://www.washingtonpost.com/blogs/erik -wemple/wp/2017/04/11/the-daily-spicer-holocaust-centers-yes-the-press-secretary -used-that-term/?hpid=hp_no-name_opinion-card-b%3Ahomepage%2Fstory&utm _term=.d736c2c1f1ea#comments.

134 Lutz, *Doublespeak,* 6, italics added.

135 Lutz, *Doublespeak,* 2–7.

136 Penelope, *Speaking Freely,* xiii.

137 Penelope, *Speaking Freely,* 146.

138 Commenting on a similar example, Penelope notes, "At a superficial level, the omission of direct and explicit reference to himself made the events seem far removed from our immediate experience, occurring in some abstract realm where human beings are not responsible for their actions" (Penelope, *Speaking Freely,* 145).

139 Chris Christie, "2014 State of the State Address," *Washington Post,* January 14, 2014, http://www.washingtonpost.com/politics/full-text-of-new-jersey-gov-chris-christies -2014-state-of-the-state-speech/2014/01/14/8fd12f08-7d55-11e3-9556 -4a4bf7bcbd84_story.html.

140 Penelope, *Speaking Freely,* 149.

141 Quoted in Roger Keren, "The Language of Gender Violence" *Middlebury Magazine,* March 15, 2012, https://www.jacksonkatz.com/news/language-gender-violence/.

142 Quoted in Keren, "The Language of Gender Violence."

143 Gerd Bohner, "Writing about Rape: Use of the Passive Voice and Other Distancing Text Features as an Expression of Perceived Responsibility of the Victim," *British Journal of Social Psychology* 40 (2001): 515–529.

144 Michel Foucault, *The Archaeology of Knowledge and the Discourse on Language,* trans. R. Sawyer (New York: Pantheon, 1972), 216.

145 Laura R. Sells, "Maria W. Miller Stewart," in *Women Public Speakers in the United States, 1825–1900,* ed. Karlyn Kohrs Campbell, 339–349 (Westport, CT: Greenwood, 1993).

146 Barbara Welter, *Dimity Convictions: The American Woman in the Nineteenth Century* (Athens: Ohio University Press, 1976).

Chapter 4
Visual Rhetoric

Not only words, but nonverbal symbolic actions, are rhetorical. For example, consider the US flag. Most people encounter a flag by looking at it. (The US national anthem begins, "Oh, say! Can you see . . . ?") A flag is much more than a piece of fabric, as anyone who has ever been presented a trifold flag at the end of a funeral knows. The flag is a symbol of the nation and its values. Supreme Court Justice John Paul Stevens once wrote, "The flag uniquely symbolizes the ideas of liberty, equality, and tolerance . . . . The flag embodies the spirit of our national commitment to those ideals."[1] To understand the flag, though, you need to ask not only what it *represents* (the United States) and what it *means* (for example, a star for every state), but also what it *does*.

Rhetorical forms that are other than language, or that include more than language, are typically referred to as "visual rhetoric." As the examples of the flag and the national anthem show, however, more than just the sense of sight is involved. You also encounter many forms of visual rhetoric through other senses: touch, taste, hearing, and smell. For example, the Vietnam Veterans Memorial illustrates that visual forms often stir more than the sense of sight. Located in the National Mall, the memorial includes a wall that lists the names of over fifty-eight thousand service members killed during the war. (A statue of three soldiers, a flag pole, and a statue of women service members are also part of the memorial.) Visitors can not only see the wall, they can touch it as they take a rubbing of a loved one's name, hear the weeping of others who visit it, smell the rain or fresh mown grass of the National Mall, and even taste the salt of their own tears.

Often, people interpret visual artifacts as representations of a reality, not as interpretations of it. They might see photographs, even photographs of the flag, as merely recording objective events. They might interpret the presence of the flag at the Vietnam Veterans Memorial as just a representation of the nation for which the people named on the wall fought and died. They might see the memorial as an objective listing of the war dead.

However, visual rhetoric can shape people's beliefs and attitudes just as verbal rhetoric does. In fact, when the design for the Vietnam Veterans Memorial was selected, outcry arose about the fact that it had no plans to include a flag. In response, the Three Servicemen statue and a flagpole were added to the design.[2] The mere presence or absence of the flag means and does a great deal.

Like the flag itself, photos of the flag are rhetorical. They are not just neutral records of reality; they *do* something to how people understand themselves and the world around them. For example, since the Vietnam War, US government officials have been aware that images of flag-draped coffins containing war dead returning home can affect public support of the war effort. Journalists coined a phrase to measure this effect: "the Dover Test." The test asks whether the US public will continue to support a war if it is faced with a stream of images of flag-draped coffins arriving at Dover Air Force base, through which, since 1955, the remains of all deceased armed forces personnel return from abroad.

The Dover Test achieved stark public awareness during President George H. W. Bush's term. In 1989, the US invasion of Panama resulted in the death of twenty-three service members. In news coverage, televisions showed a split-screen image, with one half of the screen depicting flag-draped coffins arriving at Dover and the other half showing President Bush joking with reporters during a news conference. The image created the impression that Bush was not concerned about the loss of life. In response, Bush banned media coverage of Dover arrivals during the 1991 Persian Gulf War.[3]

The ban remained in place until February 2009, when the Pentagon lifted it after President Obama asked Defense Secretary Robert Gates to review the policy.[4] Presidents' willingness to maintain the ban showed they understood the power of a photo to influence public perception of a war. Photos of flag-draped coffins arriving at Dover make present the cost of war.

Although scholars for many years confined the study of the available means of persuasion to verbal symbols, within the last few decades they have recognized the centrality of visual symbolic action to the study of rhetoric.[5] The examples we just described illustrate cultural theorists Jessica Evans and Stuart Hall's description of contemporary culture as "pervaded at all levels by a host of cultural technologies designed to disseminate viewing and looking practices through primarily visually mediated forms."[6] Photography, film, monuments, and television are some of the technologies that enable the dissemination of images. That dissemination is so constant that if people cannot see something, they may not think it matters. We presume the need and right to look.

Cultural technologies include not only the cameras that take images, but also the means of distribution. In 1991, a Sony Handycam 8-millimeter video of the police beating Rodney King became the first viral video when television news across the country broadcast it.[7] One journalist described the bystander's video as "sparking local riots and putting a spotlight on longstanding feelings of distrust toward law enforcement in minority communities," and added, "The video in particular has been credited with forcing cities to reconcile with—and sometimes reform—how they police minority neighborhoods."[8] The video led to some reforms. Police violence continued, but because recording and distribution technologies have been decentralized, a bystander with a smart phone can record an event and circulate the video online in the hope of influencing public opinion.[9] Bystander video of police violence (sometimes along with dashcam and bodycam video) against Eric Garner, Walter Scott, Dajerria Becton, Alton Sterling, Dejuan Hall, Charles Kinsey, Keith Lamont Scott, Philando Castile, and others led one commentator to argue that "the proliferation of video through smartphones, dashboard cameras, and body cameras—and social media's ability to send a video into viral overdrive—has played a major role in holding police accountable."[10] The videos put an individual face on the victim and offer a counternarrative to the one told by police. As the technology has become widely available, more videos can circulate more widely, without having to go through commercial media gatekeepers.

In this chapter, we explain how visual rhetoric creates presence (and absence) and how the ubiquity of images creates a visual culture. We discuss how to approach the study of visual rhetoric and outline three forms: photographs, bodies, and memorials. These are not *all* the forms of visual rhetoric, but each one does illustrate something unique about visual rhetoric.

PRESENCE AND ABSENCE

Dover photos are powerful because they make an event, person, or thing present. Visuals possess the characteristic of **presence** because of their *immediacy, the creation of something in the front of an audience's consciousness.* Presence, as rhetoric scholars Chaïm Perelman and Lucie Olbrechts-Tyteca would say, "acts directly on our sensibility."[11] Although Perelman and Olbrechts-Tyteca originally developed the idea of presence to explain the effects of verbal symbolism, it also helps explain the power of visual rhetoric.

Visuals may create virtual experiences in a particularly intense way, by making audience members feel as though they were present to witness an event. They offer a direct presentation instead of a discursive description.[12] They can make things that are distant in time or space feel current and close. For example, how might events at the US-Mexico border be made present to people across the United States, even those who do not live on an international border?

First, a little background. In the spring of 2018, the Trump Administration announced a "zero tolerance" policy regarding border enforcement, resulting in the criminal prosecution of all adults who enter the United States without documentation. As a result, families were separated. Parents were held while awaiting prosecution and their children were supposedly placed in shelters or foster care.

The policy of family separation was a central deterrent strategy for the administration. Thousands of children (some only four months old)[13] were separated from their parents. Many were housed in conditions that violated legally required standards of sanitation and care, in makeshift detention centers that used cage-like fencing to contain the children. An executive order on June 20, 2019, declared that children would be kept with their detained parents, but family separations continued.[14]

In June 2019, immigrant rights groups worked with street artists to create guerrilla art installations called #NoKidsInCages.[15] The campaign sought to make the detained children present in space (here) and time (now). Sculptures appeared on the streets of New York, each depicting "a small child, draped in a foil blanket and huddled on the floor of a tiny cage, with disturbing and real audio of crying children who have been separated from their families, recorded by news outlets." The sculptures made present, in the here and now, the horror of family separation and detention. Even though the detentions were occurring elsewhere in the country, the sculptures made them present at the hub of the media industry, as they appeared outside major news organization headquarters in New York. In a tweet and on their website, the campaign organizers made clear their intent to make the children present by noting that family separations were happening in the present moment, now, and not during some long past history.[16] (See Figure 1.)

You should consider not only what is given presence through visual rhetoric, but also what is made absent. As we discussed in an earlier chapter, because all rhetoric directs our attention in one direction rather than another, it selects *and* deflects reality. Something invested with presence is selected for attention. Something invested with **absence** *has attention deflected away from it, lacks immediacy, and is not in an audience's consciousness.* Prior to the #NoKidsInCages installations, the plight of children on the border was invisible, was absent. #NoKidsInCages sought to counter this absence. Presences and absences reveal much about what is valued, and not valued, in a society. As we discuss photographs, memorials, and bodies later in this chapter, think about what is made present by the visuals and what is made absent: Whose images are preserved? Who is memorialized? What bodies are visible?

THE RISE OF VISUAL CULTURE

US and global culture are becoming, in the words of Evans and Hall, a **visual culture**—*a culture distinguished by the ubiquity of visual forms of communication that appear in multiple media outlets at the same time (such as television, commercial and noncommercial web pages, tablets, cell phones, and magazines).*[17] Think about how you spend your time. You do not just read books; you watch movie adaptations of them. You do not simply phone friends; you Instagram them. You do not simply read or listen to speeches; you watch them on YouTube. Communication scholar Lawrence J. Prelli argues that the **rhetoric of display,** *rhetoric that makes ideas present through visual display,* has become the dominant mode of communication in visual culture.[18] Even a speech, a verbal form, can

FIGURE 1
#NoKidsInCages
Installation
AP Photo/Bebeto Matthews
Installation appears with
permission of Badger & Winters

be a visual event, with lavish attention paid to backdrops, clothing color, and camera angles.

Evans and Hall argue that it is impossible to understand contemporary culture without analyzing visuals, because a study of any contemporary media product—any televised or streamed show, movie, advertisement, web page, blog, or magazine—would be "incomplete" if you only analyzed the words, or if you interpreted the "images as if they only functioned as artifacts to be read rather than as sights and often exhibitionist performances to be looked at."[19] Could you really explain the power of popular culture if you only analyzed the words attached to social media posts or the scripts written for shows and movies? Could you really explain the power of fashion bloggers by studying only their words? No and no. Fashion trends and body image are influenced by the actors and images on the screens you see. People in a visual culture not only read words, they look at and interpret images.

Visuals and verbals are almost always present in symbolic action, yet they operate in ways that are both similar to and different from each other. As Evans and Hall note: "the differences between language and the visual remain significant and require further attention; that is, the different cultural technologies and industries built upon them, their characteristic forms and rhetorical devices, and the ways in which they are put to work, disseminated, and made sense of by readers and viewers."[20] You cannot explain fully the power of a Dover photo by saying it depicts a historically real event. The photo is powerful because it simultaneously captures a symbolic moment of ritual, a family's pure moment of grief, the honor of military service, a coffin containing a person, and the human costs of war. People make sense of these images by fitting them into practices of visual piety and respectful looking, cultural practices that parallel the function of visitations during funerals. Imagine if we had started the chapter by reproducing a particular Dover photo, instead of only describing Dover photos in general. Would you have had the same reaction?

Visual rhetoric was not absent prior to the age of electronic media. Most of the forms of visual rhetoric discussed in this chapter predate television and computers, although these forms have been adapted to mass and digital media. People have been using their bodies to make arguments as long as parades have crowded streets. Because electronic media make it easier to transmit images, however, and because interactive media enable everyone to be a publicist, attention to visual forms has increased.

Photography first emerged in the 1820s. It became widely accessible in the 1880s, when George Eastman developed film technology that replaced cumbersome photographic plates. With digital photography, technology is now embedded in smart phones, allowing virtually everyone to photograph anytime and anywhere. Photographs populate networked spaces such as Instagram, Facebook, Google Images, and Flickr. Because visuals dominate contemporary culture, rhetors must think about how to create rhetorical actions that can be captured visually and circulated across a range of screens.[21]

Public monuments have played a role in the United States since the inception of the nation. Monuments are literally built into the bricks and stones of the US Capitol building. Scenes commemorating Columbus's life as a discoverer appear in the massive bronze doors that lead into the Capitol rotunda. Reliefs depicting settler-Indian relations adorn the rotunda walls.[22]

The last few decades have seen a proliferation of museums, memorials, and other memory sites.[23] Visuals are now omnipresent.[24] Visual rhetoric scholar Diane S. Hope concludes that visual communication is "a foundational core within the discipline of communication. Visual artifacts provoke intended and unintended meanings for individual and collective identity."[25] Given this omnipresence, it is important to develop skills that enable you to approach visual rhetoric critically.

The interaction between mediated messages and audience interpretations is in constant negotiation, with hegemonic powers dominating in some cases and audience resistance dominating in others. The more skilled an audience is in analyzing messages, the more it is able to resist a hegemonic interpretation. Communication scholar Celeste Michelle Condit warns, "Audiences are not free to make meanings at will from mass mediated texts" because "the ability of audiences to shape their own readings . . . is constrained by a variety of factors in any given rhetorical situation," including "access to oppositional codes . . . the repertoire of available texts" and the historical context.[26] What you can say about a rhetorical artifact depends on the vocabulary you have and the questions you have been trained to ask. If the only code you have to analyze a movie is "thumbs up" or "thumbs down," you have a limited ability to provide a detailed critical analysis of it.

For any given text, Stuart Hall identifies three possible readings.[27] A **dominant reading** (or preferred, hegemonic meaning) is *a reading in which a reader (or viewer) takes the "connoted meaning . . . full and straight . . . the viewer is operating inside the dominant code."*[28] The viewer does not challenge the ideology behind the message or the way in which it maintains hegemonic power. A **negotiated reading** is *a reading in which the viewer accepts some of the hegemonic meanings, but also recognizes some exceptions.* In such a reading, the denotational meanings are understood, but some of the connotational meanings are challenged. An **oppositional reading** is *a reading in which the viewer correctly decodes the denotational and connotational meanings of a text, but challenges it from an oppositional perspective.* Because of the possible levels of reading, we find persuasive Evans and Hall's description of how visual rhetoric generates meaning:

> Meaning is constituted not in the visual sign itself as a self-sufficient entity, nor exclusively in the sociological positions and identities of the audience, but in the articulation between viewer and viewed, between the power of the image to signify and the viewer's capacity to interpret meaning.[29]

The meaning of a text is not determined solely by its author, nor is it solely contained in the text. Instead, audiences interpret meanings of visual texts in the process of looking. As images circulate across media platforms, their meanings can shift. As a result, a single text or image may have multiple meanings, meanings influenced by the audience's culture and personal interpretations. Thus, when analyzing visual rhetoric, it is important to take into consideration not only the image and its producer, but also the social context surrounding the audience's interpretation of that image, as well as how the image's meaning might shift as it circulates.

For example, American Apparel, a company that wanted to be identified as the "Made in USA—Sweatshop Free" brand,[30] ran an advertisement in *Vice* magazine. The bottom seventh of the page contains a narrative about the model, Maks, who appears in the ad. It explains that Maks was born in Dhaka, Bangladesh, and grew up "attending mosque as a child alongside her conservative Muslim parents," but moved to southern California at age four. Now an adult, Maks is a merchandiser for the company. The narrative ends by describing the jeans Maks is wearing and that they were "manufactured by 23 skilled American workers." Above the script is a picture of Maks, jeans unzipped and pulled down to expose underwear. The words "Made in Bangladesh" are emblazoned across Maks's bare chest. American Apparel's preferred reading of this advertisement is that you should buy its products because they are made in the United States and because, just as American Apparel has helped Maks "forge her own identity," it can help you forge yours. Maks may have been made in Bangladesh, but her clothes were not.

The dominant reading would suggest that the use of a woman's body to sell clothing remains unremarkable, just part of the way things are. People undertaking a negotiated reading of this image may question why a partially naked body would be used to help sell clothes, but still find the clothing attractive, partly because it is modeled by an attractive person. An oppositional reading would reject both the use of a woman's body to sell clothing and the commodification of the woman's body. The ad labels her body "made in Bangladesh" in the same way clothing is labeled, turning her into a commodity to be bought and sold just like clothing.

Oppositional reading is demonstrated by *Ms.* magazine, which, in its Summer 2014 issue, included the American Apparel ad in its "No Comment" section. *Ms.* is "the most trusted, popular source for feminist news and information." It eschews advertisements in its own pages and devotes its last page to a "No Comment" section[31] that reproduces advertisements that readers submit because they find them injurious and degrading to women. This section is both the result of oppositional readings and the cause. As communication scholar Linda Steiner explains, "*Ms.* readers call attention to [the] items in ways not encoded by their producers, precisely to make the point that *Ms.* readers are not the women inscribed in dominant media. . . . The very act of capturing these texts and setting them in an oppositional frame is an act of resistance."[32] The hope is that once others are made aware of the problematic advertisements, they will pressure companies to remove them. (The magazine includes the contact information for each company along with its advertisement.)

Although audiences may have different interpretations of the same text, often interpretations are relatively consistent. Why? The culture that constitutes the audience influences its interpretations; hence, many audience interpretations reinforce the interpretation preferred by those in power. Both media and viewers participate in the hegemonic process, in which the predominant ideology uses noncoercive forms to generate consent in the dominated. Hegemonic institutions usually influence audiences; that is what makes them hegemonic. For example, most people in the United States take the mere existence of commercial advertising in stride; the United States, as a capitalist society, sees encouragements to consume as normal.

ANALYZING VISUAL RHETORICS

The study of visual rhetoric does not stop at analyzing what an artifact means or whether it is aesthetically pleasing. The primary question of a rhetorical approach is: What does an artifact *do?* In an art class, you might analyze the color, content, spatial organization, and light in an image. You might also ask what the various elements of an image represent. Rhetoricians are interested in more than aesthetics and meaning. They want to know: What does this image tell people about what it means to be a citizen, about the costs of war, about the values of the community, about people's own place in the world, about who should be pictured and who should not? Because a central component of rhetoric is that it is addressed, you also should ask: What type of audience does this artifact address—spectators, witnesses, or participants?[33] For example, rhetorical critic Sonja K. Foss asks about the "function or functions communicated by an image"; not the rhetor's purpose, but the "action the image communicates."[34] Rhetorical critic Carole Blair, when analyzing monuments, is concerned with "not just what a text means but, more generally, what it does; and we must not understand what it does as adhering strictly to what it was supposed to do."[35]

For example, according to the National Park Service website, the World War II Memorial, which opened to the public in 2004, "recognizes the ways Americans served, honors those who fell, and recognizes the victory they achieved to restore freedom and end tyranny around the globe."[36] The dedication ceremony speakers, however, included no representatives of Allied nations and only one veteran of World War II, who was not recognized as a veteran. Instead, speakers focused on the US role in winning World War II and its then-current role in the war in Iraq. Rhetorical critics V. William Balthrop, Carole Blair, and Neil Michel argue that although the intent of the memorial intent was to celebrate service and sacrifice, the dedication ceremony makes clear that the monument actually "affirms contemporary U.S. imperialism, promotes the George W. Bush administration's highly questionable policies under the revered sign of World War II, and 'speaks' more about the present than about the past the Memorial allegedly marks."[37] Words and visuals, often in conjunction, construct reality.

Visual rhetoric scholars Kevin Michael DeLuca and Anne Teresa Demo note that visuals, just pictures, "are important not because they represent reality, but create it."[38] Thus, when people analyze visuals, the question "What do the images represent?" is insufficient; it assumes an absolute correspondence between the image and reality. In studying visual rhetoric, DeLuca and Demo say, you should also ask "What do the images want?"—meaning what attitude toward the world do these images encourage the audience to assume, and in what ways do the images direct a person's attention in one way rather than another?[39]

The rest of the chapter offers examples of what bodies, photographs, and monuments *do* rhetorically.

TYPES OF VISUAL RHETORIC

In the following sections, in the three types of communication we discuss—photographs, bodies, and monuments—the visual component is predominant and has received substantial scholarly attention. These are not necessarily the most important forms of visual rhetoric (though they are important), but they do illustrate how visual communication operates presentationally and can create presence and absence, directing attention to some things while deflecting it from others.[40]

Photographs

Photographs direct attention to a particular reality. Although people often think of photographs as exact representations of reality (assuming they are not obviously photoshopped), all visual technologies (cameras, video recorders, and smart phones) "structure images of reality."[41] Visual communication scholar Diane S. Hope explains that "what viewers see, what they do not see, and how they contextualize images depends on structural choices made by producers, and include editing, framing, sequencing, contrast, focus, illumination and grounding."[42]

Carleton Watkins's 1860s photographs of Yosemite Valley demonstrate that photographs can structure how people see the world. (See Figure 2.) The California Geological Survey began to map the valley in 1863. As part of survey head Josiah Dwight Whitney's appeal to have the valley declared a public park, the survey report included twenty-eight of Watkins's original photographs in an unprecedented use of photographs to illustrate a scientific survey. When policy-makers submitted a bill calling for President Abraham Lincoln to preserve Yosemite Valley, advocates attached some of Watkins's photographs to the bill. As the images circulated, they "became iconic of an American vision of nature itself."[43] They were central to the preservation of that area and influenced the focus of environmental movements for years to come. How?

The images are more than a simple reflection of the Yosemite Valley. They also select and highlight a particular understanding of nature, even as they deflect other understandings. DeLuca and Demo ask, in their analysis of these photos, "What vision of nature do the photographs authorize, warrant, and legitimate?"[44] For these scholars, Watkins's images are not "merely evidence in a conventional political argument;" nor are they "simply representing reality or making an argument about reality. Instead . . . the pictures are constituting the context within which a politics takes place—they are creating a reality."[45] These images influenced what it meant to be an environmentalist by equating the environment to pristine, untouched lands, rather than including all the land, sky, and water in which beings live. They also reinforced the prevailing myth that Euro-American settlers were the only people to step foot into this pristine wilderness, wiping the presence of Native Americans from public awareness. They induced people to accept a particular view of nature as untouched by human habitation. The framing of the photos meant that Native Americans were not present within the frame of reference. Watkins's images reinforced the identity of Euro-Americans as explorers and discoverers.

The centrality of photographic images to a people's understanding of their identity cannot be underestimated. When you study photographs, the questions are not limited to what meaning the image maker wants to transmit: they also include what the image does, how audiences read images, and how the rhetor calls a particular audience into being. You live in a visual culture and are bombarded by rhetorics of display. How do you develop an awareness of what images are asking of you, instead of just doing what they ask?

In a world increasingly dominated by electronic media, visual rhetoric scholars Robert Hariman and John Louis Lucaites argue that commonly viewed

FIGURE 2
Cathedral Rocks, Yosemite Valley
Carleton Watkins, Library of Congress

images can provide a sense of "shared experience." Even as public life seems impersonal, people develop a personal connection (an identification) with the people they see in pictures. In addition, "the daily stream of images in the public media . . . defines the public through an act of common spectatorship. All viewers *seem* to see the same thing."[46]

Thus, when discussing public communication, people should consider the ways visuals form what is considered public and shared. For people in the United States, a few key photos inform how citizens see themselves. Lucaites and Hariman identify these images as **iconic photographs:** "*photographic images produced in print, electronic, or digital media that are (1) recognized by everyone within a public culture, (2) understood to be representations of historically significant events, (3) objects of strong emotional identification and response, and (4) regularly reproduced or copied across a range of media, genres, and topics.*"[47] Examples of iconic photographs include Joe Rosenthal's 1945 photo of the flag raising on Iwo Jima,[48] John Filo's 1970 photo of a Kent State student shot to death by the National Guard,[49] Nick Ut's 1972 Vietnam War photo of accidental napalm,[50] and Jeff Widener's 1989 Tiananmen Square photo of a single protester. Each of these photos contributed to the way US citizens came to see themselves.

The Pulitzer Prize–winning photo of Iwo Jima, published in the midst of World War II, presents a particular understanding of citizenship and war.

(See Figure 3.) Taken by Associated Press photographer Joe Rosenthal, the photo depicts the US military seizing a Japanese observation post on the island. This image fulfills all the elements of an iconic photo: Most people in the United States would recognize it. It represents a historically significant event; in fact, it has come to represent all of World War II for many people. It creates a strong emotional identification, as citizens identify with the service members pictured, with their struggle and victory. It is regularly reproduced; in fact, it is the most reproduced photograph in history.[51] What is most significant, however, is how the photo has come to form an understanding of US public culture.

Hariman and Lucaites argue that this photo presents two arguments about what distinguishes and defines US citizens. First, it argues that war is more an act of labor than an act of killing. The marines and navy corpsman are not pictured firing weapons, but laboring to erect the flag. Second, even in an act of conquest (taking a strategic place), the soldiers work together, regardless of rank, thus enacting egalitarianism and civic pride. In depicting war and egalitarian cooperation, the photograph "reflect[s] social knowledge and dominant ideologies; . . . shape[s] understanding of specific events and periods; . . . influence[s] political action by modeling relationships between civic actors; and . . . provide[s] figural resources for subsequent communicative action."[52] As people in the United States look at this image, they come to a shared vision of who they are and why the nation fought. The photo reflects a particular image of US citizens as hardworking (not warlike), equal (rank is irrelevant, as all participants labor equally), and proud of their nation (the US flag is a primary indicator of civic pride).

Bodies

Research on body rhetoric and body argument shows that verbal messages do not exist apart from the body that creates those messages. *Who* says a message and *how* a body is made present communicate as much as *what* is said. **Body rhetoric,** then, is *rhetoric that foregrounds the body as part of the symbolic act.* Although bodies have a material component (flesh and blood), our focus is on how they are apprehended visually, particularly bodies that are watched on screens or in person and captured in photographs.

When we speak of bodies, we are not speaking of a biological entity, but of a social and individual creation, performance, and inscription. Gender, sex, ethnicity, class, sexual orientation, religion, ability, age, and a host of other identity ingredients enter the discussion. Additionally, body rhetoric is often used by people who are denied access to more traditional forms of verbal address and proof. In some cases, your body may be your only available data for a claim you want to make.

To understand the power of body rhetoric, consider the technique of **enactment,** which occurs when *the person engaging in symbolic action functions as proof of the argument they advance.*[53] As you read the following uses of enactment, think about how, if the same statement had been presented by any other person, the argument would lose some of its power, even though the words might

FIGURE 3
US Marines raising flag over Iwo Jima
AP Photo/Joe Rosenthal

be identical. The power of the visual proof presented by the body enhances the power of the words.

Barbara Jordan delivered the keynote address at the 1976 Democratic National Convention. Jordan's main argument was that the Democratic Party was the party of inclusion and opportunity, regardless of one's race, sex, or class. Jordan sought to answer the question: "[W]hat is it about the Democratic Party that makes it the instrument that people use when they search for ways to shape their future?" As proof of the claim that the Democratic Party was an instrument of positive change, she offered herself. Jordan proclaimed from her Black, female body: "[T]here is something different about tonight. There is something special about tonight. . . . I, Barbara Jordan, am a keynote speaker. . . . And I feel that notwithstanding the past that my presence here is one additional bit of evidence that the American Dream need not forever be deferred."[54]

Mary Fisher (an artist and the daughter of a major Republican fundraiser) delivered a speech on AIDS at the 1992 Republic National Convention. Fisher's main argument was "the AIDS virus is not a political creature. It does not care whether you are Democrat or Republican; it does not ask whether you are black or white, male or female, gay or straight, young or old." She believed everyone,

Democrats and Republicans, should be concerned about AIDS because it affected everyone. She proclaimed from her Republican, White, non–drug using, heterosexual, economically privileged, married-when-infected, HIV+ body: "You are at risk."[55] Fisher functioned as proof that everyone present at the convention was at risk.

In September 2010, in the wake of a number of bullying-induced suicides of LGBT youth, journalist and author Dan Savage launched the "It Gets Better Project," an online website and YouTube channel on which adults can post videos in which they "show young LGBT people the levels of happiness, potential, and positivity their lives will reach—if they can just get through their teen years."[56] What began as a social media campaign is now a "major, multi-media platform."[57] As of December 2020, over seventy thousand people had shared their stories. Each video is an example of enactment. Savage and husband Terry begin their eight-and-a-half-minute video by talking about the violence and harassment they experienced as gay youths. A little over a minute into the video, they declare: "It gets better." They spend most of the video talking about their loving parents, the beginning of their sixteen-year relationship, their thirteen-year-old son, their travels to Paris, and their skiing trips—basically describing how good, loving, and happy their lives are. They are proof that "it gets better."

These examples demonstrate that bodies can function as rhetorically powerful evidence, but they can also be the complete argument. Argument traditionalists often relegate the role of the body in argument to a means of capturing and holding attention, rather than as a central part of the substance of the argument, but their perspective lacks explanatory power when applied to contemporary activism. For example, in a study of the rhetoric of groups such as Earth First!, ACT UP, and Queer Nation, visual rhetoric scholar Kevin Michael DeLuca highlighted that the activists' bodies are "not merely flags to attract attention for the argument but the site and substance of the argument itself."[58] In the case of ACT UP and Queer Nation, two groups that focus on AIDS policy, the presence of the body *is* the argument, "for it is the body that is at stake—its meanings, its possibilities, its care, and its freedoms. In their protest actions, the activists use their bodies to rewrite the homosexual body as already constructed by dominant mainstream discourses—diseased, contagious, deviant, invisible."[59] Instead of presenting their bodies as passive, diseased, and dying, the activists present their bodies as active, healing, and living. They present integrated verbal and visual arguments about what the body means, what the government does to it, and how it is affected by disease.

The innovative "loud, demanding and in-your-face with telegenic direct action" tactics that ACT UP developed are not simply relics of the twentieth century.[60] Contemporary protest groups have sought the advice of ACT UP veterans. For example, during January 2017, Rise and Resist members were inspired by ACT UP techniques when they made brunch reservations at a range of Trump-owned properties. While others ate, they began coughing, embodying illness, and held signs saying "Trumpcare is making us sick."[61]

Grandchildren of Auschwitz survivors illustrate the ability of bodies to induce memory and to answer arguments. As the number of Holocaust survivors

FIGURE 4
M. e. Cohen cartoon
M. e. Cohen/Artizans.com

dwindles, Jodi Rudoren of the *New York Times* says, "institutions and individuals are grappling with how best to remember the Holocaust . . . after those who lived it are gone."[62] Survivors' children and grandchildren are choosing to tattoo themselves with the numbers that Nazis etched into their parents' and grandparents' arms and chests. Rhetoric scholars Linda Diane Horwitz and Daniel C. Brouwer argue that this practice resignifies the meaning of the tattoo, transforming it from a marker of power over a human to a marker of human resistance to power. They explain, "These young people articulate that they are not going to forget, and they are also going to help anyone who witnesses their tattoo in the process of never forgetting."[63] The tattoos also prove the Holocaust failed: those who Nazis sought to kill are survived by their children and grandchildren.

The power of the tattooed body as evidence is also evident in another visual form. The 2006 editorial cartoon in Figure 4 responded to Iranian past president Mahmoud Ahmadinejad, who had repeatedly called the Holocaust a "myth."[64] Ahmadinejad had also hosted a conference for Holocaust deniers, including David Duke from the United States, French lecturer Robert Faurisson, and British author David Irving.[65] The cartoon points out the overwhelming evidence of the body to refute those who deny that the genocidal Holocaust occurred.

Sometimes, body rhetoric may be the only rhetorical option available. In societies where free speech is not sanctioned, an image (a photo) and a presence (a body) may be the only way to negate a government's denial of wrongdoing. Communication studies scholar Valeria Fabj's study of the Mothers of Plaza de Mayo is an excellent example of a situation in which discursive argument was not an option and a visual form was necessary.[66] The Mothers formed in 1977 to protest the "disappearance" of their children under the repressive military regime that ruled Argentina from 1976 to 1983. Wearing as headscarves their children's nappies (diapers embroidered with the children's names and dates of disappearance) and carrying pictures of their disappeared children, they marched around the Plaza de Mayo at a time when public protest was prohibited. Fabj argues it was the very "myth of motherhood," the social beliefs attached to the women's bodies, that allowed them "to draw from their private experiences in order to gain a political voice, discover eloquent symbols, and yet remain relatively safe at a time when all political dissent was prohibited."[67] (See Figure 5.)

Bodies offer a powerful rhetorical resource. They can function as proof of an argument; they can be the argument; and they can argue when speech has been restricted.

Monuments, Memorials, and Museums

People often perceive US monuments and memorials, such as the Washington Monument and the Vietnam Veterans Memorial in Washington, DC, as neutral markers of historical figures and events, but monuments do more than simply record historic facts. They guide people in their thinking about those facts from the past, about how to act in the present, and about what possible futures to seek. Although they are inanimate objects, they are not just markers of famous locations or ways to memorialize the dead; they also constitute identity. Thus, controversy can erupt over monuments and memorials.

One controversy resulted in renaming a national monument and adding another memorial to its space. Off I-90 in southern Montana sits the Crow Indian Reservation, the site of the most famous battle in the Indian Wars, remembered not because it was a great victory for the US Seventh Cavalry under the command of Lieutenant Colonel George Armstrong Custer, but because on June 25, 1876, the Cavalry was annihilated here by the superior might of Lakota (Sioux), Hinono'eino (Arapaho), and Tsistsistas (Cheyenne) warriors. In 1879, the battlefield was dedicated as a national cemetery. In 1881, the Seventh Cavalry Memorial was erected, listing the names of all the Cavalry members and "Arikaree" (Arikara, also known as Sahnish) scouts slain in the battle. In 1925, Mrs. Thomas Beaverheart (daughter of Chief Lame White Man, a Southern Cheyenne killed in the battle) initiated Indian demands for inclusion. In 1946, the Custer Battlefield National Monument was dedicated.

After years of protest by indigenous activists, in 1991 the Custer Battlefield National Monument was rededicated as the Little Bighorn Battlefield National Monument. A national design competition was authorized for an Indian Memorial. When President George H. W. Bush signed the federal law declaring the name change, he explained: "The public interest will best be served by establishing a memorial . . . to honor and recognize the Indians who fought to preserve their land and culture."[68]

FIGURE 5
Madres de Plaza de Mayo
Horacio Villalobos/Corbis
via Getty Images

An advisory committee composed of members of all the Indian nations involved in the battle, historians, artists, and landscape architects selected the memorial's theme, "Peace through Unity," in response to the advice of elders Austin Two Moons (Northern Cheyenne) and Enos Poor Bear, Sr. (Oglala Lakota).[69] In 1997, the committee selected John R. Collins and Alison J. Towers's memorial design, which incorporated a sculpture of Spirit Warriors designed by Lakota artist Colleen "Sister Wolf" Cutschall. The Indian Memorial was dedicated on June 25, 2003.

The need for the Indian Memorial becomes clear when one considers the way Euro-Americans remembered the battle prior to the 1991 law. Not only were the sites where Indians died unmarked, a marker in the national cemetery that memorialized US officers who died in the Indian Wars told a distorted story, referring to "hostile Indians" without noting the reason for their hostility: for decades US troops had violently driven them from their homelands and onto reservations. Until the law changed the name of the battlefield and required the memorialization of the indigenous peoples who fought, only the names of Custer's soldiers, civilians traveling with the cavalry, and the three Sahnish (Arikara) Indians who scouted for the Seventh Calvary were inscribed on the monument. The deeds of the triumphant Lakota Indian chiefs Crazy Horse and Sitting Bull were not remembered in the official space, even though Native Americans kept these deeds alive in oral histories.

The evolution of the Little Bighorn site illustrates that public memory is grounded in the present rather than the past and is continually (re)made to fit the needs of the public(s) it serves. Initially, Custer Battlefield National Monument served the need to justify the westward expansion and to celebrate the actions of the military. It held Custer up as a hero who ostensibly served the cause of fighting "hostile Indians." As needs arose to account for the wrongs committed against indigenous nations, the form, content, and name of the site had to change to encompass those needs.

The Little Bighorn Battlefield is a place where the US conception of citizenship and nationhood is developed and maintained, a conception that directly implicates a particular history of Euro-American colonialists' relationship with indigenous peoples. Communication scholar Richard Morris notes in another context that "the continuous struggle to gain access to and control of America's collective memory is hardly a benign process."[70] The national monument site initially argued that only Custer and the soldiers should be remembered. As it constructed and maintained remembrances of Custer, it generated forgetfulness about the Lakota, Hinono'eino, and Tsistsistas and why they fought. The new monument argues that both soldiers and warriors should be remembered, that all the lives lost are worthy of being mourned.[71]

The question of how, and whom, to mourn is not a simple one. The Freedom Tower at Ground Zero, now called One World Trade Center, did not open until 2015. Disagreement over the form of monumental structures at the site had delayed construction until 2006.[72]

As memorials and monuments sustain public memory, they make arguments about how to think about the identities of particular groups of people. Thus monuments and memorials are rhetorical. Communication scholar Victoria J. Gallagher notes they "perpetuate values, admonish as to future conduct, and affirm or challenge existing power relations."[73] There are two reasons why they are able to perform those functions: (1) what is remembered has less to do with what happened in the past than with the needs of the present; and (2) the process of remembering always involves an act of forgetting as well, creating both presence and absence.

Memory and the architecture of memorials, monuments, and museums serve the needs of the present. Historians Peter Grey and Kendrick Oliver suggest that not only can a nation-state seek to remember key points in its history, such as wars, but "diverse and competing interest groups" can "seek to use constructions of the past to advance their agendas in the present."[74]

Research on the rhetorical power of monuments and memorials shows that architecture, itself, positions those who view the monuments in particular ways, inducing particular reactions and foregrounding particular memories. Gallagher is among the scholars who recognize that "the symbolic, architectural, and/or textual aspects of artifacts . . . impact both people who come into contact with them and the larger society of which those people are members."[75] The preferred readings of memorials and monuments call people to remember some events, and remember them in particular ways. Because some events and people are remembered, others are not; they are deflected. As monuments make some people and events present in public memory, they also make others absent.

In a 2017 speech, New Orleans mayor Mitch Landrieu explained why the city had decided to remove its Confederate memorials.[76] He first reminded the audience of New Orleans's history as the "largest slave market" in the United States, "where hundreds of thousands of souls were bought, sold and shipped up the Mississippi River to lives of forced labor, of misery, of rape, of torture." Given the history of New Orleans as a slave market, Landrieu asked, why are there "no slave ship monuments, no prominent markers on public land to remember the lynchings or the slave blocks?" He then pointed out the hypocrisy of the defenders of the Confederate monuments as historical, noting that they were "eerily silent" about the failure to remember and memorialize the history of slavery. Monuments and memorials are not a recording of objective historical fact. They solidify some things for permanent presence and praise, but in the process render others absent.

The dialectic of presence and absence complicates memorial practices. When actions by people and governments have erased the existence of a group, is it the correct memory practice to erase that erasure? How do you remember the past presence of a people without erasing their present absence? This is the memory conundrum with which Germans have grappled as they consider how to remember and memorialize the Holocaust. The Third Reich's genocidal policies sought to destroy anything associated with the Jewish people, including a fountain that had been donated to the town of Kassel by a Jewish entrepreneur named Sigmund Aschrott in 1908. Aschrott fountain, neo-Gothic in style, stood in front of City Hall. It was over thirty-six feet high and surrounded by a reflecting pool. On April 8 and 9, 1939, Nazi activists destroyed the fountain, condemning it as the "Jews' fountain." They carried it away piece by piece until, according to James Young, a professor of Judaic Studies, all that was left was "a great, empty basin in the center of the square. Two years later, the first transport of 463 Kassel Jews departed from the Central Train Station to Riga, followed in the next year by another 3,000, all murdered."[77]

In 1943, the basin was filled with soil and planted with flowers. Later, it was turned into a fountain again. By the 1960s, when people were asked what had happened to the fountain, their memory was that English bombers had destroyed it during the war. One person, who had grown up in Kassel, said, "No one wished to be reminded of the victims" nor of the collective guilt of the community. The absence of the fountain represented the desire to make the history of Kassel's role in the Holocaust absent and forgotten.[78]

In 1984, to counter this misremembering, the Society for the Rescue of Historical Monuments proposed restoring a form of the fountain as a way of recovering the memory and history of the fountain and the Jews of Kassel.[79] Horst Hoheisel, the architect of the new memorial, designed the new fountain as a mirror of the previous one. The new fountain was placed below the original as a way of recognizing it as "a wound and as an open question," focused on emboldening the residents of Kassel to ensure "such things never happen again."[80] Where the old fountain rose thirty-six feet into the air, the new fountain dives thirty-six feet into the ground. It makes the absence of the original fountain and of Kassel's Jews visible and present.

In an analysis of the new fountain, Young answers the question "How does one remember an absence?" by saying, "In this case, by reproducing it. Quite literally, the negative space of the absent monument will now constitute its phantom shape in the ground."[81] Rebuilding the fountain as it originally stood would have erased the destruction wrought by pro-Nazi members of the community. Covering the space with a new memorial would have covered the scar left by the destruction. By using negative space, however, Hoheisel was able to make an absence (of the fountain and the Jews of Kassel) present.

CIRCULATION

A recurring theme in these examples is circulation. Instead of analyzing visuals as a single image freeze-framed in a specific moment or place, **circulation** encourages critics to study *the manner in which a visual moves through space and time, sometimes unmoored from its original location of production,* and how the meaning of the artifact changes in that movement.[82] For example, Rosenthal's photograph of the Iwo Jima flag raising became iconic in part because it circulated across a range of media; it moved across space. But it also has continued to move across time. Even though the image was taken over seventy years ago, it continues to circulate in contemporary media, sometimes evolving from its original photographic form. Communication scholars Janis L. Edwards and Carol K. Winkler studied the photo and how its form (a group of humans engaged in struggle to lift something) recurred in editorial cartoons up to the late 1990s.[83] Even now the image circulates and evolves: it appeared in editorial cartoons in 2018.[84]

Similarly, the rhetoricity of bodies occurs not just in a single moment, but also across time as images of the bodies circulate. And although a monument may not move, images of it do. Even if a monument does not physically move across space, it moves across time. Little Bighorn National Battlefield, Civil War–related statues, and Aschrott's fountain all changed. How people respond to them has changed across time, too.

The point is that visuals, in fact all forms of rhetoric, circulate and, in circulation, shift and move. Particularly in the networked environment of the digital age, "images rapidly undergo change in terms of location, form, media, genre, and function."[85] The concept of image events captures the effects of circulation.

Image events are *"staged acts . . . designed for media dissemination."*[86] They may be used for protest, for example, as "mind bombs," to explode the typical ways people think about a topic.[87] They are structured to elicit the attention of media outlets, so that they appear on the public screens of television, computers, newspapers, tablets, and smartphones. Image events are premised on an understanding of circulation insofar as they are structured to induce media dissemination of their images. For an event to become an image event, images of it must circulate.

Consider the following example. In 1960, during lunch counter sit-ins at Woolworth's, college students faced violence from White onlookers. In 1961,

FIGURE 6
Firefighters turning hose on civil rights demonstrators
Charles Moore, Black Star

angry mobs confronted the Freedom Riders as police stood by and watched. In 1962, President Kennedy had to send in federal troops when James Meredith became the first Black student to enroll at the University of Mississippi and White people reacted violently. Yet, northern White people were slow to react. Then, in May of 1963, the Birmingham Children's Crusade happened. Civil rights activists had long faced violence, but not until the circulation of photos of the Birmingham civil rights march were White people's sense of themselves and the law challenged.

As civil rights activists, mostly students and children, peacefully marched, Commissioner of Public Safety Eugene "Bull" Connor ordered the police to use dogs and fire hoses to disperse them. Images of police dogs and fire hoses turned against Black protestors, widely televised and published in numerous print media, shook the conscience of the nation and made clear to moderate White people that racial equality would not be attained via a gradualist approach.[88] (See Figure 6.) Communication scholar Davi Johnson argues that a photograph of officers with police dogs attacking unresisting Black protestors constituted "a visual reversal where the traditional characteristic of the uniformed authorities are transposed into their opposites: the protector of order becomes the oppressor who brings chaotic brutality into the scene of civilization."[89] Instead of identifying with the police and accepting the ideograph of "law and order," White people were induced to break their traditional patterns of identification. The photos asked White people to identify with Black protestors who were breaking (unjust) laws.

Photographs are not the only rhetorical artifact that circulates, recirculates, and is repurposed,[90] as the Pepe the Frog internet meme illustrates.[91] In 1976, evolutionary biologist Richard Dawkins introduced the neologism "meme." Dawkins proposed that the meme was to culture what the gene was to biology. Just as humans emerged from a primordial soup of organic molecules, he believed that "the new soup is the soup of human culture" and that the new building block of cultural life is the meme.[92] He wanted "a name for the new [cultural] replicator" that captured the biological idea of replication. The Greek root for imitation, *mimēsis,* spawned "mimeme," which Dawkins shortened to "meme," which sounded like "gene."[93] Like genes, memes replicate,[94] mutate,[95] and circulate.[96] For Dawkins, a **meme** was *any building block of cultural meaning and transmission: an idea, a style, a behavior, a practice.*

The term "meme" has itself mutated to mean something specific in the digital age.[97] Asaf Nissenbaum and Limor Shifman, a graduate student and a professor of communication and journalism at the Hebrew University of Jerusalem, define **internet memes** as "*digital items with common characteristics that are imitated and reiterated around the web.*"[98]

So, how did Pepe the Frog become an internet meme and what can be learned from Pepe?

Matt Furie created Pepe the Frog in 2005 as part of a comic strip, "Boy's Club," on his MySpace page. In 2006, he published a print version of "Boy's Club" as a comic book, in which Pepe was a main character. Furie originally intended "the mellow, positive-vibed" Pepe to be "a peaceful cartoon amphibian who represents love, acceptance, and fun. (And getting stoned)."[99] In 2008, Pepe hopped from the pages of comic books into digital networks when a meme of its cropped head saying "Feels good, man" began circulating on websites such as 4chan, Imgur, Reddit, and Tumblr.[100] In 2014, the Pepe meme began circulating more widely on social media sites such as Twitter and Instagram. Even popular singers Katy Perry and Nicki Minaj posted Pepe memes.

In response, Reddit and 4chan users tried to reclaim Pepe by posting increasingly physically gross and then politically offensive pictures of Pepe.[101] Some 4chan users were probably treating racism as a joke, but members of the alt-right movement saw a serious use of Pepe: as a way to signal white supremacy and its support for Donald Trump's presidential aspirations.

On September 27, 2016, the Anti-Defamation League labeled Pepe a "hate symbol" and began working with Furie to form the #SavePepe campaign.[102] The campaign was not successful. In May 2017, Furie decided to "kill" Pepe by posting on Tumblr an image of Pepe in a casket.[103] Although news reports declared that "Pepe the Frog Is Dead: Creator Kills off Meme Absorbed by Far-Right," reports of Pepe's death were greatly exaggerated. Alt-right groups continue to use Pepe.

This example illustrates, first, that the intent of the original creator of rhetoric does not determine its meaning. Second, as rhetoric circulates across time and into new spaces, its meaning shifts. Third, to understand what a rhetorical artifact means and does, you need to study its circulation, not just its original iteration. Pepe no longer represents a mellow amphibian but instead represents white supremacy.

THE ETHICS OF LOOKING

The "social practices" of visual culture include not just the technologies that generate the ubiquity of images typifying visual culture, but also the habits people use to view those images. These habits influence not only how people look, but also the habitual default to look, rather than not to look. People tend to assume that if an image exists, it must be viewed. They do not stop and think about what their looking does. However, we want to provide a caution against the default to look and the assumption that you have a right to look.

In early 2004, the US Department of Defense began investigating allegations of prisoner abuse and torture at the US-controlled detention center at Abu Ghraib, Iraq. Army Major General Antonio M. Taguba reported that from October to December 2003, soldiers of the 372nd Military Police Company and members of the US intelligence community committed "sadistic, blatant, and wanton criminal abuses." Although some government representatives used phrases such as "enhanced interrogation" to euphemistically minimize US violence, the major general reported abuses such as

> breaking chemical lights and pouring the phosphoric liquid on detainees; pouring cold water on naked detainees; beating detainees with a broom handle and a chair; threatening male detainees with rape; allowing a military police guard to stitch the wound of a detainee who was injured after being slammed against the wall in his cell; sodomizing a detainee with a chemical light and perhaps a broom stick, and using military working dogs to frighten and intimidate detainees with threats of attack, and in one instance actually biting a detainee.[104]

Taguba cited extensive evidence and referenced "extremely graphic photographic evidence," but did not include any photos in the report. Although the US military acknowledged the abuse in early 2004, suspended seventeen soldiers in February 2004, and filed charges against six soldiers in March 2004, US media did not yet report the story widely.

Then, *60 Minutes II* acquired Taguba's classified report, including a CD-ROM containing the graphic photographic evidence of abuse, and released many of the photos on April 28, 2004, as part of its coverage.[105] Subsequently, an article by Seymour Hersh, in the April 30, 2004, *New Yorker*,[106] cited the Taguba report as its source and reprinted some of the photographs. The American Civil Liberties Union (ACLU) thought the photographs were so important that it filed a Freedom of Information Act request for the release of all of them. Over the next decade, lower courts supported the ACLU's request, but in August 2018, the US Court of Appeals for the Second Circuit ruled that the government could withhold the photos.[107] Even without official release of the photographs, however, the images used by *60 Minutes II* and the *New Yorker* circulated worldwide in newspapers, websites, and televised news coverage. Concerns about US treatment of prisoners of war were merely suspicions and rumors until images of the torture circulated and provided visual evidence of the abuse.

Although the release of the images induced a US reckoning with the torture that its soldiers committed, international relations professor Elizabeth Dauphinée offers a compelling argument that people should not look at the Abu Ghraib torture photos: Because taking the photographs was part of the torture of Abu Ghraib prisoners, viewing the photographs participates in torture. Dauphinée recognizes the important role the photos played in raising questions about US policy regarding treatment of prisoners from the war on terror, but questions the repeated showing of the images.[108]

Even if an image is placed before you, should you automatically look at it? At least in this case, Dauphinée argues that even if the images had a positive effect, to look at them is ethically questionable because "the bodies in the photographs are still exposed to our gaze in ways that render them abject, nameless and humiliated—even when our goal in the use of that imagery is to oppose their condition."[109] Although the images are available for viewing, Dauphinée argues, you should not look. Why?

These photographs are not just objective records of abuse. They were not taken for official purposes, but as titillating and amusing trophies, by the soldiers committing the criminal abuse. They were meant to intensify the prisoners' shame and degradation. The photos are about the photographers, not just about the prisoners. To look is to participate in the soldiers' abuse of the prisoners.

This example also raises the question: Why was the circulation of photographs needed to actually spark public outcry about torture? The need for photographs points to the role of visual culture and how visuals are privileged as a form of proof. As Dauphinée explains, "Images do not speak for themselves— they are made to speak for, by and about *us*."[110] In this case, the images and people's assumption that they *should* be looked at speak volumes about visual culture's default to looking, even when the looking itself commits injury.

The privileging of the image in visual culture makes it virtually impossible to avoid looking. If you read the *New Yorker* article or visit the Wikipedia page about Abu Ghraib, the pictures flow across your screen. Wikipedia uses over twenty-four images to illustrate an entry that spans eleven screens, meaning over two images per screen appear as you read.[111] Thus, to abide by Dauphinée's moral injunction, you have to actively avoid looking.

Photographs of lynching provide a second example about the ethics of looking. Although lynching was used against a variety of individuals and groups, white supremacists most often used it as a form of anti-Black domestic terrorism. White people lynched 4,743 people between 1882 and 1968, at least 3,446 of which were southern Blacks.[112] Why did white supremacists lynch Black people? Rhetoric scholar Ersula Ore argues that "lynching was a call to communion, a performance of political affiliation akin to citizenship in the way it distinguished those who belonged from those who did not."[113] White supremacists used lynching to create identification among Whites, making them an "us," while excluding Blacks from political kinship by dehumanizing them.

Both Whites and Blacks were audiences. In targeting Black audiences, Whites used lynching to terrorize Blacks. Author Richard Wright wrote, "Lynching is a terror that has many forms; there is lynching of men's spirits as well as their bodies, and spiritual lynching occurs every day for the Negro in the South."[114] All African American communities were terrorized by the threat of lynching.

Whites were also an audience, at the moment of lynching and afterward. Until the 1940s, lynching was meant to be a public spectacle, attended by hundreds and sometimes thousands of White community members and families.[115] Historian Amy Louise Wood argues that "mobs performed lynchings as spectacles for other whites" and "the rituals, the tortures, and their subsequent representations imparted powerful messages to whites about their own supposed racial dominance and superiority."[116] Those "subsequent representations" include photographs made into postcards and circulated by Whites as souvenirs to celebrate the events.[117] Hundreds of these images have been collected in James Allen's book *Without Sanctuary: Lynching Photography in America*.[118] The images are jarring because they repeatedly show not only the murdered bodies of Black people, but also crowds of White people, including families and children, smiling happily in the background. White spectators of the lynchings were not horrified: the violence committed against Black people was accepted, if not a cause for celebration and a time for White communion.

The questions that *Without Sanctuary* raises are not only whether you *should* look at these images, but if you do, *how* should you look at them? When the postcards first circulated, Whites were invited to look so their Whiteness could be reaffirmed, while Blacks were forced to look in order to terrorize them into compliance with white supremacy. In contrast, *Without Sanctuary* uses the images to protest anti-Black violence, echoing the practice of using images against their original intent pioneered by Ida B. Wells when she published an 1891 postcard of the lynching in Clanton, Alabama, in her 1894 antilynching pamphlet *A Red Record*.[119] The postcard was made to celebrate lynching; Wells published it to condemn lynching.

Does it mean something different to look at the images now than it did 80, 100, or 120 years ago? Does the fact that images of lynching exist mean that you should look at them? It depends on the looking practices in which you engage. Even when Wells and other antilynching activists such as the NAACP used these images, they carefully prepared audiences "to view the images against their intended purpose."[120] *Without Sanctuary* motivated Senators Mary Landrieu and George Allan to propose a nonbinding resolution in which the Senate formally apologized for failing to pass antilynching legislation.[121] In the resolution, the Senate noted "the recent publication of 'Without Sanctuary: Lynching Photography in America' helped bring greater awareness and proper recognition of the victims of lynching."[122]

Landrieu's advocacy for the resolution explained that the book "showed the real faces of lynching, and the images . . . unveiled began to change the way people viewed these tragic events."[123] The curating of the book and the care given to humanize the victims helped assure that people would not just glance at these images. Repeated and routine exposure to these images can normalize the violence, however, making it unremarkable. You should pause and consider what these images ask of you. To look (not just glance), in this instance, is to enact an ethical relationship.[124]

Wood argues that you need to engage in the looking practice of **witnessing,** *a practice of looking that "bears a legal, spiritual, or social consequence . . . To act as a witness is thus to play a public role, one that bestows a particular kind of social authority on the individual, at the same time that it connects that individual to a larger community of fellow witnesses."*[125] Witnesses are called to testify about what they have seen. You should resist being merely a passive spectator and instead be an active witness. You should consider and articulate your civic responsibility to address the injury recorded in these images.[126]

A third example illustrates how a civic response was enabled by photographic evidence of a lynching, but this photo was not taken by the Whites who committed the crime.

In August 1955, Emmett Till, a Black fourteen-year-old from Chicago visiting relatives in Mississippi, was accused of interacting with a White woman.[127] White supremacists used this interaction as a pretense to justify one of the most brutal and publicized racist murders in US history. We describe Till's murder in an attempt to remember and convey the violence committed, and we avoid euphemisms and truncated passives in the description because the murderers' brutality should be named.

Two White men, Roy Bryant and J. W. Milam, abducted Till from his uncle's house, beat him, mutilated him, shot him in the head, and then sank his body in the Tallahatchie River. An all-White, all-male jury found them not guilty after only an hour of deliberation, which time had been extended because the sheriff had told the jury to make the verdict "look good." Till's mutilated and bloated body was returned to his family in Chicago in a sealed casket. His mother, Mamie Till Bradley, demanded to see her son's body and then decided to hold an open-casket funeral. Photos from the funeral circulated widely, making present in public the full brutality of racism. Commenting on Bradley's choice, communication scholars Christine Harold and Kevin DeLuca note that "the photographic image of Emmett Till's corpse put a shocking and monstrous face on the most brutal extremes of American racial injustice" and "became a crucial visual vocabulary that articulated the ineffable qualities of American racism in ways words simply could not do."[128] The image of the child's vulnerable, brutalized body exposed the viciousness of racial hatred in the South, served as a catalyst for Northern Blacks to recognize they were not safe,[129] and called forth a response.

A few things distinguish Emmett Till's photograph from the Abu Ghraib photos and the lynching postcards that Whites circulated. First, Mamie Till Bradley wanted people to look: she gave her consent for people to look. Second, the looking was curated and carefully staged. During the funeral, Mamie Till Bradley chose an open casket funeral to display her son Emmett's bloated and brutalized body. On the open casket lid, she posted images of Emmett, smiling, so people could see the young boy he was. Third, the image of his body did not circulate alone. It was almost always accompanied by images of Mamie Till Bradley's grief as she wept over her child's body in the casket or her "anguished face as she watched his casket lowered into the ground."[130] People saw not only Emmett Till's body, but the searing pain of a mother whose child had been brutally murdered by white supremacists. Finally, 1955 was a unique moment for looking. By the time of Emmett Till's murder, lynching was no longer a "public spectacle" or "a community event celebrated by cheering audiences."[131] Although lynching was still common, it was conducted in secrecy and the dead body of the lynched person was "no longer a souvenir to display."[132] People were discouraged from looking at the horror of racist violence. Thus, active inducements to look and to witness the violence were necessary. All these elements—consent, staging, public grief, and the need to see—created conditions where witnessing could occur. Mamie Till Bradley demanded that all members of the audience, Whites and Blacks, witness her grief and loss.

The ethical challenges raised by lynching photos persist. Scholars have long argued that images of bodies in pain do not necessarily mobilize a productive social response. Philosopher and political activist Susan Sontag, in her book *Regarding the Pain of Others,* meditates on the power, or lack thereof, of pictures of pain to move a viewer. A failure to react to them, she argues, is a failure of "imagination, of empathy."[133] When candid images were less common, it was believed that showing painful realities would goad viewers to feel more. Writing in 2003, Sontag believed this reaction could not be taken for granted, because US society has entered an age of image fatigue, in which images of pain participate in "rote ways of provoking feeling."[134] Social science research supports her concern. Psychologists Brad J. Bushman and Craig A. Anderson conducted a series of experiments and found that mediated images of violence "make people numb to the pain and suffering of others."[135] Thus, if an image of pain is to be circulated and looked at, it must be presented in a way that invites the audience to bear witness rather than just spectate or glance.

Take a moment and think about whether you have seen an image of a dead body recently. You likely have not seen an image of a child murdered during a school shooting in the United States, but the image of the bodies of Óscar Alberto Martínez Ramírez and his twenty-three-month-old daughter Angie Valeria, both of whom died trying to cross the Rio Grande, circulated across multiple media outlets.[136] Similarly, people in the United Sates see photographs of flag-draped coffins but rarely of the bodies of dead US soldiers, although images of dead people from other countries are common.[137]

Think about recent images you have seen of war dead. You might remember seeing images of Syrians, Iraqis, Yemenis, Afghans, and Rohingya, but can you remember an image of a dead US soldier? Media scholar Sarah Sentilles notes how this differential visibility renders some people as "other":

> If the refusal to publish images of dead American service members is
> a sign of respect, then the willingness to publish photographs of other
> people's dead bodies can be read as a sign of disrespect. Publishing some
> images while suppressing others sends the message that the visible bodies
> are somehow less consequential than the bodies granted the privilege of
> privacy.[138]

A tension exists between the need to make death visible/present and the need to respect the dignity of those who have died. After years of tracking media images of the dead and noting the paucity of images of US military and civilian dead, the appearance of images of Black people killed by police in the United States struck Sentilles as noteworthy. Although photographs of Black people killed by police make present Black people's vulnerability to violence, why does US society need photos to prove police brutality exists? How many photos are needed, and how often should they be viewed? Why do people feel entitled to look, especially at another's pain and suffering?

Think about your practices of looking. When someone is looked at, it may mean they are *seen* or it may mean they are *surveilled*. Being seen is an indication of respect and recognition, but being watched can reduce a person to an object just to be stared at, or a problem that must be watched and controlled. Sentilles's point is that you should not take the looking and photography practices of visual culture for granted. Racism makes minoritized bodies "hypervisible and invisible," in that they are surveilled but not really seen.[139] The fact that looking at some dead bodies, but not others, has been normalized shows that analyzing viewing practices—what people look at, how they look, why they look, when they look, who has the right to look, where they look—is as important as analyzing the visual artifacts themselves.

What can be said about recent images of police and vigilante violence committed against Black people? Since 2013, the Black Lives Matter network (BLM) has sought to make present the state sanctioned violence committed against Black people. Using digital media, BLM has circulated video and photographic evidence of this violence. News and social media also replay these videos, leading one media commentator to cite Bushman and Anderson's research when voicing concern over "videos of black men dying on loop."[140] The circulation of the images of police brutality raised White people's consciousness and pushed police brutality onto the political agenda, in a way that Black communities saying police were violent and lawless had not.[141] The question remains, however, about whether the images should be continually shown and continually looked at. Should you default to looking?

The April 4, 2015, video of North Charleston, South Carolina, police officer Michael Slager shooting eight rounds into the back of fifty-year-old Coast Guard veteran Walter Scott provides an example. Slager claimed there had been a violent struggle and the use of deadly force was justified. Bystander video clearly showed that Scott was not a threat, that he had been running away when he was shot, and that Slager had dropped something near Scott's body, suggesting that Slager might have been trying to plant evidence of the taser he claimed they had been fighting over.[142] Slager was immediately charged with Scott's murder. He pled guilty to "Deprivation of Rights under Color of Law," as part of a plea agreement in which state murder charges would be dropped, and was sentenced to twenty years in prison.[143] This outcome probably would not have happened without the existence of the video, which "made inescapable a horrific murder, an act of outrageous injustice by a putative guardian of the law."[144]

The video was not only viewed by the family and their lawyers, law enforcement agencies investigating, and the court, however. Three days after the shooting, Charleston's *Post and Courier* posted the video online. MSNBC's Rachel Maddow devoted a twenty-minute segment to the shooting.[145] By April 8, the story had circulated, "front and center, on the home page of . . . local paper[s], the *Times,* and on the BBC, and the *Guardian,* and the *Wall Street Journal,* and thousands of other news sites, as well as hundreds of thousands of Facebook pages and Twitter feeds," leading to the question: "Should you watch the video?"[146] We remember seeing local news stations report on the shooting while the video played, on loop, in the background. The use of the video as visual wallpaper concerns us. Media's heavy reliance on visuals, even when they are unnecessary or potentially counter-productive, gives us pause.

Newsrooms debate whether to make videos available, in some cases deciding not to, as when the *New York Times* decided not to show video of jihadists executing US journalist James Foley. Even when a video is shown, there is another layer of ethical decision making. Do *you* choose to watch it? Do *you* click "play"? Do *you* click "share"? Our argument is not that you should never look at an image of a brutalized or vulnerable body, but that you should always think about for what purpose and for whose good you look.

CONCLUSION

Our goal in this chapter is to assist you in becoming a critical viewer of visual rhetoric and resisting the hegemonic pull that many images may have on you. Visual communication scholar Diane Hope explains, "Viewing audiences are not necessarily passive. Viewers select, choose, and perceive images according to the context, knowledge, and life experience they bring to the act of viewing."[147]

Because visual forms are rhetorical, and not just objective recorders of some fixed world, viewers of visual rhetoric should not ask "what do images represent?" but instead "what do the images do?" Visual rhetoric induces you to see the world one way rather than another. The more aware you are of the rhetorical aspects of visuals, the more you will be able to determine when you should assent to the arguments they advance.

In a visual culture, civic life is constituted, maintained, defined, and performed through visual rhetoric. Public bodies argue and advocate; civic identity is constituted through photographs; and national memories are maintained in monuments. Although people often think of civic life as occurring only through the medium of talk, visual rhetoric is as important to civic life as language.

When you study visual rhetoric, consider its circulation. How does where and when an image appears affect its meaning? Consider which images appear and which do not. Finally, always ask, before looking, whether you should.

DISCUSSION QUESTIONS

1. In what ways is contemporary US culture a visual culture?
2. Find an example of visual rhetoric. Identify what type it is (iconic photograph, body rhetoric, monument rhetoric, or something else). How did the visual circulate? Explore how the example induces you to accept a particular understanding of the world.

3. Find a monument or memorial in your area. Identify the symbolism (for example, what the various parts of the monument or memorial represent). Which group's memory is foregrounded? Are any groups' memories placed in the background? What cultural values or ideologies are praised? What is the message that people are meant to take away now?

4. Can you identify an iconic photograph taken in the last decade? If so, explain how it meets all the criteria of an iconic photo that Lucaites and Hariman identify. If not, is there something about contemporary US visual culture that might explain the apparent decline in iconic photographs?

5. Even though people live in a visual culture, are there instances when there is a duty *not* to look at a photograph? How does visual culture influence looking habits?

RECOMMENDED READINGS

Balthrop, V. William, Carole Blair, and Neil Michel. "The Presence of the Present: Hijacking 'The Good War'?" *Western Journal of Communication* 74, no. 2 (March/April 2010): 170–207.

DeLuca, Kevin Michael. "Unruly Arguments: The Body Rhetoric of Earth First!, ACT UP, and Queer Nation." *Argumentation and Advocacy* 36 (Summer 1999): 9–21.

DeLuca, Kevin Michael, and Anne Teresa Demo. "Imaging Nature: Watkins, Yosemite, and the Birth of Environmentalism." *Critical Studies in Media Communication* 17, no. 3 (September 2000): 241–260.

Dickinson, Greg, Carole Blair, and Brian L. Ott, eds. *Places of Public Memory: The Rhetoric of Museums and Memorials.* Tuscaloosa: University of Alabama Press, 2010. See especially the "Introduction."

Groarke, Leo, Catherine H. Palczewski, and David Godden. "Navigating the Visual Turn in Argument." *Argumentation and Advocacy* 52, no. 4 (2016). 217–235. DOI: 10.1080/00028533.2016.11821871.

Hariman, Robert, and John Louis Lucaites. "Performing Civic Identity: The Iconic Photograph of the Flag Raising on Iwo Jima." *Quarterly Journal of Speech* 88, no. 4 (November 2002): 363–392.

ENDNOTES

[1] Justice John Paul Stevens, dissent in *United States v. Eichman,* 496 U.S. 310 (1990), at 321.

[2] Allan Cromley, "Flag, Statue Added to Resolve Vietnam Memorial Controversy," *Oklahoman,* October 14, 1982, https://www.oklahoman.com/article/1998948/flag-statue-added-to-resolve-vietnam-memorial-controversy.

[3] "Lift the Veil on the Return of the Nation's War Dead," *USA Today,* February 23, 2009.

[4] "Official: Pentagon Allows Coverage of War Coffins," CNNPolitics, accessed February 26, 2009, http://www.cnn.com/2009/POLITICS/02/26/pentagon.media.war.dead/index.html; and Andrea Stone, "Ban on Photographing U.S. Troops' Coffins Lifted," *USA Today,* February 27, 2009–March 1, 2009.

[5] Charles A. Hill and Marguerite Helmers, eds., *Defining Visual Rhetorics* (Mahwah, NJ: Erlbaum, 2004); Diane S. Hope, ed., *Visual Communication: Perception, Rhetoric, and*

Technology (New York: Hampton, 2006); and Lawrence J. Prelli, *Rhetorics of Display* (Columbia: University of South Carolina Press, 2006).

[6] Jessica Evans and Stuart Hall, "What is Visual Culture?" in *Visual Culture: The Reader,* ed. Jessica Evans and Stuart Hall (London: Sage, 1999), 7.

[7] Pablo Ximénez de Sandoval, "Meet the Man Who Recorded the World's First Viral Video," *El País,* May 25, 2017, https://elpais.com/elpais/2017/05/25/inenglish /1495709209_218886.html.

[8] German Lopez, "How Video Changed Americans' Views toward the Police, from Rodney King to Alton Sterling," *Vox,* July 6, 2016, https://www.vox.com/policy-and-politics /2015/12/10/9886504/police-shooting-video-confidence.

[9] Josmar Trujillo, "#FTP Film the Police," *Extra!* 27, no. 9 (October 2014): 4.

[10] Lopez, "How Video Changed."

[11] Chaïm Perelman and Lucie Olbrechts-Tyteca, *The New Rhetoric: A Treatise on Argumentation* (Notre Dame, IN: University of Notre Dame Press, 1969), 116.

[12] Diane S. Hope, in the introduction to her edited collection of essays, *Visual Communication,* describes the way in which presence functions in visual rhetoric, referencing the works of Chaïm Perelman and Lucie Olbrechts-Tyteca. Generally, the process of "selecting certain elements and presenting them to the audience" implies that they are pertinent and important and, thus, imbues them with presence. Hope, *Visual Communication,* 116. See also Prelli, *Rhetorics of Display,* 7.

[13] Caitlin Dickerson, "The Youngest Child Separated from His Family at the Border Was 4 Months Old," *New York Times,* June 16, 2019, https://www.nytimes.com/2019/06/16 /us/baby-constantine-romania-migrants.html.

[14] Miriam Jordan, "No More Family Separations, except These 900," *New York Times,* July 30, 2019, https://www.nytimes.com/2019/07/30/us/migrant-family-separations .html.

[15] Sarah Cascone, "An Immigrant Rights Group Recruited 10 Street Artists for a Viral Campaign about Child Detention—and They Hope to Bring it to DC Next," *Artnet News,* June 14, 2019, https://news.artnet.com/art-world/no-kids-in-cages-guerrilla -art-installation-1573267

[16] RAICES, #NoKidsInCages, 2018, https://web.archive.org/web/20210308231625 /https://nokidsincages.com/.

[17] Jessica Evans and Stuart Hall, eds., *Visual Culture: The Reader* (Thousand Oaks, CA: Sage, 1999), 7.

[18] Prelli, *Rhetorics of Display,* 1–3.

[19] Evans and Hall, *Visual Culture,* 7.

[20] Evans and Hall, *Visual Culture,* 7.

[21] Kevin M. DeLuca, *Image Politics: The New Rhetoric of Environmental Activism* (New York: Guilford, 1999).

[22] Barry Schwartz, "The Social Context of Commemoration: A Study of Collective Memory," *Social Forces* 61 (December 1982): 374–402.

[23] Victoria J. Gallagher, "Memory as Social Action: Cultural Projection and Generic Form in Civil Rights Memorials," in *New Approaches to Rhetoric,* ed. Patricia A. Sullivan and Steven R. Goldzwig (Thousand Oaks, CA: Sage, 2004), 149.

[24] Diane S. Hope, ed., "Introduction: Identity and Visual Communication," in *Visual Communication,* 4.

[25] Hope, "Introduction," 5.

[26] Celeste Michelle Condit, "The Rhetorical Limits of Polysemy," *Critical Studies in Mass Communication* 6, no. 2 (June 1989): 103–104.

27 Stuart Hall, "Encoding, Decoding," in *The Cultural Studies Reader,* ed. Simon During (London: Routledge, 1993), 98–102.

28 Hall, "Encoding, Decoding," 101, italics added.

29 Evans and Hall, *Visual Culture,* 4.

30 A version of the advertisement is available at http://www.americanapparel.net /presscenter/ads/images/a9000/type3/9826_MAKS_AD_040314_LG.jpg.

31 "About Ms.," *Ms.,* http://www.msmagazine.com/about, accessed August 22, 2021.

32 Linda Steiner, "Oppositional Decoding as an Act of Resistance," *Critical Studies in Mass Communication* 5, no. 1 (March 1988): 2.

33 Lester C. Olson, Cara A. Finnegan, and Diane S. Hope, "Visual Rhetoric in Communication: Continuing Questions and Contemporary Issues," in *Visual Rhetoric: A Reader in Communication and American Culture,* ed. Lester C. Olson, Cara A. Finnegan, and Diane S. Hope (Thousand Oaks, CA: Sage, 2008), 3.

34 Sonja K. Foss, "A Rhetorical Schema for the Evaluation of Visual Imagery," *Communication Studies* 45 (Fall–Winter 1994): 213, 216–217. She also asks how well that function is communicated, given the stylistic and substantive elements of the visual, and whether the effects sought by the image are legitimate.

35 Blair encourages asking these questions: "(1) What is the significance of the text's material existence? (2) What are the apparatuses and degrees of durability displayed by the text? (3) What are the text's modes or possibilities of reproduction or preservation? (4) What does the text do to (or with, or against) other texts? (5) How does the text act on people?" Carole Blair, "Contemporary U.S. Memorial Sites as Exemplars of Rhetoric's Materiality," in *Rhetorical Bodies,* ed. Jack Selzer and Sharon Crowley (Madison: University of Wisconsin Press, 1999), 23, 30.

36 National Park Service, World War II Memorial, "Service, Sacrifice, Unity, and Victory," http://www.nps.gov/nwwm/index.htm.

37 V. William Balthrop, Carole Blair, and Neil Michel, "The Presence of the Present: Hijacking 'The Good War'?" *Western Journal of Communication* 74, no. 2 (2010): 172.

38 Kevin Michael DeLuca and Anne Teresa Demo, "Imaging Nature: Watkins, Yosemite, and the Birth of Environmentalism," *Critical Studies in Media Communication* 17, no. 3 (September 2000): 244.

39 DeLuca and Demo, "Imaging Nature," 244. See also W. J. T. Mitchell, *What Do Pictures Want?* (Chicago: Chicago University Press, 2005), especially chapter 2.

40 Prelli, *Rhetorics of Display,* 11.

41 Hope, *Visual Communication,* 17.

42 Hope, *Visual Communication,* 17.

43 DeLuca and Demo, "Imaging Nature," 242.

44 DeLuca and Demo, "Imaging Nature," 244.

45 DeLuca and Demo, "Imaging Nature," 242.

46 Robert Hariman and John Louis Lucaites, "Performing Civic Identity: The Iconic Photograph of the Flag Raising on Iwo Jima," *Quarterly Journal of Speech* 88, no. 4 (November 2002): 365.

47 John Louis Lucaites and Robert Hariman, "Visual Rhetoric, Photojournalism, and Democratic Public Culture," *Rhetoric Review* 20, nos. 1/2 (Spring 2001): 37, italics added.

48 Hariman and Lucaites, "Performing Civic Identity," 363–392.

49 Robert Hariman and John Louis Lucaites, "Dissent and Emotional Management in a Liberal-Democratic Society: The Kent State Iconic Photograph," *Rhetoric Society Quarterly* 31, no. 3 (Summer 2001): 4–31.

50 Robert Hariman and John Louis Lucaites, "Public Identity and Collective Memory in U.S. Iconic Photography: The Image of 'Accidental Napalm,'" *Critical Studies in Media*

Communication 20, no. 1 (March 2003): 35–66. Image available at http://digitaljournalist.org/issue0008/ng2.htm.

[51] Hariman and Lucaites, "Performing Civic Identity," 364.

[52] Hariman and Lucaites, "Performing Civic Identity," 366.

[53] Karlyn Kohrs Campbell, *The Rhetorical Act,* 2nd ed. (Belmont, CA: Wadsworth, 309–310.

[54] Barbara Jordan, "1976 Democratic Convention Keynote Address: Who Then Will Speak for the Common Good?" New York, NY, July 12, 1976, http://www.elf.net /bjordan/keynote.html. For an analysis of enactment in this speech, see Karlyn Kohrs Campbell and Kathleen Hall Jamieson, "Form and Genre in Rhetorical Criticism: An Introduction," in *Form and Genre: Shaping Rhetorical Action,* eds. Karlyn Kohrs Campbell and Kathleen Hall Jamieson (Falls Church, VA: Speech Communication Association, 1978).

[55] Mary Fisher, "1992 Republican National Convention Address: A Whisper of AIDS," Houston, TX, https://www.americanrhetoric.com/speeches/maryfisher1992rnc.html.

[56] It Gets Better Project, "About," accessed February 18, 2011, http://www.itgetsbetter.org /pages/about-it-gets-better-project.

[57] It Gets Better Project, "About Our Global Movement," accessed December 31, 2018, https://itgetsbetter.org/about.

[58] Kevin Michael DeLuca, "Unruly Arguments: The Body Rhetoric of Earth First!, ACT UP, and Queer Nation," *Argumentation and Advocacy* 36 (Summer 1999): 9–21, 10.

[59] DeLuca, *Image Politics* (New York: Guilford, 1999), 17.

[60] Eric Westervelt, "ACT UP at 30: Reinvigorated for Trump Fight," NPR (April 17, 2017), https://www.npr.org/2017/04/17/522726303/act-up-at-30-reinvigorated-for-trump -fight.

[61] Westervelt, "ACT UP at 30."

[62] Jodi Rudoren, "Proudly Bearing Elders' Scars, Their Skin Says 'Never Forget,'" *New York Times,* October 1, 2012.

[63] Linda Diane Horwitz and Daniel C. Brouwer, "The Progenic Trauma Tattoo as Resignification: Auschwitz 157622, A-15510, 4559, . . . ," in *Disturbing Argument,* ed. Catherine Helen Palczewski (New York: Routledge, 2014), 91.

[64] Karl Vick, "Iran's President Calls Holocaust 'Myth' in Latest Assault on Jews," *Washington Post,* December 15, 2005, http://www.washingtonpost.com/wp-dyn /content/article/2005/12/14/AR2005121402403.html.

[65] Robert Tait, "Holocaust Deniers Gather in Iran for 'Scientific' Conference," *Guardian,* December 11, 2006, http://www.theguardian.com/world/2006/dec/12/iran.israel.

[66] Valeria Fabj, "Motherhood as Political Voice: The Rhetoric of the Mothers of Plaza de Mayo," *Communication Studies* 44 (Spring 1993): 1–18.

[67] Fabj, "Motherhood as Political Voice," 2.

[68] Quoted on Friends of the Little Bighorn website, accessed June 20, 2007, http://www.friendslittlebighorn.com/Indian%20Memorial.htm.

[69] Western National Parks Association, *The Indian Memorial at Little Bighorn Battlefield National Monument: Peace through Unity* (Canada: Western National Parks Association, 2003).

[70] Richard Morris, *Sinners, Lovers, and Heroes* (Albany: State University of New York Press, 1997), 25.

[71] For more on this monument, see Ryan McGeough, Catherine H. Palczewski, and Randall Lake, "Oppositional Memory Practices: U.S. Memorial Spaces as Arguments over Public Memory," *Argumentation and Advocacy* 51, no. 4 (Spring 2015): 231–254; and Catherine H. Palczewski, "Women at the Little Big Horn: Circumferences of Memory," in *Decolonizing Native American Rhetoric: Communicating*

Self-Determination, ed. Casey Ryan Kelly and Jason Edward Black (New York: Peter Lang, 2018), 48–77.

[72] See letters to the editor, *New York Times,* July 1, 2005, http://www.triroc.com/wtc/media/freedomtower/timesletters.htm.

[73] Victoria J. Gallagher, "Remembering Together: Rhetorical Integration and the Case of the Martin Luther King Jr. Memorial," *The Southern Communication Journal* 60, no. 2 (Winter 1995): 112.

[74] Peter Grey and Kendrick Oliver, "The Memory of Catastrophe," *History Today* 51, no. 2 (February 2001): 9–15.

[75] Gallagher, "Remembering Together," 109.

[76] Mitch Landrieu, "Mayor Mitch Landrieu Gives Address on Removal of Four Confederate Statues," May 23, 2017, City of New Orleans, https://web.archive.org /web/20170524025327/https://www.nola.gov/. See also "Mitch Landrieu's Speech on the Removal of Confederate Monuments in New Orleans," *New York Times,* May 23, 2017, https://www.nytimes.com/2017/05/23/opinion/mitch-landrieus -speech-transcript.html.

[77] James E. Young, *The Texture of Meaning: Holocaust Memorials and Meaning* (New Haven, CT: Yale University Press, 1993), 43.

[78] Quoted in Horst Hoheisel, "Aschrott Fountain [Kassel 1985]," http://www.knitz.net /index.php?Itemid=3&id=30&option=com_content&task=view&lang=en. Images of the original fountain and the new memorial can be seen on this site.

[79] Young, *The Texture of Meaning,* 43.

[80] As quoted in Young, *The Texture of Meaning,* 43.

[81] Young, *The Texture of Meaning,* 45.

[82] Cara A. Finnegan and Jiyeon Kang, "'Sighting the Public': Iconoclasm and Public Sphere Theory," *Quarterly Journal of Speech* 90, no. 4 (2004): 395.

[83] Janis L. Edwards and Carol K. Winkler, "Representative Form and the Visual Ideograph: The Iwo Jima Image in Editorial Cartoons," *Quarterly Journal of Speech* 83, no. 3 (1997): 289–310.

[84] Mike Lukovich's cartoon appeared in the November 20, 2018, *Atlanta Journal and Constitution.* For more examples, see http://www.cartoonistgroup.com/subject /The-Iwo+Jima-Comics-and-Cartoons.php.

[85] Laurie E. Gries, *Still Life with Rhetoric: A New Materialist Approach for Visual Rhetorics* (Logan: Utah State University Press, 2015), 19.

[86] John W. Delicath and Kevin Michael DeLuca, "Image Events, the Public Sphere, and Argumentative Practice: The Case of Radical Environmental Groups," Argumentation 17 (2003): 315–333.

[87] Robert Hunter, quoted in Kevin Michael DeLuca, *Image Politics* (New York: Guilford, 1999), 1.

[88] Meg Spratt, "When Police Dogs Attacked: Iconic News Photographs and Construction of History, Mythology, and Political Discourse," *American Journalism* 25, no. 2 (2008): 85–105.

[89] Davi Johnson, "Martin Luther King Jr.'s 1963 Birmingham Campaign as Image Event," *Rhetoric and Public Affairs* 10, no. 1 (2007): 14.

[90] Mary E. Stuckey, "On Rhetorical Circulation," *Rhetoric & Public Affairs* 15, no. 4 (2012): 609–612.

[91] This example is deeply informed by Fernando Ismael Quinones Valdivia, "From Meme to Memegraph: The Curious Case of Pepe the Frog and White Nationalism," MA thesis (University of Northern Iowa, 2019), https://scholarworks.uni.edu/etd/949.

92 Richard Dawkins, *The Selfish Gene* (New York: Oxford University Press, 1976), 206. See also Michele Kennerly and Damien Smith Pfister, *Ancient Rhetorics and Digital Networks* (Tuscaloosa: University of Alabama Press, 2018).

93 Dawkins, *The Selfish Gene,* 206.

94 Davi Johnson, "Mapping the Meme: A Geographical Approach to Materialist Rhetorical Criticism," *Communication and Critical Cultural Studies* 4, no. 1 (March 2007): 27–50.

95 Kennerly and Pfister, *Ancient Rhetorics,* 206.

96 See Eric S. Jenkins, "The Modes of Visual Rhetoric: Circulating Memes as Expressions," *Quarterly Journal of Speech* 100, no. 4 (November 2014): 442–466.

97 Kennerly and Pfister, *Ancient Rhetorics,* 208, quoting Dawkins.

98 Asaf Nissenbaum and Limor Shifman, "Internet Memes as Contested Cultural Capital: The Case of 4chan's /b/ Board," *New Media & Society* 19, no. 4 (2015): 1–19, 1. DOI: 10.1177/1461444815609313.

99 Jacq Cohen, "The Truth about Pepe the Frog," Fantagraphics (October 6, 2016), http://fantagraphics.com/flog/truthaboutpepe/. For more on this example, see Heather Suzanne Woods and Leslie A. Hahner, *Make America Meme Again: The Rhetoric of the Alt-Right* (New York: Peter Lang, 2019); and Quinones Valdivia, "From Meme to Memegraph."

100 Jessica Roy, "How 'Pepe the Frog' Went from Harmless to Hate Symbol," *LA Times,* October 11, 2016, https://www.latimes.com/politics/la-na-pol-pepe-the-frog-hate -symbol-20161011-snap-htmlstory.html.

101 Alex Goldman, "The Grand Tapestry of Pepe," *Reply All,* September 21, 2016, https://www.gimletmedia.com/reply-all/77-the-grand-tapestry-of-pepe.

102 Anti-Defamation League, "Pepe the Frog," https://www.adl.org/education/references /hate-symbols/pepe-the-frog.

103 Daniella Silva, "Pepe the Frog is Dead: Creator Kills Off Meme Absorbed by Far-Right," NBC News, May 8, 2017, https://www.nbcnews.com/tech/social-media/pepe-frog -dead-creator-kills-meme-absorbed-far-right-n756281.

104 Quoted in Seymour M. Hersh, "Torture at Abu Ghraib," *New Yorker,* April 30, 2004, https://www.newyorker.com/magazine/20049-/05/10/torture-at-abu-ghraib.

105 Shannon L. Holland, "The Enigmatic Lynndie England: Gendered Explanations for the Crisis at Abu Ghraib," *Communication and Critical/Cultural Studies* 6, no. 3 (September 2009): 246–264.

106 Seymour M. Hersh, "Torture at Abu Ghraib."

107 Ashley Rundell, "Federal Appeals Court Rejects Release of Abu Ghraib Photographs," *Jurist,* August 22, 2018, https://www.jurist.org/news/2018/08/federal-appeals-court -rejects-release-of-abu-ghraib-photographs/.

108 Elizabeth Dauphinée, "The Politics of the Body in Pain: Reading the Ethics of Imagery," *Security Dialogue* 38, no. 2 (2007): 13155, 153, https://doi.org.10.1177 /0967010607078529.

109 Dauphinée, "Politics of the Body," 145.

110 Dauphinée, "Politics of the Body," 153.

111 "Abu Graib Torture and Prisoner Abuse," *Wikipedia,* accessed November 6, 2018, https://en.wikipedia.org/wiki/Abu_Ghraib_torture_and_prisoner_abuse#Associated _Press_report,_2003.

112 Walter T. Howard, *Lynchings, Extralegal Violence in Florida during the 1930s* (New York: Authors Choice, 2005), 18.

113 Ersula Ore, *Lynching: Violence, Rhetoric, and American Identity* (Jackson: University Press of Mississippi, 2019), 21.

114 Richard Wright, *Conversations with Richard Wright,* ed. Keneth Kinnamon and Michel Fabre (Jackson: University Press of Mississippi, 1993), 82. Thanks to Sam Perry for directing us to this quotation.

115 Amy Louise Wood, *Lynching and Spectacle: Witnessing Racial Violence in America, 1890–1940* (Chapel Hill: University of North Carolina Press, 2011), 1.

116 Wood, *Lynching and Spectacle,* 2.

117 Wood, *Lynching and Spectacle,* 75.

118 James Allen, ed., *Without Sanctuary: Lynching Photography in America* (Sante Fe, NM: Twin Palms, 2000).

119 Wood, *Lynching and Spectacle,* 186. Wells was an antilynching journalist who was threatened with lynching and forced to flee Memphis after her newspaper office was destroyed by a White mob angry at an antilynching editorial she had penned.

120 Wood, *Lynching and Spectacle,* 186.

121 "Senate Apologizes for Inaction on Lynchings," NBC News, June 13, 2005, http://www.nbcnews.com/id/8206697/ns/us_news-life/t/senate-apologizes-inaction-lynchings/#.W-3onlIkrXQ.

122 151 Cong. Rec. S6364–S6388 (June 13, 2005) (S. Res. 39 Apologizing to Lynching Victims and Their Descendants), https://www.gpo.gov/fdsys/pkg/CREC-2005-06-13/html/CREC-2005-06-13-pt1-PgS6364-3.htm.

123 151 Cong. Rec. S6364–S6388.

124 Thanks to Annie Hill for clarifying this important point and for offering other important insights on this section.

125 Wood, *Lynching and Spectacle,* 4. See also E. Cram, "'Angie Was Our Sister:' Witnessing the Trans-Formation of Disgust in the Citizenry of Photography," *Quarterly Journal of Speech* 98, no. 4 (2012): 411–438.

126 This insight is informed by Ariella Azoulay, *The Civil Contract of Photography,* trans. Rela Mazali and Ruvik Daniell (New York: Zone, 2008).

127 The exact details of the encounter are diverse and have changed over time. See Angela Onwuachi-Willig, "Policing the Boundaries of Whiteness: The Tragedy of Being 'Out of Place' from Emmett Till to Trayvon Martin," *Iowa Law Review* 102, no. 3 (2017): 1113–1185. The woman with whom Till was said to have interacted recanted her testimony. See Wade Goodwyn, "A Brutal Lynching and a Possible Confession, Decades Later," NPR: Weekend Edition Saturday, October 27, 2018, https://www.npr.org/2018/10/27/661048613/a-brutal-lynching-and-a-possible-confession-decades-later.

128 Christine Harold and Kevin M. DeLuca, "Behold the Corpse: Violent Images and the Case of Emmett Till," *Rhetoric and Public Affairs* 8, no. 2 (2005): 265.

129 Harold and DeLuca, "Behold the Corpse."

130 Harold and DeLuca, "Behold the Corpse," 265.

131 Harold and DeLuca, "Behold the Corpse," 278.

132 Harold and DeLuca, "Behold the Corpse," 278.

133 Susan Sontag, *Regarding the Pain of Others* (New York: Picador, 2003), 8.

134 Sontag, *Regarding the Pain,* 80.

135 Brad J. Bushman and Craig A. Anderson, "Comfortably Numb: Desensitizing Effects of Violent Media on Helping Others," *Psychological Science* 20, no. 3 (2009): 273–277, DOI: 10.1111/j.1467-9280.2009.02287.x.

136 See, for example, Bill Chappell, "A Father and Daughter Who Drowned at the Border Put Attention on Immigration," NPR, June 26, 2019, https://www.npr.org/2019/06/26/736177694/a-father-and-daughter-drowned-at-the-border-put-attention-on-immigration.

137 Sarah Sentilles, "When We See Photographs of Some Dead Bodies and Not Others," *New York Times Magazine,* August 14, 2018, https://www.nytimes.com/2018/08/14/magazine/media-bodies-censorship .html?smid=nytcore-ipad-share&smprod=nytcore-ipad.

138 Sentilles, "When We See Photographs."

139 Sentilles, "When We See Photographs."

140 Zach Stafford, "America's New TV Violence: Videos of Black Men Dying on Loop," *Guardian,* May 11, 2015, https://www.theguardian.com/commentisfree/2015/may/11 /when-we-watch-videos-of-black-men-dying-on-loop-it-harms-us.

141 Thanks, again, to Annie Hill for adding specificity and nuance to this argument.

142 Tierney Sneed, "Video Changes Everything in Walter Scott Shooting," *US News and World Report,* April 8, 2015, http://go.galegroup.com.proxy.lib.uni.edu/ps/i .do?&id=GALE|A489528710&v=2.1&u=uni_rodit&it=r&p=STND&sw=w.

143 Alan Blinder, "Michael Slager, Officer in Walter Scott Shooting, Gets 20-Year Sentence," *New York Times,* December 7, 2017, https://www.nytimes.com/2017/12/07/us /michael-slager-sentence-walter-scott.html; Global Plea Agreement, United States of America v. Michael Slager, Criminal No. 2:16-378, http://i2.cdn.turner.com /cnn/2017/images/05/02/slager.global.plea.agreement.pdf.

144 Philip Gourevitch, "Should You Watch the Video?" *New Yorker,* April 8, 2015, https://www.newyorker.com/news/news-desk/should-you-watch-walter-scott-video.

145 Adam Parker, "Walter Scott and the Media," *Post and Courier,* April 11, 2015, https://www.postandcourier.com/archives/walter-scott-and-the-media/article _d3478d0b-0f36-506e-a7fe-98a07a73a5fe.html.

146 Gourevitch, "Should You Watch?"

147 Hope, "Introduction," *Visual Communication,* 17.

Chapter 5
Argument

Four seventh- and eighth-grade students spoke to the Portland Public Schools Board of Education in Oregon[1] for nine minutes on May 26, 2015, testifying about the sexist and racist elements of the school dress code.[2] Jeffrey Roberts testified that the code stereotyped boys as easily distracted and that the prohibition on jerseys and sagging pants targeted specific students based on race. Haley Tjensvold and AnaLuiza Cruz testified about the double standard, which resulted in 100 percent of the students sent home being girls. Sophia Carlson declared it unacceptable that the dress code and its implementation sent the message to any girl that "hiding her body is more important than her education . . . [and that] boys are more entitled to their education than she is."[3] The students called for the formation of a committee of students, parents, teachers and administrators to create a code "fair and nondiscriminatory to all students."[4] Their arguments persuaded the school board to form a committee.[5]

Lisa Frack, president of Oregon NOW (National Organization for Women), was in the audience when the students testified. In February 2016, Oregon NOW released a model dress code that declared: "Student dress codes and administrative enforcement should not reinforce or increase marginalization or oppression of any group based on race, gender, ethnicity, religion, sexual orientation, household income, gender identity or cultural observance."[6] Carlson, Frack, and Oregon NOW vice-president Elleanor Chin were three of the members of the Board of Education committee, which met for two hours every month for a year. Responding to community input, the committee updated the dress code on the basis of the Oregon NOW Model. The Portland Board of Education adopted the new code in June 2016.

The policy changes instigated by the four students did not stop in Oregon. In August 2017, Evanston Township High School in Illinois updated its dress code to reflect the Oregon NOW model after a student advisor to the school board found it online. District superintendent Eric Witherspoon had "heard from our students that their ability to be inspired to learn was directly impacted by their daily experiences with dress code enforcement because of their gender identity or expression, racial identity, cultural or religious identity, body size, or body maturity."[7] Like the Portland school board, Evanston Township High School sought input from students. As administrators reviewed the data about who was disciplined, they found it "supported the students' claims of being disciplined disproportionately across racial and gender lines."[8]

This example illustrates a few things about argument.

First, argument matters. The students' arguments persuaded a group that had the power to change policy. As Oregon NOW president Frack recounts, the call for change "came from these kids . . . . They were seeking a solution and we just coalesced and piled on, but they really get the credit."[9]

Second, an argument requires reasons and evidence: it is not just an assertion of opinion. After Evanston students stated that the dress code was inequitably enforced against girls and racial minorities, administrators found that the evidence regarding disciplinary actions supported their statement.

Third, anyone anywhere can argue. Argument is not found solely in the halls of Congress or in front of the Supreme Court. Entities that have policy-making power exist at the local level—in school boards, city councils, county boards, and funding agencies. And it is not just members of the school board or adults who can argue. Four seventh- and eighth-graders' arguments were enough to convince the school board to begin the process of policy change.

Fourth, an argument about policy change is not resolved after a single exchange. Changing the dress code took hundreds of hours of work over months of meetings. Change is not impossible, but it usually requires deliberation, debate, input from affected parties, and careful balancing of costs and benefits.

Fifth, when engaging in argument about how to fix a problem, you do not need to attempt to solve all problems at the same time. Changing the dress code for one school or one school district will not erase all racism and sexism. As Frack said, "This isn't going to solve the world for women and girls by fixing the dress code. But it's not small. It's one answer to some giant problems. And sometimes that's how you have to solve them—chipping away at one thing at a time."[10] In this case, fixing one problem created a sense of efficacy that encouraged students to use the tools of argument to fix other problems. Seventh grader Carlson reported a sense of empowerment that resulted from replacing a sexist policy and that led to advocacy for other changes.[11]

Sixth, public policy (such as the dress code for a school district) has personal impacts. Personal experiences with policies can provide data to support changes to those policies. It is important, however, to recognize that the individual students did not simply resort to a personal solution (such as changing their clothing or having their parents talk to the principal). They identified a systemic problem and then collectively worked for institutional change.

Although it sometimes seems as though the current political climate makes reasonable argument matter less and political affiliation matter more, this example ought to give hope. It is possible for regular people to convince policy makers to change their policies.

In this chapter, we make a case for the power of argument. We want to convince you to be willing to engage in argument and put yourself at risk[12]—the risk that opening your mind to others' perspectives, information, and ideas might induce you to alter your own position. Taking this risk is necessary if democracy is to function.

Public participation in decision making distinguishes a democracy from all other forms of government. If democracy is to remain vibrant, people must be trained in the skills that enable reasoned and reasonable decision making. Harvard political scientist Danielle Allen explains that democratic skills are habits that can be taught and learned, but that must also be practiced, because these "habits of interaction give form to public space and so to our political life. . . . Ordinary habits *are* the stuff of citizenship."[13] The way people talk to and argue with others—their rhetorical practices—creates space in civic life where people can resolve disagreements, make decisions, and create identity. Some habits are more productive. Others might be destructive (for example, seeing people with whom you disagree as enemies might lead you to try to destroy them rather than work with them). Attention to the habits of interaction is important if people are to have a vibrant civic life.

Which habits are productive? Allen argues that people need to practice the habits of citizenship, of talking and listening to strangers, of interacting with others who live in their communities, in order to develop political friendship, which we discussed in chapter 1.[14] Central to these habits of citizenship is argument. In particular, speakers should give audiences opportunities to judge their arguments. They should invite others to answer and respond to their arguments.[15] They should be open to criticism and not react defensively. Listeners should seek out, and demand the chance to judge, public arguments.[16] Audience members should seek out opportunities in which they can participate in deliberation and are not merely treated as spectators. Democratic decision making and political friendship, whether at the national level or in daily interactions, require practice in order to become a habit. The habits of argument, in particular, need practice.

This chapter illustrates the necessity of public argument for civic engagement and democratic decision making. First, we define argument and discuss its role in civic life. Then, we explore Aristotle's and Toulmin's theories about how arguments persuade people. We follow by identifying three spheres of argument—personal, technical, and public—and their relationships to civic life. Next, we talk about stock issues, the themes that recur in and are necessary to making decisions about issues of common concern. For public argument to work, you must be willing to change your mind and be able to assess evidence. Thus, we end with a discussion of habits that enable you to do these things.

DEFINING ARGUMENT

The word "argument" often carries negative connotations associated with verbal altercations and interpersonal strife. That is not the type of argument we mean. We use the term **argument** to refer to *a rhetorical form that provides data for a claim.* This rhetorical form is sometimes referred to as argument$_1$. **Argumentation,** *the process of exchanging arguments,* is sometimes referred to as argument$_2$.[17]

Rhetoric scholar David Zarefsky defines argumentation as "the practice of justifying decisions under conditions of uncertainty."[18] Justifying is not providing certain or absolute proof, but rather is a process of reason-giving. Human beings must often make decisions with incomplete information and before they are certain, but argumentation allows them to make better decisions, more justified decisions, instead of acting randomly.

Argumentation is interactive, cooperative, and contingent.

The term "interactive" emphasizes that argument is as much a process as product. Although a single statement may advance a particular argument (argument$_1$), the give and take of arguments among people is also argument (the process of argument$_2$). You need a partner to engage in argumentation.

"Cooperative" emphasizes that people engaged in argumentation do not need to be unpleasant, quarrelsome, or verbally aggressive.[19] People who engage in argumentation are often trying to come to agreement about what to do. You argue *with* other people, not *against* them.

"Contingent" emphasizes that argument occurs "under conditions of uncertainty."[20] Argument does not occur when everyone is certain about what an event means, who a people are, or what should be done. Instead, it occurs when people are not certain. It provides a means to make decisions even in the face of that uncertainty.

The COVID-19 pandemic vividly illustrates the need for skills that enable people to make decisions in conditions of uncertainty, to argue under contingent conditions. Because COVID-19 was a *novel* coronavirus, not much was known during the early weeks of the pandemic about how to prevent its transmission or treat people who had been infected. Public health experts, health care providers, policy makers, and ordinary citizens had to make decisions about what to do in conditions rife with uncertainty.

Initially, emphasis was placed on preventing transmission via surfaces (rather than airborne transmission). Government officials and individual people directed their resources toward cleaning surfaces and even disinfecting food products. Masks were not encouraged (partly to make sure sufficient supplies were available to frontline medical personnel).[21] As early studies were reviewed and new data emerged, guidelines shifted. The initial data pointing to surface transmission were from studies that did not use likely real-life scenarios. For example, some studies used an extraordinary amount of virus on a surface—the amount that would be created by a hundred infected people collectively coughing on a tiny spot.[22]

Later scientific research proved that although transmission via surfaces is possible, COVID-19 spreads primarily via airborne aerosols (from breathing, speaking, and singing) and droplets (from coughs and sneezes);[23] asymptomatic people can transmit the virus; and masks can prevent transmission, both by stopping droplets and aerosols from an infected person from entering the air and by protecting uninfected people from airborne aerosols and droplets.[24] Masks do not stop 100 percent of aerosols, but they do reduce disease transmission.[25]

Thus, the emphasis shifted from surfaces (although keeping surfaces clean and hands washed is still important) and toward mask wearing and social distancing as public health measures. Scientists and policy makers debated about what to do, given the information they had. Their goal was not to wait until a perfect solution could be found, but rather to find solutions that made things better. They changed their conclusions and recommendations as new information emerged.

The changing advice about masks does not mean the scientists and public health experts were idiots or liars. Instead, it illustrates that decisions must be made, sometimes even when evidence is incomplete. When new evidence arises, decisions should change in response. Thus, the advice to wash your hands, physically distance, and wear a mask, both to protect yourself and to protect others.

ARISTOTLE'S ENTHYMEME

The ancient Greek philosopher Aristotle's approach to logic has long influenced argument studies, particularly the concept of the **syllogism,** *a statement in which a conclusion is inferred from the truth of two premises.* You may have heard of this process as deductive reasoning, which is composed of a major premise, a minor premise, and a conclusion. In a perfect syllogism, the major premise speaks to a universal truth. The minor premise speaks to a specific example of the universal. The conclusion is the result of combining the two premises.

Major premise: All human beings are mortal.

Minor premise: Ryan is a human being.

Conclusion: Ryan is mortal.

The conclusion of a formal syllogism is certain only if the premises are certain. Of course, because humans are fallible and information is often incomplete, virtually no premise can be absolutely certain.

Aristotle recognized that people typically do not speak in formal syllogisms, but rather in what he called "rhetorical syllogisms, or enthymemes."[26] Although much scholarly debate exists over exactly what Aristotle meant by the term, the definition we find most helpful is offered by communication scholar Lloyd Bitzer, who says an **enthymeme** is *"a syllogism based on probabilities, signs, and examples, whose function is rhetorical persuasion. Its successful construction is accomplished through the joint efforts of the speaker and audience, and this is its essential character."*[27] What most distinguishes the enthymeme is not its form or content, but the process through which it is constructed—jointly by the speaker and the audience. Often the speaker will leave some premises unspoken so that the audience fills them in. Bitzer argues that the process of co-construction makes the enthymeme extremely persuasive because *"the audience itself helps construct the proofs by which it is persuaded."*[28]

Enthymemes are widely used. Advertising slogans, political campaigns, and conversations with friends often rely on enthymemes. People do not systematically lay out all their premises but rely on shared beliefs and values to fill them in. For example, in 1991, Gatorade developed a marketing campaign featuring Michael Jordan, arguably the greatest basketball player of all time, with the slogan "Be Like Mike." The commercials featured highlights of Jordan playing basketball and drinking Gatorade, interspersed with images of regular people playing basketball, while the "Be Like Mike" jingle played in the background. The commercials ended with the slogan "Be Like Mike. Drink Gatorade."[29] The campaign was so successful that many people recognize the jingle more than twenty-five years later.

Because the Gatorade marketing campaign was one of the most successful in history, it is reasonable to conclude that many members of the audience completed the reasoning by filling in the premise that, if you mimic the behavior of another person, you become more like that person.[30] The power of the campaign arose largely because the reasoning was left for the audience to provide. If members of the audience had been told that by drinking Gatorade, they would become better basketball players, they would have been skeptical. When they were allowed to fill in the reasoning on their own, however, they were more likely to accept it.

TOULMIN'S MODEL

Philosopher Stephen Toulmin was troubled by the inadequacy of the syllogism as a model for actual argument in which premises are never certain.[31] For example, we do not know for certain that health care is a human right or that individuals have a responsibility to others. Argument is about the contingent and the probable, not the certain. Additionally, he realized that a person may understand the data offered and the conclusion advocated, but not why that particular data supports the conclusion. If you do not understand the science behind ice core measurements of CO_2, for example, you may not understand why it can prove global warming is happening.

Toulmin believed an explanation of the relationship between the evidence and the conclusion was needed, so he developed a description of argument patterns that are composed of the following parts: claim, data, warrant, qualifications, backing, and conditions for rebuttal. On the basis of Toulmin's work, argument scholars Wayne Brockriede and Douglas Ehninger developed a model that we adapt here:[32]

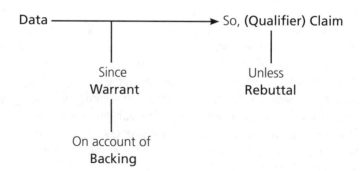

Claim

Toulmin defines the **claim** as "*the conclusion whose merits we are seeking to establish,*"[33] or what the rhetor is trying to persuade the audience to believe. Argumentation scholars distinguish between four types of claim: fact, definition, value, and policy.

A **claim of fact** is *a claim that advances an empirically verifiable statement.* Estimates of death tolls from natural disasters or pandemics are claims of fact. For example, the CDC COVID Data Tracker offers this claim of fact: In the United States, as of March 5, 2021, COVID-19 had infected 28,771,749 people and killed 522,973.[34]

A **claim of definition** is *a claim that identifies how a concept or term should be defined.* Often, when people think of a definition of a word or term, they think of its dictionary definition. Scholars of rhetoric, however, are interested in how words and terms attain these meanings (instead of others) and how they are used in argumentation. Communication scholar Edward Schiappa notes, "Definitions can be understood more productively as involving claims of 'ought' rather than 'is.'"[35] For example, he notes that different official definitions of "death" affect the possibility of organ donation. If "death" means "the cessation of cardiorespiratory functions," fewer organs are available for transplant because most people can be kept alive indefinitely with breathing support, because many organs lose viability the longer a person is on a respirator. If "death" means "the irreversible cessation of brain functions,"[36] then more viable organs can be available for transplant. The question is not what death is, but how "death" ought to be defined.

A **claim of value** is *a claim that advances a statement about what is worthy.* A claim of value may be based on arguments about what is good or bad, just or unjust, right or wrong, or beautiful or ugly. Such claims are not empirically verifiable; they are based on the audience's judgments. "During a pandemic, minor infringements on individual liberty caused by face mask mandates are outweighed by the common good that such a mandate achieves" is an example of a claim of value.

Finally, a **claim of policy** is *a claim that addresses what should be done.* A claim of policy usually contains the words "should" or "ought to," and identifies an agent and an action to be taken. "The federal government should legalize personal marijuana possession and use" is an example of a policy claim.

Making a claim might be the simplest part of making an argument, but the concept of claim, itself, is complex. Different types of claims exist, and each one requires particular forms of data to provide justification.

Data

Toulmin describes **data** as the "*information on which the claim is based.*"[37] Data are sometimes referred to as evidence or supporting materials. Forms of data include scientific research, statistics, quotations from experts, empirical examples, and personal testimony.

The need to guard against accepting a claim supported by insufficient or bad data is demonstrated by social satirist Stephen Colbert's concept of *truthiness.*

Selected by *Merriam-Webster's Dictionary* as the 2006 Word of the Year, *truthiness* is defined as:

> 1: 'truth that comes from the gut, not books' (Stephen Colbert, Comedy Central's *The Colbert Report,* October 2005) 2: 'the quality of preferring concepts or facts one wishes to be true, rather than concepts or facts known to be true' (American Dialect Society, January 2006).[38]

Colbert explains further: "It used to be, everyone was entitled to their own opinion, but not their own facts. But that's not the case anymore. Facts matter not at all. Perception is everything. It's certainty."[39] Colbert is being humorous but also is making a serious point. Too frequently, people jump to conclusions based on an impulsive reaction, without data, and sometimes even despite data to the contrary.

Warrant

Toulmin describes **warrants** as *bridges, or the generalizable "rules" and "principles" that link data to claims.*[40] A warrant shows that a jump from data to a conclusion is reasonable, that the conclusion is warranted. The warrant provides the reason that the data would lead a person to believe the claim is correct.

One difficulty in identifying warrants is that rhetors often leave them unstated. People argue enthymematically when they omit one part of an argument and leave it to the audience to fill in. For example, John once told his spouse, "I need new golf clubs (claim). The grooves on my irons are smooth (data)." To him, that was sufficient. However, his spouse did not understand the connection and asked, "What does that mean?" John then explained the warrant: grooves are what put spin on the golf ball, and the spin is what makes the ball stop on the green. Thus, when the grooves are smooth, it is time to get new clubs. (Happily, John got his new golf clubs.) Toulmin explains warrants are needed because a listener may not understand why the data provide proof of a claim.

Rebuttal

For Toulmin, **conditions of rebuttal** are *"circumstances in which the general authority of the warrant" should be set aside.*[41] Conditions of rebuttal provide reasons why the warrant may not be correct. If you have ever read a scholarly essay using scientific or social scientific methods, it probably included a section concerning the limitations of the study. This section is an example of noting conditions for rebuttal. Another example is when someone says, "I think we should go to this movie because the college paper gave it a good review, unless you think the movie critic's tastes are different from yours." The warrant is that the movie reviewer for the college paper is a good arbiter of what is a good movie; the condition of rebuttal is the "unless" statement. If you think the reviewer has odd taste, then it does not make sense to follow their advice.

Qualifier

Toulmin defines a **qualifier** as *a statement indicating the "strength conferred by the warrant."*[42] Not all claims have the same level of certainty. The level is often determined by the strength of the conditions of rebuttal. Claims can be qualified with terms such as "usually," "possibly," "likely," "in all probability," and "presumably." Notice that each qualifier represents different levels of certainty.

An example of qualifiers is contained in hurricane predictions. Meteorologists claim the hurricane will be of a particular category, follow a particular path, and make landfall at a particular time and location, on the basis of the data from weather stations, models, and radar. The warrant is that data from weather stations, models, and radar provide reliable predictions. However, the predictions are qualified because such predictions are never perfect. One media report, titled "This is Hurricane Maria's Predicted Path (So Far)," provides ample examples of qualifiers, including the "so far" and "predicted" in the title, implying that things can change and that it "*could be* a category 4 storm."[43] Because predictions are made days before a hurricane might make landfall, the National Weather Service makes clear its claims are contingent by noting: "Preliminary Data: Please, be advised that this report may be revised as additional data is received."[44]

Backing

Toulmin describes **backing** as *an assurance that the warrant is authoritative and/or current.* The backing says the warrant is supported. Usually, backing will provide an answer to the conditions of rebuttal.

Using Toulmin to Analyze Arguments

What would an argument containing the elements of the Toulmin model look like in prose form? Following is an argument that Elizabeth Cady Stanton advanced in 1892, in a speech to the Committee of the Judiciary of the United States Congress. The "Solitude of Self" speech provides a philosophical foundation for granting women the right to vote.[45] As you read the following passage, which advances a policy claim, notice how it fulfills each part of argument Toulmin identifies.

> The strongest reason for giving woman all the opportunities for higher education, for the full development of her faculties, forces of mind and body; for giving her the most enlarged freedom of thought and action; a complete emancipation from all forms of bondage, of custom, dependence, superstition; from all the crippling influences of fear, is the solitude and personal responsibility of her own individual life. The strongest reason why we ask for woman a voice in the government under which she lives; in the religion she is asked to believe; equality in social life, where she is the chief factor; a place in the trades and professions, where she may earn her bread, is because of her birthright to self-sovereignty; because, as an individual, she must rely on herself. No matter how much women prefer to lean, to be

protected and supported, nor how much men desire to have them do so, they must make the voyage of life alone, and for safety in an emergency they must know something of the laws of navigation. To guide our own craft, we must be captain, pilot, engineer; with chart and compass to stand at the wheel; to match the wind and waves and know when to take in the sail, and to read the signs in the firmament over all. It matters not whether the solitary voyager is man or woman.[46]

Stanton's argument could be broken down as follows:

> *Qualifier, Claim:* "woman [should be given] all the opportunities for higher education . . . a complete emancipation from . . . the most enlarged freedom . . . all the crippling influences of fear." In this passage, "all . . . most enlarged . . . complete" make clear the claim is unqualified; Stanton does not recognize a less than exhaustive application.
>
> *Data:* "the solitude and personal responsibility of her own individual life"
>
> *Warrant:* each person has a "birthright to self-sovereignty"
>
> *Backing:* "as an individual, she must rely on herself"
>
> *Rebuttal:* Stanton anticipates that someone might argue "women prefer to lean" on men, so she says "No matter how much women prefer to lean" they ought to experience full freedom.

Because Stanton delivered this speech after forty-five years of suffrage advocacy, she delivered the argument$_1$ in its most complete form, stating all the parts explicitly. As people engage in argument$_2$ and are challenged to explain themselves, the various parts of an argument$_1$ are filled in. In other words, argument$_2$ usually calls forth a complete argument$_1$.

A second example illustrates how the Toulmin model can help you understand an extended argument$_2$. When people argue, identifying the parts of argument can help pinpoint the exact location of disagreement.

Immediately after Category 5 Hurricane María struck Puerto Rico in September 2017, estimates indicated María caused 6 to 18 deaths. A few weeks later, the estimate rose to 34. In November, a CNN survey of funeral homes led to the estimate that María had caused 499 deaths. In December, Puerto Rican authorities declared that the official death toll was 64, while the *New York Times* said 1,052 excess deaths had been attributed to María. In May 2018, Harvard researchers published a study that estimated María caused 793 to 8,498 deaths. In August 2018, the Puerto Rican government raised the official death toll to 2,975.[47] All these estimates are claims of fact; death is empirically verifiable. What distinguishes them is how and when the data was gathered to support the claim. By assessing the data, you can determine which claim of fact is most accurate.

Hurricane María death estimates also involve a claim of definition: how should hurricane-related deaths be defined? The discrepancy in estimates arose because of different definitions of what counts as a "disaster-related death." In explaining the substantial difference between 64 and 2,975, the Milken

Institute School of Public Health (the group commissioned by the Puerto Rican government to provide an independent assessment of mortality from the storm), clarified:

> The official government estimate of 64 deaths from the hurricane is low primarily because the conventions used for causal attribution only allowed for classification of deaths attributable directly to the storm, e.g., those caused by structural collapse, flying debris, floods and drownings . . . . During our broader study, we found that many physicians were not oriented in the appropriate certification protocol. This translated into an inadequate indicator for monitoring mortality in the hurricane's aftermath.[48]

For mortality estimates to be accurate (and comparable to other storm estimates that used appropriate protocol), estimators needed to follow the Centers for Disease Control and Prevention (CDC) definition. When counting storm-related mortality, public health protocol not only counts those killed by flying debris, but also those who died as an indirect result of power failures, collapse of medical infrastructure, inability of emergency services to respond, contaminated water, disease related to hurricane conditions, and so on. When comparing death tolls of Hurricanes María, Irma, and Harvey, the same definition of hurricane-related deaths must be used or the estimates of María will be inaccurate.

Ongoing controversy over the death toll is partly a result of different definitions of "hurricane-related death." When Puerto Rican authorities claimed a death toll of 64, the only data they used were physicians' reports of cause of death in the immediate aftermath of the storm. As the Milken Institute report noted, however, physicians were not following standard protocol in determining hurricane-related causes of death. In contrast, the Milken Institute used a more systematic form of data collection. It "analyzed past mortality patterns (mortality registration and population census data from 2010 to 2017) in order to predict the expected mortality if Hurricane María had not occurred (predicted mortality) and compare this figure to the actual deaths that occurred (observed mortality)."[49] The more complete and systematically collected data supports the claim that the death toll from Hurricane María is 2,975.

When the Puerto Rican government announced its higher official estimate, on the basis of the 2018 Milken Institute report, then–President Trump responded by tweeting:

> 3000 people did not die in the two hurricanes that hit Puerto Rico. When I left the Island, AFTER the storm had hit, they had anywhere from 6 to 18 deaths. As time went by it did not go up by much. Then, a long time later, they started to report really large numbers, like 3000. . . . This was done by the Democrats in order to make me look as bad as possible when I was successfully raising Billions of Dollars to help rebuild Puerto Rico. If a person died for any reason, like old age, just add them onto the list. Bad politics. I love Puerto Rico![50]

Trump claimed "3000 people did not die" and that that the death toll was between 6 and 18, relying on the estimates from Puerto Rican authorities immediately after the storm. However, this claim disregards the fact that Puerto Rican authorities raised the toll to 2,975. Trump claimed the death toll rose "a long time later," which is not accurate; higher estimates began appearing within three months of the storm. He falsely claimed that Democrats raised the estimates, when the estimates actually came from independent researchers (such as those at Harvard and the Milken Institute). The claim that "3000 people did not die" has no data to support it and overwhelming data to the contrary to refute it.

Trump's tweet about Puerto Rican death tolls is an example of truthiness. He wished the claim that only 6 to 18 people died to be true, and so ignored the compelling data that proved 2,975 people died as a result of the hurricane. When presented with a claim, you need to ask: What data support this claim? Simply saying that you "feel" something is true is not sufficient.

Supplying incorrect or insufficient data to support a claim is bad argument. Improperly collected statistics, poorly chosen examples, or quotations that are taken out of context are some of the ways in which evidence can be incorrect. Trump's claim is based on bad data from the chaotic days following the disaster, data that was gathered using incorrect protocol.

The dispute over Hurricane María death tolls illustrates the importance of warrants. When Trump claimed "3000 people did not die," the data he cited were initial estimates. The warrants, though unstated, were that initial estimates are the most accurate and that any high estimates must be politically motivated. In contrast, when the Puerto Rican authorities adjusted their estimate up to 2,975 on the basis of the Milken Institute study, they used the warrant that data systematically collected by an independent researcher, using classifications similar to those used when making other storm estimates, result in more accurate estimates of hurricane-related deaths. Sometimes, the rhetor provides the warrant to assist the audience in understanding the argument, as the Milken Institute did.

An example of an argument (a claim of fact) relating to Hurricane María that contains all parts of the Toulmin model is:

> Results [data] from the preferred statistical model . . . estimate that excess
> mortality [warrant] due to Hurricane María using the displacement
> scenario [backing, because estimates of excess mortality that account for
> the fact populations are displaced during hurricanes are the best estimates]
> is estimated [qualifier, this is not an exact measurement] at . . . 2,975
> (95% CI: 2,658–3,290) excess deaths [claim] for the total study period of
> September 2017 through February 2018.[51]

Most researchers tend to make their warrants explicit because they are trying to present a complete argument.

Knowing the parts of an argument will help you understand what a person is arguing, become better at constructing an argument, identify where you disagree with another person, and determine whether you disagree about the data and/or about the warrants. In the Hurricane María example, people came to different conclusions about the death toll because some used data while others did not, and because some believed scientific methods of estimating total deaths were superior to haphazard reporting of deaths during the immediate aftermath of the storm. Knowing the parts of an argument also helps you analyze argument. You can understand whether someone is making a warranted argument, whether a rhetor's claim is supported by data, or whether parts of the argument are missing.

This knowledge also will help you understand when people introduce an argument that is irrelevant—that does not speak to the claim, data, or warrant, but introduces an irrelevant issue. For example, **ad hominem attacks** are *arguments against the person making the claim that are irrelevant to the claim.* During his campaign and presidency, Trump called critics names such as "crazy" Jim Acosta, "crooked" Hillary Clinton, "slippery" James Comey, and "highly overrated" Megan Kelly, suggesting that people should simply disregard anything these people had to say about him, his actions and policies, or anything else.

A statement that sounds as if it has all of the parts of a complete argument does not necessarily justify assent. It may provide bad data. A warrant may be nonsensical. A qualification may not be strong enough. The connections between the data and claim may be weak. Not only must you be able to identify the parts of an argument, you also need to be able to assess the strength of those parts.

SPHERES OF ARGUMENT

Argumentation occurs in a variety of contexts and among a range of people. The focus of this chapter is on public argument, but understanding argument about public issues such as global warming, immigration, economic policy, abortion, marijuana regulation, or police practice requires understanding the distinctions among the processes of public, personal, and technical argument. Argumentation as a process is not universal. Practices and procedures have evolved over time and become habits within particular spheres.

Defining the Spheres of Argument

Communication scholar G. Thomas Goodnight recognizes that the persuasiveness of an argument and the form it takes depend on the sphere of argument in which the argument occurs.[52] Spheres of argument are not physical places, but patterns, practices, and habits of argument. According to Goodnight, **spheres of argument** are *"branches of activity—the grounds upon which arguments are built and the authorities to which arguers appeal."*[53] Spheres are not places, but patterns, practices, and habits of argument. He defines **grounds** as *the core assumptions about how the world is organized and the basic premises on which arguments are built.* **Authorities** are *the sources of evidence that are accepted or the people who are allowed to speak as experts in that sphere.* To explain how different grounds for argument emerge, Goodnight identifies three spheres of argument: personal, technical, and public. Particular warrants and data count differently depending on the sphere in which they are used.

Think about the last time you and friends were talking. What did you talk about? Your favorite show to binge watch? Where to eat? What a friend should do about a family conflict? You may have covered a range of topics, from art to interpersonal relations. It is unlikely that any of you declared other friends incapable of speaking about a topic because they were unqualified. The next day, probably no one in your group remembered the specific arguments.

Your experience in this instance is an example of **personal sphere argument,** *informal argument among a small number of people, involving limited demands for proof, and often about topics that matter only to those involved in the conversation.* Personal sphere arguments tend to be ephemeral, meaning they are not preserved. No preparation is required. Many things count as evidence, and are pulled from memory. All topics are open to discussion even if the participants have no special knowledge about them. Expertise is not necessary; anyone can talk on any subject. The test of what constitutes a valid argument in the personal sphere is truthfulness: are the people with whom you disagree honestly representing their beliefs? The time limits imposed probably have nothing to do with the nature of the disagreement and more to do with when people need to leave.

Contrast this to **technical sphere argument,** *argument that has explicit rules and is judged by those with specific expertise in the subject.* An example of technical sphere argument is published scholarship in a specialized journal, such as the *Journal of the American Medical Association* or the *Quarterly Journal of Speech.* Technical arguments are judged by referees or peer reviewers who have special expertise in the area being discussed. When the arguments are deemed valuable, they are preserved and published. Other members of the specialized community may then join the discussion.

The function of technical sphere argument, Goodnight states, is to "advance a special kind of knowledge."[54] It takes special expertise to contribute to a technical argument. It also takes special expertise to understand it. Terms, phrasings, and the complexity of the argument make it relatively inaccessible to anyone not trained in the specialty (which explains why you might have struggled reading journal articles for classes before you were trained in the vocabulary, theories, and methods of the discipline). The argument in an essay in a technical journal may be difficult for you to follow because the data being used is unknown to you, or because the warrants were left unstated and you did not know how to provide them. Many times, the test of argument in the technical sphere is truth, either in terms of objective facts or in terms of which claim best approximates experts' understanding of the world.

In many ways, the technical and personal spheres of argument represent two extremes. **Public sphere argument** is *argument that exists "to handle disagreements transcending personal and technical disputes."*[55] Public issues are broader than the needs of a group of friends or a specialized technical community. For example, arguments about zoning, public infrastructure, or school dress codes are public sphere arguments. Generally, the issues affect a broad range of people; hence, a broad range of people may speak to the issues. The demands of proof are not as rigid as in technical argument or as fluid as in personal argument. The test of validity for a public sphere argument tends to be whether it is right, as in "just" (not as in "correct"). People, as members of a community, try to serve the interests of the community with public argument and, thus, need to assess whether they can come to agreement about what is the right thing to do.

Using Spheres to Analyze Argument

The argument about whether Pluto is a planet offers an example of the distinctions among public, personal, and technical sphere arguments, as well as of the idea of argument as contingent. When Pluto was first discovered in 1930, scientists declared the mass of rock and ice to be a planet. It was located where the scientists thought a planet should be, given the orbital path of other planets. However, Pluto is idiosyncratic: it is very small compared to the other planets; its orbit is eccentric (it crosses the orbit of Neptune) and tips more than seventeen degrees from the plane of orbit of other planets in the solar system; and other icy objects share its orbital space.[56] Pluto was demoted from planet status in 2006 when the General Assembly of the International Astronomical Union voted to accept a definition of "planet" that would exclude Pluto. Thus, the claim "Pluto is a planet" was contingent and open to revision as more information became available. But on what grounds, and on the basis of which authorities, should Pluto's planetary status rest?

In the February 1999 issue of *Natural History*, Neil deGrasse Tyson, an astrophysicist at the American Museum of Natural History and the director of the Hayden Planetarium, wrote an essay titled "Pluto's Honor" that argued:

> As Citizen Tyson, I feel compelled to defend Pluto's honor. It lives deeply in our twentieth-century culture and consciousness and somehow rounds out the diversity of our family of planets, like the troubled sibling of a large family. Nearly every schoolchild thinks of Pluto as an old friend. And there was always something poetic about being number nine. As Professor Tyson, however, I must vote—with a heavy heart—for demotion. Pluto was always an enigma to teach.[57]

Tyson recognizes that arguments that matter in the personal or public spheres (such as cultural consciousness, schoolchildren's beliefs, and the poetry of nine) are not relevant in the technical realm, where technical questions of how planets are classified are the only criteria. Children's sadness at not finding Pluto along with the terrestrial and gas giant planets in the Scales of the Universe exhibit (which portrays the relative size of things in the solar system) simply is not relevant data in a technical debate.

Other scientists also recognized the distinction among argument spheres. In a debate at the American Museum of Natural History, astronomer Jane Luu argued that Pluto was not a planet and that continuing to refer to it as a planet "would only be due to tradition and sentimental reasons. . . . So, in the end, the question goes back to this: Should science be a democratic process, or should logic have something to do with it?"[58] Luu was basically asking: Is this a technical argument or a public sphere argument? Substantial public outcry arose over the International Astronomical Union's vote to demote Pluto from planet status, but the data used by the scientific community was what mattered to the technical decision. As Tyson explains, "Science is not a democracy. As is often cited (and attributed to Galileo), the stated authority of a thousand is not worth the humble reasoning of a single individual."[59]

Scientists continue to argue, and the argument is ultimately definitional: What properties best define a planet? In March 2017, six scientists argued that the "intrinsic qualities of the body itself," such as shape and surface, rather than external factors such as orbit, should define the status of a planet, thus making Pluto one of nine (not just eight) other planets in the solar system.[60]

Interaction among Spheres

Technical and public sphere argument are related. In debates over what individuals and governments should do to combat global warming, public policy debates about the effectiveness of solutions play an important role. However, public debates over the technical claim that climate change is happening and is caused by human activity are a distraction because broad scientific consensus exists, and ample data prove, that global warming is happening and that humans are a primary cause. The 2014 report of the Intergovernmental Panel on Climate Change (IPCC) provided a summary of the scientific conclusions: "Human influence on the climate system is clear, and recent anthropogenic emissions of greenhouse gases are the highest in history. Recent climate changes have had widespread impacts on human and natural systems."[61] The IPCC relied on technical evidence, grounded its arguments in scientific method, and relied on authorities with credentials relevant to the claims of fact that had been advanced.

The strength of this technical evidence has been unjustifiably challenged in public argument. Communication scholar Leah Ceccarelli identifies "global warming skepticism" as an example of a "manufactured controversy," controversy created for public consumption that exploits "political interests . . . to achieve a particular policy objective."[62] Ceccarelli's point is that arguers manufacture some scientific disputes solely for political ends rather than because an actual technical disagreement exists. On technical issues, the norms of technical argument matter and should not be diluted with the practices of public argument.

Manufactured controversies are distinct from arguments that start in the technical sphere but that become public sphere arguments. Communication scholars Valeria Fabj and Matthew J. Sobnosky explore how HIV/AIDS activists challenged the medical establishment's drug-testing protocol (a technical issue) because it failed to serve public interests. The traditional requirements of double-blind studies to administer placebos to terminal patients magnified, rather than lessened, the public health crisis of HIV/AIDS.[63] Fabj and Sobnosky argue that public sphere deliberation was enhanced by activists' introduction of a personal and technical issue (individuals get diseases that doctors treat) into the public sphere of deliberation. Activists trained themselves in the technical language of medicine so they could persuasively argue that public concerns, and not just technical concerns, should govern drug-testing protocol.

Spheres of argument do not denote physical locations. The most technical of arguments might occur in the most private of locations: imagine two doctors debating the best treatment for a patient while in the restroom. Similarly, the most personal of arguments might occur in the most public of locations: imagine two senators having a heated personal discussion while waiting for a hearing to be called into session.

The person, topic, or location also do not determine the sphere; rather, the sphere influences who may speak on what topic and in what location. Spheres of argument do influence argumentative practices: the norms and rules that govern how the argument ought to proceed and that influence who is allowed to speak, from what location, and on what topics.

The Necessity of Argument in the Public Sphere

Although a range of forms can be used to work through public concerns, including conversation, dialogue, and discussion, public sphere argument is necessary to civic life.[64] When people discuss controversial or complicated topics, their discussions often seem to be framed not as arguments or debates, but as conversations or dialogues. Such frames may not be productive. Rhetoric scholar Mari Boor Tonn analyzes the way in which conversation and dialogue—forms appropriate to the personal sphere and typically used in therapy—can distort public sphere argument.[65]

Argument and conversation differ in two important ways. First, conversation does not require that people make a decision, whereas argument calls for reaching a conclusion. For example, you can have a conversation about what types of movies you like and your friends can all voice their personal preferences, but if you have to make a decision about what movie to watch, a decision has to be made. Because conversation does not call for a decision to be made, it can "engender inertia as participants become mired in repeated airings of personal experiences."[66] Consequently, a conversation about movies may go on for so long that you miss the start time for the movie. In contrast, argument requires that people find a way to move toward a decision: in this case, to decide which movie to watch.

Second, conversation often focuses on personal solutions ("*I* like this") whereas argument induces people to think about collective action ("*we* should do this"). Especially when people are communicating about policy, a conversational approach can divert attention from the "policy formation necessary to correct structural dimensions of social problems."[67] In conversation, people focus more on what they can do as individuals, and less on structural and institutional changes. In many ways, conversation participates in the downsizing of democracy we described in the first chapter of this book. Instead of focusing on collective decision making and civic action, conversation reduces problems to personal experiences and personal solutions.

Tonn uses the example of President William J. Clinton's 1997 Race Initiative to illustrate the differences between conversation and argument. During a commencement speech delivered at the University of California San Diego, Clinton launched "One America for the 21st Century: The President's Initiative on Race" and called for "a great and unprecedented conversation about race."[68] He said that "We must build one American community based on respect for one another and our shared values." In order to do that, he said, "We must begin with a candid conversation on the state of race relations."[69] In describing the conversation he proposed, Clinton repeatedly used terms and phrases such as "self-esteem," "honest dialogue," "emotions may be rubbed raw," and solutions coming from "the human spirit."[70] Our point here is not that conversations about race are bad, but rather that in announcing the initiative, Clinton framed it as a conversation about race whose emphasis was on individuals, not as a debate about what should be done about racist policies and institutions.

Tonn notes that the initiative "illustrated the failure of a conversation-as-counseling model to achieve meaningful social reform."[71] Communication scholars Martín Carcasson and Mitchell F. Reyes note that some of the failure of the initiative could be attributed to "the degree to which presidential scandals overwhelmed the administration's and media's time."[72] Even if media attention had remained on the initiative, however, we agree with Tonn that the use of conversation as a frame undermined the possibility of robust public sphere deliberation. Why?

Framing the initiative as a conversation placed the emphasis on personal perspectives rather than on collective decision making. During the community dialogues that the initiative sponsored, people mostly "aired personal experiences and perspectives."[73] Tonn quotes Harvard sociology professor Orlando Patterson's description of a White woman who "spent nearly five minutes of our 'conversation' . . . confessing her racial insensitivities." Instead of moving debate forward, the woman instead focused on "unburdening herself of all sorts of racial guilt feeling. There was nothing to argue about."[74] Instead of debating about how to fix racist policy, people focused on seeking personal absolution for their racism. Because conversation has no goal, talk became an end in itself; and because the rules of personal sphere argument discourage refuting another's personal perceptions, policy argument became impossible. The conversational mode meant there was no way to ask the policy question about what should be done and then debate the merits of that policy.

Tonn notes that the inertia attached to conversation became evident in the fifth month of the initiative, when "White House aides conceded no consensus had emerged even on fundamental goals: whether the initiative should formulate race-related policy or merely explore racial attitudes."[75] The conversational focus on personal experiences assumed that greater understanding of each other would lead to solutions, but understanding others' experiences does not necessarily lead to changes in structures that spawn those experiences.[76]

Contrast Clinton's conversations on race with Ta-nihisi Coates's "The Case for Reparations"[77] in the June 2014 issue of the *Atlantic*. The essay is not a conversation, dialogue, or discussion, but rather a systematic argument for reparations: Government policies prevented Black families' accumulation of intergenerational wealth via the unjustified taking of sharecroppers' land; redlining and predatory lending; and the terrorism of lynching, slavery, and segregation—practices Coates describes as spanning 395 years during which White people gave themselves "preferential treatment." Coates offers proof that a problem exists, that other solutions have failed, and that justice demands reparations.

Coates also recognizes that there might be questions about the practical issues concerning who pays reparations, who receives them, and how much they will be. So far, though, Congress has been unwilling to debate any proposal for reparations even though, as Coates notes, in every session of Congress for the twenty-five years prior to the publication of this essay, US House Representative

John Conyers, Jr., proposed a bill that would have Congress study slavery, its continuing effects, and whether reparations can be a remedy. Coates notes that if the United States were truly interested in figuring out the costs and benefits of reparations, Congressional representatives would have been eager to support Conyers's bill, but the bill had never made it out of committee for a full House debate. Coates believes this failure indicates that people are not really concerned about the practical questions relating to reparations: that the resistance to "serious discussion and debate" may stem from "something more existential." People might

> find that the country can never fully repay African Americans. But we stand to discover much about ourselves in such a discussion—and that is perhaps what scares us. The idea of reparations is frightening not simply because we might lack the ability to pay. The idea of reparations threatens something much deeper—America's heritage, history, and standing in the world.

Although people seem willing to have a conversation about race, Coates argues that they are not willing to have a public sphere argument about policy solutions to problems stemming from Whites' enslavement of Black people, the legislated segregation of Jim Crow laws, and the de facto segregation of redlining. Debates about such topics induce discomfort, but it is precisely these types of public sphere arguments that people in the United States should be having. And at last, the 117th Congress began debating the bill in January 2021.

Journalism professor Michael Schudson succinctly states that "conversation is not the soul of democracy." Conversation does not make democracy possible. Democracy requires you to move beyond the familiar, to risk yourself, to engage with people you do not know and with ideas you do not accept. For this reason, "democracy is deeply uncomfortable."[78] Debate, too, is deeply uncomfortable. It may be uncomfortable to be asked for evidence and reasons for beliefs. It is comfortable to say "Well, it's just my opinion"; it is more uncomfortable to say "This I believe, and here is why." And it is most uncomfortable to say publicly, "This is what I believe we should do," only to have others decide differently. Yet, people should be willing to take the risk, and some are willing to take it.

Public argument arises over grave issues: war and peace, life and death, justice and equality. Aristotle recognized the importance of such topics when he wrote about the subjects of political oratory in *On Rhetoric*. Ultimately, all these questions are deliberative (as opposed to epideictic or forensic): they ask what should be done. Should the United States withdraw from the Intermediate Range Nuclear Forces Treaty? Should state and federal governments abolish the use of capital punishment? Should universities consider race/ethnicity during admissions decisions? All these questions are also policy questions. To answer them, you need to understand the stock issues that recur across all policy debates.

THE STOCK ISSUES OF POLICY DEBATE

A policy claim declares that a specific agent should take a specific action. To defend such a claim, you need proof relating to four **stock issues,** *recurring* *argument themes necessary to justify assent: significance, inherency, solvency, and desirability.* Argumentation scholars George Ziegelmueller and Jack Kay referred to stock issues as *"hunting grounds for arguments"* because they name the central issues a policy advocate must prove and, hence, the areas an opponent can search for arguments against the policy claim.[79]

To illustrate the stock issues, we use snowballs, or more specifically, a policy claim that the Severance, Colorado, town board of trustees should amend its code to exclude snowballs from the century-old ordinance that made it illegal to throw or shoot missiles at people, buildings, or animals. Nine-year-old Severance community member Dane Best, in an effort to exempt snowballs from the definition of "missiles," "presented his arguments at a town board meeting . . . and members voted unanimously to lift the ban."[80] Dane Best's arguments illustrate the four stock issues that must be satisfied in a policy debate.

Significance

Significance is proven when an advocate establishes that a problem exists, and that it is of sufficient scope and intensity that action is warranted. In other words, the problem must be sufficiently important to justify action by the agent. Although you might not initially think that illegal snowball fights are a significant problem, Best argued that "today's kids need reasons to play outside" and that "research suggests that a lack of exposure to the outdoors can lead to obesity, ADHD, anxiety and depression."[81] Because snowball fights were illegal, children were deprived of an important incentive to get outside during the winter.

Solvency

After outlining a significant problem, an advocate must prove that the proposed solution can lessen or eliminate the problem. In Best's case, the problem was an ordinance banning snowball fights. Thus, overturning the law was the solution. That solution might not guarantee that children would get outside, but it would at least remove a barrier to outside play.

Inherency

Not only must one present a solution that is *sufficient* to address the problem, the solution must also be *necessary*. Inherency asks the advocate to prove the proposal is the only way or the best way to address the problem. Because the ordinance was local, only the town board had the authority to rescind it; therefore, town board action was necessary.

Desirability

Proving that a problem exists, and that your solution fixes it and is necessary to fix it despite alternatives, does not necessarily mean that people should assent to your policy claim. You also need to prove desirability: that the proposed solution will create more good than harm. The ordinance likely was enacted because windows in town were broken during snowball fights. Town trustee Dennis "Zeke" Kane voiced concerns and proposed amending the ordinance to prohibit throwing snowballs at people older than sixty.[82] Best also assured the town board that children would not target windows or throw snowballs with rocks in them. (If the snowballs did contain rocks, they would qualify as missiles and still be prohibited under the town ordinance.) Ultimately, the town board was convinced that the potential problems that might be caused by legalizing snowball fights were outweighed by the good of encouraging children to play outdoors.

We illustrate the stock issues with a playful example, but organizing arguments around the stock issues works with any policy advocacy. For example, the policy debates over global warming illustrate how these stock issues play out in national and international public argument. Arguments over significance focus on whether global warming is occurring and, if it is, what the effects of warming are. Solvency arguments assess the effectiveness of rejoining the Paris Climate Accords, the Green New Deal, cap and trade policies, or market-based carbon pricing to slow or stop greenhouse gas emissions. Inherency arguments suggest that other possible alternatives, such as seeding the atmosphere with SO_2 to create a cooling cycle, would not work as well as reducing CO_2 emissions.[83] Arguments about desirability identify the drawbacks associated with the proposal, such as the potential burden on the economy.

THREATS TO DEMOCRATIC DELIBERATION AND DEBATE

Argumentation and debate are essential for democracy, but they do not lead to better decisions if people are unwilling to change their opinions or if the evidence used in the debates is faulty. Confirmation bias might prevent people from seeing that their positions are not supported by the evidence. "Fake news" and "alternative facts" distort public debate.

Confirmation Bias

The potential for argument to resolve disagreement depends upon people being willing to change their minds as they encounter new or different evidence. Unfortunately, evidence is not always enough to get people to change their minds. Psychologists in the 1960s identified the problem of **confirmation bias,** "*the tendency for people to search for or interpret information in a manner that favors their current beliefs.*"[84] People tend to judge confirming evidence more favorably and remember it better. The corollary of confirmation bias is **disconfirmation bias,** which occurs *when people do not look for, favorably interpret, or recall evidence that is contrary to their beliefs.* The result of these two biases is that, when presented with evidence, people tend to make evidence fit what they already believe rather than allow it to challenge their beliefs.

Confirmation and disconfirmation biases also lead people to ignore information that is inconsistent with or counter to their beliefs, or to "*counterargue the contrary arguments and uncritically accept supporting arguments.*"[85] Psychologists who studied this phenomenon found that "when faced with evidence contrary to their beliefs, people try to undermine the evidence. That is, there is a bias to disconfirm arguments incompatible with one's position."[86] People are also more reluctant to question evidence that supports their beliefs.

The unfortunate effect of these biases is that people or groups who believe differently about a policy will disagree about what counts as "strong evidence." When people invest mental energy and time into refuting competing arguments, "they may become more extreme in their beliefs"[87] and the disagreement becomes even more polarized. One of the first studies of confirmation and disconfirmation biases focused on people who disagreed about capital punishment. The researchers found that "the net effect of exposing proponents and opponents of capital punishment to identical evidence—studies ostensibly offering equivalent levels of support and disconfirmation—was to increase further the gap between their views."[88] In other words, people might not only ignore evidence that contradicts their beliefs; exposure to that contrary evidence may *strengthen* their beliefs. Thus, just providing evidence to people with whom you disagree is not necessarily enough to change their views.

Bottom line: once people have formed beliefs, they tend to accept the information that supports their positions and ignore, refute, and hold to higher standards the evidence that does not support those positions. Resistance to change is a problem for the public as well as technical experts.[89] We do not mean to say that humans are doomed to wallow in the beliefs they already hold, but rather to explain why public argument can be frustrating.

If you accept the premises that human beings are fallible and that you are a human being, then you might agree that you may have sometimes embraced flawed beliefs. In other words, everyone ought to be wary of confirmation and disconfirmation biases. So, what are some suggestions you can put into practice? What habits can you develop that allow you to combat confirmation and disconfirmation biases and be open to argument?

First, consider doing a paper or speech assignment on a topic about which you do not have a strongly formed belief, so that you are more likely to assess all the evidence critically. You can train your brain to engage in the practices of assessing evidence without confirmation and disconfirmation biases. Then, you can transfer that process to evidence about beliefs you already hold. Get into the habit of carefully considering what conclusion is supported by the evidence, not just whether the evidence supports your conclusion.

Second, expose yourself consistently to a range of media, including sources that tend to take positions with which you do not agree. In one study of pre-election news coverage, communication researchers found that people who engage in "frequent habitual online news use do not exhibit a confirmation bias. However, . . . participants with infrequent online news consumption show a significant confirmation bias."[90] A pattern these researchers observed was that people might initially seek out information that confirmed their opinions, but if they were *habitual* consumers of news, they also seek out information that is contrary. People who engage in habits that make them willing to seek out and engage with the opinions of people who disagree with them tend to have less confirmation bias.

Third, "consider the opposite" by methodically thinking about which evidence is or is not persuasive. In a follow-up to the study about capital punishment, the researchers created two groups. They instructed one group to "be as *objective* and *unbiased* as possible in evaluating the studies" and the other to "ask yourself at each step whether you would have made the same high or low evaluations had exactly the same study produced results on the *other* side of the issue."[91] Those told to be unbiased experienced the same degree of confirmation bias and attitude polarization as those who received no instruction. However, those who were given a practical "corrective strategy," a new habit that changed the way they read the studies, experienced less confirmation bias.[92] In other words, wanting to be fair is not enough. You need to engage in practical actions (habits), as a critical thinker who engages with and considers opposing arguments rather than simply seeking to refute them. This strategy of habitual practical steps is used by a range of professionals, including accountants,[93] clinical researchers,[94] and police officers.[95]

Fake News and Alternative Facts

The Code of Ethics for the Society of Professional Journalists, first adopted in 1926, details the habits and conditions necessary for reporting to be fair, factual, accurate, and complete. Why was such a code needed? Prior to the 1830s, newspapers were often affiliated with political parties. Even after those affiliations ended, the papers were often more interested in making money than informing the public.

For example, in 1835, just as Halley's Comet was due to appear in the skies over North America, the *New York Sun* printed a series of six articles declaring that scientists using high-powered telescopes had discovered life on the moon. The stories described the humanoids as approximately four feet tall, with membranous wings, bodies covered in short copper-colored fur, and faces similar to an orangutan's.[96] Bipedal beavers, deer, and birds also graced the lush valleys, myriad waterfalls, and pyramids on the surface of the moon. The *Sun* illustrated its stories with lithographs depicting the fantastical scenes. Other news outlets extracted and reprinted those stories as the circulation of the *Sun* skyrocketed.[97] It took over a month for the series to be proven to be a hoax, fabricated by the publisher of the *Sun*.

We present this example to show that fake news is not unique to the digital age. Fake news has always attracted audiences because, as the introduction to the 1970s reprint of the 1835 *Sun* stories explained, people did not really like to read the news. Some of them were willing "coconspirators against reality."[98] The media dynamics of the 1830s were similar to those of today. The emergence of the penny press (mass-produced newspapers that cost only one cent), like the internet, was supposed to enable the democratization of information. Instead, it supplanted news with sensationalism and advertising that turned politics into a game.[99]

The digital age has both aided and confounded argument. Although finding research that provides data to support claims has never been easier or quicker, the speed of the internet also enables the proliferation and spread of bad data. **Fake news** is "*made-up stuff, masterfully manipulated to look like credible journalistic reports that are easily spread online to large audiences willing to believe the* *fictions and spread the word.*"[100] **Alternative facts** are *claims by political leaders that are false or made without any data.* "Alternative facts" entered the national vocabulary after presidential advisor Kellyanne Conway labeled as "alternative facts" press secretary Sean Spicer's objectively false claim that the crowds at Trump's inauguration were "the largest audience to ever witness an inauguration, ever."[101]

PolitiFact, the Pulitzer Prize–winning, nonprofit, fact-checking website, explains that journalists' definition of fake news, "fabricated content that intentionally masquerades as news coverage of actual events," is distinct from Trump's 153 uses of the term in 2017. According to Politifact, Trump's references are to "news coverage that is unsympathetic to his administration and his performance, even when the news reports are accurate."[102]

Like Politifact, we use the term "fake news" to refer to fabricated news coverage. In 2020, fake news stories circulated that dolphins had returned to Venice canals (the video was from a different area of Italy), that 5G causes COVID-19 (there is no evidence for this claim), and that massive election fraud marred the election. (Independent fact checkers, courts of law, and vote recounts have found no evidence of fraud that would have changed the outcome. Moreover, the Elections Infrastructure Government Coordinating Council and the Election Infrastructure Sector Coordinating executive committees described the 2020 election as "the most secure in American history."[103])

Fake news and alternative facts feed into confirmation bias in two ways. First, people tend to accept them when they align with their already held beliefs. Second, as bad data circulates in the form of fake news and as officials repeat alternative facts, people become more willing to accept the false information the next time they see it because it is familiar to them.[104] The effect on public discourse is magnified. Research has found that on Twitter, "Falsehood diffused significantly farther, faster, deeper, and more broadly than the truth in all categories of information."[105]

Bots accelerated the spread of fake and true news at the same rate. What made fake news spread more rapidly? Humans. As they did with the *Sun's* moon-based man-bats, people are more likely to spread fake news than true news. It takes true stories six times as long to reach the same number of people as fake stories.[106] Thus, the likelihood that people become more familiar with fake news stories than with true news is magnified.

In 2018, *USA Today* reported on an example of fake news and alternative facts interacting and gaining traction, in a story about billionaire philanthropist George Soros and what came to be called the migrant caravan. The facts were that, starting in October 2018, a group of Hondurans fled their homes because of fear of violence and lack of economic opportunity. They began a northward trek of almost two thousand miles to the United States, where they hoped to be granted asylum. Along the way, Guatemalan refugees joined them. As the number of people grew so, too, did falsehoods about them, including a conspiracy theory that, according to the *USA Today* article, claimed that "George Soros, a Jewish immigrant, is paying the migrants to make the journey—or even orchestrating it. Members of Congress and Trump's son both repeated it. Conservative celebrities, too."[107]

Cesar Sayoc, who pled guilty and received a life sentence for mailing sixteen pipe bombs to critics of Trump, and Robert Bowers, who was charged with killing eleven people at a Pittsburgh synagogue, were both inspired by false claims about the migrants and Soros. Authorities have found that in social media posts both people mentioned Soros (to whom Sayoc mailed a bomb) or the threat of a Jewish "infestation" and the caravan.[108] In other words, the conspiracy theory appears to have motivated violent actions.[109]

The *USA Today* story tracked down the evolution of the conspiracy theory. On October 14, someone called Loretta the Prole tweeted the name "Soros" and attached a *Washington Times* story about the caravan to 6000 Twitter followers. Just the name. No data. No warrant. Not even a complete sentence. The same day, during a 20-minute span, identical posts appeared in six other pro-Trump Facebook groups with a total of 165,000 members.

The unsupported claim that Soros was connected to the caravan gained traction as it circulated, illustrating that the more something circulates the more it is believed. The caravan departed Honduras on October 12. The first post linking Soros to it was on October 14. By October 16, over 2 million people had been exposed on social media to the claim that Soros had funded the caravan. On October 17, the claim broke into broader public consciousness, exposing over 60 million people on Twitter and over 15 million on Facebook. Florida Representative Matt Gaetz posted a video, claiming that it showed people in Honduras handing out small sums of money to induce migrants to join the caravan, and asking "Soros?" However, the video had actually been shot in Guatemala, not in Honduras. A Guatemalan journalist who interviewed people in the town where the video was shot reported that local merchants were giving people money, usually 13 to 26 cents.[110] Despite the incorrect information and lack of data, Gaetz's post was retweeted. By October 22, almost 275 million people on Twitter and over 98 million on Facebook were exposed to the fake claim about Soros. By October 27, the potential reach of the claim was over 479 million on Twitter and over 192 million on Facebook.

Statements by Trump and his supporters fed the circulation of this data-less claim. At a campaign rally in Missoula, Montana, on October 18, Trump claimed: "But a lot of money has been passing to people to come up and try and get to the border by Election Day, because they think that's a negative for us. . . . They have lousy policy. The one thing, they stick together, but they wanted that caravan and there are those that say that caravan didn't just happen. It didn't just happen. A lot of reasons that caravan, 4,000 people."[111] Chuck Holton of NRATV told viewers, "A bevy of left-wing groups are partnering with a Hungarian-born billionaire and the Venezuelan government to try to influence the 2018 midterms by sending Honduran migrants north in the thousands." CNN commentator Matt Schlapp said, "Because of the liberal judges and other people that intercede, including George Soros, we have too much chaos at our southern border."[112]

Again, the claim that Soros or the Democrats were funding the migrant caravan has no data to support it. As the *New York Times* declares: "There is no evidence of that."[113] In this example, people and government officials (and likely a few bots) spread fake news that claimed to provide information about the migrant caravan. That information was fabricated and simply false. Nevertheless, the story circulated throughout social media sites and across news shows. Instead of providing evidence about who was actually in the caravan and what was motivating it, Trump spread "alternative facts."

It is difficult to debate public concerns such as immigration policy when organizations and people that pretend to offer news spread claims that are supported by no data or fake data, and that uncritical media consumers then recirculate. The problem of fake news circulating and gaining credibility as it circulates was studied by the Stanford History Education Group (SHEG), which researches civic online reasoning. SHEG found that people in the United States "of all ages, from digitally savvy tweens to high-IQ academics, fail to ask important questions about content they encounter on a browser." They retweet links without reading them first, and over-rely on search engines, incorrectly thinking that what appears higher in search results is more accurate.[114]

Online gullibility[115] is a serious concern for democracy. Fake news can be spread intentionally to affect elections, as US intelligence agencies concluded Russian agents had done in 2016 and as Facebook revealed had happened before the 2018 midterm elections.[116] Fake news makes public argument far more difficult because it provides bad (false) data.

SHEG's research does not stop with identifying a problem; it also outlines solutions. Comparing how history PhDs, professional fact checkers, and undergraduates assessed the credibility of information found on the web, the researchers found that both PhDs and undergraduates made the same mistakes: they "fell victim to easily manipulated features of websites, such as official-looking logos and domain names." The researchers labeled this habit **vertical reading,** meaning that *a person stays "within a website to evaluate its reliability."* Fact checkers, in contrast, used **lateral reading,** *"leaving a site after a quick scan and opening up new browser tabs in order to judge the credibility of the original site."* Lateral reading allowed the fact checkers to arrive "at more warranted conclusions in a fraction of the time."[117] Fact checkers, as you might expect, had developed a set of habits that enabled them to assess the data presented on digital sites quickly and more accurately.

SHEG provides a series of practical steps and habits to read laterally:

1. "Take bearings": "Before diving deeply into unfamiliar content, chart a plan for moving forward."[118] Make a judgment about the credibility of the source before you embark on a trail to a destination (the conclusion to which the source would lead you). Even before reading the entire web page, leave the site and search other sources for information about its credibility. You need to take your bearings because "the web [is] a maze filled with trap doors and blind alleys, where things are not always what they seem."[119]

2. Orient information horizontally: Leaving the original website open, open new tabs next to it, creating tabs in a horizontal fashion, so you can keep track of how the information is related. The appearance

and content of the original web page is not a good indicator of its credibility. You can learn more about a website by leaving it. For example, after encountering an essay, go to the home page for the website, then the "About Us" page. Then do a search of the website's owner on a browser. Then read multiple other sources about the source.

3. Click restraint: After receiving the results of a search, take time to review the list. Do not just click on the first result. Make an informed choice about which result to click. When possible, find primary sources of information; do not just rely on others' characterizations of the original source's information or data.[120]

To these, we add:

4. Begin your search with a neutral query. Because search algorithms try to figure out what you *want* to read, a question with a conclusion embedded within it is likely to produce results that confirm that conclusion. Rather than searching "is climate change a hoax?" search "evidence about climate change."

In other words, assess all information as though it claims something with which you completely disagree (especially when you agree with it).

Argument is an essential and necessary tool for decision making in a democracy, organization, school, city, and family. Developing the habits of argument means developing habits of skepticism—a healthy doubt that recognizes the contingency of all claims (even your own). Skeptics use imagination, intelligence, and curiosity before they come to conclusions, and are willing to question those conclusions even after they have reached them. Skepticism is a series of habits to test claims. It should not be confused with cynicism, which is an attitude that sees people as generally selfish and dishonest. Cynicism doubts people. Skepticism doubts claims, others' as well as your own.

As philosopher Ariella Azoulay claims, "Civil discourse is not a fiction,"[121] but it does require an act of imagination. For us, it includes the ability to imagine (or consider) the opposite, to assess your own claims and data with as much skepticism as you assess other people's. Imagine a world in which reasons are given for decisions, evidence is given for those reasons, and, when new evidence arises, people change their minds. Just imagine.

CONCLUSION

An argument is a claim supported by data, warrant, and backing, and limited by qualifications and conditions for rebuttal. Argumentation is the process by which people engage each other in an exchange of arguments. Arguments are a central part of communication in a democratic society. The outcomes of arguments have real consequences for which campus project is funded, which job candidate is hired, which political candidate wins, whether or not a country is invaded, and so on.

Public sphere argument requires that members of a community be able to explain and justify their positions. It requires people to compare and contrast competing arguments so they can make reasonable decisions even when faced with incomplete information. Every person makes decisions every day. It is always better to make a decision based on sound evidence, strong reasoning, and warranted conclusions. When argument is conceived of as a cooperative enterprise in decision making, its utility as a way to resolve differences, rather than magnify them, becomes clear.

A good principle for arguing is to be as open to persuasion and change as you hope the person with whom you are arguing is. When you engage in argumentation, you should be willing to alter your position in the face of other arguments. Argument only works if people are willing to change their minds when they hear a sound argument or encounter new evidence.

DISCUSSION QUESTIONS

1. Does the word "argument" have a positive or negative connotation to you? Why? What would change the connotation?
2. Read an article advocating a policy, a letter to the editor, or an editorial. Diagram one of its arguments, identifying as many components of the Toulmin model as you can.
3. Identify a policy about which debate proceeds. Identify how advocates of the policy prove each of the stock issues. Identify how opponents of the policy refute the stock issues.

RECOMMENDED READINGS

Goodnight, G. Thomas. "The Personal, Technical, and Public Spheres of Argument: A Speculative Inquiry into the Art of Public Deliberation." *Argumentation and Advocacy* 18 (Spring 1982): 214–227.

Tonn, Mari Boor. "Taking Conversation, Dialogue, and Therapy Public." *Rhetoric & Public Affairs* 8, no. 3 (2005): 405–430.

ENDNOTES

[1] Evan Porter, "Tired of Being Humiliated, These Girls Fought the School Dress Code. And Won," *Upworthy*, September 1, 2016, http://www.upworthy.com/tired -of-being-humiliated-these-girls-fought-the-school-dress-code-and-won?c=ufb1.

[2] "Oregon Student Dress Codes," filmed May 26, 2015, YouTube video, posted by National Education Association, January 5, 2016, https://www.youtube.com/watch?v =r7G7KXDI4vI.

[3] Quoted in "Oregon Student Dress Codes."

[4] Quoted in "Oregon Student Dress Codes."

[5] Emily McCombs, "Sexist School Dress Codes Are a Problem, and Oregon May Have the Answer," Huffington Post, September 5, 2017 (updated September 6, 2017), https://www.huffingtonpost.com/entry/sexist-school-dress-codes-and-the-oregon -now-model_us_59a6cd7ee4b00795c2a318e5.

[6] Oregon Now, "The Oregon NOW Model Student Dress Code," February 2016, https://noworegon.org/wp-content/uploads/sites/12/2018/01/or_now_model _student_ dress_code_feb_2016__1_.pdf.

[7] Quoted in McCombs, "Sexist School Dress Codes."

[8] McCombs, "Sexist School Dress Codes."

[9] Quoted in McCombs, "Sexist School Dress Codes."

[10] Quoted in McCombs, "Sexist School Dress Codes."

[11] McCombs, "Sexist School Dress Codes."

[12] David Zarefsky, *Argumentation: The Study of Effective Reasoning,* 2nd ed., *Course Guidebook: The Great Courses* (Chantilly, VA: Great Courses, 2005), 12, https://guidebookstgc.snagfilms.com/4294_Argumentation.pdf.

[13] Danielle S. Allen, *Talking to Strangers: Anxieties of Citizenship since Brown v. Board of Education* (Chicago: University of Chicago Press, 2004), 9–10.

[14] Allen, *Talking to Strangers,* 141.

[15] Allen, *Talking to Strangers,* 158.

[16] Allen, *Talking to Strangers,* 158.

[17] Daniel J. O'Keefe, "The Concepts of Argument and Arguing," *Advances in Argumentation Theory and Research,* ed. J. Robert Cox and Charles Arthur Willard (Carbondale: Southern Illinois University Press, 1982), 3–23, esp. 3–4; and Daniel J. O'Keefe, "Two Concepts of Argument," *Journal of the American Forensic Association* 13 (1977): 121–128.

[18] David Zarefsky, "Argumentation in the Tradition of Speech Communication Studies," in *Perspectives and Approaches: Proceedings of the Third International Conference on Argumentation,* vol. 1, ed. Frans H. van Eemeren, Rob Grootendorst, J. Anthony Blair, and Charles A. Willard (Amsterdam: Sic Sat, 1995), 32–52, 43.

[19] Zarefsky, *Argumentation,* 11.

[20] Zarefsky, *Argumentation.*

[21] Holly Yan, "Top Health Officials Have Changed Their Minds about Face Mask Guidance—but for Good Reason," CNN, July 20, 2020, https://www.cnn.com /2020/07/19/health/face-masks-us-guidance/index.html.

[22] Emanuel Goldman, "Exaggerated Risk of Transmission of COVID-19 by Fomites," *Lancet Infectious Diseases* 20, no. 8 (August 2020): 892–893, doi: 10.1016/ S1473-3099(20)30561-2.

[23] Jose-Luis Jimenez, "COVID-19 Is Transmitted through Aerosols. We Have Enough Evidence, Now It Is Time to Act," *Time,* August 25, 2020, https://time.com/5883081 /covid-19-transmitted-aerosols/.

[24] Lynne Peeples, "Face Masks: What the Data Say," *Nature,* October 6, 2020, https://www.nature.com/articles/d41586-020-02801-8.

[25] Guy P. Guy, Jr., Florence C. Lee, Gregory Sunshine, et al., "Association of State-Issued Mask Mandates and Allowing On-Premises Restaurant Dining with County-Level COVID-19 Case and Death Growth Rates—United States, March 1–December 31, 2020," *Morbidity and Mortality Weekly Report,* ePub, March 5, 2021, doi: http://dx.doi.org/10.15585/mmwr.mm7010e3.

[26] Aristotle, *On Rhetoric,* 1.2 [1356], trans. George Kennedy (Cambridge, MA: Oxford University Press, 2007).

[27] Lloyd F. Bitzer, "Aristotle's Enthymeme Revisited," *Quarterly Journal of Speech* 45, no. 4 (December 1959): 408, italics added. See also Thomas M. Conley, "The Enthymeme in Perspective," *Quarterly Journal of Speech* 70 (1984): 168–187.

[28] Bitzer, "Aristotle's Enthymeme," 408.

[29] The full video is on YouTube at http://www.youtube.com/watch?v=b0AGiq9j_Ak.

[30] Darren Rovell, *First in Thirst: How Gatorade Turned the Science of Sweat into a Cultural Phenomenon* (New York: AMACOM, 2005).

[31] Stephen Toulmin, *The Uses of Argument* (Cambridge, UK: Cambridge University Press, 1969), 130.

[32] Wayne Brockriede and Douglas Ehninger, "Toulmin on Argument: An Interpretation and Application," *Quarterly Journal of Speech* 46, no. 1 (February 1960): 44–53.

[33] Toulmin, *The Uses of Argument*, 97, italics added.

[34] CDC COVID Data Tracker, accessed March 5, 2021, https://covid.cdc.gov/covid-data-tracker/#cases_casesper100klast7days.

[35] Edward Schiappa, *Defining Reality: Definitions and the Politics of Meaning* (Carbondale: Southern Illinois University Press, 2003), 5.

[36] Schiappa, "Defining Reality," 38, 47.

[37] Toulmin, *The Uses of Argument*, 97, italics added.

[38] "Truthiness," Merriam-Webster's Word of the Year 2006, http://www.merriam-webster.com/info/06words.htm.

[39] Stephen Colbert, interview by Nathan Rabin, January 25, 2006, http://www.avclub.com/articles/stephen-colbert,13970.

[40] Toulmin, *The Uses of Argument*, 98, italics added.

[41] Toulmin, *The Uses of Argument*, 101, italics added.

[42] Toulmin, *The Uses of Argument*, 101, italics added.

[43] Chris Morris, "This is Hurricane Maria's Predicted Path (So Far)," *Fortune*, September 18, 2017, http://fortune.com/2017/09/18/hurricane-maria-path/.

[44] National Weather Service, "Major Hurricane Maria—September 20, 2017," https://www.weather.gov/sju/maria2017.

[45] For an analysis of the speech, see Karlyn Kohrs Campbell, "The Humanistic Underpinnings of Feminism: 'The Solitude of Self,'" in *Man Cannot Speak for Her*, vol. 1 (New York: Praeger, 1989).

[46] Elizabeth Cady Stanton, "The Solitude of Self," in *Man Cannot Speak for Her*, vol. 2, ed. Karlyn Kohrs Campbell (New York: Praeger, 1989), 373.

[47] Ray Sanchez, "How Puerto Rico's Death Toll Climbed from 64 to 2,975 in Hurricane Maria," CNN, August 19, 2018, https://www.cnn.com/2018/08/29/us/puerto-rico-growing-death-toll/index.html; Linda Qiu, "Trump's False Claims Rejecting Puerto Rico's Death Toll from Hurricane Maria," *New York Times*, September 13, 2018, https://www.nytimes.com/2018/09/13/us/politics/trump-fact-check-hurricane.html?module=inline.

[48] Milken Institute School of Public Health, George Washington University, *Ascertainment of the Estimated Excess Mortality from Hurricane María in Puerto Rico*, August 28, 2018: 11, https://publichealth.gwu.edu/sites/default/files/downloads/projects/PRstudy/Acertainment%20of%20the%20Estimated%20Excess%20Mortality%20from%20Hurricane%20Maria%20in%20Puerto%20Rico.pdf.

[49] Milken Institute School of Public Health, *Ascertainment*, i.

[50] Quoted in Qiu, "Trump's False Claims."

[51] Milken Institute School of Public Health, *Ascertainment*, 9.

[52] G. Thomas Goodnight, "The Personal, Technical, and Public Spheres of Argument: A Speculative Inquiry into the Art of Public Deliberation," *Argumentation and Advocacy* 18 (Spring 1982): 214–227.

[53] Goodnight, "The Personal," 216, italics added.

[54] Goodnight, "The Personal," 219.

[55] Goodnight, "The Personal," 219, italics added.

[56] Neil deGrasse Tyson, *The Pluto Files: The Rise and Fall of America's Favorite Planet* (New York: Norton, 2009).

[57] Neil deGrasse Tyson, "Pluto's Honor," *Natural History* 108, no. 1 (February 1999): 82.

[58] Quoted in Tyson, "The Pluto Files," 71.

[59] Tyson, *The Pluto Files,* 127.

[60] Office of Communications, Johns Hopkins University, "Scientists Make the Case to Restore Pluto's Planet Status," news release, March 16, 2017, http://releases.jhu.edu /2017/03/16/scientists-make-the-case-to-restore-plutos-planet-status/.

[61] Intergovernmental Panel on Climate Change, *Climate Change 2014: Synthesis Report Summary for Policymakers,* 2014, http://www.ipcc.ch/pdf/assessment-report/ar5/syr /AR5_SYR_FINAL_SPM.pdf.

[62] Leah Ceccarelli, "Manufactured Scientific Controversy: Science, Rhetoric, and Public Debate," *Rhetoric & Public Affairs* 14, no. 2 (2011): 195–228, 204, 219, doi:10.1353/rap.2010.0222.

[63] Valeria Fabj and Matthew J. Sobnosky, "AIDS Activism and the Rejuvenation of the Public Sphere," *Argumentation and Advocacy* 31 (Spring 1995): 163–184.

[64] The elements of this section of the essay are drawn from Catherine H. Palczewski, "A Personal/Political Case for Debate," *Philosophy & Rhetoric* 52, no. 1 (2019), 86–92.

[65] Mari Boor Tonn, "Taking Conversation, Dialogue, and Therapy Public," *Rhetoric & Public Affairs* 8, no. 3 (2005): 405–430.

[66] Tonn, "Taking Conversation," 408.

[67] Tonn, "Taking Conversation," 408.

[68] William Jefferson Clinton, "Remarks at the University of California San Diego Commencement Ceremony in La Jolla, California," *Public Papers of the Presidents of the United States: William J. Clinton* (Washington: GPO, 1998).

[69] Clinton, "Remarks," 880.

[70] Quoted in Tonn, "Taking Conversation," 419.

[71] Tonn, "Taking Conversation," 419.

[72] Martín Carcasson and Mitchell F. Rice, "The Promise and Failure of President Clinton's Race Initiative of 1997–1998: A Rhetorical Perspective," *Rhetoric & Public Affairs* 2 (Summer 1999): 243–274, 243.

[73] Tonn, "Taking Conversation," 419.

[74] Tonn, "Taking Conversation," 419.

[75] Tonn, "Taking Conversation," 421.

[76] Tonn, "Taking Conversation," 421–422.

[77] Ta-Nehisi Coates, "The Case for Reparations," *Atlantic,* June 2014, https://www .theatlantic.com/magazine/archive/2014/06/the-case-for-reparations/361631/.

[78] Michael Schudson, *Why Democracies Need an Unlovable Press* (Malden, MA: Polity, 2008),103.

[79] George Ziegelmueller and Jack Kay, *Argumentation: Inquiry and Advocacy,* 3rd ed. (Boston: Allyn & Bacon, 1997), 172.

[80] "Boy Hits Target, Convinces Town to Scrap Snowball Fight Ban," December 4, 2018, https://www.apnews.com/f3aeb8a92a0e48f6b53672355abe0977.

[81] Quoted in Bill Chappell, "Snowball Ban Overturned in Colorado Town after Request from 9-Year-Old-Boy," NPR, December 4, 2018, https://www.npr.org/2018/12/04/673282587/snowball-ban-overturned-in -colorado-town-after-request-from-boy-9.

[82] Chappell, "Snowball Ban Overturned."

[83] "Geo-Engineering: Every Silver Lining Has a Cloud," *The Economist,* January 31, 2009, 86–87.

84 Mark E. Cowen and Michael W. Kattan, "Confirmation Bias," *Encyclopedia of Medical Decision Making* (Thousand Oaks, CA: Sage, 2009).

85 Charles S. Taber and Milton Lodge, "Motivated Skepticism in the Evaluation of Political Beliefs," *American Journal of Political Science* 50 (2006): 755–769.

86 Kari Edwards and Edward E. Smith, "A Disconfirmation Bias in the Evaluation of Arguments," *Journal of Personality and Social Psychology* 71, no. 1 (1996): 5–24, doi:10.1037/0022-3514.71.1.5.

87 Edwards and Smith, "Disconfirmation Bias."

88 Charles G. Lord, Lee Ross, and Mark R. Lepper, "Biased Assimilation and Attitude Polarization: The Effects of Prior Theories on Subsequently Considered Evidence," *Journal of Personality and Social Psychology* 37 (1979): 2098–2109, 2105, https://nuovoeutile.it/wp-content/uploads/2014/10/BIASED-ASSIMILATION-AND-ATTITUDE-POLARIZATION.pdf. See also Taber and Lodge, "Motivated Skepticism."

89 Hugo Mercier, "When Experts Argue: Explaining the Best and the Worst of Reasoning," *Argumentation* 25 (2011): 313–327, doi 10.1007/s10503-011-9222-y.

90 Silvia Knobloch-Westerwick and Steven B. Kleinman, "Preelection Selective Exposure: Confirmation Bias versus Informational Utility," *Communication Research* 39, no. 2 (April 2012): 170–193, doi:10.1177/0093650211400597.

91 Charles G. Lord, Mark R. Lepper, and Elizabeth Preston, "Considering the Opposite: A Corrective Strategy for Social Judgment," *Journal of Personality and Social Psychology* 47, no. 6 (1984): 1233.

92 Lord, Lepper, and Preston, "Considering the Opposite," 1236.

93 Benjamin L. Luippold, Stephen Perreault, and James Wainberg, "5 Ways to Overcome Confirmation Bias," *Journal of Accountancy,* February 1, 2015, https://www.journalofaccountancy.com/issues/2015/feb/how-to-overcome-confirmation-bias.html.

94 Charles Rock, "Five Ways to Take Confirmation Bias out of Your Experimental Results," *St. Jude Progress,* January 17, 2018, https://blogs.stjude.org/progress/avoiding-confirmation-bias-scientific-research/.

95 Amaury Murgado, "Dealing with Confirmation Bias," *Police: The Law Enforcement Magazine,* July 17, 2014, https://www.policemag.com/341175/dealing-with-confirmation-bias.

96 Matthew Goodman, *The Sun and the Moon* (New York: Basic Books, 2010).

97 Kevin Young, "Moon Shot: Race, a Hoax, and the Birth of Fake News," *New Yorker,* October 21, 2017, https://www.newyorker.com/books/page-turner/moon-shot-race-a-hoax-and-the-birth-of-fake-news.

98 Quoted in Young, "Moon Shot."

99 Young, "Moon Shot."

100 Angie Drobnic Holan, "2016 Lie of the Year: Fake News," PolitiFact, December 13, 2016, https://www.politifact.com/truth-o-meter/article/2016/dec/13/2016-lie-year-fake-news/.

101 Eric Bradner, "Conway: Trump White House Offered 'Alternative Facts' on Crowd Size," CNNPolitics, January 23, 2017, https://www.cnn.com/2017/01/22/politics/kellyanne-conway-alternative-facts/index.html.

102 Angie Drobnic Holan, "The Media's Definition of Fake News vs. Donald Trump's," *Politifact,* October 18, 2017, https://www.politifact.com/truth-o-meter/article/2017/oct/18/deciding-whats-fake-medias-definition-fake-news-vs/.

103 Brittany De Lea, "2020 Election 'Most Secure in American History,' Federal Election Security Officials Say," Fox News, November 12, 2020, https://www.foxnews.com/politics/2020-election-secure-history-federal-security.

[104] Katy Steinmetz, "How Your Brain Tricks You into Believing Fake News," *Time,* August 9, 2018, http://time.com/5362183/the-real-fake-news-crisis/.

[105] Sorouch Vosoughi, Deb Roy, and Sinan Aral, "The Spread of True and False News Online," *Science* 359, no. 6380 (March 9, 2018), 1146–1151, doi: 10.1126/science.aap9559.

[106] Vosoughi, Roy, and Aral, "The Spread."

[107] Brad Heath, Matt Wynn, and Jessica Guynn, "How a Lie about George Soros and the Migrant Caravan Multiplied Online," *USA Today,* October 31, 2018, https://www.usatoday.com/in-depth/news/nation/2018/10/31/george-soros-and -migrant-caravan-how-lie-multiplied-online/1824633002/.

[108] Joel Achenbach, "A Conspiracy Theory about George Soros and a Migrant Caravan Inspired Horror," *Washington Post,* October 28, 2018, https://www.washingtonpost .com/national/a-conspiracy-theory-about-george-soros-and-a-migrant-caravan -inspired-horror/2018/10/28/52df587e-dae6-11e8-b732-3c72cbf131f2_story.html; Brian Stelter, "Pittsburgh Suspect Echoed Talking Point that Dominated Fox News Airwaves," CNN Business, October 30, 2018, https://www.cnn.com/2018/10/29 /media/pittsburgh-suspect-invasion/index.html.

[109] Jonathan Albright, "The Rumor Caravan: From Twitter Reply to Disaster," *Columbia Journalism Review,* October 30, 2018, https://www.cjr.org/tow_center/the-rumor -caravan-from-twitter-reply-to-disaster.php.

[110] Linda Qiu, "Did Democrats, or George Soros, Fund Migrant Caravans? Despite Republican Claims, No," *New York Times,* October 20, 2018, https://www.nytimes .com/2018/10/20/world/americas/migrant-caravan-video-trump.html.

[111] Qiu, "Did Democrats?"

[112] Quoted in Adam Serwer, "Trump's Caravan Hysteria Led to This," *Atlantic,* October 28, 2018, https://www.theatlantic.com/ideas/archive/2018/10/caravan-lie-sparked -massacre-american-jews/574213/.

[113] Qiu, "Did Democrats?"

[114] Steinmetz, "How Your Brain."

[115] Steinmetz, "How Your Brain."

[116] Steinmetz, "How Your Brain." See also Kathleen Hall Jamieson, *Cyberwar: How Russian Hackers and Trolls Helped Elect a President: What We Don't, Can't, and Do Know* (New York: Oxford University Press, 2018).

[117] Sam Wineburg and Sarah McGrew, "Lateral Reading: Reading Less and Learning More When Evaluating Digital Information," *Teachers College Record,* 12 (2019): 1–40, tcrecord.org/content.asp?contentid=22806.

[118] Wineburg and McGrew, "Lateral Reading," 53.

[119] Wineburg and McGrew, "Lateral Reading," 23–24.

[120] Wineburg and McGrew, "Lateral Reading."

[121] Ariella Azoulay, *Civil Imagination: A Political Ontology of Photography* (New York: Verso, 2012), 3.

Chapter 6
Narrative

Historian Alfred A. Andrea notes, "Whatever the use or abuse of history, what has remained true over the ages is that history is a story, and any story that is not well told fails. . . . In *recreating* the past . . . the historian is called upon to use the art and power of words to captivate an audience."[1] When it comes to stories of people's collective pasts, it is not only historians who tell the story. As we noted in earlier chapters, the stories people tell about themselves form public and collective memory and give identity to a society. For people who were raised in the United States, numerous stories are told of its origin. Dominant stories find their start on a few different dates: in 1492 with Columbus's so-called discovery of the Americas, in 1607 with the Jamestown colony, in 1620 with Pilgrims fleeing religious persecution, in 1773 with the Boston Tea Party, and in 1776 with the Declaration of Independence.

When you start a story affects the story that is told. Do you start the history of the United States in 1492, in 15,000 BCE, or in 1142 with the formation of the Haudenosaunee (Iroquois) Confederacy ("the oldest living participatory democracy on earth"[2])? Depending on where you begin—how you set the scene in both space and time—whom you see as agents or as central characters in the story can change.

This point is demonstrated by "The 1619 Project," which the *New York Times Magazine* launched in 2019. The authors argue that the story of the United States should begin in 1619, the year the first ship of enslaved people landed in the English colony of Virginia. The goal, as the magazine described it, is "to reframe American history" by starting the story in 1619 and "plac[ing] the consequences of slavery and the contributions of black Americans at the very center of the story we tell ourselves about who we are as a country."[3] The project uses the four-hundredth anniversary of the beginning of slavery in English North America as a moment "to tell our story truthfully" as it seeks to prove "the year 1619 is as important to the American story as 1776."[4]

If we begin the story of the United States in 1619, then attention to the enslavement of Black people becomes central to understanding how the nation formed. Slavery was not an aberration; it was at the center of the stories of the founders and the founding documents. And if slavery is given attention, then the stories also begin to focus on the people who fought against slavery and inequality. The centrality of Black people to the story of the United States becomes vivid when you start the story in 1619 and accept that the nation was not founded on equality of all people and that certain segments of the population had to bear more of the burden and do more of the labor to make that promise of equality real.

The stories people tell themselves matter. When those stories start and who those stories center as major characters matter, too. If you are not convinced by our shortened version, we encourage you to visit "The 1619 Project" and read the more complete story. Our ability to use the "art and power of words" to tell you a compelling story may have failed; stories, good stories, take time and space to tell. "The 1619 Project" takes the time and space to tell a more complete story of the nation: the story of the US people. And it is brutally well told.

Stories are everywhere. Stories, or narratives, inform people's personal lives. Think about the stories you tell with your families and friends about events in which you all participated. Those shared experiences and the stories about them help bond you as a family.

Narratives also inform public life. People often vote for candidates who have life stories they find particularly appealing. Newspapers, TV news shows, and internet sites are filled with narratives about the issues and personalities of the day. Often, when people think of stories in the news, they think of gossip about celebrities, but those stories are a small fraction of the stories in public discourse. People also tell stories about the effects of inadequate health care on individuals, the effects of tariffs on farmers, the impact of student debt on college graduates, and the history of the nation. These stories play an important role in framing the way members of the public remember what has happened. Narratives are an important way to understand the world in which you live.

Quite simply, narratives are rhetorical. In the next section, we describe the form and function of narrative. We then review four criteria used to judge narratives: aesthetics, authorial intent, empirical truth, and social truth. Throughout the chapter, we examine narratives at the micro level of the individual story and at the macro level of the overarching myths that structure a culture. Our goal is to help you understand how narratives function in all areas of civic life.

FORM AND FUNCTION OF NARRATIVES

Gerald Prince, a professor of romance languages, defines **narrative** as "*the representation of at least two real or fictive events or situations in a time sequence, neither of which presupposes or entails the other.*"[5] As representations, narratives are a form of symbolic action. They are referential, meaning they depict or describe events; they are not the events themselves. Prince's reference to at least two events emphasizes the temporal component of narratives: a story moves across time as events are related to each other. The events do not presuppose or require one another. A causal or logical relationship is not necessary for the two events to exist. Instead, the narrative itself develops the relationship between them.

To be a narrative, a rhetorical action must organize people's experiences by identifying relationships among events across time. Narratives serve as retrospectives.[6] They make sense of events of your life by placing them in relation to one another, thus imbuing them with significance.[7] Whatever people are telling a story about, however, "that past story wasn't so clean or inevitable while it was happening."[8] The choices people make when they tell stories—choices about characters, their roles, the action, the scene, how the events are ordered—are part of what makes the stories rhetorical.

Narratives have several important functions, including the formation of memory and the creation of a sense of cultural identity and community.

Forming Memory

Narratives form two types of memory: personal and public. They give people a personal sense of who they are as individuals with a history, as well as a public sense of who they are as members of a community with a history.

Personal memory is *the manner in which individuals remember their own pasts.* People recollect events from their daily lives as stories they keep in their own personal memories or share with others. They remember events through the narratives they tell and that are told about them. The ability to remember narratives seems almost innate within humans. Think for a moment about what you did yesterday. The way you remember the events is most likely a narrative (unless you keep an hour-by-hour record of your activities in a journal). As you think about your more distant past, the memories become even more grounded in narratives. What do you remember from your grade school days? Probably all that you remember are narratives: events that happened one day on the playground or on a particularly memorable birthday. These memories are based on the narrative you have created about that day. They certainly do not include everything from that day.

The narratives people remember are not mental videos of their pasts. Rather, people select which bits of information they will remember. Most daily experiences are rapidly forgotten. For instance, can you remember what clothes you wore last Thursday? Probably not—unless something happened to cause you to remember exactly what you wore that day. John, one author of this text, remembers exactly the clothing he wore one day in July 2014. He was supposed to meet with high school students who were thinking about attending the University of Northern Iowa, so he wore a white shirt with an emblem of the university mascot on it. Right before the meeting, John spilled coffee on the shirt. He remembers the white shirt with the university mascot emblem because it is an important part of the story. The spilled coffee would not have mattered as much if John were not meeting with potential students.

In this story, the clothing is important. It was chosen to provide a good image of the university, but the coffee stain probably sent a different message. The memory of this day is highly selective. John cannot recall what else happened, any other meetings, or other people from that day. He selectively remembers some events of the day because of their place in the context of a narrative. The story becomes memorable because it implicates many of the author's values. John likes to make a good first impression on strangers, especially those who might consider attending the university. The story also tells you something about the author: he is likely to spill coffee and is willing to let others know that.

Just as narratives can form and maintain the memories of individual people so, too, can they form and maintain the memories of collectives of people. Maurice Halbwachs coined the term **collective memory** to clarify that memory is not simply an individual process, but *a shared and constructed creation of a group or nation.*[9] For example, a nation maintains and constructs collective memory through the narratives it tells about its founding and development. Thus, "collective memory'—as a set of ideas, images, feelings about the past—is best located not in the minds of individuals, but in the resources they share."[10]

The members of a community often participate in retelling stories and developing a collective memory of a place. For example, in May 2008 the small town of New Hartford, Iowa (population 516), was hit by a mile-wide tornado with winds of 200 miles per hour. Two weeks later, to the day, the town was flooded after a storm moved through the area and dropped over 31 inches of rain in less than three days.[11] Almost all the homes, churches, and businesses, even the school, were damaged by either the tornado or the flood.[12] As soon as the floodwaters receded, citizens of the small town began cleaning up and rebuilding the school and the town. Students, teachers, and other residents of the school district all helped. By the beginning of the school year, just a few months later, the school reopened.

The experience is encapsulated in many stories people from New Hartford tell each other and outsiders. Even those who don't have a personal memory of the tornado and flood have, as part of their memory, the experience of resilience and rebuilding. The stories are important because they represent the pride the people have in their small town, their work ethic, and their resilience, and because the stories are an important part of their collective memory. As those stories were told and retold, they began to form a collective memory of the event, shared collectively even by those who may not have been present when it happened.

As discussed in chapter 2, **public memory** is *a particular type of collective memory that combines the memories of the dominant culture and fragments of the memories of marginalized groups, and that enables people to make sense of the past, present, and future.* Communication scholar Richard Morris explains that "public memory is perhaps best conceived as an *amalgam* of the current hegemonic bloc's cultural memory and bits and pieces of cultural memory that members of other cultures are able to preserve and protect."[13] Although a particular memory may become dominant (for example, the stories of Columbus's arrival in the Americas or of the nation's founders), bits and pieces of marginalized stories persist and can be used as the basis to challenge the dominant public memory (for example, indigenous people's stories of resistance to colonization as well as African Americans' stories about their work to abolish slavery and their fight to help the United States realize its ideal of democracy). Through narratives, public memory is formed, but different groups have more or less power to have their own versions of events remembered. To study stories is to study power.

Multiple stories of a single event might seem problematic or confusing, but a single story dominating understanding is really more so, given the complexity of the world and the diversity of its peoples. Nigerian novelist Chimamanda Ngozi Adichie describes "the danger of a single story." She explains that when people base their understandings of others on a single story, they deny the full humanity of those other people. If the only story you know of Africa is of catastrophe, famine, conflict, poverty, and disease, then you cannot see the ingenuity, passion, integrity, creativeness, vibrancy, and humanity of the people who, like Adichie, populate that continent. She explains that power and narratives are related: "How [stories] are told, who tells them, when they are told, how many stories are told, are really dependent on power. Power is the ability not just to tell the story of another person, but to make it the definitive story of that person."[14] In other words, the first step in trying to understand an event or people is not to find the definitive story, but to search for all the stories. What is recalled in public memory may not be everyone's story.

One of the most important narratives for a group is its origin story, the story of how the group was first formed. That story provides meaning for the group. In families, weddings and birthdays are celebrated yearly as origin stories. In the United States, people celebrate the Fourth of July as the birthday of the nation. Fourth of July celebrations include the story of the colonies' small army taking on the superior army of King George, which suggests to members of the culture that the United States and its people can overcome great difficulties when they work together.

Sociologist Barry Schwartz explains how origin stories function:

> The magnetism of social origins resides not simply in their priority and ordering power, but in the *meaning* of this priority and ordering power, as defined by later generations and in light of their own experiences, problems, and needs. While the object of commemoration is usually to be found in the past, the issue which motivates its selection and shaping is always to be found among the concerns of the present.[15]

In other words, a public comes to understand itself in the present by telling stories of its historical past. Such stories form public memory.

In the United States, most citizens know the origin narratives of the country, including Columbus's 1492 landing in the Americas, the Pilgrims' difficult first winter in 1620–1621, and the protesters who threw tea into Boston Harbor in 1773 to protest British taxation without representation. (The narrative of throwing tea into the Boston Harbor inspired the name of a more recent political movement, the Tea Party.) Many people also know the story of Patrick Henry justifying the Revolutionary War with a speech featuring the line: "Give me liberty or give me death."[16]

Other narratives are also part of the collective memory of the United States. Schoolchildren still learn stories about Abraham Lincoln, including the story that as a young store clerk, "Honest Abe" walked miles to return a few pennies to their rightful owner. Hollywood tells the story of Lincoln's success in the 2012 movie, *Lincoln*. Many people can recite stories of heroism in the World Wars, such as those retold in the 2019 film *1917*, which is about World War I, and the 2001 television miniseries *Band of Brothers*, which is about World War II. Each of these stories assists in creating public memory. But that memory is incomplete. It centers the experiences of Euro-American settler-colonists. It decenters the stories of how native peoples of the Americas were central to the colonists' survival, as well as stories about how Haudenosaunee (Iroquois) democratic practices shaped the democratic principles of the US Constitution. As Nikole Hannah-Jones argues in "The 1619 Project," it also decenters the story of how Black Americans are "foundational to the idea of American freedom" because over the centuries their work and advocacy for abolition, emancipation, civil rights, and voting rights "have been the perfecters of this democracy."[17]

Creating Culture and Community

Members of a society understand their nation and their place in it through the stories that are told about their nation. Political scientist Eloise Buker says that narratives, whether historical or imaginative, help "celebrate our great events, but they also allow us to explore new ways of living together."[18] Narratives create culture and community by teaching cultural values, explaining causality, and entertaining.

Teaching Cultural Values. Dominant narratives imbue a culture with a set of values. For example, decades after it occurred, people still tell stories about the D-Day invasion of Normandy on June 6, 1944. Filmmakers have produced more than twenty movies and documentaries about D-Day. Authors have written numerous books and articles about it. Very few of the stories stop with the end of the day. Instead, they move past the events of June 6 in order to give meaning to the day. The official home page of the US Army describes the impact of the invasion: "The D-Day cost was high—more than 9,000 Allied Soldiers were killed or wounded—but their sacrifice allowed more than 100,000 Soldiers to begin the slow, hard slog across Europe, to defeat Adolf Hitler's crack troops."[19] To mark the seventieth anniversary of the invasion, major TV networks followed veterans to Normandy to hear their tales of heroism.

Dominant US culture remembers and retells many stories that provide a basis for its values. Think of the narratives many schoolchildren read and the values that such stories teach. What value is taught in the story of "Honest Abe" returning a few pennies to their rightful owner? In the stories of the colonists' success in the Revolutionary War and US service members' success in the World Wars?

Stories told in popular culture teach values, regardless of whether the stories are grounded in real or fictitious events. The 2019 movie *Hustlers* is adapted from a *New York* magazine story about how, in the midst of the 2007–2008 financial crisis, strippers began stealing money from stock traders by drugging them and maxing out their credit cards, knowing the men could not report them for fear of revealing that they had been duped by strippers. Although the actions portrayed are clearly in a moral gray area, the movie teaches the value of women's friendship and challenges values that preserve corporate power. Unlike other movies where strippers are treated as background wallpaper, this movie foregrounded the women's complex characters and suggests that all people should be valued.

A particular form of narrative is **myth,** which communication scholar Martha Cooper as "*a dramatic vision that serves to organize everyday experience and give meaning to life.*"[20] Myths teach cultural values as they structure how you think about yourself, other people, society, and the world around you. According to feminist scholars Sonya Andermahr, Terry Lovell, and Carol Wolkowitz, a myth is a dramatic vision because it contains a story of conflict that is not about an actual event, but is "the imagined past of a culture"[21] that guides future action.

Myths organize life because they explain people's relationships to one another. Myths justify particular actions and hierarchies. Rhetorical critic V. William Balthrop argues that myths give meaning because they provide a "cultural image of perfection."[22] They enable cultures influenced by the Abrahamic religions (Christianity, Judaism, Islam) to visualize and understand what is good or evil, right or wrong. In such cultures, myths create a norm that the world is ordered and orderly. In contrast, First Nations traditions contain myths about tricksters, who show that disorder is the norm. There is no single indigenous word for trickster; each culture has its own name for the character.[23] Depending on the nation, the trickster takes the form of a raven (the Aleuts' Qanglaagix), a rabbit (the Penobscots' Ableegumooch), a coyote (the Arikaras' Chirich), or humanlike beings (the Ojibways' Nanabozho), but always the trickster is "timeless, universal, and indestructible" as it "eludes and disrupts all orders of things," thus making clear the "necessity of disorder."[24] Tricksters contain elements of both the "sacred and scatological, of culture hero and fool, in a single figure. Coyote steals, lies, and lusts and in the process shapes and endows the world as we know it."[25]

Myths also explain people's relationship to the world. For example, dance choreographer and scholar Kariamu Welsh and African American studies professor Molefi Kete Asante note that African American myths contain main agents who are "larger-than-life heroes and heroines" and whose stories are of "triumphs and victories" that demonstrate "control over circumstance as opposed to control over nature."[26] In contrast, settler-colonialist myths about the West often contain figures who control nature: think of lumberjack Paul Bunyan or cowboy Pecos Bill. Welsh and Asante explain that "myth is important as an organizing principle in the area of human discourse." Myths organize humans' relationships with each other and with the natural world.

Myths are ethereal. People may not be aware of their presence, especially when they are taken for granted as objective reality. If, as anthropologist Clifford Geertz argues, culture is a "system of inherited conceptions expressed in symbolic forms," then myths are one of the central symbolic forms because they "communicate, perpetuate, and develop knowledge about and attitudes toward life."[27]

According to Balthrop, the meanings contained in myths constitute the essence of the culture and represent that which is taken for granted, the point at which one cannot further explain the reasons for an action or a belief.[28]

Myths help people learn values and form beliefs through the dramatic telling of social lessons. They impart an identity to people who identify with the story. Myth is not the only symbolic form that maintains culture, but it is a central and distinctly symbolic one. Myth is a narrative form whose power does not rely on truth or falsity but on its appeal to a sense of social truth.

The melting pot myth (with its metaphor) has held particular power in the United States, where citizenship is defined by rights and responsibilities rather than by a particular ethnicity or birthplace. The melting pot myth offers a story to explain who the US people are. It valorizes giving up a person's individual cultural identity for the good of the nation. In this myth, citizenship is open to people of all races, but when one becomes a US citizen, all vestiges of one's earlier culture melt away.

This story of immigration and assimilation came into general usage in 1908 with the publication of Israel Zangwill's play, *The Melting Pot*. The myth emerged during industrialization, when the form and function of a melting pot were widely understood. A melting pot is a vessel that can withstand extremely high temperatures and not lose its shape, even as its contents are melted into an indistinguishable and fluid mass. When various ores and metals are added to the pot and mixed together, they form a substance stronger than the individual ingredients. The United States was the vessel, impermeable to the high temperatures caused by the pressures of immigration; within the United States, diverse peoples represented the ores and metals that would be fused together into a strong, homogenous mass.

Historian Amy Maria Kenyon describes one particularly telling dramatization of this myth as a ritual enactment of the narrative of citizenship. Henry Ford, the founder of Ford Motor Company and the key developer of modern assembly-line techniques, sought to integrate the company's workers, many of whom were immigrants, into US culture. In 1914, Ford instituted English courses, in which the first thing workers learned to say was: "I am a good American." At the end of the course, they would participate in a "melting pot" ceremony. Of this ceremony, historian Robert Lacey says,

> "Across the back of the stage was shown the hull and deck of an ocean
> steamship at Ellis Island," described one eyewitness to the graduation
> ceremony. A gangway led down from this ship and, in the dim light, a
> "picturesque figure" appeared at the top of the gangway, dressed in foreign
> costume and carrying his possessions wrapped, Dick Whittington–like,
> in a bundle tied to a stick over his shoulder. It was the first graduate of the
> after-hours language classes, and one by one the other graduates followed
> him down the gangway into "an immense cauldron across which was
> painted the sign *Ford English School Melting Pot*." Each successful graduate
> entered the Melting Pot in his foreign costume, carrying a sign indicating
> the country he had come from. But minutes later they all emerged from

the great cauldron "dressed in American clothes, faces eager with the stimulus of new opportunities. . . . Each man carried a small American flag in his hand."[29]

Kenyon describes this myth as creating a "cultural image of perfection": "the melting pot is the 'cooking up' of social identities, a fictional process that closes the circle by constant reference back to utopia, or rather to the myth of the American people as 'colorless' (i.e., White) blend of once-present, but now mercifully absent (albeit nostalgia-laden), manifestations of ethnic difference."[30] When a single myth becomes dominant in a culture, it often defines and delimits that culture. The myth of the melting pot influences definitions of what it means to be American, declares it is the responsibility of immigrants to assimilate, and makes the predominance of White culture seem normal. Even if you do not overtly think of the melting pot, it may influence your attitudes toward and beliefs about immigration.

Implying Causation. Because a narrative relies on a chronological telling of events, the event that happened first is often seen to be the cause of later events. Literary theorist Seymour Chatman maintains that all good narratives possess the elements of causality, or at least contingency.[31] If one event in the story did not cause another, then at least the events are related in such a way that they bring into being or evoke a particular situation.[32] Even when a narrative does not explicitly offer causal reasoning, the audience members will supply that reasoning as they listen to the story. For example, the National Museum of American History website describes the end of the Cold War this way:

> Throughout the 1980s, the Soviet Union fought an increasingly frustrating war in Afghanistan. At the same time, the Soviet economy faced the continuously escalating costs of the arms race. Dissent at home grew while the stagnant economy faltered under the combined burden. Attempted reforms at home left the Soviet Union unwilling to rebuff challenges to its control in Eastern Europe. During 1989 and 1990, the Berlin Wall came down, borders opened, and free elections ousted Communist regimes everywhere in eastern Europe. In late 1991 the Soviet Union itself dissolved into its component republics. With stunning speed, the Iron Curtain was lifted and the Cold War came to an end.[33]

Notice how this narrative provides several sets of events (protracted war in Afghanistan, weakened economy, arms race, and attempted reforms) and implicitly links them to the end of the Cold War. Nowhere in the paragraph are these events called "causes," but the suggestive power of the narrative format leads the reader to identify them as causing the end of the Cold War.

This is not to say the suggestion is wrong. Indeed, most historians would agree that at least some of these events helped bring the Cold War to an end, but the identification of the causal relationship is not always accurate. The **post hoc ergo propter hoc** fallacy is *a fallacy that occurs when reasoning takes the form of "after this therefore because of this."* For example, according to the

"Super Bowl Indicator," if a team from the old American Football League (now the American Football Conference) wins the Super Bowl, the stock market will decline the next year. Conversely, if a team from the old National Football League (now the National Football Conference) wins the Super Bowl, the stock market will rise during the next year.[34] Between 1967 and 2017, the indicator was correct forty out of fifty times (although from 2007 to 2017 it was only right 50 percent of the time).[35] Still, it's obvious that no causal relationship exists between who wins the Super Bowl and the future of the stock market. Students of rhetoric should scrutinize the implied causality in a narrative.

Engaging Interest. Narratives are interesting and enjoyable, even when they are about painful events. Even the scariest or saddest narratives rivet audiences' attention because they allow people to learn about the human condition. By hearing about how other people experienced pain and how they responded in the face of overwhelming circumstances, people learn about their own limits and potentials.

For example, in February 2021, a massive winter storm hit most of the United States. Texas was hit particularly hard by ice, snow, and prolonged freezing temperatures. Media reported the loss of life, the fact that Texas has its own electricity grid, and decisions not to weatherize the infrastructure to withstand such weather. To engage interest, though, media not only reported on why the event happened, but also what it meant to the people trying to live through days of arctic temperatures with no water or heat. CNN published one news report with the headline, "A volunteer fire department ran out of water during a fire. A man searched 8 hours for food. These are the stories of the Texas storm."[36] Stories of individual Texans captured attention because readers could identify with them. The stories brought human interest to a massive and complex disaster.

Listeners find narratives easier to follow than detailed observations or complex reasoning patterns. For example, consider the State of the Union addresses that presidents deliver. The purpose of the State of the Union address is to "recommend to [Congress's] Consideration such Measures as [the President] shall judge necessary and expedient."[37] Because a laundry list of initiatives will do little to hold audience attention or move the audience to support their proposals, presidents often incorporate stories of US citizens into their speeches. It has become traditional since Reagan's time to seat those people in the balcony of the House of Representatives.

In the 2013 State of the Union Address, President Barack Obama laid out a series of proposals to try to reduce gun violence, then told this story:

> One of those we lost was a young girl named Hadiya Pendleton. She was
> 15 years old. She loved Fig Newtons and lip gloss. She was a majorette.
> She was so good to her friends they all thought they were her best friend.
> Just three weeks ago, she was here, in Washington, with her classmates,
> performing for her country at my inauguration. And a week later, she
> was shot and killed in a Chicago park after school, just a mile away from
> my house.

> Hadiya's parents, Nate and Cleo, are in this chamber tonight, along
> with more than two dozen Americans whose lives have been torn apart
> by gun violence. They deserve a vote.[38]

Why would this story fit a State of the Union Address? The proposals that Obama had listed had few specific connections to people. He told the story to make real and immediate the need to act, for Congress to vote on gun and ammunition restrictions. A mere recitation of the statistics on gun violence in the United States would have been far less effective than the story of a young girl who was killed. Many listeners know fifteen-year-old girls; many know majorettes; and many know friendly teenagers. The audience can identify with the parents and their grief. The story is engaging because it adds and a sense of humanity to Obama's speech.

Vivacity is *a sense of immediacy or presence created through the use of descriptions, imagery, and colorful language that make an idea come alive.*[39] Vivacity is one way to create presence in verbal texts. Narratives with vivacity are more compelling because they are rhetorical acts that engage the imagination of the audience and allow the audience to see the humanity of the characters portrayed. The details in narratives help listeners understand the characters' actions and reactions.

Another example of vivacity can be found in Holocaust survivor Elie Wiesel's autobiographical book *Night,* originally published in the United States in 1960. Scholars of Holocaust literature maintain that Wiesel's book is powerful because it humanizes Holocaust victims and helps readers understand the life that people in Nazi concentration camps were forced to live.

The book opens with the story of Moishe the Beadle, a poor immigrant who was in the first wave of Jewish people deported from Sighet, Wiesel's hometown. After surviving the Gestapo's mass murder of everyone else on the train, Moishe returned to Sighet. Wiesel's story makes real the suffering that Moishe had witnessed:

> Day after day, night after night, he went from one Jewish house to the
> next, telling his story and that of Malka, the young girl who lay dying for
> three days, and that of Tobie, the tailor who begged to die before his sons
> were killed.
>
> Moishe was not the same. The joy in his eyes was gone. He no longer
> sang. He no longer mentioned either God or Kabbalah. He spoke only of
> what he had seen.[40]

The power of this story comes not from statistics about train cars full of Jewish people murdered by the Nazis, but from the detailed telling of one person's story and the effect on that one person of witnessing the murders. The details engage the reader: the reader experiences the horrors of the events Moishe saw. The power also comes from naming each person—Moishe, Malka, Tobie—and thus personalizing the event for the reader.

Narratives form personal and public memory. They create a sense of culture and community by teaching cultural values, implying causation, and engaging audiences. These functions are not neutral. Stories can be extremely entertaining yet contain questionable values, or inform public memory by creating a false causal relationship. Thus, it is important to develop skill in assessing narratives.

JUDGING NARRATIVES

Narratives are sometimes presented as in contrast to the objective world, which is grounded in the empirical or the factual. Some would argue that if humans could only understand the empirical world, narratives would no longer be needed. Theoretical physicist John D. Barrow describes this view:

> Modern physicists believe they have stumbled upon a key which leads
> to the mathematical secret at the heart of the Universe—a discovery that
> points towards a "Theory of Everything," a single all-embracing picture of
> all the laws of Nature from which the inevitability of all things seen must
> follow with unimpeachable logic. With possession of this cosmic Rosetta
> Stone, we could read the book of Nature in all tenses: we could understand
> all that was, is, and is to come.[41]

We believe such an accounting of the world is unlikely as well as uninspiring. Even Barrow wonders whether the goal tells more about understanding math than about understanding the natural world. Moreover, much of scientific and mathematical understanding, itself, is grounded in narratives. In medicine, for example, patients typically describe to their physicians, in narrative form, their symptoms and when they first noticed them. Often, they will even describe what they think led to the symptoms.

Physicians are learning the importance of narratives to diagnosis. Rita Charon, an MD with a PhD in English, became convinced of the need to understand narratives better while listening to patients. In her book *Narrative Medicine,* Charon proposes that health care providers use the "narrative skills of recognizing, absorbing, interpreting, and being moved by the stories of illness."[42] Through these skills, health care providers can understand patients better. Trisha Greenhalgh, of the Royal Free and University College London Medical School, and Brian Hurwitz, of the Imperial College School of Medicine at St. Mary's in London, write:

> We "dream in narrative, daydream in narrative, remember, anticipate,
> hope, despair, believe, doubt, plan, revise, criticise, construct, gossip, learn,
> hate and love by narrative." Episodes of sickness are important milestones
> in the enacted narratives of patients' lives. Thus, not only do we live by
> narrative but, often with our doctor or nurse as witness, we fall ill, get
> better, get worse, stay the same, and finally die by narrative too.[43]

Medicine is not the only part of the objective and empirical world that is understood better through narratives. Nate Silver, a statistician, rose to fame because of the accuracy of his predictions in two presidential elections. Silver had previously developed a system for predicting how baseball players would perform in coming seasons. His book, *The Signal and the Noise,* examines how predictions are made in a variety of fields, ranging from weather forecasting to global climate change, from baseball to online gambling.[44] The book is about mathematical modeling and why it works; yet, Silver uses a narrative approach to frame discussions. He talks about the personal histories of some of the people interviewed for the book. His work on mathematical modeling becomes more understandable when it is interwoven with narratives.

If narratives are important even to our understanding of medicine and mathematical modeling, skills in reading and interpreting narratives and the surrounding empirical and mathematical results are also important. Narratives can and should be judged on several levels: aesthetics, authorial intent, empirical truth, and social truth. Assessing narratives is more than a matter of awarding a thumbs-up or a thumbs-down. It is a complex process.

Aesthetics

The narratives most capable of affecting people are typically developed in a particular way. They hold the attention of listeners through two common characteristics: plot and character development.[45]

Plot is *the "chain of causation" of events within a narrative.*[46] It is critical because it relates the meaning of the events in the narrative by laying out a story line, which is also called the arc of the story. A good plot captures the audience's attention by providing a mechanism for understanding how the narrator selected the various events and connected them to each other. Most narratives rely on plots that reveal information in a chronological manner and provide the relevance or connectedness of the information as the narratives develop. Sometimes, a plot develops in a way that the connection of the events may not be understood until the end of the narrative. Some plots use flashbacks, a technique that violates strict chronology, but most unfold chronologically to develop the connections as the story progresses. For example, a presidential candidate's biography video shown at the national convention will probably present a chain of events that makes the candidate seem destined for the presidency.

Character development, a second characteristic of good narratives, is *the process of describing the actions of and relationships among actors within the story.*[47] Characters in narratives should conform to the behaviors that the audience expects. If those behaviors are antithetical to audience expectations, the audience is likely to dismiss the narrative. Consider the way politicians attempt to portray themselves in political campaigns: they try to develop an image that corresponds to what voters desire.

Donald Trump's campaign for president in 2016, for example, relied heavily on stories of Trump as a businessperson, in real estate and on television. In his speech accepting the Republican nomination, he declared "I have made billions of dollars in business making deals—now I'm going to make our country rich again."[48] He mentioned "deals" eleven times in this speech and claimed to be able to fix all the "worst," "unfair," "disastrous" deals of other policy makers by making better deals (hearkening back to *Trump: The Art of the Deal*, a book ghostwritten by Tony Schwartz for Trump in 2015).[49] In assessing this speech, rhetorical critic Robert C. Rowland notes that the stories created a persona, or image, for Trump. All this talk of deals meant that "Trump enacted the persona of a charismatic outsider by claiming that his business experience dealing with the corrupt elites uniquely qualified him to solve problems."[50] Rhetorical critic Bonnie Dow notes that Trump's character development was central to the campaign: "Trump was famous for making deals, exercising his will ('You're fired!'), and dominating every situation he encountered."[51] Dow believes that "one explanation for Trump's unexpected victory is that voters were attracted to who he was and how he presented himself as much as or more than what he said (although what he said enabled his persona in key ways)."[52]

Within any narrative, plots and characters may be more or less complex, depending, in part, on the audience's willingness to accept the story. People often reject simplistic accounts of complex events. On the evening of September 11, 2001, for example, a five-year-old commented that it was an "unlucky day." In one sense, the child's explanation was perfectly accurate: a day on which two planes crashed into the two main buildings of the World Trade Center, another into the Pentagon, and a fourth into a field near Shanksville, Pennsylvania, would have to be considered a bad day. But this narrative was not sufficiently complex to satisfy most adults' need to understand that event. The collapse of the buildings was not the result of random unlucky motion (say, an earthquake) but human action.[53] This is an extreme example, but it demonstrates how narratives lacking in complexity may be rejected.

An audience may also reject overly complex narratives. Conspiracy theories typically offer complex explanations for events by claiming that people worked together (conspired) to produce them.[54] Such theories seem to defy simpler explanations of events and are thus rejected by the vast majority of people as implausible. One conspiracy theory, for example, suggests that Barack Obama was actually born in Kenya and that his rise to the presidency was part of a plan to have a Muslim president of the United States. For that theory to be true, however, Obama's long-form birth certificate, along with newspaper announcements, would have to have been fabricated in Hawaii at the time of his birth. The people involved in the fabrications would have to have foreseen Obama's rise to the presidency even before he was born. They would have to have had the ability to ensure his acceptance into prestigious academic institutions to prepare for a career in politics. And they would have to have known that someone who had been a US Senator for less than a full term could be elected president.[55] Such a chain of events seems, at best, improbable. Unfortunately, conspiracy theories are also an example of people accepting complex stories because they are woven into a compelling narrative.

We don't want to sound like Goldilocks, but we would suggest that narrators seek the "just right" level of plot and character development. Detail in character and plot development is necessary to create vivacity and audience engagement, but adding detail just to entertain may detract from the story's ability to transmit values and memory. It is also important to remember that just because you have told an aesthetically appealing story, you have not necessarily told an ethically *good* story. Issues of truthfulness, truth, and social truth must be considered as well.

Authorial Intent

This judgment standard calls for a critic to determine whether the rhetor intends to make factual claims.[56] Authorial intent is not always easy to determine, but there is utility in asking: Is the author attempting to tell a story grounded in events that have actually occurred? Critics should begin by determining whether a rhetor claims to be reporting facts, as well as which parts of the narrative the rhetor claims are factual. Then the audience can assess the narrative's empirical truth.

When watching a news story on television, for example, an audience believes the story is based on actual events. During the summer of 2004, Dan Rather of CBS News reported that he had received a fax documenting that George W. Bush's service in the Alabama Air National Guard had been reduced through Bush's father's influence. When Rather reported the story, the intent was to report something that had happened, but it became increasingly apparent afterward that the fax had been forged.[57] Rather's story was called into question. Despite attempts to defend the overall accuracy of the narrative, Rather ultimately stepped down as *CBS Evening News* anchor, partially because of complaints about the inaccuracy of the facts of this story.

If you were to approach Stephen King about the movie based on the novel *The Shining*, however, and say, "Excuse me, Mr. King. But Danny never said 'Red rum. Red rum,'" King would probably look at you as if you were deranged. The difference between Dan Rather and Stephen King as authors is that one is attempting to base a story on factual events while the other is not. The difficulty occurs when a rhetor mixes the factual and the invented within a given story or speech. When a rhetor attempts to make a factual claim, that claim may be judged from an empirical standpoint.

The complexity of narratives lies in the different types of truth claims that they can advance. German philosopher Jürgen Habermas identified three worlds about which claims can be made: the objective world, the subjective world, and the intersubjective world. The test of validity of a claim about the objective world is truth: can the claim be empirically verified? The test of a claim about the subjective world is truthfulness: Does the person making the claim believe it to be true? The test of a claim about the intersubjective world is moral rightness: Can reasonable people, through communication, reach agreement about what is right?[58]

Empirical Truth

What is the relationship between narratives and empirical truth? On one level, audiences should be able to expect that a narrative meant to depict actual events will report the events as accurately as possible. Audiences should ask: Did those events really happen? A paradigmatic case of uncritical acceptance of a compelling personal narrative carrying serious risks is the US Congress's acceptance of the October 1990 testimony of Nayirah, a Kuwaiti teen who claimed to have witnessed Iraqi soldiers throwing babies out of incubators. President George H. W. Bush repeated the story at least ten times in the weeks following Nayirah's testimony, significantly contributing to Congress's willingness to go to war, but the story would later be determined to be false. In 1992, Nayirah was revealed to be a member of the Kuwaiti royal family, whose testimony was part of a well-funded public relations campaign to induce the US government to fight on behalf of Kuwait. In a segment critical of the campaign, *60 Minutes* noted that Nayirah's powerful story had "mesmerized the nation and the world."[59]

Narratives based on facts, especially historical facts, can teach lessons. The 1986 movie *Hoosiers,* based on factual events, teaches much the same moral that Aesop's fable of the tortoise and the hare teaches. The empirical truth of *Hoosiers* is that a basketball team from one of the smallest towns in Indiana can beat every team in the state if it works hard enough and has enough persistence. The 2007 movie *The Great Debaters* tells a similar story about a group of African American debaters from Wiley College in Texas, who defeated the national championship team from Harvard University by working hard, overcoming incredible racism, and speaking a truth learned not only from books but also from their own personal stories.[60] The 2012 movie *Lincoln,* based on Doris Kearns Goodwin's book *Team of Rivals: The Political Genius of Abraham Lincoln,*[61] tells a story that suggests Lincoln was successful because he included in his presidential cabinet some of the political figures who were most strongly opposed to his policies. The lesson from the film is that it is important to seek out diverse opinions. Alan Jackson's song "Where Were You when the World Stopped Turning," about people's reactions to the events of 9/11, shows that some responses to those events are personal rather than political, and argues that those personal emotions and responses are equally legitimate.

A complication to the empirical truth test is that rhetors may be completely truthful, telling events as known through their subjective experiences, yet not be telling the empirical truth. For example, witness misidentification in trials is the leading cause of wrongful convictions. The witnesses believe what they say and are trying to do the right thing, but still contribute to the incarceration of an innocent person.[62]

A second complication is that it is possible for a narrative to be based entirely on factual statements, and yet to be false as a whole. When children, teens, and politicians are suspected of doing things they should not be doing, they often base the narratives that explain their actions on numerous factual statements. How can the narrative then be false? First, it can omit significant details. At some point, for example, someone may have asked you, "What did you do last night?" You may have given a complete account. If you omitted some events, the story you told was not exactly false, but it was certainly not the most accurate account of what you did. Second, the narrative can incorporate the correct events and details, but fashion them in a way that leads to a false inference. For instance, the Internal Revenue Service (IRS) was involved in a scandal in late 2013 and 2014 because it investigated certain nonprofit groups that received contributions from people who were taking tax deductions for those contributions. It is illegal for such nonprofits to be political groups. The IRS certainly did target groups—everyone agreed on that—but there was significant disagreement about what types of groups were targeted. Republicans claimed the IRS only targeted conservative groups.[63] Democrats noted that the IRS also investigated groups associated with liberal and progressive issues.[64] Both sides based their claims on facts, but their conclusions were very different.

The IRS example points to an important conclusion about empirical truth. For any given set of facts, incompatible narratives may be created. Most historians recognize that there will always be evidence that is inconsistent with a given narrative. Philosopher Michael Krausz writes: "Yet, no matter how widely one might cast the evidential net—no matter how richly the evidence may be described—it may still underdetermine any one single interpretation."[65] Krausz's point is that the world is extremely complex. Narratives attempt to simplify that world so it can be understood, but the process of simplification means that no narrative can account for all the empirical facts that might be relevant. Narratives about Christopher Columbus's discovery of the Americas exemplify how incompatible narratives can be based on the same evidence. No one disputes the evidence historians use when discussing Columbus's voyages, but assessments vary, viewing Columbus as the "first American" for his willingness to explore,[66] as a genocidal imperialist,[67] or as lucky for becoming famous for being so lost that he thought Cuba was Japan.[68]

Facts never fully determine the validity of a narrative. Incompatible narratives may be derived from the same facts. People may even believe a narrative when they are confronted with evidence that is incompatible with it. At this point, you may fear a form of total relativism in which no narrative can make claims to any type of truth and all narratives are equally true, but such a conclusion would be incorrect. In judging competing narratives, says historian Peter Stansky, a historian must "take all the available 'facts,' which are often contradictory, and judge which interpretation [or narrative] of them may seem the most [right and] 'truthful.'"[69] The same is true of audiences.

Many narratives are possible, but not every possible narrative is equally correct; nor must every possible narrative be considered. Sometimes, writes histori-ographer Donald Spence, narratives are "just plain wrong."[70] Some, however, contain social truth. Narratives supporting the existence of the Easter Bunny, Santa Claus, and the Tooth Fairy lack an empirical basis. Most people over the age of ten know that they are just plain false, but the stories persist because of the social truths they possess. Young children who insist on the existence of Santa, the Easter Bunny, and the Tooth Fairy are being truthful.

One might argue that we should only believe stories if they are empirically true; if the events recounted in the story actually happened, in the order told; and if the actions were done by the people to whom they were attributed. This is the standard to which histories are held, but empirical truth as a standard for all stories, imaginative and historical, is not enough.

Social Truth

The relationship between narratives and truth is complex. Historians, literary critics, philosophers, and rhetoricians have argued about that relationship at least since the time of Aristotle. Mark Twain explained the relationship between imaginative fictional stories and historical stories: "Truth is stranger than fiction, but it is because Fiction is obliged to stick to possibilities; Truth isn't."[71] Twain's point is that fictional stories must be consistent with listeners' expectations of the way the world works. By conforming to expectations, fictional narratives can be quite effective and speak to social, if not empirical, truths. For example, Ta-Nehisi Coates's fantasy novel *The Water Dancer* is having a profound impact on readers. Why? Coates explains "Novels don't impact in the direct way," for instance, by spurring people to enact policies or march; nevertheless, "the novel and narrative is extremely powerful . . . the long term impact of books should not be underestimated."[72] Narratives enable political imagination when they remember pasts that seem impossible because they have been forgotten, as well as when they imagine futures made possible by reimagining the scene, the agents, and the actions that are possible.

We use the concept of **social truth** to refer to *those beliefs and values that do not refer to some objective reality, but to social reality—those beliefs about what is right that people have arrived at together.* An example of a social truth is that individual liberty is one of the United States' highest values; that it is guaranteed and should be preserved. The Declaration of Independence declares "all men are created equal, that they are endowed by their Creator with certain unalienable Rights, that among these are Life, Liberty and the pursuit of Happiness." The story behind this declaration is that a creator endowed "men" (at the time meaning men and not women, and only White men) with the right to liberty. The value of liberty is a social truth because it cannot be empirically proven or demonstrated. In fact, cultures that are more collectivist in nature are less likely to value liberty. The value of liberty is established primarily through communication, including the stories that are told within the culture to help establish that value. Through communication, people can reach an intersubjective idea (an idea they have accepted that is neither fixed and objective, nor totally random or completely subjective) of what is right. The nature of that intersubjective social truth is complex.

Narratives play an important role in forming memory and values. The social truth of a narrative does not necessarily lie in the objective truth of the individual statements that compose the narrative, but in the meaning of the story. Examples abound of fictive narratives that teach social truths. Aesop's fables are fictive narratives: Animals do not really talk; hares and tortoises do not really race; foxes do not really reject unreachable grapes as sour; and wolves do not really don sheep's clothing; but the fables teach lessons such as "slow and steady wins the race" and "appearances are deceptive." Moral philosophy professor Jonathan L. Gorman notes that "Plots have a truth, but it is not a scientific one"; it is "not a truth about the subject the plot purports to be about."[73] But social truths are important. Joan Didion's book *We Tell Ourselves Stories in Order to Live* summarizes the importance of narratives in its title.[74]

Even simple children's stories can teach important lessons. Dr. Seuss's *Oh, The Places You'll Go* has been read to and by children for more than three decades.[75] Its lesson is that all people have unique abilities and can succeed. The book is obviously fictional, but Dr. Seuss meant for it to teach a lesson to children and people of all ages.

As these examples show, the traditional distinction between fiction and nonfiction (or historical and imaginative) stories is too simple: the relationship between the two is highly complex. Like Mark Twain, scholars of narrative typically maintain that fiction actually must be truer than nonfiction, in the sense that the events must be believable. Nonfiction, on the other hand, ultimately resorts to the claim that the events actually happened. If someone had created a fictive narrative a few years ago of a man who was born of a Kenyan father and a Kansan mother, grew up in Hawaii and Indonesia, went to college at Columbia and Harvard, was elected to the Senate from Illinois in 2004, was elected president of the United States in 2008, won the Nobel Peace Prize in 2009, and was reelected in 2012, most people would have concluded that the story was fanciful and rejected it out of hand. However, these events comprise a portion of the narrative of Barack Obama.

Just as fictive narratives can be socially true, stories based in facts always have elements of fiction because the rhetors create the stories. The events recounted in narratives have no necessary starting or ending point. Narrators select the beginning and ending points according to the ideas they are trying to communicate. In addition, the rhetors determine what counts as facts.

Think about how different people tell different stories about the same person, event, or place, as is often the case with families. Filmmaker Sarah Polley, in the 2012 documentary *Stories We Tell*, set out to examine the stories her family tells of her deceased mother, Diane Polley. The people interviewed—Sarah's siblings; Sarah's father and Diane's husband; Sarah's biological father and Diane's distant, extramarital lover; and Diane's friends—all tell quite different stories. Some stories begin with meeting Diane; others before meeting her. They include different events, interpret the same events in different ways, and conclude very differently. Yet, each story claims to be true. Film critic Manohla Dargis notes that the differing stories are not an endorsement of relativism. Rather, the documentary tells stories from different perspectives. "Everyone has his or her memories . . . but most adhere to the communally accepted facts. . . . What matters . . . is how each person organizes those memories, with love, humor, regret, self-interest."[76] Dargis's point is that the narrators choose facts and frame those facts in ways that are consistent with their narratives. All narratives are not equally true, nor are narratives necessarily grounded in relativism, but our narratives must provide reasonable explanations of the facts.

Another example of competing narratives grounded in the same set of historical events is the debate over the effect of the New Deal in the 1930s. Looking at the same set of historical events, narratives differ about the impact of President Franklin Delano Roosevelt's economic policies. Traditionally, historians have held that the New Deal stimulated the economy. Historian William Edward Leuchtenburg's famous treatise on the New Deal argues that FDR's decisive policies ended the Great Depression.[77] Historian Burton W. Folsom, Jr., however, argues that the New Deal actually exacerbated it.[78] Both narratives are grounded in historical evidence, but each emphasizes different aspects of the historical record. Readers must evaluate each narrative on the basis of the historical evidence, plot, and character development it presents.

Sophisticated audiences evaluate the narratives they hear. As we discussed when we talked about social truth, audiences must be able to do two things. First, they must be able to assess which narratives are just plain wrong. Second, they must be able to employ standards that will assist them in determining which narratives are better, even in the face of multiple, incompatible narratives, all of which could be plausible.

Several aspects of narratives can help us assess their social truth claims: narrative fidelity, narrative probability, and the narrative's frame. These aspects are not at issue in evaluating the empirical or factual claims of the narrative, only in evaluating the social truth claims.

Narrative Fidelity and Narrative Probability.

Rhetorical critic and narrative theorist Walter Fisher identified two standards for evaluating narratives: narrative fidelity and narrative probability. **Narrative fidelity** asks *whether the events included in the story correspond to the audience's experiences and understanding of reality.*[79] This standard focuses on the external consistency of the story by asking people to look at "whether the stories they experience ring true with the stories they know to be true in their lives."[80] **Narrative probability** asks *the question "what constitutes a coherent story?"*[81] *or, more simply, does the story hang together?* This standard focuses on the internal consistency of the story, requiring people to look at the development of characters and plot, and asking whether the characters react the way we would expect people to react. Fisher writes, "Formal features are attributes of narrative probability: the consistency of characters and actions, the accommodation of auditors, and so on."[82] Narrative probability and fidelity can be used to judge both fiction and nonfiction.

A narrative should have both narrative fidelity and narrative probability, but it may have one and lack the other, or it may lack both. For example, one of the authors has a son who broke his arm. When the author asked how that happened, the son replied, "I was rollerblading in my friend's driveway. I was going slowly. I lost my balance and fell in the grass." The story lacked fidelity because the author knew people generally do not break their arms after falling on grass, because it is a forgiving surface. The story did not make sense internally because it was not probable that the athletically gifted son would fall when going slowly. Thus, the author suspected there was more to the story, and asked, "Were you going off a ramp?" The son coyly responded: "That part of the story has not come out yet."

Certain types of narratives may be more likely than others to exhibit strengths in either narrative fidelity or narrative probability. Narratives of trauma survivors, for instance, sometimes lack narrative probability (they might lack internal consistency because trauma, by definition, is unusual and extraordinary) while having a great deal of narrative fidelity (they report what actually happened). For example, one author of this book was once in a very bad van accident. His story about the accident is that he was sleeping, felt the van swerve, woke up, asked what was happening, was told a deer had run in front of the van, turned in his seat, and went back to sleep before being thrown from the van. Given the speed at which the accident would have happened, it does not seem likely that all those events took place during the accident. The story lacked narrative probability, but the passengers' injuries and the destroyed van give it narrative fidelity.

A story may be true and yet lack narrative fidelity. For example, Invisible Children is an organization seeking to "end the use of child soldiers in Joseph Kony's rebel war and restore Northern Uganda to peace and prosperity."[83] One difficulty the organization faces is that the stories of children being abducted and forced to serve as soldiers, while empirically true, lack narrative fidelity for many people in the United States, who find it difficult to understand that anyone would force children to fight to the death in a war. Consequently, Invisible Children has relied on activism, peaceful protests such as sit-ins, and videos. The videos, in particular, present stories with strong narrative probability.

Representative Anecdotes. A **representative anecdote** is *a narrative that summarizes a person, thing, or situation.* The concept, developed by Kenneth Burke, helps critics understand the appropriateness of the narrative.[84] If a narrative claims to speak to a social truth, then it should be representative of the social truth. Burke developed his notion of the representative anecdote as a response to the behaviorist argument, which dominated the first half of the twentieth century, that the world—even human behavior, as complex as it is—could eventually be understood through science and mathematics. Burke rejected such notions. His discussion of the representative anecdote borrows some of the language of the social sciences, but he redefines those terms for his own uses. Social scientists use the term "representative," for instance, to discuss how a sample should be drawn from a population. Burke writes of a representative anecdote: "*It must have scope. Yet it must also possess simplicity; in that it is broadly a reduction of the subject-matter.*"[85] For Burke, the issue was not whether the anecdote was statistically representative; rather, he believed that a single powerful anecdote could represent a complex human experience.

The representative anecdote is not subject to the tests of statistics and the social sciences. Rather than examining the statistical accuracy of the sample, for instance, Burke argues that an appropriate representative anecdote will contain, in a nutshell, the essence of the item being represented. Think about your family or the household in which you grew up. If someone were to ask you about the way you were raised or your family life, you might tell a story that would summarize or encapsulate your experiences. You would not tell your entire life history, but you might pick a moment from when you were five years old, or ten, or fifteen. It would not be representative from a social scientific perspective—indeed, the story might be about an atypical and unrepeated moment or event—but it would demonstrate the essence of your childhood to the listener.

This notion of the representative anecdote leads to two important criteria. First, the narrative must be relevant to the point being made, not simply interesting. Second, the narrative must capture or summarize the most important aspects of the subject it is meant to represent, even though it may not be typical of that subject. For instance, in the aftermath of the Sandy Hook Elementary School shootings, blogger David Waldman began a series on the progressive website Daily Kos about gun accidents. The initial post, "Today in GunFail News," grew into a weekly series[86] in which Waldman described press reports of gun accidents. These reports are representative anecdotes, although the stories are not typical, in a statistical sense, of what happens when people have guns in their homes or in their possession. People who have guns in their homes typically have the proper motives, Waldman concedes. They do not want to get involved in dangerous situations, nor do they want to use their guns. Most gun owners have the "best of intentions." Nevertheless, sometimes bad things happen and "often people die because of it. These are the stories you should think about every time you handle a weapon."[87] Waldman's stories are intended to show the dangers of guns in a way that a statistical analysis cannot.

Burke suggests that one way to test a narrative is by determining whether it is representative. When Waldman tells of the gun accidents each week, he is claiming that they are representative of the dangers of guns, regardless of how seldom such accidents occur.

Comic and Tragic Frames. The final aspect of a narrative that is useful in assessing its social truth claims is its frame, or narrative worldview. The frame of a narrative positions its audience to see the world and the people in it in a particular way.

We turn to Kenneth Burke's description of tragic and comic frames.[88] In general, a **comic frame** is *a viewpoint that would have you see others as mistaken rather than as evil*. If a person does something you perceive as wrong, then the solution is not to destroy the person, but to correct them. As part of recognizing the inherent fallibility of humanity, a comic frame would also induce you to ask whether you are as mistaken as those with whom you disagree. The comic orientation ultimately asks for humility, not in the face of some higher power, but in the face of the human condition.

In contrast, the **tragic frame** is *a viewpoint that would have you see others as vicious and evil rather than as mistaken*. Because "evil" implies that a person has an inherent defect, correction is not possible as a solution. Destruction is the only solution to a wrong action, the only way to rid the world of evil. The tragic frame also induces humility, but only because if you become too arrogant, a higher power will put you in your place. As Burke explains, the tragic "frame of acceptance admonished one to 'resign' [oneself] to a sense of [one's] limitations."[89]

Imagine, for example, that a friend passes you in the hallway but does not say "Hi." With friends, people tend to operate in a comic frame, creating a story to explain the event that assumes the best of them. You might construct a story containing the explanation that your friend was probably having a bad day, or was really busy and may not have seen you. Your friend did not intentionally snub you, but instead made a mistake, a mistake you are just as likely to make in similar circumstances. In contrast, imagine that someone you do not really like passes you in the hallway and does not say "Hi." In this case, you might operate in a tragic frame and construct a story that attributes pernicious motives to the person. You might conclude that the person was being rude, snubbed you, intentionally ignored you, or was just being vicious. Your story assumes the worst of the person, even though the action was the same as your friend's. The point of the comic frame is to induce you to give people the benefit of the doubt, to think about the reasons they might take actions and not immediately attribute malicious motives to them. As Burke explains: "Like tragedy, comedy warns against the dangers of pride, but its emphasis shifts from *crime* to *stupidity*."[90]

Highlighting the differences between the comic and tragic frames in terms of meanings, attitudes, and characters, Burke concludes that a comic frame offers the most humane equipment for living: "The progress of humane enlightenment can go no further than in picturing people not as *vicious,* but as *mistaken*. When you add that people are *necessarily* mistaken, . . . you complete the comic circle, returning again to the lesson of humility that underlies great tragedy."[91] The comic frame is preferable because it "should enable people *to be observers of themselves, while acting*. Its ultimate would not be *passiveness,* but *maximum consciousness.* One would 'transcend' [oneself] by noting [one's] own foibles."[92] In other words, a key characteristic of the comic frame is self-reflexivity, meaning that you would turn whatever criticism you lodge against someone else back against yourself to see whether you engage in the same action or had contributed to the other person's mistaken deeds.

The comic frame might sound as though it involves frivolity or comedy, but that is not the case. The comic is no less serious than the tragic. Religious studies professor John Morreall explains: "Comedy is not 'time out' from the world; rather it provides another perspective on the world, a perspective no less true than the tragic perspective."[93] Frames structure responses to events in the world. If you operate in the tragic frame, you tend to construct stories about evil, which must be destroyed. If you operate in the comic frame, you tend to construct stories of mistakes from which everyone can learn. In a comic frame, disagreement is a sign that someone is mistaken, and you are just as likely as the other person to be mistaken. In a tragic frame, a disagreement is usually seen as evidence that another person is being vicious, if not evil.

As Burke constantly reminds us, a name for something often contains within it an attitude toward that thing and, thus, also contains "cues of behavior."[94] Thus, how you name someone else is influenced by your frame, and that the name influences the actions toward the other person. As Burke explains, "Call a [person] a villain, and you have the choice of either attacking or cringing. Call [them] mistaken, and you invite yourself to attempt setting [them] right. Contemporary exasperations make us prefer the tragic (sometimes melodramatic) names of 'villain' and 'hero' to the comic names of 'tricked' and 'intelligent.'"[95] As you might expect, the First Nations trickster tales we described earlier fit under the comic frame.

When Burke was writing, "contemporary" meant 1937. The preceding years had seen the United States emerging from the Great Depression; Japan leaving the League of Nations; Adolf Hitler coming to power in Germany, stripping German Jews of their citizenship rights, and creating with Mussolini the Rome-Berlin Axis; Italy invading Abyssinia (Ethiopia); the Spanish Civil War breaking out; and

King Edward VIII's abdication rocking Great Britain. Still, Burke's comment remains apt over seventy years later.

The 1990s through the current time saw a host of events that appear to be the handiwork of villains and that are often rhetorically presented as evidence of evil in the world. In April 1999, a *New York Times* editorial said the mass shooting at "Columbine . . . was about evil."[96] After another mass shooting in April 2007, Columnist Cal Thomas remarked, "My prayers are with the Virginia Tech community that had this evil unleashed upon them."[97] In May 2014, when a young man opened fire in Isla Vista, California, killing six people and injuring thirteen before killing himself, a commentator described the shooter as "a narcissistic, evil man whose sex desires got in the way of his humanity."[98] In June 2016, President Obama described the Orlando nightclub mass shooting as "an evil, hateful act."[99] In October 2017, President Trump described the Las Vegas mass shooting as "an act of pure evil."[100] In February 2018, Florida Governor Rick Scott described the Parkland high school mass shooting as "just absolutely pure evil."[101]

Rhetoric about the war on terror has caused communication scholars to consider the invocation of evil. President George W. Bush's speech on the evening of September 11, 2001, described the acts of that day as evil, declaring: "Thousands of lives were suddenly ended by evil, despicable acts of terror. . . . Today our nation saw evil, the very worst of human nature. . . . The search is underway for those who were behind these evil acts."[102] From that evening on, every speech Bush delivered about the events of September 11 would refer to "evil." Not only would the term "evil" be used to describe the actions (for example, "evil, despicable acts of terror"), evil itself would become an entity. His address from the Cabinet Room on September 12 concluded, "This will be a monumental struggle of good versus evil, but good will prevail."[103] His remarks on September 14, during a National Day of Prayer and Remembrance ceremony, used the tragic frame, asserting that evil cannot be corrected, but must be obliterated: "Our responsibility to history is already clear: to answer these attacks and rid the world of evil."[104] Bush would eventually expand the scope of "evil" to apply to more than those who perpetrated 9/11. His January 2002 State of the Union address declared that the countries of Iran, Iraq, and North Korea "constitute an axis of evil." Toward the conclusion of the speech, Bush said, "We've come to know truths that we will never question: evil is real, and it must be opposed."[105]

Despite Bush's invocation of evil as a verifiable fact, the reality is that "evil" is an evaluative word, not a statement of fact.[106] Many political science and communication scholars have discussed Bush's use of the word. Political science journals such as *International Affairs* and communication studies journals such as *Rhetoric and Public Affairs* published special issues exploring "how 'evil' is produced, deployed, used, and misused in public discourse."[107]

Our point is not that tragedies do not happen. They do happen, in part because people operate in a tragic frame. Even in the face of tragedy, however, a comic frame may be more humane. When an act of violence occurs, do not assume that locking up the person who committed it will end all violence. Instead, ask: What have I done to contribute to a world in which tragedies occur; and how can I change the world—the institutional structures, the culture, the rhetorical formations—so that such acts are less likely to happen again?

CONCLUSION

Narrative, in the most basic sense, places two or more events in a time sequence. The human instinct to structure thinking and communication sequentially has several ramifications for rhetoric. The narrative structure leads audiences to perceive causation, helps them to remember, and entertains them. Sometimes, because these functions of narratives are so powerful, audiences are more susceptible to accepting narratives that are wrong, in either the factual or ethical sense.

It is vital for members of an audience to understand what the narrative is teaching about the nature of living through its character development and structure. As a member of an audience, however, you also must remain vigilant in applying the standards for evaluating narratives.

Narratives, the stories people tell each other, are central to civic life. They maintain public memory and teach cultural values. They are part of the warp and woof that holds the fabric of civic life together. They help place people in relation to one another, and to the history of the group, the nation, and the culture. Even as stories aid in memory, however, they can induce forgetting. One must resist the allure of the simple story or the single story.

DISCUSSION QUESTIONS

1. Identify a story that members of your family tell over and over. Why is that story repeated? What does it tell you about your family's values? Use the standards identified in this chapter to judge the narrative.
2. Think about your favorite superhero. How does the superhero's origin story influence your understanding of the character?
3. Novels and songs often tell narratives that affect people's lives and values. Identify a novel or song that has affected you. Why did it have such an effect on you?
4. People often describe TV news coverage and newspaper articles as "stories." Given the definition of narrative in this chapter, are they stories? Why?
5. Pick a current controversy on your campus or in your state or nation. Describe it, using the comic frame and the tragic frame.

RECOMMENDED READINGS

Braden, Waldo W. "Myths in Rhetorical Context." *The Southern Speech Communication Journal* 40 (Winter 1975): 113–126.

Fisher, Walter R. "Narration as a Human Communication Paradigm: The Case of Public Moral Argument." *Communication Monographs* 51 (1984): 1–22.

Rowland, Robert C., and Kirsten Theye. "The Symbolic DNA of Terrorism." *Communication Monographs* 75, no. 1 (March 2008), 52–85.

ENDNOTES

1 Alfred J. Andrea, "History as Story," *The Historian* 54, no. 1 (Autumn 1991), 183.

2 Terri Hanson, "How the Iroquois Great Law of Peace Shaped U.S. Democracy," PBS, December 13, 2018, https://www.pbs.org/native-america/blogs/native-voices/how -the-iroquois-great-law-of-peace-shaped-us-democracy/.

3 Jake Silverstein, "Editor's Note," "The 1619 Project," *New York Times Magazine,* August 18, 2019, https://pulitzercenter.org/sites/default/files/full_issue_of_the_1619 _project.pdf.

4 Nikole Hannah-Jones, "The 1619 Project," August 14, 2019, https://www.nytimes.com /interactive/2019/08/14/magazine/black-history-american-democracy.html.

5 Gerald Prince, *Narratology: The Form and Functioning of Narrative* (New York: Mouton, 1982), 4, italics added.

6 J. B. Schneewind, "Virtue, Narrative, and Community: MacIntyre and Morality," *Journal of Philosophy* 79 (1982): 659.

7 Barbara DeConcini, *Narrative Remembering* (Lanham, MD: University Press of America, 1990), 112.

8 Jennifer Garvey Berger, *Unlocking Leadership Mindtraps* (Stanford, CA: Stanford University Press, 2019), 17.

9 Maurice Halbwachs, *On Collective Memory* (Chicago: University of Chicago Press, 1992).

10 Iwona Irwin-Zarecka, *Frames of Remembrance: The Dynamics of Collective Memory* (New Brunswick, NJ: Transaction, 1994), 4.

11 Eilene Guy, "American Red Cross Stands Up for Iowa Tornado, Flood Victims," *ReliefWeb,* July 16, 2008, http://reliefweb.int/report/united-states-america/american -red-cross-stands-iowa-tornado-flood-victims.

12 Josh Hinkle, "Floods Ravage New Hartford Weeks after Deadly Tornado," KCRG.com, June 9, 2008, http://www.kcrg.com/news/local/19684209.html.

13 Richard Morris, *Sinners, Lovers, and Heroes* (Albany: State University of New York Press, 1997), 26.

14 Chimamanda Ngozi Adichie, "The Danger of a Single Story," TEDGlobal 2009, July 2009, http://www.ted.com/talks/chimamanda_adichie_the_danger_of_a _single_story#t-584723.

15 Barry Schwartz, "The Social Context of Commemoration: A Study in Collective Memory," *Social Forces* 61 (1982): 395.

16 Patrick Henry, "Give Me Liberty or Give Me Death," March 23, 1775, at Henrico Parish Church, Richmond, Virginia, Second Virginia Convention, http://www.americanrhetoric.com/speeches/patrickhenrygivemeliberty.html.

17 Hannah-Jones, "The 1619 Project."

18 Eloise Buker, *Politics through a Looking-Glass: Understanding Political Cultures through a Structuralist Interpretation of Narratives* (New York: Greenwood, 1987), 1.

19 US Army, "D-Day: June 6, 1944," accessed September 6, 2010, http://www.army.mil/d-day.

20 Martha Cooper, *Analyzing Public Discourse* (Prospect Heights, IL: Waveland, 1989), 161.

21 Sonya Andermahr, Terry Lovell, and Carol Wolkowitz, *A Glossary of Feminist Theory* (New York: Oxford University Press, 2000), 174.

22 V. William Balthrop, "Culture, Myth, and Ideology as Public Argument: An Interpretation of the Ascent and Demise of 'Southern Culture,'" *Communication Monographs* 51 (December 1984), 341.

[23] Shannon Thunderbird, "Art and Magic of Indigenous Storytelling," accessed January 2, 2008, at http://www.shannonthunderbird.com/art_of_indigenous_storytelling.htm. See also Lawrence William Gross, "The Comic Vision of Anishinaabe Culture and Religion," *The American Indian Quarterly* 26, no. 3 (Summer 2002): 436–459.

[24] Barbara Babcock and Jay Cox, "The Native American Trickster," in *Handbook of Native American Literature*, ed. Andrew Wiget (New York: Garland, 1996), 99.

[25] Babcock and Cox, "The Native American Trickster," 100.

[26] Kariamu Welsh and Molefi Kete Asante, "Myth: The Communication Dimension to the African American Mind," *Journal of Black Studies* 11, no. 4 (1981): 388–389.

[27] Clifford Geertz, *The Interpretation of Cultures* (New York: Basic Books, 1973), 48, 89.

[28] Balthrop, "Culture, Myth, and Ideology," 342.

[29] Robert Lacey, *Ford: The Men and the Machine* (New York: Little, Brown, 1986), 126.

[30] Amy Maria Kenyon, *Dreaming Suburbia: Detroit and the Production of Postwar Space and Culture* (Detroit: Wayne State University Press, 2004), 126.

[31] Seymour Chatman, "Towards a Theory of Narrative," *New Literary History* 6 (1975): 318.

[32] Seymour Chatman, *Coming to Terms: The Rhetoric of Narrative in Fiction and Film* (New York: Cornell University Press, 1990), 9.

[33] National Museum of American History, "Cold War Timeline: The End of the Cold War," 2000, http://americanhistory.si.edu/subs/history/timeline/end.

[34] "The Super Bowl Indicator," Snopes.com, April 15, 2011, http://www.snopes.com/business/bank/superbowl.asp.

[35] Will Kenton, "Super Bowl Indicator," *Investopedia,* January 24, 2019, https://www.investopedia.com/terms/s/superbowlindicator.asp.

[36] Amir Vera, Paul P. Murphy, and Alisha Ebrahimji, "A Volunteer Fire Department Ran Out of Water during a Fire," CNN (February 18, 2021), https://www.cnn.com/2021/02/17/us/texas-winter-storm-vignettes-trnd/index.html.

[37] US Constitution, Article II, Section 2.

[38] Barack Obama, "Remarks by the President in the State of the Union Address," February 12, 2013, http://www.whitehouse.gov/the-press-office/2013/02/12/remarks-president-state-union-address.

[39] George Campbell, *The Philosophy of Rhetoric* (Edinburgh, Scotland: George Ramsey, 1808; Google Books), 163–165.

[40] Elie Wiesel, *Night,* rev. ed. (New York: Hill and Wang, 2006), 7.

[41] John D. Barrow, *New Theories of Everything,* 2nd ed. (Oxford, UK: Oxford University Press, 2007), 1–2, http://site.ebrary.com/lib/rodlibrary/docDetail.action?docID=10183335.

[42] Rita Charon, *Narrative Medicine* (New York: Oxford University Press, 2006), 4.

[43] Trisha Greenhalgh and Brian Hurwitz, "Why Study Narrative?" The BMJ, 1999, http://www.bmj.com/content/318/7175/48.1?variant=full-text. Internal quotation is attributed to B. Hardy, as quoted in G. Widdershoven, "The Story of Life: Hermeneutic Perspectives on the Relationship between Narrative and Life History, in The Narrative Study of Lives, ed. R. Josselson and A. Lieblich (London: Sage, 1993).

[44] Nate Silver, *The Signal and the Noise: Why So Many Predictions Fail—But Some Don't* (New York: Penguin, 2012).

[45] Although most scholarly works devoted to narratives identify a number of additional characteristics, such as narrator and setting, the two most important are plot and character development. See, for instance, Paul Cobley, *Narrative* (London: Routledge, 2001).

[46] Cobley, *Narrative,* 239, italics added.

47 Ronald Jacobs, "Narrative, Civil Society and Public Sphere," in *Lines of Narrative: Psychological Perspectives,* ed. Molly Andrews, Shelley Day Sclater, Corinne Squire, and Amal Treacher, 18–35 (New York: Routledge, 2000).

48 "Full Text: Donald Trump 2016 RNC Draft Speech Transcript," *Politico,* July 21, 2016, https://www.politico.com/story/2016/07/full-transcript-donald-trump-nomination -acceptance-speech-at-rnc-225974.

49 Donald Trump, "Full Text."

50 Robert C. Rowland, "The Populist and Nationalist Roots of Trump's Rhetoric," *Rhetoric & Public Affairs* 22, no. 3 (2019): 343–388, 364.

51 Bonnie J. Dow, "Taking Trump Seriously: Persona and Presidential Politics in 2016," *Women's Studies in Communication* 40, no. 2 (2017): 136–139.

52 Dow, "Taking Trump Seriously."

53 Robert C. Rowland and Kirsten Theye, "The Symbolic DNA of Terrorism," *Communication Monographs* 75, no. 1 (March 2008): 52–85.

54 G. Thomas Goodnight and John Poulakos, "Conspiracy Rhetoric: From Pragmatism to Fantasy in Public Discourse," *Western Journal of Speech Communication* 45, no. 4 (Fall 1981): 299–316.

55 Robert Schlesinger, "Obama's Birth Certificate Release Won't End Conspiracy Theories," *US News & World Report,* April 27, 2011, http://www.usnews.com/opinion/blogs/robert-schlesinger/2011/04/27/obamas -birth-certificate-wont-end-conspiracy-theories.

56 This standard is derived partially from the work of John R. Searle, "The Logical Status of Fictional Discourse," *New Literary History* 6 (1975): 319–332.

57 William Safire, "First, Find the Forger," *New York Times,* September 22, 2004, http://query.nytimes.com/gst/fullpage.html?res =9A02E5DE1339F931A1575AC0A9629C8B63.

58 Jürgen Habermas, *Reason and the Rationalization of Society,* vol. 1, *The Theory of Communicative Action* (Boston: Beacon, 1984).

59 Morley Safer, "Iraqis Stealing Incubators from Babies May Have Been a Fraud," *60 Minutes,* January 19, 1992, LexisNexis: CBS News Transcripts.

60 This movie illustrates how historical narratives can be changed to achieve narrative truth. Although the movie depicts a debate between Wiley and Harvard, the debate that actually occurred was between Wiley and the University of Southern California, the national championship team in 1930.

61 Doris Kearns Goodwin, *Team of Rivals: The Political Genius of Abraham Lincoln* (New York: Simon & Schuster, 2005).

62 See Elizabeth Loftus and Katherine Ketcham, *Witness for the Defense* (New York: St. Martin's, 1991), reprinted at http://www.pbs.org/wgbh/pages/frontline/shows /dna/photos/eye/text_06.html as part of *Frontline,* "What Jennifer Saw," 1997, http://www.pbs.org/wgbh/pages/frontline/shows/dna.

63 John Hayward, "House GOP Report: The IRS Did Not Target Progressive Groups," *Human Events,* April 7, 2014, http://humanevents.com/2014/04/07/ house-gop-report-the-irs-did-not-target-progressive-groups.

64 Abby Ohlheiser, "New Documents Show the IRS Targeted 'Progressive' and 'Tea Party' Groups for Extra Scrutiny," *The Wire,* April 23, 2014, http://www.thewire.com /politics/2014/04/new-documents-show-the-irs-targeted-progressive-and-tea-party -groups-for-extra-scrutiny/361125.

65 Michael Krausz, *Rightness and Reasons: Interpretation in Cultural Practices* (Ithaca, NY: Cornell University Press, 1993), 47.

66 Samuel Eliot Morison, *Admiral of the Ocean Sea: A Life of Christopher Columbus* (Boston: Little, Brown, 1942).

67 Noam Chomsky, *Year 501: The Conquest Continues* (Boston: South End, 1993).

68 Helen Wallis, "What Columbus Knew," *History Today* (May 1992): 17–23.

69 Peter Stansky, "The Crumbling Frontiers of History or History and Biography: Some Personal Remarks," *Pacific Historical Review* 59 (1990): 6.

70 Donald Spence, "Saying Good-Bye to Historical Truth," *Philosophy of the Social Sciences* 21 (1991): 247.

71 Mark Twain, *Following the Equator: A Journey around the World Part 2* (Hartford, CT: American, 1897), 156.

72 "Ta-Nehisi Coates on His Debut Novel," NPR, October 1, 2019, https://www.npr.org /2019/10/01/766075978/ta-nehisi-coates-on-his-debut-novel.

73 J. L. Gorman, review of *Writing History,* by Paul Veyne, *History and Theory* 26 (1987): 99–114, 110, 113.

74 Joan Didion, *We Tell Ourselves Stories in Order to Live* (New York: Knopf, 2006).

75 Dr. Seuss, *Oh, The Places You'll Go* (New York: Random House, 1990).

76 Manohla Dargis, "Family Opens Its Diary, with Mother as Subject," *New York Times,* May 9, 2013, http://www.nytimes.com/2013/05/10/movies/stories-we-tell-written -and-directed-by-sarah-polley.html.

77 William Edward Leuchtenburg, *Franklin D. Roosevelt and the New Deal, 1932–1940* (New York: Harper and Row, 1963).

78 Burton W. Folsom, Jr., *New Deal or Raw Deal: How FDR's Economic Legacy Has Damaged America* (New York: Threshold, 2008).

79 Walter Fisher, "Narration as a Human Communication Paradigm: The Case of Public Moral Argument," *Communication Monographs* 51 (1984): 8.

80 Fisher, "Narration," 8.

81 Fisher, "Narration," 8, italics added.

82 Fisher, "Narration," 16.

83 Invisible Children, http://www.invisiblechildren.com/home.php.

84 Kenneth Burke, *A Grammar of Motives,* rev. ed. (Berkeley, CA: University of California Press, 1945 and 1969), esp. part 3. For a detailed description of this standard, see Arnie Madsen, "Burke's Representative Anecdote as a Critical Method," in *Extensions of the Burkeian System,* ed. James W. Chesebro, 208–229 (Tuscaloosa: University of Alabama Press, 1993).

85 Burke, *A Grammar of Motives,* 60.

86 David Waldman, "Today in GunFail News," DailyKos.com, January 19, 2013, http://www.dailykos.com/story/2013/01/19/1180131/-Today-in-GunFail-News.

87 Waldman, "Today in GunFail News."

88 Kenneth Burke, *Attitudes toward History,* 3rd ed. (Berkeley: University of California Press, 1937 and 1984).

89 Burke, *Attitudes toward History,* 39.

90 Burke, *Attitudes toward History,* 41.

91 Burke, *Attitudes toward History,* 41.

92 Burke, *Attitudes toward History,* 171.

93 John Morreall, *Comedy, Tragedy, and Religion* (Albany: State University of New York Press, 1999), 3.

94 Burke, *Attitudes toward History,* 4.

95 Burke, *Attitudes toward History,* 4–5.

96 Alan Wolfe, "Littleton Takes the Blame," *New York Times,* May 2, 1999.

[97] In Bob Beckel and Cal Thomas, "What about the Guns?" *USA Today,* April 19, 2007.

[98] Joel Mathis, "Can 'Culture' Explain the Isla Vista Shootings?" *Desert Sun* (Palm Springs, CA), May 30, 2014, http://www.desertsun.com/story/opinion/columnists/2014/05/31/red-blue-america-isla-vista-shooting/9803497.

[99] Quoted in Halimah Abdullah and Erik Ortiz, "President Obama: Nation and Orlando 'Shaken by an Evil, Hateful Act,'" NBC News, June 16, 2016, https://www.nbcnews.com/storyline/orlando-nightclub-massacre/president-obama-traveling-orlando-stand-solidarity-after-shooting-n593551.

[100] Quoted in Christina Wilkie, "Trump: Las Vegas Shooting 'Was an Act of Pure Evil,'" CNBC, October 2, 2017, https://www.cnbc.com/2017/10/02/trump-las-vegas-shooting-was-an-act-of-pure-evil.html.

[101] Quoted in Elizabeth Chuck, Alex Johnson, and Corky Siemasko, "17 Killed in Mass Shooting at High School in Parkland, Florida," NBC News, February 14, 2018, https://www.nbcnews.com/news/us-news/police-respond-shooting-parkland-florida-high-school-n848101.

[102] George W. Bush, "9/11 Address to the Nation: A Great People Has Been Moved to Defend a Great Nation," September 11, 2001, http://www.americanrhetoric.com/speeches/gwbush911addresstothenation.htm.

[103] George W. Bush, "The Deliberate and Deadly Attacks . . . Were Acts of War," September 12, 2001, http://www.americanrhetoric.com/speeches/gwbush911cabinetroomaddress.htm.

[104] George W. Bush, "Remarks at the National Day of Prayer and Remembrance," September 14, 2001, http://www.americanrhetoric.com/speeches/gwbush911prayer&memorialaddress.htm.

[105] George W. Bush, "State of the Union Address," January 29, 2002, http://www.whitehouse.gov/news/releases/2002/01/20020129-11.html.

[106] William Casebeer, "Knowing Evil when You See It: Uses for the Rhetoric of Evil in International Relations," *International Relations* 18, no. 4 (2004): 441–451.

[107] Dana L. Cloud, "Introduction: Evil in the Agora," *Rhetoric & Public Affairs* 6, no. 3 (2003), 509.

Part III

Generators of Symbolic Action

Chapter 7
Rhetors

On June 25, 2013, Wendy Davis, a Texas state senator, engaged in an eleven-hour-long filibuster on the floor of the Texas Senate Chamber.[1] Speaking from 11:18 a.m. to 10:07 p.m., Davis sought to stop passage of Senate Bill 5 (SB 5), a law that would create additional restrictions on abortion access and likely result in closing thirty-seven of the forty-two Texas clinics that provide abortions as part of their services.[2] During a filibuster, Texas Senate rules prohibit a person from eating, drinking, or having a bathroom break, and require that person to stand when speaking and confine "remarks to the bill before the Senate."[3] If ruled out of order three times, the senator must yield the floor and the filibuster ends.

To stop the vote on SB 5, Davis had planned to speak until midnight, the end of that special legislative session. She turned to Twitter to declare her intention to speak for the women of Texas even if the legislature was unwilling to listen to women. Davis, and people around the nation, began using #SB5 and #txleg to allow Twitter users to follow the filibuster.[4] As Davis prepared to speak for up to thirteen hours, she asked people following the event on social media (for example, Twitter and Davis's website) to provide crowdsourced stories to share.[5] They did so. One commentator noted, "The internet was hugely involved in Davis's effort, with thousands of testimonials pouring in through her website."[6] Davis's filibuster included newspaper articles, seven statements from medical professionals and organizations, sixty-two statements from her constituents (fifty-four from women), and lengthy exchanges with other senators. Davis viewed her filibuster as a collective work relying on the words of Texans to oppose the Texas legislature's action.[7]

Over 200,000 people watched the filibuster on *The Texas Tribune*'s YouTube live stream.[8] People who did not watch could access the filibuster in 140-character tweeted fragments from people in the gallery and lawmakers on the floor.[9] A newspaper reporter tweeted images of Davis in tennis shoes as the filibuster began. As it progressed, President Obama's Organizing for American Twitter account sent out a special message supporting Davis and picking up on the trending hashtag #StandWithWendy.[10] That hashtag alone amassed more than 547,000 Tweets.[11] Davis's personal Twitter account jumped from 6,000 to 48,000 followers throughout the day. Allies used Twitter to recruit people to fill the Senate Chambers.

Throughout the filibuster, as out-of-order strikes were called on Davis, supporters in attendance chanted, "Let her speak!"[12] When Lieutenant Governor David Dewhurst assigned Davis a third "out of order" at 10:07 p.m., other senators sought to delay the vote by making points of order that Twitter users, consulting *Roberts Rules of Order*, provided to them.[13] At 11:45 p.m., when Senator Leticia Van de Putte's motion to adjourn was not recognized, she asked, "At what point does a female senator have to raise her hand in order to be recognized over a male senator?" In response, the crowds filling the rotunda shouted so loudly that order could not be restored until after midnight.[14]

The role of social media in this event cannot be underestimated. "Through it all," the *Daily Dot* reported, "Twitter chronicled the debate in dramatic images, humor, and emotion."[15]

This social media event did not arise serendipitously or accidentally. Like Davis's speech, it was organized and planned, and not by Davis alone. NARAL Texas used Facebook to arrange rides for supporters. Annie's List, a Progressive women's group, live-tweeted from the gallery.[16] As allies tweeted about the event and other groups retweeted, the tweetstorm grew in strength.[17] The rhetorical action did not end with the chaotic postmidnight vote. Activists around the country, reacting to other state legislators restricting access to reproductive services, have reread large portions of Davis's filibuster at pro-choice protests around the nation.[18]

If you were asked to name the rhetor in this example, who would it be? Davis? The crowd? The people who were tweeting the filibuster? The organizations who organized the crowd? The people whose testimonies Davis read? The newspaper reporters whose stories she read? People who have reread Davis's words? This filibuster raises interesting questions about the rhetor in a multimodal world of social media.

First, it demonstrates the need for flexible thinking about who counts as a rhetor delivering a text. Davis's text cannot be attributed to a single rhetor. Second, it complicates what counts as a text. The transcript of the filibuster, its retweeted fragments, the crowd noises that delayed the vote, and the actions of other senators are all part of the text of the filibuster; and again, multiple rhetors are involved. Third, it shows that no simple, objective standard determines which rhetors garner attention from broadcast news networks. As the social media statistics demonstrate, "Twitter and Facebook were aflame with arguments over the filibuster as it was happening, while TV news networks generally paid little or no attention, at least at first."[19] During the tumultuous conclusion of the filibuster, CNN's Anderson Cooper and Piers Morgan conversed about the calorie count of blueberry muffins; MSNBC and Fox News aired reruns.[20] For breaking news, one might do better to rely on the internet than on twenty-four-hour news channels. As one commentator noted, "The coverage of the filibuster itself marks a clear example of social media's ability to provide viewers with accurate information in real time—however disjointed it might have been,"[21] given the variety of people tweeting about the filibuster. Finally, this filibuster establishes that rhetors can rise to national prominence as a result of their rhetorical actions. A *New York Times* story explains, "[Davis] was a state senator Tuesday morning. By Wednesday, she was a political celebrity known across the nation."[22]

In this chapter, we discuss the rhetor as an essential participant in any symbolic action. As rhetors produce symbolic action, they are also produced by it. To explore this process, we outline the general concept of "persona," then discuss its various facets: ethos, roles, identity, and image. An analysis of a speech on climate change during a United Nations Climate Action summit illustrates these concepts. We end with a consideration of the complexities of the rhetor.

PERSONA AS PERFORMANCE

During her filibuster, Wendy Davis (and the people and media recirculating the filibuster) created a complex persona. In the first few minutes, Davis claimed authority as a legislator, critiquing the decision to depart from past Senate procedure to discuss SB 5 in a special session. But she quickly moved from that role to claiming an identity as a Texan and an amplifier for Texan voices: "I'm rising on the floor today to humbly give voice to thousands of Texans who have been ignored."[23] Davis also claimed that part of her character was defined as a representative of a "minority voice" as a Democratic senator, and that, as a member of the minority party, she had a special obligation to speak. Later during the filibuster, Davis assumed the role of a lawyer, discussing the details of the *Roe v. Wade* decision, then returned to a legislative role as she conducted a "bill analysis bit-by-bit." Davis assumed many personas.

The rhetorical **persona** is *the ethos, roles, identity, and image a rhetor constructs and performs (or that others construct for a rhetor to perform) during a rhetorical act.* Central to this definition is an understanding that a persona is something a rhetor does, not something a rhetor innately has. A rhetor, through symbolic action, constructs and performs a persona, which the audience perceives to be the source of the symbolic action. As a result, as communication scholar James Jasinski notes, the persona becomes "a human presence that saturates a text."[24]

For example, commentators describe how former President Trump "[took] on contrasting personas, showcasing divergent traits with flourishes," sometimes in a span as short as forty-eight hours.[25] At Fort Myer military base, in front of a uniformed military audience, he played the role of commander in chief; the next morning, in Phoenix, while talking about immigration, he assumed the role of "the divider"; and that night in Reno, at a "Make America Great Again" rally, he was "the uniter."[26]

Our definition of persona is informed by English literature scholar Wayne Booth's examination of authorial persona. Booth drew a distinction between the actual identity of the author of a work of fiction and the identity that the author performed in that work. In his book *The Rhetoric of Fiction,* Booth refers to that performed identity as the author's "second self" or an "implied author" who "chooses, consciously or unconsciously, what we read; we infer [that person] as an ideal, literary, created version of the real [person]; . . . the sum of [their] own choices."[27] Booth sought to raise awareness of the fact that works of literature did not reflect an authentic authorial self, but were rhetorical. An authorial persona is performed when a person presents particular elements to the world as definitive of who they are: it is not just a neutral reflection of the person.

Narratives, whether in a novel or in an explanation of why you need a homework extension, attempt to influence an audience to see an event in a particular way. Your narratives are told from a particular perspective—your persona. Personas appear not only in works of fiction, but in every rhetorical action. Because every act of communication contains its own drama, it also contains characters, including the persona of the rhetor.

Sociologist Erving Goffman uses a drama metaphor to explain how people in social situations perform roles. He defines a **performance** as *"all the activity of a given participant on a given occasion which serves to influence in any way any of the other participants."*[28] When you give a public presentation, you engage in a performance. You not only present your speech; you also enact a role. Your choice of what to wear, whether to speak from the front of the room or from your seat, what level of formality to display, what evidence to use, and what attitude to take toward the audience and topic all influence the way others perceive you and your message. Thus, in order to completely understand how rhetoric works, you must recognize how persona invites assent both to the request made and to the person making it. Communication scholar Randall Lake notes that "arguments seek assent not only to the claim stated but also to the claim enacted."[29] Your symbolic actions seek affirmation of what you say and as whom you say it.

When people think of a performance, they may think of an actor who memorizes a script and performs it in front of an audience. A person's daily interactions with others, as well as the public interactions of a rhetor with an audience, are not scripted (although they might sometimes be rehearsed); however, they are still a performance. When you try to persuade your professor to give you an extension on an assignment, you probably plan what you will say: you produce a loose script to make the request in a way that is consistent with the professor's expectations and the image you wish to convey. A script is not written for you, but you may draft one in your head, rehearse it, edit it, and then finally perform it for its target audience.

Why do you feel the need to rehearse? You want to perform a persona that enhances your persuasiveness by directing the audience's interpretation of the message. The message will also inform the audience's perception of you. Depending on how you make your request, your professor may perceive your character as trustworthy because you displayed the identity of a hardworking student, or as lacking because you appear to be a procrastinator. The professor may grant your request because you played the role of student and asked politely, or refuse it because you played the role of superior and demanded an extension, thus assuming an authority you do not possess.

Although a persona is rhetorically constructed, an archetypal form for the persona may preexist the rhetorical action in which it is performed. Communication scholars B. L. Ware and Wil A. Linkugel clarify that "*persona* does not refer to the personality" of the actor as a person, but to "the characteristics assumed by the actor when [they] don the mask."[30] A rhetor does not create a persona out of nothing; rather, the persona can "reflect the aspirations and cultural visions of audiences."[31] For example, when you perform the role of good student, you do not create from scratch the characteristics and habits of a good student. Instead, a prototype of the good student already exists within cultural expectations. The university culture generally agrees that the qualities of a good student include being prepared, serious, engaged, focused, and interested, as well as being a critical thinker. You bring individual characteristics to the role, but the archetype existed prior to your performance of the persona.

FACETS OF PERSONA

To highlight the ways in which persona is performed and is itself a symbolic action, we describe the various facets of persona in the following sections. Ethos, roles, identity, and image are interlocking parts, or facets, of a person's persona. We use the metaphor "facets" because they are interconnected parts of a larger whole. Each facet offers a distinct perspective, although the distinctions are not absolute. In addition, people perceive that particular identities fit particular roles better. For example, people's perceptions of sex roles make female nurses and elementary school teachers less remarkable than male nurses or teachers. All these facets of persona have two things in common: (1) skillful choices about each facet can enhance symbolic action, and (2) each facet is produced by symbolic action.

Ethos

Ethos is *that which is "in the character of the speaker"; more specifically, it is the character of a rhetor performed in the rhetorical act and known by the audience because of prior interactions.* This understanding of ethos is informed by two classical scholars: Aristotle and Cicero.

Aristotle defined ethos as an appeal based on a rhetor's "presentation of character" within a persuasive act.[32] For Aristotle, ethos is created by the rhetor and comprises three dimensions: practical wisdom, virtue, and goodwill.[33] Rhetors demonstrate practical wisdom (*phronesis*) through the display of common sense and sound reason. For example, if a rhetor attempts to persuade an audience with arguments that the audience perceives to be irrational, unbelievable, or unrealistic, the rhetor's character is harmed and the audience will probably not be persuaded. Rhetors are perceived to possess virtue (*arête*) when they share the values the audience considers worthy of merit. Virtue is defined by the culture and the situation, so the values that an audience esteems determine whether a rhetor is perceived to be virtuous. Rhetors who possess goodwill (*eunoia*) are perceived as being motivated by their audiences' best interests and as putting the needs of their audiences ahead of their own interests and motives, much as a friend would. If an audience perceives a rhetor to be trustworthy and to possess the character qualities and virtues it esteems, it will be more open to the rhetor's message.

Roman rhetorician and statesperson Cicero described ethos as composed of elements of character outside the rhetorical act.[34] He included "the customs, the deeds, and the life" of the rhetor of which the audience was already aware.[35] For Cicero, the rhetor's character known from previous acts was more important to demonstrating ethos than the appeals a rhetor made in the speech.

Ethos is developed both prior to and within a rhetorical act. For example, on August 15, 2018, then–President Trump revoked former CIA director John Brennan's security clearance. He justified the move by claiming that Brennan had made "a series of unfounded and outrageous allegations" and posed a security risk.[36] Trump later admitted that he had revoked Brennan's security clearance because Brennan was responsible for Special Counsel Robert Mueller's investigation of Russian interference in the 2016 election.[37]

In response, politicians and intelligence community leaders declared that the revocation was an unprecedented and abnormal action, motivated not by concern for national security but by political animus.[38] On August 16, "thirteen former leaders of the Pentagon, the C.I.A. and the F.B.I." wrote and signed a statement,[39] which began by referencing their experience "as former senior intelligence officials."[40] Because of their experience, they possessed practical wisdom. Because they had served in the highest intelligence roles, and done so with distinction, they could claim virtue. Because they were intelligence officials, who typically are seen as above politics, they could claim goodwill; they were not considered to be motivated by personal political gain. By August 20, 175 former US officials had added their names to the statement.[41]

On August 16, retired four-star Navy admiral William H. McRaven added his name. In a *Washington Post* opinion column titled "Revoke My Security Clearance, Too, Mr. President,"[42] McRaven defended Brennan's character, writing that Brennan "is a man of unparalleled integrity, whose honesty and character have never been in question, except by those who don't know him."[43] A biography attached to the column noted why McRaven was credible: he had served in the Navy, achieved the rank of admiral, and commanded the US Joint Special Operations Command; in 2011, he oversaw the Navy SEAL raid that killed Osama bin Laden.[44] If McRaven is not credible on national security, who is? And if he thought his own security clearance should also be revoked, then clearly revocation is not about security but about politics. The question for audience members is: Who has more ethos regarding who constitutes a national security risk?

Roles

People perform various roles in their daily lives and across their lifetimes. On any given day you probably assume several roles, each having particular functions, qualities, characteristics, and communication patterns. Suppose you make three requests during a day: You ask your professor to extend the deadline on a paper, your friend to let you borrow something, and your subordinate at work to perform a required task. In each of these situations, you play a different role: student, friend, or manager. You perform different personas, each calling for different attitudes toward the audience. As a student, you are a subordinate to the audience, as friend a peer, and as manager a superior. You are the same person, but the role you perform to make the request influences the tone of the request. At the same time, the nature of the request places you in a particular role. By becoming aware of social roles and the way they affect perceptions of the rhetor, you can become more aware of the factors that influence reception of rhetorical acts.

If the rhetor plays a role that is held in high regard and consistent with the values of the society, Goffman explains, the audience may be more receptive to the message.[45] During performances, Goffman says, individuals "tend to incorporate and exemplify the officially accredited values of the society."[46]

One way to play a role is to don its costume. People dress up for job interviews because US society equates professional dress with a professional work attitude. A potential employer can see you more easily in the role of worker if you perform the role of a worker. Thus, when you interview for a professional job, you likely dress in a way you think others perceive to be professional, rather than in blue jeans, flip-flops, and a ripped T-shirt; you speak in a professional manner, using complete sentences and limited slang; and you move in a professional way, sitting up in your chair rather than slouching with your feet on the table.

That you *perform* the role of professional has become evident with a new wardrobe item: the "Zoom shirt." During the COVID pandemic, businesses, organizations, and schools shifted from in-person to remote meetings, most using the video conferencing platform Zoom, which tends to show only people's heads and torsos. Because people were connecting from home, they could wear sweatpants, leggings, or pajama bottoms. But because they wanted to appear professional, they needed to wear tops that appeared more business-like. Hence, the idea of the Zoom top, and the motto "business on the top, party on the bottom."[47] As one etiquette expert noted, such a shirt allows you to play the role of professional without having to wear the whole costume and even while sitting at your kitchen table.[48]

People also can perform roles in ways that challenge the society's values in order to highlight unspoken (and sometimes contradictory) norms attached to particular social roles. For example, in discussing third-wave feminism, feminist philosophers Rita Alfonso and Jo Trigilio note that Riot Grrls (members of the underground feminist punk movement) dressed "in baby doll dresses, usually worn with combat boots, colorful but torn stockings, and any number of tiny plastic hair barrettes, but writing 'slut' on their bodies to preempt society's judgment of them."[49] Riot Grrls intentionally performed contradictory roles: young children in feminine baby doll dresses and tough adults in masculine combat boots, innocent girls wearing plastic barrettes and adult women with torn stockings. Riot Grrls played with roles because they wanted to challenge the officially accredited social values.

When a persona pushes at the social expectations attached to the body performing it, the audience may reject the performance as unauthorized. It is hard for some audiences to see some bodies playing particular roles. Because not all rhetors have equal authority to perform a role, analysis of performances should focus on the power to perform, rather than on the truth of a performance. As Goffman states: "Sometimes when we ask whether a fostered impression is true or false we really mean to ask whether or not the performer is authorized to give the performance in question, and are not primarily concerned with the actual performance itself."[50] Even though personas are performances, people are not free to play any role they wish.

For example, during the 2018 election, Oregon state representative Janelle Bynum was knocking on doors around 5 p.m. in the suburban Portland area she represents. Someone in the neighborhood called the police to report a "'suspicious person' who might be a burglar" and who appeared to be "casing the neighborhood."[51] Bynum, who happens to be the only Black member of the Oregon House of Representatives, had been canvassing the neighborhood and using a cellphone to take notes about constituent concerns. The caller apparently did not think Bynum could perform a role that would allow a person access to neighbors and use of a cell phone without suspicion. Fortunately, Representative Bynum reports, the deputy "'responded professionally' and thanked her for her service after she explained who she was."[52]

When women activists struggled for their rights during the 1960s and 1970s, they sought to perform a new form of womanhood, but they were not totally free to perform "womanhood" in any way they wanted, free from social sanction. Communication scholar Karlyn Kohrs Campbell notes that the social status of women placed them at odds with the persona of "rhetor," which called for "self-reliance, self-confidence, and independence."[53] If women performed the persona of "woman," then they did not enact the persona of "rhetor;" if they performed the persona of "rhetor," they might not be perceived as enacting "woman." Campbell argues that feminist rhetoric during this era, "no matter how traditional its argumentation, how justificatory its form, how discursive its method, or how scholarly its style, . . . attacks the entire psychosocial reality, the most fundamental values, of the cultural context in which it occurs."[54]

A person's gender expression (tending toward feminine, tending toward masculine, or a creative mix of both; tending toward conforming or nonconforming) is a performance. People perform gender roles. Although each person has a gender identity, or an internal and individual experience of their own gender, in terms of understanding rhetors it is useful to think of gender as something people do, not something they are—a performance; a series of repeated actions, postures, and statements. Rhetoric professor Judith Butler aptly describes the relationship between gender and perceptions of identity: "Gender is the repeated stylization of the body, a set of repeated acts within a rigid regulatory frame that congeal over time to produce the appearance of substance, of a natural kind of being."[55] Consider the ways you do gender through your stylization of your body: your dress, hairstyle, body posture, movements, language choice, hand gestures, areas of interest, and so on. When humans (consciously or unconsciously) behave in gendered ways, they construct, maintain, and transform their own and others' notions of gender. These performances are repeated so frequently they become nonconscious, if not involuntary, and might even appear natural and determined rather than performed. Yet, they are still actions, not some inherent identity a person possesses.

Butler explains that even though "gender is a kind of doing, an incessant activity performed, in part, without one's knowing and without one's willing," it is not "automatic or mechanical."[56] Butler asks people to think about gender as "a practice of improvisation within a scene of constraint."[57] It is a performance, but one where the actor maintains only some level of control over the content of the scene. When you wake up every day, you make choices about how to "do gender"; about how to dress, move, sit, and talk. You could choose to do gender differently, but first you would have to see other choices as options. If a man wanted to do gender differently, he might need to see wearing a dress and heels as a viable option; most men do not. Although women can now wear pants and still be perceived as feminine (which was not true until the latter half of the twentieth century), a man who decided to wear a skirt would face serious social censure. Thus, the performance of gender is constrained; the script has already been written with only limited space for improvisation. Some bodies have the authority to perform some genders. Some genders are perceived as more acceptable performances.

Identity

Identity refers to *the physical and/or behavioral attributes that make a person recognizable as a member of a group.* Identity ingredients that have attained social significance and functioned as the basis for group identification include, but are not limited to, the social categories of race, class, sex, sexual orientation, gender, veteran status, religion, nationality, citizenship status, ability or disability, education, and profession. Your answer to the question "who/what are you?" provides a clue about how you understand identity.

Identity as Rhetorical. Assuming an identity when speaking is not a politically neutral act. When people say they are speaking as members of a race, class, sex, sexuality, nationality, profession, or other group, they are assuming personas. For example, the signatories of the letter condemning revocation of Brennan's security clearance opened their statement with "As former senior intelligence officials," and ended with their signatures, followed by the roles they had played as directors of the CIA or National Intelligence. They did not include the fact that among them were also a circuit court judge, a professor, a Republican congressional representative, a CNN analyst, a White House chief of staff for a Democratic president, and so on. They foregrounded in their identities their roles as intelligence officials.

Rhetoric involves not only *what* people communicate (the words and images), but also *as whom* they communicate—the identities they foreground. Beyoncé offers a vivid example: her public identity evolved over time from apolitical female pop star to unapologetic Black feminist. Angelica Jade Bastién, staff writer for *Vulture,* declares, "To watch Beyoncé Giselle Knowles-Carter is to take a master class in image construction."[58] Bastién describes how Beyoncé "evolved dramatically," from 2011 to 2020, working through a range of images: mother, reluctant speaker, political leader, capitalist, representational force, cautious revolutionary, matriarch, goddess, royalty. The image of unapologetic revolutionary Black feminist was made most evident in 2016, which saw the release of her album *Lemonade*[59] and the Super Bowl halftime performance of "Formation."[60]

In an analysis of *Lemonade,* African diaspora studies professor Omise'eke Natasha Tinsley describes how Beyoncé's "triumphant, blinged-out persona" celebrates the feminine in a way that makes clear Black women can be both feminine and powerful, even though dominant perceptions of gender and sex roles have long seen femininity as a domain of White women and power the domain of White men.[61] The halftime performance of "Formation" celebrated the fiftieth anniversary of the founding of the Black Panthers: performers wore berets; dancers referenced Malcolm X when they formed an X; and lyrics celebrated ethnic-racial pride when they referenced natural hair.[62] Linguistic scholars Maeve Eberhardt and Madeline Vdoviak-Markow note, "As Beyoncé has moved steadily away from popular expectations for representations of Black womanhood, language is a central tool that she uses strategically in the evolution of a newly transgressive persona."[63] Beyoncé uses dress, movement, topic choices, and language to perform and transform her identity.

Although the range of personas available to a rhetor is constrained by the various identities in which the rhetor can participate, identities are not fixed, immutable, or one-dimensional. In fact, scholars argue that identity should be understood as intersectional. Legal scholar Adrien Katherine Wing defines **intersectionality** as *the nature of identity as "multiplicative" rather than additive.*[64] This definition enables a more complex understanding of identity at the individual and systemic level. Intersectionality is a theory of power and identity that enables analysis of communication at both the "micropolitical level of everyday life and at the macropolitical level of social structures, material practices, and cultural norms." As women's and gender studies professor Vivian M. May explains, intersectionality "approaches lived identities as interlaced and systems of oppression as enmeshed and mutually reinforcing."[65] To understand Beyoncé's identity, as well as the positive and negative reactions to it, you need to consider how her race, class, ethnicity, age, gender, sex, and color intersect, and how each infuses and influences the others.

Identity makes more sense if you think of its ingredients as intermixed and interwoven parts of a single whole, rather than as the addition of each element on top of another. The way a person performs "man" is influenced by race, gender, sexuality, religion, education, and class. The way people perform "White" is influenced by the same characteristics. For example, Beyoncé is never just a woman or just a Black person. Instead, the way her sex and gender are performed and perceived is always infused by Blackness, and her Blackness is always infused by her sex and gender.

The metaphor of "ingredients" helps explain intersectionality.[66] Just as a cake is composed of discrete parts (eggs, flour, milk, sugar, and so on), the parts become inextricably intertwined when they are melded together through the alchemic process of cooking. The interaction among the initially discrete ingredients makes a cake a cake. Similarly, the interaction among identity ingredients as they meld together makes a person a person. You cannot understand what it means to have a certain identity without examining how all of a person's identity ingredients interact with and infuse each other.

For example, studies of motherhood show how a woman's identity as mother intersects with the social categories of race and class. Many people think of "mother" as a gentle soul who provides unconditional love and protective nurturing. In contrast, sociologist Patricia Hill Collins describes a form of motherhood that develops among women who have had to prepare children to face discrimination. Hill Collins shows that many working-class people and African Americans think of "mother" not as the gentle nurturer who soothes all wounds, but as the person who gave them the strength and the ability to handle life's hard knocks. Communication scholar Mari Boor Tonn labels this identity as "militant motherhood."[67]

Militant motherhood appears not only in families, but also in public discourse. Tonn's study of labor activist Mary Harris "Mother" Jones describes how militant motherhood uses "assertive, even aggressive, modes of presentation. Militant mothers not only confront their children's enemy, but must also train their children to do likewise if the threat they face is ongoing and systematic."[68] Militant motherhood is not sweet and gentle, but uses "bawdy, rowdy, and irreverent personal expression . . . . Such mothers also may bait, tease, and otherwise provoke children in order to acclimate them to attack, to provide practice at fighting back, and to sharpen their emotional control."[69] The way a woman performs the identity of "mother" is influenced by race and class. That identity is not static and fixed: multiple performances of "mother" exist. Thus, multiple "mother" personas exist.

Intersectionality theory highlights the unique combinations of characteristics that make up each individual and calls attention to the ways interlocking forms of privilege marginalize members of some groups. Legal scholar Kimberlé Crenshaw first used the word "intersectionality" to explain why existing civil rights law, which treats race and sex discrimination as two discrete forms of discrimination, did not work for Black women. Crenshaw explains, "Because the intersectional experience is greater than the sum of racism and sexism, any analysis that does not take intersectionality into account cannot sufficiently address the particular manner in which Black Women are subordinated."[70] Black women were not discriminated against simply because they were Black, or simply because they were women, but because they were Black women.

As feminist philosopher Sandra Harding points out, one should remember "that it is not just the marginalized who have a gender, race, and so on."[71] Intersectionality explains the complexity of all people's identities. "Man" is as much an identity as "woman"; "middle class" is as much an identity as "poor"; and "White" is as much an identity as "Black" or "Hispanic" or "Asian." People who belong to a dominant identity, however, do not perceive it to be an identity. Because it is the norm, the dominant identity becomes invisible. In their article on Whiteness as a strategic rhetoric, communication scholars Thomas K. Nakayama and Robert L. Krizek identify the ways Whiteness is created and maintained rhetorically as (1) closely tied to power, (2) the norm, (3) natural, (4) indicative of nationality and citizenship, (5) beyond the necessity of racial identity labels, and

(6) consciously tied to White people's European ancestry.[72] To illustrate the hidden nature of race, think about references you may have heard to "the Asian doctor," "the Hispanic lawyer," or the "Black accountant." Some people may suggest that these are only objective descriptions, but consider "White" as a descriptor: "the White doctor," "the White lawyer," or the "White accountant." Do these phrases sound strange? The fact that they might sound odd suggests that "White" is an identity that receives preference for positions of power and authority. A complex interaction among audience, the rhetor, and identity exists, a relationship that calls for an analysis of power.

Feminist scholar Paula M. L. Moya, among others, recognizes that identities are fluid even as the performance of those identities are constrained by the existing relationships among social groups and "the historically produced social facts which constitute social locations."[73] The social roles that people are allowed to play and the level of social authority that they are granted are constrained by their identities. For example, a 2014 study conducted by three business scholars found that professors were less likely to respond to prospective students' requests to discuss research opportunities if the students' names signaled their sex as female and/or their race as not White. Emails, identical save for the names of the senders, were sent to "over 6,500 professors at top U.S. universities drawn from 89 disciplines and 259 institutions."[74] The researchers found "that faculty ignored requests from women and minorities at a higher rate than requests from Caucasian males, particularly in higher-paying disciplines and private institutions." Professors in business colleges ignored requests from women and minorities at 2.6 times the rate of requests from White males.[75] In other words, female and minority students' identities, as indicated only by their names, marked them as less deserving of responses, regardless of the messages' performance of student.

Audiences read rhetors' personas through the identities they apply to the rhetors (there is never a "blank canvas") and often do not recognize that identities are intersectional. Thus, when some people look at US Representatives Sharice Davids and Deb Haaland, the first Native American women elected to the US Congress and, later, the first Native American cabinet secretary, they might see only Native American or woman, rather than US citizen, Ho-Chunk or Laguna Pueblo, lawyer, child of military veterans, or college educated.[76] In the United States, people who are categorized as Black, Latinx, Native American, Muslim, or Asian are subjected to stereotypes on the basis of those categories.

People often assume they know a rhetor's persona even before the rhetor performs it. These social assumptions are why identity matters: identities have real effects on how people live their lives. Moya argues that the external construction of peoples' identities influences their experiences, which then inform what they know and how they know it. Moya urges everyone to remember that although "people are not *uniformly* determined by any *one* social fact, . . . social facts (such as gender and race)" do influence who people are.[77] Even if identities are fictions, those fictions matter because they influence how people understand others based on their identities.

Although social imposition of an identity may limit the range of persona options, identity is not fixed. It can be both an obstacle and an opportunity in constructing a persona. Communication scholar Karlyn Kohrs Campbell explains that one may have the opportunity to choose to speak from an identity that has been accorded authority, or to face the obstacle of speaking from an assigned identity that lacks authority. For Campbell, the concept of persona captures the "shifting but central character of the roles that we assume in the plays in which we participate."[78] Barack Obama had both an obstacle and an opportunity arising from his status as the first US president of African descent. The obstacle arose from the 5 percent of the electorate who said they would never vote for a Black candidate;[79] they might never see Obama as the legitimate president even though he was the president. However, Obama's race also provided an opportunity. He could use a personal life history as proof of the promise of the United States of America. In his first inaugural address, he stated:

> This is the meaning of our liberty and our creed—why men and
> women and children of every race and every faith can join in
> celebration across this magnificent mall, and why a man whose
> father less than sixty years ago might not have been served at a local
> restaurant can now stand before you to take a most sacred oath.[80]

President Obama foregrounded racial identity in order to make a point about the nation's progress toward equality. He spoke the oath for the highest office in the land in a city that, years earlier, had used Jim Crow segregation laws to deny equal treatment to people like his father.

Many rhetors call forth particular ingredients in their identities, just as President Obama did with race, to form their personas in particular speech acts. Rhetors may speak as and for women, men, women of color, African Americans, Whites, immigrants, Muslims, patriots, US citizens, and so on. Even though each of those identity ingredients may be fluid and shifting, the rhetor chooses to fix on one ingredient momentarily in order to speak from the social location attached to that identity. Claiming and performing that identity become a strategic part of the communication act.

Strategic Essentialism. The differences among races and between women and men are not nearly as extensive as most popular culture literature would have you believe, but people often treat each other as being more different from each other than they really are. When others label you with an identity that is perceived as essential, meaning that it is fixed and immutable, how might you use that identity? If you have been assigned an identity by the larger society, thus limiting your range of personas, how might you use that assigned identity to enhance your communicative actions? A rhetor may have limited power because of sex, race, class, or nationality, yet still find creative and artistic ways to communicate.

Literary critic Gayatri Chakravorty Spivak describes **strategic essentialism** as *the process of making an identity ingredient the core part of one's persona, which legitimizes the right to speak.*[81] The process is strategic because it is an intentional construction of persona based on that single identity ingredient: a rhetor consciously picks an identity ingredient to foreground. That choice is essentialist because it positions one element of identity as fixed and determinative of the rhetor's identity, and because it seeks to create group identification through the appeal to that one shared identity ingredient. Strategic essentialism chooses to ignore intersectionality and, instead, focuses on a single identity ingredient. For example, in the 1960s and 1970s, African Americans appealed to the single identity ingredient of race with their slogan "Black Power";[82] women appealed to the single identity ingredient of sex with their proclamation that "Sisterhood is Powerful";[83] and Native Americans appealed to their nationality/race with "Red Power."[84] Marginalized groups are more likely to employ strategic essentialism because they are fighting misrepresentations of their group identity and struggling for a right to speak with authority.

Strategic essentialism as a rhetorical technique has two important characteristics. First, the ostensibly essential attributes of the group are defined by the group members themselves. The members of a marginalized group accept their identity as a group but seek to control how they are defined. Instead of passively accepting labels imposed by the dominant group, they actively take possession of an identity and define it in their own terms. "Black" does not mean powerless and enslaved, but powerful. "Sisterhood" means women are not divided cat-fighting individuals, but unified and powerful. Native American identity is not extinct, but vibrant and alive. Second, even as the group members engage in essentialism, they recognize that identity is always artificially constructed. Spivak recognizes that strategically appealing to an essential understanding of identity can sometimes be politically productive, but it must be done "in a scrupulously visible political interest."[85] Thus, people must consciously appeal to an essential identity in order to achieve a particular goal for their group; once that goal has been achieved, they should consciously question that essentialism. If they are to have agency or some degree of control over persona production, they must consciously perform and question that persona.

Throughout this discussion, we have tried to make clear that as identities are used to form personas, they should be critically examined. Sometimes, people strongly embrace an identity ingredient in order to create a sense of belonging. Other times, identity ingredients are de-emphasized so alliances can be built on the basis of other ingredients. Identities can be defined in order to create unification, but the process creates divisions. If a group unifies on the basis of a common ethnic background, it excludes those who do not share that background. Thus, the deployment of identity must be carefully considered in order to avoid creating a permanent division. Chicana author, scholar, and activist Gloria Anzaldúa offers an elegant metaphor for the complex process of identity negotiation in her essay "Bridge, Drawbridge, Sandbar or Island: Lesbians-of-Color *Hacienda Alianzas*."[86] Groups who build bridges to other groups find, at times, that moments of separation are needed, and raise the drawbridge. Sometimes no bridge is built, because the group needs the isolation of an island. Sometimes permanent bridges are built so the connections to others can always be maintained.

Identity is performed. Thus, when people are seeking to present a particular persona by strategically foregrounding an identity ingredient, they should remember that a persona is a mask, which can become suffocating if it is fixed and permanent.

Image

If we asked you to describe the image of a "G-man," the colloquial term for an FBI agent, you could probably come up with a description. Regardless of whether you agree with FBI politics and policy, you would probably describe the agent as straightlaced, short-haired, stern, physically fit, and wearing a pantsuit. All these characteristics are associated with masculinity. This image is not an accident, but the result of decades of image work.[87] The same year the FBI opened its training academy, the movie *G-Men* premiered. It starred James Cagney, who was known for a string of roles as tough guys. This movie was part of official and unofficial attempts in newspapers, newsreels, movies, and pulp literature to create an image of the FBI that would counter the attractive image of "elusive male bandits and their sexy, aggressive molls," such as Bonnie and Clyde. The image was of a "new kind of cop": "the scientific, hardworking, masculine G-man."[88] An image was born. FBI agents were masculine, rational, and independent.

Other elements can also contribute to a masculine image. Research has demonstrated that a person who is tall and has a strong jaw is considered more masculine.[89]

You might think James Comey, who served as director of the FBI from 2013 to 2017, would have no trouble maintaining a masculine image. A former prosecuting attorney standing 6 feet 8 inches tall, Comey easily met the characteristics associated with a masculine image, especially because he had long "cultivated an image of purity as a lawman who stood above politics and politicians."[90]

On May 9, 2017, President Trump fired Comey, ostensibly because of Comey's handling of the investigation into Hillary Clinton's use of a personal email server while she served as Secretary of State.[91] In an interview days later, however, Trump told NBC's Lester Holt, "When I decided to just do it [fire Comey], I said to myself, I said 'you know, this Russia thing with Trump and Russia is a made-up story, it is an excuse by the Democrats for having lost an election that they should have won.'"[92] This comment confirmed suspicions that Trump fired Comey because of his work investigating Russian interference in the 2016 election.

Regardless of the reason for the firing, it is clear the Trump administration and its supporters had long had a problem with the FBI Director. What is interesting is the way critics tried to transform the image of the masculine, rational lawman: They described Comey as feminine and emotional. Political science professor Bonnie Honig collected a few instances:

> Laura Ingraham claimed that Comey is a "drama queen" who writes in an unmanly way. Comey, says Charles Payne, is . . . "emotional . . . and vindictive" . . . . Amy Holmes thinks the fired FBI director is "like a 13 year old girl," while a CNN commentator offered that Comey couldn't ". . . man up."
>
> Then there is this from the President's son, Donald Trump, Jr.: "So if he was a 'Stronger guy'. . . ."[93]

Media Matters, a progressive website that critiques media coverage, provides clips and screen shots of tweets that implied Comey was homosexual, "brag[ged] about being beta," and was "a pearl-clutching senior [citizen]."[94]

So what is James Comey's image now? It depends. *New York Times* columnist David Leonhardt says that "his reputation has whipsawed" from "villain" to "savior" to a "bizarre combination of the two, depending on your political views."[95] As this example shows, images are rhetorical constructions that can be created by one's self or others.

An **image** is *a verbal and visual representation, emphasizing particular qualities and characteristics, that creates a perception of the rhetor in the audience's minds.* Image is an aspect of persona, but also an effect of it. Across time, an image is created by the performance of persona. An image is most persuasive, according to historian Daniel Boorstin, when it builds a reputation and does not outrage common sense.[96]

In *The Image,* a book critiquing the rise of hollow images and pseudo-events, Boorstin identifies several characteristics of an image. For Boorstin, an image is (1) synthetic, (2) believable, (3) passive, (4) vivid and concrete, (5) simplified, and (6) ambiguous.[97] His purpose in analyzing images is to condemn them, but these characteristics can be useful in studying how images work generally.

By "synthetic," Boorstin means that an image is "planned: created especially to serve a purpose, to make a certain kind of impression."[98] Comey planned to create an image when telling Congress of a March 2004 showdown with the Bush/Cheney administration, while he was a deputy Attorney General, over the legality of NSA surveillance.[99] Instead of keeping the disagreement internal to that administration, Comey publicized it to create an image of independence.

Yet an image must be perceived as authentic to be effective. It must be *believable.* As Boorstin explains, an image "serves no purpose if people do not believe it."[100] The believability of the image is not determined simply by the rhetor's ability to project an image, but also by the audience's willingness to accept it. Comey's image of masculine independence had long been accepted, especially within legal circles, where Comey was "a revered figure."[101] After Trump fired him, however, Comey became a household name. With a broader audience, his image was harder to control.

Although images are actively constructed, they are most believable when they appear passive—not something the rhetor strives for but that occurs naturally. Leonhardt noted this dialectic between the naturally occurring and the actively constructed, explaining that even though Comey's "independence and integrity" were real, he also "cultivated" them as part of his "persona."[102] At the point at which an image or persona appears to have been cultivated, or intentionally fostered, it loses its credibility. Thus, Comey's image worked until people started pointing out that it was cultivated and made conspicuous by his own actions.

In order for constructed images to influence an audience, they must be vivid and concrete, yet simplified. Because the images are meant to invite identification, they must be ambiguous enough for multiple audiences to feel similarity, yet vivid enough to give them a sense of who the rhetor is. Comey's image worked for a long time because it seemed to fit within the popular image of the G-man.

Images are not always positive creations meant to enhance a rhetor's appeal. Sometimes, negative images are imposed on a rhetor. Critics sought to change Comey's image from "rational, masculine lawman" into "emotional, feminine, and weak."

Although Boorstin is extremely critical of images (especially as deployed by those with power), contemporary scholars find that image events have a productive role in contemporary protest. Movements, groups, and organizations outside the mainstream political order can also construct images. Images not only conform, keep things the way they are, and squelch dissent, they also shake things up. Particularly in an increasingly multimediated world, rhetors recognize the need to have their images appear on the public screen. (See discussion of image events in chapter 4.)

RHETOR ANALYZED

In September 2019, sixteen-year-old Swedish climate activist Greta Thunberg spoke to the United Nations Secretary General, heads of state, civil society representatives, and government leaders at a UN Climate Action Summit. Why was a teenager speaking to this audience?

After convincing her parents to make changes that reduced the family's carbon footprint, in August 2018 Thunberg started protesting outside the Swedish parliament, holding a sign that said "SKOLSTREJK FÖR KLIMATET," which translates to "School Strike for Climate." Coupling the tactic of a school strike with direct protest at a policy-making body, Thunberg called for action on climate change. Each day, more students joined her protest. She continued this protest every Friday and, under the hashtag #FridaysForFuture, called for students around the world to strike with her.[103] Thunberg's actions inspired school strikes around the world. By December 2018, more than 20,000 students participated in the school strike. In March 2019, 1.6 million students participated in 2,200 strikes in over 125 countries.[104] In May 2019, another 1,600 strikes occurred in over 150 countries.[105] In September 2019, 4,500 strikes occurred.

Thunberg got the idea of a school strike from the Parkland students who protested against school shootings, the same students we introduced you to in the first pages of this textbook.[106] On the heels of her first (of two) nominations for the Nobel Peace Prize, Thunberg was invited to speak to the United Nations. The panel moderator asked: "What's your message to world leaders today?" Thunberg responded with the speech below.

Greta Thunberg
United Nations Climate Action Summit
New York, New York
September 23, 2019

1. My message is that we'll be watching you.

2. This is all wrong. I shouldn't be up here. I should be back in school on the other side of the ocean. Yet, you all come to us young people for hope. How dare you!

3. You have stolen my dreams and my childhood with your empty words and yet I'm one of the lucky ones. People are suffering. People are dying. Entire ecosystems are collapsing. We are in the beginning of a mass

extinction and all you can talk about is money and fairy tales of eternal economic growth. How dare you!

4. For more than 30 years, the science has been crystal clear. How dare you continue to look away and come here saying that you're doing enough when the politics and solutions needed are still nowhere in sight.

5. You say you hear us and that you understand the urgency, but no matter how sad and angry I am, I do not want to believe that. Because if you really understood the situation and still kept on failing to act then you would be evil and that I refuse to believe.

6. The popular idea of cutting our emissions in half in 10 years only gives us a 50 percent chance of staying below 1.5 degrees and the risk of setting off irreversible chain reactions beyond human control.

7. Fifty percent may be acceptable to you, but those numbers do not include tipping points, most feedback loops, additional warming hidden by toxic air pollution or the aspects of equity and climate justice.

8. They also rely on my generation sucking hundreds of billions of tons of your CO_2 out of the air with technologies that barely exist.

9. So a 50 percent risk is simply not acceptable to us, we who have to live with the consequences.

10. How dare you pretend that this can be solved with just business as usual and some technical solutions? With today's emissions levels, that remaining CO_2 budget will be entirely gone within less than eight and a half years.

11. There will not be any solutions or plans presented in line with these figures here today, because these numbers are too uncomfortable and you are still not mature enough to tell it like it is.

12. You are failing us, but the young people are starting to understand your betrayal. The eyes of all future generations are upon you and if you choose to fail us, I say: We will never forgive you.

13. We will not let you get away with this. Right here, right now is where we draw the line. The world is waking up and change is coming, whether you like it or not.

14. Thank you.[107]

David Murray, editor of the monthly magazine *Vital Speeches of the Day*, indicated that had the speech been submitted for publication by an "anonymous environmental activist," it would not have been published. The words on the page were not remarkable. What made the speech remarkable was that it was delivered by someone who had captured the world's attention for over a year, spoke through tears, and "whose whole being was behind it."[108] Murray published the speech "because rhetoric isn't just words. It's the humanity of the people who speak them." Thus, it is as important to analyze the rhetor, to watch and hear the speaker, as it is to analyze the words (You can find a video of the speech at https://www.youtube.com/watch?v=KAJsdgTPJpU, or search "Greta Thunberg" and "United Nations Climate Action Summit.")[109]

Prior to the speech, Thunberg had earned credibility. Her commitment to climate solutions had been established by a commitment to action that inspired others to act. In fact, in order to get to the United States to deliver the speech, Thunberg made sure to do so with the smallest carbon footprint. Instead of flying, she took a two-week-long voyage to New York from Plymouth, England, on an emission-free yacht.

Within the speech, Thunberg established ethos by demonstrating knowledge and practical wisdom about the topic with reference to the technical concepts of tipping points, feedback loops, and specific statistics on the effect of carbon reduction effect on temperature. She established the most important element of persona, however, by naming herself as one of "us young people," just a teenager.

As a teenager, Thunberg was not out for political gain, but for the best interests of her audience and her fellow youth. The creativity editor at *Ad Age* noted that Thunberg was an ideal rhetor for the message because of her ability to present goodwill: "Thunberg . . . has no apparent ulterior motive for speaking out and is obviously uncomfortable in crowds and onstage. But she speaks with a single-mindedness and clarity of purpose."[110]

Thunberg's youthful persona is apparent in her appearance, words, and expression of teen outrage at the inaction of adults. Dressed in grey leggings, tennis shoes, and a pink collarless shirt, and wearing her hair in a long braid, Thunberg looked like a teenager. She spoke as a teenager, stating that she should not be on the platform alongside three adults but that instead she should be in school. As one description of her said, with her "Pippi Longstocking braids . . . she looks younger than her years," but that it might be precisely "her extreme teenager-ness" that is "key to her influence."[111] Thunberg spoke as a teenager and for other youth, using "we" and "us" pronouns. When condemning leaders who had long failed to act to stop climate change, she spoke on behalf of "my generation . . . who have to live with the consequences."

Thunberg did not present a persona that was detached or try to hide the tears in her voice. Instead, she said she was "sad and angry." Her anger came through in every passage. Even though she was decades younger than the audience members and had far less power, she spoke to them as an equal, not asking but repeatedly accusing: "How dare you!" Like a typical teen, Thunberg was focused on fairness and was willing to let adults see her emotions. Her concern, though, was not with some personal slight but rather with the incredible unfairness that adult inaction meant for all youth.

RHETORS IN A POSTMODERN WORLD

To end the chapter, we want to reiterate the complex role the rhetor plays in symbolic action. Just as rhetors may be inventors of symbolic action, they are invented by symbolic action. The very idea of an author/rhetor may be a rhetorical invention, because rhetors' identities are constructed within the play of larger social forces. Thus, we offer four caveats about studying "the rhetor": (1) authorial intent does not determine the meaning of a text; (2) no text has a single author; (3) rhetors, themselves, may be the rhetorical constructions of others; and (4) in a networked age, algorithms, rather than people, may author the web content you see.

These insights are informed by postmodern theory. **Postmodernism,** broadly defined, is *the theory that places into question singular explanations, metanarratives, categories, and the certainty of supposedly objective interpretations of the world.* Because human beings only access the world through the symbols they use, those symbols tend to limit explanations. In particular, postmodernism induces questioning the definition of the rhetor as possessing a stable identity and as the sole origin of the meaning of a text. We have taken a postmodern perspective throughout this textbook, for example, when we asked whether Wendy Davis was *the* rhetor in the chapter's opening example, when we noted how race and nation are rhetorically constructed, and when we noted that meaning is co-created by rhetors and audiences.

Authorial intent does not determine the meaning of a rhetorical action. The most extreme version of this argument can be dated to a 1967 essay by French literary theorist Roland Barthes, "The Death of the Author."[112] Barthes proposes that the author of a text does not determine the meaning of a text, because "to give an Author to a text is to impose upon that text a stop clause, to furnish it with a final signification, to close the writing."[113] Instead, Barthes proposes, the audience determines the meaning of a text:

> a text consists of multiple writings, issuing from several cultures and
> entering into dialogue with each other, into parody, into contestation;
> but there is one place where this multiplicity is collected, united, and
> this place is not the author . . . but the reader.[114]

The readers (or audiences), Barthes argues, provide meaning to the text through the experiences (including other works they have read) they bring to their interpretations. He warns against relying on an author's intent or biography to determine the meaning of a text. The centrality of audiences to making meaning led communication theorist Michael McGee to declare "*text construction is now something done more by the consumers than by the producers of discourse.*"[115]

Communication scholar Karlyn Kohrs Campbell declares, however, that "reports of the death of the author are greatly exaggerated."[116] Although we agree that audiences are central to understanding rhetorical action, we also believe rhetors still carry ethical responsibilities with them when they engage in rhetorical action.

An example that illustrates the limit of intent is the use of the derogatory term for Native Americans, the "R-word," as the name for the Washington, DC, football team. Every dictionary definition of the term calls it a racial slur. For decades, every major Native American group has called for athletic teams to drop the use of American Indian names and mascots unless the team is connected to an American Indian school. In 2006, the NCAA began banning their use in postseason tournaments.[117] In 2013, the Oneida nation launched an advertising campaign on radio and the internet to induce Washington team owner Dan Snyder and league Commissioner Roger Goodell to change the name of the Washington football team. In 2013, the Leadership Conference on Civil and Human Rights adopted a resolution that demanded the Washington team change its name.[118]

In May 2014, after fifty US Senators sent a letter to Goodell asking the commissioner to change the name,[119] NFL spokesperson Brian McCarthy defended the team's name, saying it was intended to be complimentary to and respectful of Native Americans.[120] Clearly, though, and regardless of the NFL and team's intent, the term is perceived as disrespectful and derogatory. On June 18, 2014, the US Patent Office cancelled six federal trademark registrations that the team owned because the name was "disparaging to Native Americans."[121] (The team appealed. After the Supreme Court struck down the disparagement clause as unconstitutional in another case in 2017, Native American petitioners and the Justice Department dropped their case.)[122]

Where does meaning reside? Barthes critiqued the idea that the rhetor's intent determines the meaning of a text. One insight of contemporary rhetorical and communication theory is that meaning does not really reside in the intent of the author (if one can be identified) or in the text, but in the interaction between an audience and a text. Media studies have extensively theorized this relationship because many mass-mediated texts (such as reality TV shows, movies, dramas, and situation comedies) do not have a single author to whom intent could be attributed; the writers, directors, actors, and editors all play a part in creating meaning in such shows.

Media scholar John Fiske argues that the meanings of texts are open to multiple interpretations by audiences, and that audiences are not just passive recipients—they are able to create their own meanings.[123] Fiske believes people actively and creatively engage with media, using a range of tactics to make media meet their needs. He also believes that diverse readings are possible because media messages have multiple meanings. He uses the term **polysemous** ("poly" meaning "many" and "sema" referring to "sign" or "symbol") to describe *the multiple meanings of a single text.*[124]

Fiske claims that mediated messages are not open to an endless range of interpretations, but some scholars think Fiske does not devote enough time to the things that limit interpretations. A mediated message does not occur in a vacuum, but in a particular place, at a particular time, and to particular audiences. Communication scholar Celeste Michelle Condit explains that a rhetorical approach reminds the researcher that "audiences are not free to make meanings at will from mass mediated texts" because "the ability of audiences to shape their own readings . . . is constrained by a variety of factors in any given rhetorical situation," including "access to oppositional codes . . . the repertoire of available texts," and the historical context.[125] In other words, people should be trained to engage in critical reading. Condit argues that instead of the concept of polysemy (multitude of meanings) researchers should use **polyvalence,** meaning *multitude of valuations,* which "occurs when audience members share understandings of the denotations of a text but disagree about the valuation of these denotations to such a degree that they produce notably different interpretations."[126] Polysemy implies that audiences interpret different denotative meanings from a text, while polyvalence implies that they extract different connotational meanings.

The reactions to Beyoncé's 2016 Super Bowl halftime performance of "Formation" illustrate polyvalence. Although everyone agreed on the meaning of some of the symbolism—the X and Black Panther berets—not everyone agreed on whether those references should be praised. Some celebrated the performance as a defiant call to action; others as an overt criticism of police.[127] Some saw it as a powerfully artistic performance; others, such as politician Rudy Giuliani, described it as "outrageous," "ridiculous," and just "a bunch of people bouncing around and all strange things."[128]

The concepts of polysemy and polyvalence challenge the idea that the rhetor determines the meaning of a text. Different audience members might come away from the same rhetorical event with radically different interpretations of what the event meant. Thus, for students of rhetoric, the goal of analysis "is not to locate *the* message" a rhetor might have intended, but to identify "the multiple, frequently conflicting, messages."[129] Given postmodern insight into the creation of multiple meaning, a singular, unitary reading of the meaning of a text is inaccurate.

Nevertheless, people should not manipulate a text in a way that refuses to recognize another person's creative intent. For example, in 2014, the world was horrified by the story of Boko Haram kidnapping more than 250 girls from their boarding school in Nigeria and auctioning them to the highest bidder. The attack on a school was not accidental, nor was it the first. (The name Boko Haram roughly translates to "Western education is forbidden.")[130] Little effort was made to find the girls, even as television networks devoted seemingly endless coverage to a "major international search" for a missing Malaysian airliner.[131] But the girls' parents persisted. With other protestors, they marched in the capital to pressure Nigerian President Goodluck Jonathan to do something.[132] In support, a social media campaign was launched on Change.org, Facebook, and the White House website: #BringBackOurGirls. Eventually, the Nigerian government began accepting assistance from other countries in the search for the girls. (Four years after the abduction, only a hundred had been freed or escaped; more than a hundred were still in captivity, and at least twelve of the girls were presumed dead. Even those who were no longer under Boko Haram control were still not completely free; their access to their families and children was limited.[133])

As part of the #BringBackOurGirls campaign, three photographs of girls were tweeted and retweeted thousands of times.[134] The problem: the photos were not of the girls who had been kidnapped; in fact, the girls in the photographs were not even from Nigeria. The photos had been taken by photojournalist Ami Vitale of girls from Guinea-Bissau (which is over a thousand miles from Nigeria). Whoever created the tweets had taken the photos from Vitale's website or from another website.

Although supportive of the campaign, Vitale was deeply concerned about the misuse of these photos, explaining:

Can you imagine having your daughter's image spread throughout the world as the face of sexual trafficking? These girls have never been abducted, never been sexually trafficked.[135]

An additional concern was that Vitale's project had focused on the beauty of Africa, which existed between the dominant narratives of it as a war-torn wasteland or an exotic land of safari. Vitale's photographs were of girls who "are not victims," but these girls had now become the international face of victimization. Unfortunately, the photographs were misused in this campaign and in many others. If you search for "crying little Black girls," Vitale's photographs come up, and might then be used in a variety of ways.

No text has a single author. Although we often talk of *the* rhetor, all symbolic actions are actually the creation of multiple rhetors. Some of the rhetors can be identified; others cannot. In some cases, a multitude of authors is easy to recognize, as when a politician works with a speechwriter, a social movement generates a website or protest action, a group creates and solicits signatures for a petition on Change.org, or a campus group advocates for increased funding from the student government.

Even when a speech seems to be authored by a single individual, multiple authors are present. Rhetors knit together recognized turns of phrase, metaphors, ideographs, narratives, myths, and public vocabularies. As Campbell notes, because rhetors "are linked to cultures and collectivities" they cannot create meaning independently. Instead, they are inventors, "points of articulation" who link together the components of symbolic action as they invent speeches, personas, identities, and communities.[136]

Rhetors may be rhetorically constructed by others. Who people think a rhetor is, sometimes even the words that are attributed to that rhetor, are constructions. You may have heard of Sojourner Truth and the 1851 speech "Ain't I a Woman?" that is attributed to Truth,[137] and that is extensively read in middle school and high school curricula. According to Campbell, the way Truth's speech was perceived and recorded provides insight into how power and privileges affect the perception of a rhetor's persona.[138]

What is known is that Truth was born into slavery in upstate New York sometime in 1797 and freed in 1827. Truth spoke English as a second language, having been owned by a Dutch master; thus, her accent was likely Dutch rather than Southern Black dialect. She was involved with a range of religious, socialist, transcendental, women's rights, and antislavery groups. According to rhetoric scholar Roseann M. Mandziuk, your perception of Truth might be any of the following: "tragic victim of slavery, a religious pilgrim, a comic caricature, and a fiery orator and advocate for women's rights."[139]

Most people came to know Truth through the 1851 speech, but even it is a construction. The transcript of the speech, by Frances Dana Gage, a White woman suffrage and abolition advocate, was not created until twelve years later. It still defines how the speech is remembered, but both the content and the dialect preserved in Gage's version are vastly different from reports of the speech published in papers at the time.[140] The transcript uses speech styles found in racist caricatures and blackface minstrel shows; it does not reflect what historians know of how Truth spoke.[141] Truth's persona, as preserved in Gage's version of the speech, imposed on Truth the social perceptions of slaves as ignorant. Although illiterate, Truth was not ignorant, and there is no certainty that the speech attributed to Truth is anything like the words she actually spoke.

Truth is unquestionably a historically significant rhetor. Nevertheless, who you think Truth was is a rhetorical construction; and that construction has an effect. Rhetorical scholars Mandziuk and Suzanne Pullon Fitch, in "The Rhetorical Construction of Sojourner Truth," compellingly argue that "paradoxically, because the colorful and complex crusader for multiple causes effectively is reduced to a single, false rhetorical moment in contemporary invocations of her, Truth's persona and power actually are diluted and diminished."[142]

The very idea of a rhetor is also constructed. For years, the study of public address assumed that the rhetor of a text was a stable, singular entity. But as the example that opened this chapter illustrates, what we think of as the rhetor may not be so simple. Wendy Davis's filibuster was composed not only of her words, but also scores of other people's words. In addition, many people's access to Davis's speech was not the speech itself but the fragments other people tweeted. For the people who followed only the tweets, their understanding of the filibuster came through other people's judgments about what was relevant to tweet.

In a networked age, algorithms, rather than people, may author the web content you see. If you use Google to conduct your internet searches (as of June 2021, nearly 88 percent of all internet searches were conducted on Google),[143] who is the author of those results? The author is as much you (or at least a combination of information about you that the Google algorithm used) as it is the organizations and people who wrote the documents that the algorithm thought might interest you. What you find when you search the Web is not some universal or objective result. Instead, it is the result of an algorithm specific to you, the audience.

In 2005, Google announced on its official blog that the results of its searches were now "customized search results for you based upon 180 days of search activity linked to an anonymous cookie in your browser."[144] Fifty-seven signals (including location, previous searches, bookmarked sites, and type of computer) would influence the search results. In 2009, Google refined this algorithm with its "social search" feature, which highlighted results from people you knew.[145] In 2012, it proclaimed "We're transforming Google into a search engine that understands not only content but also people and relationships" by adding additional personalization features.[146] The result: when two people use exactly the same search terms, they do not receive the same search results. You, the audience, determine the content you receive.

Internet activist Eli Pariser, author of *The Filter Bubble*, provided the following illustration. When the Deepwater Horizon Oil Rig exploded in 2010 and began "spewing crude oil into the Gulf of Mexico," he asked two friends to conduct a search. Even though they were similar in terms of sex, location, education, and politics, their results were remarkably different: one saw "investment information about BP. The other saw news. For one, the first page of results contained links about the oil spill; for the other, there was nothing about it except for a promotional ad from BP."[147] This discovery led Pariser to title the second chapter of his book "The User is the Content."

The networked, digital age demands rethinking the relationship between the rhetor and the audience, recognizing that sometimes people are simultaneously neither and both. Media studies professor Siva Vaidhyanathan argues that people need to think of themselves not as Google's "customers," but "its product. We—our fancies, fetishes, predilections, and preferences—are what Google sells to advertisers."[148] Instead of reading what Google offers you as only the results of other rhetors' work, recognize that it is also a creation of you (or at least of Google's records of your past computer activities). Vaidhyanathan urges people to be critical of Google's "claims of omniscience, omnipotence, and benevolence" and quit granting its search results "inordinate and undeserved power."[149] That critical perspective is important when you participate in civic life. To embrace "global civic responsibility,"[150] people must resist Google's pressures to be enclaved in increasingly personalized search worlds, where they see only that with which they already agree.

CONCLUSION

Understanding the rhetor is central to understanding rhetoric. Conceiving of the rhetor through the concept of persona enables you to recognize that the rhetor simultaneously invents and is invented by rhetorical action.

As a civic actor, you play various roles even as other people's rhetoric constructs your role as a civic actor. Thus, when you contemplate producing a rhetorical action, pay attention to the way you produce yourself as rhetor in that action. Because seeking agreement with a claim invites assent not only to what was said, but who says it, attention to persona is central to understanding how rhetoric operates.

Persona is a holistic term referring to the ethos, role, identity, and image that a rhetor performs during a rhetorical act. When you communicate, you may do so from a range of personas. You can develop ethos, play a role, embrace an identity, or project an image.

Regardless of where you find the resources for your performance, a persona is something you do, something you perform, not merely something you are. You possess agency not only in relation to what you say, but as whom you say it. Despite this agency, rhetors are not free to construct just any persona, because audiences and societies place meaning and value on characteristics such as gender, sex, race, socioeconomic status, and ethnicity.

Even as you consider your responsibilities as a rhetor, do not assume a rhetor (even if you can identify that individual) is the sole determinant of a symbolic action's meaning or content. Authorial intent alone does not determine the meaning of a rhetorical message. Multiple rhetors are always involved in the production of a single symbolic action. Personas may be constructed by others and imposed on rhetors. Nonhuman agents (such as algorithms) may be restricting the rhetoric to which you are exposed.

DISCUSSION QUESTIONS

1. What identity ingredients are available to you as you perform a persona? In what ways do you have the privilege (or opportunity) to choose between multiple personas? In what ways do the identities that others assign to you present an obstacle to your communication acts?
2. Give an example of a person's character getting in the way of a persuasive message. How did the person's persona create obstacles for persuasion? What could the person have done to correct these obstacles?
3. Think about the examples of Wendy Davis, Greta Thunberg, and Beyoncé. Did any of these rhetors engage in strategic essentialism? Why do you think they did—or did not? If they did, give examples.
4. How might you describe how meaning is created in a postmodern world? For example, who is the rhetor in a contemporary song, a streaming show, or a web page? How might this description affect how you understand your own agency?

RECOMMENDED READINGS

Campbell, Karlyn Kohrs. "Agency: Promiscuous and Protean." *Communication and Critical/Cultural Studies* 2, no. 1 (March 2005): 1–19.

Ceccarelli, Leah. "Polysemy: Multiple Meanings in Rhetorical Criticism." *Quarterly Journal of Speech* 84, no. 4 (1998): 395–415.

Mandziuk, Roseann M., and Suzanne Pullon Fitch. "The Rhetorical Construction of Sojourner Truth." *Southern Communication Journal* 66, no. 2 (Winter 2001): 120–138.

Nakayama, Thomas K., and Robert L. Krizek. "Whiteness: A Strategic Rhetoric." *Quarterly Journal of Speech* 81 (August 1995): 291–309.

ENDNOTES

[1] Wendy Davis, "Texas Senate Filibuster of SB5 (06-25-2013) Transcript," transcribed Ana Mardoll, 2013, https://docs.google.com/document/d/1c0xuAFFc _6klQ1nrnQ72Qd9Y-o_uG8rSykO4wDgNqFQ/edit?pli=1. We would like to thank Zoe Russell for her research assistance on this example.

[2] Heather Kelly, "Texas Filibuster on Abortion Bill Rivets Online," CNN, June 26, 2013, http://www.cnn.com/2013/06/26/tech/social-media/texas-filibuster-twitter. This article contains many powerful images of the filibuster.

[3] *Senate Rules,* adopted by the 83rd Legislature (January 9, 2013): 10, State Resolution No. 4, http://www.senate.state.tx.us/rules/SenateRules83.pdf.

[4] Wendy Davis, @WendyDavisTexas, https://twitter.com/WendyDavisTexas/status/349377951877443584.

[5] As cited in Kelly, "Texas Filibuster."

[6] Aja Romano, "How the Internet and Abortion Rights Won in Texas," *Daily Dot,* June 26, 2013, http://www.dailydot.com/politics/wendy-davis-filibuster-texas-sb5.

[7] Wendy Davis, "Wendy Davis: Why I Stood Up for Texas Women," *Washington Post,* July 15, 2013, http://www.washingtonpost.com/opinions/wendy-davis-why-i-stood-up-for-texas-women/2013/07/15/07bc14fa-eb67-11e2-aa9f-c03a72e2d342_story.html.

[8] Carl Franzen, "Why Did Networks Fail at Covering Wendy Davis's Epic Abortion Bill Filibuster in Texas?" *The Verge,* June 26, 2013, http://www.theverge.com/2013/6/26/4468130/wendy-davis-tx-abortion-bill-filibuster-media-fail.

[9] Romano, "How the Internet."

[10] Kelly, "Texas Filibuster."

[11] Caitlin Dewey, "Wendy Davis 'Tweetstorm' Was Planned in Advance," *Washington Post,* June 26, 2013, http://www.washingtonpost.com/blogs/the-fix/wp/2013/06/26/this-tweetstorm-was-planned-in-advance.

[12] Romano, "How the Internet."

[13] Romano, "How the Internet."

[14] Jennings Brown, "Wendy Davis' Filibuster by the Numbers," *Esquire,* June 26, 2013, http://www.esquire.com/blogs/politics/wendy-davis-filibuster-by-the-numbers-062613.

[15] Romano, "How the Internet."

[16] Dewey, "Wendy Davis 'Tweetstorm.'"

[17] Dewey, "Wendy Davis 'Tweetstorm.'"

[18] Craig Jarvis, "Activists Will Read Aloud Texas Sen. Wendy Davis' Filibuster," NewsObserver.com, November 2, 2013, http://www.newsobserver.com/2013/11/01/3331338/activists-will-read-aloud-texas.html.

[19] Scott Collins, "Wendy Davis' Filibuster Ignites Twitter; Fans Rip News Networks," *Los Angeles Times,* June 26, 2013, http://articles.latimes.com/2013/jun/26/entertainment/la-et-st-wendy-davis-filibuster-20130626.

[20] Franzen, "Why Did Networks?"

[21] Franzen, "Why Did Networks?"

[22] Manny Fernandez, "In Texas, A Senator's Stand Catches the Spotlight," *New York Times,* June 26, 2013, http://www.nytimes.com/2013/06/27/us/politics/texas-abortion-bill.html?pagewanted=all.

[23] Davis, "Texas Senate Filibuster."

[24] James Jasinski, "Persona," in *Sourcebook on Rhetoric: Key Concepts in Contemporary Rhetorical Studies* (Thousand Oaks, CA: Sage, 2001), 429.

[25] Philip Rucker, "Trump's Whiplash: Three Personas in Three Speeches, but the Same President," *Washington Post,* August 23, 2017, https://www.washingtonpost.com/politics/trumps-whiplash-three-roles-in-three-speeches-but-the-same-president/2017/08/23/.

[26] Rucker, "Trump's Whiplash."

[27] Wayne Booth, *The Rhetoric of Fiction* (Chicago: University of Chicago Press, 1961), 74–75.

[28] Erving Goffman, *The Presentation of Self in Everyday Life* (New York: Anchor, 1959), 15, italics added.

[29] Randall Lake, "The Implied Arguer," in *Argumentation Theory and the Rhetoric of Assent,* ed. David C. Williams and Michael D. Hazen (Tuscaloosa: University of Alabama Press, 1990), 83.

[30] B. L. Ware and Wil A. Linkugel, "The Rhetorical *Persona:* Marcus Garvey as Black Moses," *Communication Monographs* 49 (1982): 50.

31 Ware and Linkugel, "The Rhetorical *Persona,*" 50.

32 George A. Kennedy, *A New History of Classical Rhetoric* (Princeton, NJ: Princeton University Press, 1994), 57–60.

33 Aristotle, *On Rhetoric,* trans. George A. Kennedy (New York: Oxford University Press, 1991), 2.1 [1378a].

34 James M. May, *Trials of Character: The Eloquence of Ciceronian Ethos* (Chapel Hill: University of North Carolina Press, 1988).

35 Cicero, *On the Ideal Orator (De Oratore),* trans. James M. May and Jakob Wisse (New York: Oxford University Press, 2001), 2.182.

36 Donald Trump, "Trump's Full Statement about Why He Revoked Brennan's Security Clearance," NBC News, August 15, 2018, https://www.nbcnews.com/politics /donald-trump/trump-s-full-statement-about-why-he-revoked-brennan-s-n901066.

37 Mike Calia, "Trump Cites Russia Probe as a Reason for Revoking Former CIA Chief John Brennan's Security Clearance," CNBC, August 16, 2018, https://www.cnbc.com/2018/08/16/trump-cites-russia-probe-as-reason-for-revoking-john-brennan-clearance.html.

38 See for example Peter Feaver, "The Real Reasons Trump Was Wrong to Revoke Brennan's Clearance," *Foreign Policy,* August 21, 2018, https://foreignpolicy.com /2018/08/21/trump-was-wrong-to-strike-john-brennans-security-clearance/; Kathryn Watson, "Critics Blast Revoking of John Brennan's Clearance as 'Authoritarian,'" CBS News, August 15, 2018, https://www.cbsnews.com/news/critics-react-to-trumps -dangerous-decision-to-revoke-brennans-clearance/.

39 Tom Weiner, "Trump is Not a King," *New York Times,* August 17, 2018, https://www.nytimes.com/2018/08/17/opinion/cia-brennan-trump-letters.html.

40 "Statement from Former Senior Intelligence Officials," August 16, 2018, https://drive.google.com/file/d/1F7pZ8oP2KpIK8x-yI0RbescPzP3RK2S4/preview.

41 Maegan Vasquez, "175 Former US Officials Added to List Denouncing Trump for Revoking Brennan Security Clearance," CNN Politics, August 20, 2018, https://www.cnn.com/2018/08/20/politics/john-brennan-more-intelligence-officials -statement/index.html.

42 William H. McRaven, "Revoke My Security Clearance, Too, Mr. President," *Washington Post,* August 16, 2018, https://www.washingtonpost.com/opinions/revoke-my -security-clearance-too-mr-president/2018/08/16/8b149b02-a178-11e8-93e3 -24d1703d2a7a_story.html.

43 McRaven, "Revoke My Security Clearance."

44 McRaven, "Revoke My Security Clearance."

45 Goffman, *The Presentation of Self,* 6.

46 Goffman, *The Presentation of Self,* 35.

47 Chrissy Callahan, "How Zoom Shirts Became the New Work-from-Home Wardrobe Staple," *Today,* July 2, 2020, https://www.today.com/style/what-are-zoom-shirts -why-are-they-so-popular-t185763.

48 Priya Elan, "'The Zoom Shirt': How the Pandemic Changed Work Dress Codes," *Guardian,* July 20, 2020, https://www.theguardian.com/business/2020/jul/20 /the-zoom-shirt-how-the-pandemic-changed-work-dress-codes.

49 Rita Alfonso and Jo Trigilio, "Surfing the Third Wave: A Dialogue between Two Third Wave Feminists," *Hypatia* 12, no. 3 (Summer 1997), 13, 7–16.

50 Goffman, *The Presentation of Self,* 59.

51 Mihir Zaveri, "A Black Oregon Lawmaker Was Knocking on Doors. Someone Called the Police," *New York Times,* July 5, 2018, https://www.nytimes.com/2018/07/05/us/janelle-bynum-police-portland.html.

[52] Zaveri, "A Black Oregon Lawmaker."

[53] Karlyn Kohrs Campbell, "The Rhetoric of Women's Liberation: An Oxymoron," *Quarterly Journal of Speech* 59 (February 1973): 75.

[54] Campbell, "The Rhetoric of Women's Liberation," 75.

[55] Judith Butler, *Gender Trouble* (New York: Routledge, 1990), 33.

[56] Judith Butler, *Undoing Gender* (New York: Routledge, 2004), 1.

[57] Butler, *Undoing Gender,* 1.

[58] Angelica Jade Bastién, "What Beyoncé Tells Us without Saying a Word," *Vulture,* July 31, 2020, https://www.vulture.com/2020/07/beyonce-images-close-read.html.

[59] Beyoncé, *Lemonade,* 2016, https://www.beyonce.com/album/lemonade-visual-album/.

[60] Beyoncé, "Formation," YouTube, February 6, 2016, https://www.youtube.com/watch?v=LrCHz1gwzTo&feature=emb_logo.

[61] Omise'eke Natasha Tinsley, *Beyoncé in Formation: Remixing Black Feminism* (Austin: University of Texas Press, 2018), 10.

[62] Rachel D. Davidson and Catherine A. Dobris, "Social Activism in Popular Culture: A Critical Review of Disparate Responses to Beyoncé's 2016 Super Bowl Performance and Kendrick Lamar's 2016 Grammy Performance," *Women & Language* 39, no. 2 (Spring 2017): 115–20, http://search.ebscohost.com.proxy.lib.uni.edu/login.aspx?direct=true&db=ufh&AN=124204815&site=ehost-live.

[63] Maeve Eberhardt and Madeline Vdoviak-Markow, "'I Ain't Sorry': African American English as a Strategic Resource in Beyoncé's Performative Persona," *Language & Communication* 72 (May 2020): 68–78, https://doi.org/10.1016/j.langcom.2020.03.003.

[64] Adrien Katherine Wing, "Brief Reflections toward a Multiplicative Theory of Praxis and Being," in *Critical Race Feminism: A Reader,* ed. Adrien Katherine Wing, (New York: New York University Press, 1997).

[65] Vivian M. May, *Pursuing Intersectionality, Unsettling Dominant Imaginaries* (New York, NY: Routledge, 2015), 5, 3.

[66] The inspiration for the metaphor of ingredients comes from Audre Lorde, *Sister Outsider* (Trumansburg, NY: Crossing, 1984), 120.

[67] Mari Boor Tonn, "Militant Motherhood: Labor's Mary Harris 'Mother' Jones," *Quarterly Journal of Speech* 82 (February 1996): 1.

[68] Tonn, "Militant Motherhood," 5.

[69] Tonn, "Militant Motherhood," 6.

[70] Kimberlé Crenshaw, "Demarginalizing the Intersection of Race and Sex: A Black Feminist Critique of Antidiscrimination Doctrine, Feminist Theory and Antiracist Politics," *University of Chicago Legal Forum* (1989): 59.

[71] Sandra Harding, "Subjectivity, Experience, and Knowledge: An Epistemology from/for Rainbow Coalition Politics," in *Who Can Speak? Authority and Critical Identity,* ed. Judith Roof and Robyn Weigman (Urbana: University of Illinois Press, 1995), 121.

[72] Thomas K. Nakayama and Robert L. Krizek, "Whiteness: A Strategic Rhetoric," *Quarterly Journal of Speech* 81 (August 1995): 291–309.

[73] Paula M. L. Moya, "Postmodernism, 'Realism,' and the Politics of Identity: Cherríe Moraga and Chicana Feminism," in *Feminist Genealogies, Colonial Legacies, Democratic Futures,* ed. M. Jacqui Alexander and Chandra Talpade Mohanty, 125–150 (New York: Routledge, 1997), 127.

[74] Katherine L. Milkman, Modupe Akinola, and Dolly Chugh, "What Happens Before? A Field Experiment Exploring How Pay and Representation Differentially Shape Bias on the Pathway into Organizations," April 23, 2014, available at Social Science

Research Network: http://ssrn.com/abstract=2063742
or http://dx.doi.org/10.2139/ssrn.2063742.

[75] Milkman, Akinola, and Chugh, "What Happens Before?" 35.

[76] "First Muslim Elected to Congress," MSNBC, November 7, 2006,
http://www.msnbc.msn.com/id/15613050.

[77] Moya, "Postmodernism," 132.

[78] Karlyn Kohrs Campbell, "Agency: Promiscuous and Protean," *Communication and Critical/Cultural Studies* 2, no. 1 (March 2005): 5.

[79] New York Times/CBS News Poll, "Whites, Race and the Election," August 9, 2008,
http://www.nytimes.com/imagepages/2008/08/09/opinion/09blow_art.ready
.html?scp=3&sq=whites%20race%20election&st=cse.

[80] Barack Obama, Presidential Inaugural Address, "What is Required: The Price and the Promise of Citizenship," January 20, 2009, http://www.americanrhetoric.com
/speeches/barackobamabarackobamainauguraladdress.htm.

[81] Gayatri Chakravorty Spivak, *The Spivak Reader,* ed. Donna Landry and Gerald MacLean (New York: Routledge, 1996), 159, 214.

[82] Stokely Carmichael, "Black Power," October 1966, http://www.americanrhetoric.com
/speeches/stokelycarmichaelblackpower.html.

[83] Robin Morgan, ed., *Sisterhood Is Powerful* (New York: Random House, 1970).

[84] Vine Deloria, Jr., and Daniel R. Wildcat, *Power and Place: Indian Education in America* (Golden, CO: Fulcrum, 2001).

[85] Spivak, *The Spivak Reader,* 214.

[86] Gloria Anzaldúa, "Bridge, Drawbridge, Sandbar or Island: Lesbians-of-Color *Hacienda Alianzas,*" in *Bridges of Power: Women's Multicultural Alliances,* ed. Lisa Albrecht and Rose M. Brewer (Philadelphia: New Society, 1990).

[87] Richard Gid Powers, *G-Men: Hoover's FBI in American Popular Culture* (Carbondale: Southern Illinois University Press, 1986).

[88] Claire Bond Potter, *War on Crime: Bandits, G-Men, and the Politics of Mass Culture* (New Brunswick, NJ: Rutgers University Press, 1998), 6.

[89] Carlota Batres, Daniel E. Re, and David I. Perrett, "Influence of Perceived Height, Masculinity, and Age on Each Other and on Perceptions of Dominance in Male Faces," *Perception* 44, no. 11 (2015): 1293–1309,
https://doi.org/10.1177/0301006615596898.

[90] Julie Hirschfeld Davis and Jonathan Martin, "James Comey's Attacks on Trump May Hurt a Carefully Cultivated Image," *New York Times* (International Edition), April 16, 2018, Lexis.

[91] Michael D. Shear and Matt Apuzzo, "F.B.I. Director James Comey Is Fired by Trump," *New York Times,* May 9, 2017,
https://www.nytimes.com/2017/05/09/us/politics/james-comey-fired-fbi.html.

[92] Quoted in James Griffiths, "Trump Says He Considered 'This Russia Thing' before Firing FBI Director Comey," transcribed from video, CNN Politics,
https://www.cnn.com/2017/05/12/politics/trump-comey-russia-thing/index.html.
However, a tweet from the president on May 31, 2018, contradicted this earlier statement. Veronica Stracqualursi, "Trump, Again, Denied Firing Comey over Russia Despite Saying Exactly That at the Time," CNN Politics, May 31, 2018,
https://www.cnn.com/2018/05/31/politics/trump-russia-investigation/index.html.

[93] Bonnie Honig, "He Said, He Said: The Feminization of James Comey," *Boston Review,* June 10, 2017, http://bostonreview.net/politics-gender-sexuality/bonnie-honig
-he-said-he-said-feminization-james-comey.

94 Bobby Lewis, "Conservative Media Deflect from James Comey's Testimony by Attacking His Sexuality and Gender," *Media Matters for America,* June 8, 2017, https://www.mediamatters.org/research/2017/06/08/conservative-media-deflect-james-comeys-testimony-attacking-his-sexuality-and-gender/216846.

95 David Leonhardt, "The Tragedy of James Comey," *New York Times,* April 8, 2018, https://www.nytimes.com/2018/04/08/opinion/james-comey.html.

96 Daniel J. Boorstin, *The Image: A Guide to Pseudo-Events in America,* 25th anniversary ed. (New York: Athenaeum, 1987), 188–189.

97 Boorstin, *The Image,* 185–193.

98 Boorstin, *The Image,* 185.

99 Garrett M. Graff, "The Political Isolation of Jim Comey," *Politico,* May 9, 2017, https://www.politico.com/magazine/story/2017/05/09/the-political-isolation-of-jim-comey-215120.

100 Boorstin, *The Image,* 188.

101 Leonhardt, "The Tragedy of James Comey."

102 Leonhardt, "The Tragedy of James Comey."

103 "Greta Thunberg: Who Is She and What Does She Want?" BBC News, February 28, 2019, https://www.bbc.com/news/world-europe-49918719.

104 "School Strike for Climate: Protests Staged around the World," BBC News, May 24, 2019, https://www.bbc.com/news/world-48392551.

105 Suyin Haynes, "Students from 1,600 Cities Just Walked out of School to Protest Climate Change. It Could Be Greta Thunberg's Biggest Strike Yet," *Time,* May 24, 2019, https://time.com/5595365/global-climate-strikes-greta-thunberg/.

106 Amy Goodman Interview of Greta Thunberg, "School Strike for Climate: Meet 15-Year-Old Activist Greta Thunberg, Who Inspired a Global Movement," *Democracy Now!,* December 11, 2018, https://www.democracynow.org/2018/12/11/meet_the_15_year_old_swedish.

107 Greta Thunberg, "Transcript: Greta Thunberg's Speech at the U.N. Climate Action Summit," NPR, September 23, 2019. Video available at https://www.youtube.com/watch?v=KAJsdgTPJpU.

108 David Murray, "Greta Thunberg's UN Speech: A Rhetorical Analysis," *Pro Rhetoric,* 2019, https://prorhetoric.com/greta-thunbergs-un-speech-a-rhetorical-analysis/.

109 Greta Thunberg's Full Speech to World Leaders at UN Climate Action Summit, *PBS News Hour,* September 23, 2019, https://www.youtube.com/watch?v=KAJsdgTPJpU.

110 I-Hsien Sherwood. "Marketer of the Year 2019: Greta Thunberg No. 8," *Advertising Age* 90, no. 23 (December 9, 2019): 24.

111 Robinson Meyer, "Why Greta Makes Adults Uncomfortable," *Atlantic,* September 23, 2019, https://www.theatlantic.com/science/archive/2019/09/why-greta-wins/598612/.

112 Roland Barthes, "The Death of the Author," translated by Richard Howard, *Aspen* 5–6 (1967), reprinted at http://www.tbook.constantvzw.org/wp-content/death_authorbarthes.pdf.

113 Barthes, "Death of the Author," 5.

114 Barthes, "Death of the Author," 6.

115 Michael Calvin McGee, "Text, Context, and the Fragmentation of Contemporary Culture," *Western Journal of Speech Communication* 54, no. 3 (Summer 1990): 288.

116 Campbell, "Agency," 5.

117 "NCAA American Indian Mascot Ban Will Begin Feb. 1," ESPN College Sports, August 12, 2015, http://sports.espn.go.com/ncaa/news/story?id=2125735.

118 "Resolution on the Washington, D.C., Football Team Name," December 12, 2013, http://www.changethemascot.org/wp-content/uploads/2013/12/Leadership -Conference-on-Civil-and-Human-Rights-Resolution.pdf.

119 Marc Weinreich, "Redskins Name Controversy: 50 Senators Sign Letter to Roger Goodell Urging Name Change," *Sports Illustrated,* SI Wire, May 22, 2014, http://tracking.si.com/2014/05/22/washington-redskins-senators-urge-name-change.

120 Darren Rovell, "U.S. Senators Send Letters to Goodell," ESPN NFL, May 22, 2014, http://espn.go.com/nfl/story/_/id/10968190/senators-puts-pressure-washington -redskins-nfl.

121 United States Patent and Trademark Office, "Amanda Blackhorse, Marcus Briggs-Cloud, Philip Gover, Jillian Pappan, and Courtney Tsotigh v. Pro-Football, Inc.," Cancellation No. 92046185, June 19, 2014, 2.

122 Erik Brady and Megan Finnerty, "Washington Redskins Appeal Decision to Cancel Trademark," *USA Today,* August 14, 2014; Ian Shapira and Ann E. Marimow, "Washington Redskins Win Trademark Fight over the Team's Name," *Washington Post,* June 29, 2017.

123 John Fiske, "Television: Polysemy and Popularity," *Critical Studies in Mass Communication* 3 (1986): 391–408; John Fiske, *Television Culture* (New York: Methuen, 1987).

124 Fiske, "Television: Polysemy and Popularity."

125 Celeste Michelle Condit, "The Rhetorical Limits of Polysemy," *Critical Studies in Mass Communication* 6, no. 2 (June 1989): 103–104.

126 Condit, "Rhetorical Limits of Polysemy," 106.

127 Randall Roberts, "Beyoncé Draws Outrage and Praise for Super Bowl Set," *Los Angeles Times,* February 8, 2016, https://www.latimes.com/entertainment/music/posts/la-et -ms-beyonce-super-bowl-reaction-20160208-story.html.

128 Roberts, "Beyoncé Draws Outrage."

129 Carole Blair, Marsha S. Jeppeson, and Enrico Pucci, Jr., "Public Memorialization in Postmodernity: The Vietnam Veterans Memorial as Prototype," *Quarterly Journal of Speech* 77 (1991): 263–288, 269.

130 "Waging War in Nigeria, and Seeking New Battlegrounds," *New York Times,* May 7, 2014, http://www.nytimes.com/2014/05/08/world/africa/boko-haram-seeks-new -battlegrounds.html.

131 Nicholas Kristof, "'Bring Back Our Girls,'" *New York Times,* May 3, 2014, http://www.nytimes.com/2014/05/04/opinion/sunday/kristof-bring-back-our-girls .html?smid=pl-share.

132 Adam Nossiter, "Nigerians Hold Second Day of Protests over Mass Abductions," *New York Times,* April 30, 2014, http://www.nytimes.com/2014/05/01/world/africa /nigerians-hold-second-day-of-protests-over-mass-abductions.html.

133 Dionne Searcey, "Why the Chibok Girls Returned by Boko Haram Are Still Not Entirely Free," *The Independent,* May 1, 2018, https://www.independent.co.uk/news/long_reads/boko-haram-girls-kidnapped -freed-return-nigeria-campus-children-babies-a8307866.html.

134 James Estrin, "The Real Story about the Wrong Photos in #BringBackOurGirls," *New York Times,* Lens, http://lens.blogs.nytimes.com/2014/05/08/the-real-story -about-the-wrong-photos-in-bringbackourgirls/?_php=true&_type=blogs&_php =true&_type=blogs&smid=fb-nytimes&WT.z_sma=LE_TRS_20140508&bicmp =AD&bicmlukp=WT.mc_id&bicmst=1388552400000&bicmet=1420088400000& _r=3&.

135 Quoted in Estrin, "The Real Story."

[136] Campbell, "Agency," 5.

[137] Sojourner Truth, "On Women's Rights," Ohio Women's Rights Convention, Akron, OH, 1851, available at http://people.sunyulster.edu/voughth/sojourner_truth.htm.

[138] Campbell, "Agency."

[139] Roseann M. Mandziuk, "Commemorating Sojourner Truth: Negotiating the Politics of Race and Gender in the Spaces of Public Memory," *Western Journal of Communication* 67, no. 3 (Summer 2003): 275.

[140] Roseann M. Mandziuk and Suzanne Pullon Fitch, "The Rhetorical Construction of Sojourner Truth," *Southern Communication Journal* 66, no. 2 (Winter 2001): 129. Thanks also to Bonnie Dow for insights concerning this example.

[141] Campbell, "Agency."

[142] Mandziuk and Fitch, "Rhetorical Construction of Sojourner Truth," 135.

[143] "Worldwide Desktop Market Share of Leading Search Engines from January 2010 to June 2021," Statista, July 2021, accessed August 23, 2021, https://www.statista.com /statistics/216573/worldwide-market-share-of-search-engines/.

[144] Bryan Horling and Robby Bryant, "Personalized Search for Everyone," *Official Google Blog,* December 4, 2009, http://googleblog.blogspot.com/2009/12/personalized -search-for-everyone.html.

[145] "Introducing Google Social Search: I Finally Found My Friend's New York Blog," *Official Google Blog,* October 26, 2009, http://googleblog.blogspot.com/2009/10 /introducing-google-social-search-i.html.

[146] "Search, Plus Your World," *Official Google Blog,* January 10, 2012, http://googleblog.blogspot.com/2012/01/search-plus-your-world.html.

[147] Eli Pariser, *The Filter Bubble* (New York: Penguin, 2011), 1–3.

[148] Siva Vaidhyanathan, *The Googlization of Everything (And Why We Should Worry)* (Los Angeles, CA: University of California Press, 2011), 3.

[149] Vaidhyanathan, *The Googlization of Everything,* 3.

[150] Vaidhyanathan, *The Googlization of Everything,* 3.

Chapter 8
Audiences

On May 17, 1954, the United States Supreme Court issued the *Brown v. Board of Education* decision, authored by Chief Justice Earl Warren, ordering the desegregation of public schools. Typically, judges write decisions in a style appropriate for members of the legal profession, focusing their attention on either of two types of questions: questions of fact or questions of law. Trial courts focus on questions of fact to determine what happened, who was involved and to what degree, and whether there were extenuating circumstances. Appellate courts, including the Supreme Court, address questions of law to determine whether the court has jurisdiction, whether the legal process was followed, which precedents and legal principles apply, whether the law is constitutional, and how the law should be interpreted.[1] Given the specialized audience and evidentiary requirements, legal decisions tend to participate in technical (rather than public) argument.

In *Brown v. Board of Education,* the Court clearly articulated the technical question of law at hand: "Does segregation of children in public schools solely on the basis of race, even though the physical facilities and other 'tangible' factors may be equal, deprive the children of the minority group of equal educational opportunities?"[2] The *Brown* decision was unique. Examining whether the "separate but equal" doctrine established by *Plessy v. Ferguson*[3] in 1896 violated the equal protection clause of the Fourteenth Amendment, the Court did not present the decision in the typical legal style. Read aloud in its entirety from the bench, the decision overtly declared that precedent alone did not govern the Court's interpretation of the Constitution. The decision was short, deliberately written in a length that could be reproduced on a single page of newsprint and understood by the general public. (The *Brown* decision was approximately 1,775 words. By comparison, the 1973 *Roe v. Wade* decision was approximately 11,667 words.)

The *Brown* decision engaged in public argument, rather than technical legal argument. The Court explained its reliance on social factors rather than on legal precedent:

> Segregation of white and colored children in public schools has a detrimental effect upon the colored children. The impact is greater when it has the sanction of the law, for the policy of separating the races is usually interpreted as denoting the inferiority of the negro group. A sense of inferiority affects the motivation of a child to learn. Segregation with the sanction of law, therefore, has a tendency to [retard] the educational and mental development of negro children and to deprive them of some of the benefits they would receive in a racial[ly] integrated school system.
>
> Whatever may have been the extent of psychological knowledge at the time of *Plessy v. Ferguson,* this finding is amply supported by modern authority. Any language in *Plessy v. Ferguson* contrary to this finding is rejected.[4]

Compared to most court decisions, this one is easily understood by a general audience. It avoids the use of legal jargon, focuses on the question of right and wrong, and refuses to be governed by *stare decisis* (the legal principle that says that, in deciding a case, a court should be governed by the precedents set in earlier decisions). The decision refers to the psychological effects of the 1896 *Plessy* decision on schoolchildren, a type of evidence unexpected in an appellate court ruling that typically would look to legal precedents (not their effects) to guide the present case.

What induced Chief Justice Warren to write such an atypical decision? In a memoir written two decades after the ruling, he explains: "It was not a long opinion, for I had written it so it could be published in the daily press throughout the nation without taking too much space. This enabled the public to have our entire reasoning instead of a few excerpts from a lengthier document."[5] By addressing the decision to the US public, and not just the technical sphere of the law, the Court participated in the public discussion about race and segregation.

Much debate ensued. Appellate judge and judicial philosopher Learned Hand derided the decision because it failed to follow precedent and did not exhibit judicial restraint.[6] Judge Hand's reaction can be explained in part because the decision was not written to persuade a fellow legal expert and, thus, violated the technical rules of legal argument.

Not everyone in the public was persuaded, however. In 1956, 101 southern senators and congressional representatives wrote a Southern Manifesto that "pledged the signers to exert 'all lawful means' toward reversing the Supreme Court's desegregation decision."[7] In response, Warren pointed out that the decision did not seek to end desegregation by court decree but to give Congress and the public the ability to act politically to end segregation.[8] By targeting its discourse to a wider audience, the Court also helped persuade the general public of the social and political importance of desegregation. Separate could not be equal.

This example illustrates the important role of the audience in rhetoric. The Supreme Court was a rhetor possessing considerable power, but it did not rely solely on that power to persuade the country. "Because we say so" was not enough to persuade the public. The Court realized its decision, alone, could not create the necessary social change if only other lawyers and judges understood the decision: the society as a whole had to change.

In this chapter, we examine the complex relationship among audiences, rhetors, and symbolic actions. First, we discuss how rhetoric is adapted to audiences. Because rhetoric is addressed to other people, understanding audience is central to rhetoric. Second, we analyze audience agency, recognizing that not all audiences possess the same degree of power to effect change in the world. Third, we discuss how audiences can be adapted to rhetoric and how rhetoric can constitute, or bring into being, a particular audience.

ADAPTING RHETORIC TO AUDIENCES

Audience is the element that distinguishes rhetoric from purely expressive forms of communication (such as shouting "ouch" when you stub your toe, or drawing for the pure pleasure of artistic creation). Rhetorical scholar Kenneth Burke identifies the central element of rhetoric as "its nature as *addressed*, since persuasion implies an audience."[9] He describes rhetoric as "the use of words by human agents to form attitudes or to induce actions in other human agents."[10] We would expand Burke's definition to include the use of any symbolic action, but we embrace his emphasis on rhetoric as addressed to other people—an audience. In the next section, we explain what we mean by "rhetoric as addressed." We then outline three means of adaptation: identification, pathos, and public emotion.

Rhetoric as Addressed

Recognizing that rhetoric is addressed to an audience is not as simple as it might first appear. **Audience** can mean *any person who hears, reads, or sees a symbolic action; the group targeted by a message, even if it is not present; or the group capable of acting in response to the message.* Multiple audiences may exist for any given symbolic action.

In interpersonal interactions, the audience is usually easy to identify: it is the person to whom you are speaking (unless—in a particularly middle-school moment—you are hoping that person will pass along what you said to your intended audience, or you are subtweeting). Identifying the audience is more complicated in public rhetoric. The group of people who might encounter public rhetoric is large and diverse. Its members may carry conflicting expectations. Sometimes, everyone present is the intended recipient of the symbolic action; other times, only some of those present are the intended audience.

When you speak to a large group, not every member may be part of the **rhetorical audience,** or *the audience that "consists only of those persons who are capable of being influenced by discourse and of being mediators of change."* In this definition, rhetoric scholar Lloyd F. Bitzer distinguishes a rhetorical audience from all those who might hear a speech.[11] For Bitzer, a rhetorical audience pre-exists the rhetorical action; it is empirically real and already possesses the ability to implement the change that the rhetor calls for. In Bitzer's approach, rhetors and critics need to analyze the audience members who are agents capable of bringing about the action, not just anyone who might receive the message.

Bitzer's understanding of the rhetorical audience finds its roots in the classical tradition, which defined the audience as the people who were capable of acting in response to a message. Aristotle points out, "A speech consists of three things: a speaker and a subject on which he speaks and someone addressed, and the objective of the speech relates to the last."[12] Aristotle argues that rhetoric is persuasive to a *particular* audience, which he defines as those who make judgments concerning the issue or issues at hand. The objective of the speech is, in turn, determined by the audience, as the audience holds the power to act on the message.[13]

Philosophers Chaïm Perelman and Lucie Olbrechts-Tyteca[14] note that the classical rhetorical tradition emphasizes "the discursive ways of acting upon an audience, with a view to winning or increasing its adherence to the theses that were presented to it for its endorsement."[15] They agree with Aristotle, explaining: "It is indeed the audience which has the major role in determining the quality of argument and the behavior of orators."[16] Whenever you consider the function of symbolic action, it is essential to assess the audience to whom the rhetor addresses the message. For example, in a graduation ceremony, the students may appreciate a commencement address that their parents condemn.

You can probably recall times when you made rhetorical choices according to the audience to whom you spoke; that is, you adapted to the rhetorical audience. For example, when requesting an extension on a paper due for a class, you probably tailor your request to the professor from whom you are requesting the extension. Some professors might be more persuaded by a pity appeal, while others would only be persuaded if you proved you had not procrastinated. You might not even make such a request to some professors because you believe they are not likely to grant the request. In all these instances, you frame your message to speak to the particular audience. You adapt because your audience determines and delimits the objective of your symbolic action.

When identifying the audience(s) for a rhetorical act, remember that multiple audiences may be targeted. For example, consider New Orleans Mayor Mitch Landrieu's speech about removing Confederate monuments from the city.[17] Two years earlier, the murder of nine Black people at a church in South Carolina by a self-avowed white supremacist had catalyzed a debate about Confederate symbols; in response, several cities began removing monuments.[18] When New Orleans decided to remove four Confederate monuments, the workers tasked with the job wore body armor, helmets, and face coverings because they feared for their safety.[19]

Mayor Landrieu addressed the public controversy in a speech after the monuments had been removed. He spoke to numerous audiences:

- "Self-appointed defenders of history and the monuments," whom Landrieu challenged by pointing out they were silent about the lack of monuments or markers remembering the city's history of slave ships, auction blocks, or lynchings.

- People who may have been unaware that the statues were not erected immediately after the Civil War to honor particular leaders but decades later, by people who sought to remember the war as a just and heroic cause. The movement that is sometimes called the cult of the Lost Cause used Confederate statues as a form of "terrorism," meant to show Blacks that Whites controlled the city.

- Proponents of removal who fear this will be where debates about race will end, whom Landrieu assured the statue removal was "not a naïve quest to solve all our problems."

- The people of New Orleans, in whom Landrieu evoked pride in the traditions of food, music, architecture, Mardi Gras, and jazz the city has "given to the world."[20]

The speech addressed the distinct audiences who populate the city and who disagree about the removal of the monuments, with most of the speech addressed to those who oppose, or were neutral, about the removal.

The speech went viral even though Landrieu "intended" the speech "for a local audience."[21] Why? Because it spoke to national themes about identity, memory, and the stories people tell about US history. Landrieu spoke to multiple audiences and attempted to create identification with all of them by celebrating the identity of New Orleans and the national commitment to equality.

Appealing to an Audience

How might you go about adapting to an audience? You could draw on a range of overlapping rhetorical techniques. First, you can seek to create identification, or a sense of commonality between you and the audience. Second, you can employ *pathos* appeals, trying to put the audience members in a state of mind where they are most open to the arguments offered. Third, you can try to harness public emotion.

Identification. The concept of identification plays a central role in describing the relationship between rhetors and audiences. As we discussed in chapter 1, **identification** is *a communicative process through which people are unified into a whole on the basis of common interests or characteristics.*[22] Through identification, you make a connection with the audience on a psychological level, not simply on a demographic level. On the surface you might identify with another student simply because of the shared demographic characteristic—the other person is also a student. However, identification can be deeper if you do not take it for granted, but actively produce it through rhetoric. If you wanted to create identification on the basis of shared student status, for example, you would not simply take for granted that other students would agree with you. Instead, you would use evidence based on experiences students share, speak from the persona of a student, and emphasize values and concerns that are prominent in students' lives.

Rhetors and audience members are both similar and different. Identification can be achieved by emphasizing similarities even while respecting differences. Burke explains that "two persons may be identified in terms of some principle they share in common, an 'identification' that does not deny their distinctness."[23] Notice that Burke does not reduce identification to shared demographic characteristics but argues that a shared principle must be identified. These moments of **consubstantiality,** in which *two distinct things momentarily become part of a whole,* are at the heart of persuasion and rhetoric. Burke posits, "Here is perhaps the simplest case of persuasion. You persuade [people] only insofar as you can talk [their] language by speech, gesture, tonality, order, image, attitude, idea, *identifying* your ways with [theirs]."[24] If you are connected to people in some way, you probably have a better chance of persuading them than if you were a stranger or completely alien to them.

Understanding the process of identification is central to understanding rhetoric as addressed. Thus, critics need to explore how rhetors seek to create identification with their audiences. In a 2009 speech at Cairo University in Egypt, President Obama[25] sought to create identification with each of several audiences. He opened by identifying with Muslims, using the customary Muslim greeting "Assalaamu alaykum."[26] He reaffirmed that identification by outlining other personal connections to Islam: "My father came from a Kenyan family that includes generations of Muslims. As a boy, I spent several years in Indonesia and heard the call of the azaan at the break of dawn and at the fall of dusk. As a young man, I worked in Chicago communities where many found dignity and peace in their Muslim faith."[27] Obama identified with Christians by testifying "I'm a Christian."[28] He highlighted the identification of political interests between the United States and Israel: "America's strong bonds with Israel are well known. This bond is unbreakable. It is based upon cultural and historical ties, and the recognition that the aspiration for a Jewish homeland is rooted in a tragic history that cannot be denied."[29] Finally, he created identification between the United States and Arab countries by recognizing the common interests they have in stopping the suffering of Palestinians:

> On the other hand, it is also undeniable that the Palestinian people—
> Muslims and Christians—have suffered in pursuit of a homeland. For more
> than 60 years they've endured the pain of dislocation. Many wait in refugee
> camps in the West Bank, Gaza, and neighboring lands for a life of peace
> and security that they have never been able to lead. They endure the daily
> humiliations—large and small—that come with occupation. So let there
> be no doubt: The situation for the Palestinian people is intolerable. And
> America will not turn our backs on the legitimate Palestinian aspiration for
> dignity, opportunity, and a state of their own.[30]

Even though President Obama spoke to audiences with different, if not conflicting, interests and identities, he was able to create the impression that he as a person, and the United States as a nation, were consubstantial with Muslims and Christians, Arabs and Israelis. Obama's need to create identification with multiple audiences can be explained by the various audiences' abilities to effect change.

Pathos. Aristotle defined *pathos* as proof *that leads the audience "to feel emotion."* More specifically, pathos appeals lead audience members to particular emotional states of mind. Aristotle's treatment of human emotions was perhaps the earliest systematic treatment of psychology.[31] Aristotle placed emotions in contrasting pairs: anger/calmness; friendliness/enmity; fear/confidence; shame/shamelessness; kindness/unkindness; pity/indignation; envy/emulation. The pairs were not meant to imply that one emotion was good and the other bad. Even anger, an emotion people are often told they should suppress, has a place. Communication scholars Kenneth S. Zagacki and Patrick A. Bolyn-Fitzgerald explain that Aristotle's theory of rhetoric "maintains that there are some rhetorical situations where the public expression of anger is appropriate and where its absence is morally blameworthy."[32] Nevertheless, political communication scholar Martin J. Medhurst notes, "Until quite recently, appeals to the emotions or feelings of an audience were regularly condemned but seldom studied."[33]

Aristotle explained that rhetors must consider the emotional state of the audience[34] because people make judgments differently depending upon their state of mind.[35] You have thought about the emotional state of your audience when you have considered someone's mood before initiating a difficult conversation. Suppose you want to talk to a housemate about redistributing chores. If you ask a mutual friend what kind of mood your housemate is in before you talk, you are considering the emotional state of the audience. You might even choose not to make the request that day if you conclude that your housemate is not in the appropriate state of mind to consider your request, or you might think about how to alter your housemate's state of mind to be more open to a conversation about shared housework. Pathos appeals recognize the effect of emotion on an audience's receptiveness, so they are chosen to induce particular emotions in order to enhance persuasive appeals. For example, fear is a strong emotion that can lead people to make particular choices. For Aristotle, fear is "pain or agitation derived from the imagination of a future destructive or painful evil."[36] But fear cannot be triggered merely by saying "Be afraid, be very afraid!" According to rhetorical scholar Michael William Pfau, Aristotle posited that "one must believe that a destructive or painful event or object is likely to affect oneself, and that the object of fear is near at hand—both temporally and spatially."[37] But not all fear appeals are the same.

In a review of the classical literature on fear appeals, Pfau offers a useful distinction between generic fear appeals that can undermine deliberation and **civic fear appeals** that *"potentially contribute to effective public deliberations about challenges facing the community of citizens"* because they are *"generative of needed public discussions and debates."*[38] A fear appeal might make people freeze, or become so afraid they think nothing can be done. In contrast, civic fear appeals

move beyond just instilling fear. They include four other elements: (1) an identification of an "unrecognized or underappreciated" object of fear; (2) a description
of the object of fear as "contingent" because audience members can take action to
ameliorate the danger; (3) a constitution of the audience members as courageous,
and thus able to act in the face of their fears to preserve their community; and
(4) a goal of opening space for deliberation about ways to address the fear.[39]

Not all fear appeals are bad. The test is whether a fear appeal is meant to close
off deliberation or to encourage it. For example, throughout the 2016 presidential
campaign, the media repeatedly reported that candidate Trump appealed to fear.
A story in the *Atlantic* said, "Trump is a master of fear, invoking it in concrete
and abstract ways, summoning and validating it. More than most politicians, he
grasps and channels the fear coursing through the electorate."[40] When accepting
the Republican nomination, after declaring "a moment of crisis for our nation"
which included "attacks on our police, and terrorism in our cities, [that] threaten
our very way of life," "crime and violence," and "new illegal immigrant families,"
Trump declared that "nobody knows the system better than me . . . I alone can
fix it."[41]

Fear appeals also figured prominently in Trump's inaugural address, which
described "American carnage," including "rusted out factories scattered like
tombstones across the landscape of our nation," "radical Islamic terrorism," and
"infrastructure . . . fallen into disrepair and decay." Trump also declared: "There
should be no fear. We are protected and we will always be protected. We will be
protected by the great men and women of our military and law enforcement. And
most importantly, we will be protected by God."[42] In other words, the audience
members cannot act to lessen fear; instead, authority figures protect the audience
from the fearful thing.

The fear appeals continued during the 2018 midterms. *Time* reported
that "Trump keeps using fear,"[43] and "no President has weaponized fear quite
like Trump."[44] A *New York Times* opinion piece labeled the president "The
Commander of Fear,"[45] a play on the presidential role of commander in chief.
Things to fear included radical Islamic terrorism, persecution of Christians in
the Middle East, "illegal immigrants," the "fake news media," crime, and "urban
gangs." CNN described the core of Trump's rhetorical appeal: "He foments fear
and casts the world as a very, very dangerous place—and then promises that" as
long as the people provide approval in polls and votes in elections "he will take
care of everything."[46]

Trump's rhetoric used fear appeals about a variety of threats that are temporally and spatially near by describing the United States as in a crisis *now*, amid
threats at the borders flooding into airports and into US cities. However, these
fear appeals did not do the work necessary to be *civic* fear appeals. They did not
induce civic deliberation. In fact, they tended to cut it off. For example, debates
over the variety of ways to improve border security were shut off, as Trump
declared a "national emergency" that expanded presidential powers to access
funds that Congress had refused to allocate.[47] In addition, the rhetoric did not
empower audience members to be agents of change, nor were they encouraged
to exhibit courage to act. Instead, they were encouraged to hand over agency to

the president ("I alone can fix it") and other higher powers (the military, police, and God).

In contrast, much of NIAID (National Institute of Allergy and Infectious Diseases) director Anthony Fauci's rhetoric about COVID attempted to create a civic fear appeal. Fauci repeatedly declared that the rate of infection had to be controlled, that "we are all in this together," that everyone had a role to play, and that the solution is "in our hands" and "it can be done."[48] Fauci sought to make clear (1) the full danger of COVID, in response to some people downplaying the pandemic; (2) the steps audience members could take to lessen the danger (for example, social distancing, wearing masks, washing their hands, getting vaccinated); (3) the American people's courage and, thus, their able to act; and (4) the space available for continued deliberation as more information was gathered. By talking about COVID as a public health crisis, Dr. Fauci made clear that all community members had a responsibility to do what they could. Although an audience might want a speaker to talk with absolute certainty, the reality is that argument is contingent. Even in the face of fear, changing information, and evolving data, however, Fauci emphasized that audiences can, and should, be empowered to act.

Public Emotion. Rhetors can both express emotion and induce emotions in audiences. Rhetors and audiences can display emotions such as anger, passion, or disgust. Such display, unjustifiably, is often thought of as undermining public deliberation. Rhetoric scholars Robert Hariman and John Louis Lucaites note that both rhetorical and political theory have "constructed, studied, and policed . . . emotional display" through "general suppression or suspicion."[49] If emotional display is suppressed in public deliberation, however, "then emotional display can become a mode of dissent"[50] against a purely rational approach to decision making. For example, the emotional displays behind the "Black Lives Matter" protests, following the deaths of young Black people in police custody, powerfully demonstrate the value and humanity of Black lives. The public displays of emotion have moved a nation.

Scholars have begun to attend to the importance of **public emotions,** which, according to Hariman and Lucaites, are *collective expressions of feeling that are "crucial elements of democratic deliberation, judgment, and action" that "comprise a language for collective life."*[51] To understand rhetoric in civic life, you need to understand the role of emotion in civic life. Hariman and Lucaites emphasize that "public reason has to be underwritten by public emotion" and that "if citizenship is to be an embodied identity, an actual mode of participation in decision making . . . , then it has to be articulated in a manner that encourages emotional identification with other civic actors."[52] Identification is not simply a rational calculation that another person shares an interest; it is an emotional connection through which a person *feels* connected to another.

Public emotion moves beyond Aristotle's theory of pathos "as an individual subjective state" and instead treats emotions as "shared (intersubjective) moods created by" rhetorical action.[53] For example, when speaking about the 2012 killing of seventeen-year-old Trayvon Martin by a person who used Florida's "stand your ground" laws as a defense, President Obama employed identification and spoke to a public grief: "Obviously this is a tragedy. I can only imagine what these parents are going through. When I think about this boy I think about my own kids and I think every parent in American should be able to understand why it is absolutely imperative that we investigate every aspect."[54] He created identification with parents on the basis of shared grief over the loss of a child.

As another example, consider public vigils such as those held after twenty-six people were killed in a shooting at Sandy Hook Elementary School in Newtown, Connecticut, in 2012;[55] six people in Isla Vista, California, near the University of California, Santa Barbara, campus in 2014;[56] nine people at the Emanuel African Methodist Episcopal Church in Charleston, South Carolina, in 2015;[57] forty-nine people at the Pulse night club in Orlando, Florida, in 2017;[58] fifty-eight people at the Route 91 Harvest music festival in Las Vegas in 2017;[59] and twenty-six people at the First Baptist Church in Sutherland Springs, Texas, in 2017.[60] As rhetoric scholar E. Cram notes, "Public vigils are a rich site to explore how local, regional, or national publics respond to and publicize acts of violence." They exemplify how people coming together to grieve the loss of community members form a political community.[61]

Cram's study of the vigils held for Angie Zapata, a transwoman murdered by an acquaintance, highlights an "emotional politics of visuality" in which Angie's self-portraits were displayed on T-shirts worn at community vigils and by her family members sitting in the courtroom during her murderer's trial. The family's and community's public displays of grief countered the defense team's attempt to exclude Angie from the community because she was trans. Cram notes that family, friends, and allies participated in citizenship as "a category of embodied sociality, public emotionality, and performative enactment."[62] They wore images of Angie on their bodies, close to their hearts. They displayed public grief for a person whom the prosecution tried to present as deserving of disgust rather than mourning. And they performed their belief that Angie was part of their community by keeping her images alive in their midst.

Historically, the word "vigil" has referred to a prayer service held the day before a funeral. The vigils for shooting victims, like traditional vigils tend to happen before funerals and are confined to a discrete moment in time. But "vigil" also refers to the practice of staying awake when you typically sleep in order to stay alert, guard, or engage in devotional watching. In many ways, Angie's family's vigil combines both senses of the word. They are mourning the loss of their daughter *and* they are standing watch at court.

This expansion of the time and purpose of "vigil" also can be found in the activism of Black Lives Matter, which combines the act of public grieving with the idea of standing watch, on guard to prevent further "state-sanctioned violence and anti-Black racism."[63] The "SayTheirNames"[64] and #SayHerName[65] projects participate in the memory and memorial aspects of prefuneral vigils. All these projects use expressions of public grief to induce changes in policies and practices that result in the deaths of Black people.[66]

When studying emotion, do not reduce it to a mere supplement to persuasive appeals. According to Hariman and Lucaites, one should recognize that public emotion is part of civic life, "intricately woven into the material fabric of a society" because "emotions flood language and all other symbolic media in a society."[67] Public reason and public emotion are central to civic life.

Of course, not every emotional display, nor every attempt to induce an emotional reaction, is good for civic life. Just as with any rhetorical action, you need to assess not only the effectiveness of the action, but also its ethics. Jon Stewart's *Daily Show* pointed out the tensions that exist in a world filled with public fear. On June 5, 2014, Stewart aired a segment titled "Keep Gun and Carry On" in response to "open carry" demonstrations during that spring. The segment explored the problem posed by open carry advocates, who feared erosion of their Second Amendment rights, and who also tended to be "stand your ground" advocates who believed they had the right to use deadly force in fear-inducing situations.[68] Opponents said the open carry advocates induced fear themselves, by displaying weapons in restaurants and other public places. The *Daily Show* asked, when open carry advocates enter a place, and the other people in the place perceive a threat, what are the other people to do? The conclusion: "We are at the intersection of open carry road and stand your ground place." Stewart then showed a series of clips of people declaring their need to use their rights or lose them, as well as their fear of groups of armed people in public places. The series also included an explanation of stand your ground laws and a criticism of the legal "duty to retreat to avoid danger." Stewart showed the National Rifle Association arguing that you have the right to carry a weapon that terrifies another person, while the terrified person has the right to respond with deadly force, thus creating a "perpetual violence machine" of public fear.

AUDIENCE AGENCY

Audiences are not passive recipients of a message: they are active participants in the process of rhetoric. Audiences matter. A rhetor who is seeking to induce some sort of action in an audience must consider the limits of audience agency, of the audience's ability to take the action. You can try to adapt rhetoric to an audience in order to create a desired change, or you can try to adapt the audience to your rhetoric.

The concept of audience agency explains why rhetors must sometimes adapt audiences to rhetoric. Recall, from chapter 1, that Karlyn Kohrs Campbell defines **rhetorical agency** as "*the capacity to act, that is, to have the competence to speak or write [or engage in any form of symbolic action] in a way that will be recognized or heeded by others in one's community.*"[69] We have extended Campbell's definition (in square brackets) to include competence in visual rhetoric, as well as in the verbal forms of speaking and writing.

Both rhetors and audiences possess agency. Just as rhetors may possess various degrees of agency, depending on their positions in the socioeconomic order, cultural norms, or ideologies, so, too may audiences possess various degrees of agency, or various capacities to act on or respond to rhetors' symbolic actions. Campbell argues that traditional understandings of the audience, as the group to whom a symbolic action is addressed and who is capable of enacting the called-for change, are overly limiting. Not all audiences who are addressed already possess agency; some are not yet rhetorical audiences, but must be constituted as such. In some cases, rhetors may need to construct audiences as agents of action.

For example, in the women's liberation that emerged in the 1960s and 1970s, a central goal of the rhetoric was empowerment: convincing women that they could, indeed, be agents of change. Campbell argues, "The [traditional] concept of the audience does not account for a situation in which the audience must be *created under the special conditions* surrounding women's liberation."[70] Women activists faced the challenge of figuring out how to perform the public role of rhetor when social demands on how to perform the role of woman pushed them to stay out of public affairs. In addition, although women were not equal under the law, not all women perceived inequality to be a problem. Many of those who did were not sure they had the ability to effect change in the law or culture. As women appealed to other women to act, they had to make clear that audience members possessed the agency with which to act. They had to construct audiences as having agency as one of the characteristics of audiences.

Given the complexities associated with the interplay of rhetoric and audience, you need to decide whether the audience is (1) the group of people who happened to receive the symbolic action, (2) the group or groups targeted by the rhetor, (3) the group with whom the rhetor sought to create identification, or (4) the audience called into being by the rhetoric. We now turn to an analysis of this last form of audience.

ADAPTING AUDIENCES TO RHETORIC

Audiences, even those already capable of acting, are molded by the rhetoric addressed to them. Rhetoric scholar Barbara Biesecker suggests that identities of audiences and of rhetors are not fixed; that rhetorical action is "an event that makes possible the production of identities and social relations."[71] Rhetors can call audiences into being. An audience can be understood not only as Bitzer's objectively identifiable empirical audience that is capable of acting, but also as a rhetorical creation.

A rhetor addresses an audience in the hope of affecting that audience in some way. Often, however, people simply assume that the audience is the people who receive the message. Think about your preparations for a speech in class. How much time do you spend thinking about who your audience is? Do you just assume it is your classmates? Or your instructor? In other words, do you assume that an audience preexists the message? Or do you think about how you could actually change the character of the class with your message, how you could target your message to only some people in your class, or even how you might address an audience who is totally absent? Your audience might come into being because of your message.

Examples of bringing an audience into existence are found in scholarly examinations of "the people." Political discourse often takes for granted that a group known as "the people" exists, and directs discourse to that group. For example, Speaker of the House John Boehner attempted to delay implementation of the

Affordable Care Act (ACA) in 2013, declaring "It's time for the Senate to listen to the American people just like the House has listened to the American people and to pass a one-year delay of ObamaCare and a permanent repeal of the medical device tax."[72]

The ACA, signed into law in 2010, expanded health care coverage by improving the affordability of health insurance, expanding coverage of adult children under their parents' plans, increasing access to insurance for people with preexisting conditions, expanding Medicaid, subsidizing low-income people's insurance plans, and creating health care exchanges. The law also contained an individual mandate: everyone must have health insurance or pay a penalty. In order to stop full implementation of the individual mandate, House and Senate Republicans attempted to link an ACA implementation delay to a vote on whether to fund the government. The Republican-controlled House passed three funding bills, each of which denied funding to the ACA or delayed its implementation. When the Democrat-controlled Senate would only consider a funding bill that did neither of those things, a government shutdown ensued. Boehner, attempting to induce the Senate to act, argued that a delay was what "the American people" wanted, but what people was he talking about? Polls from that period indicate that 59 to 63 percent of respondents did not think it was right to shut down the government in order to stop the ACA.[73]

Who, then, are "the people?" Communication scholar Michael Calvin McGee points out that the concept of "the people" is a rhetorical construction. McGee explains that "'the people,' even though made 'real' by their own belief and behavior, are still essentially a mass illusion. In purely objective terms, the only human reality is that of the individual; groups, whether as small as a Sunday school class or as big as a whole society, are infused with an artificial identity."[74] The individuals who compose an audience are real, but the belief that the collection of individuals represents a unit called "the people" is a social construction. To say an audience is a social construction does not mean, however, that it is illusory or meaningless. How an audience is constructed matters to how it acts. Rhetoric matters.

Silvio Waisbord, a professor of media and public affairs, enumerates recent cases of populist leaders invoking "the people":

> Appeals to "the people" are ubiquitous in contemporary populist discourse. Just as Turkey's Recep Tayyip Erdoğan affirmed "Enough is enough, sovereignty belongs to the people," Venezuela's Hugo Chavez stated "Here I am standing. The people should order me, I know how to obey. I am a soldier of the people, you are my boss." In the aftermath of Trump's successful presidential run, Hungary's Orban exulted: "We are moving back to reality, which means [respecting] the views of real people and what they think, how they approach these questions—not to educate them, but accept them as they are, because they are the basis of democracy." Populism conceives "the people"—what UKIP leader Nigel Farage often described as "ordinary," "little," "real," "decent" people during the 2016 "Brexit" campaign, as the pure and noble embodiment of democratic politics, the true manifestation of the collective soul.[75]

Waisbord argues that such appeals simplify complex collections of individuals; leave distinctions among "the people," "the elites," and others "open to political calculations"; and promote a "binary, conflict-centered view of politics."[76] Rarely does "the people" refer to everyone. Instead, according to sociologist Bart Bonikowski, it narrows the public into a "subset . . . that qualifies as a legitimate source of political power" and breeds vilification of any who are not included in "the people."[77]

Just as McGee analyzes "the people," scholars have explored the rhetorical creations of other groups. Such a creation is not the result of a single rhetorical act, but the repeated invocation of that group across multiple messages. When a rhetor constructs an audience as a group of people who identify with one another, a second persona has been created. Yet, whenever identification is created within a group, division is also created. Thus, an assessment of the third persona, the excluded or denied audience, is necessary. The rhetor may also create an audience that is indirectly or surreptitiously addressed.

Second Persona

The **first persona** is *the author implied by the discourse*. Rhetorical theorist Edwin Black posits that just as the rhetor may construct a persona for the "I" who is speaking, so too may a rhetor create a **second persona** for the "you" to whom the rhetor speaks, *the implied audience for whom a rhetor constructs symbolic actions*.[78] (Here, think about the grammatical constructs of first, second, and third person: I/we, you, he/she/they.) Black challenges critics to look beyond the immediate audience and to recognize the larger social context in which symbolic action worked.

At the beginning of this chapter we discussed the Supreme Court decision in *Brown v. Board of Education,* which was written for the general public. The use of public reasoning rather than legal precedent pointed to the wider public as the implied audience, the second persona, rather than to the narrower legal community. In this case, the public is composed of a particular type of person—one who is called to accept the equal humanity of all people. When analyzing the audience from this perspective, a critic does not ask: To what group of individuals does a rhetor speak? Instead, the more pertinent question is: What auditor is implied in the rhetorical discourse? Identifying the implied auditor is important, Black says, because "the critic can see in the auditor implied by a discourse a model of what the rhetor would have [their] real auditor become."[79]

For example, who is the implied audience of mainstream commercial newspapers? It is no longer everyone who can read. By analyzing the advertising and content in newspapers, as well as how newspapers sold themselves to advertisers, media scholar Christopher Martin documents that in the late 1960s, newspaper companies "made a significant and devastating shift from targeting a mass audience to targeting an upscale audience" because advertisers were most interested in the upscale demographic.[80] The result: newspapers no longer addressed the working class. Martin details how this "purposeful shift" changed what newspapers covered (most no longer have a reporter on the "labor beat") and how they covered it (instead of aligning with workers, stories positioned readers against workers who hurt the interests of the upscale news consumer). Workers were no longer part of the collective "we" addressed by print media. Martin explains that "with the working class bereft of journalism that spoke to their lives, the emerging conservative news filled a gap, but only for the White working class." Conservative talk radio hosts (for example, Rush Limbaugh), FOX news, right-wing websites (such as Breitbart News Network), and eventually presidential candidate Donald Trump explicitly addressed the "working class"—a group that mainstream newspapers no longer addressed. In the process, they constituted an identity for who counted as a real American: "white, working-class men."[81]

Politicians often say that "we" need to do something, or that "we" as a nation believe in particular values, when in reality they are referencing a particular segment of the population who, they hope, will vote for them. Granted, it is extremely easy to fall into using "we," especially when a person wants to create a sense of identification and community. As Burke points out, however, whenever identification is used, one must "confront the implications of *division*.... Identification is compensatory to division."[82] When a group says "we are alike," it implies that others are not like them.

For example, Manuel Miranda (a former aide to Senator Bill Frist), in a Heritage Foundation luncheon explaining how conservatives could woo the Hispanic vote, said: "Hispanic polls, Hispanic surveys, indicate that Hispanics think just like everyone else. We're not like African-Americans. We think just like everybody else."[83] By identifying Hispanics with "everybody else," then dissociating African Americans from that group, Miranda suggests that "everyone else" as a group does not literally include everyone else. Instead, Miranda's rhetoric says "everyone else" means Whites. Whenever a rhetor seeks to create identification among group members, disidentification is a necessary counterpart. If you create an "us," you also create a "them." From this dialectic relationship comes the reality of a third persona, an "it" who not only is excluded from address, but whose humanity is questioned.

Third Persona

If rhetors can call an audience into being, they can construct other people as lacking being. Rhetoric scholar Philip Wander labels these people the **third persona:** "*audiences not present, audiences rejected or negated through the speech and/or the speaking situation.*"[84]

Recognition of such an audience is essential in tracking the ways in which rhetoric enacts ideology. Thus, whenever you study the audience that is present in the rhetorical action, you should also ask about the people who have been excluded from being addressed. Wander explains that "what is negated through the Second Persona forms the silhouette of a Third Persona—the 'it' that is not present, that is objectified in a way that 'you' and 'I' are not.... The potentiality of language to commend being carries with it the potential to spell out being unacceptable, undesirable, insignificant."[85] The third persona is the group treated as an object and dehumanized, while the second persona is recognized or commended. If the first persona is an "I," and the second persona a "you," then the third persona is an "it."

The construction of a third persona involves more than speaking to one group of people rather than another. A rhetor cannot speak to all people all the time. In some instances, messages really are meant for a particular audience. In many cases, however, constituting one audience by including some people necessarily excludes other people. For Wander's purposes, the third persona

> refers not merely to groups of people with whom "you" and "I" are not to identify, who are to remain silent in public, who are not to become part of "our" audience or even be allowed to respond to what "we" say. Beyond its verbal formulation, the Third Persona draws in historical reality, so stark in the twentieth century, of peoples categorized according to race, religion, age, gender, sexual preference, and nationality, and acted upon in ways consistent with their status as non-subjects. The Third Persona directs our attention to beings beyond the claims of morality and the bonds of compassion.[86]

In other words, by calling some groups into being, rhetoric also can deny the existence of others, or erase them.

A contemporary example of the construction of a third persona can be found in the debates over immigration. Communication scholars who study rhetoric about immigration have noted that instead of addressing people who immigrate without documentation by attempting to persuade them not to cross the border illegally, critics of illegal immigration turn them into a third persona, dehumanizing them by describing them as a "flood," "tide," "pollutant," "infestation," "infection," and "disease."[87] Such language was revivified during the Trump administration. Then–President Trump tweeted that Democrats want "illegal immigrants . . . to pour into and infest our Country,"[88] and said during a White House meeting, "These aren't people. These are animals."[89] Once denied humanity, immigrants are also denied compassion. They become an infestation to be fought, a tide to be held back, a pollutant in need of cleansing.

A third persona can be created even when a speaker appears to use inclusive language. Political scientist Jane Mansbridge analyzes the use of the collective "we" in political discourse to represent a particular few by making invisible a distinct other. She explains, "'We' can easily represent a false universality, as 'mankind' used to."[90] Thus, "the very capacity to identify with others can easily be manipulated to the disadvantage of" a subordinated group because "the transformation of 'I' into 'we' brought about through political deliberation can easily mask subtle forms of control."[91] The earlier example from Manuel Miranda is one illustration.

The perniciousness of a falsely universal "we" is evident even in a speech that was meant to celebrate inclusion. In 1998, President Bill Clinton delivered a speech announcing the Race Initiative, a series of national conversations and policy initiatives meant to counter racism in the United States. Clinton's speech provides a review of history, which uses the inclusive language of "we," but actually excludes some groups by their absence from the historical occurrences outlined. As you read this passage, ask yourself: who is "we"?

> *We* were born with a Declaration of Independence which asserted that *we* were all created equal and a Constitution that enshrined slavery. *We* fought a bloody Civil War to abolish slavery and preserve the Union, but *we* remained a house divided and unequal by law for another century. *We* advanced across the continent in the name of freedom, yet in so doing *we* pushed Native Americans off their land, often crushing their culture and their livelihood. *Our* Statue of Liberty welcomes poor, tired, huddled masses of immigrants to our borders, but each new wave has felt the sting of discrimination. In World War II, Japanese-Americans fought valiantly for freedom in Europe, taking great casualties, while at home their families were herded into internment camps. The famed Tuskegee Airmen lost none of the bombers they guarded during the war, but their African-American heritage cost them a lot of rights when they came back home in peace. [emphasis added][92]

The first "we" most likely does not refer to everyone, even though Clinton had earlier noted that the audience was composed of people of "many backgrounds." It refers only to White US citizens of European descent, the group granted rights by a "Constitution that enshrined slavery." Clearly, not everyone was born equal under the nation's founding documents. Although Clinton does recognize that "we" drove Native Americans off their lands, such a use of "we" is interesting because US citizens of European descent were primarily responsible for the genocide against Native Americans. This statement also implies that "they" (Native Americans) are not part of "us" (Americans).

Clinton's use of "we" is complicated further by the use of truncated passives. In the first few sentences, a "we" is present. Yet, when Clinton begins to describe specific examples of discrimination, the agent of those acts becomes invisible. Clinton explains that each new wave of immigrants "felt the sting" of discrimination but does not identify who discriminated against them. Japanese families were "herded into internment camps," but he does not identify who herded them. Finally, their "African-American heritage cost" the Tuskegee Airmen their rights; the bigotry of White people ("we") did not deny them their "inherent dignity." Thus, responsibility either lies with no one or with the heritage of those who faced racism. Although Clinton's historical narrative might attempt to expose the hypocrisy of the dominant myths of democracy, exploration, and equality, it fails to unmask the agency of White Americans.

Indirectly Addressed Audiences

Thus far, we have explored the first persona (the implied author, the "I"), the second persona (the implied audience, the "you"), and the third persona (the excluded and dehumanized audience, the it). However, an audience type is missing from this list: the covertly or indirectly addressed audience. Scholars have written about two types of indirectly addressed audiences: the fourth persona and an eavesdropping audience.

The **fourth persona** is *an audience who recognizes that the rhetor's first persona may not reveal all that is relevant about the speaker's identity, but maintains silence in order to enable the rhetor to perform that persona.* A rhetor's persona may require an act of passing: convincing an audience that the rhetor's persona participates in an acceptable identity category. Gays and lesbians sometimes attempt to pass as straight. Historically, some light-skinned Black people passed as White. During the Holocaust, some Jewish children passed as Christian.

Passing, "*performing a privileged identity . . . in order to mask non-privileged identities*"[93] is a fraught way to perform persona. Communication scholars Catherine R. Squires and Daniel C. Brouwer note that passing can both "enact psychological or physical suffering" because it might be motivated by "self-hatred and disloyalty" to the group one is passing out of *and* enact "creative identity play for the passer," who challenges rigid identity categories.[94] Passing is rhetorically interesting because it shows how a rhetor's persona is dependent on the perceptions of audiences and because "passing and catching someone in a pass make clearly visible the web of individual, state, society, and culture involved in maintaining identities."[95] Communication scholar Marcia Alesan Dawkins explains that passing is rhetorical because it directs attention to some things and away from others: "Passing demands that we think hard about issues of identity and rhetoric, of the public and the private, in ways that most of us are privileged enough to ignore if we so choose."[96] Understanding passing and the fourth persona are central to rhetoric in civic culture.

When rhetors engage in rhetorical passing, some members of the audience are usually aware of the attempt to pass. Rhetoric scholar Charles E. Morris III posits that rhetors enact passing "by means of the *fourth persona:* a collusive audience constituted by the textual wink. Similar to its counterpart, the second persona, the fourth persona is an implied auditor of a particular ideological bent."[97] Passing only works if a person who knows otherwise, one whom Amy Robinson labels the "in-group clairvoyant,"[98] enables the rhetor to perform the passing persona. Thus, identity is less about some innate characteristic of the rhetor and more about what is intelligible to an audience.

Passing is a voluntary action that hides a person's identity. However, some pressures force people to downplay their identities. For people with nondominant identities, immense pressure exists to conform to hegemonic norms. Legal scholar Kenji Yoshino refers to such conforming not as passing, but as **covering,** which involves *downplaying an identity rather than hiding it* (as it is in passing).[99]

"Covering" responds to the social pressures, not to change one's identity, but to minimize it; for example, to "act White," to not "flaunt" one's sexuality, or to downplay childcare responsibilities if you are a woman.[100] It is a demand for code-switching—adjusting your appearance, speaking style, behaviors, and mannerisms in order to make your audience feel comfortable. Basically, it is a demand to perform a different persona.[101] Code-switching is exhausting because you must remain hyperaware during every interaction.[102] As Yoshino wrote of his own acts of covering during law school and academic career, "I soon grew tired of such performances" because they "mute my passion for gay subjects, people, and culture."[103]

Any time you perform a persona that does not comport with the persona with which you operate most often, you rely on those people who know you differently not to interfere with your performance. You call an audience to silence. Because they do not say anything, they assist in the construction of the fourth persona; they enable passing.[104] Audiences are as important to the fourth persona as the rhetor.

An **eavesdropping audience** is *an audience whom the rhetor desires to hear the message despite explicitly targeting the message at a different audience.*[105] A rhetor might use this indirect form of address for either of two reasons: (1) to limit room for response by, or the agency of, the eavesdropping audience or (2) to allow the eavesdropping audience to feel empowered because it is not being criticized even as it hears criticisms against others.

In the first instance, by constructing the audience as an eavesdropper, the rhetor limits the options available to the audience members; they were not being addressed, so how can they answer or participate in the discussion? A rhetor uses such a technique to center attention on one audience in order to maximize its agency while limiting the agency of the eavesdropping audience. One powerful example is Gloria Anzaldúa's "Speaking in Tongues: A Letter to Third World Women Writers," originally written for *Words in Our Pockets,* the Feminist Writers' Guild handbook, and later appearing in two other books, *This Bridge Called My Back* and *Speaking For Ourselves: Women of the South.* All three books bring the letter to an audience broader than the one addressed in its title.[106]

Although the letter is addressed to third world women writers, first world women are an audience. In the introduction to their edited volume, *This Bridge Called My Back,* Cherríe Moraga and Anzaldúa note that the book was created "to express to all women—especially to white middle-class women—the experiences which divide us as feminists."[107] They exhort teachers to use the book in the classroom, again recognizing that White people are an audience. In the foreword to the second edition of the book, Anzaldúa further clarifies the existence of a complex audience: "We have come to realize that we are not alone in our struggles nor separate nor autonomous but that we—white black straight queer female male— are connected and interdependent. We are each accountable for what is happening down the street, south of the border or across the sea."[108] Anzaldúa knows first world White people will read the letter, and wants them to.

Despite (or because of) the broader audience, Anzaldúa titles the letter as being addressed to a specific group of women, "third world women," not to all women (and not to any men). Anzaldúa linguistically and symbolically reinforces and expands this group by beginning the first and last sections with "Dear mujeres de color" ("women of color"),[109] thus placing first world White women (and men) in the position of reading mail that is not intended for them. The letter moves first world White women (and all men) to a borderland by not addressing the letter to them, while empowering third world women and women of color by literally addressing them as the primary subjects. First world White women are written about. Men are just absent; they are not written to, nor do they write. Men and first world White women are uninvited eavesdroppers and, hence, suspended from a critical position. They are reminded of their difference. They are reminded that they constantly tokenize third world women and women of color and deny differences among women. The letter reverses power relationships so that first world White women are allowed access without input, a condition that third world women and women of color often experience.

The exclusive address of the letter operates heuristically; it creates, for people who are not third world women or women of color, an experience of exclusion from which they can learn. Men and White women are made to feel like outsiders, much as women of color are made to feel in US culture. They learn, through experience, what it means to be marginalized, and why marginalization might make people angry. When the letter addresses third world women and women of color, it knocks first world readers out of the position that assumes White, Western, and male is the norm.

At the same time that the letter marginalizes men and first world White women, it creates a community in which third world women and women of color are foregrounded. It quotes numerous third world women and women of color and thereby centers them physically and mentally. They are written to and they write. They are visualized early in the letter: "Black woman huddles over a desk. . . . [A] Chicana fanning away mosquitos. . . . Indian woman walking to school or work. . . . Asian American, lesbian, single mother, tugged in all directions by children, lover or ex-husband, and the writing."[110] The letter reminds third world women and women of color of their worth and ability, and of their identification with Anzaldúa, when she refers to her "brown hand clutching the pen."[111] Third world women and women of color are present throughout the letter in the examples, thus proving that third world women and women of color *do* write. The letter form also operates as empowerment by eliciting a response, encouraging third world women and women of color to write back—to answer the letter.[112]

The second function, empowerment, points to another way that eaves-dropping can be used. Criticisms can be targeted at one audience, in the hope that another audience overhears them and feels empowered. Communication scholars Michael Leff and Ebony A. Utley argue that Martin Luther King, Jr., did just this in the "Letter from Birmingham Jail."[113] Although the letter is addressed to "My Dear Fellow Clergymen"—meaning White moderates—it also indirectly speaks to all Black people in the United States as King attempts to persuade them to risk their bodies in nonviolent civil disobedience in civil rights protests. White moderates appear unwilling to act, so it is other African Americans who must be persuaded to push for social change. Leff and Utley argue that King's persona in the letter is one

> that black readers can use as a model for becoming effective actors on the American scene. Like King, they can view themselves as agents who need not and will not suffer the indifference of white moderates, who can break free of external restraints without losing self-restraint, and who can work from within American society to make fundamental changes in the way they conceive themselves and are conceived by others.[114]

Eavesdroppers' agency was not limited, but enhanced, as King modeled for them how to be an agent of action.

These examples demonstrate that the overtly addressed audience is not necessarily the only, or even the most important, audience. A careful analysis of symbolic acts is required to understand the range of audiences to whom a rhetor speaks and the ways in which the rhetoric positions that audience.

CONCLUSION

Rhetoric is always addressed to another. Thus, a rhetor must consider ways to create identification with the audience or to construct the audience in such a way that it is capable of being an agent of action. Audience members should consider whether they are, indeed, the audience spoken to (the second persona), simply bodies that are present, or people who are excluded from address. The concept of audience is much more complex than just the random group of people who may be gathered to hear a message. Rhetors actively create audiences, active recipients who are able to accept, question, and reject messages.

Civic engagement means engaging with another, an audience, but rhetoric may also exclude people. If the ideal civil society is, in principle, open to the participation of all people, then rhetoric that excludes people works against civic ideals.

DISCUSSION QUESTIONS

1. Advertisers market their products to particular audiences. Find an advertisement and figure out who its audience is. Does the advertisement construct an audience? How? Does it create audience agency? Does it use identification or pathos?
2. When you attempt to persuade someone, how does your audience frame and alter your message? What is an example of a particular audience that was difficult for you to persuade?
3. We discussed fear as an example of a public emotion. Hope is another emotion often found in public discourse. Can you find examples of rhetorical appeals to hope? Clues: President Clinton's campaign video was titled *The Man from Hope,* President Obama titled one of his books *The Audacity of Hope,* the Chicks released the song "I Hope" in 2006, and climate activists debate the utility of optimism versus hope (see Diego Arguedas Ortiz's January 9, 2020, essay for the BBC titled "Is It Wrong to be Hopeful about Climate Change?").
4. Find a symbolic action and identify the audiences. Who is the second persona? Who is the third persona?
5. Politicians frequently refer to "the people." Find examples of these references and explain how the rhetor is defining and conceptualizing "the people." Who is the second persona in the reference to "the people?" Who is the third persona? What does the politician's use of "the people" tell you about the rhetor and the issue?

RECOMMENDED READINGS

Balthrop, V. William. "Culture, Myth, and Ideology as Public Argument: An Interpretation of the Ascent and Demise of 'Southern Culture.'" *Communication Monographs* 51 (December 1984): 340–352.

Black, Edwin. "The Second Persona." *The Quarterly Journal of Speech* 56 (April 1970): 109–119.

McGee, Michael Calvin. "In Search of 'The People': A Rhetorical Alternative." *The Quarterly Journal of Speech* 61 (1975): 235–249.

Wander, Philip. "The Third Persona: An Ideological Turn in Rhetorical Theory." *Central States Speech Journal* 35 (Winter 1984): 197–216.

ENDNOTES

[1] Stephen Toulmin, Richard Rieke, and Allan Janik, *An Introduction to Reasoning,* 2nd ed. (New York: Macmillan, 1984), 306–307.

[2] Earl Warren and Supreme Court of the United States, *U.S. Reports: Brown v. Board of Education, 347 U.S. 483,* 1953, https://www.loc.gov/item/usrep347483/.

[3] *Plessy v. Ferguson,* 163 U.S. 537 (1896).

[4] *Brown v. Board of Education.*

[5] Earl Warren, *The Memoirs of Earl Warren* (New York: Doubleday, 1977), 3.

[6] Ed Cray, *Chief Justice: A Biography of Earl Warren* (New York: Simon and Schuster, 1997), 351; and Learned Hand, *The Bill of Rights* (Cambridge, MA: Harvard University Press, 1958).

[7] "The Southern Manifesto," *Time,* March 26, 1956, http://www.time.com/time/magazine /article/0,9171,824106,00.html; Jim Newton, *Justice for All: Earl Warren and the Nation He Made* (New York: Riverhead, 2006), 339–340; and Ed Cray, *Chief Justice,* 320, 342–347.

[8] Warren, *Memoirs,* 297.

[9] Kenneth Burke, *A Rhetoric of Motives* (University of California Press, 1969), 38.

[10] Burke, *A Rhetoric of Motives,* 41.

[11] Lloyd F. Bitzer, "The Rhetorical Situation," *Philosophy and Rhetoric* 1 (1968): 7, italics added.

[12] Aristotle, *On Rhetoric,* trans. George A. Kennedy (New York: Oxford University Press, 1991), 47 [1.3.1; 1358b].

[13] Aristotle, *On Rhetoric,* 1.2.11 [1356b], 47 [1.3.1; 1358b].

[14] Lucie Olbrechts-Tyteca's contributions to this work often are undervalued. For a discussion of her scholarship, see Barbara Warnick, "Lucie Olbrechts-Tyteca's Contribution to *The New Rhetoric,*" in *Listening to Their Voices: The Rhetorical Activities of Historical Women,* ed. Molly Meijer Wertheimer (Columbia: University of South Carolina Press, 1987), 69–85.

[15] Chaïm Perelman, "Rhetoric and Philosophy," *Philosophy and Rhetoric* 1 (1968): 15.

[16] Chaïm Perelman and Lucie Olbrechts-Tyteca, *The New Rhetoric,* trans. John Wilkinson and Purcell Weaver (Notre Dame, IN: University of Notre Dame Press, 1969), 24.

[17] Mitch Landrieu, "Mayor Mitch Landrieu Gives Address on Removal of Four Confederate Statues," May 23, 2017, City of New Orleans, https://web.archive.org /web/20170524025327/https://www.nola.gov/. See also Mitch Landrieu, "Mitch Landrieu's Speech on the Removal of Confederate Monuments in New Orleans," *New York Times,* May 23, 2017, https://www.nytimes.com/2017/05/23/opinion/mitch -landrieus-speech-transcript.html.

[18] "Confederate Monuments are Coming Down across the United States. Here's a List," *New York Times,* August 28, 2017, https://www.nytimes.com/interactive/2017/08/16 /us/confederate-monuments-removed.html.

[19] Christopher Mele, "New Orleans Begins Removing Confederate Monuments, under Police Guard," *New York Times,* April 24, 2017, https://www.nytimes.com/2017/04/24/us/new-orleans-confederate-statue.html.

[20] Mitch Landrieu, "Mayor Mitch Landrieu Gives Address on Removal of Four Confederate Statues," May 23, 2017, City of New Orleans, https://web.archive.org/web/20170524025327/https://www.nola.gov/. See also "Mitch Landrieu's Speech on the Removal of Confederate Monuments in New Orleans," *New York Times,* May 23, 2017, https://www.nytimes.com/2017/05/23 /opinion/mitch-landrieus-speech-transcript.html.

[21] "Landrieu on 'Meet the Press': Monuments Speech Meant for 'Local Audience,' Surprised It Went Viral," *The New Orleans Advocate,* May 26, 2017, https://www.theadvocate.com/new_orleans/news/article_fae5423c-424d-11e7- bea7-5ff644459524.html.

[22] Burke, *A Rhetoric of Motives,* 20.

[23] Burke, *A Rhetoric of Motives,* 21.

[24] Burke, *A Rhetoric of Motives,* 55.

[25] Barack Obama, "A New Beginning: Speech at Cairo University," June 4, 2009, http://www.americanrhetoric.com/speeches/barackobama/ barackobamacairouniversity.htm.

[26] Stephen Prothero, "In Egypt, a Theologian in Chief," *USA Today,* June 8, 2009.

[27] Obama, "A New Beginning," para. 7.

[28] Obama, "A New Beginning," para. 7.

[29] Obama, "A New Beginning," para. 29.

[30] Obama, "A New Beginning," para. 31.

[31] George A. Kennedy, *Classical Rhetoric and Its Christian and Secular Tradition,* 2nd ed. (Chapel Hill: University of North Carolina Press, 1999), 89.

[32] Kenneth S. Zagacki and Patrick A. Bolyn-Fitzgerald, "Rhetoric and Anger," *Philosophy and Rhetoric* 39, no. 4 (2006): 292.

[33] Martin J. Medhurst, "A Tale of Two Constructs," in *Beyond the Rhetorical Presidency,* ed. Martin J. Medhurst, xi–xxv (College Station: Texas A&M Press, 1996), xvii.

[34] Aristotle, *On Rhetoric,* 2.1.2 [1378a].

[35] Aristotle, *On Rhetoric,* 1.2.5 [1356a].

[36] Aristotle, *On Rhetoric,* 2.5.1. For a discussion of Aristotle's theorizing of fear appeals, see Michael William Pfau, "Who's Afraid of Fear Appeals? Contingency, Courage, and Deliberation in Rhetorical Theory and Practice," *Philosophy and Rhetoric* 40, no. 2 (2007): 216–237.

[37] Pfau, "Who's Afraid of Fear Appeals?", 222.

[38] Pfau, "Who's Afraid of Fear Appeals?," 228, 229.

[39] Pfau, "Who's Afraid of Fear Appeals?," 229, 232.

[40] Molly Ball, "Donald Trump and the Politics of Fear," *Atlantic,* September 2, 2016, https://www.theatlantic.com/politics/archive/2016/09/donald-trump-and-the -politics-of-fear/498116/.

[41] Donald Trump, "Read Donald Trump's Acceptance Speech at the Republican Convention," *Time,* July 22, 2016, http://time.com/4418493/republican-convention-donald-trump-transcript/.

[42] Donald Trump, "Read Donald Trump's Full Inauguration Speech," *Time,* January 24, 2017, http://time.com/4640707/donald-trump-inauguration-speech-transcript/.

43 Tessa Berenson, "Trump Keeps Using Fear. But Is It Helping Republicans?" *Time,* November 4, 2018, http://time.com/5444213/donald-trump-midterms-fear/.

44 Alex Altman, "No President Has Spread Fear Like Donald Trump," *Time,* February 7, 2017, http://time.com/4665755/donald-trump-fear/.

45 Charles M. Blow, "The Commander of Fear," *New York Times,* August 29, 2018, https://www.nytimes.com/2018/08/29/opinion/trump-fear.html.

46 Chris Cillizza, "How Donald Trump Uses Fear and Reassurance to Build Allegiance," CNN, July 3, 2018, https://www.cnn.com/2018/07/03/politics/donald-trump-north -korea-nuclear-war-tweet/index.html.

47 Peter Baker, "Trump Declares a National Emergency, and Provokes a Constitutional Clash," *New York Times,* February 15, 2019, https://www.nytimes.com/2019/02/15/us/politics/national-emergency-trump.html.

48 Quoted in Kevin B. O'Reilly, "Dr. Fauci Outlines 5 ways to Blunt COVID-19 Pandemic's Resurgence," American Medical Association, August 4, 2020, https://www.ama-assn.org/delivering-care/public-health/dr-fauci-outlines-5-ways -blunt-covid-19-pandemic-s-resurgence.

49 Robert Hariman and John Louis Lucaites, "Dissent and Emotional Management in a Liberal-Democratic Society: The Kent State Iconic Photograph," *RSQ: Rhetoric Society Quarterly* 31, no. 3 (Summer 2001): 6.

50 Hariman and Lucaites, "Dissent and Emotional Management," 6.

51 Robert Hariman and John Louis Lucaites, *No Caption Needed: Iconic Photographs, Public Culture, and Liberal Democracy* (Chicago: University of Chicago Press, 2007), 139.

52 Hariman and Lucaites, *No Caption Needed,* 161.

53 Hariman and Lucaites, *No Caption Needed,* 162.

54 Barack Obama, "President Obama Statement on Trayvon Martin Case," CNN, March 23, 2012, http://whitehouse.blogs.cnn.com/2012/03/23/president-obama -statement-on-trayvon-martin-case.

55 Bill Chappell, "In Grief-Stricken Newtown, Vigils and Support for Victims and Families," National Public Radio, December 14, 2012, http://www.npr.org/blogs/thetwo-way/2012/12/14/167293608/in-grief-stricken -newtown-vigils-and-support-for-victims-and-families.

56 Adam Poulisse and Susan Abram, "Thousands Mourn Slain UC Santa Barbara Students in Public Vigil," *Los Angeles Daily News,* May 27, 2014, http://www.dailynews.com/general-news/20140527/thousands-mourn-slain-uc -santa-barbara-students-in-public-vigil.

57 "Prayer Vigil for Charleston Church Shooting Victims," C-SPAN, June 18, 2015, https://www.c-span.org/video/?326645-1/prayer-vigil-charleston-church-shooting -victims.

58 Associated Press, "Raw: Vigil for Orlando Pulse Nightclub Victims," streamed live on June 12, 2017, YouTube video, https://www.youtube.com/watch?v=KPdBY8UttLM.

59 "Las Vegas Mourns Victims of Mass Shooting with Vigils and Tributes," ABC News, October 5, 2017, https://abcnews.go.com/US/las-vegas-mourns-victims-mass -shooting-vigils-tributes/story?id=50301247.

60 Eleanor Dearman, "Vigil Honors Sutherland Springs Church Shooting Victims," *USA Today,* November 5, 2017, https://www.usatoday.com/story/news/nation-now/2017 /11/05/vigil-honors-sutherland-springs-church-shooting-victims/834762001/.

61 E. Cram, "'Angie Was Our Sister': Witnessing the Trans-Formation of Disgust in the Citizenry of Photography," *Quarterly Journal of Speech* 98, no. 4 (November 2012): 416.

62 Cram, "Angie Was Our Sister," 417.

[63] Black Lives Matter, "What We Believe," accessed February 24, 2019, https://blacklivesmatter.com/about/what-we-believe/.

[64] "SayTheirNames: Shifting the Narrative about Victims of Police Brutality," accessed February 24, 2019, http://saytheirnames.org/.

[65] #SayHerName, accessed February 24, 2019, http://www.aapf.org/shn-campaign.

[66] Keeanga-Yamahtta Taylor, *From #BlackLivesMatter to Black Liberation* (Chicago: IL: Haymarket, 2016); Patrisse Khan-Cullors and asha bandele, *When They Call You a Terrorist: A Black Lives Matter Memoir* (New York: St. Martin's, 2018).

[67] Hariman and Lucaites, *No Caption Needed,* 162.

[68] John Stewart, "Keep Gun and Carry On," *Daily Show,* June 5, 2014, http://thedailyshow.cc.com/videos/mplvs5/keep-gun-and-carry-on.

[69] Karlyn Kohrs Campbell, "Agency: Promiscuous and Protean," *Communication and Critical/Cultural Studies* 2 (2005): 3, italics added.

[70] Karlyn Kohrs Campbell, "The Rhetoric of Women's Liberation: An Oxymoron," *The Quarterly Journal of Speech* 59 (February 1973): 85.

[71] Barbara Biesecker, "Rethinking the Rhetorical Situation from within the Thematic of *Différance*," *Philosophy and Rhetoric* 22 (1989): 126.

[72] John Boehner, "Speaker Boehner: Time for the Senate to Listen to the American People," Speaker.gov, September 30, 2013, http://www.speaker.gov/speech/speaker-boehner -time-senate-listen-american-people.

[73] Adam Wollner, "Government Shutdown? Not over Obamacare, Polls Say," NPR: It's All Politics, September 24, 2013, http://www.npr.org/blogs/itsallpolitics /2013/09/23/225510362/government-shutdown-not-over-obamacare-polls-say.

[74] Michael Calvin McGee, "In Search of 'The People': A Rhetorical Alternative," *Quarterly Journal of Speech* 61 (1975): 242.

[75] Silvio Waisbord, "Why Populism Is Troubling for Democratic Communication," *Communication Culture & Critique* 11, no. 1 (2018): 21–34, 26–27.

[76] Waisbord, "Why Populism Is Troubling," 27–30.

[77] Bart Bonikowski, "Three Lessons of Contemporary Populism in Europe and the United States," *Brown Journal of World Affairs* 23, no. 1 (Fall 2017): 9–24, 11.

[78] Edwin Black, "The Second Persona," *Quarterly Journal of Speech* 56 (April 1970): 109–119.

[79] Black, "The Second Persona," 113.

[80] Christopher Martin, *No Longer Newsworthy: How the Mainstream Media Abandoned the Working Class* (Ithaca, NY: Cornell University Press, 2019), 18.

[81] Martin, *No Longer Newsworthy,* 19.

[82] Burke, *A Rhetoric of Motives,* 22.

[83] Think Progress, accessed August 23, 2021, https://archive.thinkprogress.org/manuel -miranda-latinos-are-not-like-african-americans-we-think-just-like-everybody-else -5f93f0a70362/.

[84] Philip Wander, "The Third Persona: An Ideological Turn in Rhetorical Theory," *Central States Speech Journal* 35 (Winter 1984): 209, italics added.

[85] Wander, "The Third Persona," 209.

[86] Wander, "The Third Persona," 216.

[87] J. David Cisneros, "Contaminated Communities: The Metaphor of 'Immigrant as Pollutant' in Media Representations of Immigration," *Rhetoric and Public Affairs* 11, no. 4 (Winter 2008): 569–602; Anne Demo, "Sovereignty Discourse and Contemporary Immigration Politics," *Quarterly Journal of Speech* 91 (2005): 291–311; Hugh Mehan, "The Discourse of the Illegal Immigration Debate: A Case Study in the Politics of Representation," *Discourse and Society* 8 (1997): 249–270; Kent A. Ono and

John M. Sloop, *Shifting Borders: Rhetoric, Immigration, and California's Proposition 187* (Philadelphia: Temple University Press, 2002); and Otto Santa Ana, *Brown Tide Rising: Metaphors of Latinos in Contemporary American Public Discourse* (Austin: University of Texas Press, 2002).

88 Donald J. Trump, [tweet] @realDonaldTrump, June 19, 2018, https://twitter.com /realDonaldTrump/status/1009071403918864385?ref_src=twsrc%5Etfw%7Ctwcamp %5Etweetembed%7Ctwterm%5E1009072619805724672&ref_url=http%3A%2F %2Ftime.com%2F5316087%2Fdonald-trump-immigration-infest%2F.

89 Quoted in Gregory Korte and Alan Gomez, "Trump Ramps Up Rhetoric on Undocumented Immigrants," *USA Today,* May 16, 2018, https://www.usatoday.com/story/news/politics/2018/05/16/trump-immigrants -animals-mexico-democrats-sanctuary-cities/617252002/.

90 Jane Mansbridge, "Feminism and Democracy," in *Feminism and Politics,* ed. Anne Phillips, 142–158 (New York: Oxford University Press, 1998), 152.

91 Mansbridge, "Feminism and Democracy," 143.

92 William Jefferson Clinton, "Remarks at the University of California San Diego Commencement Ceremony in La Jolla, California," *Public Papers of the Presidents of the United States: William J. Clinton* (Washington: GPO, 1998), 877, italics added.

93 Catherine R. Squires and Daniel C. Brouwer, "In/Discernible Bodies: The Politics of Passing in Dominant and Marginal Media," *Critical Studies in Media Communication* 19, no. 3 (September 2002): 283–310, 283.

94 Squires and Brouwer, "In/Discernible Bodies," 286.

95 Squires and Brouwer, "In/Discernible Bodies," 287.

96 Marcia Alesan Dawkins, *Clearly Invisible: Racial Passing and the Color of Cultural Identity* (Waco, TX: Baylor University Press, 2012), xi.

97 Charles E. Morris III, "Pink Herring and the Fourth Persona: J. Edgar Hoover's Sex Crime Panic," *Quarterly Journal of Speech* 88, no. 2 (May 2002): 228–244, 230.

98 Amy Robinson, "It Takes One to Know One: Passing and Communities of Common Interest," *Critical Inquiry* 20, no. 4 (Summer 1994): 715–736, 716.

99 Kenji Yoshino, *Covering: The Hidden Assault on Our Civil Rights* (New York: Random House, 2006).

100 Yoshino, *Covering,* xi.

101 Courtney L. McCluney, Kathrina Robotham, Serenity Lee, Richard Smith, and Myles Durkee, "The Costs of Code-Switching," *Harvard Business Review,* November 15, 2019, https://hbr.org/2019/11/the-costs-of-codeswitching.

102 Madeleine Holden, "The Exhausting Work of LGBTQ Code-Switching," *Vice,* August 12, 2019, https://www.vice.com/en/article/evj47w/the-exhausting -work-of-lgbtq-code-switching.

103 Yoshino, *Covering,* 17.

104 Morris, "Pink Herring," 230.

105 This concept of audience is discussed extensively in James L. Golden and Richard D. Rieke, *The Rhetoric of Black Americans* (Columbus, OH: Charles E. Merrill, 1971).

106 Gloria Anzaldúa, "Speaking in Tongues: A Letter to Third World Women Writers," in *This Bridge Called My Back,* 2nd ed., ed. Cherríe Moraga and Gloria Anzaldúa (New York: Kitchen Table, 1981), 165–173.

107 Cherríe Moraga and Gloria Anzaldúa, "Introduction," *This Bridge,* xxiii.

108 Moraga and Anzaldúa, *This Bridge,* iv.

109 Anzaldúa, "Speaking in Tongues," 165, 171.

110 Anzaldúa, "Speaking in Tongues," 165.

111 Anzaldúa, "Speaking in Tongues," 169.

[112] This analysis is adapted from Catherine Helen Palczewski, "Bodies, Borders and Letters: Gloria Anzaldúa's 'Speaking in Tongues: A Letter to 3rd World Women Writers,'" *Southern Communication Journal* 62, no. 1 (Fall 1996): 1–16.

[113] Martin Luther King, Jr., "Letter from Birmingham Jail," April 16, 1963, http://www.africa.upenn.edu/Articles_Gen/Letter_Birmingham.html.

[114] Michael Leff and Ebony A. Utley, "Instrumental and Constitutive Rhetoric in Martin Luther King Jr.'s 'Letter from Birmingham Jail,'" *Rhetoric and Public Affairs* 7, no. 1 (2004): 37–51.

Part IV
Contexts for Symbolic Action

Chapter 9
Rhetorical Situations

KEY CONCEPTS

conformity

constraints

contextual reconstruction

deliberative discourse

desecration

epideictic discourse

exigence

fitting response

forensic discourse

genres

hybrid response

nonparticipation

rhetorical audience

rhetorical ecology

rhetorical situation

On June 23, 1957, Reverend Douglas Moore and six members of the Asbury Temple United Methodist Church of Durham, North Carolina, entered the Royal Ice Cream parlor, sat down together, and ordered ice cream. (Some of the six were teenagers; the oldest were in their late thirties.) The owner of the store called the police. All seven were arrested for trespassing, found guilty by an all-White jury, and fined $433.25.[1] Their crime? They sat in a section of the ice cream parlor labeled "Whites Only," and they were not considered to be White. This was the first sit-in to protest race-based segregation.

Civil disobedience is now widely accepted as a form of protest, but at the time it was not. Even members of the local African American community were disturbed and viewed Moore and the church members as troublemakers.

Almost three years later, on February 1, 1960, four first-year college students sat at the lunch counter in the Greensboro, North Carolina, Woolworth's store, whose policy was to serve only Whites.[2] When Woolworth's employees denied the students service because they were not considered to be White, they refused to move. They stayed until the store closed and returned the next day with twenty-five more students from local colleges who were dressed in their ROTC uniforms or Sunday best. By February 5, three hundred students were engaging in sit-ins at Woolworth's and other Greensboro businesses.[3] They, too, were arrested. During the Greensboro sit-ins, Moore and the lawyer who defended the Royal Seven went to Greensboro to help train the students and develop a strategy to make sit-ins a central tactic against anti-Black segregation. As news coverage of the sit-ins intensified, this form of embodied direct action appeared to have a far more profound effect on segregation than verbal appeals to end it. Moore invited Martin Luther King, Jr., to come to Greensboro. King accepted the invitation.

King's speech in Greensboro, "A Creative Protest," was his first explicit endorsement of nonviolent civil disobedience. King encouraged the audience not to be afraid of jail and to answer the threat of arrest "by saying that we are willing and prepared to fill up the jails of the South. Maybe it will take this willingness to stay in jail to arouse the dozing conscience of our nation."[4] Nevertheless, he reassured everyone that "We're not rabble rousers; we're not dangerous agitators, nor do we seek political dominance" and reassured Whites in particular that the Civil Rights movement was "not going to take bombs into your communities. . . . We will not turn to some foreign ideology. Communism has never invaded our ranks."[5]

How were sit-ins an appropriate response to segregation? How did they become an effective and increasingly accepted response? Why did the students wear the clothing they did? Why students? Why did Moore invite King to speak? Why did King feel called to speak? Why did King need to provide reassurances when college students were sitting peacefully at a lunch counter? The protestors and King faced a complicated set of circumstances, challenged hegemonic beliefs, and appealed to a range of audiences. As a result, they had to make careful rhetorical choices.

This moment was a pivotal moment for the Civil Rights Movement. Would it embrace civil disobedience? King had to navigate a complex array of audiences, including young activists who were ready to risk jail and older leaders who thought direct action risked too much. Endorsing civil disobedience meant that King had to convince activists to risk bodily harm from physical violence (from white supremacists who would pour scalding hot coffee on them and burn their backs with lit cigarettes, as well as the social stigma of jail.[6] King and the activists also had to convince White audiences that civil disobedience was not a precursor to physical violence: 57 percent of the White population thought the sit-ins actually hurt the cause of integration. Many worried that communism had infiltrated the Civil Rights movement.[7] Without an understanding of the rhetorical situation presented by the topic, the audiences, and perceptions of the students and King, it is impossible to understand the sit-ins or King's speech, nor how these actions, themselves, altered the situation.

We will begin exploring the idea of the rhetorical situation by reviewing classical theories about it. We will then compare a more recent theory that claims "rhetoric is situational" to a theory that argues "situations are rhetorical." Each of these theories, taken alone, has limits, so we combine the most insightful parts of both theories to explore how situations and rhetoric constantly interact with and affect each other. Situations can limit a rhetor's rhetorical choices; moreover, a rhetor's rhetorical choices can (re)define the situation. We will then reconsider which rhetorical actions constitute a fitting response to a situation, as well as why rhetors sometimes may not want to provide a fitting response at all. We will conclude the chapter by considering how contemporary media technologies challenge static understandings of the rhetorical situation. Because symbolic action circulates and recirculates, a fluid understanding of rhetorical situations is necessary.

CLASSICAL UNDERSTANDING OF THE RHETORICAL SITUATION

Aristotle's definition of rhetoric as "an ability in each [particular] case, to see the available means of persuasion,"[8] makes clear that the options open to rhetors and the demands placed on them differ from situation to situation.[9] Communication does not occur in a vacuum, but in a particular place, at a particular time, about a particular topic, as part of a particular socioeconomic and cultural context, and with a particular audience. Some situations recur, however, and rhetors learn from their recurrence. The challenge to a rhetor is to determine what options exist to communicate a message in a particular situation.

Aristotle offered an early description of the interplay of audience, topic, and rhetor in a situation. For Aristotle, the composition of the audience determined the rhetorical situation because the audience determines the expectations the rhetor will need to fulfill.

He divided rhetoric into three situational classifications: deliberative, forensic, and epideictic.[10] **Deliberative discourse** is *rhetoric that addresses broad public audiences and concerns the merits of proposals for future courses of action.* It responds to policy issues such as those concerning ways and means, war and peace, and legislation. **Forensic discourse** is *rhetoric that occurs when a designated audience (such as a jury) judges the arguments about events in the past and accusations of wrongdoing.* The language of forensic discourse tends to be "accusation" or "defense" (apologia).[11] **Epideictic discourse** consists of *speeches of praise or blame, usually delivered to audiences assembled during ceremonial occasions, and oriented to the present moment, while calling on the past to inform the future.* Its focus on praise or blame means the audience is called to determine the fittingness of the values that the rhetor uses and to judge the virtues and vices of the rhetor's subject.

Each of these three classifications has a distinct audience, as well as a particular form, style, and range of arguments. In addition, Aristotle explains, "Each of these has its own 'time': for the deliberative speaker, the future . . . ; for the [forensic] speaker in court, the past . . . ; in epideictic, the present is the most important; for all speakers praise or blame in regard to existing qualities, but they often also make use of other things, both reminding [the audience] of the past and projecting the course of the future."[12]

For most of the history of rhetorical studies, Aristotle's model was the dominant perspective on rhetorical situations, but more complex theories have evolved.

RHETORIC AS SITUATIONAL

More recently, communication scholar Lloyd F. Bitzer argues that "rhetoric is situational."[13] He proposes that rhetoric is produced at a specific time, for a particular audience, and in response to a particular issue. He distinguishes the "meaning-context" formed by previous communication from the "rhetorical situation" formed by a particular event.

"Context" and "situation" are not synonymous for Bitzer.[14] For instance, when voting rights activist Fannie Lou Hamer delivered testimony to the 110 members of the 1964 Democratic National Convention Credentials Committee, she was asking the Democratic Party Convention to recognize and seat the Mississippi Freedom Democratic Party as the official delegation from Mississippi, instead of the already recognized, all-White, anti–civil rights, regular Democratic Party delegation. As Hamer detailed police violence in response to Blacks' attempts to vote and to register others to vote, she had to consider much more than the setting and immediate audience. The rhetorical situation included expectations attached to convention speeches; Hamer's relationship to the Civil Rights Movement, the Mississippi Freedom Democratic Party, and the Democratic Party; the audiences Hamer hoped to influence, ranging from the Credentials Committee to other African Americans and the nation as a whole; the social and cultural history of voting rights for African Americans; and her own reputation as an activist and vice-chair of the Mississippi Freedom Democratic Party.[15]

As this example illustrates, and Bitzer points out, all messages occur in a context, but only a rhetorical situation demands a rhetorical response, insofar as "rhetorical discourse . . . obtain[s] its character-as-rhetorical from the situation which generates it."[16] For Bitzer, rhetoric is instrumental, or pragmatic; and its intent "is always persuasive."[17] People engage in rhetorical action to respond to some external and preexisting problem, such as the Credentials Committee refusing to seat a delegation.

Bitzer believes that rhetorical situations are distinct from contexts because they should elicit particular responses from rhetors. Knowing the historical context of a speech gives you an understanding of its contextual meaning. Knowing the rhetorical situation helps you understand the rhetorical choices that the rhetor made in response to it. Accordingly, Bitzer defines the **rhetorical situation** as *"a complex of persons, events, objects, and relations presenting an actual or potential exigence which can be completely or partially removed if discourse, introduced into the situation, can so constrain human decision or action as to bring about the significant modification of the exigence."*[18]

Bitzer identifies three elements of any rhetorical situation: exigence, audience, and constraints. These elements are present prior to any rhetorical act and compose the "situation which calls the discourse into existence."[19] According to Bitzer, a rhetor should consider these elements when constructing a rhetorical act. When critically analyzing a rhetorical act, critics should begin by identifying the components of the rhetorical situation to which the rhetorical act responds.

Exigence

Bitzer defines **exigence** as *"an imperfection marked by urgency; it is a defect, an obstacle, something waiting to be done, a thing which is other than it should be."*[20] The exigence calls for, or demands, a rhetorical response. If rhetoric cannot create a change in the exigence, then the situation is not a rhetorical situation. Although a hurricane is a problem, for example, it is not a rhetorical exigence because rhetoric cannot stop the onslaught of wind and water. People's reactions to a hurricane (usually panic) do present an exigence.

Rhetorical appeals not to panic, to prepare, to shelter in place, and to evacuate in an orderly manner can alter the exigence. When Hurricane Ike threatened the Gulf Coast during the Atlantic storm season of 2008, Texas officials asked Houston residents not to evacuate and instead to remain in Houston and shelter in place, even though hundreds of thousands of Texans who were living in low-lying areas were told to evacuate or face certain death. All Texans faced the same storm, but different exigences presented themselves to disaster officials. Evacuation from less populated areas could occur in an orderly manner, but in more densely populated areas, as the experience with Hurricane Rita in 2005 demonstrated, more people might die from the evacuation than from the storm itself.[21]

Bitzer believes that rhetoric "comes into existence as a response to a situation, in the same sense that an answer comes into existence in response to a question, or a solution in response to a problem."[22] The situation invites and guides rhetors' responses.[23] In many cultures, for example, discourse is expected in response to someone's death, such as eulogies, sympathy cards, expressions of condolences to family and friends, and obituaries. The situation gives the rhetorical acts their significance. When a situation has importance, the persuasive responses to that situation are given importance.

Bitzer also explained that although "rhetors enter a situation to clarify it, structure it, or otherwise hasten" the need to act, "competing rhetors, who see a different exigence, can . . . obscure and weaken a situation" and thus suppress the need to act.[24] Different rhetors may also see different exigences.

On September 11, 2001, when planes crashed into the Twin Towers of the World Trade Center, the Pentagon, and a field in Pennsylvania, events demanded a response. Public reactions to the events created an evolving exigence. President George W. Bush delivered three statements throughout the day. His first statement (lasting 68 seconds), immediately after the Twin Towers were hit, was from Emma E. Booker Elementary School in Sarasota, Florida, where he was visiting when the attack began. The second statement (lasting 130 seconds), after the Pentagon was hit, was from Barksdale Air Force Base in Louisiana,.[25] Finally, on the evening of September 11, when it appeared the attacks were over, President Bush delivered a seven-minute address to the country from the Oval Office to make sense of the day's events. The magnitude of the developing events motivated him to respond rhetorically to the situation three times in one day. In each speech, he responded to the urgency of the situation at that moment—the exigence.

President Bush had choices regarding how to respond. One choice could have been to ignore the events and not deliver any public statements. He probably felt compelled to speak about the events immediately, because to ignore them could have created additional problems that would have been more damaging than the risks he faced in responding. If he had not responded, people would have believed he failed to see the magnitude of the events,[26] or they would have seen the president as out of touch, incompetent, or afraid. Rhetorical theorist Bruce E. Gronbeck explains that the very unexpectedness of events "calls for particular messages at particular times . . . . the unexpectedness of impending harm produces public uncertainty, especially if the event is unique rather than cyclical; public uncertainty produces public fear, which consequently calls for explanation [and] reassurance."[27] In this case, President Bush sought to calm people's initial fears and uncertainties through his rhetorical acts.

Most rhetors have an inherent sense of exigence, recognizing a need to say something in response to unexpected events. They feel they are "invited" or "called" to respond to the situation. The feeling that you must say something is an indication that an out-of-the-ordinary event has occurred that demands an immediate (urgent) response. Of course, urgency must be defined relative to the situation. Explaining why you might be late to a party is less urgent than explaining to your boss that you will be late for work. If you are going to be late to a party, you might not feel that you must contact the hosts immediately, even though you might call as a courtesy. If you are late for work, however, you probably feel a greater sense of urgency.

The second component of the rhetorical situation is the **rhetorical audience** (discussed in chapter 8), which Bitzer defines as *an audience that "consists only of those persons who are capable of being influenced by discourse and of being mediators of change."*[28] He distinguishes the entire group of people who might hear a speech or read an essay from the rhetorical audience, the group to whom a rhetor targets a message because that group is composed of agents of change who can respond. Just because you are reading or watching a speech does not mean that you are the rhetorical audience for the speech. You would have to have the ability to remedy the exigence in order to be part of the rhetorical audience.

Electoral politics provide an example of how audience is an essential part of the rhetorical situation. Candidates argue that if they are not elected, an imperfection will persist. They respond to the imperfection—the exigence—by attempting to mobilize voters. Voters are a rhetorical audience because they are capable of being influenced and have the power to act to remedy the exigence, but candidates do not perceive all voters as being equally open to influence or capable of action.

How candidates identify who constitutes the rhetorical audience has shifted over time. From the 1980 presidential campaign (which saw the emergence of the Reagan Democrats) until 2004, presidential campaigns tended to focus on wooing swing voters because voters without a strong party identification could swing a presidential election in favor of one side or another. After the 2000 election, Republican campaign strategist Matthew Dowd studied eligible voters and discovered that "independents or persuadable voters in the last 20 years had gone from 22 percent of the electorate to 7 percent of the electorate in 2000." Using this information, campaign strategists for the 2004 Republican election campaign developed what came to be known as "the base strategy" which attempted "to focus on delivering votes from reliable Republicans."[29] These strategists saw the Republican Party's base as the key agents of change. As a result, the Republican presidential campaign limited rallies to invitation-only events and only gave tickets to people willing to state their allegiance to George W. Bush.[30] The campaign redefined the rhetorical audience by suggesting that the key to winning elections (the exigence) was not about persuading undecided or centrist voters, but about mobilizing dedicated party supporters to go to the polls.

In contrast, the 2008 Republican campaign saw the rhetorical audience as broader than its base, so it used a mix of appeals to the base (including the selection of Sarah Palin as the vice presidential candidate) and to independents (including the emphasis on John McCain as a maverick). The 2008 Democratic campaign also redefined the rhetorical audience. Instead of simply looking at registered voters as the audience, the Obama campaign focused on all those who were eligible to vote. On April 25, 2008, the Democrats launched a fifty-state voter registration drive to attract first-time voters, targeting youth and minority voters who might have felt disenfranchised by politics in the past.

The 2012 presidential election saw another evolution. Journalist Sasha Issenberg reports that, using big data and advanced analytics, forgoing focus groups, and relying on "empirical testing in the real world," the Democratic campaign sent out multiple messages via direct mail and followed up with survey calls to learn which message had resonated with which voters (based on age, sex, race, and so on). As a result, the campaign targeted "unexpected population[s]"; for example, the campaign "found that voters between 45 and 65 were more likely to change their views about the candidates after hearing Obama's Medicare arguments than those over 65, who were currently eligible for the program." The campaign also emphasized one-on-one contact to encourage people to register and then to vote. In a comprehensive assessment of this strategy, Issenberg concluded, "Few events in American life other than a presidential election touch 126 million adults . . . Obama did so by reducing every American to a series of numbers." The Obama campaign used those numbers to capture more information by measuring how each person had the potential to "change politics," rather than by merely placing that person within traditional demographics.[31]

The results of the 2016 election might be partly explained by the candidates' different understandings of who constituted the rhetorical audience. Statistician Nate Silver, in an analysis of the election, posits that Hillary Clinton "focused too much on *close states* rather than *tipping-point states*"[32]—those "states most likely to provide the decisive vote in the Electoral College."[33] Because Electoral College votes, not popular vote totals, determine the outcome of presidential elections, the goal is not to win the most popular votes but rather the votes that will tip key states' Electoral College votes in a candidate's direction. In contrast, Donald Trump saw rhetorical audiences in states in which Republicans had often not spent much time campaigning—Wisconsin, Michigan, and Pennsylvania. These were tipping-point states.

Constraints

The third component of a rhetorical situation, according to Bitzer, is **constraints,** *"persons, events, objects, and relations which are parts of the situation because they have the power to constrain decision and action needed to modify the exigence."*[34]

Constraints restrain and enable choices that a rhetor might make in response to the exigence, audience, and the rhetor's own history. They do not determine or dictate a specific response to a situation; rather, they limit and provide opportunities for the rhetor's persuasive choices.[35] An impending election imposes a temporal constraint. Additional constraints in an election campaign include the opposing candidates and PACs, as well as the candidate's history and favorability ratings.

People who come from marginalized groups as a result of the social categories of sex, race, or class often face greater rhetorical constraints and have fewer rhetorical opportunities than do people from privileged groups. In the 1960s, for example, when engaging in lunch counter sit-ins to protest Jim Crow segregation laws, young Black women and men would dress conservatively and ask politely to be served. The simple reality of Black and White people eating together was so radical and confrontational, the protesters had to moderate all their other actions. They also had to counteract White people's irrational perceptions that Black people were violent and unruly. Civil rights activist and later US Congressman John Lewis, who was one of the participants in the Nashville sit-ins, explains, "It was like going to Church, I guess. You would put on your church-going clothes, Sunday clothes, and we took books and papers and did our homework at the lunch counter, just quiet and trying to be as dignified as possible."[36]

As a counterexample, consider performance artist Bill Talen's character of Reverend Billy. Located in New York, Talen uses street theatre to protest the rise in consumerism and the invasion of Times Square by transnational corporations such as Disney and Starbucks.[37] Reverend Billy begins his sermon in a local theatre but takes it directly into a store to challenge shoppers. He preaches to them about the evils of consumption or whispers in their ears that the cute stuffed Dumbo was made by sweatshop labor. His race, sex, and class provide him an opportunity, rather than a constraint. He recognizes that as a White man, he is able to get away with more. As he explains: "I don't suffer from racial profiling. If a cop stops me, he knows immediately that I have a college education and dental work."[38] He is able to gain access to spaces and command attention from people who might otherwise dismiss the message.

Communication scholars Karlyn Kohrs Campbell and Susan Schultz Huxman provide a more expansive assessment of constraints in their examination of "the rhetorical problem."[39] Adapting their work and applying it to the framework of the rhetorical situation, we can see constraints stemming from the exigence, audience, and rhetor.

Constraints arising from the exigence include the complexity of the exigence and its cultural history.[40] The exigence can be more or less complex; the level of expertise needed to understand it varies from subject to subject. In the case of the student requesting an extension, the exigence is fairly straightforward and clear. The student's reasons for the extension might make the exigence more complex, but the obstacles that the student must overcome include the professor's stated (or unstated) deadline policies and the academic culture of the institution or department.

In contrast, some exigences are extremely complex. When the United States was in the throes of the Great Depression, following the 1929 stock market collapse, President Franklin Delano Roosevelt faced the daunting task of explaining to the public what was happening, why it was happening, and how the government would respond. When he was inaugurated on March 4, 1933, five thousand banks had already folded; ten million people in the United States had lost their savings; 25 percent were unemployed; hundreds of thousands of families had lost their homes; and farmers were leaving crops to rot in the fields because commodity prices had fallen so far that the farmers could not afford to harvest.[41] On March 12, 1933, via the relatively new medium of radio, Roosevelt delivered his first presidential fireside chat. The subject was banking.[42] He sought to explain the federal "banking holiday" he had declared, in terms that would be understood by "the average citizen."[43] He faced the exigence of an extremely complex and volatile situation, which called forth rhetoric that would explain and calm. In an interesting parallel, as the economic crisis that had begun in October 2008 intensified during early 2009, many commentators encouraged President Barack Obama to respond to his complex exigence in the same way Roosevelt had. Mary Kate Cary of *U.S. News and World Report* argued that "one-on-one talks with the American people explaining the crisis and the government's response—as well as a go-get-'em confidence builder at the end—might work wonders."[44]

According to Campbell and Huxman, constraints arising from the rhetorical audience—the audience that is capable of acting—include whether the rhetor can reach it, as well as whether it is likely to misinterpret or misperceive the message, can be motivated to act despite potential costs, perceives itself as an agent of change, and has control over the action asked of it.[45] Even if the rhetor is able to deliver the message to the audience, the audience must perceive and interpret the situation as described in the message in a way that is consistent with how the rhetor interprets and perceives it. Further, audience members must be motivated and believe they can make a change, that they have agency to act on the exigence. In some cases, responding to an exigence will present costs to the audience, which could include money, time, or the risk of social disapproval.

When a student asks for an extension, the professor clearly is an audience with agency. Control is not the most significant constraint arising from this audience, but rather the cost, which from the professor's perspective might be the perception of unfairness to other students or the time the professor needs to grade the assignment. (If the extension is granted, the professor has less time to evaluate the assignment.)

Constraints can also arise from audience agency. If you are trying to encourage other students to join a protest against building a road through a campus green space, you might encounter apathy. You might need to persuade them that they can make a difference. You might need to motivate them to become involved, even if they agree the road should not be built.

Finally, Campbell and Huxman say, constraints arising from the rhetor include the rhetor's reputation, ability to create identification with the audience, and social power.[46] These characteristics can also present opportunities for the rhetorician, however. A rhetor who has credibility with an audience can use that credibility to persuade it. For example, as Roosevelt's term in office progressed, he developed credibility with the public. His fireside chats and constant communication instilled confidence to such an extent that, in their letters to him, people described him as "a gift from God, and a 'friend-next-door,' a supreme being and a real fellow who did not talk down to the public."[47] Because of his reputation, Roosevelt was able to persuade audiences by relying on his relationship with them. Conversely, rhetors who have negative images or tarnished reputations would have to overcome them in order to persuade their audiences.

Fitting Response and Genre

Bitzer concludes that although a rhetorical situation invites a response, not all responses are fitting. A **fitting response** is *a response that meets the expectations of the rhetorical situation.* Bitzer points out that "every situation prescribes its fitting response; the rhetor may or may not read the prescription accurately."[48] A successful persuasive message is appropriate for the exigence, audience, and constraints of the rhetorical situation.

To be fitting, a response must also meet the expectations established by responses to preceding situations that the audience perceives to be analogous. Rhetoric scholars Karlyn Kohrs Campbell and Kathleen Hall Jamieson argue that when a rhetorical situation (or a particular interaction of audience, exigence, and constraints) repeatedly recurs, stylistic and substantive expectations become attached to that situation.[49] Stylistic expectations can involve the formality of language, the attitudes toward the subject and audience, and the structure of the speech. Substantive expectations include the types of subjects and evidence.

The determination of what is fitting need not occur anew with every act. When a type of situation recurs, rhetors can look to previous responses to identify general types of form and content that seem to work. They can respond to common elements in exigences, contexts, responses, and audiences. These responses often lead to the formulation of **genres**, *rhetorical forms created by recurrent elements of rhetorical situations, which create clusters of discourse that share style, substance, and purpose.* Genres create constraints and opportunities for rhetors as they respond to situations. Thus, it is not solely the present situation that generates constraints on and resources for a rhetor, but also, according to Jamieson, the previous situations that create—"the chromosomal imprint of ancestral genres."[50]

Even if you have never given or heard a eulogy, you probably have a general sense of what it should include. As Campbell and Jamieson note, Western audiences expect that a eulogy "acknowledges the death, transforms the relationship between the living and the dead from present to past tense, eases the mourners' terror at confronting their own mortality, consoles them by arguing that the deceased lives on, and reknits the fabric of the community."[51] What people expect to hear in a eulogy is determined not just by the particular death but by all the eulogies that have gone before. If someone were to give a speech that did not even mention the person who had died, people would probably not see that speech as fitting and say, "It wasn't really a eulogy."

Campbell and Jamieson explain that genres are "a fusion of elements, formed from a constellation of forms."[52] First, a genre is a *fusion* of elements, not just a collection of individual elements.[53] The chemical concept, fusion, emphasizes that the way components are combined is more important to examine than whether the same elements appear in multiple forms. When fusion occurs, discrete parts are combined in such a way that their discreteness is no longer observable. Second, their emphasis on "constellation" highlights that the parts of a symbolic action, like stars, are connected by human perception. The shapes we see in the stars—the Big Dipper or Orion—are not inherent in the organization of the stars; rather, people perceive relations between stars, imbue them with meaning, and create constellations symbolically. Once a constellation has been accepted, people use it to identify the stars and to navigate. Genres of discourse are human constructions, just as constellations are. The constraints that develop from these genres guide rhetorical choices just as constellations guide navigational choices.

Genres guide rhetorical action because they provide a pattern to follow. Even when rhetors are presented with unprecedented situations, they tend to look to established genres to guide their responses. When President Richard Nixon resigned from office and Gerald Ford was sworn in, Campbell and Jamieson point out, Ford's speech as president occurred in an "unprecedented rhetorical situation." Ford was not elected: he had replaced Spiro Agnew as vice-president after Agnew pleaded no contest to a felony charge and resigned, making Ford the first appointed vice president in the nation's history. Subsequently, Ford replaced Nixon, who had resigned from the presidency in the face of three articles of impeachment from the House Judiciary Committee. Because the situation was unprecedented, Ford did not have a ready-made blueprint for how to respond to that exigence, yet he had a resource on which to rely—the established expectations of an inaugural address.

In his first speech after taking the oath of office and assuming the presidency on August 9, 1974, Ford stated it was "Not an inaugural address, not a fireside chat, not a campaign speech—just a little straight talk among friends."[54] Yet, Campbell and Jamieson argue, Ford delivered a classic inaugural, as the speech "established that the office had been vacated, constituted the audience as the people, rehearsed basic constitutional principles, invited investiture, and previewed Ford's approach to the presidency."[55] These elements constitute the stylistic and substantive expectations attached to presidential inaugural speeches in the United States. Ford's speech reflected all the formal elements of the inaugural genre and relied on that genre to guide his response to an unprecedented situation.

In some cases, a situation may call for a response that includes elements of multiple genres. Jamieson and Campbell call *symbolic actions that combine elements of two different genres* a **hybrid response**.[56] The fusion of genres can come about when a rhetor is trying to respond to a rhetorical situation that has competing demands. For example, Lyndon Baines Johnson's first address as president, five days after the assassination of President John F. Kennedy, had to both mourn Kennedy and invest Johnson with the powers of the presidency. As Campbell and Jamieson explain, "Before Johnson could tell the audience where he would lead it, the office of the presidency had to be vacated rhetorically and its former occupant laid to rest in a eulogy."[57] Johnson responded to this need by playing off Kennedy's inaugural theme of "let us begin," with the theme "let us continue." After noting that "the greatest leader of our time has been struck down by the foulest deed of our time" and recounting Kennedy's accomplishments, Johnson declared: "Today in this moment of new resolve, I would say to all my fellow Americans, *let us continue.* This is our challenge—not to hesitate, not to pause, not to turn about and linger over this evil moment, but to continue on our course so that we may fulfill the destiny that history has set for us."[58] He then listed the policy initiatives that demanded congressional action: passage of the Civil Rights Bill, a tax bill, and education bills. As Campbell and Jamieson note, this approach allowed him to explain what the Kennedy presidency had meant and to what a Johnson presidency would be committed.

Rhetors are not required to follow general guides, however. Ronald Reagan often responded to deliberative occasions by using epideictic discourse celebrating the people of the United States. He initiated the presidential practice of inviting "citizens who have distinguished themselves in some field of service or endeavor to be his personal guests in the gallery" and then highlighting them as part of the State of the Union address, which responds to a deliberative situation.[59] The result, as Campbell and Jamieson explain, was that Reagan's yearly addresses tended to be "short on policy proposals, sharply tilting the character of the address toward ceremonial and away from the deliberative."[60] As Jamieson notes: "Genres should not be viewed as static forms but as evolving phenomena. . . . While traditional genres may color rhetoric they do not ossify it."[61]

You've likely witnessed this blending of genres when you have watched film and television award winners use the epideictic occasion of winning to make deliberative appeals. For example, when John Legend and Common won an Oscar for best original song in 2015, they used the moment to argue for voting rights. Comparing the struggle for voting rights now to the struggle for the Voting Rights Act fifty years earlier, as depicted in *Selma,* the movie for which they wrote the song, Legend encouraged the audience to fight for voting rights. After noting that voting rights were being "compromised" today, he declared that "the struggle for freedom and justice is real."[62] Legend sought to convince the audience they should fight for voting rights (a deliberative appeal) even as he participated in the epideictic moment of an award presentation.

Analysis: The *Challenger* Explosion

President Ronald Reagan's speech after the explosion of the *Challenger* space shuttle illustrates how a rhetor responds to a rhetorical situation and how critics can use the concept of the rhetorical situation to analyze a rhetorical act.

On January 28, 1986, NASA launched the *Challenger* in what it believed to be a routine mission, even though there had been five liftoff delays. On board were seven astronauts: Gregory Jarvis, Christa McAuliffe, Ronald McNair, Ellison Onizuka, Judith Resnik, Dick Scobee, and Michael J. Smith. NASA had been plagued by declining public interest in its space missions, but many people in the United States, particularly schoolchildren, watched the launch live because of schoolteacher Christa McAuliffe, the first member of the Teacher in Space Project. A little over a minute after the launch, the shuttle exploded in flight, killing all seven astronauts. Although the only live coverage of the launch was on newly formed CNN and via a satellite feed of NASA TV targeted at schools, one study reported that 85 percent of those surveyed had heard the news within an hour of the explosion as a result of the extensive media coverage.[63]

The vivid imagery of the explosion shocked the nation.[64] Within minutes, the networks replaced regular programming with the news coverage. The nation watched in horror as their televisions repeatedly showed the shuttle exploding and debris raining down. Despite all the news coverage in the hours after the explosion, the public was left with a void of meaning. People did not know what had happened or why. They could have interpreted the explosion as proof that NASA was inept and the benefits of space exploration were not worth the costs, or as an inexplicable and irredeemable loss of human life. Knowing that the situation demanded a response, President Reagan cancelled his scheduled State of the Union address to speak to the country about the *Challenger* disaster.

President Ronald W. Reagan
The Space Shuttle *Challenger* Tragedy Address
Oval Office
January 28, 1986

1. Ladies and Gentlemen, I'd planned to speak to you tonight to report on the state of the union, but the events of earlier today have led me to change those plans. Today is a day for mourning and remembering. Nancy and I are pained to the core by the tragedy of the shuttle *Challenger*. We know we share this pain with all of the people of our country. This is truly a national loss.

2. Nineteen years ago, almost to the day, we lost three astronauts in a terrible accident on the ground. But we've never lost an astronaut in flight. We've never had a tragedy like this. And perhaps we've forgotten the courage it took for the crew of the shuttle. But they, the *Challenger* Seven, were aware of the dangers, but overcame them and did their jobs brilliantly. We mourn seven heroes: Michael Smith, Dick Scobee, Judith Resnik, Ronald McNair, Ellison Onizuka, Gregory Jarvis, and Christa McAuliffe. We mourn their loss as a nation together.

3. For the families of the seven, we cannot bear, as you do, the full impact of this tragedy. But we feel the loss, and we're thinking about you so very much. Your loved ones were daring and brave, and they had that special grace, that special spirit that says, "Give me a challenge, and I'll meet it with joy." They had a hunger to explore the universe and discover its truths. They wished to serve, and they did. They served all of us.

4. We've grown used to wonders in this century. It's hard to dazzle us. But for twenty-five years the United States space program has been doing just that. We've grown used to the idea of space, and perhaps we forget

that we've only just begun. We're still pioneers. They, the members of the *Challenger* crew, were pioneers.

5. And I want to say something to the schoolchildren of America who were watching the live coverage of the shuttle's take-off. I know it's hard to understand, but sometimes painful things like this happen. It's all part of the process of exploration and discovery. It's all part of taking a chance and expanding man's horizons. The future doesn't belong to the fainthearted; it belongs to the brave. The *Challenger* crew was pulling us into the future, and we'll continue to follow them.

6. I've always had great faith in and respect for our space program. And what happened today does nothing to diminish it. We don't hide our space program. We don't keep secrets and cover things up. We do it all up front and in public. That's the way freedom is, and we wouldn't change it for a minute.

7. We'll continue our quest in space. There will be more shuttle flights and more shuttle crews and, yes, more volunteers, more civilians, more teachers in space. Nothing ends here; our hopes and our journeys continue.

8. I want to add that I wish I could talk to every man and woman who works for NASA, or who worked on this mission and tell them: "Your dedication and professionalism have moved and impressed us for decades. And we know of your anguish. We share it."

9. There's a coincidence today. On this day three hundred and ninety years ago, the great explorer Sir Francis Drake died aboard ship off the coast of Panama. In his lifetime the great frontiers were the oceans, and a historian later said, "He lived by the sea, died on it, and was buried in it." Well, today, we can say of the *Challenger* crew: Their dedication was, like Drake's, complete.

10. The crew of the space shuttle *Challenger* honored us by the manner in which they lived their lives. We will never forget them, nor the last time we saw them, this morning, as they prepared for their journey and waved goodbye and "slipped the surly bonds of earth" to "touch the face of God."

11. Thank you.[65]

President Reagan was called to give this speech instead of the planned State of the Union address because of the rhetorical situation. In Bitzer's terms, people's reaction to and public witnessing of this event established an exigence, "an imperfection marked by urgency." The unexpected explosion and the magnitude of the tragedy created urgency for President Reagan to respond. The uniqueness of the tragedy created public uncertainty about the meaning of the event and the safety of the NASA space program, and called for explanation and reassurance.

President Reagan clearly identified the exigence when he said that "the tragedy of the shuttle *Challenger*...is truly a national loss," making it a day "for mourning and remembering," but that the march of progress and the call for exploration gave meaning to that loss of life. According to Reagan, the members of the space shuttle crew had "a hunger to explore the universe" and were part of a long line of explorers. The examples of the 1967 *Apollo I* fire and the 1596 death of Sir Francis Drake offered similar historical events that helped make the loss of life during exploration seem normal and expected. As Reagan explained to schoolchildren: "It's all part of the process of exploration and discovery."

The audiences in the situation were composed of people who shared the need for reassurance and the sentiment that exploration defines the character of the people of the United States: the astronauts' families, schoolchildren, NASA workers, and the public as a whole.[66] President Reagan provided them with an explanation, not of the actual accident, but of exploration. Thus, he identified the meaning of the situation and offered a response that suggested both a time of mourning and a continued faith in exploration in general, and in NASA more specifically.

President Reagan faced constraints in the situation. The exigence was unique because it was the first time a space shuttle had exploded. Death is a recurring part of the human condition, however. The genre of eulogy represented a constraint but also offered a resource, as Reagan was able to mirror the stylistic and substantive expectations attached to eulogies to structure the speech. He also faced limits and opportunities as a rhetor. A president could not react in a purely personal way, but Reagan was a popular president and played the role of a grandfather, targeting a specific message to schoolchildren. This role provided an opportunity because he could come across as a caring and comforting leader responding to a constraint: the audiences' need for reassurance about the space program.

Reagan situated the loss of the *Challenger* crew not as an aberration but as a normal part of exploration and discovery, practices that define the US spirit. He reminded the audience that the crew members "were aware of the dangers" and faced them bravely. He gave meaning to an event that seemed devoid of meaning.[67] Reagan's response to the exigence defined the situation in such a way that it did not mark the end of NASA, but rather was a justification to continue funding the space program—not as proof of NASA's failure, but as proof of the undying exploratory impulse in the US spirit: "The future doesn't belong to the fainthearted; it belongs to the brave. The *Challenger* crew was pulling us into the future, and we'll continue to follow them." Reagan used a eulogy of the astronauts to call for a policy of continued support of the space program, thus creating a hybrid response of eulogizing (epideictic) and advancing a policy (deliberative).[68]

This case illustrates the components of a rhetorical situation. The rhetor, President Reagan, responded to an exigence by speaking to particular audiences in a way that accounted for constraints in the situation. However, this analysis also shows that the rhetorical situation is not as objectively knowable and fixed as Bitzer suggests. People knew an explosion had happened, but they did not know what it meant. President Reagan not only responded to a situation, he also attempted to define exactly what it meant. The complexity of this speech illustrates the need for an alternative view of the relationship between rhetoric and situations.

SITUATIONS AS RHETORICAL

Numerous scholars have critiqued Bitzer's formulation.[69] In an essay that systematically responds to Bitzer, communication scholar Richard Vatz concludes: "situations are rhetorical."[70] He contends that Bitzer's claim that rhetoric is situational is inaccurate. He writes:

> The essential question to be addressed is: What is the relationship
> between rhetoric and situations? It will not be surprising that I take
> the converse position of each of Bitzer's major statements regarding this
> relationship. For example: I would not say "rhetoric is situational," but
> situations are rhetorical; not " . . . exigence strongly invites utterance,"
> but utterance strongly invites exigence; not "the situation controls the
> rhetorical response . . . " but the rhetoric controls the situational response;
> not " . . . rhetorical discourse . . . does obtain its character-as-rhetorical
> from the situation which generates it," but situations obtain their character
> from the rhetoric which surrounds them or creates them.[71]

Vatz argues that rhetoric constructs the situation because "meaning is not discovered in situations, but *created* by rhetors."[72] The meaning, or the definition of a situation, is not always clear. Consequently, the demand for a response is not necessarily self-evident to the audience or the rhetor. Instead, people's responses to situations make those events meaningful. Thus, rhetors are "responsible for what [they choose] to make salient."[73]

Summarizing the differences between the two approaches, writing, rhetoric, and digital studies professor Jenny Edbauer-Rice explains that in Bitzer's view, "the rhetor discovers exigencies that already exist" while "Vatz argues that exigencies are created for audiences through the rhetor's work."[74] Bitzer argues that "the situation is objective, publicly observable, and historic [which means] that it is real or genuine."[75] In Bitzer's perspective, a fitting response would not attempt to alter or (re)define the situation.

Bitzer's approach is overly limiting. Sometimes, the exigence is not clear or even known. The audience members may not perceive the urgency until the rhetor introduces the problem to them. For example, in 1962 Rachel Carson, a scientist who worked for the US Fish and Wildlife Service, wrote *Silent Spring* in order to galvanize action to ban the pesticide DDT.[76] Having researched and written several articles on ecologies, Carson became concerned at the rapidly increasing use of chemical pesticides. She wrote *Silent Spring* to challenge their use and warn the public of their dangers.[77]

Prior to the publication of Carson's book, people had not known about the dangers of chemical pesticides or recognized the urgency of the problem. They did not perceive an exigence. Technological progress was accepted as an unassailable good. Few people believed that nature was vulnerable to human intervention. Carson's book created a firestorm of controversy over pesticide use, an exigence to which chemical industries and the government had to respond, ultimately by banning DDT. Carson's rhetorical actions helped create the meaning and importance of the exigence to which the audience responded.

Another example of defining an exigence can be seen in President Reagan's *Challenger* speech. Reagan began by calling the event a "national tragedy" and clarified the exigence by stating "We're still pioneers. They, the members of the *Challenger* crew, were pioneers." In this way, he gave meaning to the disaster: the accident was part of the US pioneer spirit, not an indication of the failure of NASA or the end of space travel.

A SYNERGISTIC UNDERSTANDING OF RHETORIC AND SITUATIONS

The rhetorical situation is complex. Symbolic action constructs human beings' understanding of reality and, hence, their understanding of situations. This statement does not mean that nothing exists outside of symbolic action, but that the meaning of the material world is always mediated through symbols and language. A synergistic relationship emerges between rhetoric and situation, one in which situations guide rhetorical responses *and* rhetoric constructs situations. Events happen, but their relative importance is given to them through interpretations, which are rhetorically constructed.

Although we recognize the importance of Bitzer's work, we question the assumption of an objectively knowable situation. Although Vatz makes some good points, we recognize that rhetoric does not occur in a vacuum. A rhetor does not, all alone, define a situation. Human beings do not come to understand situations unmediated by discourse. Rhetors do not come to situations with only their own discourse as the means of mediation. Other rhetors may have already responded; a subject's cultural history may have developed across time; individuals may have watched an event on television or the internet.

Rhetoric scholars Robert J. Branham and W. Barnett Pearce point out that rhetoric gets its meaning from the situation, but it also influences and helps create the situation.[78] For example, when you speak in class, you are aware that you are in a classroom with other students and a professor, so you probably speak differently from the way you do when you are at lunch with your friends. Once you speak in class, however, your communication shapes the class, helping to set a tone for the discussion. As people interact, the interaction begins to define the situation. Consequently, we believe a synergistic understanding of the rhetorical situation is needed.

Definition of the Situation

Argumentation theorist Robert Cox points out that a rhetor's definition of the situation determines which responses appear to be reasonable, rational, and coherent.[79] Cox argues that "actors' *definitions of the situation* emerge in their symbolic interactions with their environment"; they are not predetermined by the situation.[80] The way a rhetor defines a situation determines the exact nature of the exigence and, hence, what appear to be reasonable judgments about it and actions responding to it. Instead of the situation containing rules and conventions that the rhetor must discover, Cox suggests, the rhetor's proposed definition of the situation provides the "contextual rules for interpreting choices as rational, reasonable, or justified."[81]

The various elements of the rhetorical situation are connected in complex ways. For instance, how rhetors define rhetorical situations determines how they respond to them. Events beyond a rhetor's control may demand a response, but rhetors can also influence which responses are perceived as reasonable and which situations rise to a level that demand a response. As an illustration, we offer various responses to the events of 9/11.

Analysis: 9/11 Defined as an "Act of War"

The events of September 11, 2001, demonstrate how a rhetorical situation can be defined in multiple ways. The situation created uncertainty: the public needed answers as to why the attacks had happened, who was responsible, and whether the country was safe. Media coverage of the burning and collapse of the Twin Towers and of the smoldering wreckage of the Pentagon was so immediate, constant, intense, and evocative, it called for a response from the government, specifically, the president.

Initial responses were complicated by the fact that no one really knew how to name the situation. In the first few hours, the event was called a terrorist attack, an act of war, an accident, a hijacking, a tragedy, a bombing, a breach of international and domestic law, and so on. A situation with an uncertain or equivocal meaning creates a need for a response to define the situation. When media and government officials began to define the events as terrorist attacks and acts of war, people began to understand them in a particular way. President Bush could have chosen to define the rhetorical situation other ways. The choices were neither automatic nor obvious. In fact, they were based on ambiguous and incomplete information. Naming the event was a central rhetorical act, but the situation appeared to be unparalleled, creating undefined exigences and a complex set of constraints. No perfect precedent existed.

The confusion invited a response that would clarify and comfort. Thus, when the president delivered an address to the nation on the evening of September 11, people were seeking not only consolation for the lives lost and the havoc wreaked, but also explanations of the meaning of the attacks.[82] (For a complete text and a video of the speech, visit http://www.americanrhetoric.com/speeches /gwbush911addresstothenation.htm, or search "Bush," "9/11," and "address to the nation.")

In the beginning of the speech, Bush described the attacks as "evil," "acts of terror" and "acts of mass murder," but not yet as "acts of war." Still, he established a rhetorical trajectory that made clear a military response was planned by declaring halfway through the speech "Our military is powerful, and it's prepared," and, a few sentences later, stating that the US would "win the war against terrorism."

Not until September 12 did President Bush specifically refer to the attacks as acts of war.[83] Naming them as acts of war and also declaring a "war against terrorism" defined the situation differently from the way it would have been defined if he had named them as criminal acts, violations of international law, or crimes against humanity. Because President Bush was able to convince the public that the situation was an act of war in which terrorism was attacking freedom, a definition that media coverage echoed,[84] the course of action that appeared reasonable was a military response. He stretched the definition of an act of war to encompass acts of terrorism that, although they were believed to be sponsored by another country, were perpetrated by nonstate actors. By declaring a war against terrorism, he expanded the idea of war to targets beyond aggressive nation states.

President Bush's definition of the situation framed the types of evidence that were admissible (only US sources counted because the attackers were evil) and the information that was relevant (the "war" began on 9/11, and no earlier). By defining the attacks as acts of war, Bush limited the appropriate response. An act of war requires some sort of military response.

The rhetorical response, the rhetorical situation, the rhetor, and the audiences all influence each other, bringing into existence a situation at their nexus. Once a rhetor crafts a definition of the rhetorical situation and calls a particular audience into being, the rhetorical situation is defined for present, as well as future, rhetors. Events clearly happened on September 11, 2001, but what they meant was open to interpretation. Depending on that interpretation, rhetors could defend particular reactions as the most reasonable. As events unfold, however, rhetorical action ensues and the rhetorical situation evolves, eliciting different interpretations. Definitions do not go unanswered or unchallenged. Competing definitions of the situation can sustain and generate arguments about what the appropriate rhetorical response is.

Analysis: 9/11 Redefined

Now, years later, given how deeply the US public has been immersed in rhetoric declaring 9/11 an act of war, it seems unreasonable to think about whether a nonmilitary response would have been appropriate. At the time, over 80 percent of US citizens approved of the US-led invasion of Afghanistan as part of its "war on terror."[85] The US government declared that the Afghanistan government harbored the people who masterminded the 9/11 attacks. Afghanistan was controlled by the Taliban, who supported Osama bin Laden, who claimed credit for the 9/11 attacks.

The interpretation of 9/11 as an act of war is not the only way to understand it, however.[86] Pope John Paul II offered a different definition of the situation. In a papal audience on September 11 one year after the attacks, the Pope stated clearly that the attacks were unjustified, but that defining them as an act of war was unacceptable.[87] (For a complete text of the speech, visit http://www.vatican.va/holy_father/john_paul_ii/audiences/2002/documents/hf_jp-ii_aud_20020911_en.html, or search "Pope" and "September 11, 2002.")

The Pope described terrorism as unjustified "inhuman ferocity," "savage," "barbaric and cruel," but did not define the attacks as an act of war. Thus, the reasonable response is not war, but rather "political and economic initiatives that" can ameliorate "the scandalous situations of injustice and oppression."[88] The Pope defined the 9/11 rhetorical situation as tragedy, which must be understood and prevented through dialogue. In 2004, to explain this position further, he declared that terrorism must be confronted with "firmness and decision, in fighting the workers of death," but that "war must always be considered a defeat: a defeat of reason and of humanity."[89]

Pope John Paul II defined the attacks as an act of terrorism, but unlike President Bush, he did not define them as an act that requires another act of violence—a war. Specifically, he referred to war as a choice, meaning the situation did not automatically and necessarily require military action. He provided the rules for interpreting the choice for war in this case as irrational, unreasonable, and unjustified, and argued that the correct response to terrorism is reason and love.

Additionally, he argued that underlying problems create the conditions for people to "fall prey to the temptations of hatred and violence." In this way, he challenged assumptions about why the attacks had happened and declared a global responsibility to ensure that all people have access to basic rights. He argued that the response to terrorism should not be war but removing the conditions that generate terrorism.

Philosopher Judith Butler offered another challenge to prevailing definitions of the situation. She mused on the very question of what 9/11 came to mean for the United States by suggesting people "ask what, politically, might be made of grief besides a cry for war."[90] Her goal was not to argue that the grief over the attacks was unwarranted or to minimize the moral abhorrence people might feel toward them. Instead, her argument was that

> neither moral outrage nor public mourning [should] become the occasion
> for the muting of critical discourse and public debate on the meaning
> of historical events. One might still want to know what brought about
> these events, want to know how best to address those conditions so
> that the seeds are not sown for further events of this kind, find sites of
> intervention, help to plan strategies thoughtfully that will not beckon
> more violence in the future. One can even experience that abhorrence,
> mourning, anxiety, and fear, and have all of these emotional dispositions
> lead to a reflection on how others have suffered arbitrary violence at the
> hands of the US, but also endeavor to produce another public culture and
> another public policy in which suffering unexpected violence and loss and
> reactive aggression are not accepted as the norm of political life.[91]

Butler's call for a nonviolent ethics that understands the precariousness of life is at odds with the public discourse that defined US reactions to 9/11. Her point is that invasion should not be perceived as the only option. Instead of constituting the audience as vengeful citizens of an attacked nation, she called on people to be empathic citizens of the world. If the audience members accepted Bush's definition of the situation as war, however, it would be difficult to persuade them to redefine the situation, as Butler attempted to do.

Ultimately, Butler argued that dissent is important, including dissent against definitions of situations that lead to labeling dissent as anti-American or, worse, treason. Recognition that situations are rhetorically defined is essential if people are to recognize the possibility of challenging the definition of a situation.

Redefining a situation is not easy. Once an audience accepts a definition of a situation, it can be difficult to change that definition. When the US public accepted the definition of 9/11 as an act of war against the United States and identified another country as sharing responsibility, US support for military action was strong. Such strong support should not have meant that people who disagreed were anti-American or did not support the troops, but the definition of the situation became stable and, hence, presented a particular exigence to anyone who might question the US response.

Analysis: 9/11 Redefined, Again

On May 15, 2014, the 9/11 Memorial Museum was dedicated. Its 110,000-square-foot exhibition space is located at the center of the World Trade Center site. The memorial space includes reflecting pools in the footprints of the two towers, surrounded by bronze plaques on which are inscribed the names of every person who died in the 2001 attack (except for the hijackers) and in an earlier, 1993, attack on the Towers. During the dedication, President Barack Obama delivered remarks during the dedication.[92] (For a complete text of the speech, visit http://www.whitehouse.gov/the-press-office/2014/05/15/remarks-president-911-museum-dedication, or search "Obama," "dedication," and "9/11 Memorial Museum.")

What is remembered in Obama's speech is not the moment the planes hit the towers, but the aftermath: the heroism of coworkers, first responders, and passengers who stopped a fourth plane from reaching its target. The situation to which President Obama responds is not one of terror, fear, or grief. Instead, he defines "the true spirit of 9/11" as "love, compassion, sacrifice."

This situation is marked by the dedication of the 9/11 museum, and as such, is constrained by the genre of dedications. The museum sustains public memory about the events, using events of the past to meet the needs of the present. The nearly thirteen years of temporal distance between the dedication of the museum and the events of 9/11 enabled Obama to focus on the values of love, compassion, and sacrifice.

Obama does not confine his remarks to what the lesson of the museum might be, but to what the spirit of 9/11 is. He uses a representative anecdote, a narrative that summarizes a situation, by telling the story of Welles Crowther, who worked in the South Tower and who died while helping others escape from the building. Crowther was known for wearing a red bandana, and several survivors reported that a young man wearing a red bandana led them to safety. This story connects the artifacts in the museum (in this case, the red handkerchief) to the heroism Obama praises. The speech calls forth a national audience dedicated to service, selflessness, and a commitment to others.

FITTING RESPONSES RECONSIDERED

Identifying the components of a rhetorical situation and recognizing when symbolic actions have attempted to define the situation are useful steps in understanding how rhetoric functions. If the situation is defined more expansively, then the issues to be considered become broader as well. As Butler asks about 9/11, do people mourn only the loss of US life, or all life? If the situation is defined expansively, it might call for a radically different response, such as the Pope's call to respect all human life and to reflect on and correct the underlying conditions that might lead people to violence. If defined narrowly, the situation tends to demand a focused response. A focus on the loss of US lives constructs a definition of the situation that suggests armed conflict is necessary to protect US lives. As time passes, the situation and the fitting response continue to alter and expand. Obama's response included a memorialization of the heroes on the day of the tragic events.

In the next section, we identify possible influences on whether responses are fitting, including cultural variations in historical context and conscious decisions on the part of rhetors to challenge what is considered to be a fitting response.

Cultural Variations and Historical Context

Although the rhetorical situation is more than the historical context, placing a rhetorical act in its historical context can help you understand the choices available to a rhetor. Not all rhetors have equal access to the full range of persuasive possibilities. Moreover, meaning is not only in texts but in the audiences who interpret the texts. Various audiences' social norms influence what they consider appropriate, even during a single historical moment.

Understanding the historical context is a necessary, but not sufficient, condition for understanding how a response fits a rhetorical situation. Communication scholars Robert J. Branham and W. Barnett Pearce point out that an audience interprets a rhetorical text within the rhetorical situation.[93] If you read the Gettysburg Address without knowing the rhetorical situation of the speech, for example, you might read it as a piece of literature and miss how it responds to a very particular situation. Knowing that it was given on the battleground of the bloodiest battle in the US Civil War gives meaning to the speech and the persuasive choices President Lincoln made.

The context is more than the historical facts and events surrounding a persuasive response. It also includes the participants' cultural orientations and how they influence interpretations of the events and facts. What today might be viewed as unfitting or as inappropriate language, form, topic, style, or approach might have been viewed as acceptable or fitting response when a speech was first delivered. For example, expectations concerning the appropriate length of speeches have changed dramatically. In 1841, William Henry Harrison delivered a 105-minute inaugural speech. After the advent of radio in the 1920s, most speeches lasted no more than an hour. By the 1940s, the 30-minute speech was the norm; almost all major political speeches were reprinted in their entirety in newspapers. Now, most political speeches average about 20 minutes in length. Barack Obama's 2013 inaugural was barely 20 minutes long. Speakers hope to receive evening news coverage with 5-, 10-, or 15-second sound bites.[94]

The length of speeches is not the only thing that has changed. What you might take for granted as appropriate now could have been extremely shocking in a different era. For example, political communication scholar Kathleen Hall Jamieson traces how a style that was once condemned as effeminate (soothing, ornamental, personal, self-disclosing, and using dramatic narratives) became the norm for contemporary politicians speaking in an electronic age.[95] Television is a medium in which the visual elements combine intimately with the verbal elements.[96] It has also given the public a closer view of their leaders, and people expect the words from speakers who are close-up to be intimate and personal.[97] Additionally, television gives people the illusion that the rhetor is speaking to them individually, rather than to a large audience. Hence, television invites a more personal style than did the oratorical contexts of a pretelevision age.[98]

With the emergence of digital technologies, the issue of style is complicated further. As communication scholar Bruce Gronbeck notes in an assessment of citizen voices in a networked culture, "Many web messages are both oral and literate in tone and form, sometimes chatty, at other times formal, and they can—but need not—rely on visual technologies for controlling meaning-making by the way they're laid out."[99] Tweets and emails can be highly personal, addressed to you personally, even when they address broad public concerns.

Responses to Rhetorical Situations

How does one explain persuasive responses that, at first glance, do not appear to fit the rhetorical situation, but still persuade an audience? Sometimes a rhetor might respond in an "unfitting" way in order to draw attention to an issue or shock an audience into awareness. Civil rights activists' lunch counter sit-ins of the 1960s and AIDS activists' die-ins of the 1980s did not persuade in a conventional way.[100]

A rhetor may choose to respond in an unconventional way if they do not interpret the situation in a conventional way. As Branham and Pearce explain, "not all texts are conventional, not all contexts are stable, and not all situations imply recognizable techniques or consensual standards of interpretation."[101] These scholars offer four ways in which a rhetor can respond to a rhetorical situation: conformity, nonparticipation, desecration, and contextual reconstruction. We begin with their description of conformity, which echoes Bitzer's idea of the fitting response to the rhetorical situation.

Conformity. Rhetors use **conformity** when they employ *a conventional response to a situation*.[102] Reagan's *Challenger* speech conformed insofar as it fulfilled the expectations attached to a eulogy: it was somber in tone, recognized the deaths, transformed the audience's relationship with the astronauts from the present to the past, and sought to reknit the community. Conformity adapts the persuasive message to the norms and expectations of the audience it addresses.

Societal norms affect what is considered a conforming response. Audiences have expectations that rhetors may decide to follow in order to have their messages heard and accepted. Much of our everyday communication conforms. For example, when you attempt to persuade your professor to alter an assignment that you think is too difficult or time consuming, you probably make an argument in a polite way, offering support for your position. You probably suggest alternatives to the assignment or ways to make the assignment more workable for you and your classmates. You are attempting to persuade your professor conventionally, using a style and arguments that are expected in this situation.

Nonparticipation. Some rhetors may choose not to respond to situations within the established contexts because they do not believe the contexts are legitimate. According to Branham and Pearce, **nonparticipation** is *a response that denies the legitimacy of the rhetorical situation.*[103]

In the summer of 2019, as the US Women's National Soccer Team was in the midst of an undefeated run to its fourth, and second consecutive, World Cup championship, a video from team captain Megan Rapinoe from earlier in the year went viral in June. In an interview, Rapinoe indicated (in some decidedly forceful language) that should the team win the World Cup, she would not go to any White House celebration for the championship. The reason: She believed Trump's policies and rhetoric excluded people.[104] In an interview with CNN'S Anderson Cooper, Rapinoe indicated that other team members agreed. The team had spent the years and months leading up to the World Cup advocating for equal pay and equal treatment for the Women's National Team, whose international success was unparalleled. The team had garnered media and public attention for the equal pay issue and, according to Rapinoe, chose not to participate in a White House reception because to do so would have let the "platform that we've worked so hard to build, and the things that we fight for, and the way that we live our life . . . be co-opted or corrupted" by the Trump administration.[105] When the team received a private invitation to the White House after their victory, they declined; they chose nonparticipation.[106]

Desecration. While nonparticipation refuses to grant legitimacy to a situation by participating in it, **desecration** is *a response that violates what would be considered an appropriate response; it participates, but in a way that overtly challenges expectations.* The rhetor ridicules the situation and/or those who take part in it. This response, according to Branham and Pearce, violates norms and conventions in order to question the legitimacy of the situation.[107]

The Russian punk rock group Pussy Riot illustrates symbolic desecration. The group engages in various forms of protest in unusual public places and has often videotaped its actions and uploaded music videos to YouTube.[108] Wearing balaclavas to cover their faces and remain anonymous, the members of the group staged protests against Russian President Vladimir Putin's policies and his apparent ties to the Russian Orthodox Church.[109] On February 21, 2012, five members entered Moscow's Cathedral of Christ the Saviour and performed a forty-second-long "punk prayer."[110] They began "bowing and crossing themselves in the manner of ardent believers" while singing a prayer calling on "the Lord to oust Russian President, Vladimir Putin."[111]

Although the women did not destroy, deface, or endanger church property, three of them (Nadezhda Tolokonnikova, 22; Maria Alyokhina, 24; and Yekaterina Samutsevich, 29) were arrested for "hooliganism with religious hatred" and sentenced to prison.[112] US Representative Steve King told reporters in Moscow that Pussy Riot's actions had "desecrated" the cathedral. He defended the prison sentences.[113] The patriarch of the church, at a liturgy delivered in Moscow's Deposition of the Robe Cathedral, condemned the performance for making fun of religion.[114] Pussy Riot mirrored the form of prayer, but by including lyrics informed by their punk sensibility, they also desecrated what was considered appropriate prayer in that space. They challenged expectations by demanding that Putin be ousted, offering a political prayer, and delivering a prayer whose words were more punk than religious.

Contextual Reconstruction. Contextual reconstruction is *a response in which a rhetor attempts to redefine the situation.* Such a response might appear to conform to the situation, but actually challenge the expectations of what it is meant to achieve, sometimes quite overtly, as part of the rhetorical act. In these instances, Branham says, "Speaking itself is both the subject and object of such discourse."[115] According to Branham and Pearce, instead of "accepting the rhetorical situation as presented," a rhetor "dismantles and then reconstructs it."[116] In contextual reconstruction, the rhetor recognizes the traditional meaning of the rhetorical situation, but seeks to redefine it.

Branham and Pearce offer President Abraham Lincoln's Gettysburg Address as an example of contextual reconstruction.[117] Lincoln had been invited to make "a few appropriate remarks"[118] to dedicate a cemetery for the soldiers who had died fighting a horrific Civil War battle that saw fifty-one thousand casualties during a three-day period in July 1863.[119] Lincoln acknowledged that such a situation asked him to look backward, stating: "We are met on a great battle-field of that war. We have come to dedicate a portion of that field, as a final resting place for those who here gave their lives that that nation might live. It is altogether fitting and proper that we should do this."[120] He reinterpreted the exigence, however, by stating that the assumed exigence was not accurate: "But, in a larger sense, we can not dedicate—we can not consecrate—we can not hallow—this ground." Instead of only looking backward in consecration, Lincoln shifted the orientation to the future. He reinterpreted the situation by creating a new exigence of renewal.[121]

Harkening back to Pericles's funeral oration, delivered 2,394 years earlier,[122] President Lincoln questioned whether a verbal response was even fitting: "The brave men, living and dead, who struggled here, have consecrated it, far above our poor power to add or detract. The world will little note, nor long remember what we say here, but it can never forget what they did here." Finally, he solidified a reconstruction of the situation to a future orientation, calling for a renewed commitment to the war effort:

> It is for us, the living, rather, to be dedicated here to the unfinished work which they who fought here have thus far so nobly advanced. It is rather for us to be here dedicated to the great task remaining before us . . . that from these honored dead we take increased devotion to that cause for which they gave the last full measure of devotion; that we here highly resolve that these dead shall not have died in vain; that this nation, under

> God, shall have a new birth of freedom; and that government of the people, by the people, for the people, shall not perish from the earth.

On one level, the Gettysburg Address, considered by many to be one of the greatest speeches in US history, was not a fitting response because the purpose of the gathering was to consecrate part of the battlefield as a cemetery. Yet, as Branham and Pearce point out, President Lincoln reconstructed the situation and offered a new interpretation to the audience[123] that focused on renewal, not consecration. Lincoln was faced with eulogizing the largest number of US soldiers ever killed in one battle, a tragedy that could have a demoralizing effect on Union supporters, especially because not all of the North was committed to the war effort. Lincoln's interpretation of the meaning of the situation transformed the understanding of the battle and the memorial.[124]

RETHINKING THE RHETORICAL SITUATION IN A DIGITAL AGE

In the examples we have discussed thus far, the rhetorical situation appears to be bounded in space and time. The *Challenger* explosion, 9/11, and Gettysburg could each be defined as a discrete event that required a presidential response. Each presidential speech also occurred at a specific time and place. Although the speeches recirculated in the news media, the messages remained relatively stable. Fragments also circulated, but each address was preserved in its entirety; moreover, the fragments were tethered to a relatively stable text (the speech) and a relatively stable rhetor (the president). Contemporary rhetoric, however, is dominated by tweets, images, and videos that anyone can create and then recirculate. Because single rhetorical agents have been displaced by networks of rhetors (supplemented by bots), the rhetorical situation must be rethought.

Writing, rhetoric, and digital studies professor Jenny Edbauer-Rice urges a move away from focusing on the singular rhetorical situation and to "rhetorical ecologies."[125] Ecology is a branch of science that studies the complex interactions through which organisms and environments constantly affect one another. Studying a **rhetorical ecology** entails considering *the "mixture of processes and encounters" as rhetoric moves across space and time and interacts with other rhetorical actions to grow its meaning.*[126] This definition induces critics to consider the movement and mutability of rhetoric. Neither texts nor rhetors nor situations are stable. As rhetoric circulates across media platforms and among people, the compositions of the text, rhetor, and situation shift and change. Interconnected situations form a complex web of rhetorical challenges. Rather than studying rhetorical situations as single moments, or as simple cause and effect, taking an ecological approach means recognizing that rhetorical actions circulate and are generated by multiple rhetorical agents; that they affect and are affected by the situation. Consequently, the situation is constantly changed by the rhetoric in it.

All rhetoric circulates, mutates, and replicates. To study rhetoric, critics need to explore how it emerges, is distributed, and then continues to circulate long past its moment of emergence.[127] For example, what Pepe the Frog meant when circulating in a comic is different from what Pepe meant as a meme is different from what Pepe means when displayed on the lapel of a white supremacist.

Digital rhetoric scholar Eric Jenkins echoes the need to attend to circulation and its effect on the rhetorical situation. In a study of memes, Jenkins notes, "As images circulate, their meaning changes. . . . Circulation continually alters situations and contexts by varying the rhetors, audiences, exigencies, and constraints."[128] Rather than looking for *one* exigence or *one* rhetorical situation, consider instead what rhetoric will do in the many rhetorical situations through which it circulates. The issue is not just that meanings change because the audience or the rhetor changes. With memes, for example, the actual text changes. The distinction between rhetor and audience blurs because meme-makers are often both audience members (who receive one version of a meme) and rhetors (who remake and recirculate the memes for their own purposes). Thus, it is hard to answer the question "Did the rhetor provide a fitting response to the situation?" because "circulation multiplies rhetors and objects to the point where origin and motivation become uncertain."[129]

Practically, what might all this mean for you? In some cases, you might confront a relatively discrete rhetorical situation. For example, when you request an extension on an assignment, the exigence is relatively clear, as are the audience and constraints you might face as a rhetor. You think about whether it is generally acceptable to ask for an extension for an assignment and whether your professor has rules about late assignments. You may consider your particular relationship with the professor, your performance in the class, and whether you have asked for an extension in the past.

In other cases, you confront not a rhetorical situation but a rhetorical ecology. For example, before you post a photo on social media, you might want to consider all the ways that image might circulate, how it might be used (or misused) by others, and whether the humor that presently is attached to an image of you doing something slightly stupid might dissipate when that image is viewed years later by a prospective employer. The situation changes as the message circulates across different spaces and time, as does the meaning of the photo. Moreover, you are no longer the sole rhetor; others who recirculate the photo do so for their own purposes. Although you might think of the image as yours, others can put that image to use in ways you never intended or desired. Similarly, before you distribute or share someone else's image, you should consider the way in which your circulation of that image mutates it.

CONCLUSION

As far back as Aristotle's time, students of rhetoric have recognized that rhetors make rhetorical choices when responding to a rhetorical situation. Those choices include the rhetor's definition of the situation and indicate how the rhetor wants the audience to interpret and respond to it. The rhetor's choices do not determine the situation alone, however. A situation comes into existence as a result of the interplay between rhetor, audience, and context. As a result, the range of rhetorical choices available to a rhetor are limited.

When analyzing a rhetorical act, a critic must recognize the reflexive relationship between text and context to understand whether and how the response functioned as the rhetor wished. In addition, the critic must recognize that some rhetorical actions are called forth by recurrent rhetorical situations, which then influence audience expectations.

When analyzing the rhetorical situation, you must examine the cultural and historical context, as well as the interpretations of the context, to assess whether a response is fitting. Branham and Pearce advise an approach that "assumes neither that all contexts are 'fittable' nor that texts should necessarily 'fit' the contexts in which they occur."[130] They conclude that "rhetorical competence" is not based solely on "conformity to audience expectations or to standardized models of acceptable performance."[131] Sometimes, rhetoric that seems to fit a situation least is the rhetoric that is most eloquent, ethical, and elegant. In an interactive digital world, media technologies require the rhetorical competence of understanding rhetorical ecologies.

When rhetors participate in civic life, whether they use deliberative rhetoric about policy or epideictic rhetoric that constitutes identity, they do not add their symbolic actions to a blank slate. Other rhetors have spoken before them. Audiences carry expectations with them. Rhetors, themselves, have histories; and their rhetoric may be taken up and moved in ways they never intended. Symbolic actions are woven into already existing rhetorical situations. Rhetors reconstruct those situations by bringing particular audiences into being and by redefining exigences. Rhetorical action and the situation of civic life are synergistic.

DISCUSSION QUESTIONS

1. Think of a time when you had no idea how to respond to a situation. Was the situation difficult to define? Were you unclear about what was expected? Did the participants in the event create discourse that was confusing?
2. Think about a recent crisis to which an organization or politician needed to respond. What was the exigence to which they were responding? Who was the audience? Who was the rhetorical audience? How were the two audiences different? Think about a particular tweet or speech or email. What was the context of the rhetorical action? What were the constraints the rhetor faced? What choices did the rhetor make?
3. Identify the generic expectations in each of the following situations:
   You are asked to deliver a speech at your best friend's wedding.
   You are selected to deliver the commencement speech at your graduation.
   You are asked to speak at a funeral.
   What are the similarities and differences among these situations? How do these similarities and differences suggest similar and different responses?
4. Identify a rhetorical action that you believe failed to fulfill its purpose. Were there elements of the rhetorical situation that led to this failure? Did the rhetor present an unfitting response? What could the rhetor have done to respond to the situation or to (re)define it?

RECOMMENDED READINGS

Biesecker, Barbara. "Rethinking the Rhetorical Situation from within the Thematic of *Différance*." *Philosophy and Rhetoric* 22 (1989): 110–130.

Bitzer, Lloyd F. "The Rhetorical Situation." *Philosophy and Rhetoric* 1 (1968): 1–14.

Branham, Robert J., and W. Barnett Pearce. "Between Text and Context: Toward a Rhetorical Contextual Reconstruction." *Quarterly Journal of Speech* 71 (1985): 19–36.

Campbell, Karlyn Kohrs and Kathleen Hall Jamieson. *Presidents Creating the Presidency: Deeds Done in Words*. Chicago: University of Chicago Press, 2008.

Jenkins, Eric S. "The Modes of Visual Rhetoric: Circulating Memes as Expressions." *Quarterly Journal of Speech* 100 (2014), 442–466.

Stuckey, Mary E. *Slipping the Surly Bonds: Reagan's Challenger Address* (College Station: Texas A&M Press, 2006)

Vatz, Richard E. "The Myth of the Rhetorical Situation." *Philosophy and Rhetoric* 6 (1973): 154–161.

ENDNOTES

[1] Details about this sit-in come from Victoria J. Gallagher, Kenneth Zagacki, and Jeff Swift, "From 'Dead Wrong' to Civil Rights History: The Durham 'Royal Seven,' Martin Luther King's 1960 'Fill Up the Jails' Speech, and the Rhetoric of Visibility," in *Like Wildfire: The Rhetoric of the Civil Rights Sit-Ins*, ed. Sean P. O'Rourke and Lesli K. Pace (Columbia: University of South Carolina Press, 2020).

[2] For more on the sit-ins, see Susan Leigh Foster, "Choreographies of Protest," *Theatre Journal* 55, no. 3 (October 2003), 395–412, https://doi.org/10.1353/tj.2003.0111.

[3] Rebekah J. Kowal, "Staging the Greensboro Sit-Ins," *The Drama Review* 48, no. 4 (Winter 2004), 135–154.

[4] Martin Luther King, Jr., "A Creative Protest," in *The Papers of Martin Luther King, Jr., Volume V*, ed. Clayborne Carson, Tenisha Armstrong, Susan Carson, Adrienne Clay, and Kieran Taylor (Berkeley: University of California Press, 2005), 369.

[5] King, "A Creative Protest," 370.

[6] Jimmy Hart, "A New Challenge Awaits," *The Jackson Sun*, October 1960, http://orig.jacksonsun.com/civilrights/sec3_sitins.shtml.

[7] Jeanne Theoharis, "Don't Forget That Martin Luther King Jr. Was Once Denounced as an Extremist," *Time*, January 12, 2018, http://time.com/5099513/martin-luther-king-day -myths/; and Roper Center for Public Opinion Research, "Public Opinion on Civil Rights," July 2, 2014, https://ropercenter.cornell.edu/blog/public-opinion-civil-rights -reflections-civil-rights-act-1964-blog.

[8] Aristotle, *On Rhetoric*, trans. George A. Kennedy (New York: Oxford University Press, 1991), 1.2.1 [1355].

[9] Aristotle, *On Rhetoric*, 1.3.1 [1358].

[10] Aristotle, *On Rhetoric*, 1.3.1 [1358b].

[11] Aristotle, *On Rhetoric*, 1.3.1 [1358b], italics added.

[12] Aristotle, *On Rhetoric*, 1.3.1 [1358b].

[13] Lloyd F. Bitzer, "The Rhetorical Situation," *Philosophy and Rhetoric* 1 (1968): 3.

[14] Bitzer, "The Rhetorical Situation," 3.

[15] For a full description of Hamer's activism, see Kay Mills, *This Little Light of Mine: The Life of Fannie Lou Hamer* (New York: Dutton, 1993), esp. chapter 6. A transcript and audiotape of Hamer's testimony is available at http://www.americanrhetoric.com /speeches/fannielouhamercredentialscommittee.htm.

[16] Bitzer, "The Rhetorical Situation," 3.

[17] Bitzer, "The Rhetorical Situation," 4.

[18] Bitzer, "The Rhetorical Situation," 6, italics added.

[19] Bitzer, "The Rhetorical Situation," 2.

[20] Bitzer, "The Rhetorical Situation," 6, italics added.

[21] Tom Leonard, "Hurricane Ike: Houston Residents Ordered Not to Evacuate as Deadly Storm Hits," *The Telegraph* (London), September 12, 2008, http://www.telegraph.co.uk/news/worldnews/northamerica/usa/2824891/Hurricane -Ike-Houston-residents-ordered-not-to-evacuate-as-deadly-storm-hits.html.

[22] Bitzer, "The Rhetorical Situation," 5.

[23] Bitzer, "The Rhetorical Situation," 5–6.

[24] Lloyd F. Bitzer, "Functional Communication: A Situational Perspective," in *Rhetoric in Transition: Studies in the Nature and Uses of Rhetoric,* ed. Eugene E. White (University Park: Pennsylvania State University Press, 1980), 35.

[25] David Kohn, "The President's Story: The President Talks in Detail about His Sept. 11 Experience," *60 Minutes,* September 10, 2003, http://www.cbsnews.com/stories/2002/09/11/ 60II/main521718.shtml.

[26] Some people perceived failure to respond. After President Bush was informed that the second tower had been hit, he continued to listen to sixteen second-graders take turns reading *The Pet Goat.* The perception of a failure to respond is most detailed in Michael Moore's controversial documentary, *Fahrenheit 9/11* (2004).

[27] Bruce E. Gronbeck, "Rhetorical Timing in Public Communication," *Central States Speech Journal* 25 (1974): 91.

[28] Bitzer, "Rhetorical Situation," 7, italics added.

[29] Matthew Dowd, "Interview from 'Karl Rove—The Architect,'" *Frontline,* January 4, 2005, posted April 12, 2005, http://www.pbs.org/wgbh/pages/frontline/shows/architect/interviews/dowd.html.

[30] Tim Harper, "It's Very Difficult to Ambush Bush: 'Bush Bubble' Keeps Fans in Line for Hours, Campaign Events Strictly Limited to Loyal Republicans," *NewsCenter,* September 24, 2005, http://www.commondreams.org/headlines04/0925-24.htm. In response to the strict control of access to campaign events, professors at Allegheny College in Meadville, Pennsylvania, created the Soapbox Alliance (http://cpp .allegheny.edu/soapboxalliance/ index.php). See Oren Dorell, "College Criticizes Invitation-Only Political Rallies," *USA Today,* updated November 19, 2007, http://www.usatoday.com/news/politics/election2008/2007-11-19-soapbox_N.htm. The invitation-only strategy continued during Bush's presidency. See Michael A. Genovese and Lori Cox Han, "The 'Invitation Only' Presidency of George W. Bush," *HistoryNewsNetwork,* December 5, 2005, http://hnn.us/articles/18302.html.

[31] Sasha Issenberg, "A More Perfect Union: How President Obama's Campaign Used Big Data to Rally Individual Voters," *MIT Technology Review,* December 19, 2012, http://www.technologyreview.com/featuredstory/509026/how-obamas-team-used-big -data-to-rally-voters.

[32] Nate Silver, "Donald Trump Had a Superior Electoral College Strategy," FiveThirtyEight, February 6, 2017, https://fivethirtyeight.com/features/donald-trump-had-a-superior -electoral-college-strategy/.

[33] Walt Hickey, "Which Tipping-Point States Favor Trump," *FiveThirtyEight,* November 2, 2016, https://fivethirtyeight.com/features/which-tipping-point-states-favor-trump/.

[34] Bitzer, "The Rhetorical Situation," 8, italics added.

[35] Martha Cooper, *Analyzing Public Discourse* (Prospect Heights, IL: Waveland, 1989), 22.

[36] John Lewis, "John Lewis," in *My Soul is Rested: The Story of the Civil Rights Movement in the Deep South,* ed. Howell Raines (New York: Penguin, 1977), 99.

[37] For examples, see Reverend Billy's website, The Church of Stop Shopping, http://www.revbilly.com.

[38] Quoted in Jill Lane, "Reverend Billy: Preaching, Protest and Postindustrial Flânerie," *The Drama Review* 46, no. 1 (Spring 2002): 71.

[39] Karlyn Kohrs Campbell and Susan Schultz Huxman, *The Rhetorical Act,* 3rd ed. (Belmont, CA: Thomson/Wadsworth, 2003), 184–198, 206–214, 224–236.

[40] Campbell and Huxman, *The Rhetorical Act,* 207–212.

[41] H. W. Brands, "15 Minutes That Saved America," *American History* 43, no. 4 (October 2008): 34–41.

[42] David Michael Ryfe, "Franklin Roosevelt and the Fireside Chats," *Journal of Communication* 49, no. 4 (Autumn 1999): 80–103.

[43] Franklin D. Roosevelt, First Fireside Chat, "The Banking Crisis," March 12, 1933, http://www.americanrhetoric.com/speeches/fdrfirstfiresidechat.html. For a detailed analysis of this speech, see Amos Kiewe, *FDR's First Fireside Chat: Public Confidence and the Banking Crisis* (College Station: Texas A&M Press, 2007).

[44] Mary Kate Cary, "Obama Should Make Roosevelt-Style Fireside Chats on the Banking Crisis," *U.S. News and World Report,* March 12, 2009, http://www.usnews.com/blogs/mary-kate-cary/2009/3/12/obama-should-make-roosevelt-style-fireside-chats-on-the-banking-crisis.html.

[45] Campbell and Huxman, *The Rhetorical Act,* 184–198, 212–214.

[46] Campbell and Huxman, *The Rhetorical Act,* 224–236.

[47] Ryfe, "Franklin Roosevelt," 99.

[48] Bitzer, "The Rhetorical Situation," 10.

[49] Karlyn Kohrs Campbell and Kathleen Hall Jamieson, "Form and Genre in Rhetorical Criticism: An Introduction," in *Form and Genre: Shaping Rhetorical Action,* ed. Karlyn Kohrs Campbell and Kathleen Hall Jamieson (Falls Church, VA: Speech Communication Association, 1978), 19.

[50] Kathleen M. Jamieson, "Antecedent Genre as Rhetorical Constraint," *Quarterly Journal of Speech* 61 (1975): 406.

[51] Karlyn Kohrs Campbell and Kathleen Hall Jamieson, *Deeds Done in Words* (Chicago: University of Chicago Press, 1990), 37.

[52] Campbell and Jamieson, "Form and Genre," 23.

[53] Campbell and Jamieson, "Form and Genre," 21.

[54] Gerald R. Ford, "Address upon Taking the Oath of the U.S. Presidency," August 9, 1974, East Room of the White House, Washington, DC, http://www.americanrhetoric.com/speeches/geraldfordpresidentialoath.html.

[55] Campbell and Jamieson, *Deeds Done in Words,* 47.

[56] Kathleen Hall Jamieson and Karlyn Kohrs Campbell, "Rhetorical Hybrids: Fusions of Generic Elements," *Quarterly Journal of Speech* 68 (1982): 146–157.

[57] Campbell and Jamieson, *Deeds Done in Words,* 38.

[58] Lyndon Baines Johnson, "Let Us Continue," *American Rhetoric,* November 27, 1963, http://www.americanrhetoric.com/speeches/lbjletuscontinue.html.

[59] Michael Kolakowski and Thomas H. Neale, "The President's State of the Union Message: Frequently Asked Questions," CRS Report for Congress, March 7, 2006, 5, http://www.senate.gov/artandhistory/history/resources/pdf/stateoftheunion.pdf.

[60] Campbell and Jamieson, *Deeds Done in Words,* 70.

[61] Kathleen Hall Jamieson, "Generic Constraints and the Rhetorical Situation," *Philosophy & Rhetoric* 6, no. 3 (1973): 168.

[62] Quoted in Sam Rullo, "John Legend & Common's Oscar Speech Was Inspiring," video, *Bustle,* February 22, 2015, https://www.bustle.com/articles/65840-transcript-of-john-legend-commons-oscar -acceptance-speech-proves-glory-has-a-timeless-message-video.

[63] Daniel Riffe and James Glen Stovall, "Diffusion of News of Shuttle Disaster: What Role for Emotional Response," *Journalism Quarterly* 66 (Autumn 1989): 551–556.

[64] You can watch footage of the explosion on YouTube: "*Challenger* Disaster Live on CNN," streamed live on January 28, 1986, http://www.youtube.com/watch?v=j4JOjcDFtBE.

[65] Ronald W. Reagan, "The Space Shuttle 'Challenger' Tragedy Address," January 28, 1986, http://www.americanrhetoric.com/speeches/ronaldreaganchallenger.htm. A video of the speech is available on this site.

[66] The Soviet Union was probably also an audience, especially considering Reagan's thinly veiled reference to the Soviet penchant for secrecy in paragraph 6.

[67] For additional analysis, see "Special Issue: The Space Shuttle *Challenger,*" *Central States Speech Journal* 37 (Fall 1986). For analysis of the interactions between the visuals of the explosion and Reagan's rhetoric, see Kathleen Hall Jamieson, *Eloquence in an Electronic Age: The Transformation of Political Speechmaking* (New York: Oxford University Press, 1988), esp. pp. 126–133.

[68] For an excellent, detailed analysis of the *Challenger* speech, see Mary E. Stuckey, *Slipping the Surly Bonds: Reagan's Challenger Address* (College Station: Texas A&M Press, 2006).

[69] See for example Barbara A. Biesecker, "Rethinking the Rhetorical Situation from within the Thematic of Différance," *Philosophy & Rhetoric* 22, no. 2, 110–130; Scott Consigny, "Rhetoric and Its Situations," *Philosophy & Rhetoric* 7, no 3 (1974), 175–186; and Elizabeth Ervin, "Rhetorical Situations and the Straits of Appropriateness: Teaching Feminist Activism," *Rhetoric Review* 25, no. 3 (2006): 316–333.

[70] Richard E. Vatz, "The Myth of the Rhetorical Situation," *Philosophy and Rhetoric* 6 (1973): 159.

[71] Vatz, "The Myth," 159.

[72] Vatz, "The Myth," 157.

[73] Vatz, "The Myth," 159.

[74] Jenny Edbauer-Rice, "Unframing Models of Public Distribution: From Rhetorical Situation to Rhetorical Ecologies," *Rhetoric Society Quarterly* 35, no. 4 (Fall 2005): 6.

[75] Bitzer, "The Rhetorical Situation," 11.

[76] Rachel Carson, *Silent Spring,* 40th anniversary ed. (New York: Mariner, 1962/2002).

[77] Linda Lear, "The Life and Legacy of Rachel Carson," 1998, http://www.rachelcarson.org/Biography.aspx.

[78] Robert J. Branham and W. Barnett Pearce, "Between Text and Context: Toward a Rhetorical Contextual Reconstruction," *Quarterly Journal of Speech* 71 (1985): 19.

[79] J. Robert Cox, "Argument and the 'Definition of the Situation,'" *Central States Speech Journal* 32 (1981): 197–205, esp. 200.

[80] Cox, "Argument," 197. Although Cox disagrees with Bitzer, his position is not identical to Vatz's. For Cox, the definition of the situation refers not only to individual

interpretations, but also to broader, culturally formulated, and shared perceptions. See Cox, "Argument," 199.

[81] Cox, "Argument," 200.

[82] George W. Bush, "9/11 Address to the Nation," September 11, 2001, http://www.americanrhetoric.com/speeches/gwbush911addresstothenation.htm. A video of the speech is available on this site.

[83] George W. Bush, "Remarks by the President in Photo Opportunity with the National Security Team," September 12, 2001, http://www.whitehouse.gov/news/releases/2001/09/20010912-4.html.

[84] Kenneth Mentor, "Crime or Act of War?—The Media, 9-11, and Iraq," Presentation at the November 2002 Annual Meetings of the American Society of Criminology, Chicago, IL, http://critcrim.org/critpapers/911_iraq.htm; and John Domke, David Hutcheson, Andre Billeaudeaux, and Philip Garland, "U.S. National Identity, Political Elites, and a Patriotic Press Following September 11," *Political Communication* 21, no. 1 (January/March (2004): 27–50.

[85] The Pew Research Center for People and the Press, "Americans and Europeans Differ Widely on Foreign Policy Issues," April 17, 2002, http://people-press.org/reports/display.php3?ReportID=153.

[86] Many responses to 9/11 have been penned, including Noam Chomsky, *9-11* (New York: Open Media, 2001); Sara Ruddick, "The Moral Horror of the September Attacks," *Hypatia* 18 (2003): 212–222; and Gayatri C. Spivak, "Terror: A Speech after 9-11," *Boundary 2* 31 (2004): 81–111.

[87] John Paul II, "General Audience of John Paul II," September 11, 2002, http://www.vatican.va/holy_father/john_paul_ii/audiences/2002/documents/hf_jp -ii_aud_20020911_en.html.

[88] John Paul II, "General Audience."

[89] "Pope Opposes Military Response to Terrorism," *Catholic World News,* http://www.cwnews.com/news/viewstory.cfm?recnum=32004.

[90] Judith Butler, *Precarious Life: The Powers of Mourning and Violence* (London: Verso, 2004), xii.

[91] Butler, *Precarious Life,* xiv.

[92] Barack H. Obama, "Remarks by the President at 9/11 Museum Dedication," May 15, 2014, http://www.whitehouse.gov/the-press-office/2014/05/15/remarks-president -911-museum-dedication.

[93] Branham and Pearce, "Between Text and Context," 20.

[94] Jamieson, *Eloquence in an Electronic Age,* 9–10.

[95] Jamieson, *Eloquence in an Electronic Age,* 67–89.

[96] Jamieson, *Eloquence in an Electronic Age,* 13.

[97] Jamieson, *Eloquence in an Electronic Age,* 62–63.

[98] Jamieson, *Eloquence in an Electronic Age,* 44.

[99] Bruce Gronbeck, "Citizen Voices in Cyberpolitical Culture," in *Rhetorical Democracy: Discursive Practices of Civic Engagement,* ed. Gerard A. Hauser and Amy Grim, 17–31 (Mahwah, NJ: Erlbaum, 2004), 27.

[100] For an exploration of these tactics, see Susan Leigh Foster, "Choreographies of Protest," *Theatre Journal* 55 (2003): 395–412.

[101] Branham and Pearce, "Between Text and Context," 19.

[102] Branham and Pearce, "Between Text and Context," 28.

[103] Branham and Pearce, "Between Text and Context," 28–29.

[104] Caroline Kelly, "Megan Rapinoe to Trump: 'Your Message Is Excluding People,'" CNN, July 10, 2019, https://www.cnn.com/2019/07/09/politics/megan-rapinoe-anderson -cooper-trump-cnntv/index.html.

[105] Megan Rapinoe interview by Anderson Cooper, "Rapinoe's Message to Trump: You Need To Do Better for Everyone," CNN, July 9, 2019, https://www.youtube.com/watch?v=8X5ixs8Nsd0.

[106] Jenna West, "USWNT Received Private Invite from White House to Visit after World Cup," *Sports Illustrated,* December 19, 2019, https://www.si.com/soccer/2019/12/09/uswnt-white-house-visit-invite-megan-rapinoe.

[107] Branham and Pearce, "Between Text and Context," 29.

[108] Henry Langston, "Meeting Pussy Riot," *Vice,* March 12, 2012, http://www.vice.com/read/A-Russian-Pussy-Riot.

[109] Carole Cadwalladr, "Pussy Riot: Will Vladimir Putin Regret Taking on Russia's Cool Women Punks?" *Guardian,* July 28, 2012, http://www.theguardian.com/world/2012/jul/29/pussy-riot-protest-vladimir-putin-russia.

[110] *Pussy Riot: A Punk Prayer,* dir. Mike Lerner and Maxim Pozdorovkin, HBO Documentaries, 2013, http://www.hbo.com/documentaries/pussy-riot-a-punk-prayer.

[111] Thom Nickels, "Pussy Riot and Sacred Spaces," HuffPost Religion, November 25, 2013, http://www.huffingtonpost.com/thom-nickels/pussy-riot-and-sacred-spa_b_4334415.html.

[112] Nickels, "Pussy Riot."

[113] Quoted in Julian Pecquet, "Rep. Steve King Defends Jail Sentence for Russian Pro-Democracy Activists," The Hill, June 3, 2013, http://thehill.com/policy/international/303029-rep-steve-king-raises-conservative-ire-with-pro-putin-comments-during-moscow-trip.

[114] Quoted in "Pussy Riot Reply to Patriarch," RT, March 27, 2012, http://rt.com/art-and-culture/pussy-riot-clash-patriarch-567.

[115] Robert J. Branham, "Speaking Itself: Susan Sontag's Town Hall Address," *Quarterly Journal of Speech* 75, no. 3 (August 1989): 259–276, 259–260.

[116] Branham and Pearce, "Between Text and Context," 32.

[117] Branham and Pearce, "Between Text and Context," 32–33.

[118] David Wills, a prominent citizen, invited Lincoln to speak. See "Gettysburg," http://www.medalofhonor.com/civilwar/gettysburg.html.

[119] Abraham Lincoln, Gettysburg Address, November 19, 1863 (Chicago: Sherwood Lithograph, c. 1905).

[120] All references to the speech are to Abraham Lincoln, "Gettysburg Address," November 19, 1863, http://www.loc.gov/exhibits/gadd/images/Gettysburg-2.jpg.

[121] Branham and Pearce, "Between Text and Context," 33.

[122] Garry Wills, *Lincoln at Gettysburg: The Words That Remade America* (New York: Simon and Schuster, 1992), 56.

[123] Branham and Pearce, "Between Text and Context," 32.

[124] Branham and Pearce, "Between Text and Context," 32–33.

[125] Edbauer-Rice, "Unframing Models."

[126] Edbauer-Rice, "Unframing Models," 13.

[127] Edbauer-Rice, "Unframing Models," 13.

[128] Eric S. Jenkins, "The Modes of Visual Rhetoric: Circulating Memes as Expressions," *Quarterly Journal of Speech* 100, No. 4 (November 2014), 442–466, 445.

[129] Jenkins, "Modes of Visual Rhetoric," 445.

[130] Branham and Pearce, "Between Text and Context," 33.

[131] Branham and Pearce, "Between Text and Context," 33.

Chapter 10
Publics and Counterpublics

KEY CONCEPTS

counterpublics

enclaved publics

networked public screen

networked publics

oscillating publics

public

public screen

public sphere

strong publics

weak publics

In January 2017, the city council of Iowa City debated a resolution that codified a longstanding practice: not allocating local resources toward immigration law enforcement on the grounds that the "power to regulate immigration is exclusive to the federal government."[1] In the days before the vote, hundreds of phone calls and written comments came into city hall. Some were from people who did not live in Iowa City. Many were inspired by robocalls from Priorities for Iowa, a group that claimed the resolution meant Iowa City was declaring itself a sanctuary city.[2] During the vote, community members filled the meeting room and spilled into the hallway. Fifteen people spoke, including Marcela Hurtado, a member of an immigrant advocacy group called Center for Worker Justice of Eastern Iowa.[3] All fifteen spoke in support of the resolution, which passed unanimously. The mayor explained that the local government was committed to keeping the Iowa City community "a safe and welcoming place for all of its residents and visitors."[4]

This example likely describes what you think of when you imagine debate over public policy: concerned citizens and government officials in a town hall exchanging arguments that oppose or support a specific policy. As this example also illustrates, however, public debates do not only happen in city halls or the halls of Congress, but also in phone calls, letters, and news articles. Not just elected officials, but also community members, participate in public debates. Disagreements occur not just over policy, but also over identity: What does it mean to be a member of a community? Public controversies can span days or months or years, not just the length of a single meeting.

Legislative attempts to limit immigration have occurred throughout US history, even though the United States of America was founded as a nation of immigrants and the Statue of Liberty declares:

Give me your tired, your poor,

Your huddled masses yearning to breathe free,

The wretched refuse of your teeming shore.

Send these, the homeless, tempest-tost to me,

I lift my lamp beside the golden door!

Despite this welcome, immigration restrictions have, over time, targeted Asian, Eastern European, Southern European, and Latinx people. In 1882, Congress passed the Chinese Exclusion Act, which prohibited people from immigrating from China to the United States for ten years. The Immigration Act of 1917 restricted the amount of immigration from Asia generally. During the first two decades of the 1900s, more than 14 million people immigrated to the United States, mostly from Southern Europe, Eastern Europe, and Asia. In response, the Immigration Act of 1924 sought to lock in the then-current ethnic distribution. In 1954, the United States Immigration and Naturalization Service launched "Operation Wetback," which forcibly deported 1.2 million migrant workers, mostly from Mexico. In 1994, California passed Proposition 187, which eliminated public health, education, and welfare provisions for undocumented workers.

The spring of 2006 saw public demonstrations in response to Congressional debates over immigration policy.[5] Pro-immigration rallies occurred in 140 cities across the country from March to May 2006, including gatherings of 500,000 in Los Angeles, 350,000–500,000 in Dallas, and 400,000 in Chicago. The Minuteman Project, which opposes illegal immigration, held a 13-city campaign tour, culminating in a rally outside the US Capitol building.

Between October 2013 and July 2014, more than 52,000 unaccompanied children, "many who were fleeing gang violence in Guatemala, El Salvador and Honduras," were detained after crossing the US-Mexico border without legal documentation.[6] A humanitarian crisis arose when Texas facilities were overwhelmed. Immigration officials dispersed the immigrants to other places so they could be processed, to be either deported or united with family living in the United States.

In 2015, presidential candidate Donald Trump appealed to people who held anti-immigration sentiments in an announcement address that clearly differentiated the second persona of the addressed audience ("you") from the third persona into which immigrants were cast:

When Mexico sends its people, they're not sending their best. They're not sending you. They're not sending you. They're sending people that have lots of problems, and they're bringing those problems with us. They're bringing drugs. They're bringing crime. They're rapists. And some, I assume, are good people.[7]

Throughout the presidential campaign, crowds chanted "Build the wall." Results from the American National Election Study found that "immigration was central to the [2016] election, and hostility toward immigrants animated Trump voters." As a candidate, Trump rallied not only those who opposed undocumented immigration but also those who opposed all immigration.[8]

In April 2018, Trump deployed troops to the US-Mexico border and announced a "zero tolerance" policy that resulted in children being separated from their parents. In May 2018, he said of "people coming into the country or trying to come in": "These aren't people. These are animals."[9] Again, public rallies responded. In June 2018, hundreds of rallies, coast to coast, sought reversal of the family separation and zero tolerance policy.[10] In February 2019, President Trump declared a state of emergency in order to circumvent congressional inaction on funding for his border wall.[11]

The debates over immigration illustrate several things about publics and public deliberation.

First, they illustrate how people constitute a public as they present their concerns for public consideration. For our purposes, a **public** is formed by *people coming together to discuss common concerns, including concerns about who they are and what they should do.* The **public sphere** is *the civic space created when people (publics) engage in "collective, democratic opinion formation"*[12] *and where political participation is enacted through rhetorical action.* The goal of public deliberation is not always consensus; sometimes it is to unsettle existing agreement. Regardless of the goal, publics use rhetoric to discuss matters of common concern (including determining what those concerns are), constitute identity, and construct their shared reality.

Second, debates about immigration illustrate how public discourse includes both deliberative debates about policy (For example, is a border wall the best way to secure the border?) and cultural debates about civic identity (Who is part of the "community?" Who can and should participate in public deliberations about national policy and national identity?). Communication scholar Anne Demo notes that anxiety has grown "over the nation's changing ethnic demographics, characterized in the popular press as 'the browning of America.'"[13] As a result, according to several other communication scholars, these debates are not just about immigration policy, but also about what it means to be a US citizen, how to define the country's identity, and what power and privilege comes with citizenship.[14]

Third, these debates show that "public" is a term with diverse meanings. News reports noted various ways in which the 2006 rallies and debates had a public character. Some described the gatherings as a "wave of public protests."[15] Other people talked about the public as an audience. US Representative Tom Tancredo, for example, said, "Millions of people are flaunting the fact that they are here illegally and are demanding special treatment. I don't think that flies with John Q. Public."[16] In response, rally organizers encouraged protestors to carry more US flags because they "did not want to alienate the broader public."[17]

Public opinion became a thing to be moved. Reports noted that "immigrant groups face several hurdles in their attempt to sway politicians and public opinion."[18] Other stories examined whether the rallies were a possible influence on "the public debate on immigration."[19] Those who sought to limit undocumented immigration argued that immigrants were "invading" the United States and creating economic problems such as job loss, and that "illegal aliens bring diseases and drain public services."[20] Ultimately, media reports said a congressional bill was unlikely to pass because of "deep public divisions."[21]

The public continues to play a role in more recent debates over immigration policy. Media reports declared the June 2018 "Families Belong Together" rallies created "public pressure" that forced the "Trump administration to shift course on family separation."[22] In a 2019 White House roundtable discussion on border security in California, a person representing Immigration and Customs Enforcement (ICE) claimed "America is also facing a public safety crisis."[23] Newspapers reported that "the public sees through Trump's national emergency lies."[24] In these descriptions, the term "public" describes a range of things—the rallies, a place, a people, policy, opinion, services, safety, and nonpoliticians.

Fourth, the immigration debates show that understanding the meaning of publicity and publics is central to understanding the role of rhetoric in civic life. Which issues are considered worthy of public consideration? What discussions are part of public discourse? Which people are given access to the public sphere? Who is included in the public?

Fifth, these debates show that a multitude of voices are present in the public sphere and that public deliberation does not occur only in official spaces such as the floors of legislatures. Various perspectives and actions emerged on the issue, including the Minuteman Project's frustrations with the lack of federal enforcement of immigration law; the United Constitutional Patriots (a militia group) taking it upon themselves to unlawfully detain migrants in April 2019; the work of La Raza, a Hispanic civil rights organization, on immigrants' rights; and various governors' concerns about the fiscal impact of illegal immigration policies on state budgets. Other emergent perspectives included those of presidents defending their policies, ICE agents, crowds at rallies, and people who attended political rallies.

Rhetoric scholar Gerard A. Hauser notes that such diversity is central to the public sphere, for "it is only when a multitude of voices is heard that social actors begin to realize that they can do more than respond; they can choose."[25] Thus, it is important to pay attention to rhetoric in what writing, rhetoric, and digital studies professor Jenny Rice describes as "ordinary spaces of encounter," such as social media platforms or dinner tables, as well as "nonofficial spaces" such as city parks or coffee shops. It is in the communicative exchanges in those places that you can hear and see the emergence of publics.[26]

This chapter introduces you to the idea of publics and the role rhetoric plays in them, but we do not end the discussion there. As with all communication, power also plays a role. Not all people have equal rhetorical power, nor do all publics. Some publics are dominant because they have the power to amplify their voices and enact policies. Others are marginalized because they are denied access to the public sphere. Thus, the question arises: if a group is not represented in the dominant public, how can its members develop a vocabulary that articulates their identity, interests, and needs? To answer this question, we explore the concept of *counter*public spheres—arenas of public deliberation that arise in response to exclusions from the dominant public sphere. We also explore the increasing role of the internet and the challenges it poses to the very idea of what is public. Finally, we discuss the expanding roles of visual rhetoric and social media, and why they call for reconsidering the public sphere as a panmediated networked public screen.

THE PUBLIC SPHERE

Most contemporary understandings of the public sphere rely on German sociologist Jürgen Habermas's groundbreaking work.[27] Habermas studied nations such as Britain, France, and Germany that shifted from monarchical and feudalistic forms to democratic societies during the eighteenth and early nineteenth centuries. These societies had in common the emergence of a bourgeois public sphere, composed of people (artisans and tradespeople who formed guilds and companies) who influenced culture and had control over the means of production, and who engaged in practices that enabled them to serve as intermediaries between the state (the executive power of official government) and society (associational activity among private individuals). Habermas believed that the needs and interests of individuals can come together in a public to check the exercise of state power and make sure that power always acts in the interest of those it governs.

In chapter 5, we defined the public sphere as the argument sphere that exists "to handle disagreements transcending personal and technical disputes." That definition is consistent with Habermas's definition of the public sphere as "a domain of our social life in which such a thing as public opinion can be formed" and that "is constituted in every conversation in which private persons come together to form a public."[28] By "public opinion," Habermas does not mean the survey responses that Roper tracks or the call-in polls your local evening news conducts. Instead, public opinion is formed only when "a public that engages in rational discussion exists" to create informed opinion, which Habermas contrasts to "mere opinions."[29] As an illustration, Habermas describes the coffeehouses that opened in Britain and Germany between 1680 and 1730 and served as places where a variety of people (mostly men) could meet and talk about contemporary moral, literary, and political issues.[30] London, alone, had three thousand coffee houses, each with its own regulars. For Habermas, the conversations in these coffee houses were central to the formation of a public sphere.

Notice that Habermas defines the public sphere in terms of *communication*. A public sphere is not brought into being by a particular group of people, a location, or a set of topics. Instead, it is constituted by the *conversations* (rhetorical acts) of people as they discuss and debate topics of general interest.[31] Political and social theorist Nancy Fraser describes Habermas's public sphere as an arena of discourse "in which political participation is enacted through the medium of talk" as people come together to "deliberate about common affairs."[32]

Habermas's definition is both descriptive and prescriptive. It describes public discourse as enabled and constrained within a society by institutions, legal rights, and norms. It also prescribes an ideal to work toward. An ideal public sphere is (1) "open in principle to all citizens," (2) addresses "matters of general interest," and (3) is free from coercion.[33] This ideal of the public sphere is central to democracy. Free and open communication, in which anyone can participate, about issues that transcend personal interest, is essential to a fully functioning democracy and open society.

It is challenging to point to an example of a public sphere because it is difficult to identify a specific place or arena of discourse. Instead, one knows a public sphere has come into being because one can identify trace elements of it in rhetoric. The immigration rhetoric described earlier in this chapter is an example of public sphere discourse. People enacted political participation through their rhetorical acts (debates, speeches, parades, signs, tweets, blog posts, letters to the editor, and meetings) about an issue of common concern. Although the hope was that public opinion, and not merely a collection of individual opinions, was formed, it would be wrong to describe all the rhetorical acts in these debates as "rational discussion." Still, the debates suggest the existence of a public sphere.

Another example of public sphere activity is the February 2011 debate in Wisconsin over the collective bargaining rights of public employee unions. In response to record state budget deficits, Governor Scott Walker proposed a "budget repair bill"[34] that would cut public workers' compensation and eliminate almost all collective bargaining rights for most public employees except police, firefighters, and the state patrol. The rhetoric about the bill provides ample trace evidence of a public sphere, as citizens talked about issues of common concern: the budget deficit, the vitality of public unions, and the legislative impasse caused when fourteen Democratic state senators fled the state in order to deny a quorum to Republican senators seeking to pass the bill.

A public sphere was constituted in protests as tens of thousands of citizens filled the Wisconsin state capitol square and rotunda; as union members, citizens, and students took part in public hearings; as state representatives and senators, as well as the governor, talked in various media outlets and during legislative debates; and as citizens around the state talked to each other about the bill. The constitution of the public sphere was not confined to the events at the capitol building or the statements of lawmakers. It also occurred in coffee shops such as the Coffee Vault in Dousman[35] and EVP Coffee in Madison. In the tradition of Habermas's European coffeehouses, many regulars at EVP Coffee (including public sphere scholar Robert Asen) engaged in conversations about public affairs, including the governor's bill. The protests, testimony, media interviews, and coffee shop conversations across the state enacted political participation through talk.

Habermas's ideal of open, public, and coercion-free communication may never have existed in reality,[36] but more recent scholars herald it as an ideal toward which democratic societies should strive.[37] Civic engagement requires open and reasoned communication between informed citizens. Imagine if the public debates about health care were open only to those who are already covered by health insurance. A part of the citizenry would be voiceless about an issue that deeply affects them. Or imagine that during debates, people who voiced disagreement with the government were jailed or threatened, as happened in Russia in

2014. The day after the Winter Olympics ended, a judge sentenced eight people to two and a half years to four years in prison. Their crime: they had participated in a protest on the eve of Russian President Vladimir Putin's inauguration. They were not the leaders of the protest but "ordinary people, selected from the demonstration apparently at random." Even though the Russian constitution promises "Everyone shall be guaranteed the freedom of ideas and speech," it appears that people who disagreed with Putin were selected for prosecution "for the crime of expressing their opinions."[38]

We want to warn you against conflating and confusing the complex meanings of "public" identified in the introduction to this chapter.[39] When you think of "public," you might think of anything outside the domestic sphere or family. In this common understanding, that which is public is not private and that which is private is not public. This common understanding is reflected in phrases such as "public officials" (people who work for the state), "public opinion" (as polled by Roper), and "public figures" (people whom a substantial portion of the population can identify). Fraser argues that this common understanding of "public" collapses four analytically distinct ideas: (1) the state, (2) the economy, (3) arenas of public discourse, and (4) people to whom the state should be accountable.[40] When discussing public spheres in this chapter, we use Habermas's ideal as referenced in Fraser's third sense—arenas of public discourse. The public sphere is distinct from the state; ideally, discourse in the public sphere can critique and challenge state actions. The public sphere is also distinct from the economy; it is not a location in which to buy and sell, but to deliberate about policy and form collective identities. Finally, although people's discourse forms the public sphere, the people are not identical to it. Just because many people are present does not mean that a public sphere has formed.

The boundaries of the public sphere are not static. As communication scholars Robert Asen and Daniel C. Brouwer explain, "'public' and 'private' are not fixed, content-specific categories that structure the public sphere prior to discourse."[41] What counts as an issue of general interest can change over time. The question of what counts as a public issue is, itself, a topic to be discussed and debated in the public sphere. Communication scholars Valeria Fabj and Matthew J. Sobnosky note, for example, that for many years HIV/AIDS was perceived to be a personal issue, a "gay disease." As a result of public activism, it was recognized as a public health issue about which everyone should be concerned and to which the state should respond.[42]

Habermas's description of the role of public sphere rhetoric in civil society is the foundation of more nuanced descriptions of civic participation. Because power plays a role in rhetoric, we will now explore how power affects publics.

Strong and Weak Publics

Although Habermas held out the ideal of an overarching public sphere that could represent universal human interests in an arena distinct from the state, other scholars have noted that it makes more sense to speak of multiple publics, the way representative assemblies of the state can function as publics, and the interactions among publics.[43] In contrast to Habermas's description of the state as distinct from the public sphere, some scholars note, democratic parliaments and legislative assemblies can participate in public sphere discourse.

Fraser distinguishes between weak publics and strong publics. **Weak publics** are "*publics whose deliberative practice consists exclusively in opinion formation and does not also encompass decision making.*"[44] **Strong publics** are "*publics whose discourse encompasses both opinion formation and decision making.*"[45] "Strong" and "weak" here refer to the power to make decisions or legislate, not to the general ability to dominate public opinion. In the example of the immigration rallies and debates, both the Minuteman Project and immigrants' rights groups are weak publics. They cannot pass laws, but they seek to affect the opinions of politicians, who are members of strong publics. A weak public also participates in the formation of identity for those who are part of it. Communication scholars Kent A. Ono and John Sloop document how the discourse of the strong public (politicians) and the dominant media, both for and against California's Proposition 187, constructed an identity of undocumented immigrants and Latinx people as prone to criminality, diseased, and of value only as an economic commodity (as workers).[46] In response, according to rhetoric scholars Marouf Hasian, Jr., and Fernando Delgado, the weak public of immigrants' rights groups sought to redefine their identity by celebrating immigrants' contributions to the United States, creating unity around a conception of La Raza ("the people"), and developing counterhistories of immigration law.[47] For example, immigrants' rights groups repeatedly used the slogan, "we didn't cross the border, the border crossed us," to highlight that much of the western United States once belonged to the very people who are now considered to not belong there.[48]

Strong publics engage in instrumental acts of governance. Governing bodies made up of representatives of the people (such as the US Congress or a parliament) are examples of strong publics. Where a democratically elected body exists through which the people's will can be voiced, Fraser says, it can function not as an arm of the state but as "the site for the discursive authorization of the use of state power."[49] Thus, democratically elected representative bodies begin to blur the distinction that Habermas draws so clearly between the state and civil society. Strong publics are important because "the force of public opinion is strengthened when a body representing it is empowered to translate such 'opinion' into authoritative decisions."[50] When it implements public policy (on health care, immigration, or taxes, for example), the US Congress transforms what it perceives to be public opinion into laws.

Although strong publics possess decision-making powers, weak publics also have power to create change. They can exert influence on people in decision-making roles. For example, if a school board is considering curriculum changes, a weak public can exert pressure on the school board members (a strong public) by participating in public hearings and making public comments. If the school board Members are elected, then the weak public could exert pressure because board members might be concerned about reelection.

Another example of a weak public is Black Twitter, a community of primarily Black users who focus their rhetoric on public issues affecting Black people.

Numerous scholars note that Black Twitter is a set of discourses that enables a weak public sphere to emerge because it invites people to network, engage, and connect with others as they resist being treated as invisible and insignificant.[51] Young Black people, in particular, form a public as they use Twitter in a unique way: readily retweeting, following, and @ing each other; and, in so doing, directly responding and reacting to each other.[52] Across hashtags such as #BlackLivesMatter, #SayHerName, #OscarsSoWhite, and #BlackOnCampus, users employ rhetoric to formulate deliberative discourse that can appeal to the strong public of policy makers. Black Lives Matters organizers on Black Twitter, after months of sustained protest, focused on passage of the BREATHE Act, a four-part proposal to redirect money away from incarceration and policing and toward community building and community safety.[53] They also supported a House resolution that would create a committee to study reparations (the same House resolution we described in chapter 5). Although even a Democratic-controlled House was unlikely to pass the BREATHE Act, the advocacy for it influenced policy makers to explore other criminal justice reform policies.[54]

Identity Formation in Publics

The immigration issue demonstrates that debates about laws are also debates about identity, as is highlighted by people who attended Trump rallies and declared Trump is "trying to keep us as Americans. He's pro-American."[55] Hasian and Delgado note that the debate, which began as a general discussion of the dangers of a foreign "other" illegally immigrating to the United States, "transformed into a complex debate regarding the meaning of American citizenship and the social and political power that comes from belonging to particular racial categories in the U.S."[56] Hasian and Delgado's insight highlights that the public sphere may not just mediate between the state and society; it is also a sphere in which people develop understandings of their role in society.[57]

Rhetoric that forms identity and rhetoric that forms policy are equally important. Rhetoric exploring what it means to be a US citizen is as much a part of the public sphere as rhetoric defending a policy. Thus, rhetoric in the public sphere includes epideictic and forensic rhetoric about identity as well as deliberative rhetoric about policy. Hauser clarifies the link between rhetoric, the public sphere, and social reality: "Public spheres . . . are discursive spaces where society deliberates about normative standards and even develops new frameworks for expressing and evaluating social reality."[58]

PUBLICS AND COUNTERPUBLICS

Publics are not equally powerful. A dominant public tends to emerge, one that has the strength to translate its beliefs into actions affecting even people who do not share its beliefs. Unfortunately, the power of a dominant public often masks the existence of other publics and makes it more difficult to recognize that not everyone's needs and interests are being represented. Literature professor

Michael Warner explains, "Some publics . . . are more likely than others to stand in for *the* public, to frame their address as the universal discussion of the people."[59] For example, scholars argue that a Black public sphere exists in the United States,[60] constituted by media, aesthetic forms, and memories that are owned by and targeted to Black people. The existence of a Black public sphere demonstrates that there is more than one public sphere, and that what is thought of as *the* public sphere does not represent universal human concerns.

Scholars have identified several limits to Habermas's original formulation of the public sphere: A single universal public does not explain actually existing democracies. The state is no longer the sole site of sovereign power, given the rise of corporate power. The economy, itself, can become a site of public contestation and action. Thus, scholars have expanded the study of *the* public to studies of multiple publics and counterpublics.

Counterpublics

A dominant public tends to focus only on the interests and needs of the dominant group and, in the process, to subordinate those groups of people who are disempowered. Even in fourth and fifth century BCE Athens, a civilization often upheld as an ideal of democracy, the very notion of citizenship was defined by exclusion. Only citizens (free Athenian men) were allowed to participate. Women, slaves, and foreigners were excluded.[61] They had identities, interests, and needs, but they had to find alternative locations and means to articulate them. For example, in 415 BCE, when the boldest Greek military offensive since the Trojan War was launched, statues of the god Hermes were mutilated. Classicist Eva Keuls argues that the women of Athens performed that act to protest yet another war.[62]

To call attention to a multiplicity of publics and to publics that are alternatives to the dominant public, scholars developed the concept of **counterpublics,** which Fraser defines as "*parallel discursive arenas where members of subordinated social groups invent and circulate counterdiscourse to formulate oppositional interpretations of their identities, interests, and needs.*"[63] Counterpublics expand not only the space for argument but also what counts in argument. Fraser's critique of Habermas notes that "these counterpublics emerge in response to exclusions within dominant publics, they help expand discursive space. In principle, assumptions that were previously exempt from contestation will now have to be publicly argued out."[64] New topics are introduced to deliberation; so, too, are new tests for argument. Literary theorist Rita Felski proposes that counterpublics can challenge norms of argument and what is considered to be useful evidence.[65] Who can speak, what can be spoken about, and how it can be discussed can all be topics of public discussion. Consequently, some issues not previously considered public can become public as a result of deliberation and argument.

Counterpublics create safe spaces in which participants: (1) develop alternative norms for public argument and what counts as evidence; (2) regenerate their energy to engage in argument in the political and public spheres; (3) enact identities through new idioms and styles; and (4) formulate oppositional interpretations of identities, interests, and needs through the creation of new language. A counterpublic is far more than a group calling for change. It creates the conditions for people to see themselves as part of a group, to identify the need for change, and to amass the energy to work for that change.

Some publics emerge as a counter to a dominant public and can eventually effect change in public policy. Prior to the 1970s, for example, workplace sexual harassment as a concept did not exist, even though the activity did. During slavery, African American women were sexually used by their White masters. During industrialization, immigrant women were forced by economic necessity to acquiesce to their employers' demands. In contemporary times, women are subjected to work environments where their sex is used as a basis of ridicule, often in the hope of driving them from the workplace. People who violate gender expectations are often harassed and ridiculed. Historically, a workplace that was hostile, abusive, and violent to women and gender-nonconforming people was attributed to a "bad boss," dismissed as just the way things were, or explained as further proof that women did not belong in the rough world of the workplace.

With the burgeoning of women's movements in the 1970s, however, women had a physical and discursive space in which they could come together to develop ways to make their interests understood. The Women's Center at Cornell University held the first speak-out (a new form and style of public argument) in 1975. Women from around the country came together to name and refuse to accept these experiences. Women's experiences began to count as evidence of a public harm. Women would name their experiences "sexual harassment" and articulate the harm in terms of sex discrimination, whether it occurred in the form of a hostile environment or quid pro quo demands for sex as the price for keeping a job. Harvard legal scholar Catharine A. MacKinnon describes sexual harassment as "the first legal wrong to be defined by women," believing "it took a women's movement to expose these experiences as systematic and harmful in the first place, a movement that took women's point of view on our own situation as significantly definitive of that situation."[66] Attention to sexual harassment was revivified in 2017 with the tweet by Alyssa Milano that spawned the hashtag #MeToo.[67]

Women as private citizens came together to formulate opinions about a subject of concern. To do so, they had to articulate an understanding of their shared identity, interests, and needs that countered dominant perceptions of women as primarily sexual beings who belonged in the private sphere. In the process, they constituted a counterpublic sphere of discourse, in which they came to understand their identity as workers deserving of rights, their interest in creating harassment-free workplaces, and their needs as human beings. They contested existing norms of argument that only counted men's perspectives as correct. Women's perceptions of harassment came to matter. Women developed a vocabulary that enabled them to name an act that previously had been invisible. In 1986, the US Supreme Court recognized sexual harassment as a violation of Title VII of the Civil Rights Act.

A counterpublic sphere is a public sphere, even if it is not perceived to be *the* public sphere. To understand the full range of symbolic action happening in contemporary US society, you need to listen to and watch not just the rhetoric occurring in the strong publics of legislatures and in the dominant/hegemonic public sphere but rhetoric emerging across multiple publics.

Enclaved and Oscillating Counterpublics. As the last example demonstrates, counterpublics can both focus inward (for example, when attempting to articulate identity, interests, and needs) and oscillate outward (for example, when marshaling broader public support to make demands on the state for changes in law). Counterpublics serve different functions depending on their audiences. When members of a counterpublic speak among themselves, the emphasis is on identity formation. When they speak to dominant publics, the emphasis is on opinion formation about potential state action.

Communication scholar Catherine Squires explains a corresponding distinction between enclaved and oscillating counterpublics. **Enclaved publics** are *publics that conceal their "antiestablishment ideas and strategies in order to avoid sanctions, but internally produc[e] lively debate and planning."* By contrast, **oscillating publics** are *publics that exist to "engage in debate with outsiders and to test ideas."*[68] Sometimes a counterpublic is internally focused, developing alternative discourses that are relatively independent of the dominant public. Other times, it oscillates outward, engaging in debate with other publics. This turning outward is most evident when a counterpublic engages with the dominant public.

When they are enclaved, counterpublics create safe spaces for discourse that are necessary to the possibility of oppositional ideas and actions. When they focus on their own participants and foreground their perspectives, alternative interpretations of identities and needs become possible. A counterpublic sphere provides a location in which rhetoric can empower the group. As a group constitutes itself as a counterpublic, it forms an understanding of members' identity, interests, and needs that symbolically rejects the dominant public's description of them.

Encapsulating the role of the counterpublic and the need for an oppositional discourse, bell hooks, an African American cultural critic,[69] explains: "The most important of our work—the work of liberation—demands of us that we make a new language, that we create the oppositional discourse, the liberatory voice."[70] Rhetoric plays a central role in counterpublics. People cannot challenge the way things are unless they can see another way to be, and then develop a language to articulate that alternative vision.

Examples of enclaved counterpublic discourse include the consciousness-raising groups of 1960s and 1970s feminism, the discussions in Black churches about the immanent humanity of all people that fed into the activism of the Civil Rights movement, and the identity formation and needs identification in the farmworkers' organizations that Dolores Huerta, Larry Itliong, and César Chávez founded. In each case, people who had been rendered silent by the dominant public talked back. They demanded recognition of their immanent humanity and opposed dominant perceptions of women as people who should be confined to the domestic arena, Black people as second-class citizens who should be segregated from White people, and Hispanics as laborers who deserved atrocious workplace treatment.

If a counterpublic remains enclaved, its participants risk speaking only to each other and failing to make others understand their new language. Public sphere scholars Robert Asen and Daniel C. Brouwer argue that talking only to others of like mind generates the dangers of "breeding of intolerance for others, difficulty of translating interests, [and] detachment from healthy criticism."[71] Political scientist Jane Mansbridge agrees that if counterpublic participants speak only to each other, "they do not learn how to put what they want to say in words that others can hear and understand."[72] Thus, engaged argument with those with whom the members of a counterpublic disagree is an essential element of a healthy counterpublic. In terms of the immigration debates, Hasian and Delgado say that people must find and analyze "the bridges as well as the walls that have been built at contested borderlands."[73] Rhetors should search for places of agreement, not just places of difference.

Oscillation also has practical benefits for a counterpublic. In a study of ACT UP and its participation in congressional hearings concerning AIDS, Brouwer identifies a number of benefits. Oscillation can (1) garner national attention for a group and, thus, enhance its credibility; (2) open a forum for the repetition and recognition of the group's message; (3) push for implementation of the group's recommendations that require institutional support (the support of a strong public); and (4) enable the counterpublic to "push for access to strong publics."[74] Historically, counterpublics have used their specialized newspapers both to speak to members and to oscillate outward. For example, in the early 1900s, the National Association Opposed to Woman Suffrage's newspaper (*The Woman Patriot*) shifted from a single-issue focus against woman suffrage to a broader challenge to what it saw as emerging radical rhetoric.[75] Additional examples of oscillating counterpublic discourse include second-wave feminists' 1968 "No More Miss America" protest against the pageant, including their ten-point brochure outlining their arguments; the Civil Rights movement's 1955 Montgomery Bus Boycott and ensuing legal challenges to segregation; and the United Farm Workers' grape boycott and public education campaign in the late 1960s, as well as their 2010 "Take Our Jobs" campaign,[76] which Stephen Colbert publicized when he took a farm worker's job for a segment and then testified to Congress.[77]

Counterpublic theory challenges the idea that a single, universal public sphere is an ideal toward which a diverse society should strive. Although Habermas initially bemoaned the erosion of the public sphere as a multiplicity of publics emerged, Fraser argues that multiplicity is not necessarily a bad thing. For people who are excluded from access to the dominant public sphere, articulation of their needs becomes nearly impossible. A universal public sphere intensifies the subordination of those needs. In addition, multiple publics are more likely to promote participation. According to Fraser, forcing all deliberation into the dominant public "will tend to operate to the advantage of dominant groups and to the disadvantage of subordinates" because "members of subordinated groups would have no arenas for deliberation among themselves about their needs, objectives, and strategies. They would have no venues in which to undertake communicative processes that were not . . . under the supervision of dominant groups."[78]

Subordinated social groups need a space to develop language to articulate their identities, interests, and needs.

A counterpublic's orientation oscillates; its primary audience shifts. According to Asen and Brouwer, a counterpublic shifts back and forth between the formulation of its identities, interests, and needs within the relative safety of its protected enclaves, where the primary audience is the counterpublic, and its participation in deliberation about administrative state action, where its audience is the strong, dominant public.[79]

Identity as a Public or Counterpublic. Publics engage in deliberative discourse about policy and civic culture, about who they are and what they need. Although identity formation is an element of all public discourse, counterpublic sphere theories clarify the importance, to disempowered peoples and groups, of identity creation and self-expression. Before people can participate in deliberation over public issues, they need to see themselves as capable of deliberation, their interests and needs as worthy of discussion. The focus on identity in counterpublics, according to Felski, becomes apparent insofar as they are "directed toward an affirmation of specificity in relation to gender, race, ethnicity, age, sexual preference, and so on."[80] According to rhetoric scholar Lisa Flores, the specificity allows people to develop and explore their own identities, and to counter repressive characterizations.[81] For example, immigrant groups seek to define themselves in contrast to dominant public and media depictions of them as diseased masses and an undifferentiated flood overwhelming the United States. Otto Santa Ana, in a book about metaphors used to describe Latinx people in contemporary public discourse, observes that countermetaphors emerge. Instead of a flood, immigrants have become a "stream that makes the desert bloom," a flow of workers who could quench the thirst for labor, or the "lifeblood" of the California economy.[82]

Counterpublic discourse that contributes to identity creation is as important as the outward-directed rhetoric that contributes to policy making, as literary critic Michael Warner discusses in his book *Publics and Counterpublics*. To say a group of people is a "public" or "counterpublic" is more than merely descriptive; it also constructs an understanding of who that group is and how to interact with it. When people identify themselves as members of a public or counterpublic and participate in it, their "identities are formed and transformed."[83] Warner's model of the circulation of identities within public discourse is referred to as the circulatory model of counterpublics.

The naming of a public and the construction of identity can be linked to our earlier discussions of language, persona, and audience. Naming can construct social meaning and understanding. How marginalized groups are named affects how, and whether, they participate in the dominant public. In the 1800s, women fought against being named chattel (personal property owned by another) and asserted their full humanity and right to participate in public discourse. In the 1960s, African Americans fought against racist names and declared their interests to be public interests. In the 1980s, ACT UP worked with researchers to rename GRID (Gay Related Immune Deficiency) as AIDS (Acquired Immune Deficiency Syndrome) and define it as a public health issue of general concern.

More recently, undocumented workers resist the name "illegal" because it reduces them to a single act and deflects recognition of them as contributing members of the economy.

The power of language is also evident in the naming of "the public." As Warner points out, sometimes *a* public comes to be perceived as *the* public that represents "the people." However, "the people" is a rhetorical construction, an ideograph that itself is used to warrant the use of power. "The public" is also an ideograph. In the process of creating identification among themselves, members of "the public" also create divisions, excluding people who are not part of the falsely universal "we." In other words, some publics claim to represent more people than they actually do, but it is their claimed universality that is false, not their existence.

Publics, Counterpublics, and the Economy

In Habermas's formulation, the public sphere is distinct from the state and the economy, which is why many scholars tend to focus on the distinctions between publics and the state, but communication scholar Dana Cloud claims that the economy must also be considered.[84] For example, communication scholars Joshua P. Ewalt, Jessy J. Ohl, and Damien Smith Pfister point out that the 2011 Occupy protests occurred in over fifteen hundred cities around the world. Millions of people organized, gave time and money, and attempted to change political and economic systems.[85] Though the protests originated in Liberty Square in Manhattan's Financial District, they were not just in one country, or directed at one government; they challenged a transnational economic system. Protestors from various countries with distinct identities used common economic interests to counter the dominant economic powers. The Occupy Wall Street movement's criticism targeted large banks, international corporations, and Wall Street investment practices for creating the "greatest recession in generations."[86]

Cloud argues that because the state, the dominant public sphere, and the economy are intertwined, and because the public sphere and state are often in service to the economy, one must challenge all three through identity circulation (for example, by challenging racist, sexist, or class constructions) and through a focus on the state structure as well as on the institutions of the economy (such as the banks and corporations). The state is not a neutral arbiter of class interests.

The interweaving of publics, the state, and the economy gives rise to two related points emerge about rhetoric in civic life. First, collective economic action can be a form of civic action. Second, civic action cannot be reduced to personal economic choices.

Communication scholar Phaedra C. Pezzullo argues that "consumer-based advocacy campaigns" such as boycotts ("a concerted refusal to spend money") and buycotts ("a concerted effort to make a point of spending money" to support businesses with which the consumer group is aligned) are "significant tactics worth engaging during a political period in which . . . 'impure politics' have become the norm."[87] Even if people are concerned about how the US culture of consumption contributes to ecological problems, they might need to engage in consumption through buycotts in order to induce a corporation to change its practices. For example, one store began delivering purchases on bicycles rather than in cars as a way to reduce its carbon footprint. Customers supported the store through a buycott as a means of encouraging other stores to follow that example. Particularly if you believe "transnational corporations . . . have become more or equally as powerful as at least some nation-states,"[88] then an economic mechanism becomes a necessary civic mechanism. Pezzullo examines consumer-based advocacy campaigns that address global ecological crises (such as rainforest depletion, mistreatment of agricultural workers, and global warming) and concludes that the collective action of buycotts and boycotts shows "that everyday people can become successful agents of change in the world when they can identify" a specific example of a larger problem, at a specific place, and "mobilize a public to respond."[89] Notice, however, that she is praising *collective* economic action that is announced, organized, publicized, and visually made present through demonstrations or pickets.[90]

Relationships among Publics

To understand how publics function, you need to consider not only their relationships to the state and economy but also to each other. Counterpublics may exist counter to the state or the economy, but they can also replicate some of the more oppressive elements of the state or economy. In other words, counterpublics are not counter to everything for which dominant society stands. Exclusions based on sex, race, class, and sexual orientation can be found in counterpublics, even as they attempt to counter other social problems.

For example, consider the emergence of the environmental movement. Early members of environmental groups came together as individuals to articulate new understandings of humans' relationship to the environment. In the 1800s, arguments were made to preserve nature. In 1864, Lincoln signed a bill granting Yosemite Valley and the Mariposa Grove of Giant Sequoias to California as an inalienable public trust. In 1872, Yellowstone was designated the first national park. New understandings of the environment were integrated into the public vocabulary repertoire, but they tended to reinforce a notion that the environment was something other than where human beings lived. It was to be visited, preserved, and kept separate from human intervention.

The reality is that *all* human beings live in environments. Not all environments are the same. Some environments are less pristine and have large amounts of pollution. Polluted environments are not equally distributed. People of color and poor people are more likely to live near plants that produce toxic wastes and emissions. New toxic disposal sites tend to be sited closer to where the poor and people of color already live.[91]

Preservation of pristine parks that socioeconomically privileged people could visit represented an incomplete understanding of humans' relationship to the environment. African American civil rights leader Dr. Benjamin Chavis coined the phrase "environmental racism" in the early 1980s.[92] To counter environmental racism, most environmental groups now seek environmental justice and recognize that all of the environment must be valued.

Our point is that just because a counterpublic is *counter* does not mean it is without flaws. Privileges and ideologies weave themselves deeply into people's psyches. The process of testing assumptions is not done easily, nor without the danger of replicating some of the very inequalities people might seek to counter.

PUBLICS IN THE INTERNET AGE

"Public," as an adjective and a noun, represents a concept central to discussions of US democracy. The tradition of public deliberation is typified by the New England town meeting, where members of a community come together to debate, face-to-face, about issues of common interest. The vitality of such public deliberation has long concerned political and rhetorical theorists in the United States. John Dewey, in his 1927 book *The Public and Its Problems,* wrote about issues with which US society continues to grapple. How does a group come to have an identity as a public? What role does public discourse play in democratic politics? How can public apathy be lessened? How can experts and the general public interact productively to resolve controversies?[93]

Dewey worried that "increasing social complexity threatened the collective perception and practical judgment of a functioning public of citizens."[94] In particular, he was concerned about the effects that technological change would have on public deliberation. (In the 1920s, technological change meant the emergence of the telephone, cheap reading material, movies, telegraph, railways, and newspapers.) Dewey worried that new entertainment technologies would distract people from discussing issues of public concern and change how people interacted.[95] This concern persists and perhaps intensifies with digital technologies, social media, and the internet.

Although you might not be able to conceive of a world without the internet and interactive digital communication technologies, they are relatively recent phenomena. Not until the late 1980s did email become privatized and commercially available. The World Wide Web was created in 1989. Cell phones were not widely used until the early 1990s, when they became small enough to carry in a jacket pocket. The internet became widely available in the mid-1990s, when the US government allowed commercialization of the networking technologies that enabled mass participation. At this point, the internet was primarily used for email (one-to-one communication) and web pages (one-to-many communication). The White House went online in 1994. Although it was not the first search engine, Google launched its first version in August 1996, revolutionizing how people searched the growing information available on the internet. Microsoft began marketing FrontPage in 1996 and Macromedia created Dreamweaver in 1997, enabling people without programming skills to create web pages. All these events represent Web 1.0, which simply allowed the early internet to replicate noninteractive print communications.

A variety of new software programs enabled the creation of Web 2.0, supporting interactive many-to-many communication and truly enabling a networking of communication. Wikipedia was launched in 2001. In 2002, LinkedIn was launched. Blogs became popular when blogging software became widely available. Facebook was launched in 2004. YouTube and Reddit were created in 2005. Twitter was created in 2006. Tumblr, a short-form microblogging platform, was launched in 2007, the same year Apple released its first iPhone. In 2008, Apple released its second-generation iPhone and opened its App Store, allowing phone owners to buy and install applications created by third parties. In 2010, Pinterest and Instagram were launched. In July 2011, Snapchat (then called Picaboo) was launched. By 2012, Facebook had one billion active users worldwide *per month;* by December 2020, it had 1.62 billion active users *per day.*[96] By 2011, 35 percent of US people owned a smart phone; by 2013, 56 percent; and by 2020, 81 percent.[97] By 2019, 73 percent of US adults used YouTube; 69 percent used Facebook; 37 percent used Instagram; 28 percent used Pinterest; 27 percent used LinkedIn; 24 percent used Snapchat; and 22 percent used Twitter.[98]

The important role interactive digital technology can play in enabling publics to form is evident in the 2011 protests in Tunisia (and then in Egypt, Bahrain, Libya, Jordan, and Algeria). When Tunisian police let loose with real bullets, killing hundreds of protestors, the state-controlled media showed no images of the bloodshed. Facebook did. With 20 percent of Tunisians on Facebook, the information spread.[99] In Egypt, the sacrifices of the protesters, who literally put their bodies on the line in public spaces (with hundreds if not thousands losing their lives), were documented and communicated via the internet and cell phones. In response to protesters' reliance on digital communication technologies, the Egyptian government cut off all cell phone use and internet access.

In response to governments' efforts to control protest by controlling communication technology, then–Secretary of State Hillary Clinton delivered a speech outlining the administration's "Internet Freedom Agenda" at George Washington University. She declared:

> The internet has become the public space of the 21st century—the world's town square, classroom, marketplace, coffeehouse, and nightclub. . . . The goal is not to tell people how to use the internet any more than we ought to tell people how to use any public square, whether it's Tahrir Square or Times Square. The value of these spaces derives from the variety of activities people can pursue in them, from holding a rally to selling their vegetables, to having a private conversation. These spaces provide an open platform, and so does the internet.[100]

The internet is not itself the public sphere, but interactive digital technologies enable the formation of publics. Like the coffeehouses of previous centuries, websites and cell phones enable people to converse about current events and plan public action. Examples of publics enabled by digital technology include Black Lives Matter, me too, #NoDAPL, and #GirlsLikeUs.[101]

To explore the role of interactive digital technologies on public deliberation, we next examine how the very concept of "public" is made more complicated by interactive communication technologies. Second, we discuss ways in which digital technologies affect public activism, taking into account inequalities in access. Finally, we explore the possibility of networked publics.

The Meaning of "Public" in the Internet Age

Reflect on the spaces in which you use the internet. You get online in your bedroom or kitchen, in a coffee shop, and in your car (not while driving, we hope). You access the Web, one of the most open and accessible of forums, from some of the most private and personal physical spaces. You might post on Facebook while lounging on your sofa, Instagram a selfie taken in your bathroom mirror, or tweet from your bedroom.

Your images and statements might be about your most personal activities and feelings, yet (depending on the security of your password protocol) they are now potentially accessible to everyone; they are as public as you can get. The internet presents a conundrum: it offers a medium in which you think you are narrowcasting (to only the friends you admit to your page) the most private of moments (about what you just ate, how you broke up with a romantic partner, or where you are going to listen to music tonight), yet in reality it is the broadest of broadcast media. If you become angry about a public policy, you can create a Facebook group to challenge it. To plan a protest, you can tweet about it. To share images of an event, you can use Instagram or Periscope.

The forms of communication on the internet challenge the understanding of the demarcation between public and private, and require rethinking what is public and what is private. The concept of a public sphere relied on a spatial metaphor (spheres are a geometric concept), so the concept of networked space becomes relevant. Media theorist Vivian Sobchack notes that the idea of a public sphere is problematic in the digital age because people's access to others through computers, and now through mobile technology such as tablets and smartphones, has redrawn the boundaries of public and private. Sobchack writes that people's notions of public space and private space have "been transformed so that even to pose the notion of a 'public sphere'—as opposed to a 'private sphere'—is problematic in the age of electronic pervasion."[102]

In the process of gaining access to other people's private space through webcams and digital uploads, your own private space may also have been reduced. Just as you can access others' private spaces, they may be able to access yours. Think about the differences between a generation raised in the world of Web 2.0 and earlier generations. Many people in the Web 2.0 generation think little of publicly posting their most interior thoughts on the internet. Consider sexting: A meta-analysis of studies published in *JAMA Pediatrics* in 2018 found that among youth ages twelve to seventeen, 14.8 percent had sent sexts and 27.4 percent had received them. Although the consensual exchange of sexts may be unremarkable, these statistics are worrisome when you consider that 12 percent of youth had forwarded sexts without consent and 8.4 percent had had sexts they sent forwarded without their consent.[103] What was initially narrowcast to one other person may be broadcast to everyone with a simple "share."

In addition to the development and maintenance (and destruction) of social relationships, public deliberation and civic participation take place over the internet. People are mobilized to support political candidates. Citizens organize themselves to protest government policy. Groups come together to articulate identities, interests, and needs. In the process, the very boundary between public and private is challenged. Are you really engaging in political action when you "friend" a political candidate on Facebook? Are people's understandings of political participation affected by the format in which it occurs? When is expression on a blog an act of civic culture and identity formation, and when is it just the expression of an individual's interior thoughts on a screen that everyone can see? Scholars and users are just beginning to answer these questions.

Digital Participation and Access

The 2008 election campaign was the first time that more than half (55 percent) of the voting-age population went online to get involved in election year politics.[104] The 2012 presidential campaign continued this trend and expanded the use of digital technology from computers to mobile technology. Because 88 percent of registered voters were using cell phones,[105] campaigns had to adapt to mobile technology. The Obama campaign devoted 10 percent of its "advertising budget on outreach through Facebook, Google, and Bing," thus allowing "the campaign to engage in highly targeted outreach and reach people beyond the traditional electorate."[106]

During the 2016 campaign, candidates shifted from using interactive websites to using social media, albeit in a way that let them control the message, "leaving fewer ways overall for most voters to engage and take part."[107] During their campaigns, Jeb Bush and Hillary Clinton used Instagram and Snapchat to communicate with voters. Donald Trump and Bernie Sanders used Twitter. Researchers at the Brookings Institute said "The use of social media in the presidential election has created a new normal for what we expect from candidates."[108] In particular, the researchers analyzed each candidate's "activity network," or the likes, shares, and comments they received on Facebook. They found that Trump's network was three times larger than Sanders's or Clinton's and that the people in Trump's network interacted with each other more. The analysis demonstrated that "social media platforms have become a new means of communication between politicians and the public" and among members of the public.[109] Because the 2020 election occurred during the COVID-19 pandemic, the role of digital campaigning was even larger, with most campaign events happening virtually.[110]

The increasing centrality of digital networks during political campaigns highlights three key contributions to publics that the internet provides: a platform on which people can express political opinions, a forum in which publics can form and interact, and an outlet for information. Each of these functions, though, carries risks or limits. Political expressions might only be voiced in an echo chamber or attract trolls. Online activism might devolve into slacktivism (where "likes" take the place of donations, talking to others, contacting government representatives, or voting). Online information may be fake or lacking. Underlying all discussions of digital participation are concerns about access.

Expressing Political Opinions. A June 2018 Pew Research survey found that 53 percent of adults in the United States had done at least one of five civic activities on social media within the previous year: 34 percent had "taken part in a group that shares an interest in an issue/cause"; 32 percent had "encouraged others to take action on issues important to them"; 19 percent had "looked up information on local protests/rallies"; 18 percent had "changed a profile picture to show support for a cause"; and 14 percent had "used hashtags related to a political/social issue."[111] Politics on the internet can be public discourse in which citizens are actively engaged, and not just a spectator sport.

Civic action includes not only participation in institutionalized politics (such as "friending" a presidential candidate or emailing a legislator) but also broader forms of discursive internet activities (such as providing narratives to a state representative to include in a filibuster, tweeting in response to the #MeToo hashtag, or sharing a video that seeks to raise awareness about a social issue).[112] Many scholars, politicians, and analysts limit discussions and proposals to questions concerning administration and governance, even when they recognize the interactive nature of the internet. They also tend to ignore the role that online publics can play in identity formation.[113]

Some analysts fear that the participation that occurs on the internet will result in increasing fragmentation, because people are able to seek out only that information with which they most agree and to avoid any meaningful interaction with people who have different perspectives. The effect is a kind of echo chamber. Legal scholar Cass R. Sunstein argues forcibly for this fear: "If people on the internet are deliberating mostly with like-minded others, their views will not merely be reinforced; they will instead be shifted to more extreme points. . . . With the internet, it is exceedingly easy for each of us to find like-minded individuals."[114] The very ability of the internet to assist in identity formation also enables it to participate in polarization, as differences are identified and then intensified. Instead of being a site where public deliberation can occur despite time and distance constraints, the internet can result in polarization and lead to an erosion of a sense of common cause.

Not everyone is as pessimistic as Sunstein. People tend to seek reinforcement rather than challenges, and the internet may contribute to the creation of deliberative enclaves, but it can also be a way to open up those enclaves and allow for the development of community. For example, research indicates that LGBTQ youths living in rural communities once felt extremely isolated, but now the internet provides them an opportunity to belong to a virtual community and seek social support outside their own geographic locations.[115] Communication scholar Lincoln Dahlberg claims that "the internet is being used by many people [to] encounter difference that they would not normally encounter in everyday life."[116] Instead of functioning as an echo chamber, the internet can provide access to information that at least some people may not be able to access otherwise.

When judging the internet, do not compare it to some ideal world of civic discourse but to a noninternet world. Using the 2004 presidential election as a basis for analysis, the Pew Internet & American Life Project discovered that internet users were exposed to a wider range of information about the candidates and the political arguments than were nonusers, "including those that challenge their candidate preferences and their positions on some key issues."[117]

If you are willing to express an opinion to people who do not already agree with you, however, you risk being misunderstood or, worse, targeted by trolls. Leslie Jones, the star of *Ghostbusters,* was driven off Twitter after trolls targeted her with racist and hate-filled tweets inspired by a Breitbart movie review.[118] Trolls targeted feminist media critic Anita Sarkeesian for criticizing the sexism of the video game industry, spawning the online harassment group with the hashtag #GamerGate.[119] The fact that these targets were not White men is no accident. *The Guardian* newspaper analyzed the seventy million comments left on its digital news site since 2006 and found that "of the 10 most abused writers eight are women, and the two men are black."[120] The ten writers who received the *least* abuse were men. The *Guardian*'s analysis provided clear quantitative proof that "articles written by women attract more abuse and dismissive trolling than those written by men."[121] Not only celebrities or journalists are targets. Trolls have targeted 20 percent of internet users.[122]

Forming Publics and Political Activism. Recent writings about citizen activism on the internet discuss myriad parallels among digital activism, social movements, and counterpublics. Just as social movements can mobilize others of like mind, virtual communities are a way in which "the creative powers of controversy can spread beyond local communities"[123] as people form connections with others who share their interests, even with people who live in other states or countries.[124]

For example, the Harry Potter Alliance (HPA), describes itself as "a 501c3 nonprofit that takes an outside-of-the-box approach to civic engagement by using parallels from the Harry Potter books to educate and mobilize young people across the world toward issues of literacy, equality, and human rights."[125] The HPA tries "to make civic engagement exciting by channeling the entertainment-saturated facets of our culture toward mobilization for deep and lasting social change" among its "worldwide network of enthusiastic fan activists who are connected via the internet and social media." The HPA uses fans' love of the series to motivate people to engage in collective action relating to climate change, racial justice, gender equity, and immigrants' rights. Digital technologies make activism and engagement easy.

A concern is that digital activism may only be slacktivism, a hollow form of activism that does more to make people feel good than to correct a problem. An example is a Facebook "like." Instead of educating others about an issue, donating time or money to a cause, or working to change institutions or laws, a Facebook "like" is simply clicking a button, reducing civic activism to slacktivism. In 2013, in response to rising concerns that slacktivism was displacing real activism, UNICEF Sweden launched a campaign urging people to make real monetary contributions rather than merely expressing support through social media.[126] The campaign reminded people that liking or upvoting items on social media leads to no real action. No children will receive polio vaccines because of social media comments. Real action requires money and volunteer efforts.[127] For people to take action, their awareness must be raised; but if social media action is limited to raising awareness, is that enough?

Recent cyberactivism seems to demonstrate that it can be combined with brick-and-mortar activism and appeals to legislatures for policy change.[128] For example, the 2017 Women's March was born online, then became the largest single-day protest in history, then inspired a range of women to run for office. After the 2018 shooting at Marjorie Stoneman Douglas High School, students launched the hashtags #NeverAgain and #EnoughIsEnough *and* went to the state capitol in Tallahassee to argue for gun control *and* planned the March for Our Lives.

Access to Information. The internet plays an important role in transmitting information that can inform public decision making and debates. Although a majority (57 percent) of people often get their news from television, 38 percent often get their news online. Almost 50 percent of people aged nineteen to forty-nine often get their news online. Between 20 to 29 percent of people who are fifty or older often use online news sources.[129] As of 2018, 68 percent of US adults got some news from social media (20 percent often, 27 percent sometimes, and 21 percent hardly ever).[130]

The rise of fake news on the internet during the 2016 election cycle is a concern. One study of 171 million tweets identified 30 million that contained a link to a news outlet. Of these 30 million, 25 percent "spread either fake or extremely biased news."[131] One quarter of all news-related tweets contained false-hoods, lies, and fake stories. Bots (automated Twitter accounts) also played a significant role. Bots can make a story appear more popular and, thus, induce humans to "trust it and share it more widely."[132] According to an intelligence community assessment, Russian hackers, trolls, and bots, at the direction of Russian president Vladimir Putin, sought to interfere in the 2016 election by "undermin[ing] faith in the US democratic process" and hurting Hillary Clinton's "electability and potential presidency."[133]

Although it is hard to determine the exact effect of fake news on the 2016 election, many studies have generally found that social media directed people to fake news sites more than to real news sites; more than 25 percent of voting-age adults visited fake news sites during the final weeks of the campaign; and 10 percent of people in the United States accounted for 60 percent of the visits.[134]

In a comprehensive assessment, political communication scholar Kathleen Hall Jamieson enumerates the reach of Russian interference in the 2016 election: on Facebook, 126 million users saw Russian-influenced content; on Twitter; 1.4 million read and/or retweeted content generated by Russian trolls and bots; print and television news media shared content stolen by Russia via hacks of campaign servers; and Russian agents hacked the electoral systems of at least 21 states.[135] Jamieson is convinced that this Russian act of cyberwar, "whose messaging was strategically adept" by targeting selective audiences,[136] affected the election by "shaping the agenda and framing of news media; reweighting the message environment in news and social media; priming and reinforcing anti-Clinton content; capitalizing on timing consistent with short-term effects; and relaying and creating content designed to mobilize and demobilize key constituencies."[137] Although messaging may not change most people's votes, some voters were susceptible to change.[138] The extent of Russian interference in the 2020 election, however, appears to have been far less.[139]

In addition, there is concern about good information disappearing. Whenever one presidential administration transitions to another, the content of the federal government website changes. Recognizing the extensive information that is found on government websites, members of the International Internet Preservation Consortium and the National Digital Infrastructure and Preservation Program began the "End of Term Web Archive" project in 2008.[140] They did not always capture all the data sets compiled as a result of government-sponsored research, however. Recognizing a particular concern relating to climate change data, the Environmental Data & Government Initiative (EDGI) was created in November 2016 to "archive[e] vulnerable environmental data," monitor changes to government websites, interview federal employees, and generate "Environmental Data Justice."[141]

EDGI organized over 30 "data rescue" missions "to preserve publicly accessible and potentially vulnerable scientific data and archive web pages from EPA, DOE, NOAA, OSHA, NASA, USDA, DOI, and USGS."[142] In total, EDGI archived over 200 terabytes of government websites and data, including over 250 million URLs and files, 70 million html pages, and 40 million pdfs.

In writing about the archive-a-thon in which they participated on inauguration day in 2017, UCLA students Morgan Currie and Britt S. Paris said, "The need for such work quickly became palpable. Within hours of Trump's inauguration ceremony, official statements on anthropogenic, or [human]-made, climate change vanished from governmental websites."[143] The students understood that this preservation of data intersected with publics in various ways:

> By treating federal scientific data as a public utility, data rescues create an occasion for community and political resistance. In fact, we might find that the importance of mirroring federal climate data lies less in rescuing data sets for the scientific community . . . but instead in creating spaces for community dialogue and wider public awareness of the vulnerabilities of politically contentious scientific work. By building communities around web mirroring, data rescues already play a political role.[144]

Although the data was generated by participants in technical spheres, its utility was essential to public sphere argument. Data can be a public good. Information is necessary for good public debate.

The Digital Divide. For digital participation to be democratic, all people must have access to the internet. Unfortunately, not all people do. Although the internet is theoretically open to all, material barriers to participation exist. Digital divides also exist among countries. In 2017, between 77 and 80 percent of people in Sweden, Netherlands, Spain, Australia and the United States own smartphones.[145] In contrast, in Poland, Hungary, and Greece, between 46 and 52 percent own smartphones.

Digital divides also exist within countries. Of the countries surveyed, people who are younger, have more formal education, and have an income above the national median "are more likely to own a smartphone compared with older, less educated and poorer members of their societies."[146] Globally, around 48 percent of the population has online access, but regional variations are great. In Europe, 79.6 percent of people have internet access, as do 67.7 percent in the Commonwealth of Independent States in Eurasia and 65.9 percent in the Americas; but only 43.9 percent in Asia and the Pacific, 43.7 in Arab states, and 21.8 percent in Africa.[147] As of 2016, 3.9 billion people in the world are offline. These people are "disproportionately female, elderly, less educated, lower income, and rural."[148]

Where people around the world have had access to communication technologies such as cell phones, web pages, and blogs, they have used that access to supplement and sustain civic engagement and political action. If marginalized groups are not represented on the internet, however, then cyberspace cannot expand the discursive arena. Instead, in Fraser's words, it merely replicates the "modes of deliberation that mask domination"[149] as it absorbs the less powerful into a dominant "we." The internet creates an appearance of deliberation, but a series of monologues transversing the Web do not substitute for critical engagement. Inequitable internet access should be troubling, not only because it mirrors other inequalities in society, but also because it masks the existence of those inequalities. It is difficult to recognize the absences of some groups if you cannot even identify who is present.[150]

Networked Publics

Theories emphasizing multiple publics, as opposed to a unitary public, encourage thinking about how networks of communication constitute civic life.[151] Networks emerge among publics, discursive arenas, people, institutions, and organizations. Our use of "networked" in this section reflects both the multiple publics that make up civic life and the way in which those publics are connected. Internet technology enhances the networked features of publics by allowing the interactive exchange of ideas across multiple media and among multiple rhetors.

Two specific features of networked publics deserve attention. First, digital media technologies enable bidirectional flows of communication. In the pre-internet, mass-mediated public sphere, in journalist A. J. Liebling's unique phrasing, "freedom of the press [was] guaranteed only to those who own one."[152] In the internet age, however, the flow of communication is no longer in only one direction, from professional communicators such as journalists to everyday people. Second, the flow of communication has become less vertical (from the powerful few to the less powerful many) and more horizontal (from many to many, regardless of power position). Before the internet, mass media controlled the agenda: what was discussed and who got to comment on the major stories of the day. It also fulfilled an editorial function, vetting stories for accuracy. In the internet era, however, a range of people introduce topics for discussion, comment on stories, and spread or make news (fake and real) through social networking sites.[153]

An example of the internet displacing commercial mass media's function as agenda setter and sole informer occurred in December 2002. Then–US Senate Majority Leader Trent Lott toasted Senator Strom Thurmond, a long-time advocate of segregation, on his hundredth birthday by saying: "I want to say this about my state: When Strom Thurmond ran for president, we voted for him. We're proud of it. And if the rest of the country had followed our lead, we wouldn't have had all these problems over all these years either."[154] Initially, communication scholar Damien Pfister notes, the toast celebrating Thurmond's advocacy of segregationist policies was "barely covered by the institutional press. Only after bloggers started connecting the toast to Thurmond's past deeds did the press pick up on the story and eventually generate public pressure for Lott to resign his Senate Majority post."[155] Similarly, when commercial media did not cover Wendy Davis's 2013 filibuster, citizens covered it through Twitter. And when official cameras were turned off during the 2016 House of Representatives sit-in, participants used smartphones to generate video feed.

With the emergence of interactive digital communication technologies, people no longer participate in a "mass-mediated public sphere" where their role is only as information consumers, but in a "networked public sphere" where they perform the roles of producers and consumers.[156] **Networked publics** are *interconnected publics and counterpublics formed or strengthened as a result of the communication practices enabled by the internet and social media.* In networked publics, digital media technologies change patterns of public participation. Law professor Yochai Benkler says that "the social practices of information and discourse allow a very large number of actors to see themselves as potential contributors to public discourse and as potential actors in political arenas, rather than mostly passive recipients of mediated information who occasionally can vote their preferences."[157] Because everyone is potentially a contributor, creative participatory activities burgeon, including generating memes, blogging, creating parodic video mashups, and culture jamming. As Pfister notes, "The networked public sphere isn't a dour, stale site of elite public deliberation but is in fact a lively, participatory, dynamic arena where creativity thrives (for better or for worse)."[158]

For an example of the speed and power of networked advocacy, consider what happened in June 2014. On June 6, the US Food and Drug Administration (FDA) announced a new rule regarding cheese making that banned the use of wooden shelves, on which artisan cheeses are aged. The result would have been the end of artisanal cheeses in the United States. Foregoing its usual "comment rule-making" process, the FDA simply announced the new rule.[159] Nevertheless, within days, a "We the People" petition on the White House website had thousands of signatures. People emailed the FDA directly. Twitter hashtags emerged, including #Savethecheese and #Speakcheesies (referring to the speakeasies of the Prohibition era, in which alcohol was illegal). By June 11, the FDA had backed down from its ruling.[160]

For a less cheesy example, consider the Zapatista movement in Chiapas, Mexico, and its support of prodemocracy reforms.[161] Formed in 1983, the EZLN (Ejército Zapatista de Liberación Nacional) demanded autonomy for the indigenous people of Chiapas when increasing governmental and economic pressures threatened their communal lands, diverse local cultures, and languages.

The movement expanded to the internet on January 1, 1994, when supporters launched a digital campaign using networks created during an earlier international campaign against the North American Free Trade Agreement (NAFTA).

The transition to networked space was not easy. The Zapatistas were transmitting messages from villages that did not have electricity, much less modems. Communiqués were delivered via courier to newspapers in cities within twelve hours of creation and circulated internationally within twenty-four hours. Supporters translated the messages from Spanish and sent them to email list subscribers on networks such as Peacenet, the internet, and Usenet. The speed with which the world heard about and mobilized to support this struggle by a small band of indigenous peoples was unprecedented.[162] Even before Web 2.0, the Zapatistas showed the potential of the internet to create networks of activism.

The protest was not solely digital. Real bodies were put at risk, even as information was distributed electronically. On the same day the group's demands went digital, elements of the EZLN seized several towns, with some reports indicating "at least 145 people died in the ensuing battle with state troops."[163] Supporters flocked to Chiapas to document and protest the Mexican government's attempts at military repression. Hundreds of thousands demonstrated in the streets of Mexico City and other cities and towns, eventually forcing the government to shift from overt military attacks on the EZLN to political negotiations and covert repression. Once again, human rights activists from around the world came to Chiapas to observe, report, and constrain government actions.

The Mexican government tried to quash the uprising by limiting press coverage by the state-controlled television network Televisa, but the world heard about it because of messages posted on websites and sent over the internet. Economics professor Harry Cleaver explains that the pro-Zapatistas' use of electronic and computer communications made it difficult for the government to isolate and silence the movement:

> Despite its initial defeat, a key aspect of the state's war against the Zapatistas (both in Mexico and elsewhere) has been its on-going efforts to isolate them, so that they can be destroyed or forced to accept co-optation. In turn, the Zapatistas and their supporters have fought to maintain and elaborate their political connections throughout the world. This has been a war of words, images, imagination and organization in which the Zapatistas have had surprising success.
>
> Vital to this continuing struggle has been the pro-Zapatista use of computer communications. While the state has all too effectively limited mass media coverage and serious discussion of Zapatista ideas, their supporters have been able, to an astonishing degree, to circumvent and offset this blockage through the use of electronic networks in conjunction with the more familiar tactics of solidarity movements: teach-ins, articles in the alternative press, demonstrations, the occupation of Mexican government consulates and so on.[164]

Instead of having to rely on traditional commercial or state-controlled media to broadcast their message, the group was able to speak to the world directly through email and then, increasingly, through dozens of supporters' web pages, across the globe and in many languages. A small group of activists supporting indigenous Mayan farmers in Chiapas against repressive policies of the Mexican government were able to take their message global, speaking not just to the "strong public" of the Mexican government or the "weak public" of Mexican citizens, but to a "transnational public" of global citizens, demonstrating that publics are not bound by national boundaries. The publics to which the Zapatistas spoke were far larger than those within the nation's borders, and those publics sustained their interest across the years. During periods of renewed military repression in early 1994 and again in early 1995, supporters demonstrated at Mexican embassies and consulates in over forty countries.

The early use of the networked public sphere to communicate with a transnational public was only the first step. The Zapatistas, with the help of supporters, used digital communication technologies to engage in a variety of protests. Early in 1994, internet-based organizing brought together thousands of prodemocracy advocates in a Zapatista village, for a National Democratic Convention to discuss how to get beyond the essentially one-party rule in Mexico. In 1995, the Zapatistas called for, and their supporters organized, a Plebiscite for Peace and Democracy that had over a million attendees. Internet technology enabled international participation. In 1996, internet connections provided the main vehicle to organize the Intercontinental Encounter for Humanity and against Neoliberalism, which brought together thousands of grassroots activists from around the world.

We can trace a direct line from the Intercontinental Encounter in 1996 in Chiapas villages and the rise of the antiglobalization/anti-WTO movement. The 1996 global meeting gave rise to People's Global Action, which organized the 1998 anti-WTO protest in Geneva and participated in the 1999 anti-WTO protest in Seattle. Indymedia, "a grassroots network committed to using media production and distribution as tools for promoting social and economic justice,"[165] began to emerge during the Zapatista support experience. Indymedia was fully developed "in late November of 1999, to allow participants in the anti-globalization movement to report on the protests against the WTO meeting that took place in Seattle."[166] Ultimately, Zapatistas and their supporters have used "the internet as a means to build a global grassroots support network" not bound by time or space.[167] Since 1994, using the most basic of digital technologies (cell phones and listservs), you can find discussions of Zapatistas on blogs.[168] The EZLN and Zapatistas are on Facebook and Twitter, and have hashtags on Instagram.

Supporters have sometimes acted autonomously, using digital forms of protest that have generated controversy within the pro-Zapatista movement. In 1998, a small group organized a virtual sit-in in Mexico. It sent email instructions to supporters, calling on them to connect to the websites for five Mexican financial institutions and hit "reload" several times during the hour in order to overload the sites and stop all business, just as US civil rights sit-ins sought to stop commerce at targeted businesses. This action was controversial because many in the Zapatista support movement were afraid that the state, which was much better equipped, would counterattack by shutting down supporters' websites or block their listservs.

Networked publics should be able to fulfill all the functions of counterpublics, even as they face similar challenges. Networked movements can contest existing norms and develop alternative validity claims. Just as counterpublics often renegotiate the distinctions between the public and private, so may internet activism. Stephen Wray, a member of the Electronic Disturbance Theatre (EDT), sees an inherent potential for digital activism to challenge dominant validity claims but cautions that digital activism should be considered carefully: those engaging in it do not, alone, create the rhetoric about it and are not the only ones who can engage in it. Wray would like to see attempts at electronic civil disobedience redefine "infowar" and make it a plausible form of activism, because "we need to seriously question and abandon some of the language that the state uses to demonize genuine political protest and expression."[169] Wray and the EDT have provided software, such as FloodNet, that enables people to stage nonviolent mass protests (virtual sit-ins) in networked space.[170] In many ways, protest in the public sphere is being supplemented and/or replaced by protest on a networked public screen.

In addressing serious social and political issues, digital activism can also be creative, productive, and even joyful. In fact, some scholars argue, "A sense of playfulness [is] common to new media environments."[171] Alt Twitter handles and Facebook pages illustrate this sense of playfulness, as well as ways in which counterpublic discourse can emerge from actors positioned within the state.

Donald Trump was inaugurated as president on January 20, 2017. Immediately, the administration began purging any mention of climate change on government websites and banned all press releases, blog updates, or social media posts by the Environmental Protection Agency and the Departments of Health and Human Services, Agriculture, and the Interior (in which the National Park Service is a federal bureau).[172] Although a temporary communication embargo is typical during administration transitions, purging all mentions of an issue is not.[173] On January 23, Golden Gate National Park tweeted that 2016 was the hottest year on record.[174] On January 24, between 11:40 a.m. and 12:25 p.m., the official social media division of Badlands National Park sent four tweets stating facts about gasoline's production of CO_2, the concentration of CO_2 in the atmosphere, and ocean acidity. By 5:35 p.m., the tweets had been blamed on a former employee and removed, but people had already screen-captured them.[175] Soon after, the Theodore Roosevelt Inaugural Site sent a tweet quoting Roosevelt, declaring, "Free Speech, exercised both individually and through a free press, is a necessity in any country where the people are free."[176]

Almost immediately, fifty-one renegade Twitter sites associated with government agencies appeared, including altEPA, RogueNASA, AltNASA, Alt USDA, Alternative CDC, Alternative HHS, AltNIH, AltFDA, and AltNOAA, and AltUSNatParkService (which within two days gathered twice as many followers as the official NPS site).[177] AltUSNationalParkService (AltNPS) has its own Facebook site and web page, which declared that the new administration might have shut down the social media accounts of the agencies, but could not shut down the internet or what government employees did with their own time.[178] The Facebook page engages in both serious contributions to public debates about the environment and playful responses such as posters of Smokey Bear declaring "Resist!

Only you can prevent fascism." On January 29, 2017, AltNPS tweeted an image of the Badlands with a poem superimposed (borrowing language from the famous Pastor Niemöller quotation about the Holocaust), noting that first the administration sought to silence scientists, but the NPS said "LOL. No." Describing the NPS as "going rogue," the tweet called on popular culture references by identifying park rangers as leading "the resistance" even though such a scenario was unlike any of the dystopian teen novels popular at the time.[179]

During the March for Science on April 23, 2017, the AltNPS tweet moved from the digital to the analog world when it appeared on a handwritten sign repeating the tweet describing the NPS as "going rogue."[180] On August 19, 2017, the Badlands image recirculated on the AltNPS Facebook page.[181] Other playful forms of internet activism included editorial cartoons depicting mild-mannered park rangers representing the "Bad[ass]lands" and Facebook pages for the "Badasslands National Park."[182] Aragorn (the ranger character in *Lord of the Rings*) inspirational speech memes played on a double meaning of the term "ranger" by expressing surprise that *park* rangers (rather than Tolkien's mythical northern wandering people of Eriador) were leading the resistance.[183]

THE PANMEDIATED NETWORKED PUBLIC SCREEN

Historically, public sphere discourse was associated with the type of discussion that happens in a brick-and-mortar public place: the town square or the town hall. Prior to the emergence of electronic mass media, the discourse that consists of reasoned exchanges of opinion could only occur in such settings. Media such as newspapers served a subsidiary role: they provided the information with which (and sometimes the medium in which) members of the public advanced their arguments.

The evolution of media such as television and the internet challenge such a simple role for media in public discourse. Media no longer transmit information that is primarily verbal. We live in an age in which visuals play a dominant role. People in the United States live in a visual culture. Once you begin to recognize the power of visuals and the places where they appear, you need to expand the forms and modes of rhetoric to which you respond critically.

Thinking about the public sphere has evolved rapidly, along with the rapid evolution of electronic and digital technologies. Communication scholars Kevin Michael DeLuca and Jennifer Peeples offer the concept of the public screen as an alternative concept of public discourse. The **public screen** is composed of *the constant circulation of symbolic action enabled by the relatively new media technologies of television, computers, photography, film, internet, and smart phones.* DeLuca and Peeples encourage people to recognize "that most, and the most important, public discussions take place via 'screens'—television, computer, and the front page of the newspaper."[184] These scholars recognize that we live in a primarily visual culture. Meaning is shaped and guided by the images people see rather than strictly (or even primarily) by words.[185] Television and the videos people watch on the internet are prime examples of a discourse grounded in images and the visual. Thus, when studying public communication, the focus should not only be on public speeches, but also on "image events," which are now the primary mode of communication to a public that is characterized by its reliance on commercial, professional communication on public screens.[186]

DeLuca and Peeples's point is not that the visual rhetorics of the public screen are superior to the verbal discourses of the traditional public sphere, nor that everyone should engage in image events instead of public discourse.[187] Instead, they argue that you cannot really understand the complete dynamics of contemporary public controversies unless you account for the role of the visual. As they explain, "the public screen is the essential supplement to the public sphere. In comparison to the rationality, embodied conversations, consensus, and civility of the public sphere, the public screen highlights dissemination, images, hypermediacy, spectacular publicity, cacophony, distractions, and dissent."[188] The public screen does not share the ideals of consensus formation and civility that typifies descriptions of the ideal public sphere, but neither does other public communication, as is demonstrated by the confrontational rhetoric of British and US suffrage advocates of the late 1800s and early 1900s, as well as the antiwar protests of the 1960s and 1970s. The concept of the public screen emphasizes that public discourse, as it exists, is diffuse, messy, loud, vivid, and immediate. In many cases, it does more to generate controversy than to generate consensus.

Because media technology is no longer confined to mass media such as television and newspapers, communication scholars Joshua P. Ewalt, Jessy J. Ohl, and Damien Smith Pfister argue that rhetoricians need to expand the concept of the public screen. They explain,

> **"networked public screens"** better captures how *image events, iconic and everyday, are produced and circulated in a networked mediascape.* Images and text hop from screen node to screen node, following the developing logics of social networking and algorithmic culture. Unlike a conventional public address or formal screen presentation . . . with a specific context, internal coherence, and a sequential development, images on networked public screens are often decontextualized, random, and bricolaged.[189]

In response, and noting the ubiquity of portable screens (on smart phones and tablets), communication scholars Elizabeth A. Brunner and Kevin Michael DeLuca proposed a concept of *panmediated* networked public screens. Reinforcing our earlier discussion of circulation, they argue that people need to "understand images as things in motion in a network" and analyze "their movement and force."[190] In proposing "panmediated," they emphasize that "people are networked to others and to objects via online platforms that can transmit a wide array of information, including images, and do so ceaselessly at great speeds."[191] They cite statistics indicating that billions of views occur daily of the 300 hours of video that are uploaded to YouTube every minute, and that Instagram's 180 million users upload 58 million photos daily. Their point is not just that everyone is networked to visual media, but that you are networked to visual media all the time and in all the places where you can get a signal. The International Telecommunications Union reports that "people no longer *go* online, they *are* online."[192] In other words, "public screens are scenes of remediation and hypermediacy" as rhetoric is shared on one medium but then circulated on other media, creating a sense that you are closer to rhetorical events than physical space might indicate.[193]

For example, on March 19, 1979, as cable television channels expanded, Brian Lamb launched C-SPAN as a nonprofit public service to televise sessions of the US Congress and, when Congress was not in session, other public affairs programs. C-SPAN enabled people to watch congressional debates on a public screen (television) rather than having to attend in person or read debate transcriptions in the *Congressional Record*. In January 1997, C-SPAN began streaming content on its website, bringing video of congressional debates to the networked public screen. By its twenty-fifth anniversary in 2004, C-SPAN had broadcast 24,246 hours of floor debates in the House of Representatives.[194]

Another example of the networked public screen becoming panmediated occurred June 22–23, 2016. Speaker of the House Paul Ryan refused to allow debate on Democrat-sponsored gun legislation in the wake of the Pulse nightclub shooting in Orlando. In response, Democratic House representatives held signs containing the names of victims of gun violence and began chanting as Representative John Lewis, who had organized civil rights sit-ins in the 1960s, began a sit-in on the House floor.[195] C-SPAN showed footage of the sit-in being announced before Ryan gaveled the session into recess. C-SPAN cameras were turned off because the House's procedure is to only keep the cameras rolling when the House is in session, [196] but the visual of the sit-in was not absent from networked public screens.

The *Atlantic*'s Live Blog began posting reportorial updates and copies of tweets from representatives participating in the sit-in.[197] Representative Scott Peters, in violation of House rules, used Periscope's live video feed to share the event on digital platforms. C-SPAN then broadcast the Periscope feed after it was shown on commercial network news shows. The House sergeant-at-arms asked those who were sitting in to stop taking photos and videos, but they continued to record.[198] Representative Mark Takano used a phone to livestream the event on Facebook. He placed the phone in front of the podium from which people were speaking before leaving the chamber to appear on CNN. Representative Jared Huffman declared that "far more people" were watching the "pirated" Periscope video than normally watch C-SPAN.[199] The sit-in lasted for over 24 hours, with usually 10 to 20 people on the House floor, and as many as 170 legislators participating at times. News media reported the sit-in as a "social media happening": Periscope links were tweeted 1.4 million times.[200]

Access to this event on the floor of the House was enabled because recording technology is diffused and the internet enables easy distribution. The video appeared on networked public screens, enabling Periscope's live video feeds to travel across tweets, through Facebook, and to commercial television news, eventually landing at C-SPAN even though the House cameras feeding video to C-SPAN had been turned off. The fact that people had access to these events even when broadcast media did not have video access demonstrates the networked public screen is panmediated.

When you think about rhetoric in civic life, recognize that (1) both visual and verbal rhetoric are involved, so the public sphere is also a screen on which rhetoric is viewed and felt as much as heard; (2) with the shift from mass to networked communication, rhetoric, people, organizations, and actions are networked, so circulation across audiences is as important as delivery to the initial audience; and (3) impact must be considered differently, as the effect of circulation in mass media may be less important than the effect of circulation in social media created by individuals.[201] Rhetoric in civic life is not simply a dialogue. It is a messy, vibrant, confounding, sometimes cacophonous multilogue, in which everyone can be involved as a producer and a consumer, a rhetor and an audience, an activist and a bystander, all at the same time.

CONCLUSION

Defining "public" is complicated. A group of people that exists prior to a rhetor's message does not come into being as a public until it is constituted through rhetoric. Further, publics are fluid, coming into and out of existence. An understanding of multiple public spheres reveals the multifaceted relationships among rhetors, audiences, public spheres, power, economy, and state.

Habermas's ideal public sphere is "open to all citizens," addresses "matters of general interest," and is free from coercion,[202] but this ideal is not a reality. Not everyone is accorded access to the public sphere. Not everyone's words are given the same weight as others. Power differentials matter.

When people perceive that they are outside of the dominant public and that their issues and concerns are not being addressed, they may construct counterpublic spheres in which they define their identities and concerns, countering the perspective of the dominant public sphere. The internet provides a place in which counterpublic spheres can form, as well as a space for participation in the dominant public sphere and in the strong public of the state.

The concept of the public sphere has been expanded to include networked publics and the networked public screen, as well as both visual and verbal messages, because modern media have changed the ways people communicate and obtain messages. Not all public rhetoric achieves the high ideals of reasoned face-to-face communication that theorists such as Habermas and Dewey imagined. Communication on the panmediated networked public screen can appear to be emotional, something other than rational, and disruptive. Still, argument and controversy are signs of a healthy democratic society and central to civic engagement. Disagreement opens space for argument, challenges norms, and urges people to consider which arguments make sense.

Civic engagement occurs whenever a public sphere is brought into being through discourse. People participate in individual and collective action to develop solutions to social, economic, and political challenges in their communities, states, nation, and the world. In any democratic society, change and maintenance of social, political, and economic structures is accomplished through civic engagement, which is accomplished through rhetoric. Civic engagement is a process with many different forms, all of which involve rhetoric.

DISCUSSION QUESTIONS

1. In chapters 1 and 2, we defined civic engagement not as a single thing you do, but as a process. Identify all the ways you participate in civic life. How many of those forms of participation require collective and coordinated action? How many are individual and personal? What do your answers tell you about the health of public spheres in contemporary society?
2. Identify publics to which you belong. What identifies you as a member of that public? How has your participation in that public developed your own identity?
3. For much of the Covid pandemic, many people worked from home, took classes from home, and seldom left their houses. How did the isolation impact the creation of publics? Did it change the nature of those publics?

SUGGESTED READINGS

Asen, Robert, and Daniel C. Brouwer. "Introduction: Reconfigurations of the Public Sphere." In *Counterpublics and the State,* edited by Robert Asen and Daniel C. Brouwer, 1–32. Albany: State University of New York Press, 2001.

Brunner, Elizabeth A., and Kevin Michael DeLuca. "The Argumentative Force of Image Networks: Greenpeace's Panmediated Global Detox Campaign." *Argumentation and Advocacy* 52, no. 4 (Spring 2016): 281–299.

Fraser, Nancy. "Rethinking the Public Sphere." In *Habermas and the Public Sphere,* edited by Craig Calhoun, 109–137. Cambridge, MA: MIT Press, 1992.

Mansbridge, Jane. "Using Power/Fighting Power: The Polity." In *Democracy and Difference: Contesting the Boundaries of the Political,* edited by Seyla Benhabib, 46–66. Princeton, NJ: Princeton University Press, 1996.

Pfister, Damien Smith. *Networked Media, Networked Rhetorics: Attention and Deliberation in the Early Blogosphere.* University Park: Penn State University Press, 2014.

ENDNOTES

[1] For a full text of the resolution, see https://www8.iowa-city.org/weblink/0/edoc/1565536/2017-01-17%20Resolution.pdf.

[2] Andy Davis, "Iowa City Adopts Limited Role in Immigration Enforcement," *Des Moines Register,* January 17, 2017, https://www.desmoinesregister.com/story/news/local/2017/01/17/iowa-city-adopts-limited-role-immigration-enforcement-sanctuary-city/96684972/.

[3] "Iowa City Council Unanimously Approves Resolution Concerning Local Police, Immigration Enforcement," *Gazette* (Cedar Rapids, IA), January 17, 2017, https://www.thegazette.com/subject/news/government/iowa-city-council-unanimously-approves-resolution-concerning-local-police-immigration-enforcement-20170117.

[4] Quoted in Davis, "Iowa City Adopts."

[5] The Sensenbrenner Bill, officially known as House Resolution 4377: Border Protection, Antiterrorism, and Illegal Immigration Control Act of 2005, passed in the House in December 2005, catalyzing the Spring 2006 protests. It did not pass in the Senate.

[6] Lindsey Bever, "Protesters in California Block Busloads of Immigrant Children and Families," *Washington Post,* July 2, 2014, http://www.washingtonpost.com/news/morning-mix/wp/2014/07/02/protesters-in -california-block-busloads-of-immigrant-children-and-families.

[7] Donald Trump, "Here's Donald Trump's Presidential Announcement Speech," *Time,* June 1, 2015, http://time.com/3923128/donald-trump-announcement-speech/.

[8] Philip Klinkner, "Yes, Trump's Hard-Line Immigration Stance Helped Him Win the Election—but It Could Be His Undoing," *Los Angeles Times,* April 17, 2017, https://www.latimes.com/opinion/op-ed/la-oe-klinker-immigration-election -20170417-story.html.

[9] Gregory Korte and Alan Gomez, "Trump Ramps up Rhetoric on Undocumented Immigrants: 'These Aren't People. These Are Animals,'" *USA Today,* May 16, 2018, https://www.usatoday.com/story/news/politics/2018/05/16/trump-immigrants -animals-mexico-democrats-sanctuary-cities/617252002/.

[10] Dakin Andone, "Coast-to-Coast Protests Denounce Trump Immigration Policies," CNN, June 30, 2018, https://www.cnn.com/2018/06/30/us/june-30-immigration-protests/index.html.

[11] "Timeline of Federal Policy on Immigration, 2017–2020," Ballotpedia, January 8, 2019, https://ballotpedia.org/Timeline_of_federal_policy_on_immigration,_2017–2020.

[12] Damien Pfister, *Networked Media, Networked Rhetorics* (University Park: Pennsylvania State University Press, 2014), 48.

[13] Anne Demo, "Review Essay: Policy and Media in Immigration Studies," *Rhetoric and Public Affairs* 7, no. 2 (2002): 216.

[14] Richard D. Pineda and Stacey K. Sowards, "Flag Waving as Visual Argument: 2006 Immigration Demonstrations and Cultural Citizenship," *Argumentation and Advocacy* 43 (Winter and Spring 2007): 164–174; and Kent A. Ono and John M. Sloop, *Shifting Borders: Rhetoric, Immigration, and California's Proposition 187* (Philadelphia: Temple University Press, 2002).

[15] Nina Bernstein, "In the Streets, Suddenly, an Immigrant Groundswell," *New York Times,* March 27, 2006.

[16] Quoted in Rick Klein, "Immigrants' Voice: 'We're in the Fight,'" *Boston Globe,* April 11, 2006.

[17] Ralph Ranalli and Yvonne Abraham, "O'Malley Urges Policy Reform Based on Respect: Immigration Backers Stream through Hub," *Boston Globe,* April 11, 2006.

[18] Amanda Paulson, "Rallying Immigrants Look Ahead," *Christian Science Monitor,* May 3, 2006.

[19] Stephen Dinan, "The Washington Times," *Washington Times,* May 4, 2006.

[20] Keyonna Summers, "End of Minuteman Tour Marked by Confrontations; Demonstrators Compare Group to Klan," *Washington Times,* May 13, 2006.

[21] Richard Sammon, "Immigration Bill Still a Long Shot," *Kiplinger Business Forecasts* 2006, No. 0505, May 1, 2006, LexisNexis.

[22] Jen Kirby and Emily Stewart, "Families Belong Together Protest Underway in More Than 700 Cities," *Vox,* June 30, 2018, https://www.vox.com/2018/6/18/17477376 /families-belong-together-march-june-30.

[23] Quoted in "President Donald Trump Holds Roundtable Discussion on Border Security in California," *CQ Transcriptions,* April 5, 2019, NEXIS-UNI.

[24] Greg Sargent, "The Public Sees through Trump's National Emergency Lies" (blog), *Washington Post,* February 19, 2019, Nexis-Uni.

[25] Gerard A. Hauser, "Features of the Public Sphere," *Critical Studies in Mass Communication* 4, no. 4 (December 1987), 440.

[26] Jenny Rice, *Distant Publics: Development Rhetoric and the Subject of Crisis* (Pittsburgh: University of Pittsburgh Press, 2012), 19.

[27] James Jasinski, *Sourcebook on Rhetoric: Key Concepts in Contemporary Rhetorical Studies* (Thousand Oaks, CA: Sage, 2001), 474. Jürgen Habermas's writings include *The Structural Transformation of the Public Sphere: An Inquiry into a Category of Bourgeois Society,* trans. Thomas Burger (Boston: MIT Press, 1991); *Reason and the Rationalization of Society,* vol. 1, *The Theory of Communicative Action,* trans. Thomas McCarthy (Boston: Beacon, 1984); and *Lifeworld and System: A Critique of Functionalist Reason,* vol. 2, *The Theory of Communicative Action,* trans. Thomas McCarthy (Boston: Beacon, 1987).

[28] Jürgen Habermas, "The Public Sphere," in *Jürgen Habermas on Society and Politics: A Reader,* ed. S. Seidman, 231–236 (Boston: Beacon, 1989), 230, italics added.

[29] Habermas, "The Public Sphere," 232.

[30] Habermas, *Structural Transformation,* 32–41.

[31] Robert Asen, "The Multiple Mr. Dewey: Multiple Publics and Permeable Borders in John Dewey's Theory of the Public Sphere," *Argument and Advocacy* 39 (Winter 2003): 174–188; Robert Asen, "A Discourse Theory of Citizenship," *Quarterly Journal of Speech* 90, no. 2 (May 2009): 189–211.

[32] Nancy Fraser, "Rethinking the Public Sphere," in *Habermas and the Public Sphere,* ed. Craig Calhoun (Cambridge, MA: MIT Press, 1992), 110.

[33] Habermas, "The Public Sphere," 231.

[34] "Read Gov. Walker's Budget Repair Bill," wisconsinrapidstribune.com, February 24, 2011, http://www.wisconsinrapidstribune.com/article/20110224/WRT0101 /110224063/Read-Gov-Walker-s-budget-repair-bill.

[35] Judy Keen, "Wisconsin Budget Crisis Has Folks Talking," *USA Today,* February 24, 2011.

[36] Although Habermas points to eighteenth- and early nineteenth-century Europe for an example of the emergence of a public sphere, other scholars have noted that his bourgeois public sphere was premised on exclusions based on sex and class. See Mary P. Ryan, "Gender and Public Access: Women's Politics in Nineteenth-Century America," and Geoff Eley, "Nations, Publics, and Political Cultures: Placing Habermas in the Nineteenth Century," in *Habermas and the Public Sphere,* ed. Craig Calhoun, 259–339 (Cambridge, MA: MIT Press, 1992). Habermas recognizes such exclusion. See Jürgen Habermas, "Further Reflections on the Public Sphere," in Calhoun, *Habermas and the Public Sphere.*

[37] Melanie Loehwing and Jeff Motter, "Publics, Counterpublics, and the Promise of Democracy," *Philosophy and Rhetoric* 42, no. 3 (2009): 220–241.

[38] Editorial Board, "Putin's Repression Resumes, Now That the Olympics Have Ended" (editorial), *Washington Post,* February 25, 2014, http://www.washingtonpost.com /opinions/putins-repression-resumes-now-that-the-olympics-have-ended/2014/02 /25/071f010a-9e5a-11e3-b8d8-94577ff66b28_story.html.

[39] Fraser, "Rethinking the Public Sphere," 110.

[40] Fraser, "Rethinking the Public Sphere," 111.

[41] Robert Asen and Daniel C. Brouwer, "Introduction: Reconfigurations of the Public Sphere," in *Counterpublics and the State,* ed. Robert Asen and Daniel S. Brouwer (Albany: State University of New York Press) 10. See also John Dewey, *The Public and Its Problems* (1927; repr. Athens, OH: Swallow, 1954).

[42] Valeria Fabj and Matthew J. Sobnosky, "AIDS Activism and the Rejuvenation of the Public Sphere," *Argumentation and Advocacy* 31 (Spring 1995): 163–184.

[43] The authors thank Robert Asen for his useful distinction between universality and multiplicity.

[44] Fraser, "Rethinking the Public Sphere," 134, italics added.

[45] Fraser, "Rethinking the Public Sphere," 134, italics added.

[46] Ono and Sloop, *Shifting Borders*. See also J. David Cisneros, "Contaminated Communities: The Metaphor of 'Immigrant as Pollutant' in Media Representations of Immigration," *Rhetoric and Public Affairs* 11, no. 4 (2008): 569–602; Otto Santa Anna, *Brown Tide Rising: Metaphors of Latinos in Contemporary American Public Discourse* (Austin: University of Texas Press, 2002).

[47] Marouf Hasian, Jr., and Fernando Delgado, "The Trials and Tribulations of Racialized Critical Rhetorical Theory: Understanding the Rhetorical Ambiguities of Proposition 187," *Communication Theory* 8, no. 3 (August 1998): 259.

[48] Matthew Webster, "The Border Crossed Us," *Nonviolent Migration*, posted October 18, 2007, http://nonviolentmigration.wordpress.com/2007/10/19/the-border-crossed-us; and Rubén Martínez, "Fighting 187: The Different Opposition Strategies," *NACLA: Report of the Americas* 29, no. 3 (November/December 1995): 30.

[49] Fraser, "Rethinking the Public Sphere," 134.

[50] Fraser, "Rethinking the Public Sphere," 134–135.

[51] Jennifer L. Borda and Bailey Marshall, "Creating a Space to #SayHerName: Rhetorical Stratification in the Networked Sphere," *Quarterly Journal of Speech* 106, no. 2 (2020): 133–155, https://doi.org/10.1080/00335630.2020.1744182; Sara Florini, "Tweets, Tweeps, and Signifyin': Communication and Cultural Performance on 'Black Twitter,'" *Television & New Media* 15, no. 3 (2013): 223–7, https://doi.org/10.1177/1527476413480247; and Marc Lamont Hill, "'Thank You, BlackTwitter': State Violence, Digital Counterpublics, and Pedagogies of Resistance," *Urban Education* 53, no. 2 (2018): 286–302, https://doi.org/10.1177/0042085917747124; Roderick Graham and Shawn Smith, "The Content of Our #Characters: Black Twitter as Counterpublic," *Sociology of Race and Ethnicity* 2, no. 4 (2016): 433–49, https:///doi.org/10.1177/2332649216639067; and Catherine R. Squires, "Rethinking the Black Public Sphere: An Alternative Vocabulary for Multiple Public Spheres," *Communication Theory* 12, no. 4 (2002): 446–68, https://doi.org/10.1111/j.1468-2885.2002.tb00278.x.

[52] Farhad Manjoo, "How Black People Use Twitter," *Slate,* August 10, 2010, https://slate.com/technology/2010/08/how-black-people-use-twitter.html; Meredith Clark, "Black Twitter: Building Connection through Cultural Conversation," in *Hashtag Publics,* ed. Nathan Rambukkana (New York: Peter Lang, 2015), 205–217.

[53] The BREATHE Act, https://breatheact.org/wp-content/uploads/2020/07/The-BREATHE-Act-PDF_FINAL3-1.pdf.

[54] Maya King, "Black Lives Matters Goes Big on Policy Agenda," *Politico,* August 28, 2020, https://www.politico.com/news/2020/08/28/black-lives-matter-breathe-act-403905.

[55] Quoted in Andrew Kragie, "Inside the Alternative Universe of the Trump Rallies," *Atlantic,* November 6, 2018, https://www.theatlantic.com/politics/archive/2018/11/donald-trump-stokes-fear-immigrants-his-rallies/574984/.

[56] Hasian and Delgado, "Trials and Tribulations," 262.

[57] Fraser, "Rethinking the Public Sphere," 136.

[58] Hauser, "Features of the Public Sphere," 439.

[59] Michael Warner, *Publics and Counterpublics* (New York: Zone, 2002), 117.

[60] The Black Public Sphere Collective, ed., *The Black Public Sphere* (Chicago: University of Chicago Press, 1995).

[61] George A. Kennedy, *Classical Rhetoric and Its Christian and Secular Tradition from Ancient to Modern Times,* 2nd ed. (Chapel Hill: University of North Carolina Press, 1999): 20.

[62] Eva C. Keuls, *The Reign of the Phallus* (New York: Harper and Row, 1985), 391.

[63] Fraser, "Rethinking the Public Sphere," 123, italics added.

[64] Fraser, "Rethinking the Public Sphere," 124.

[65] Rita Felski, *Beyond Feminist Aesthetics* (Cambridge, MA: Harvard University Press, 1989), 12.

[66] Catharine A. MacKinnon, *Women's Lives, Men's Laws* (Cambridge, MA: Harvard University Press, 2005), 111.

[67] Emma Frances Bloomfield, "Rhetorical Constellations and the Inventional/Intersectional Possibilities of #MeToo," *Journal of Communication Inquiry* 43, no. 4 (2019): 394–414, https://doi.org/10.1177/0196859919866444.

[68] Catherine Squires, "The Black Press and the State: Attracting Unwanted (?) Attention," in *Counterpublics and the State,* ed. Robert Asen and Daniel C. Brouwer, 111–136 (Albany: State University of New York Press, 2001), 132, n. 1, italics added. In addition to discussing enclaved and oscillating publics, Squires offers two additional levels of distinction: a counterpublic "engages in mass actions to assert its needs . . . utilizing disruptive social movement tactics to make demands on the state," and parallel publics "work in conjunction with other [publics] on equal footing." For our purposes, her discussion of oscillation and enclaved publics is the most useful.

[69] bell hooks does not capitalize her name. Her birth name is Gloria Jean Watkins. She chose the name of bell hooks in remembrance of her lineage (she took her great-grandmother's name), as well as to distinguish her voice from Gloria Watkins's. The pseudonym and the lowercase letters signify the importance of her ideas and writing instead of her socially constructed identity.

[70] bell hooks, *Talking Back: Thinking Feminist, Thinking Black* (Boston: South End, 1989), 29.

[71] Asen and Brouwer, "Introduction: Reconfigurations," 8.

[72] Jane Mansbridge, "Using Power/Fighting Power: The Polity," in *Democracy and Difference: Contesting the Boundaries of the Political,* ed. Seyla Benhabib, (Princeton, NJ: Princeton University Press, 1996), 58.

[73] Hasian and Delgado, "Trials and Tribulations," 259.

[74] Daniel C. Brouwer, "ACT-ing UP in Congressional Hearings," in *Counterpublics and the State,* ed. Robert Asen and Daniel C. Brouwer, (Albany: State University of New York Press, 2001), 132, n. 1.

[75] Kristy Maddux, "When Patriots Protest: The Anti-Suffrage Discursive Transformation of 1917," *Rhetoric and Public Affairs* 7, no. 3 (Fall 2004): 283–310.

[76] United Farm Workers, *Take Our Jobs,* 2010, http://www.takeourjobs.org.

[77] United Farm Workers, "Stephen Colbert & Farmworkers Take Fight to Congress," 2010, http://action.ufw.org/page/s/colbert92410.

[78] Fraser, "Rethinking the Public Sphere," 99–100.

[79] Asen and Brouwer, "Introduction: Reconfigurations," 20.

[80] Felski, *Beyond Feminist Aesthetics,* 166.

[81] Lisa A. Flores, "Creating Discursive Space through a Rhetoric of Difference: Chicana Feminists Craft a Homeland," *Quarterly Journal of Speech* 82 (1996): 142–156.

[82] Santa Ana, *Brown Tide Rising,* 298–299.

[83] Warner, *Publics and Counterpublics,* 57.

[84] Dana Cloud, "Connection and Action in Public Sphere Studies: Conversations about What We Do and Why We Do It" (presentation at the National Communication Association preconference, Chicago, November 15, 2006).

[85] Joshua P. Ewalt, Jessy J. Ohl, and Damien Smith Pfister, "Activism, Deliberation, and Networked Public Screens: Rhetorical Scenes from the Occupy Movement in Lincoln, Nebraska (Parts 1 and 2)," *Cultural Studies <=> Critical Methodologies* 13, no. 3 (2013): 184.

[86] Occupy Wall Street, "About," accessed July 7, 2014, http://occupywallst.org/about.

[87] Phaedra C. Pezzullo, "Contextualizing Boycotts and Buycotts: The Impure Politics of Consumer-Based Advocacy in an Age of Global Ecological Crises," *Communication and Critical/Cultural Studies* 8, no. 2 (June 2011): 125–126.

[88] Pezzullo, "Contextualizing Boycotts and Buycotts," 131.

[89] Pezzullo, "Contextualizing Boycotts and Buycotts," 140.

[90] Pezzullo, "Contextualizing Boycotts and Buycotts," 129.

[91] Clifford Rechtschaffen, Eileen Gauna, and Catherine O'Neill, *Environmental Justice: Law, Policy & Regulation,* 2nd ed. (Durham, NC: Carolina Academic Press, 2009), esp. excerpt from Vicki Been.

[92] Benjamin Chavis, "Concerning the Historical Evolution of the 'Environmental Justice Movement' and the Definition of the Term: 'Environmental Racism,'" September 4, 2009, http://www.drbenjaminchavis.com/pages/landing?Concerning-the-Historical -Evolution-of-t=1&blockID=73318&feedID=3359.

[93] For an explanation of Dewey's position, see Asen and Brouwer, "Introduction: Reconfigurations," 1.

[94] Asen and Brouwer, "Introduction: Reconfigurations," 1.

[95] Dewey, *The Public and Its Problems,* 30.

[96] Sarah Aboulhosn, "18 Facebook Statistics Every Marketer Should Know in 2020," *SproutSocial,* August 3, 2020, https://sproutsocial.com/insights/facebook-stats-for-marketers/.

[97] Pew Research Center, "Mobile Fact Sheet," February 5, 2018, https://www.pewinternet.org/fact-sheet/mobile/.

[98] Andrew Perrin and Monica Anderson, "Share of U.S. Adults Using Social Media, Including Facebook, Is Mostly Unchanged since 2018," Pew Research Center, April 10, 2019, https://www.pewresearch.org/fact-tank/2019/04/10/share-of-u-s -adults-using-social-media-including-facebook-is-mostly-unchanged-since-2018/.

[99] Bob Simon, "How a Slap Sparked Tunisia's Revolution," *60 Minutes,* February 20, 2011, http://www.cbsnews.com/stories/2011/02/20/60minutes/main20033404.shtml.

[100] Hillary Clinton, "Internet Rights and Wrongs: Choices and Challenges in a Networked World," February 15, 2011, http://www.state.gov/secretary/rm/2011/02/156619.htm.

[101] Sarah J. Jackson, Moya Bailey, and Brooke Foucault Welles, *#Hashtag Activism: Networks of Race and Gender Justice* (Boston: The MIT Press, 2020).

[102] Vivian Sobchack, "Democratic Franchise and the Electronic Frontier," in *Cyberfutures: Culture and Politics on the Information Superhighway,* ed. Ziauddin Sardar and Jerome R. Ravetz (New York: New York University Press, 1996), 82.

[103] Sheri Madigan, Anh Ly, Christina L. Rash, et al., "Prevalence of Multiple Forms of Sexting Behavior among Youth: A Systematic Review and Meta-Analysis," *JAMA Pediatrics* 172, no. 4 (2018): 327–335, https://doi.org/10.1001/jamapediatrics.2017.5314.

[104] Aaron Smith, "The Internet's Role in Campaign 2008," Pew Internet & American Life Project, April 15, 2009, http://www.pewinternet.org/Reports/2009/6—The-Internets -Role-in-Campaign-2008.aspx.

[105] Aaron Smith and Maeve Duggan, "The State of the 2012 Election—Mobile Politics," Pew Research Internet Project, October 9, 2012, http://www.pewinternet.org/2012/10 /09/the-state-of-the-2012-election-mobile-politics.

[106] Darrell M. West, "Communications Lessons from the 2012 Presidential Election," Brookings.edu, November 6, 2012, http://www.brookings.edu/blogs/up-front/posts /2012/11/06-election-communications-west.

[107] "Election 2016: Campaigns as a Direct Source of News," Pew Research Center, July 18, 2016, https://www.journalism.org/2016/07/18/election-2016-campaigns-as-a-direct -source-of-news/.

108 Saud Alashri, Vikash Bajaj, Srivatsav Kandala, and Kevin C. Desouza, "Tracking Presidential Campaigns on Facebook," Brookings Institute, April 13, 2016, https://www.brookings.edu/blog/techtank/2016/04/13/tracking-presidential -campaigns-on-facebook/.

109 Alashri, Bajaj, Kandala, and Desouza, "Tracking Presidential Campaigns."

110 Jon Swartz, "The Election Is Being Fought on Social Media amid the Pandemic," *MarketWatch,* October 12, 2020, https://www.marketwatch.com/story/the-election -is-being-fought-on-social-media-amid-the-pandemic-11602529760.

111 Monica Anderson, Skye Toor, Lee Rainie, and Aaron Smith, "Public Attitudes toward Political Engagement on Social Media," Pew Research Center, July 11, 2018, https://www.pewinternet.org/2018/07/11/public-attitudes-toward-political -engagement-on-social-media/.

112 Brenda Chan, "Imagining the Homeland: The Internet and Diasporic Discourse of Nationalism," *Journal of Communication Inquiry* 29, no. 4 (October 2005): 336–368; and Peter Dahlgren, "The Internet, Public Spheres, and Political Communication: Dispersion and Deliberation," *Political Communication* 22, no. 2 (April/June 2005): 147–162.

113 See, for example, Graeme Browning, *Electronic Democracy: Using the Internet to Influence American Politics* (Wilton, CT: Pemberton, 1996); Lawrence K. Grossman, *The Electronic Republic: Reshaping Democracy in the Information Age* (New York: Viking, 1995); Kevin A. Hill and John E. Hughes, *Cyberpolitics: Citizen Activism in the Age of the Internet* (Lanham, MD: Rowman and Littlefield, 1998); and Jay Kinney, "Is There a New Political Paradigm Lurking in Cyberspace?" in *Cyberfutures: Culture and Politics on the Information Superhighway,* ed. Ziauddin Sardar and Jerome R. Ravetz, 138–153 (New York: New York University Press, 1996).

114 Cass R. Sunstein, *Going to Extremes: How Like Minds Unite and Divide* (New York: Oxford University Press, 2009), 81.

115 Christopher J. Stapel, *No Longer Alone: A Resource Manual for Rural Sexual Minority Youth and the Adults Who Serve Them* (pamphlet), National Youth Advocacy Coalition, http://www.nyacyouth.org/docs/ruralyouth/NoLongerAlone.pdf.

116 Lincoln Dahlberg, "Rethinking the Fragmentation of the Cyberpublic: From Consensus to Contestation," *New Media and Society* 9, no. 5 (2007): 830.

117 John Horrigan, Kelly Garrett, and Paul Resnick, *The Internet and Democratic Debate,* Pew Internet & American Life Project, 2004, http://www.pewinternet.org/Reports /2004/The-Internet-and-Democratic-Debate.aspx.

118 Bridget Blodgett and Anastasia Salter, "*Ghostbusters* is for Boys: Understanding Geek Masculinity's Role in the Alt-Right," *Communication Culture & Critique* 11, no. 1 (2018): 133–146.

119 Shira Chess and Adrienne Shaw, "A Conspiracy of Fishes, or, How We Learned to Stop Worrying about #Gamergate and Embrace Hegemonic Masculinity," *Journal of Broadcasting & Electronic Media* 59, no. 1 (2015): 208–220, https://doi.org/10.1080/08838151.2014.999917.

120 Becky Gardiner, Mahana Mansfield, Ian Anderson, Josh Holder, Daan Louter, and Monica Ulmanu, "The Dark Side of Guardian Comments," *Guardian,* April 12, 2016, https://www.theguardian.com/technology/2016/apr/12/the-dark-side-of-guardian -comments?CMP=share_btn_link.

121 Gardiner, et al., "The Dark Side."

122 Alexandra Samuel, "How to Live with Internet Trolls," *JSTOR Daily,* September 20, 2016, https://daily.jstor.org/how-to-live-with-internet-trolls/.

[123] Patty Riley, James Klumpp, and Thomas Hollihan, "Democratizing the Lifeworld of the 21st Century: Evaluating New Democratic Sites for Argument," in *Argument and Values,* ed. Sally Jackson (Annandale, VA: National Communication Association, 1995), 259.

[124] Patty Riley, Thomas Hollihan, and James Klumpp, "The Dark Side of Community and Democracy: Militias, Patriots and Angry White Guys," in *Argument in a Time of Change: Definitions, Frameworks, and Critiques,* ed. James F. Klumpp (Annandale, VA: National Communication Association, 1997), 205.

[125] Harry Potter Alliance, "What We Do," 2014, http://thehpalliance.org/what-we-do.

[126] Amar Toor, "UNICEF Says Facebook 'Likes' Won't Save Children's Lives," *Verge,* May 3, 2013, http://www.theverge.com/2013/5/3/4296194/unicef-facebook -activism-ad-campaign-likes-dont-save-lives.

[127] Brendan Rigby, "Slacktivists Take Note: We Don't Like Your Likes," WhyDev.org, July 15, 2013, http://www.whydev.org/slacktivists-take-note-we-dont-like-your-likes.

[128] AJ Willingham, "Slacktivism Is Over: The #NeverAgain Movement Is about What's Next," CNN, March 25, 2018, https://www.cnn.com/2018/03/25/us/march-for-our -lives-slacktivism-trnd/index.html; and Nicole Gallucci, "America's Youth Could Put Slacktivism behind Us Once and for All," *Mashable,* March 27, 2018, https://mashable.com/2018/03/27/trump-era-end-of-slacktivism/#LY_55rvAZgq4.

[129] Amy Mitchell, Michael Barthel, Elisa Shearer, and Jeffrey Gottfried, "Pathways to News," *The Modern News Consumer,* Pew Research Center, July 7, 2016, https://www.journalism.org/2016/07/07/pathways-to-news/.

[130] Katerina Eva Matsa and Elisa Shearer, "News Use across Social Media Platforms 2018," Pew Research Center, September 10, 2018, https://www.journalism.org/2018/09/10 /news-use-across-social-media-platforms-2018/.

[131] Alexandre Bovet and Hernán A. Maske, "Influence of Fake News in Twitter during the 2016 US Presidential Election," *Nature Communications* 10 (2019), https://www.nature.com/articles/s41467-018-07761-2.

[132] Maria Temming, "How Twitter Bots Get People to Spread Fake News," *Science News,* November 20, 2018, https://www.sciencenews.org/article/twitter-bots-fake-news-2016-election.

[133] Office of the Director of National Intelligence, "Russia's Influence Campaign Targeting the 2016 US Presidential Election," Intelligence Community Assessment, January 6, 2017, https://www.dni.gov/files/documents/ICA_2017_01.pdf.

[134] Danielle Kurtzleben, "Did Fake News on Facebook Help Elect Trump? Here's What We Know," NPR, April 11, 2018, https://www.npr.org/2018/04/11/601323233/6-facts -we-know-about-fake-news-in-the-2016-election.

[135] Kathleen Hall Jamieson, *Cyberwar: How Russian Hackers and Trolls Helped Elect a President* (New York: Oxford University Press, 2018).

[136] Jamieson, *Cyberwar,* 28.

[137] Jamieson, *Cyberwar,* 39.

[138] Jamieson, *Cyberwar,* 63.

[139] Scott Jasper, "Why Foreign Interference Fizzled in 2020," Atlantic Council, November 23, 2020, https://www.atlanticcouncil.org/blogs/new-atlanticist/why -foreign-election-interference-fizzled-in-2020/.

[140] "Project Background," End of Term Web Archive, http://eotarchive.cdlib.org/background.html.

[141] "About," Environmental Data & Justice Initiative, https://envirodatagov.org/about/.

[142] "Archiving Data," EDGI, https://envirodatagov.org/archiving/.

143 Morgan Currie and Britt S. Paris, "How the 'Guerrilla Archivists' Saved History—and Are Doing It Again under Trump," *The Conversation,* February 21, 2017, https://theconversation.com/how-the-guerrilla-archivists-saved-history-and-are -doing-it-again-under-trump-72346.

144 Currie and Paris, "How the 'Guerrilla Archivists.'"

145 Jacob Poushter, "Smartphones Are Common in Advanced Economies, but Digital Divides Remain," Pew Research Center, April 21, 2017, https://www.pewresearch.org/fact-tank/2017/04/21/smartphones-are-common -in-advanced-economies-but-digital-divides-remain/.

146 Poushter, "Smartphones Are Common."

147 Phillippa Biggs and Youlia Lozanova, *The State of Broadband 2017: Broadband Catalyzing Sustainable Development,* UNESCO, September 2017, 12, https:// www.itu.int/dms_pub/itu-s/opb/pol/S-POL-BROADBAND.18-2017-PDF-E.pdf.

148 International Telecommunications Union, *Measuring the Information Society Report,* 2016, 179, https://www.itu.int/en/ITU-D/Statistics/Documents/publications /misr2016/MISR2016-w4.pdf.

149 Fraser, "Rethinking the Public Sphere," 123.

150 Catherine Helen Palczewski, "Cyber-Movements, New Social Movements, and Counterpublics," in *Counterpublics and the State,* ed. Robert Asen and Daniel C. Brouwer, 161–210 (Albany: State University of New York Press, 2001), 171–172.

151 Asen and Brouwer, "Introduction: Reconfigurations," 6.

152 A. J. Liebling, "Do You Belong in Journalism?," *New Yorker,* May 14, 1960, 105.

153 The authors thank Damien Pfister for his assistance in working through this explanation.

154 Trent Lott, "Toast Delivered at Sen. Strom Thurmond (R-SC) 100th Birthday Celebration," December 5, 2002, transcribed from http://web.archive.org/web /20021207064833/www.c-span.org/politics.

155 Damien Pfister, "The Logos of the Blogosphere: Flooding the Zone, Invention, and Attention in the Lott Imbroglio," *Argumentation and Advocacy* 47, no. 3 (Winter 2011), 142–3.

156 Yochai Benkler, *The Wealth of Networks: How Social Production Transforms Markets and Freedom* (New Haven, CT: Yale University Press, 2006), 10, http://www.benkler.org/Benkler_Wealth_Of_Networks.pdf.

157 Benkler, "The Wealth of Networks," 220.

158 Damien Pfister, personal correspondence with Catherine Palczewski, June 2, 2014.

159 Carly Ledbetter, "Here's Why the FDA's New Cheesemaking Ban is Terrible News for Artisans," Huffington Post, June 10, 2014, http://www.huffingtonpost.com/2014/06 /10/fda-banning-aging-cheese-_n_5479816.html; and Jeanne Carpenter, "Game Changer: FDA Rules No Wooden Boards in Cheese Aging," *Cheese Underground,* June 7, 2014, http://cheeseunderground.blogspot.com/2014/06/game-changer-fda -rules-no-wooden-boards.html.

160 Ledbetter, "Here's Why."

161 For more information, see *Zapatistas in Cyberspace,* a website maintained by economics professor Harry M. Cleaver, Jr., http://indigenouspeople.net/zapatist.htm. We are particularly thankful to Professor Cleaver for his expert feedback on the discussion in this section of the events in Chiapas.

162 Harry M. Cleaver, Jr., "The Chiapas Uprising and the Future of Class Struggle in the New World Order," February 14, 1994, la.utexas.edu/users/hcleaver/kcchiapasuprising.html.

163 Donna Kowal, "Digitizing and Globalizing Indigenous Voices: The Zapatista Movement," in *Critical Perspectives on the Internet,* ed. Greg Elmer, 105–126 (Lanham, MD: Rowman and Littlefield, 2002), 111.

164 Harry Cleaver, "The Zapatistas and the Electronic Fabric of Struggle," la.utexas.edu/users/hcleaver/zaps.html.

165 "Mission Statement," indymedia.us, accessed January 26, 2011, http://indymedia.us/en/static/mission.shtml.

166 Indybay, "Indymedia and Indybay History," accessed August 22, 2021, http://www.indybay.org/newsitems/2005/03/11/17262451.php.

167 Jill Lane, "Digital Zapatistas," *Drama Review* 47, no. 2 (2003): 135.

168 Jesus Barraza, "Celebrating 15 years of Zapatista Struggle," January 5, 2009, http://www.justseeds.org/blog/2009/01/celebrating_15_years_of_zapati.html. Postings also have appeared on the *De Tod@s Para Tod@s* (blog) (see for example http://detodos-paratodos.blogspot.com/2010/05/april-2010-chiapaszapatista-news. html), *the new internationalist* (blog) (see for example http://www.newint.org /blog/majority/2008/06/09/zapatistas-threatened), and *The Frugal Traveler* (blog) (see for example http://frugaltraveler.blogs.nytimes.com/2008/12/09/in-the-village -of-the-zapatistas).

169 Stephen Wray, quoted in B. Paquin, "Hacktivism: Attack of the E-Guerrillas!" *Straits Times* (Singapore), December 13, 1998, 32–33, LexisNexis.

170 Jill Lane, "Digital Zapatistas," *Drama Review* 47, no. 2 (Summer 2003): 129–144.

171 Aaron Hess, "Resistance up in Smoke: Analyzing the Limitations of Deliberation on YouTube," *Critical Studies in Media Communication* 25, no. 5 (December 2009): 427.

172 Coral Davenport, "Federal Agencies Told to Halt External Communications," *New York Times,* January 25, 2017, https://www.nytimes.com/2017/01/25/us/politics/some -agencies-told-to-halt-communications-as-trump-administration-moves-in.html. For a copy of the memo, see "Trump Admin Orders EPA Media Blackout and Contract Freeze," CBS News, January 24, 2017, https://www.cbsnews.com/news /president-trump-administration-orders-epa-media-blackout-contract-freeze/.

173 Davenport, "Federal Agencies Told to Halt."

174 Davenport, "Federal Agencies Told to Halt."

175 Christina Capatides, "Badlands National Park Twitter Account Goes Rogue, Starts Tweeting Scientific Facts," CBS News, January 24, 2017, https://www.cbsnews.com /news/badlands-national-park-twitter-goes-rogue-starts-tweeting-facts-about-the -environment; and Katie Reilly, "A Rogue National Park is Tweeting Out Climate Change Facts in Defiance of Donald Trump," *Time,* January 24, 2017, http://time.com/4645927/badlands-national-park-climate-change-tweets/.

176 Davenport, "Federal Agencies Told to Halt."

177 David Morgan, "Government Science Goes Rogue on Twitter," CBS News, January 26, 2017, https://www.cbsnews.com/news/government-science-goes-rogue-on-twitter-resist/.

178 "A Message for President Trump," accessed April 22, 2019, https://www.altnps. org/.

179 AltUSNatParkService, Twitter, accessed January 29, 2017, https://twitter.com/AltNatParkSer.

180 http://i.imgur.com/4iOsin7.jpg?fb, accessed August 22, 2021.

181 AltNPS, Facebook, accessed August 19, 2017, https://www.facebook.com/AltUSNationalParkService/photos/a.1742440909417307 /1868946893433374/?type=3&theater.

182 Badasslands National Park, Facebook, accessed August 22, 2021.

183 Aragorn inspirational speech meme, *Meme Generator,* accessed August 22, 2021, https://memegenerator.net/instance/75054012/aragorn-inspirational-speech-rangers -shall-lead-the-resistance-park-rangers.

184 Kevin Michael DeLuca and Jennifer Peeples, "From Public Sphere to Public Screen: Democracy, Activism, and the 'Violence' of Seattle," *Critical Studies in Media Communication* 19, no. 2 (June 2002): 129, 131, italics added.

185 DeLuca and Peeples, "From Public Sphere," 132.

186 DeLuca and Peeples, "From Public Sphere," 144.

187 DeLuca and Peeples, "From Public Sphere," 147.

188 DeLuca and Peeples, "From Public Sphere," 145.

189 Joshua P. Ewalt, Jessy J. Ohl, and Damien Smith Pfister, "Activism, Deliberation," 187.

190 Elizabeth A. Brunner and Kevin Michael DeLuca, "The Argumentative Force of Image Networks: Greenpeace's Panmediated Global Detox Campaign," *Argumentation and Advocacy* 52, no. 4 (Spring 2016): 281–299, 284.

191 Brunner and DeLuca, "The Argumentative Force," 285.

192 International Telecommunications Union, "Measuring the Information Society," 179.

193 Brunner and DeLuca, "The Argumentative Force," 285.

194 "C-SPAN by the Numbers," *Washington Post,* March 14, 2004, Nexis-UNI.

195 Thanks to Theodore F. Sheckels for introducing us to this example.

196 Josh Feldman, "Here's Why Democrats' Gun Control Sit-In Isn't Being Broadcast on C-SPAN," *Mediaite,* June 22, 2016, Nexis-UNI; and Amber Phillips, "The Real Reason C-SPAN Cameras Aren't Showing Democrats' Gun Control Sit-In," *Washington Post Blogs,* June 22, 2016, Nexis-UNI.

197 "A Sit-In on the House Floor over Gun Control," *Atlantic* live blog, June 22, 2016, https://www.theatlantic.com/liveblogs/2016/06/house-democrats-gun-control -sit-in/488264/.

198 Rep. John Yarmuth, "A Sit-In," Twitter, June 22, 2016, https://twitter.com/RepJohnYarmuth/status/745645886366191616.

199 "A Sit-In," Nore Kelly blog post, June 22, 2016, 3:06 pm.

200 Deirdre Walsh, Manu Raju, Eric Bradner, and Steven Sloan, "Democrats End House Sit-In Protest over Gun Control," CNN Politics, June 24, 2016, https://www.cnn.com /2016/06/22/politics/john-lewis-sit-in-gun-violence/index.html.

201 Ewalt, Ohl, and Pfister, "Activism, Deliberation."

202 Habermas, "The Public Sphere," 231.

Appendix

Appendix
Rhetorical Traditions and Democracy

KEY CONCEPTS

arête

dissoi logoi

ethos

isonomia

kairos

logos

paideia

pathos

sophist

techne

to prepon

The connections between rhetoric and civic life run deep. From the first emergence of democratic communities in ancient Greece and in the Americas, rhetoric has played a central role. Classicist George A. Kennedy explains that rhetoric was a civic art in ancient Greece and is a phenomenon of all human societies.[1] This appendix explains some of the roots of the modern rhetorical tradition and their connections to democracy in the United States.

Because the term "rhetoric" emerged in ancient Greece, we begin by exploring the cultural context that gave rise to its study. Teachers from the classical Greek tradition, including the sophists, Aspasia, Plato, Isocrates, and Aristotle, have had a profound influence on education, government, and the study of rhetoric in the United States. The classical influences have been both productive and problematic, and Western democratic traditions have inherited both the good and bad. This appendix describes the contributions of the classical Greek era, as well as ways in which they have perpetuated civic inequality. We end with a discussion of the ways that the creation of US democracy was influenced by classical thought and by another democratic tradition: the Haudenosaunee Confederacy.

THE EMERGENCE OF RHETORIC IN CLASSICAL GREECE

The ability to persuade people was essential to life in ancient Greece, just as it is today. Throughout the sixth century BCE, Athenians passed a variety of laws that undermined wealthy aristocrats' power and placed greater power in the hands of all Athenian citizens: men who were neither foreigners nor enslaved. Instead of appointed officials, juries of citizens judged trials. Political decisions, instead of being made by a king, were decided by citizens' votes in the assembly. (This was one of the first times in the history of rhetoric when citizenship as a concept was infused into rhetoric.) All free-born Athenian men had a right to cast their votes on political decisions.[2] Although the Greek model was a step toward democracy, the exclusion of women, enslaved people, and anyone not born in Athens (and these three groups comprised the majority of people living in the city-state) meant Athenian democracy was incomplete. Contemporary democracies continue to grapple with the legacy of these exclusions.

Speaking was central to this early experiment in democracy. Each day, the same ceremonial question opened the gathering of citizens: "Who of those above fifty years of age wishes to address the assembly?"[3] After citizens older than fifty had spoken, all other Athenian citizens who wished to speak were invited to do so. The assembly served as a forum in which male Athenians could speak as equals and debate matters of shared concern, such as alliances, trade, public construction projects, or wars. Because the ancient Greek city-states were constantly feuding, the stakes of these decisions could be life or death. A water clock ensured that every speaker received the same amount of time. Finally, each citizen would vote. The outcome was determined by a simple majority, and all decisions were final.

Because Athenian men considered married women to be suitable only for childbearing and housekeeping, women "were not regarded as fit to partici-pate in serious discussions" and "were denied access to all those places where the boys and men discussed and learned about civic and intellectual affairs."[4] In earlier times, women married to citizens might have visited the agora—an open public space for trade and discussion—to shop and fetch water. During the fifth and fourth centuries BCE, however, classical historian Sarah B. Pomeroy explains that "because fetching water involved social mingling, gossip at the fountain, and possible flirtations," communication from which women married to citizens were ostensibly to be protected, "slave girls were usually sent on this errand."[5] There were women innkeepers and merchants in the agora, but it is not clear from the historical evidence whether they were Athenians, resident foreigners, or enslaved. The only time women married to citizens could uncontroversially move in public was during religious rituals.[6] Enslaved people could participate in many cultural and economic activities (for example, they could be physicians, musicians, and teachers), but they were prohibited from participating in politics in the assembly.

Athens was only one of many Greek city-states. How did a quasi-democratic civic culture take hold in Athens, when most of its neighbors were governed by tyrants (single rulers) or aristocrats (wealthy elites)? Cultural, intellectual, and economic exchanges with other nations and city-states throughout the ancient world played an important part. After a surprising victory over the Persian navy in the Battle of Salamis, Athens suddenly controlled the entire Mediterranean Sea, allowing Athenian merchants to trade goods across southern Europe, northern Africa, and the Middle East. As Athens became a trading hub, merchant ships from across the ancient world stopped in its ports, bringing not only goods to trade, but also new ideas, languages, customs, and religions. Athens became increasingly cosmopolitan as the influx of new ideas challenged existing norms and conventional wisdom.[7] Athens opened itself to strangers in ways that more insular city-states did not.

The growing wealth of Athens that resulted from trade contributed to the development of civic culture. As the Athenian middle-class grew, however, so did the number of citizens able to dedicate time to participating in politics. This growing middle class had an ever-increasing stake in the laws and decisions made in the assembly and, thus, had an incentive to participate actively in government. As in the contemporary United States, however, it was more difficult for poor citizens to participate in political processes. Then, as now, many people who technically had the right to do so could not afford to spend time away from their work to attend the assembly and vote.

By creating a society in which citizens had the power to address their peers as part of collective decision making, as well as the responsibility to represent themselves in court, Athenians created a situation in which rhetoric was a necessary part of public life. High-stakes decisions were made by persuading a majority of one's peers. Rhetorical skill could transform ordinary citizens into powerful leaders or change the outcome of court cases. Thus, "the advanced education of a boy concentrated on the art of rhetoric, with the aim of delivering persuasive speeches at public meetings and winning a fine reputation among men."[8]

The growing number of men able to participate in politics put those who could teach rhetoric in high demand. Rhetoric teachers from across Greece and beyond came to Athens to offer lessons to those who could pay for them. The rhetorical tradition and US democracy have inherited much, both good and bad, from these teachers' lessons.

The importance of rhetoric in Athens also led to its careful study. It also led to disagreements about its role, which continue to the present time: What is the fundamental nature of rhetoric? Is rhetoric good, evil, or indifferent?

The Sophists: Exploring the Possibilities of Rhetoric

Today, the term "sophist" is almost always used in a negative way, connoting lying, trickery, or misleading arguments. Originally, however, the term simply meant a person who was wise or skillful. (Note: both "sophist" and "philosophy," or the love of wisdom, come from the Greek word *sophia,* meaning wisdom or skill.)[9] In fifth century BCE, the term **sophists** referred to *teachers who were wise and skillful in the art of writing and delivering speeches.*

The sophists taught people how to be better public speakers and, on occasion, wrote speeches for people who needed to give them.[10] They maintained that the study of rhetoric was essential to citizenship in the Athenian democracy. They described rhetoric as "the art which seeks to capture in opportune moments that which is appropriate and attempts to suggest that which is possible."[11] Sophists such as Protagoras and Gorgias believed rhetoric could both delight and induce belief. The right thing spoken at the right time could entertain, even as it formed people's knowledge.

Prior to the establishment of Athenian democracy and the growth of a vibrant middle class, the only people who received formal education were elite members of the wealthiest aristocratic families, who could afford to hire tutors who lived in their homes. Because sophists offered to teach anyone who could pay for a lesson, not just those who could afford live-in tutors, they democratized education. For one of the first times in the ancient world, middle- and even working-class people had access to formal education, putting the average citizen on a more equal footing with aristocrats in the courts and assemblies. Because of the sophists' egalitarian belief in education, comparative literature professor Susan C. Jarratt argues, they posed a real "threat . . . to members of the aristocracy eager to undo democratic reforms and return to oligarchic or monarchic government."[12] Unlike Athenian elites, who believed only they themselves possessed innate virtue, "the sophists argued for the most diverse range of human potentialities capable of cultivation by society, for which process public discourse, including the teaching of civic virtue, was essential."[13]

The sophists' convergence in Athens brought together a variety of rhetorical techniques from across the ancient world.[14] Through competition and imitation, they built upon one another's ideas. Thus began the formal study of rhetoric as a **techne,** *an art that could be learned through study and practice and taught to others.* The sophists shared a fundamental belief that through learning the techne of rhetoric, humans could control their destinies and change the conditions of their lives and communities. This belief was revolutionary at the time. In a culture that believed the gods assigned humans their destinies at birth, the sophists claimed that rhetoric allowed practitioners the possibility of building lives and communities of their own choosing.[15]

An essential element of Athenian society was the pursuit of **arête,** or *excellence.* Raised on stories of Homeric heroes such as Achilles, Athenian men were intensely competitive. Their culture valued standing out from peers through bravery and excellence. The creation of a democratic culture and the thoroughly public nature of the assembly gave men another space where they could prove their excellence. In order to help their students stand out as rhetors, the sophists treated rhetoric as a competition that could be won by the person who best understood the circumstances in which they spoke.

Three concepts were central to sophistic teachings on rhetoric: *dissoi logoi, to prepon,* and *kairos.*

Dissoi Logoi. A growing trade empire meant Athenians interacted with people from a variety of cultures. The sophists noticed that people's beliefs differed.[16] Because humans came from various cultures and had various individual perceptions, multiple perspectives existed on every issue. **Dissoi logoi** is the idea that *for every argument, there are one or more opposing arguments.* The sophist Protagoras often receives credit for developing this idea, although it was introduced by an unknown author, who pointed out that beliefs that are deeply held in one culture may be opposed in another. For example "to the Spartans it is seemly that young girls should do athletics and go about with bare arms and no tunics, but to the Ionians this is disgraceful . . . And to [the Spartans] it is seemly for their children not to learn music and letters but to the Ionians it is disgraceful not to know all these things."[17] A practice might be viewed as good or just by some cultures, evil or unjust by others.

The sophists embraced the idea of dissoi logoi, as well as the belief that people decided which argument was right. They did not worry about whether the majority might choose unwisely or oppress the minority, because as long as people maintained a commitment to democracy and public argument, the minority perspective would have many opportunities to be argued more skillfully.[18] Sophists promised to teach their students how to convince audiences which argument to believe. They also promised to teach them how to make the weaker argument into the stronger, leading many, such as Plato, to accuse the sophists of trickery and deceit. (This is one reason that "sophist" is sometimes used in a negative way.) To the sophists, however, the weaker argument was not an argument that was less true, but rather the argument that fewer people believed. In other words, the sophists claimed the ability to change peoples' minds. A rhetor, the sophists believed, could take a position with which people disagreed and convince the majority to support it.

By sophistic standards, what is the weaker or stronger argument is constantly subject to change. For example, in May 1940, only 10 percent of US citizens supported joining the fight against Nazi Germany. Those who argued that the United States should enter the war were making the weaker argument at that time. Today, US people generally think entering World War II was a good decision not only because of the attacks on Pearl Harbor, but as a necessary action to protect the United States, US allies, and people victimized by the Nazi regime.[19] More recently, attitudes about same-sex marriage have shifted. In 2004, only 30 percent of US people supported same-sex marriage equality; in 2019, that number rose to 61 percent.[20] The sophists would view both these shifts as victories of the supposedly weaker argument over the stronger.

Athenian sophists recognized that an argument might sometimes be weaker and sometimes stronger because for many issues about which arguments are made, absolute certainty is not possible. People gather the best information they can, identify the competing perspectives, and determine which conclusion is best. For such an issue, rhetoric is essential. Lacking certainty, the sophists turned to probability and asked: Which argument is most likely to be correct? They would then organize their arguments to demonstrate that their positions were more likely or that their opponents' positions were less likely. Protagoras famously claimed, "Of all things the measure is Man."[21]

Gorgias, one of the most famous sophists, provided an example of making the weaker argument prevail in *The Defense of Palamedes*. Everyone in ancient Greece would have known that Palamedes, a character in Homer's poem *The Iliad*, was executed for betraying the Greeks to the Trojans in exchange for money. In other words, Gorgias defended the innocence of someone every Greek knew was guilty. Gorgias's defense of Palamedes demonstrated how the weaker argument could prevail. How?

Gorgias first argued that Palamedes could not have committed the act without witnesses, yet there were no witnesses. Gorgias then asked, even if Palamedes could have found a way to commit the act without witnesses, how could he have been paid? No one would sell out their country for only a small amount of money, but transporting great amounts of money to Palamedes would surely have been noticed. Next, Gorgias argued that even if the money could have been transported, Palamedes already had more than a person needs. Once a person has more money than they need, that person does not want more money; they most desire glory and honor from their peers. Yet, a traitor would receive no such honor and would lose whatever honor and glory they previously had. Again and again, Gorgias repeated this pattern.

Gorgias's case amounts to the following: If there is no proof of guilt, what are the odds that a person would attempt a crime that would be nearly impossible to commit, in exchange for compensation they cannot receive or do not need, and at the cost of that which is most important to them? With every possibility Gorgias considered, the probability of Palamedes's guilt seems lower. *The Defense of Palamedes* shows how the sophists used probability to guide audiences in the absence of certainty, as well as Gorgias's impressive talents at making the weaker argument seem the stronger.

To Prepon. *To prepon* (in Greek, or decorum in Latin, and translated as proper) means *to recognize the circumstances in which you are speaking and select a rhetorical response appropriate to those circumstances.* What determines what is or is not appropriate? Ultimately, the appropriateness of a rhetorical response is determined by the audience's expectations. What a particular audience perceives as appropriate may differ according to the occasion (a joke that may be appropriate at a wedding toast might be received differently at a funeral) or the subject (certain topics may not be wise to joke about at all). In teaching to prepon, sophists recognized that most speaking situations recur and that audiences' expectations for how a rhetor should speak in these situations are based on how such situations have been addressed in the past.[22] Whether in formal speaking situations such as a commencement address or informal situations such as apologizing to a friend, definitions of what is appropriate come from past experiences. We explore the classical emphasis on the appropriate later in this appendix and in chapter 9, about the rhetorical situation.

Kairos. The sophists also recognized that listeners' responses are influenced not just by the occasion in which rhetoric occurs, but also by the time at which it occurs. *Kairos* is *saying the right thing at the right time.* Notice that this definition has two components: *what* is said and *when* it is said. Rhetoric scholar James L. Kinneavy defines kairos as the "right or opportune time to do something, or right measure in doing something."[23] In other words, kairos has a "dimension of time to it, but also . . . a dimension of measure."[24]

You have probably experienced saying the right thing but at the wrong time, or saying something because you felt that you had to say something, but saying the wrong thing. For example, when people die, you ought to say something to those who loved them to recognize the loss. *When* you say this can depend on how well you knew the person who died and how well you know the person who is grieving: Do you immediately contact the person to express your condolences, or do you wait until you interact with them as part of your regular schedules? Compounding the problem of people's discomfort with writing a sympathy note or talking to a person who has suffered loss is uncertainty about *what* to say, even though you know you should say something. Many helpful guides illustrate what should be said (for example, "I am sorry for your loss" or "I am here for you").

Aspasia

Although Athenian women were kept out of public life, Aspasia's presence indicates that some women were rhetoricians during the Greek classical era. Aspasia was from Miletus (a Greek colony in what is now Turkey), educated, and part of Pericles's inner circle. (Pericles was an influential Athenian statesperson and general.) She taught Athenian boys and girls philosophy and writing sometime after 450 BCE. Because she was a free foreigner, she was able to distinguish herself as a rhetorician and political theorist in a way that Athenian women could not.[25]

As is the case with Socrates, scholars have nothing written by Aspasia from which they might glean a rhetorical theory; they rely on secondary sources and fragments.[26] Despite evidence of Aspasia's influence on contemporaries (including Plato), "writers who would have resisted the idea of a public intellectual and woman such as Aspasia portrayed her almost exclusively as a *hetaera*," a high-class courtesan who is sexualized as primarily a man's companion who is not his wife.[27] Although other sources belittled Aspasia, Socrates counted her as one of the people from whom he learned rhetoric. It also seems likely that Aspasia and Protagoras originated what became known as the Socratic method: a way of arguing and teaching that uses probing questions to clarify assumptions and induce critical thinking.[28] Aspasia is a central figure in the rhetorical tradition, not only because she influenced Plato and Socrates, but also because she demonstrates that one's influence in the public sphere should not be tied to the legal status of citizenship.

Plato: The Dangers of Rhetoric

Although the sophists contributed ideas and techniques that have influenced rhetoric for centuries, many people—both past and present—have criticized their ideas. Plato was the most famous of these critics. Plato, who came from a family of wealthy aristocrats, believed many of the sophists' ideas were useless at best and dangerous at worst. Unlike the work of the sophists, which has survived only in fragments, the majority of Plato's writings survive. His dialogues portray Socrates, his own teacher, as having conversations or arguments with other intellectual figures in Athens. Several dialogues respond to the sophists in general; two depict Socrates arguing with prominent sophists Gorgias and Protagoras. Plato was deeply skeptical of many of the ways the sophists taught and practiced rhetoric, although he eventually did articulate what rhetoric ought to be.

Plato maintained that rhetoric was for the most part evil. He and Socrates believed that people used rhetoric to obscure truth and justice, and that one could only come to know the truth through the use of philosophical methods, such as the Socratic method captured in Plato's dialogues. In these dialogues, Socrates said people often used rhetoric to make the weaker case seem the stronger. Socrates and Plato both maintained that rhetoric could be used to avoid a just punishment or lead a democracy to make poor decisions. Partially as a result of his teachings, and partially as a result of the rhetoric used against him in his trial, Socrates was convicted and sentenced to death.[29]

To understand why Plato was so critical of the sophists, it is important to know a bit about the life and death of Socrates. Socrates lived when Athens was at its most powerful. He served in the Athenian military through three campaigns in its wars with Sparta. He later became a critic of the direction Athenian democracy had taken and argued against multiple unjust jury rulings. As Athens—once the most powerful city-state in Greece—began to lose its long conflict with Sparta, Athenians began turning on each other and looking for someone to blame. After a storm destroyed twenty-five Athenian naval ships, Athenians blamed the generals who left the bodies rather than risk more lives to the storm. A proposal to execute all ten generals was supported unanimously save for one dissenter: Socrates.

Socrates often spoke out against the majority and argued with peers. After the Oracle at Delphi, an important priestess, said that no one was wiser than Socrates, he set out to prove the Oracle wrong. Unlike many of the teachers and political leaders of Athens, he was willing to admit to ignorance, so he wandered through the city and sought out fellow citizens who were believed to be wise. He would begin asking them question after question (in the questioning method likely influenced by Aspasia) to see whether they were as wise as people perceived them to be. No one was. Many respected citizens found themselves confused and flummoxed by Socrates's endless and incisive questions. To make matters worse, Socrates had also begun teaching philosophy to young Athenian students, who followed him when he went out to interrogate Athenian citizens. It is easy to see how the most influential and respected citizens of Athens would be aggravated when their trips to the market were interrupted by Socrates questioning their wisdom and making them look like fools in front of a crowd of young people.

Looking for scapegoats after their defeat by the Spartans, Athenians turned on Socrates, who had repeatedly questioned their judgment. At the trial, three skilled speakers (who had likely been trained by sophists) accused him of two crimes: impiety (not believing in the gods) and corrupting the youth. The sentence for these crimes was death. You might expect Socrates would have used all available rhetorical techniques. Instead, he began his defense with a contrast to the accusers' rhetorical approach, saying, "From me you shall hear the whole truth: not, however, delivered after their manner, in a set oration duly ornamented with words and phrases. No indeed! but I shall use the words and arguments which occur to me at the moment."[30] Even facing death, Socrates resisted using sophistic techniques.

In such a trial, the person accused would typically deny the charges, swear never to offend again, and/or beg for mercy from the court. Not Socrates, who promised never to stop and suggested that constant questioning, arguing, and irritating Athenians was a gift from the gods to help the intellectually lazy Athenians. Socrates told them:

> I am a sort of gadfly, given to the state by the God; and the state is like a great and noble steed who is tardy in his motions owing to his very size, and requires to be stirred into life. I am that gadfly which God has given the state and all day long and in all places am always fastening upon you, arousing and persuading and reproaching you. And as you will not easily find another like me, I would advise you to spare me. [31]

Socrates even went so far as to tell the jury that an appropriate sentence would be to provide him with free meals for life.

This was not a winning defense. Socrates was found guilty and sentenced to death. His trial and death were formative to Plato, whose understanding of rhetoric was shaped by its potential to sway a jury to execute one of their peers for so little an offense. Plato also believed that voters in the Assembly had been persuaded to enter a war with the Spartans that had led Athens to ruin. He concluded that the masses were ignorant. He became deeply skeptical of the use of rhetoric to persuade them and openly hostile to the sophists who taught it.

Plato rejected the sophists' claims that learning rhetorical techniques could help students become more powerful or better people. All his critiques assume one thing about sophistic rhetoric: that the sophists lack knowledge of the Truth. Unlike the sophists, Plato believed that Truth could be known about most topics. Plato suggested that because the sophists claimed they could speak convincingly on any topic, their expertise lay in talking about things rather than knowing things. They were able to speak so convincingly on topics about which they had no expertise by telling audience members what they wanted to hear. Plato concluded that the sophists' rhetoric was focused on flattering an audience rather than telling them the Truth.

The idea that learning rhetoric could make any person more powerful and influential seems uncontroversial, and explains why so many students paid sophists to teach them. Yet, Plato rejected the sophists' claims to offer power by declaring that (1) rhetoric, at least as the sophists practiced it, was not a techne, a skill of artful making or doing, that the sophists were capable of mastering and teaching; (2) audiences were mostly ignorant; and (3) rhetors were bound by the will of those audiences.

Plato suggested that rhetoric could not be taught; that it was just a knack that some people possessed. He rejected the idea that the sophists could offer anything of value. In *Gorgias,* he suggested that techne requires a deep knowledge of the object underlying that craft. A doctor, for example, must have a deep knowledge of the human body. Gorgias, however, claimed to be able to speak persuasively on every topic, and that expertise in speaking would allow him to be more persuasive on issues of health than a doctor. Plato used this medical analogy to contrast rhetoric with philosophy, suggesting that both should be concerned with the wellbeing of people. He then made a series of comparisons: between philosophy and rhetoric, medicine and cookery, and gymnastics and cosmetics. The art of medicine is concerned with health, and doctors—who know the nature of human health—may recommend unpleasant treatments in order to heal their patients. A cook—who does not know the nature of human health—may offer a food that will temporarily make a patient feel better but not truly improve their condition. Similarly, while gymnastics improves the body and makes it stronger, cosmetics temporarily make the body look more attractive without actually changing it. Plato compared the rhetorician to the baker and the cosmetic artist, claiming that they lack knowledge of what is good for people and offer a more pleasant, but less beneficial, path than philosophy does.

Plato thought most people prefer the easy and pleasant to the necessary and good, because they are too ignorant to understand the difference. Whether because he grew up in one of Athens's wealthiest families, because of what happened to Socrates, or because of general observations, Plato had a low opinion of the average person. He was deeply suspicious of democracy, believing the masses lacked the knowledge necessary to guide a state wisely. He believed most people were ignorant and primarily concerned with satisfying their immediate desires. It is these people, Plato suggested, for whom rhetoric is persuasive: when people know little about a topic, it is easy for a skillful speaker to persuade them. It is far more difficult to persuade experts who are knowledgeable about a topic. Plato agreed with Gorgias's claim that a sophist would be more persuasive on medical issues than a doctor, though he thought the doctor would be more persuasive to other doctors. He suggested people who are knowledgeable are more persuasive to others who are knowledgeable, while the ignorant are more persuasive to other ignorant people. Plato thought that what most rhetoric offers is the ability to persuade the ignorant masses by telling them what they want to hear.

But is this ability not still a form of power? If the majority of people are ignorant, doesn't the ability to persuade them make the rhetor powerful? Plato said the opposite is true. He claimed that because rhetoric relies on flattery, telling people what they want to hear, most rhetors could only lead people where they already wanted to go. The masses had supported going to war with Sparta, so it is easy to understand why Plato thought the will of the people was unwise and dangerous. He suggested that if a speaker goes against the desires of an audience, that audience will either ignore them or turn on them. Think back to Socrates, who challenged the beliefs and desires of Athenians and was put to death for it. Plato argued that rhetors frequently attempt to gain power from their audiences, but actually become beholden to the whims of those they seek to lead. Rather than becoming more powerful, Plato said, rhetors are the least powerful people in the state.

Despite his criticisms of both democracy and rhetoric, Plato eventually recognized that those who knew Truth could use rhetoric as a tool to guide the masses to live better lives. In the absence of benevolent dictators who could simply order people to do the right things, rhetoric offered a means through which people with knowledge might convince those without it to live better. In later writings, Plato offered insights into what good rhetoric might look like.[32] He suggested that a True rhetoric has several requirements: speakers must know the Truth of the topic about which they are speaking, understand audiences, employ appropriate delivery, and possess a moral purpose.[33]

Again, when Plato references a speaker, that person is presumed to be male. Although Socrates had some of the most inclusive views on women at the time, believing men's and women's virtue to be the same, Plato's depictions of women were "extremely deprecating."[34] Although Plato saw a role for women and thought those of the elite classes should be taught, it was not because women could possess virtue or possess knowledge, but because they could be a conduit through which knowledge passed to their male children.

At this point, we have reviewed two classical perspectives on rhetoric. The sophists understood rhetoric as an art to be learned. They identified a variety of techniques to help their students become effective rhetors. They believed rhetorical techniques enabled individuals to succeed in their businesses and have a voice in the decisions of their cities. Thus, rhetoric was not simply a good thing, but an essential one for all citizens who wanted a chance to control their own destinies. In contrast, Plato saw rhetoric as a dangerous practice that only worked through flattery. By telling the masses what they want to hear, Plato believed, rhetors could inflame the passions of the ignorant. Bound by the desires of the masses, rhetoric was incapable of offering people the power that the sophists promised. Instead, it forced a culture down the road to ruin by pursuing the desires of the ignorant masses rather than encouraging them to follow wise leaders.

In addition to Plato and the Sophists, two people influenced the study of rhetoric in late fourth-century BCE Athens. Isocrates sought to moderate the excesses of sophistic rhetoric because rhetoric was an important part of civic education. Aristotle, Plato's most famous student, developed a different view of rhetoric that was based on some of Plato's thoughts. He believed that rhetoric was a necessary part of politics and tried to create a systematic approach to it.

Isocrates and Rhetorical Education

Isocrates, a contemporary of Plato, was one of the most important rhetorical thinkers who succeeded the sophists. Unlike the sophists, who moved from place to place teaching, Isocrates created what was possibly the first brick-and-mortar school, several years before Plato founded his academy. Isocrates became the wealthiest and most influential teacher in Athens.[35] During his lifetime, "and well into later classical antiquity, Isocrates was a more central figure in discussions of civic education, and especially the role of rhetorical training in civic education, than Aristotle ever was."[36]

Many scholars see Isocrates as following in the sophists' footsteps and offering significant corrections to some of their ideas. Like the sophists, Isocrates taught for money. He believed rhetoric itself was neither moral nor immoral, and that students (rather than teachers) were responsible for the manner in which rhetoric was used.[37] Unlike the sophists, he argued that rhetoric was a practical tool. His teachings and writings focused on two central aspects of rhetoric: the thematic and the pragmatic.[38] In emphasizing the thematic, he emphasized that rhetoric should focus on important topics. The sophists, by contrast, sometimes gave speeches on trivial matters simply to entertain audiences and display their oratorical abilities. In emphasizing the pragmatic, he emphasized that rhetoric should be used to benefit its listeners and not just the person using it. The sophists, by contrast, often trained students to advance their own interests effectively, sometimes at the expense of their neighbors. In short, Isocrates argued that rhetoric should focus on matters of shared concern and benefit the broader community.[39] According to rhetoric scholar John Poulakos, Isocrates considered that the goal of teaching rhetoric was to educate "pupils to see beyond their own interests and to serve Athens . . . selfishlessly [*sic*]."[40]

Isocrates's *Against the Sophists* offers a concept of rhetoric that corrects what he considered to be the mistakes of the sophists.[41] Whereas the sophists were largely relativists who perceived different cultures and cultural practices as equal, Isocrates believed that the Greeks were ethically superior.[42] The sophists believed that learning a variety of tricks and techniques was a valuable way to become a more effective rhetor; Isocrates believed that many of the sophists' verbal displays were useless in addressing the important challenges facing Athens. The sophists were mostly mercenaries who worked for the sake of attaining money and fame, but Isocrates sought to teach a rhetoric that would benefit Athens.

Like Plato, Isocrates lived at a time when Athens, formerly the most wealthy, powerful, and influential of the Greek city-states, had declined after the war with Sparta. Like many other Athenians, Isocrates believed the sophists had played a role in diminishing Athens, but he also believed rhetoric would play an essential part in returning the city to glory. He argued that rhetoric was the essential human activity: that the ability to persuade one another and come to an agreement on common action is what separates humans from other animals. He recognized the many challenges of democratic self-governance, and believed that the best way to face these challenges was to train citizens to be skillful rhetors.

Isocrates's focus on the thematic and the pragmatic aspects of rhetoric[43] led to an embrace of the Greek notion of **paideia,** *an education intended to produce people capable of excellence.*[44] Rhetorical education was an essential part of this training because "teachers of discourse are able to advance their pupils to a point where they are better men and where they are stronger in their thinking."[45] Like the sophists, Isocrates promised to teach students effective oratory. Unlike the sophists, he claimed the value of such training was not simply in getting one's way in the assemblies and courts, but in the greater good it brought to one's country. By learning to argue effectively, Isocrates believed, people would be able to deliberate wisely and come to more beneficial decisions.

Unlike Plato, who believed a person ought to know the Truth about a topic before engaging in rhetoric, Isocrates recognized that certainty was impossible on some topics. Contemporary society faces topics that pose a similar challenge: What is the government's role in providing healthcare? What is an appropriate amount of gun regulation? What drugs should be legalized for recreational use? These are topics for which there is no absolute Truth to know. Isocrates recognized that people often face situations in which they do not or cannot know with certainty, but still need to act. He believed the best solution to these topics was to train capable rhetors who could skillfully debate the details of such issues and challenge one another's arguments in order to find the best possible solution for their communities.

Aristotle's Treatise *On Rhetoric*

Perhaps no person has had a greater impact on the contemporary study of rhetoric than Aristotle. An extremely influential philosopher and scientist, Aristotle is considered one of the founders of Western philosophy. One of the most influential writings on rhetoric in ancient Greece was his fourth-century BCE treatise, *On Rhetoric*.[46]

Unlike Plato, who was born into one of Athens's wealthiest families, Aristotle immigrated to Athens as a teenager. Despite coming from a less prominent background than Plato, with whom he studied, he became a private tutor to the young prince who was later known as Alexander the Great. Whereas Plato explored topics within philosophy, Aristotle wrote about virtually every topic imaginable, including philosophy, biology, physics, psychology, astronomy, economics, logic, and poetry. The stunning depth and breadth of his writing was influential in both Christian and Muslim intellectual traditions. Historically, Catholic scholarship referred to Aristotle simply as "The Philosopher." Muslim philosophy referred to him as "The First Teacher."[47] In the modern study of rhetoric, Aristotle's shadow still looms large. For much of the twentieth century, analyses of rhetoric relied on applying his ideas to speeches or essays.[48]

Because rhetoric had utility, Aristotle systematized it. He defined rhetoric as "an ability in each [particular] case, to see the available means of persuasion."[49] Notice that this definition says that rhetoric is an *ability to see*. Thus, the use of rhetoric requires analysis of a situation in order to determine how to persuade. For Aristotle, a rhetorical situation "consists of three things: a speaker and a subject on which he speaks and someone addressed, and the objective of the speech relates to the last."[50] In other words, rhetoric is addressed to particular people, on particular occasions, in particular times and societies, about particular issues. Because it is specific to each particular situation, rhetoric is distinct from philosophy, which studies universals.

Persuasion plays a prominent role in Aristotle's definition insofar as a rhetor uses rhetorical proofs to persuade an audience. Aristotle identified three types of artistic proofs used in persuasion: ***ethos,*** *proofs that are "in the character of the speaker";* ***pathos,*** *proofs that lead the audience "to feel emotion";* and ***logos,*** *proofs that rely on "argument itself, by showing or seeming to show something."*[51] He said ethos was the most effective form of proof because an audience who trusted the rhetor would be more receptive to the message. Conversely, if an audience did not trust the rhetor, the rhetor's use of logos and pathos would be ineffective. Aristotle also pointed out that audiences make decisions based on their states of mind, not only on the basis of reasoned appeals. Because emotions play a significant role in the human experience, pathos appeals are an important part of rhetoric. Many decisions people make are based on emotions, taste, and individual preferences.

These decisions are not necessarily irrational. A person's favorite color is based on personal preference. All the logical arguments in the world may not change that preference, but that does not make the preference logically wrong.

Some of Aristotle's most influential writings focused on ethics (how to live a good life). Aristotle believed that politics was a subset of ethics, and that rhetoric was essential to ethical and effective politics. He also believed rhetoric was necessary for political judgment, when people decide how to act in particular circumstances.[52] Part scientist and part philosopher, Aristotle drew on empirical observation to build theories. He set out to examine rhetoric in a way that was more systematic than the sophists' and more practical than Plato's. Aristotle's teaching on rhetoric, simply titled *On Rhetoric,* remains among the most in-depth treatments of the topic. The work describes persuasive proofs and audience analysis, as well as broader philosophical questions about teaching rhetoric and the relationship between rhetoric and practical knowledge.

Aristotle argued for the benefits of knowing your audience and matching your rhetoric to them. He talked extensively about different types of audiences and what motivates each. Whereas Plato suggested that different people are motivated by different aspects of their souls and left it up to rhetors to decide what types of audiences they are addressing, Aristotle claimed audience analysis could be done through observable demographic characteristics. For example, he argued that age can provide clues into what audience members desire. He believed young people are more dominated by their desires than older people, while older audience members are guided less by emotions and more by reason. Where young people are motivated by imagining the future, he said, older people think more of the past. He repeated this sort of analysis for various other types of audiences. Aristotle believed that such distinctions could help rhetors construct their messages more effectively by recognizing what excites and motivates a particular group of people.

Aristotle also addressed some of the philosophical issues that the sophists, Plato, and Isocrates articulated. He rejected Plato's claim that rhetoric is not a techne that can be learned and taught. He combined, developed, and supplemented rhetorical techniques that the sophists identified, and studied rhetoric more systematically than Plato or Isocrates did, proving that it was a techne. To Aristotle, rhetoric is the techne that sought to identify all the available means of persuasion in any given situation.[53] The art lies in the ability to see the particulars of a case, as well as how they interact with more general rhetorical principles. The art of rhetoric requires recognizing what is unique about a particular situation, as well as what recurs (such as genres of speech and types of audience), and choosing an appropriate response.

Like Isocrates, Aristotle believed political deliberation generally happens around issues that do not lend themselves to certainty. In contrast to Plato, who believed rhetors needed to know the Truth before engaging in rhetoric, Aristotle believed that effective rhetoric could help people discover wise paths of action, particularly in situations where certainty and Truth were unavailable. Aristotle discussed practical wisdom as the ability "to deliberate well about what is good and expedient . . . to the good life in general,"[54] then noted that "the man who is capable of deliberating has practical wisdom."[55]

Aristotle did not use "man" generically; he meant *man,* and a very particular type of man. Like Socrates and Plato, he asserted that women and enslaved people were inferior and should be ruled by privileged men.[56] He rejected Socrates's argument that men and women possessed the same virtue, approvingly quoting the poet who asserted that "silence is a woman's glory" and claiming "this is not equally the glory of a man." Aristotle asserted that men should rule because "the slave has no deliberative faculty at all, the woman has, but it is without authority."[57] Although women and enslaved people were subordinated in Greek society long before Plato and Aristotle lived, their influence on political, philosophical, and rhetorical theories "provided a *conceptual* ground for centuries' more exclusions."[58]

Despite his limitations, Aristotle was correct in saying that the ability to judge wisely based on incomplete information is essential to a functioning democracy. Sometimes, action is necessary even in the absence of certainty. Aristotle believed that deliberation can move people closer to truth and certainty, claiming "things that are true and things that are just have a natural tendency to prevail over their opposites, so that if the decisions of judges are not what they ought to be, the defeat must be due to the speakers themselves."[59] In other words, he believed that if ideas are presented and evaluated by rhetorically skilled community members, what is more true and just will win out over competing ideas. When the wrong idea wins out in a political debate, it is a result of a failure to effectively advocate for the better idea. Aristotle's perspective echoes Isocrates's belief in the value of providing a rhetorical education for citizens.

Contemporary Echoes of Sophistic and Platonic Debates

The disagreement between sophists and Platonists persists in contemporary times. You have probably heard someone refer to an argument as "sophistry" or "mere rhetoric." Presidential rhetoric and Supreme Court decisions have been called "sophistry."[60] Plato's attacks gave the sophists and rhetoric a bad name, but contemporary understandings of rhetoric are much closer to that of the sophists and Isocrates than to Plato's. We, the authors, find ourselves closely aligned with the sophistic definition of rhetoric as the art of capturing the right thing to say in the right moment, of determining what is appropriate and possible, and of being able to teach people to use and understand rhetoric better. We are also aligned with Isocrates's notion that rhetoric is a practical tool.

The controversy between the Platonists and the Sophists over the nature of truth also continues today. Some people maintain that an absolute truth exists and simply needs to be discovered. For instance, some people believe the Bible is the inerrant word of God and contains absolute truth by which all people should live. Other people view truth and justice as things that change, based on conditions and the times. The fact that divorce is now acceptable to many people, but once was not, is an example of changing ethical standards. Given our discussion of social reality in chapter 1, you will not be surprised that we have difficulty with Plato's notion of fixed and immutable truth.

The sophists, Isocrates, Plato, and Aristotle do seem to agree that rhetoric is important in a democracy. (This was one reason Plato rejected democracy as the ideal form of government.) History has demonstrated that where democracy is strong, the study of rhetoric is vibrant. Where nondemocratic government prevails, the study of rhetoric either disappears or is taught as merely a form of entertainment.

RHETORIC AND US DEMOCRACY

The legacy of classical ideas about civic culture extends to the foundation of the United States. In mustering popular support for the American revolution, speakers and pamphleteers frequently drew on Aristotle and Cicero (a later Roman states-person).[61] In the public debates over the creation and ratification of the US Constitution, Alexander Hamilton, John Jay, and James Madison published a series of letters, now known as the Federalist Papers, supporting the Constitution. These authors not only drew on classical ideas about civic culture, they actually signed them "Publius," after one of the founders of the Roman republic.

In 1791, Thomas Paine wrote that "what Athens was in miniature, America will be in magnitude."[62] The Fourteenth Amendment to the Constitution, which guarantees equal protection under the law, echoes the Greek idea of *isonomia,* or *equality of political rights.*[63] The English language even has Greek civic attitudes hidden in everyday words. For example, words such as "tyranny" and "idiot" have clear negative connotations in English. No one wants to live under tyranny or be thought of as an idiot. Yet, these words began as simple Greek words. "Tyranny" comes from the word for a government run by a single ruler. "Idiot" comes from the word for a private person who does not speak or participate in civic life. Thousands of years later, the terms for governments that do not allow civic engagement and for people who do not participate in it remain common ways of insulting governments or people.

As the colonists who settled in what came to be known as North America looked for unions on which to model their constitution, they looked not only to classical times, but also to the nearby Haudenosaunee (Iroquois) Confederacy of the Mohawk, Seneca, Onondaga, Oneida, and Cayuga nations.[64] Although debate amongst historians continues about the scope of its influence,[65] they agree that the Haudenosaunee (Iroquois) Confederacy is the world's oldest living participatory democracy[66] and that it influenced the fledgling democracy of the United States.[67] Unlike in classical democracies, women could vote in the Haudenosaunee Confederacy and participate in council meetings, although men whom the women selected spoke most often in the meetings. Women could not serve as council representatives, but in this matrilineal society they had a strong role in defining economic, political, social, and spiritual norms. It was they who nominated men for leadership positions and oversaw their performance.[68] Thus, long before the Nineteenth Amendment to the US Constitution was ratified in 1920, women voted and participated in civic culture in North America. The influence of the Haudenosaunee tradition highlights how problematic and hypocritical it was for the US government to disenfranchise Native Americans. Nearly two hundred years passed before the US government fully ended its "denial of Indian suffrage"; still, efforts to abridge Native American voting rights continue.[69]

The differences between the classical and Haudenosaunee democracies regarding who was allowed to participate in civic culture merit attention to the negative legacies of exclusion, inequality, and oppression, as well as the positive legacies of the classical influences. US democracy and rhetorical practice have work to do to realize the full promise of rhetoric in civic life.

Decades of activism, numerous constitutional amendments, and a Civil War were needed to begin to correct these exclusions and oppressions. The *New York Times*'s "1619 Project," a public memory project designed to mark the four hundredth anniversary of the first ship of enslaved people landing in the English colony of Virginia, has shown that Black people played a central role in demanding US democracy fulfill its promise. Journalist and "1619 Project" creator Nikole Hannah-Jones writes, "Our democracy's founding ideals were false when they were written. Black Americans have fought to make them true."[70]

The work of building a true and inclusive democracy continues. It is work that everyone must do every day. Harvard political science professor Danielle Allen writes that "A constitution is more than paper; it is a plan for constituting political rights and organizing citizenship, for determining who has access to the powers of collective decision making that are used to negotiate a community's economic and social relations."[71] Allen argues that "the United States has had several foundings" and that individuals continue to constitute the nation in every one of their civic interactions.[72] For Allen, the correction to the exclusions and errors in the Constitution can be found in the Declaration of Independence, with its insistence on equality as a necessary condition for freedom. To correct the flaws of the written Constitution, individual members of a community must reconstitute themselves as a people on a daily basis, in daily interactions, by developing habits of civic engagement. Allen argues that "the Declaration of Independence matters because it helps us see that we cannot have freedom *without* equality. It is out of an egalitarian commitment that a people grows—a people that is capable of protecting us all collectively, and each of us individually, from domination."[73]

Allen believes rhetoric plays a central role in the formation of a civic people. The Declaration of Independence demonstrates that "language is one of the most potent resources each of us has for achieving our own political empowerment."[74] She believes that people and institutions need "to cultivate the capacity of citizens to use language effectively enough to influence the choices we make together. The achievement of political equality requires, among other things, the empowerment of human beings as language-using creatures."[75] In other words, democracy and equality require the study of rhetoric because political equality is not just about securing individual liberty; it is also about "engag[ing] all members of a community equally in the work of creating and constantly re-creating that community."[76]

Just as it took work to build and maintain inequalities, it takes persistent work to deconstruct and remedy them. Democracy is not something that is created once and then endures. Instead, for the United States to realize true democracy, it needs liberty *and* equality. Both of these take work to maintain and grow. Democracy requires habits of rhetoric, interaction, argumentation, and debate.

Just as the classical tradition influenced government, it has deeply influenced the study of rhetoric, and not always in productive ways. Rhetoric scholars Martin Law and Lisa Corrigan note that they "understand and appreciate the importance of the Greeks in introducing the vocabulary of citizenship, democratized participation, cultural memory, and the ideals of rhetorical practices into the West," but they also caution against overly tethering rhetoric to that tradition because the Greeks were "unconcerned with or silent about" many important phenomena.[77] According to these scholars, the Greeks were overly concerned with appropriateness and decorum and provided little that helps people understand rhetors "whose ideas, voices, or bodies are considered inherently inappropriate," those rhetors who are disruptors and "reject tactics like persuasion, identification, and political engagement."[78]

Although we are striving to convince you to develop a civic attitude—an openness to argument and a willingness to think about issues and interests beyond your own—we hope you do not hear us as admonishing you to always be appropriate. Those in power tend to define what is appropriate; rhetorical actions that challenge power tend to be deemed inappropriate or lacking in civility. Rhetoric scholars Kristiana Báez and Ersula Ore point out that "civility as a democratic good," grounded in Greek traditions of appropriateness, "cannot be divorced from its historical usage and meaning," despite contemporary praise of that ideal. Citizenship, civility, and civilized society were presumed to be White, in contrast to the "nonwhite 'savage' and 'slave.'"[79] People in power use admonitions to "be civil" against marginalized people who, because they are marginalized, are presumed to be uncivil. Accusations of incivility are used to dismiss those who have good points because powerholders do not like the way the points were made. Conversely, civility is reduced to politeness, which is enacted by avoiding conflict and, hence, avoiding people with whom you might disagree.[80]

Civis is Latin for "citizen" of ancient Rome but also the root word for city. Our embrace of the civic is an embrace of the city, not of notions of civility or citizenship that are built on the exclusion and subordination of others. It embraces the messy, loud interactions with strangers and the need to learn to work with others to improve everyone's lives in a world bound by uncertainty. Civis is about striving toward wholeness, not oneness.

RECOMMENDED READINGS

Báez, Kristiana L., and Ersula Ore. "The Moral Imperative of Race for Rhetorical Studies: On Civility and Walking-in-White in Academe." *Communication and Critical/Cultural Studies* 15, no. 4 (2018): 331–336.

Jarrett, Susan C. *Rereading the Sophists: Classical Rhetoric Refigured.* Carbondale: Southern Illinois University Press, 1998.

Johansen, Bruce E. *Forgotten Founders: Benjamin Franklin, the Iroquois, and the Rationale for the American Revolution.* Cambridge, MA: Harvard Common Press, 1982.

Kennedy, George A. *A New History of Classical Rhetoric.* Princeton, NJ: Princeton University Press, 1994.

ENDNOTES

[1] George A. Kennedy, *Classical Rhetoric and Its Christian and Secular Tradition,* 2nd ed. (Chapel Hill: University of North Carolina Press, 1999), 1–2; George A. Kennedy, *Comparative Rhetoric: A Historical and Cross-Cultural Introduction* (New York: Oxford University Press, 1998), 1–28.

[2] Sarah B. Pomeroy, *Goddesses, Whores, Wives, and Slaves: Women in Classical Antiquity* (New York: Schocken, 1975), 74.

[3] Aeschines, "Against Timarchus," *The Speeches of Aeschines* (New York: Putnam, 1919), 23.

[4] Susan Moller Okin, *Women in Western Political Thought* (Princeton, NJ: Princeton University Press, 1979), 19.

[5] Pomeroy, *Goddesses, Whores, Wives, and Slaves,* 72.

[6] Susan I. Rotroff and Robert D. Lamberton, *Women in the Athenian Agora* (Athens, Greece: Athenian School of Classical Studies, 2006), 13–15.

[7] Thomas B. Farrell, *Norms of Rhetorical Culture* (New Haven, CT: Yale University Press, 1995), 52.

[8] Pomeroy, *Goddesses, Whores, Wives, and Slaves,* 74.

[9] Edward Schiappa, *Protagoras and Logos: A Study in Greek Philosophy and Rhetoric,* 2nd ed. (Columbia: University of South Carolina Press, 2003), 4.

[10] Kennedy, *Classical Rhetoric,* 1–5, 29–30.

[11] John Poulakos, "Toward a Sophistic Definition of Rhetoric," *Philosophy and Rhetoric* 16, no. 1 (1983): 37.

[12] Susan C. Jarratt, "The First Sophists and Feminism: Discourses of the 'Other,'" *Hypatia* 5, no. 1 (Spring 1990): 27–41, 28.

[13] Jarratt, "The First Sophists," 28.

[14] Though sophists taught on a variety of topics, the name eventually became synonymous with teachers of speech.

[15] Harald R. Wohlrapp, *The Concept of Argument: A Philosophical Foundation* (New York: Springer, 2014), 396.

[16] Susan C. Jarrett, *Rereading the Sophists: Classical Rhetoric Refigured* (Carbondale: Southern Illinois University Press, 1998), 11.

[17] Rosamond Kent Sprague (trans.), "Dissoi Logoi or Dialexis," *Mind* 77, no. 306 (April 1968): 155–167, 157–158.

[18] John Poulakos and Takis Poulakos, *Classical Rhetorical Theory* (Boston, MA: Houghton Mifflin, 1999), 38.

[19] United States Holocaust Memorial Museum, "How Did Public Opinion about Entering World War II Change between 1939 and 1941?," *Americans and the Holocaust,* accessed August 22, 2021, https://exhibitions.ushmm.org/americans-and-the -holocaust/us-public-opinion-world-war-II-1939-1941.

[20] Pew Research Center, "Attitudes on Same-Sex Marriage," May 14, 2019, https://www.pewforum.org/fact-sheet/changing-attitudes-on-gay-marriage/.

[21] Wohlrapp, *The Concept of Argument,* 396.

[22] John Poulakos, "Toward a Sophistic Definition," 35–48

[23] James L. Kinneavy, "Kairos: A Neglected Concept in Classical Rhetoric," in J. D. Moss, ed., *Rhetoric and Praxis: The Contribution of Classical Rhetoric to Practical Reasoning* (Washington, DC: Catholic University Press), 80. See also James L. Kinneavy and Catherine R. Eskin, "Kairos in Aristotle's *Rhetoric,*" *Written Communication* 17, no, 3 (July 2000): 432–444.

[24] James Kinneavy and Roger Thompson, "Kairos Revisited: An Interview with James Kinneavy," *Rhetoric Review* 19, no. 1/2 (Autumn 2000): 75–76.

[25] Kathleen Ethel Welch and Karen D. Jobe, "Aspasia of Miletus," in *Classical Rhetoric and Rhetoricians,* eds. Michelle Baillif and Michael G. Moran (New York: Greenwood, 2005), 65–68.

[26] The complexities involved in doing history about Aspasia are detailed in Xin Liu Gale, "Historical Studies and Postmodernism: Rereading Aspasia of Miletus," *College English* 62, no. 3 (2000): 361–386.

[27] A. Cheree Carlson, "Aspasia of Miletus: How One Woman Disappeared from the History of Rhetoric," *Women's Studies in Communication* 17, no. 1 (1994): 26–44.

[28] Susan C. Jarratt and Rory Ong, "Aspasia: Gender, Rhetoric, and Colonial Ideology," in *Reclaiming Rhetorica: Women in the Rhetorical Tradition,* ed. Andrea A. Lunsford (Pittsburgh: University of Pittsburgh Press, 1995), 15. See also Cheryl Glenn, "Remapping Rhetorical Territory," *Rhetoric Review* 13, no. 2 (Spring 1995): 287–303.

[29] I. F. Stone, *The Trial of Socrates* (New York: Anchor, 1989); and Plato, *Apology,* trans. Benjamin Jowett, *The Internet Classics Archive,* para. 1, http://classics.mit.edu/Plato/apology.html.

[30] Plato, *Apology.*

[31] Plato, *Apology.*

[32] This happens most directly in the dialogue *Phaedrus,* although Plato addresses rhetoric in the *Symposium* and *Republic.* See Nathan Crick and John Poulakos, "Go tell Alcibiades: Tragedy, Comedy, and Rhetoric in Plato's Symposium," *Quarterly Journal of Speech* 94, no. 1 (2008): 1–22.

[33] Joe Sachs, *Plato Gorgias and Aristotle Rhetoric* (Newburyport, MA: Focus, 2009).

[34] Okin, *Women in Western Political Thought,* 21–22.

[35] Andrew Ford, "The Price of Art in Isocrates: Formalism and the Escape from Politics," in *Rethinking the History of Rhetoric,* ed. Takis Poulakos (Boulder, CO: Westview), 37.

[36] David Depew and Takis Poulakos, *Isocrates and Civic Education* (Austin: University of Texas Press, 2004), 2.

[37] John Poulakos, *Sophistical Rhetoric in Classical Greece* (Columbia: University of South Carolina Press, 1995), 113.

[38] Werner Jaeger, *Paideia: The Ideals of Greek Culture,* 3 vols., trans. Gilbert Highet (New York: Oxford University Press, 1939–1944), 60–61.

[39] Poulakos, *Sophistical Rhetoric,* 132–133.

[40] Poulakos, *Sophistical Rhetoric,* 135.

[41] Niall Livingstone, "Writing Politics: Isocrates' Rhetoric of Philosophy," *Rhetorica: A Journal of the History of Rhetoric* 25, no. 1 (2007): 15–34.

[42] Richard Leo Enos, *Greek Rhetoric before Aristotle,* rev. and expanded ed. (Anderson, SC: Parlor Press, 2011).

[43] Werner Jaeger, *Paideia: The Ideals of Greek Culture,* 3 vols, trans. Gilbert Highet (New York: Oxford University Press, 1939–1944), 60–61.

[44] The notion of paideia precedes Isocrates and is at least as old as Homer. For more on Isocrates's version of paideia, see Kathryn A. Morgan, "The Education of Athens: Politics and Rhetoric in Isocrates (and Plato)," in *Isocrates and Civic Education,* ed. David Depew and Takis Poulakos (Austin: University of Texas Press, 2004), 125–154.

[45] Isocrates, *Antidosis,* vol. 2, trans. George Norlan (New York: Putnam, 1928), 289.

[46] Aristotle, *On Rhetoric,* trans. George A. Kennedy (New York: Oxford University Press, 1991). See Kennedy's "Prooemion," x–xi.

[47] Cristina D'Ancona, "Greek Sources in Arabic and Islamic Philosophy," *Stanford Encyclopedia of Philosophy,* February 23, 2017, rev. November 28, 2017, https://plato.stanford.edu/entries/arabic-islamic-greek/.

[48] Edwin Black, *Rhetorical Criticism: A Study in Method* (Madison: University of Wisconsin Press, 1978).

[49] Aristotle, *On Rhetoric,* 1.2.1 [1355].

[50] Aristotle, *On Rhetoric,* 1.3 [1358b].

[51] Aristotle, *On Rhetoric,* 1.2 [1356a–60], italics added.

[52] Danielle S. Allen, *Talking to Strangers: Anxieties of Citizenship since Brown v. Board of Education* (Chicago, IL: University of Chicago Press, 2004), 141.

[53] Aristotle, *On Rhetoric,* 1.2 [1355 b-26]

[54] Aristotle, *Nichomachean Ethics,* 7.4 [1340a-25]

[55] Aristotle, *Nichomachean Ethics,* 7.4 [1340a-30]. Despite believing in the power of teaching effective rhetorical practices, Aristotle also believed practical wisdom is a virtue that not everyone can possess.

[56] Okin, *Women in Western Political Thought,* 79, 81; and Pomeroy, *Goddesses, Whores, Wives, and Slaves,* 74, 230.

[57] Aristotle, *Politics,* 1254b3–1277b25, in Mary R. Lefkowitz and Maureen B. Fant, *Women's Life in Greece and Rome: A Source Book in Translation* (Baltimore, MD: Johns Hopkins University Press, 1982), 64.

[58] Jarratt, "The First Sophists," 28.

[59] Aristotle, *On Rhetoric,* 1.1 [1355a-25].

[60] Ted Abram, "Obama and UNIVISION: Sophistry and Missed Questions," States News Service, September 27, 2012, LexisNexis; and "Supreme Court Sophistry," *New York Post,* June 29, 2012, LexisNexis.

[61] Bernard Bailyn, *The Ideological Origins of the American Revolution* (Cambridge, MA: Belknap, 1992), 23.

[62] Thomas Paine, *The Rights of Man* (New York: Eckler, 1892), 172.

[63] W. G. De Burgh, *The Legacy of the Ancient World* (Baltimore: Penguin, 1963).

[64] "Iroquois Constitution: A Forerunner to Colonists' Democratic Principles," *New York Times,* June 28, 1987, https://www.nytimes.com/1987/06/28/us/iroquois-constitution -a-forerunner-to-colonists-democratic-principles.html.

[65] Louis Jacobson, "Viral Meme Says Constitution 'Owes Its Notion of Democracy to the Iroquois,'" *Politifact,* December 2, 2014, https://www.politifact.com/truth-o-meter/statements/2014/dec/02 /facebook-posts/viral-meme-says-constitution-owes-its-notion-democ/.

[66] Congress has officially recognized the role of the Haudenosaunee Confederacy as a model for the structure of U.S. government. See Terri Hansen, "How the Iroquois Great Law of Peace Shaped U.S. Democracy," PBS, December 13, 2018, https://www.pbs.org/native-america/blogs/native-voices/how-the-iroquois -great-law-of-peace-shaped-us-democracy/#3.

[67] Bruce E. Johansen, *Forgotten Founders: Benjamin Franklin, the Iroquois, and the Rationale for the American Revolution* (Cambridge, MA: Harvard Common Press, 1982); and Lester C. Olson, *Benjamin Franklin's Vision of American Community: A Study in Rhetorical Iconology* (Columbia: University of South Carolina Press, 2004), 18, 36, 122.

[68] Nancy Shoemaker, "The Rise or Fall of Iroquois Women," *Journal of Women's History* 2, no. 3 (Winter 1991): 39–57.

[69] Daniel McCool, Susan M. Olson, and Jennifer L. Robinson, *Native Vote: American Indians, the Voting Rights Act, and the Right to Vote* (New York, NY: Cambridge University Press, 2007). See also "Securing Indian Voting Rights," *Harvard Law Review* 129, April 8, 2016, 1731+, https://harvardlawreview.org/2016/04/securing-indian-voting-rights/.

[70] Hannah-Jones, "The 1619 Project."

[71] Danielle Allen, *Talking to Strangers: Anxieties of Citizenship since Brown v. Board of Education* (Chicago: University of Chicago Press, 2004), 6.

[72] Allen, *Talking to Strangers,* 6.

[73] Danielle Allen, *Our Declaration* (New York: Liveright, 2014), 21.

[74] Allen, *Our Declaration*, 21.

[75] Allen, *Our Declaration*, 21.

[76] Allen, *Our Declaration*, 34.

[77] Martin Law and Lisa M. Corrigan, "On White-Speak and Gatekeeping: or, What Good Are the Greeks?," *Communication and Critical/Cultural Studies* 15, no. 4 (2018): 327.

[78] Law and Corrigan, "On White-Speak."

[79] Kristiana L. Báez and Ersula Ore, "The Moral Imperative of Race for Rhetorical Studies: On Civility and Walking-in-White in Academe," *Communication and Critical/Cultural Studies* 15, no. 4 (2018): 331.

[80] Dreama Moon, "White Enculturation and Bourgeois Ideology: The Discursive Production of 'Good (White) Girls,'" in *Whiteness: The Communication of Social Identity,* ed. Thomas K. Nakayama and Judith N. Martin (Thousand Oaks, CA: Sage, 1999), 177–197; C. Kyle Ruddick and Kathryn B. Golsan, "Civility and White Institutional Presence: An Exploration of White Students' Understanding of Race-Talk at a Traditionally White Institution," *Howard Journal of Communications* 29, no. 4 (2018): 335–352, https://doi.org.10.1080/10646175.2017.1392910; and Nina Lozano-Reich and Dana Cloud, "The Uncivil Tongue: Invitational Rhetoric and the Problem of Inequality," *Western Journal of Communication* 73, no. 2 (2009): 220–226, https://doi.org.10.1080/10570310902856105.

Credits and Acknowledgments

This page is an extension of the copyright page.

Grateful acknowledgment is made for permission to use the following:

Excerpts on pages 89 and 112 from Carole Blair, "Contemporary U.S. Memorial Sites as Exemplars of Rhetoric's Materiality," in *Rhetorical Bodies,* ed. Jack Selzer and Sharon Crowley (Madison: University of Wisconsin Press, 1999). Reproduced with permission of University of Wisconsin Press.

Excerpt on page 120 from Eric Witherspoon quoted in Emily McCombs, "Sexist School Dress Codes Are a Problem, and Oregon May Have the Answer," Huffington Post, September 6, 2017, reprinted by permission of Eric Witherspoon.

Excerpts on page 120 from Lisa Frack quoted in Emily McCombs, "Sexist School Dress Codes Are a Problem, and Oregon May Have the Answer," Huffington Post, September 6, 2017, reprinted by permission of Lisa Frack.

Definition on page 126 of "Truthiness," Merriam-Webster's Words of the Year 2006. By permission. From *Merriam-Webster Online © 2011* by Merriam-Webster, Incorporated (www.Merriam-Webster.com).

Excerpt on page 133 from Neil deGrasse Tyson, "Pluto's Honor," From *Natural History* 108, no. 1 (February 1999): 82; copyright © Natural History Magazine, Inc. 1999. Reproduced by permission of Natural History.

Speech on pages 201 and 202, "The World is Waking Up (UN General Assembly, NYC 9/23/19)" from NO ONE IS TOO SMALL TO MAKE A DIFFERENCE by Greta Thunberg, copyright © 2018, 2019 by Greta Thunberg. Used by permission of Penguin Books, an imprint of Penguin Publishing Group, a division of Penguin Random House LLC. All rights reserved.

Excerpts on pages 222, 251, 252, 253, 254, 255, 258, and 264 from Lloyd F. Bitzer, "The Rhetorical Situation," *Philosophy and Rhetoric* 1, 1968. Reproduced with permission of Pennsylvania State University Press.

Excerpts on pages 231 and 232 from Silvio Waisbord, "Why Populism is Troubling Democratic Communication," *Communication Culture & Critique* (2018) 11, 1: 21–34, by permission of International Communication Association.

Excerpts on page 233 and 234 from Philip Wander, "The Third Persona: An Ideological Turn in Rhetorical Theory," *Central States Speech Journal* 35 (Winter 1984). Reprinted by permission of Central States Communication Association, www.csca-net.org.

Excerpts on page 264 from Richard E. Vatz, "The Myth of the Rhetorical Situation," *Philosophy and Rhetoric* 6 (1973). Reproduced with permission of Pennsylvania State University Press.

Excerpt on page 304 from Harry Potter Alliance, "What We Do," 2014, http://thehpalliance.org/what-we-do. Reproduced with permission of the Harry Potter Alliance.

Excerpt on page 308 from Damien Pfister, personal correspondence with Catherine Palczewski, June 2, 2014. Reproduced with permission of Damien Pfister.

Excerpt on page 309 from Harry Cleaver, "The Zapatistas and the Electronic Fabric of Struggle," la.utexas.edu/users/hcleaver/zaps.html. Reproduced with permission of Harry Cleaver.

Credits for figures appear in the figure captions.

Index

About the Authors

Catherine Helen Palczewski is professor of communication and media, former director of debate, and an affiliate faculty member of women's and gender studies at the University of Northern Iowa. She received her BS, MA, and PhD from Northwestern University. She teaches courses in social protest, rhetorical criticism, argumentation, and gender in communication. She has served as coeditor of *Argumentation and Advocacy*. She has served on the editorial boards of and published essays in the *Quarterly Journal of Speech, Women's Studies in Communication, Argumentation and Advocacy, Communication Studies,* and the *Southern Communication Journal.* She received the Francine Merritt Award for Outstanding Contributions to the Lives of Women in Communication, the Iowa Regents Award for Faculty Excellence, the George Ziegelmueller Outstanding Debate Educator Award, and the Rohrer Award for the Outstanding Publication in Argumentation. She has served as the keynote speaker at the AFA/NCA Summer Conference on Argumentation, directed the conference, and edited its selected works (*Disturbing Argument,* 2020).

Richard Ice is professor of communication and provost at the College of St. Benedict and St. John's University. He received an AB from Wabash College and his MA and PhD from the University of Iowa. He has taught courses in rhetoric, freedom of speech, public address, group communication, and organizational communication. He has published essays in *Management Communication Quarterly* and *Communication Quarterly.* He received the St. John's University Robert L. Spaeth Teacher of Distinction Award and the College of St. Benedict / St. John's University Academic Advisor Award.

John Fritch is professor of communication and media at the University of Northern Iowa, and dean of the College of Humanities, Arts and Sciences. He received his BA from the University of Nebraska–Lincoln and his MA and PhD from the University of Kansas. He has taught courses in rhetoric and ethics. He has coedited *Argumentation and Advocacy* and published essays in that journal and in *A Century of Transformation: Studies in Honor of the 100th Anniversary of the Eastern Communication Association.* Previously, he was director of forensics at Southwest Missouri State University. He received the Outstanding Teaching Award from the College of Arts and Letters and the Outstanding Graduate Faculty Member in Communication Studies Award from Southwest Missouri State University. The Eastern Communication Association has recognized him as a Centennial Scholar.

Ryan McGeough is professor of communication and media at the University of Northern Iowa, director of the oral communication course, and head of the department. He received his BA and MA from the University of Northern Iowa and his PhD from Louisiana State University. He teaches courses in oral communication, political communication, and rhetoric. He has published essays in *Argumentation and Advocacy* and *Communication Education* and is the author of *The Essential Guide to Visual Communication* (2019). He received the Rohrer Award for the Outstanding Publication in Argumentation, the Robert Bostrom Young Scholar Award, and the Dwight L. Freshley Outstanding New Teacher Award.